THIRD EDITION

Research Methods

DONALD H. MCBURNEY
University of Pittsburgh

with the assistance of
Patrick Middleton

Brooks/Cole Publishing Company
Pacific Grove, California

I(T)P ™ The trademark ITP is used under license.

Brooks/Cole Publishing Company
A Division of Wadsworth, Inc.

Printed in the United States of America

10   9   8   7   6   5

Library of Congress Cataloguing-in-Publication Data
McBurney, Donald, 1938–
    Research methods / Donald H. McBurney. — 3rd ed.
        p.   cm.
    Rev. ed. of : Experimental psychology. 2nd ed. c1990.
    Includes bibliographical references and index.
    ISBN 0-534-17646-1
    1. Psychology, Experimental—Methodology.   2. Psychology—
Research—Methodology.   I. McBurney, Donald H., 1938–
Experimental psychology.   II. Title.
BF181.M22   1994   93-5651
150'.72—dc20   CIP

Sponsoring Editor: Jim Brace-Thompson
Editorial Associate: Cathleen S. Collins
Production Editor: Nancy L. Shammas
Production: Cecile Joyner, The Cooper Company
Manuscript Editor: Margaret C. Tropp
Permissions Editor: May Clark
Interior Design: Terri Wright
Cover Photo: Ed Young
Cover Design: Roy R. Neuhaus
Interior Illustration: Lotus Art
Typesetting: Graphic World, Inc.
Cover Printing: Southeastern Color Graphics
Printing and Binding: Arcata Graphics/Fairfield

THIS BOOK IS PRINTED ON ACID-FREE RECYCLED PAPER

BRIEF CONTENTS

It is of the essence of teaching that it seeks to render itself superfluous.

Dietrich Bonhoeffer
The Cost of Discipleship

CONTENTS

4 Tabular and Graphical Description of Data 83

5 Validity 119

8

Nonexperimental Research, Part 2: Survey Research   193

9

True Experiments, Part 1: Single-Factor Designs   221

10   True Experiments, Part 2: Factorial Designs   248

11   Single-Subject Experiments   276

12   Quasi Experiments   298

13   Reporting the Results   330

14   Ethics in Research   371

15   Biases and Limitations of
Experimental Psychology   394

PREFACE

THIS BOOK IS INTENDED TO SERVE AS A TEXT FOR COURSES IN RESEARCH METHODS IN PSYCHOLOGY AT the undergraduate level. It is the third edition of *Experimental Psychology* (the first two were published by Wadsworth Publishing Company). The new title, *Research Methods*, reflects the increased attention this edition gives to nonexperimental research. The previous chapter on nonexperimental research has been expanded into two: one on observational, archival, and case-study methods and another devoted to surveys and questionnaires. In addition, there are sections on meta analysis, developmental designs, and program evaluation in various chapters.

Following the emphasis of the earlier editions on practical matters of doing research, I have expanded the chapter on variables into two chapters, resulting in more emphasis on graphs and tables and a new section on data reduction. Although the book assumes that students have had a course in statistics, Appendix A now provides a more complete review of the basic concepts of both descriptive and inferential statistics.

Other changes are also evolutionary. There are more exercises and problems; the more involved ones are found in the sections entitled "A Case in Point." Along with the sections entitled "Reading between the Lines," they provide a vehicle for a problem-solving approach to teaching research methods. I believe that this is the most realistic and effective way to teach this subject matter. It is also in line with the current emphasis on critical thinking.

The features that made the first edition distinctive have been retained. First is to put psychological research into a larger scientific context. Other books on the topic provide too little emphasis on how psychology fits into the scientific approach to understanding the world. Given the debate that exists among the behavioral, dynamic, humanistic, Marxian, and other types of psychologies, as well as the confusion about the nature of science evidenced by the many popular and fringe psychologies, it is not surprising that undergraduate students have questions about how scientific psychology should be done. The first section of the book therefore deals with psychology as a science, emphasizing the similarities between psychology and the other sciences on the one hand and the differences between science and pseudoscience on the other.

A second goal is to separate the discussion of research methods from its traditional dependence on statistical procedures. Many experimental psychology books are organized around particular statistical methods, especially the analysis of variance. In contrast, I have organized this book around the general problems of validity and how to control for the various threats to validity. The later chapters on true experiments, quasi experiments, and single-subject designs give examples of solutions to the problems of validity, rather than a catalog of statistical applications. With this goal in mind, it made sense to have early chapters that discuss the types of variables encountered in psychological research and how data are represented graphically.

A third goal, closely related to the second, is to convey the idea that designing and conducting research is an exercise in problem solving that can be exciting and creative. I have avoided giving the impression that psychological research involves following a set of cut-and-dried rules or selecting one of a fixed number of available designs. My belief is that the best research derives from solving particular threats to the validity of a contemplated piece of research and only then asking what kind of design has resulted. Throughout the book I have emphasized the considerations that are involved in designing and conducting research.

Fourth, I have chosen from the psychological literature a wide variety of problems in research and their solutions. Generally I have avoided nonpsychological examples and artificial data.

Finally, I have tried to convey a feeling for all of the stages of research, from choosing the problem to publishing the results. I have discussed the literature search, the nuts and bolts of research protocols, research ethics, and the publication process. The only major step omitted is statistical analysis, which is left to a prerequisite or corequisite course or to supplementary material, according to the instructor's choice.

Many colleagues and friends have contributed to this project. Among others, Seymour Antelman, Craig Brown, Anthony Caggiula, Lynn Cooper, Michael Cross, Martin Greenberg, James Greeno, James Holland, Peter Holland, Robert Jewell, Russell Jones, John Levine, Peter Mechamer, Scott Monroe, Richard Moreland, Merle Moskowitz, Walter Schneider, Janet Schofield, Valerie Shalin, Mark Strauss, Edward Stricker, and Eva Vaughan all provided helpful suggestions and/or discussion. Special thanks go to

Janneane Gent for drafting the boxes on statistics that appear in Chapters 9 and 10, as well as for making other important contributions to the book. The idea for the Reading between the Lines exercises came from Schuyler Huck and Howard Sandler's book, *Rival Hypotheses: Alternative Explanations of Data-Based Conclusions*. Many of the exercises are the work of Patrick Middleton, who also assisted greatly in the preparation of the manuscript.

I thank the following colleagues who reviewed the manuscript and provided detailed suggestions for the first edition that improved the book greatly: Mark Kinnucan of St. Michael's College, Nancy Kirkland of Trinity College, John Knight of Central State University, Virgil Nylander of the University of Wisconsin, Howard Orenstein of Western Maryland College, Walter Pieper of Georgia State University, Thomas Rowe of the University of Washington, Timothy Salthouse of the University of Missouri at Columbia, W. Scott Terry of the University of North Carolina, and Ronald Ulm of Salisbury State College. I would also like to thank the following reviewers of the manuscript for the second edition for their valuable comments and suggestions: Robert L. Breckinridge of Northwestern State University of Louisiana, Linda L. Faldetta of Fort Lewis College, Albert Katz of the University of Western Ontario, Horace Keller of Glassboro State College, Ruth Maki of North Dakota State University, Michael Perone of West Virginia University, and Paul Schulman of the State University of New York Institute of Technology at Utica–Rome.

I am further indebted to the reviewers for the third edition: L. Joseph Achor of Baylor University, Michael Biderman of the University of Tennessee at Chattanooga, Tom Brigham of Washington State University, John Crosbie of West Virginia University, Hill Goldsmith of the University of Wisconsin at Madison, Tim Goldsmith of the University of New Mexico, Gui-Young Hong of the University of Tennessee at Chattanooga, William Jacobs of the University of Arizona, Donald Leitner of St. Joseph's University, and Paul Schulman of the State University of New York Institute of Technology at Utica–Rome. They made many valuable suggestions on emphasis, clarity, and tone.

I would like to give a special word of thanks to Ken King, psychology editor at Wadsworth, who saw this book through the first two editions and the formative stages of the third edition. His valuable advice and suggestions have improved this book greatly. I miss working with him, and I miss his unique editing style. Jim Brace-Thompson and all the other people at Brooks/Cole have been a pleasure to work with.

—Donald H. McBurney

1

Psychology and Science

Experimental psychology is a science essentially like any other. Between psychology and biology, chemistry, or anthropology, there may be considerable difference in subject matter, but the essentials are common to all. The differences are fairly obvious: Because animals are more complex than trees, psychological theories may be more complicated than botanical theories; because the behavior of animals varies more than that of rocks, psychology uses statistics more than does physics. On the other hand, the similarities may not be as easy to grasp. For this reason we will devote this chapter to discussing psychology as a science. First let us put psychology in context by talking about ways of looking at behavior.

WAYS OF KNOWING ABOUT BEHAVIOR

The point to stress here is that there is more than one way to learn about the behavior of animals. Every day all of us use several methods to learn about behavior. We can divide these methods into two broad categories: empirical methods and nonempirical methods. The term **empirical** simply means based on experience.

empirical
based on
experience

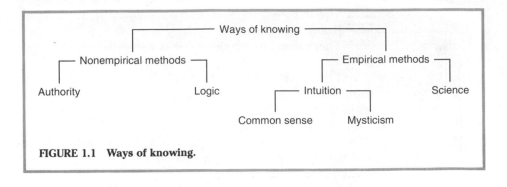

FIGURE 1.1   Ways of knowing.

■ Nonempirical Methods

First we will consider two nonempirical methods: authority and logic. Then we will consider the empirical methods.

Authority

We may believe something because some respected person told us it is true. Religious authorities proclaim the will of God to us about various matters, the government tells us that we should not drive over 55 miles per hour, and our parents tell us that we will catch cold if we get our feet wet. Because these authorities often disagree among themselves, we are inclined to reject authority as a way of knowing. How do you know that Neil Armstrong walked on the moon on July 20, 1969? You were not there. Perhaps you watched it on television if you were born before then. Yet there are people who believe that no man ever has walked on the moon and that the moon walk was a gigantic propaganda hoax perpetrated by the United States government. If you believe that Neil Armstrong walked on the moon, you do so because of your faith in the credibility of the government, the news media, and the books you have read. These sources all serve as authorities for you if you believe what they say. Yet authority has major limitations as a way of knowing. Authorities often are wrong, even when they assert their beliefs most forcefully. Galileo suffered grievously for daring to hold that the earth goes around the sun. That the history of science is in large part a struggle for intellectual freedom from the dogmas of authority is a continuing theme in the history of science from Galileo in the 16th century to the recent Soviet dissidents. If you did not have any faith in authority, though, you would not be reading this book or taking a research methods course from a college professor.

Logic

Logic is an important way of helping us know about behavior. Take the following set of statements:

The behavior of all animals is subject to the laws of natural science.
Humans are animals.
Therefore, human behavior is subject to the laws of natural science.

These statements are logical. That is, if the first two are true, then the third follows logically. Use of logic is often crucial in drawing correct conclusions about the world.

Yet, as important as reasoning logically is, logic has limitations as a way of knowing. Logic can tell you that a statement is false because it draws an improper conclusion. But a statement can be logically valid and still not be true because it assumes something to be the case that is not. Suppose that the behavior of all animals is not, in fact, subject to the laws of natural science. Then the conclusion that human behavior is subject to the laws of natural science would be false.

Take another example. Suppose I say "If it rains, then there will be no baseball game." If I look out the window and see it is raining, it is valid for me to say "It is raining; therefore there will be no baseball game." But the truth of the statement depends on the fact that it is raining. If it is, in fact, not raining, then the statement is false.

Logic is extremely important to science, but it cannot substitute for making the observation that it is raining, or proving that the behavior of all animals is subject to the laws of natural science. In other words, there is no substitute for empirical evidence. As any reader of science fiction can attest, there are many logically possible worlds. Logic alone cannot tell you which world actually exists.

■ Empirical Methods

Just as we divided ways of knowing into empirical and nonempirical on the basis of whether or not they depended on experience, we can divide the empirical methods into two categories: intuitive and scientific.

Intuition

intuition
spontaneous
perception or
judgment not
based on
reasoned mental
steps

We size up strangers within the first few seconds of meeting them. We do this by **intuition,** a way of knowing based on spontaneous, "instinctive" processes rather than logic or reasoning. Intuition has a powerful effect on our beliefs about other people. We may distrust a person who seems too sincere to be true. This sizing up has sometimes been called "women's intuition"; today we are more likely to say that someone gives off "bad vibes." We use intuition continuously in making the myriad decisions necessary during the course of a day. Think for a moment how you decide whether to step off the curb in front of an oncoming car at a traffic light. You make a life-or-death decision in a split second. How do you do it? Probably your decision is based on a number of factors, including whether the traffic light has changed to red, whether the driver looks you in the eye, whether the car is decelerating, and so forth. Somehow you take all of these factors into account. That somehow is what we call intuition.

There are two important varieties of intuition: common sense and mysticism.

common sense
practical intelligence shared by a large group of persons

Common sense.   **Common sense** is a kind of intuition because of its dependence on informal methods. It has the additional characteristic of emphasizing the agreement of a person's judgment with the shared attitudes and experiences of a larger group of people. We are familiar with the example of a recent college graduate who starts working with people who lack formal education. The graduate wants to apply his scientific knowledge to the job. The old hands may resist the ideas that don't agree with common sense. After all, their methods worked well before the newcomer arrived.

Common sense as a way of knowing has two basic limitations. First, standards of common sense differ from time to time and from place to place according to the attitudes and experiences of the culture. Years ago a commonsense method of trying suspects for crimes was having them attempt to chew dry grain. It was believed that if they were innocent, they would be able to eat the grain without difficulty; if they were guilty, their mouths would be too dry to permit swallowing. In reality, this practice does have some scientific basis: A guilty person is likely to be scared spitless. We now know, however, that innocent people can be just as nervous as guilty ones, so today we are usually more scientific in our trial practices. Again, common sense may tell us not to trust a person who will not look us in the eye. In another culture, though, the same behavior may be a sign of respect.

The second limitation of common sense as a way of knowing lies in the fact that the only criterion common sense recognizes for judging the truth of a belief or practice is whether or not it works. The old hand will tell the college graduate to forget his scientific ways because the old ways work well enough. According to the commonsense method, no systematic attempt is made to test the theoretical explanation of a practice and see whether it is true. As long as a certain practice works, that practice is maintained and the theory behind it considered true. This principle can be useful at times. Child-rearing practices for thousands of years were based on commonsense notions. Perhaps most children turned out reasonably well on this basis. Only in recent years have scientists advocated child-rearing methods that were an improvement over folk practices. Yet following a practice simply because it works does not permit any basis for predicting when the practice will work and when it will not. Commonsense notions of child rearing do not help in dealing with autistic children, for example.

More important, because common sense has only practical success as its criterion of truthfulness, it cannot predict new knowledge. Later we will discuss in some detail the idea that science aims at a theoretical explanation of phenomena. Here we will only point out that the absence of theory as a principal goal of common sense is one of the major limitations of this method of knowing.

Given that common sense has these two basic limitations—that it changes with time and circumstance and that it is pragmatic rather than theoretical—it is not surprising that scientific knowledge often contradicts commonsense knowledge. We may speak of a scientific result as being **counterintuitive**; that is, it goes against our notions of common sense. In fact, we consider a scientific theory to be good if it predicts something that we did not expect.

counterintuitive something that goes against common sense

For example, a recent theory of obesity in humans says that overweight persons are controlled more by external cues (sight of food or a clock that indicates dinnertime) and less by internal signals (hunger pangs) than are other people. This theory makes the counterintuitive prediction that there should be situations in which overweight people eat less than normal-weight people. True to prediction, overweight people do eat less if they have to make a special effort to obtain the food. If there is plenty of food in front of them, however, they will eat more than other people.

In one experiment by Richard Nisbett (1968), sandwiches were placed in front of subjects who were told to eat all they wanted and to help themselves to more from the refrigerator if they desired. Half of the subjects had only one sandwich in front of them, and the other half had three. Subjects of average weight tended to eat about the same in either condition. That is, they would get more from the refrigerator in the one-sandwich condition but leave food on the plate in the three-sandwich condition. Overweight subjects, however, tended to eat whatever was there, either the small amount or the large amount, and not go to the refrigerator.

Even though science frequently contradicts common sense, we must not go to the extreme of concluding that we throw away common sense when we start doing science. In fact, science ultimately rests on common sense. There may be several different theories that could explain a given phenomenon. One of them may be rejected by scientists because it strains their common sense. Often scientists say that such and such a theory seems plausible, meaning that it agrees with their notion of common sense. Scientists choose among theories on a number of bases, but the theory that is finally accepted must satisfy the common sense of the scientific community. The crucial point here is that the scientist's common sense is different from the layperson's. Scientists' background in similar problems trains them to think in terms of a particular scientific theory. Laypersons have different backgrounds that may make the theory of the scientists seem ridiculous. Their ideas of common sense will differ precisely because they do not have common backgrounds.

mysticism belief in insight gained by means of a private experience such as an altered state of consciousness

Mysticism. **Mysticism** is an intuitive way of knowing based on direct insight, associated with an altered quality of consciousness. The mystical approach to knowing is like common sense in not using logical reasoning. In addition, the mystical experience has a quality about it that sets it apart from ordinary experience. We may describe it as an altered state of consciousness, a transcendental experience, a spiritual encounter, or more simply, a high or a trip. Although we tend to think of mystical experiences as being the province of the yogi, medieval monk, or drug user, research shows that 36% of Americans have had an experience of this type (Greely, 1975). The mystical experience is triggered by such ordinary experiences as listening to music, praying, or looking at a sunset. The most common interpretation of the mystical experience is "a feeling of deep and profound peace," "a certainty that all things would work out for the good," or "a sense of the need to contribute to others" (Greely, 1975, p. 65).

The value of these experiences for those who have them should not be underestimated. Such persons may be led to dedicate their lives to serving their fellow humans. Certain problems exist, however. First, conveying the message received during the experience is hard because of the difficulty of describing the experience in a convincing way. Second, the message itself may be invalid. The person who feels that everything will work out for the good may have a serious disease that could be cured by medical care. Therefore, although mystical experiences may be significant for certain people, they have limitations as ways of knowing.

Science

In addition to authority, logic, and intuition, the fourth major way of knowing about behavior is science. In the sections that follow, we will consider what science is, how it differs from other ways of knowing, and how psychology fits into the scientific approach to knowing.

WHAT IS SCIENCE?

To attempt to define science for a book of this type may seem either totally unnecessary, highly presumptuous, or both. Every reader of this book will have had exposure to science at the high school level, if not in college, which included some study of the scientific method. At this point there are three reasons why we must discuss the nature of science. First, there is not *a* scientific method; rather, there are scientific methods. Somewhere you probably learned that the scientific method consisted of executing the following steps: (1) defining the problem, (2) forming a hypothesis, (3) collecting data, and (4) drawing conclusions. This recipe is usable, if you understand that it is greatly simplified. Research is sometimes done according to these steps, but more often it involves modification of this procedure. As our discussion progresses, the need for modification will become apparent.

The second reason for discussing the nature of science in this book is that even persons who have developed a basic idea of how to do science that involves biology, chemistry, or physics often have difficulty seeing how to go about the science of psychology. To many people it seems that psychology should follow different rules from other sciences because psychology appears by definition to deal with mental events. If you have trouble seeing how psychology can be like the other sciences, don't be discouraged. The experts on psychology took a long time to come to a tentative consensus about how psychology should be done, and the debate is not settled by any means.

A third reason for defining science in an introductory discussion of experimental psychology is that beginning psychology students sometimes feel that they have become amateur psychologists by virtue of observing human and animal behavior for a lifetime. When you took chemistry, you probably had not spent much time thinking about how atoms combine to form molecules. Yet you may have had a lifetime interest in why people are friendly or unfriendly, moody or not moody, and so forth. Sometimes, too, you know exactly why you do things: "I wore a certain style of clothes in order to be accepted by my fellow students." So your very experience with people may make it more difficult for you to think about human behavior scientifically. Studying human behavior might seem easier if you were the mythical Martian sent to spy on the behavior of earthlings. We often are more aware of the customs of a slightly different culture than we are of our own.

To tell the truth, it is impossible to define science neatly because it is too complex an enterprise. It is not like defining a bachelor as an unmarried male. We can characterize science, however, somewhat the way we might characterize happy families by listing their typical attributes: parental interest in children's progress, many shared activities, stable lifestyle, and so on. These are useful in describing a typical happy family even though any one we might mention could be true of some unhappy family, and any one might be missing from some happy family. So we will state several important characteristics of science that tend to distinguish it from all other ways of knowing.

■ Characteristics of Science

Science Is Empirical

You probably have heard the expression "I got it from the horse's mouth." Years ago, some philosophers are said to have argued at great length about how many teeth a horse had. After many logical arguments were presented on various sides of the question, someone suggested looking into a horse's mouth to find out. Although that suggestion seems obvious to us in today's scientific age, it was not clear to the scholastic mind of the Middle Ages that observation could be as good as logic in reaching a conclusion. For example, suppose that the horse was not typical in some respect: It had not yet grown all its teeth, or some had fallen out. The scientific attitude is to rely on experience more than on authority, common sense, or even logic.

Although empiricism is an essential characteristic of science, it is important to note that not all empirical ways of knowing are scientific. The intuitive methods we discussed—common sense and mysticism—were empirical, but not scientific.

Science Is Objective

The most important characteristic of **science** is that it is a way of obtaining knowledge based on objective observations. The key word in this brief definition is *objective*. Objective observations are those made in such a way that any person having normal perception and being in the same place at the same time would arrive at the same observation. Objectivity in science is a concept that is often misunderstood. It does not mean that scientists are coldly detached from their subject matter. It does not mean that they treat people as objects rather than persons. Nor does it mean that what they observe is necessarily what actually happened. Objectivity simply means that other persons would have seen the same things had they been looking over the shoulder of the scientist who made the observation.

In addition, when observations are objectively made and carefully reported, they serve as a sort of recipe for others to follow. Other scientists can repeat the procedures to see if they observe the same things. For this reason, careful records and clear, accurate reports are a crucial part of science. Such documentation permits others to bridge the gaps of space and time and peer over the shoulder of the scientist, making his or her observations objective.

The opposite of objective observations are subjective observations. These are the observations that a person makes that another person is not required to accept as true. Ann may say, "I taste salt." This statement by Ann is subjective because no one else is required to believe that she actually experienced a salty taste. She might have tasted nothing, because the salt was too weak, and said "salt" out of perverseness. On the other hand, the statement "Ann reported tasting salt" is objective, because anyone else present in the room could verify the fact that Ann made such a statement. So the experimenter can report objectively about Ann's subjective report. It is the experimenter's report that becomes the object of scientific discussion.

The need for objective observations explains the importance that scientists place on proper research methods. Great care is taken to specify the exact conditions under which observations are made so that other scientists can repeat the observations, if they desire, and try to obtain the same results.

Objectivity is the single most important characteristic that tends to set science apart from what is not science. Science deals with phenomena that are available to anyone. It cannot deal with phenomena that only one person or a few persons can observe. This fact distinguishes science from all systems of knowledge based on authority—religion, politics, nationalism, or whatever. Objectivity is what makes science the one universal means of achieving understanding, because it eliminates from consideration at the outset any phenomenon that cannot command the agreement of every person. This is not to say that there are no scientific controversies or nationalistic scientists. Far from it. But science as a whole is remarkably free from parochialism precisely because it deals only with those phenomena that are available to any person.

Science Is Self-Correcting

Because science is an empirical enterprise, it follows that new evidence is constantly being discovered that contradicts previous knowledge. Science is characterized by a willingness to let new evidence correct previous beliefs. This makes science different from perhaps every other human enterprise. Courts appeal to the Constitution of the United States, religions appeal to the writings of prophets, and institutions appeal to their traditions. Science, however, is characterized by openness to change. A notable example is provided by the French Academy of Science, which had a debate in the 18th century as to whether stones fell from the sky. When the Academy concluded, on the basis of the best evidence at the time, that stones did not fall from the sky, museums discarded priceless collections of what we now know to be meteorites. Today the existence of meteorites is common knowledge, as a direct result of more empirical evidence.

A psychological example concerns the relative influence of heredity and environment on behavior. Most psychologists in the middle years of this century emphasized the role of environment in behavior, including personality. Recent evidence (for example, Bouchard, 1990) suggests, however, that heredity has a considerable degree of influence on personality and other behavioral characteristics. This has led to rewriting of psychology textbooks to a remarkable degree. The willingness of scientists to change their opinions is a hallmark of science.

Science Is Progressive

From the fact that science is empirical and self-correcting, it follows that it is also progressive. Other areas of human activity may change, but it is difficult to argue that they progress. Consider fashions in clothes. What is in fashion today may have been the latest thing 50 years ago and completely out of fashion last year. The arts and humanities change, but it is difficult to argue that they progress. Literature, music, and painting are different today from what they were a hundred years ago, to be sure, but whether they are better is a matter of taste, not a matter that could be settled by any empirical test. Comparison of science textbooks over the years, however, shows remarkable progress in the amount and quality of knowledge they contain.

Science Is Tentative

What we have just said makes it obvious that science must be tentative. Science never claims to have the whole truth on any question, because new information may make current knowledge obsolete at any time. Because of the progressive nature of science, however, we can be reasonably confident that we are increasingly approaching the truth, rather than simply changing our ideas according to fashion or whim.

Science Is Parsimonious

According to the dictionary, *parsimony* means stinginess. This may seem a peculiar trait to claim as a desirable characteristic of science. In the case of science, the principle of parsimony holds that we should use the simplest explanation possible to account for a given phenomenon. If we want to explain why a mother cat licks and cleans her kittens of the fluids and membranes that cover them when they are born, we could say that she knows that she must clean them up or they will become cold and will not survive. Alternatively, we could suggest that she does so because that stuff tastes good to her. The first explanation may be more appealing to us, and attribute more dignity to the cat, especially if we are cat lovers, but the second explanation is closer to the truth as well as simpler. A good scientist will always prefer a simpler explanation to a more complex one, other things being equal. In our example, the explanation in terms of taste preferences is simpler than attributing to the cat sophisticated mental processes.

This principle of parsimony was advocated by William of Ockham (also spelled Occam), a philosopher who was active in the 14th century. He became so associated with this concept that it is often called "Occam's razor."

Science Is Concerned with Theory

Science shares the characteristic of empiricism with the intuitive methods. It is distinguished from mysticism by its emphasis on objectivity. How it differs from common sense, however, is not so obvious. Recall that we said that one of the limitations of common sense was that its only criterion of acceptability of an idea is that it works. As we will see in Chapter 2, one of the major concerns of science is the development of a theory of how something works.

The difference between these two goals can be illustrated by contrasting science and technology. These are similar enterprises, and historically the two have developed together. People were concerned with how to grow corn, for example. Techniques of growing better corn tended to lead to understanding of what made the corn grow. This, in turn, led to better technology. Even today we often hear science and technology mentioned together, and they sometimes appear together in the names of magazines, colleges, and other institutions. But technology has the goal of making something work, whereas science has the task of understanding why it works. Often the technology is far ahead of the science.

A good example is the development of automatic controls. During the early days of the industrial revolution, the invention of the steam engine made work much easier. But it was necessary for someone to watch the earliest steam engines constantly, decreasing the supply of steam to the engine when it went too fast, and increasing it when it went too slow. This was no doubt a boring task, albeit better than turning the wheels by hand. Eventually someone decided there had to be a better way to control the supply of steam, and invented the automatic governor. Years later, scientists understood that the principle of feedback by which the automatic governor maintains the constant speed of the steam engine is the same principle by which an animal's internal environment is kept constant, also called homeostasis. Technology gave us the automatic governor long before scientists understood that it represented a general theoretical principle.

■ The Relation between Science and Nonscience

We have noted that science is not uniquely different from other ways of knowing. In fact, we stated that logic and common sense have important roles to play in science. At the same time, science and technology share a number of common characteristics, including empiricism and progress. We should point out that by emphasizing science we are not saying that we must reject other ways of knowing. Scientists are, after all, human, and therefore subject to all of the frailties of humankind. They begin their inquiry on the basis of the actual beliefs that they hold at the time, as influenced by authority, logic, and common sense. What makes scientists different is the fact that their method of inquiry causes them to change those beliefs based on objectively obtained empirical evidence.

Mysticism, on the other hand, has a sharply reduced role in the workings of science. Mysticism can only have the role of motivating people as single individuals. The private nature of the mystical experience rules it out as evidence to be considered by the scientific community as a whole. Certainly, many scientists have been motivated by mystical experiences or religious ideas. Nevertheless, they cannot urge a mystical experience or a religious doctrine as scientific evidence for the consideration of other scientists. For example, Gustav Fechner, the founder of psychophysics and a pioneer in experimental psychology, pursued his science as a way of proving his belief in panpsychism. His scientific work, however, has been evaluated on its own merits.

Authority also has a reduced role in science. In virtually every human enterprise, there are people who serve as guardians of orthodoxy. Even in the most democratic organization, a majority vote can render certain opinions heretical. Although a power structure is by no means absent from science, authority plays a different role than it does in other human activities. A clear example can be seen in almost any meeting of a large scientific organization. Anyone who meets minimal requirements—an undergraduate, graduate student, or new PhD—can present a paper that challenges the theories of even the most illustrious scientist. Although the challenger may suffer trepidation, and the senior scientist's arguments may receive more careful attention, the focus of the discussion will be on the soundness of the research methods and on the logic of the challenger's position. If the challenger has presented a sound argument based on acceptable methods of observation, other scientists will be motivated to try to repeat the observations. If these repeated observations are successful, the illustrious scientist's ideas are replaced by the challenger's.

This process of challenging repeats itself so often that it is commonplace in scientific activity. Still, it is a characteristic unique to science and stems from the fact that the only basis for authority in science is the objective evidence that any person can evaluate. True, the editors of journals and the reviewers of grants and journal articles do wield authority of a sort. Their authority, though, is that of peer review—that is, review by a person's equals. No scientific courts exist where truth is established for all to accept. A scientist must convince the entire scientific community, not just a jury of authorities. That is why we often read statements like the following: "Most workers in the field believe that . . . " or "It is generally accepted that . . . " People who serve as reviewers for articles and grants are chosen because of their expertise, and so they are authorities in a sense. Yet they serve as authorities because, and as long as, they are able to convince their peers that they are in fact better informed on the subject than are other persons.

PSYCHOLOGY AS SCIENCE

Our discussion so far has assumed that psychology is a branch of science essentially on the same basis as any other science. This idea has not always held sway and is still somewhat controversial. Before World War I psychology was often conceived as a mental science, concerned with events inside the head that were different in kind from those in the physical world. It followed that a mental science would need techniques different from those of the physical sciences. An important technique for the study of psychology by mentalistic psychologists was **introspection**, a method of examining the contents of one's own consciousness practiced by carefully trained observers. Introspection was a reasonably useful technique, but it ran into a basic problem: Two observers would introspect about a question and come to opposite conclusions.

introspection observation of one's own thoughts and feelings

Suppose one observer introspected about the color orange and concluded that orange was a unique sensation, different from red or yellow. Another might conclude that orange was a mixed sensation made up of red and yellow sensations. How would you decide which observer was correct? Observers could introspect about their own experience and no one else's. No one else could take an independent look at the introspection of the two observers and decide which one was correct. This situation occurred frequently enough to cause long and fruitless debates on many topics.

behaviorism a view that the objective study of behavior constitutes psychology

Eventually, experimental psychology converted to the doctrine of **behaviorism** put forth by John Watson. Watson argued that the behavior of organisms, not their consciousnesses, provided the basic data of psychology. Only behavior could be observed, not sensations or mental images. Behaviorism was a radical doctrine in 1913 and is still widely misunderstood. Behaviorists do not deny that there is such a thing as consciousness or that it has an important role in human or even animal behavior. Behaviorism says that the events we study must be things that can be observed by anyone: They must be objective, public events.

Recall our example of Ann tasting salt. Ann's sensation of saltiness is a private event accessible only to Ann. Ann can introspect at length about what salt tastes like, and only Ann has access to her own introspection. But Ann's saying "I taste salt" is an event that can be observed by anyone; it is objective and public rather than subjective and private. Behaviorists can count the number of times Ann says that a particular concentration of salt tastes salty. They can compare this with the number of times John says that the same solution tastes salty. They can use the frequency of the verbal reports as data to compare Ann with John, or Ann on Day 1 with Ann on Day 2.

Until recently, behaviorism was the dominant theoretical orientation in psychology. Although mental events were not denied to have taken place, the focus was on the objective data of behavior, and this led to vigorous and successful science. On the other hand, there were psychologists who felt that the baby of consciousness had been thrown out with the bathwater of introspectionism. Eventually, many psychologists returned to an interest in consciousness and the mental events that lay behind the behavior they had been studying.

cognitive psychology
the study of behavior in terms of internal processes such as perceiving or reasoning

Thus, we have seen the rise of **cognitive psychology** in the 1960s and 1970s. Cognitive psychology is characterized by the attempt to explain behavior in terms of internal events such as images, short-term memories, and other processes that cannot be observed directly. However, cognitive psychology represents an elaboration of behaviorism rather than a rejection of it. The presence of these internal events is inferred from the objective behavior of the subject.

A common way of inferring internal events from behavior is to measure how long it takes to perform a response. For example, suppose you show a person a list of numbers to remember. Immediately after the list is removed, you ask whether a certain number is in the list. The time required to decide whether the number is in the list turns out to be a linear function of how many numbers the list has. In other words, each additional number in the list requires a certain additional amount of time for deciding whether the asked-for number is there. From this experiment an internal, unobserved process is inferred to take place that requires about 40 milliseconds for each item in the list that must be searched (S. Sternberg, 1966). Although cognitive psychology is more interested in internal events than is strict behaviorism, it can be considered an extension of behaviorism because it relies on objective, public data.

humanistic psychology
a philosophy that emphasizes feelings, con-sciousness, and other human values in contrast to the objec-tiveness of behaviorism

Another approach to psychology is that of **humanistic psychology**, a branch that is difficult to define. Having developed in large part as a reaction to the narrowness of behavioristic psychology, it encompasses a wide variety of viewpoints (Shaffer, 1978). As a movement, however, humanistic psychol-ogy has several characteristic features. First, it is critical of the scientific emphasis on objective behavior at the expense of feelings, fantasies, and the like. Second, it places great importance on human conscious experience. Third, it emphasizes the freedom and autonomy of human action. Fourth, it is careful to include a concern with human values in the science of psychology. Behaviorism tends to downplay these four areas because studying them objectively is difficult.

In Chapter 15 we will evaluate humanistic psychology further by discussing some of the limitations and biases of scientific psychology. At this point, we will simply say that developing a science of psychology that can satisfy all the concerns of humanistic psychology will be an accomplishment, if it can be done. Science has been spectacularly successful in answering certain kinds of questions precisely because it has limited itself to dealing with evidence that can command the agreement of every person as meeting the criterion of objectivity. We can wish the humanistic psychologists every success, but we will stick to the methods common to all sciences because they have worked. We will cheerfully admit that this rules out many interesting questions for the psychologist to study. As someone has said, science is the substitution of small problems that can be solved for important ones that cannot. Remember that science is one way of knowing among many. We must realize that each way has its limitations, and we must be grateful for the balance thus brought to human understanding of ourselves and of the world.

WORKING ASSUMPTIONS OF SCIENCE

To most of us who have come through our Western educational system, science seems an obvious way to learn about the world. The rise of the counterculture in the 1960s, though, and the interest in non-Western modes of thought in recent years have reminded us that there are certain assumptions about the world that lie behind the scientific approach. Let us discuss these briefly.

■ The Reality of the World

realism
the philosophy that objects perceived have an existence outside the mind

Most scientists agree that one of science's fundamental assumptions is the reality of the world. Philosophers call this assumption the doctrine of **realism**—the notion that the objects of scientific study in the world exist apart from their being perceived by us. The scientist assumes, for example, that a rat does not stop being reinforced in a Skinner box simply because the experimenter fell asleep or went out for coffee or the recorder ran out of paper. This point may seem obvious to you, but there are a number of philosophers and some scientists who would argue fiercely on this point. They are concerned with the valid and difficult question of how we know what the nature of the world really is. For example, how can we know our senses are not deceiving us when we observe that a piece of coal is black?

In general, scientists have little interest in philosophical debates about the reality of the world. They assume that the world is there, and they go about studying it as best they can. We must note, however, that they do avoid one variety of realism that is known as commonsense realism, or naive realism. Commonsense realism is the philosophy of the person in the street who never wondered why coal looks black because anybody knows that coal is black. Commonsense realism says that things are just the way they seem: Coal looks black because it is black. The failure of commonsense realism in many situations actually contributed to the development of science, psychology in particular. For example, under some conditions, coal can look not black but light gray. Students of perception devoted a good deal of energy to solving the problem of why a piece of coal can look black at one time and gray at another.

Although the scientist and the layperson both believe in the existence of a real world, the world that the scientist believes in is different from the one the layperson believes in. The layperson's world may contain persons who are lazy or hardworking, good or evil. The scientist's world, on the other hand, is more likely to consist of people who are influenced by stimuli, reinforcers, and drives. The scientist and the layperson both assume that there is only one reality, but they differ as to what that reality is.

■ Rationality

rationality
a view that reasoning is the basis for solving problems

Another crucial assumption of science is **rationality**—that the world is understandable by way of logical thinking. If the world were irrational—if it could not be understood by using principles of logic—then there would be no point in trying to understand it by any means whatever. We would simply throw up our hands and try to get along as best we could without trying to understand the world around us.

■ Regularity

regularity
a belief that phenomena exist in recurring patterns that conform with universal laws

The reality and rationality of the world would not be much use to science without the assumption of **regularity**. Regularity means that we assume that the world follows the same laws at all times and in all places. We pick up a book confident that it will not have become explosive since we last used it. We go to sleep at night without worrying that we will wake up in the morning as a giant cockroach. The reason regularity is so important for science is that it says that the laws of science are the same today as they were yesterday or a thousand years ago, and they will be the same tomorrow and a thousand years from now. If a new clothing style were to sweep the country tomorrow, a scientist would try to explain it using the same principles as would explain the fad for the flapper style of the 1920s or the punk style of the 1980s. A scientist believes that "there is nothing new under the sun." It is true that the causes of these events may be complex and that we may never have all the facts necessary to explain a particular event in detail, but science assumes that nothing about human behavior falls outside the laws of nature, wherever or whenever the behavior occurs.

■ Discoverability

Not only do scientists assume that the world is real, rational, and regular, they believe that it is possible to find out how it works. There is a difference between this assumption and the others. It is possible that the world is entirely rational but that we could never find the key to the puzzle unless it were revealed to us. The scientist assumes that we can discover the way the world works without having a holy person or book reveal it to us. This belief in **discoverability** is the difference between a puzzle and a mystery. A puzzle can be solved by a person using ordinary means. A mystery, using the word in the strict sense, cannot be understood by human means but must have its solution revealed by someone who knows the mystery. Science treats the world as a gigantic puzzle that is mysterious in the loose sense of leading to wonder but is not mysterious in the strict sense of not being solvable by human means.

discoverability
the belief that it is possible to learn solutions to questions posed

This belief in the discoverability of the world by scientific methods must be tempered by an appreciation of the difficulty of the task. Many scientific puzzles have intrigued people throughout recorded history. Nature gives up its secrets reluctantly. Many books on experimental methods in psychology give the false impression that by a straightforward application of simple methods, the pieces of the psychological puzzle will slowly and steadily fall into place. Far from it. Many fascinating examples exist that show how solutions to scientific problems require great ingenuity and effort. In a fascinating autobiographical article, B. F. Skinner (1956) describes the processes that led him to become the founder of operant psychology. The basic belief in discoverability is one of the characteristics of science that motivates people to make the effort necessary to carry on experimental work for large parts of a lifetime.

■ Causality

In order to do science, it is necessary to assume that events do not just happen by themselves or for no reason. Thus, the idea that every event has a cause is a basic tenet of science. In fact, some have defined science as a search for causes of events.

determinism
the doctrine that all events happen because of preceding causes

A belief that all events are caused is called **determinism**. A strict determinist holds that if it were possible to know all laws of behavior and the exact condition of persons, together with everything that was influencing them at a particular time, it would be possible to predict exactly what they would do next. Others say that because the laws of behavior cannot be stated with certainty, the possibility of free will cannot be ruled out.

The problem of determinism and free will is a thorny one that we can leave to the philosophers. We do not have to decide whether people's behavior is strictly determined or whether we have free will, or whether both positions can be true at the same time. We are only stating that scientists use the concept of causality as a working assumption. People who believe in free will send their children to school because they expect the school to change the children's behavior in a predictable way. Therefore, they believe in determinism to some extent. Similarly, scientists seek causes for behavior without necessarily making the assumption that they will ever completely learn the causes of behavior, or that the idea of free will is an illusion.

While we are discussing causality, we should note that some events may be considered causes of other events even if the relationship between them is less than constant. These events may be considered probabilistic. The classic example is the conclusion that smoking is a cause of lung cancer even though not every person who smokes contracts lung cancer. Similarly, poverty is a probabilistic cause of crime. Even though every poor person does not become a criminal and not all criminals are poor, there is a statistical association between poverty and crime.

We must not leave the topic of the assumptions of science without pointing out that these need only be methodological, or working, assumptions, not assertions of ultimate truth. All scientists operate under such assumptions in the laboratory and in their writing about science. Outside the laboratory, however, some of them make different assumptions. At home they may doubt the existence of the real world. They may believe that human behavior is irrational, that miracles sometimes happen, or that the world really is mysterious in the strict sense. The point is that persons are scientists when they are doing science, and in order to do science, they must make the assumptions we have discussed.

✳ NUTS & BOLTS ✳

Almost every chapter in this book has a section titled "Nuts & Bolts." These sections are intended to bridge the gap between the material in the earlier part of the chapter and the carrying out of research, or between theory and practice.

Choice of a Problem

You would be surprised to learn how many scientists have chosen by accident the problem they make their life's work. Perhaps they enrolled in psychology so they would not have to walk too far between classes. They liked the course and subsequently majored in psychology, then went to the graduate school recommended by their instructor, were assigned to an adviser, and began working on whatever that person was doing. Their interest in the area grew until it consumed their working hours. Because this process is little appreciated, students become anxious when they must choose a problem for an experimental psychology class. How do they find the right project on which to spend a whole term?

Ideas will be found in several likely places. Previous psychology courses may have covered topics that especially interested you. Most psychology textbooks and lectures contain statements of unsolved problems and suggestions for future research. Everyday observation is another source of research problems. For instance, you may have wondered what caused a certain type of behavior. The list of sources is perhaps endless, including such possibilities as dormitory bull sessions and newspaper articles.

A valuable source is your instructor or adviser. He or she has been thinking about research for a number of years and can often respond to an idea with a key reference or a suggestion. You would be wise to ask what problems your instructor is interested in and pick one that appeals to you. The advantage in this procedure is that, by virtue of background knowledge in the area, your instructor can give you sound advice and will be more motivated to do so than if you chose an unfamiliar problem.

The Literature Review

Before you can design a study that will contribute to psychological knowledge, you need to have a good idea of what is known already. Newcomers to a field often tend to display one of two opposite tendencies. The first is to act as though one were the first intelligent person ever to have contemplated this particular problem, and to plunge right into designing the study. The second tendency is to be overwhelmed by the number of books in a particular field, and conclude that every conceivable study must have been thought of already.

How do you steer a course between these two extremes? Avoiding the first involves realizing that thoughtful people have considered most of the important issues that we confront for thousands of years, albeit frequently without the benefit of modern methods to guide them. Discovering the results of their labors may be difficult, however. As someone has said, "more is known than is known is known." There is, in fact, a considerable amount of information in libraries that has been forgotten or overlooked. It happens with some regularity that someone with a historical bent will show that a researcher many years ago found the same thing that is now being presented as brand new. It takes hard work to keep knowledge from being forgotten and to assure that scientific knowledge actually is cumulative. This is the purpose of conducting research literature reviews.

Avoiding the opposite extreme of being overwhelmed by the sheer bulk of what is known requires knowing some techniques for cutting the literature down to manageable size. If you pick a problem suggested by your adviser, that person no doubt will suggest a few references with which to begin your search of the literature. If you select a problem of your own, you may be able to start with a reference from a textbook you have studied. Otherwise, you may have to start from scratch in the library. The first source to check for books in the area is the card catalog or electronic catalog. If you do not find any books on your topic, consult one of the many handbooks that provide broad coverage of most areas. These books and handbooks should give you access to the literature you need. Skim as many of these books as are available to you to get an overview of your topic. After you have an initial idea of the scope of what is known in your field, you are ready to dig a little deeper.

An indispensable tool is *Psychological Abstracts*. This publication contains abstracts of most psychological articles published. The extensive index lists articles by subject areas and gives a short description of each. A careful review of *Psychological Abstracts* will eventually lead you to virtually all of the literature in an area. Two aspects of your search in *Psychological Abstracts* may be frustrating, however. First, the subject headings are broad, so it is necessary to sift through many irrelevant articles to find the ones you want. Second, you have no way of telling which article will be a gold mine of information and which will be a minor note.

Another powerful bibliographic tool exists in the form of the *Science Citation Index* and the similar *Social Science Citation Index*. These publications may not be in your library, but you should know about them because of their great usefulness. They do not contain abstracts of articles, and they are not arranged according to topic. Rather, they contain references to articles and books that have been cited by any other article or book in a given year, along with the references for the articles that did the citing. They permit you to do something that is impossible to do with *Psychological Abstracts*: You can move forward in time, following the development of a field by tracing the influence of particular articles on later ones. You can start with any article from any date. The *Citation Index* will then tell you whether anyone has referred to that article in a particular year. The process is similar to taking a key article and then looking up the articles in its reference list. Only, using the *Citation Index*, you can find any other article (a) that was published after the article you started with and (b) that cites your initial article in its reference list. By using this method, you can trace what has happened to a field *after* your initial article was written. Thus, you follow pertinent articles and are not distracted by the many articles that may sound relevant to your topic but are not. If the *Science Citation Index* is available at your school, by all means use it. If it is not, you may be able to find it at a nearby institution.

Current Contents/Social & Behavioral Sciences is a widely used aid in finding the latest articles in psychology. *Current Contents* is a weekly publication that essentially consists of the contents pages of journals in psychology and related areas. Over time, more than 1,000 journals are covered as they are published. The authors' addresses are listed in an index so you can write for reprints, or you may order articles by telephone or facsimile. Because the subject index to *Current Contents* is rather rudimentary, this source is mainly of use when you have mastered the literature in an area and wish to keep up with articles as they appear.

Many bibliographic tools now exist in computerized form. These include *PsycLIT/PsycINFO*, *SCISEARCH*, and *SOCIAL SCISEARCH*, which are the computerized forms of *Psychological Abstracts*, *Science Citation Index*, and *Social Science Citation Index*, respectively. (*PsycLIT* is a CD-based system, whereas *PsycINFO* is an on-line system. *PsycINFO* is the more comprehensive of the two.) On some campuses, the databases may be commonly referred to by the names of the suppliers, such as *SilverPlatter* or *Dialog*.

Although the computerized versions of the bibliographic tools generally contain the same information as the bound versions, the computer permits you to search essentially instantaneously and to focus your search much more directly. All computerized databases allow you to search for articles that satisfy several criteria at once, not just one at a time as is possible in the bound version. For example, suppose you were interested in the learning of English as a foreign language by adults. If you were to look in *Psychological Abstracts* under foreign language learning, you would find hundreds of listings in the past few years. If you go to *PsycLIT* or *PsycINFO*, on the other hand, by typing in FOREIGN LANGUAGE LEARNING AND ENGLISH AND ADULT IN PO[pulation] you would instantly narrow your search down to fewer than two dozen references. The details of computerized searches are best learned by going to the library and using the on-line tutorial for the particular database.

On some campuses library users conduct their own database searches, and on others a librarian conducts the search for them. End-user searching, as the first method is called, is more convenient and flexible than mediated searching once you have mastered a few skills.

Whereas some smaller libraries may not have computerized database capabilities, *Inter-Library Loan* is a service that all libraries provide. If you find a reference to a book or journal that your library does not have, your librarian can generally obtain a copy within a few days. The combination of database searching with *Inter-Library Loan* can make a small library almost as useful as a large one and save a long trip.

Once you have identified most of the key articles in your field, you should begin to read them. Pay particular attention to the introductions to the articles: What was known at the time the authors began their work? What are the major theories? What are the major unsolved problems? At this point, do not worry about the details of the methods and results. Read the abstract and the conclusion, if there is one, to learn the basic results. Skim the rest. Check the reference list for articles you may have missed. In this way, you will begin to get a grasp of the subject area. You will find that certain experiments are the key ones in the field.

After this initial review, you can begin to focus on the methods of these key experiments. What are their strengths and weaknesses? Remember that well-trained scientists can make mistakes and sometimes overlook important problems of design. Some of these problems will be pointed out by other authors; some you may think of yourself. All experiments are not created equal. The fact that they are published in major journals does not make them perfect. In addition to the author, as few as three people may have read a particular paper—the editor and two reviewers. In any case, you will find that there are some unsolved problems, some theories to be tested, some conflicting results to be resolved. These may give you an idea for your own study.

Style Guide for Written Assignments

(Your instructor may have different guidelines.)

1. All papers should be typewritten, although you may turn in hand-written papers if you have excellent handwriting.
2. Papers must not exceed the assigned length. (Assigned length is based on typewritten papers, which have approximately 250 words per page.)
3. All assignments should be prepared in APA style; see Chapter 13 and the *Publication Manual of the American Psychological Association* (1983).
4. Use standard-size (8 1/2-by-11-inch) paper with smooth edges. Do not use erasable paper. Do not use a cover or cover sheet. Fasten pages with paper clips, not staples.
5. For all assignments (except for a complete paper in APA format), the following information should be placed in the upper right-hand corner of the first page:

   Title of Project
   Your Name
   Lab Section/Instructor
   Date

   The assignment should follow immediately (not on the next page).
6. The page number should appear in the upper right-hand corner of every page.
7. Leave a 1 1/2-inch margin at the top and bottom and on both sides.
8. Double-space *everything*.
9. Keep a photocopy of everything you submit.
10. Part of your grade will be based on grammar, spelling, and other basic writing skills.
11. Papers must be submitted on time, except with prior permission.
12. Papers may be resubmitted within one week of their being returned to you with all errors corrected and comments accounted for.   ❏

SUMMARY

1. Psychology is a science essentially like any other science.
2. There are four ways of knowing about behavior: authority, logic, intuition, and science.

3. Authority plays a diminished role in science compared with other social institutions.

4. Logic plays an important role in science but is secondary in importance to observation.

5. Intuitive methods of knowing about behavior include common sense and mysticism.

6. Common sense is limited in its usefulness to science because it changes from time to time and place to place and cannot predict new knowledge.

7. Scientific knowledge often contradicts common sense, but ultimately it rests on a certain kind of common sense.

8. Mystical experiences are of limited usefulness in science because they are difficult to convey to another person and their insights are often invalid.

9. There is not one scientific method but many scientific methods.

10. Science is a way of obtaining knowledge based on objective observations.

11. Characteristics of science are that it is empirical, objective, self-correcting, progressive, tentative, parsimonious, and concerned with theory.

12. Psychology used to be considered a science that dealt with mental events but is now usually considered to deal with observable events and those that may be inferred from observable events.

13. Humanistic psychology attempts to deal with aspects of human experience that are slighted by the rest of psychology but does so at the expense of scientific rigor.

14. Science has five major working assumptions: the reality, regularity, and rationality of the world; the discoverability of how the world works; and the operation of causality.

15. Scientists assume that the world is real, but they do not assume that it is just the way it appears to be.

16. The assumption of rationality means that the world is believed to be understandable via logical thinking.

17. The assumption of regularity means that the world is believed to follow the same laws in all times and places.

18. The assumption of discoverability means that scientists believe that it is possible to find out how the world works.

19. The assumption of causality means that all events are believed to have causes.

20. Sources for the literature review include textbooks, handbooks, *Psychological Abstracts*, *Science Citation Index*, *Current Contents*, and computerized databases such as *PsycLIT/PsycINFO*.

21. Written assignments should be prepared according to the guidelines in the chapter and in the APA *Publication Manual*.

Suggestions for Further Reading

CAMPBELL, N. (1953). *What is science?* New York: Dover. This book, originally published in 1921, is a classic introduction to the nature of science. It is brief and particularly clear in its discussion of the nature of scientific laws and theories.

CONANT, J. B. (1961). *Science and common sense.* New Haven, CT: Yale University Press. This book shows by examples from the natural sciences how science grew out of a concern with practical problems and how science differs from technology in its emphasis on speculative knowledge to satisfy curiosity about the world.

REED, J. G. (1992). *Library use: A handbook for psychology* (2nd ed.). Washington, DC: American Psychological Association. This very useful book is designed for undergraduates who are doing library work in psychology for the first time.

ⅢⅢ➡ A CASE IN POINT ⬅ⅢⅢ

Each chapter in this book has a case study that illustrates at least one issue raised in the text. These cases are generally more complex than an exercise and usually have no single best solution. You will need to use your judgment to complete the case, and different people will often come to different justifiable conclusions.

Mike's Research Project

Mike was a sophomore psych major at State University. One weekend when he was home, he and his family got into a discussion of his experimental psychology project, which concerned the reasons why teenagers use drugs. Mike said that he suspected that teenagers who use drugs are seeking a substitute for the satisfactions others get through close personal relationships. He was describing what he had found so far in his library search when his father suggested that he read an interesting article in last week's Sunday supplement from the local paper. "It quoted several persons who worked with drug users, each of whom explained drugs on the basis of their own personal experiences, some as past drug abusers, and all with teenagers. The article said that it was obvious why kids used drugs: too much money and free time, television, and the breakdown of the family."

Mike's mother had a different idea. "It's all a reaction to the Vietnam War. There was much less drug use before Vietnam; now there's a lot. It's a simple matter of logic."

Mike's little sister, Jennifer, had been listening to the conversation. "All the people I know who use drugs are just weird, and there's no point in trying to figure them out; they're just different from everyone else. If you want to know why they use drugs, you'll have to become a pothead and try it for yourself."

This suggestion got his mother's attention in a hurry. "I'm worried enough about your being down there at the university as it is without your getting involved with drugs. There are some things we can never know because we aren't supposed to. You should just pick another topic—or better yet, another major."

Mike's father said, "I think Jennifer has a point. Psychology may be a science, but because it deals with the mind, it can't be done the way chemistry is. You can't put the mind in a test tube. You need to use different methods. You should ask drug users why they do it."

Later, as he drove back to school, Mike realized that he had not been able to answer their arguments. He reread the first chapter in his textbook and wrote a letter to his parents.

REQUIRED: Compose Mike's letter for him.

≡ READING BETWEEN THE LINES ≡

One of the most important goals of an experimental-psychology course is to develop skills in critically evaluating published studies and other claims made on the basis of evidence. Any set of data always has alternative explanations, but some are more plausible than others. Students need to develop a healthy skepticism for claims made about data. The problems that will be presented in this section contain conclusions that are questionable. Study each one to see what other hypotheses might account for the data.

Some of the problems are fairly easy; others are very difficult. Because all involve actual cases, they also involve questions of interpretation that authorities of one sort or another have differed on. Most of these examples have been published in the scientific literature, passing through the peer review process with their original interpretations. In some cases, the problem of interpreting was so difficult that scientists worked for years to find the proper interpretation of the results. In other cases, the results are still debated. So don't feel discouraged if you cannot see immediately what is questionable about the interpretation of the data. Study each problem to see what other interpretations might be possible. Begin to learn to read between the lines. The answers are given in Appendix D.

1.1 GUNS DON'T KILL PEOPLE; PEOPLE KILL PEOPLE

The gun lobby says that guns don't kill people; people kill people. This argument is used to refute the desirability of stricter gun-control laws. On the other hand, it is known that the presence of a gun makes it more likely that a given situation will result in a death. Analyze the gun lobby's slogan. What assumption does it make about the causes of human behavior? What would you suggest as an answer to the slogan?   ■

1.2 IS PRAYER EFFECTIVE?

Sir Francis Galton wanted to know whether prayer changes things. He reasoned that the royalty would be prayed for by more people and should therefore live longer than average. He found, instead, that royalty lived 64 years, intellectuals lived 68, and gentry lived 70, on the average (Webb, Campbell, Schwartz, & Sechrest, 1966). What do you think of Galton's reasoning? What way or ways of knowing about behavior did Galton use?   ∎

✓ EXERCISES

1.1 WHICH WAY OF KNOWING?

Read the following statements, and identify the way of knowing that best characterizes which method Professor Martin uses in each case.

Topic

a. After puzzling over a novel that discusses traveling backward in time, he concludes that the notion implies that a person would have to be alive before he or she was born.

Common Sense

b. He decides after a life-threatening illness that he should devote more time to his teaching and less to research.

Authority

c. His colleague, an expert in statistics, advises him to use a certain type of test to analyze his data.

Science

d. He concludes from the results of his first test in perception that those students who had previously taken a course in research methods scored 10 points higher than those who had not.

1.2 USING THE *PSYCHOLOGICAL ABSTRACTS*

The purpose of this exercise is to enable you to learn to use the *Psychological Abstracts* to do a library search.

a. Choose a topic to research. This may be a topic that you have been interested in, or it may be one assigned by your instructor. Do not worry too much about whether this is the best topic to study. You may feel that there are too many interesting topics, or none that interests you enough. The best solution is to take one and dig in. You will likely find that it becomes more interesting as you get into it, or you will decide quickly that it is the wrong one. The most important thing is to get started. At this stage you will probably be looking through textbooks and handbooks.

b. Try to narrow the topic down to a manageable size. Say you start out with an interest in developmental psychology. You will find that this is a very large topic in itself. If you turn to an introductory psychology text, you will find at least an entire chapter devoted to the topic. Looking through the chapter, you will find sections devoted to smaller divisions, such as Piaget's theory. Even this covers a lot of ground, so look for more manageable sections. You may find a heading on moral development that discusses Kohlberg's theory, which grew out of Piaget's thinking. Reading that section, you will find that Carol Gilligan has suggested that Kohlberg's theory does not apply to women. So you may narrow your interest to gender differences in moral development. If possible, make your topic a specific question: Does the moral thinking of women depend more on social responsibilities, whereas men's is based on rights?

Now you are ready to go to the *Psychological Abstracts*. Starting with the most recent complete volume, you will find that the volume is bound in various sections. One or more sections will contain the Subject Index. This section contains an alphabetical listing of topics covered in the *Abstracts*. You will find a listing for moral development, which contains a series of one- or two-line descriptions, each followed by a number. Each description concerns a different article or book, and the number is the key to the article. Find which descriptions sound relevant to your topic, and write down their numbers.

Then turn to the sections that contain the abstracts of the articles. These are listed in numerical order and contain, usually, the actual abstract as it appears in the original article, together with the complete reference, including the authors' names. After you have gone through the most recent several years' volumes, you will generally have enough articles to begin to see the general shape of your topic.

Now look up the articles or books that are on your list. Skim them to see if they are actually relevant. Make up a list of about ten references in APA style (including alphabetical order). Turn them in, together with a statement of the question or topic that you are researching.

1.3 USING THE *SCIENCE CITATION INDEX*

It is good to do this exercise after the *Psychological Abstracts* exercise. If you do so, you may use one or more of the references from that search as the starting reference. In that way, you will see how the *Science Citation Index* can supplement the *Abstracts* search. (But note that if the starting reference you chose is too recent, you may find that it has not yet been cited by anyone.)

a. Go to the library and locate the *Science Citation Index*.

b. Take one of the annual volumes labeled *Citation Index* and turn to the inside cover. Read the instructions on the use of the index.

c. Take an article or book referred to in some standard psychology text. (So that people will use different articles, you should choose one whose author's name starts with the same letter as yours.) We will call this the starting reference.

d. Find references to several articles or books that refer to the starting reference. We will call these "citing articles." Continue until you have at least five references to your starting reference. You may have to use more than one starting reference in order to get five citing articles. Example: On page 131 of a certain book, an article by Weisstein and Bisaha (1972) is cited. Turning to the references in the back of the book, we find:

> Weisstein, N., & Bisaha, J. (1972). Gratings mask bars and bars mask gratings: Visual frequency response to a periodic stimuli. *Science, 176,* 10047–10049.

Turning to the 1976 *Citation Index*, we find that this article was cited by four authors:

> Fiorenti, A. *Vision Research, 16,* 1303, 1976.
> Kulikows, J. J. *Vision Research, 16,* 1419, 1976.
> May, J. G. *Science, 192,* 145, 1976.
> White, C. W. *Perception and Psychophysics, 19,* 281, 1976.

(The names are truncated to a maximum of eight characters.) Turning now to the volume marked *Source Index*, we find under "Fiorenti, A." that the full reference is:

Fiorenti, A., Siretean, R., & Spinelle, D. (1976). Lines and gratings: Different inter-
ocular aftereffects. *Vision Research, 16,* 1303–1309.

e. Turn in a list containing a complete reference to the article cited in the book and complete references to five articles that cite it. (If there aren't five articles that cite the one starting reference, you may use two or more starting references.)   ❏

2

The Goals of Science

In Chapter 1 we discussed what science is and what its working assumptions are. From this you may already have an idea of what the goal of science is. Broadly speaking, the goal of any science is simply to understand the world. Of course, such a broad statement requires elaboration. The purpose of this chapter is to discuss in some detail how scientists go about trying to understand the world. Before we start to talk about science, however, we will discuss pseudoscience, because oftentimes it is easier to understand what something is by contrasting it with something else.

PSEUDOSCIENCE

Pseudoscience is whatever attempts to be science but is not. Philosophers have struggled to define the difference between science and pseudoscience in a rigorous way. Because science itself is so difficult to define, they have generally come to the conclusion that there are no demarcation criteria between the two. In other words, there is no single criterion or set of criteria that will always separate science from pseudoscience.

Although there is no way of definitively separating science from pseudoscience, certain endeavors are clearly science, others are clearly pseudoscience, and for still others the jury is out. Pseudosciences generally lack certain characteristics of science. The following checklist is useful in deciding whether an endeavor is science or pseudoscience. You will see that each one is the negative of one characteristic of science discussed in these two chapters. You may also notice that some areas of psychology do not fare especially well on one or another of the items on the checklist. We must admit that not all areas of psychology are equally scientific.

pseudo-psychology
any of various disciplines or movements mistakenly regarded as psychology but not meeting the criteria of psychology

A list of all the **pseudopsychologies** that exist today would be long and controversial, but many people would include parapsychology, biorhythms, astrology, and much of the human potential movement. Their popularity warrants our discussing the marks of a pseudoscience. We will use parapsychology, the most popular of the pseudopsychologies, to illustrate our points.

Lack of Objectivity or Concern with Measurement

One can read the parapsychological literature in vain to find careful measurement of conditions in an experiment. This is especially significant when one considers that the purpose of parapsychological research is to rule out normal sensory means of perceiving a stimulus. I have never seen a paper in which the possibility of sound being conducted between a sender and a receiver in a mental telepathy experiment has been measured according to normal physical standards—that is, in terms of decibels. One paper said that normal means of communication were impossible because the wall between the subjects was "thick." In a report published in the most scientifically respectable journal in which a parapsychology paper has ever appeared, Puthoff and Targ (1974) studied the alleged psychic powers of Uri Geller. Part of the experiment involved sending messages through a "shielded room." Puthoff and Targ did not specify anything about the room except that it was double walled, was made of steel, and had double doors. Researchers in hearing know that no room is totally soundproof, so they commonly specify the acoustic properties of a room, explicitly stating by how many decibels the walls of the room will reduce a sound that passes through it. This elementary information was omitted from Puthoff and Targ's report.

Concepts Are Not Disconfirmable

Because it is impossible to specify who has paranormal powers or when they are present, it is impossible to disconfirm the paranormal hypothesis by negative evidence. Believers in the paranormal may say that psychic ability is spontaneous or that it is subject to "negative vibes" when skeptics are present. This is called the "shyness effect." The result of this immunizing strategy is that belief in parapsychology continues after a century of negative evidence.

Lack of Formal Logic and Mathematics

Although there is much philosophical speculation present in parapsychological writings, some of it very sophisticated, it is fair to say that formal logic and mathematics are completely absent.

Isolation from the Rest of Science

Parapsychologists generally publish their findings in their own journals and do not interact with other scientists. The parapsychologists would say that the reason for their isolation is the hostility of scientists, which forces them to start their own societies and journals. The scientists would say that the parapsychological work does not warrant inclusion in the standard journals.

The parapsychologists' social isolation is related to their intellectual isolation. By and large, the theoretical discussions of parapsychology do not relate to neighboring sciences.

Lack of Progress

After more than a century of work on the paranormal, researchers are still trying to prove that ESP, telepathy, and so forth, even exist. It is a useful exercise to read the introductions to articles in parapsychology. A large number of them state that the purpose of the paper is to prove the existence of a paranormal phenomenon.

Attempts to Answer Ultimate Questions

It has been said that science is the substitution of unimportant questions that can be solved for important ones that cannot. In any case, science avoids dealing with ultimate questions, such as the meaning of life. Parapsychology largely rejects this property of science. J. B. Rhine, for example, had originally intended to be a minister. In college, he began to have doubts about religion and went into botany instead. After hearing a lecture by Sir Arthur Conan Doyle on spiritualism, he dedicated his life to psychic research.

Lack of Precise Definition of Terms

A good example of imprecise definition is the term *occult* as used by many to define an area of study. The term simply means hidden or poorly understood. Those who use it do not indicate why the subject is occult or whether the information once was known and now is lost, whether it is known only to a special class, or whether nobody understands it.

Definition of Terms by Exclusion

A good example of definition by exclusion is extrasensory perception. Because perception, as normally understood, involves the senses by definition, the term *extrasensory perception,* strictly speaking, is absurd. If it means perception by means of receptors that now are not known or understood, such a definition would include many other processes of little interest to parapsychologists, such as bird migration. Psychic scientist Thelma Moss defines parapsychology as "anything for which we do not have a material explanation" (Allan, 1975, p. 5). Taken seriously, this definition would include most of the phenomena studied by scientists in all fields.

Lack of Lawfulness

As we will discuss later in this chapter, a science that has discovered no laws is no science at all. Extrasensory perception (ESP) is such a nonscience. In brief, there is no convincing evidence that ESP even exists. In 1882, the year of the founding of the (British) Society for Psychical Research, Henry Sidgwick, its first president, spoke of the task of finding convincing evidence for ESP. "We must drive the objector into the position of being forced either to admit the phenomena as inexplicable, at least by him, or to accuse the investigators either of lying or cheating or of a blindness or forgetfulness incompatible with any intellectual condition except an absolute idiocy" (Hansel, 1966, p. 27).

Nearly 100 years later Martin Johnson, chairman of the Parapsychology Laboratory of the University of Utrecht, Netherlands, speaking to an audience in Chapel Hill, North Carolina, one of the world centers of ESP research, said, "At this stage, parapsychology is badly in need of a repeatable experiment" (1976, p. 151). Similar statements can be found in almost any issue of the *Journal of Parapsychology* or the *Proceedings of the American Society for Psychical Research.* R. A. McConnell says, "The result [of the psychological nature of ESP] is a poor record on repeatability" (1977, p. 430).

If there are no repeatable experiments, it follows that no lawful relationships can be stated about the occurrence of ESP. It is not possible to state the conditions under which ESP occurs. There are no personality types, age groups, or nationalities that tend to show ESP. Distance is not a factor in ESP performance.

These circumstances could be interpreted as proving that ESP does not conform to the usual physical laws as expressed, for example, by the law of the decrease in effectiveness of a signal with distance. More reasonable is the notion that there is no regularity of any sort to be found and, hence, no statable law. Some persons believe that a condition of quiet rest is conducive to ESP; others maintain that ESP works best under states of extreme stress. Some say that ESP is a primitive ability that we are evolving away from as our senses become keener; others believe that ESP is an evolutionarily advanced form of communication that will become more prominent over evolutionary time.

Lack of Theoretical Agreement

Theories are developed to explain lawful regularities. It follows that pseudosciences might be short on theories because they are short on facts. Actually the reverse is true. Literally dozens of theories of parapsychology exist, but they bear little relation to one another and, more important, to the rest of science. They are largely castles in the air. A standard handbook reviews current parapsychology theories and states: "We cannot produce a theory of psi (parapsychology) which is both comprehensive and credible. The field is strewn with dead and dying hypotheses and desperate expedients" (Chari, 1977, p. 806). The article concludes that there is "a complete lack of anything remotely like an explanatory theory of ESP (extra-sensory perception) and PK (psychokinesis)" (p. 819). This is a fair and modest assessment. Dozens of theories of ESP exist, every one as capable of explaining the data as any other. Ramakrishna Rao surveyed 20 of them and concluded: "While none [of the theories] is entirely satisfactory in explaining psi, each of them seems to contain some fruitful ideas. . . . The need of the day is for theory and research to go hand in hand" (1977, p. 344). It is unheard of for a scientific field to have dozens of theories, each of which is equally well supported by evidence. The absence of theory and empirical laws is the main reason most scientists conclude that ESP is a pseudoscience.

Exaggerated Importance of a Few People

Although there are leaders in every field of endeavor, pseudosciences are characterized by the dominance of one person or a few persons whose work is taken as revolutionary and fundamental to further progress in the field. A science that is the province of one or a few persons is almost certain to be a pseudoscience. Most sciences have a historical continuity with science as a whole and have enough people working in the field to prevent domination by one person. This characteristic of dominance is not as typical of parapsychology as it is of, say, dianetics, which is the brainchild of L. Ron Hubbard, or the orgonomy of Wilhelm Reich. Nevertheless, J. B. Rhine was the virtual guru of the parapsychology movement for many years. In addition, a few "gifted" people like Uri Geller have received attention because they have been able to produce certain effects without admitting to the use of magic.

In summary, pseudoscience differs from science by violating a number of its chief characteristics: objectivity and concern with measurement, disconfirmability, use of formal logic and mathematics, unity of science, progress, lack of interest in ultimate questions, precise definition of terms, avoidance of definition by exclusion, lawfulness, theoretical coherence, and collegiality.

THE SCHOOLTEACHER WHOSE CAR WOULDN'T START

This is a true story about a certain schoolteacher who had a car that often refused to start. We tell this story to make some important points about how scientists work. This teacher was neither a scientist nor a mechanic, nor was she particularly interested in cars. When this car of hers would fail to start, it would act completely dead: it would not crank, let alone cough a few times. This would happen when it had plenty of gas and the battery was charged and even when the car had just been running fine.

The schoolteacher's mechanic poked around a while and diagnosed the problem as a poor connection between the battery terminal and the clamp on the cable that led from the battery. Without mentioning his diagnosis, he just told her that whenever the problem arose, she should take some object and strike the clamp sharply. When she tried this, the car promptly started and ran perfectly.

One day her car failed to start in the parking lot of a shopping center. She got out of the car, raised the hood, took off her shoe, and gave the battery clamp a few good whacks. This greatly amused a man who was sitting in the car next to her, waiting for his wife to come back with their groceries.

His laughter stopped abruptly when the car roared to life and the woman drove off with an air of satisfaction. The schoolteacher's approach to the problem with the car was intelligent, but to this point it was not what we would call scientific. She beat on the battery clamp because it made the car start, and that was all she cared about, so long as it worked. This is the commonsense approach to a problem that we discussed in Chapter 1.

Over time, the woman developed a rule to guide her actions in this situation that went as follows: If the car fails to crank and the battery has a good charge, beating on the battery clamp will cause the car to start. This rule worked almost every time. (Of course, there are other possible causes of a car's failing to start.)

Eventually, she asked the mechanic why this worked. He explained that corrosion built up between the battery terminal and the cable clamp. This corrosion, which did not conduct electricity, prevented the electricity from flowing out of the battery, through the cable, and to the starter. Beating on the clamp usually got rid of enough corrosion that the electricity would flow to the starter.

Then, one day, the car would not start, and beating on the battery clamp did not work. The schoolteacher reasoned that if there was too much corrosion on the terminal to be freed by simply hitting the clamp, perhaps she could create a better electrical connection if she removed the clamp and scraped away the corrosion with sandpaper. Sure enough, after she cleaned off the terminal, the car roared to life.

What she had done was develop a prediction based on her understanding of the principle behind her rule. She tested this prediction and found it to be true.

The steps in her understanding are the same steps that scientists often take.

1. Observe that there is a problem: The car won't start.
2. Start with some rule of thumb that will generally solve the problem: If the engine will not crank, beat on the battery clamp.
3. Develop a more formal rule: If the battery is charged and the engine will not crank, beat on the battery clamp.
4. Develop an understanding of the principle behind the problem: Corrosion on the battery terminal prevents the flow of electricity to the rest of the car.

5. Based on your understanding of the situation, make new predictions to take into account those situations in which your rule fails: If the corrosion is removed, the car will start.
6. Test your predictions to see if they come true.

Our schoolteacher went through the basic steps that scientists use in understanding a problem. In the light of this example, let us turn to a further elaboration of these steps. We may group them into two larger goals: the discovery of regularities and the development of theories.

THE DISCOVERY OF REGULARITIES

The subgoal of discovering regularities can be considered in three ways: the description of behavior, the discovery of lawful relationships among aspects of behavior, and the search for causes. For convenience we will consider them separately, even though they are three aspects of the same subgoal.

■ Description

The first step in any science is to describe the phenomena considered to be important for the science to deal with. We must define events and entities such as stimuli and responses, drives and motives, or neuroses and psychoses. This step seems so modest that often we are tempted to skip it and go on to the next one, the discovery of laws. We must have some agreement, though, on just what it is that we are going to study. Before we can find out what causes a person to become a sociopath, we must carefully describe the behavior of the sociopathic person and find out what sociopaths have in common. Only when we have a fairly clear description of the sociopathic personality can we look for factors in a person's background or physiology that caused him or her to become sociopathic.

The importance of description illustrates the close relationship between psychology and the biological sciences. For many years a chief occupation of biologists was the description and classification of living forms. This process is still important today, but only recently have biologists been able to get beyond the descriptive level to study the mechanisms of life processes. Because psychology is a young science, much descriptive work still remains to be done. Perhaps nowhere is this more evident than in the area of personality, where there is fundamental disagreement about the way to go about describing personality. Several quite different approaches to personality description currently exist.

Type theories attempt to classify persons into particular categories or types, much as a botanist would classify a plant. Trait theories, on the other hand, see people as differing in amount, rather than kind, on various traits that all persons share to a greater or lesser extent. Social-learning theories play down the personal causes of behavior in favor of situational causes.

Besides these theories, there are others. Without judging the relative merits of the various theories, we may observe that the large number of conflicting approaches to describing personality reflects a relatively primitive state of science.

Lest anyone think we are emphasizing one area of psychology over another, let us consider an example from perception. Complete lack of agreement exists about the classification of odor qualities. Many odor classification schemes have been proposed over the centuries, but to the present none has demonstrated its superiority over the others. It is fair to say that the absence of a satisfactory odor classification has severely hampered the development of satisfactory theories of smell and lawful relationships among variables.

Description of phenomena is crucially important to a science because it defines the subject matter for which laws are sought and theories are developed. If the descriptive phase of a science is skipped or done carelessly, it may become necessary to return to square one and start over again. All too often experimenters, yielding to the temptation to skip the difficult descriptive phase, jump into the next phase of developing laws. You might say, "I have noticed that my cat seems aggressive at certain times, fighting often with other cats and killing lots of mice. I will study the conditions under which this behavior occurs and look for its causes." What you have overlooked is that fighting with other cats and killing mice are two different kinds of behaviors. The cat that is fighting hisses, arches the back, and erects the fur. The cat that is hunting and killing a mouse has sleek fur, slinks quietly, and generally shows a different behavior pattern from that of a cat that is fighting. A careful description of the behaviors in these two situations will reveal that they are not the same class of behaviors at all. This kind of mistake is made frequently in psychology. Unfortunately, there is no simple way to avoid it. You must be alert to the danger and diligent in describing behavior thoughtfully.

Not only does description of behavior define the subject matter of a science, it can also be thought of as *creating* the subject matter. An example is the use of the electroencephalograph (EEG) to describe dreaming. Since antiquity people had reported dreams, and for many years psychologists and others had studied them. Yet some scientists denied that dreams were a separate stage of sleep, stating that those who reported having dreams were merely describing a mental activity that was more or less continuous throughout sleep. In 1953 Eugene Aserinsky and Nathaniel Kleitman, while studying the EEG of sleeping persons, noticed occasional periods of a distinct type of eye movement they called rapid eye movement, or REM for short. They also noted that REM was associated with particular types of EEG activity. When subjects were awakened during a bout of REM, they usually reported that they had been dreaming. When they were awakened during non-REM sleep, they generally reported they had not been dreaming. This discovery led to further research on dreaming that has been both exciting and informative. The direct observation of the response of dreaming by the measurement of REM and related EEG activity has been important in the study of dreaming, and few people today deny that there is such a state as the dream.

Many other examples exist. For years sexual behavior was not studied in the laboratory because of strong taboos. A widely held belief was that women could experience two kinds of orgasm, vaginal orgasm and the so-called clitoral orgasm, depending on the method of stimulation and other factors. William Masters and Virginia Johnson began taking photographs and other measurements of people engaged in sex. Their research made clear that only one kind of female orgasm existed. Years of myth flew out the window. Another belief was that women did not respond to erotica as men did. Yet when suitable measuring devices were built to record the activity of the vagina, women were shown to respond to erotic stimuli in much the same way as men did (Fisher & Byrne, 1978). The women, however, were not aware of their vaginal behavior and so did not interpret their response as sexual arousal.

■ Discovering Laws

law
a statement that certain events are regularly associated with each other in an orderly way

As the describing of behavior progresses, various regularities appear among behavioral events. These regularities form laws of behavior. A **law** is simply a statement that certain events are regularly associated. The frustration-aggression law states that frustration causes aggression. (This law is commonly known as the frustration-aggression hypothesis for reasons that do not concern us here.) In other words, the occurrence of frustration is regularly associated with aggression. Psychology has many examples of laws, because any time a regular association between two variables exists you have a law.

It is not necessary to have a perfect relation between the two variables in order to have a law. As we noted earlier in the discussion of causality, some laws are probabilistic; that is, there is a regularity between two variables, but the regularity is not such that every time one variable is present the other is too. Because of the complexity of behavior, laws of behavior are often stated in statistical form.

Laws do not have to state cause-effect relationships between events; any regular relationship is a law. When we described the behavior of a fighting cat, we noted that the cat hisses, arches its back, and has its fur erect. These events are regularly associated together when a cat fights and so can be considered a law. Thus, description and discovery of laws are actually part of a single activity; we have separated them in our discussion only for the purpose of exposition. In our earlier example, description of the sociopathic personality produces a statement of a lawful relationship among the various characteristics of people we call sociopaths.

By extension of this idea, discovery of a law becomes not the capstone of scientific activity but one of the early steps. In our example of the schoolteacher whose car would not start, her rule—if the engine would not crank and the battery was charged, beating on the battery clamp would permit the car to start—was a kind of law. She developed this law of the car's behavior before she had any theoretical understanding of why it worked. The meaning of the term *law* will become clearer later as we contrast law and theory.

■ The Search for Causes

We have said that the goal of science is to understand the world. Another way of putting this is to say that scientists search for the causes of the events that we observe. If we know the causes of child abuse, for example, then we believe that we understand child abuse. The search for causes is so important that all the other goals of science that we will talk about can be considered as subgoals of it.

John Stuart Mill was a 19th-century philosopher who wanted to clarify how we can go about making valid claims about causality. We will discuss three of the methods he proposed.

The Method of Agreement

Mill's method of agreement looks for the cause of an event by trying to find a single circumstance that is common to all occurrences of some event. Consider the discovery of the part of the brain responsible for speech.

The extent to which the brain acts as a single unit rather than having specialized parts that perform particular functions was a major controversy in the 19th century. Paul Broca was a French physician of the time. Several of his patients experienced strokes that left them unable to speak, a condition now known as expressive aphasia. A stroke is lay terminology for damage to brain tissue caused by interruption of blood flow to parts of the brain, either by clots that block blood vessels or by a leak in a blood vessel. In an attempt to determine the part of the brain that might be responsible for speech, he performed autopsies on these patients after they died. It happens that strokes are highly variable in their extent and location in the brain. Some are very large, and others are quite small; they can affect any part of the brain. All of Broca's aphasic patients had strokes that affected the left hemisphere of the brain, but they varied in location and extent. By carefully comparing the brains of all his aphasic patients, he found that one particular area of the frontal cortex was involved in all patients whose strokes left them unable to speak.

For purposes of illustration, let us suppose that he had three aphasic patients whose strokes affected more than one part of the left hemisphere of the brain:

CASE	AREAS OF LEFT HEMISPHERE OF BRAIN AFFECTED	APHASIC?
1	Frontal, Parietal, Temporal	Yes
2	Frontal, Parietal	Yes
3	Frontal, Temporal	Yes

We can see that all three cases of expressive aphasia had damage to the frontal area of the left hemisphere. By Mill's method of agreement, we can conclude that the frontal area of the left hemisphere is responsible for speech. (Actually, the area concerned is only a small part of the frontal area, now known as Broca's area.)

The Method of Difference

The second of Mill's methods that we will consider is the method of difference. This method looks for the cause of an event by trying to find a single difference between cases that share some characteristic and those that do not.

Suppose that Broca had two stroke victims, one of whom had aphasia and one of whom did not. Then he could look for what was different between the two patients. He might have found the following pattern:

CASE	AREAS OF LEFT HEMISPHERE OF BRAIN AFFECTED	APHASIC?
4	Frontal, Parietal, Temporal	Yes
5	Parietal, Temporal	No

Here there is a difference between the aphasic case and the other: only the aphasic case had damage of the frontal area. Therefore, Broca could conclude that frontal-area damage is responsible for aphasia.

The Method of Concomitant Variation

The third of Mill's methods that we will talk about is the method of concomitant variation. This method looks for the cause of an event by trying to find some circumstance or condition that varies together with the rate or degree of some event.

The method of concomitant variation is useful when the cause of some event is present in all individuals in the population to varying degrees. For example, we know that all people experience stress in their lives. Because all members of the population experience the potential cause, it is not possible to use the methods of agreement or difference to determine if stress causes illness. We can, however, see if there is *concomitant variation* between stress and illness. In other words, we can see if the likelihood of illnesses is greater in a group of individuals who experience more stress than in another, less stressed group. The method of concomitant variation can be schematized as follows:

GROUP	POSSIBLE CAUSES	ILLNESS?
1	Less stress, germs, flu season	Little
2	More stress, germs, flu season	Much

Of course, the method of concomitant variation may also be applicable in cases where a greater amount of the causal agent is associated with *less* of the event we are concerned about: more money for schools may be associated with lower dropout rates, for example.

You may recognize that the method of concomitant variation is another name for correlation. Correlational techniques will be discussed later in this book.

Problems in Applying John Stuart Mill's Methods

The three methods we have discussed are very useful in helping us discover causes for events in the world. They have distinct limitations, however.

Consider Brian, a college student who goes out to the local campus bar three Friday nights in a row. This bar provides complementary pretzels to its customers. The first night Brian drinks beer and eats pretzels, and the next day he wakes up with a hangover. The second night he drinks wine coolers and eats pretzels, and the next day he wakes up with a hangover. The third night he drinks scotch and soda and eats pretzels, and the next day he wakes up with a hangover. After waking up feeling terrible the third Saturday in a row, he begins to wonder what is causing his hangover. Using Mill's method of agreement, he reasons that he consumed different drinks each time, but he always ate pretzels. Because pretzels are common to all three incidents, he concludes that pretzels cause hangovers.

Use of Mill's method of agreement led Brian to commit two fallacies. First, in concluding that pretzels cause hangovers, he *confused cause with coincidence*. Pretzels were only associated with his hangover by chance. He might have eaten potato chips with his drinks instead of pretzels, or even nothing at all, and still have gotten a hangover. The association of pretzels with hangover was pure coincidence. The second fallacy Brian committed was to *overlook a common causal factor* that was present every time he had a hangover: alcohol. Mill's methods will never find the true cause if it is not in the list of candidate causes in the first place.

The method of difference is subject to the same two limitations as the method of agreement. Consider Susan, a college student who usually does well on tests. After she did poorly on her research methods test, she realized that she had forgotten to wear her lucky sweatshirt. Using Mill's method of difference, she attributed her low grade to her not wearing the sweatshirt, because she believed that she had done everything the same as always, except for wearing the sweatshirt. Mill's method of difference led Susan to commit the fallacies of *confusing coincidence with cause* and *ignoring a possible cause*. Susan overlooked a number of possible causes: The material being tested might have been more difficult than usual, or the fact that she studied for the test together with her boyfriend might have made her less attentive to the material. She considered the lack of the sweatshirt to be a cause, when it was only coincidentally associated with performance.

Finally, the method of concomitant variation can lead one to *overlook a common causal factor*. Jonathan is a fourth-grader whose father keeps up on the latest scientific methods of improving his children's school performance.

After reading that boys who wear longer pants tend to have larger vocabularies, he suggests to his wife that they start buying longer pants for Jonathan. In this case, Jonathan's father overlooked something that was a cause of both long pants and larger vocabularies: age. He also committed the fallacy of ignoring a possible cause: What he thought was a cause was itself caused by a third event that he had overlooked.

In all of these examples where the true cause was ignored, the individuals overlooked the well-known adage that *correlation does not prove causation.*

There is no simple way of avoiding these fallacies. Brian, Susan, and Jonathan's father all used Mill's methods as Mill intended them to be used. The problem is that the methods are not foolproof. The best antidote is general knowledge of the phenomenon being studied, which will prevent one from making silly mistakes, as in these examples.

Let us return to Broca for a moment to illustrate this point. Suppose that all of Broca's aphasic patients suffered their strokes while fighting with their spouses. The factor of fighting with one's spouse was common to all cases, and therefore is a candidate cause of aphasia. Before we conclude that fighting with a spouse is a cause of aphasia, however, we would want to know why that should cause aphasia instead of some other type of stroke. In other words, our general knowledge of strokes and aphasia would guide us in selecting candidate causes for consideration. In the absence of some theoretical connection between aphasia and fighting with one's spouse, we would tend to ignore this candidate cause.

Further, Broca's background as a physician gave him understanding that led him in the right direction. He thought to do autopsies on the patients, to look specifically at their brains, and to notice that one particular small area of the frontal lobe was affected. Others who were not physicians no doubt had observed stroke patients who showed aphasia, but they had not done the autopsies.

THE DEVELOPMENT OF THEORIES

The ultimate goal of science is the development of a theory to explain the lawful relationships that exist in a particular field. We will define the concept of theory shortly. For now we can briefly say that a theory is a set of statements that organize a large body of facts (laws) into a single explanatory system. In a nutshell, a theory is an explanation for a set of facts.

■ Everyday Uses of the Term *Theory*

Before we can understand the importance of theory building, however, we must point out some very common misconceptions surrounding the idea of theory. There are some everyday uses of the term that are very different from the scientific usage. These uses can cause misunderstanding of the true significance of theory in science.

Theory and Fact

We often hear theory used in distinction to fact. For example, someone might say, "Is it a fact that Lee Harvey Oswald acted alone in assassinating President Kennedy, or is it only a theory?" This usage confuses a theory with a hypothesis, which is proved either to be a "fact" or to be wrong. (See the discussion of hypotheses on pages 47–48). Actually, theories never "grow up and become facts" even when they are accepted as true by everyone.

Take the duplicity theory of vision. This theory was developed to account for a large number of facts about vision having to do with the differences between the functions of structures in the eyes known as rods and cones: color vision versus black-and-white, day vision versus night, and so forth. The term *duplicity* means that the retina is duplex; that is, it has two separate systems, the rod system and the cone system.

Now, duplicity theory is universally accepted as true (to be a "fact" in the everyday sense). Still, it has the status of a theory because it serves a theory's function of organizing a large body of facts (laws) into a single explanatory system. To go back to Oswald, if it were ever proved beyond a shadow of a doubt that he acted alone, we would then say that the single-assassin theory has been proved to be true.

Theory and Practice

Another popular usage of the term *theory* is in statements like the following: In theory, students should learn better if they expect unannounced quizzes, but in practice, it doesn't work that way. This usage drives a wedge between theory and the real world, as if theories exist in books and practice exists in the real world. The hope of any theorist is to explain events in the real world. The problem in the quiz example arises because the real-world situation contains complications not accounted for by the theory. The theory behind giving unannounced quizzes is true, but other factors in the real classroom situation make the prediction of the theory uncertain for that case.

■ What Is a Theory?

We can define the concept of theory either broadly or narrowly. Broadly speaking, a theory is a statement or set of statements about the relationships among variables. If the statements concern only a single relationship between variables, we are speaking of a law. However, sometimes a number of laws are tied together into a more general set of statements, which is called a theory. An example is Skinner's theory of operant conditioning, which makes statements about the effects of various reinforcement schedules on response rates, among other things. Skinnerian theory avoids using nonobserved

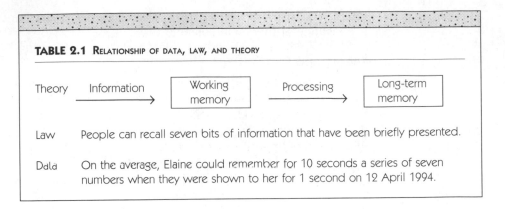

TABLE 2.1 RELATIONSHIP OF DATA, LAW, AND THEORY

Theory	Information $\longrightarrow$	Working memory	Processing $\longrightarrow$	Long-term memory

Law   People can recall seven bits of information that have been briefly presented.

Data   On the average, Elaine could remember for 10 seconds a series of seven numbers when they were shown to her for 1 second on 12 April 1994.

theory
a statement or set of statements explaining one or more laws, usually including one indirect concept needed to explain the relationship

concepts such as habit strength in favor of simply stating lawful relationships among directly observed variables. This is what Skinner meant when he said that theories of learning are not necessary (1950). In other words, he did not find it necessary to develop theoretical concepts that went beyond observable laws. Skinner's system, however, is a theory in the broader sense of a set of interrelated laws.

More often, the term **theory** is used in a second and stricter sense. According to this view, a theory is a statement or a set of statements about relationships among variables that includes at least one concept that is not directly observed but that is necessary to explain the relationship among the variables. Refer to Table 2.1. The statement at the bottom, about Elaine's ability to remember a series of numbers, concerns a specific set of observations on one person at one time under particular conditions. This statement has no generality. The middle statement is about the behavior of people in general under similar conditions. This is a general statement that is true whenever certain conditions obtain; therefore we are justified in calling it a law. At the top is a statement that is different from the middle or the bottom one. Depicted here is a brief outline of a theory of memory. This theory introduces concepts, such as working memory, that are not present at the level of law. These new concepts are theoretical concepts because they are invoked to explain the relationship between the variables in the middle statement. Specifically, the theory introduces the concept of working memory, which is said to be a stage in the processing of information into permanent form. All information to be remembered is held for a while in working memory before being transferred into long-term memory. Working memory is a theoretical concept because it is not seen or measured directly but must be inferred from behavior. This stage of processing can be inferred from several bases. Among the more important is the fact that only about seven items can be held briefly in memory after they have been presented together once, as when we remember a telephone number that we have just looked up. If more than about seven numbers are presented together, some of them are lost. In our long-term memory, on the other hand, no such limitation exists on the number of things we can recall. Thus, working memory is clearly different from long-term memory in its limited capacity to hold information. Psychology makes use of a number of unobservable concepts such as working memory in developing theories of behavior.

Note that working memory is never observed directly. No single way of measuring its effects defines the concept completely. Theoretical concepts are not observed directly; they can be defined only indirectly by reference to events that are directly observed. A theoretical concept is an invention of the scientist to account for laws of behavior. To take an example from physics, no one has ever seen an electron. It is a theoretical concept invented to account for particular laws of physics.

■ Theories Must Be Testable

The comic strip character Lucy once said that she had a perfect theory—it could not be proven right or wrong. This may seem like a good idea to Lucy, but to a scientist such a theory is worse than useless. A good theory must be capable of a clear test. It must make a definite prediction that can be proven right or wrong. The reason for this is the empirical nature of science. If science is based on empirical evidence, its theories must be capable of empirical testing. A theory of how people would behave in space colonies would not be a scientific theory because we cannot test it. Some day we may have space colonies, and such a theory would then be scientific because it could then be tested.

Not only must a theory be testable, it must be capable of being proven wrong. When most people attempt to test a theory, they try to prove that it is true. But in fact, the most fruitful test of a theory is to set up a condition in which it can fail. You may have heard the joke about the person who kept snapping his fingers in order to keep the elephants away. When his friend objected that there were no elephants around, he said "See, it works." Snapping his fingers as a test of this theory was nearly useless. There are many reasons other than finger snapping why there may be no elephants in a particular area: climate, food supply, and so forth. A far more useful test would be *not* snapping his fingers. That test would permit his theory to be proven wrong.

This notion is based on the work of the philosopher Sir Karl Popper, who said that a scientific theory can never be proven true because there are many false theories that can predict any given outcome. Popper would say that no matter how many times the predicted result occurs, there might still be another theory that actually is the true one. What would be informative would be a disconfirmation, or a result that contradicted the theory. According to Popper, we make up theories and try to knock them down. The ones that survive the testing process can tentatively be accepted as true by a process of elimination. We can never prove the theory to be true for certain, but we gain more confidence in the theory the more tests it survives.

THE ROLE OF THEORIES

We have emphasized the development of theories as a major goal of science. But why are theories so important? Theories play three crucial roles in the development of a science: (1) organizing knowledge and explaining laws, (2) predicting new laws, and (3) guiding research.

■ Organizing Knowledge and Explaining Laws

First, theories serve to organize knowledge and explain laws. In the absence of a theory, we simply have a collection of descriptions and some laws. The theory pulls these together into a unified framework. According to philosophers of science, this relating of individual events to laws and laws to theories constitutes scientific explanation. The individual fact is explained by being shown to be an instance of a general law. In turn, the law is explained by its relation to the theory. We explain Elaine's inability to remember more than seven numbers as an instance of the law of the limited nature of working memory. We can go up one level and explain the limited nature of working memory in terms of the way information is processed from a working store into a permanent form according to memory theory. Explanation is a process of relating more particular concepts to more general concepts. The theory serves to explain the laws that have been found.

The better the theory, the more events and laws it can explain. We would have little interest in a theory that explained the behavior of only a few individuals under a limited set of circumstances. In addition, the more specific and precise the explanation, the better the theory is. For this reason, theories that are stated mathematically are considered better than theories that state relationships only in general terms. Of course, these two considerations are often in conflict. A broad general theory can explain more laws and instances but with less precision than a less ambitious theory. During the first half of this century, psychology was characterized by many broad theories, such as those of Freud, Hull, and others, that were designed to encompass much of behavior. More recently, psychologists have devoted themselves to theories that are less ambitious in scope but have greater explanatory precision, such as theories of speech perception or problem solving.

■ Predicting New Laws

The second role of theories is to predict new laws. A fruitful theory not only will explain many different laws that were previously unrelated, but will suggest places to look for new laws as well. A particularly good example of a new law or phenomenon predicted by a theory is provided in an experiment by Mark Lepper, David Greene, and Richard Nisbett (1973). According to self-perception theory, people understand their own behavior on much the same basis as would other persons—by observing the behavior and attributing it to observable causes. In a common experimental situation, a person is underpaid for participating in a dull task. Afterward, this person tends to report enjoying the task more than a person who was paid adequately for doing it. According to the theory, the person says something like the following: "I did that task for only $1. It really must have been interesting." Lepper, Greene, and Nisbett concluded that the theory should also predict the opposite effect: if a person were paid to do something that was fun, it would become less fun. To test this prediction, they had nursery school children color with Magic Markers. Some expected to be rewarded for coloring, and others did not. Those who expected a reward were found in a later test to have lost interest in coloring. The other children lost interest to a lesser degree. Thus, self-perception theory predicted a law that later was found to be true: Rewarding a person for having fun can make it less fun.

This example is notable because the effect was counterintuitive; that is, it would not have been predicted by common sense. For generations teachers have been giving gold stars to students for good work. The results of this experiment suggest that rewarding good schoolwork may actually make school more boring.

■ Guiding Research

Theories also serve to guide research. Most researchers will say that they work within a certain theoretical framework, such as the self-perception theory just described. A good theory will suggest new experiments and help researchers choose alternative ways of performing them. This role of theory in guiding research goes hand in hand with its role in predicting new laws. When scientists use a theory to predict a new law, they also use the theory to suggest new experiments to perform in order to establish that new law. Lepper et al. were guided in their research by self-perception theory when they derived a prediction from the theory that led them to study the effect of rewarding children for coloring on those children's interest in coloring.

■ Theories and Experiments

Talking about theories sometimes seems—well—theoretical. We do experiments in order to understand the world and to develop theories. But how do experiments and theories relate to one another? Actually, the relationship is quite close, as shown in Figure 2.1, which is based on a similar figure by Coombs, Raiffa, and Thrall (1954). We start with the real world at the top center of the figure. From the real world we make two abstractions. Going to the right, we devise some theory, however primitive. Then we make predictions by logical deductions from the theory. Going to the left, we begin with the real world and abstract from it an experimental design. Then, putting the design into effect, we carry out the experiment and obtain the empirical data. The next step is to compare the results of the experiment to the predictions of the theory. If they match, we say that the theory is confirmed; if they do not, the theory is disconfirmed. Although this might seem the end

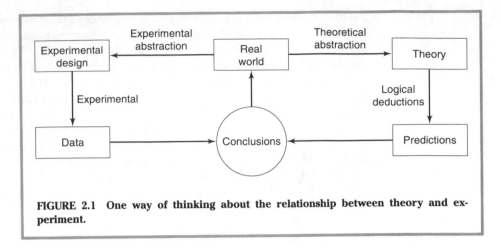

FIGURE 2.1 **One way of thinking about the relationship between theory and experiment.**

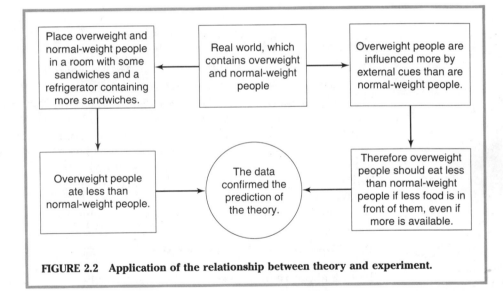

FIGURE 2.2 **Application of the relationship between theory and experiment.**

of the process, ordinarily it represents only one cycle in a continuous process. If the theory is confirmed, then other predictions of the theory may be tested in another experiment, or the theory may be elaborated to generate other testable predictions. Figure 2.2 illustrates how this model applies to Nisbett's experiment on the eating behavior of overweight people discussed earlier.

If the theory is disconfirmed, again there are two options. The theory may be modified to account for the new data, or the experiment may be changed to make it a more sensitive test of the theory. In any case, we can see that after the conclusions have been drawn from any experiment, the next step is to go back to the real world and decide whether to modify the theory or the experimental method or both. So the arrow going from the conclusions back to the real world represents the fact that science is a continuous process.

Seldom, if ever, does a single experiment settle all questions about a scientific problem. Scientists continuously develop theories to account for phenomena in the real world, and they continuously test these theories by conducting experiments. Figure 2.1 illustrates that science cannot be either purely theoretical or purely empirical. An interest in both must be present for science to progress. To be sure, sometimes there is very little theory to guide research and we experiment more or less randomly. At other times, a well-developed theory may not be capable of being tested by today's methods. Most of the time, however, there is a continuous interplay between the development of experimental data and theory.

■ Other Goals

We have stressed theoretical explanation as the ultimate goal of science. On the other hand, many books say that the goals of psychology are description, prediction, and control. We have already discussed description as a goal. Prediction and control actually are part of the describing process. If we have done our job of description well, we have established laws of behavior. The knowledge of these laws will allow us to predict the occurrence of behavior. If we can predict behavior, we are also able to control it if we have control over the events that cause it. So description, prediction, and control are three aspects of the goal of discovering regularities of behavior.

HYPOTHESES IN SCIENCE

If developing laws and theories is the goal of science, how do we go about that process? Let us return for a moment to the example of self-perception theory, which deals with how people interpret their own behavior. Lepper et al. said that if people are paid to do something that is fun, it will become less fun. What Lepper et al. did was to propose a **hypothesis.** A hypothesis is a statement that is assumed to be true for the purpose of testing its validity. A hypothesis can be put in the form of an if-then statement: If A is true, then B should follow. The statement must be one that is either true or false: After people are paid to do something that is fun, it either will or will not become less fun; it cannot be both less fun and not less fun.

hypothesis
a provisional assertion assumed to be true for the purpose of testing its validity

A scientific hypothesis is of the following form: If we make certain observations under particular conditions, and a given theory is correct, then we should find the following results. In other fields, such as mathematics, hypotheses can be tested logically; but a scientific hypothesis must be capable of empirical testing and, as a result, empirical confirmation or disconfirmation.

In the instance of Lepper et al., the hypothesis concerned a law that was predicted from the theory. In other cases, the theory may be the focus of the hypothesis. Take an example from law enforcement. Police may hypothesize that the butler did it. This is a hypothesis that states a theory to be tested: We are working on the theory that the butler did it. In actuality, however, we must not suppose that a particular hypothesis can concern only a theory or a law, to the exclusion of the other. A hypothesis about a law involves certain assumptions about the theory underlying the law. Conversely, it is impossible to test a theory without also testing some lawful prediction of the theory. Lepper et al. might well have said, "If the theory of self-perception is correct, and if people are paid to do something that is fun, then it will become less fun." This statement contains one hypothesis about the theory and another one about the law. If the prediction is not confirmed when it is tested empirically, either the law or the theory—or both—may be false.

Most scientific research, then, is designed to test at least one hypothesis. Much of the rest of this book can be considered a discussion of how one makes and tests scientific hypotheses in the field of psychology.

DEFINING THEORETICAL CONCEPTS

We said earlier that science seeks to develop theoretical explanations of phenomena that occur in the world. Developing theoretical explanations is such a complex activity that breaking down the processes into definite steps is difficult. Sometimes we start with a theory and look for phenomena that should occur if the theory is true. At other times we begin with a phenomenon for which we have no explanation and try to develop a satisfactory theory. We now take up the question of how we build theories.

The first and most important question is, How do we go about inferring the existence of the theoretical entities, such as working memory, that we develop to account for the facts of behavior? On what basis, that is, are we permitted to construct theoretical concepts such as working memory, learning, hunger, and so forth? How do these supposedly scientific concepts differ from nonscientific concepts?

To answer these questions, we must recall that science deals with objective knowledge—those events that are available to every person. **Operationism,** which is associated with physicist Percy Bridgman, states that scientific concepts must be public in the same way that scientific data are public. According to Bridgman, a theoretical concept must be tied to observable operations that any person can observe or perform. If a concept cannot be tied to particular operations, then it is not a scientific concept. Take the concept of the will of God. If we say that everything that happens is the will of God, then the concept is without operational meaning. If it should rain tomorrow, we might say the rain was God's will. On the other hand, if it should not rain tomorrow, we likewise conclude that not raining was God's will. We have no way to define which future events would be according to God's will

operationism
a view that scientific concepts must be defined in terms of observable operations

and which would not. Few persons would say that God's will is a scientific concept.

Let us consider another example. Some people believe that psychic ability (for example, extrasensory perception) is a scientific concept. Here the problem is that the only way of defining psychic ability is for certain types of unlikely data to occur. No conditions are known that are favorable or unfavorable to the demonstration of psychic ability; that is, no operations exist that increase or decrease the probability of an event that would be defined as reflecting psychic ability. Psychic perceptions take place according to no lawful operations. Most psychologists conclude that the concept of psychic ability has no operational definition and, therefore, is not a scientific concept. Operationism, then, strictly limits the kind of concepts with which science can deal. If there is no way of defining the concept according to observable operations, the concept is barred from science.

Operationism has a further, more specific, meaning—namely, that scientific concepts are defined according to the operations by which they are measured. If you were to read the report of an experiment on the effect of hunger on learning in rats, you probably would want to know what the author meant by hunger. In the methods section of the paper, you might read that rats were made hungry by being deprived of food for a certain number of hours, perhaps 23. You would say to yourself, "Ah, when the author says the rats were hungry, he means that they had no food for 23 hours." The statement of what the experimenter did to induce hunger is called an **operational definition** of hunger. Of first and crucial importance in an operational definition is to state a procedure, or operation, that specifies what the concept means. For the purposes of the experiment, the particular way of producing hunger in the rat defines the concept of hunger.

operational definition
a statement of the precise meaning of a procedure or concept within an experiment

As important as an operational definition of a concept is, it has been misunderstood and misused in psychology. The principal misuse is to take a trivial definition of a concept and attempt to build a theory on it. You may believe that twiddling a button on one's clothing is a sign of anxiety. However, this would probably not be as good a measure of anxiety as the galvanic skin response or the Taylor Manifest Anxiety Scale. Experiments that relied on the button-twiddling measure probably would not be as good tests of an anxiety theory as those that used one of the other measures.

Another misuse of the concept of operational definition is to consider that every measure of a concept is independent of every other measure. According to this view, making a rat hungry by starving it for 23 hours is a different type of hunger from making the rat hungry by feeding it just enough to maintain 80 percent of its ad lib weight (the weight it would maintain without any restriction on its eating). It is true that these two operational definitions of hunger may produce somewhat different results in particular situations because of peculiarities inherent in the methods of depriving the animal. Yet by using different methods of producing hunger, we hope that a common core of knowledge about hunger will result. Using different ways of homing in on a concept via different operational definitions is called

converging operations
using different operational definitions to arrive at the meaning of a concept

converging operations. Each new way of producing the concept of hunger will rule out one possible objection to the explanation, until a high degree of confidence can be reached. The method of converging operations is much like the way a surveyor locates a point on the ground. The point is marked from two or more independent locations in order to get a good fix on it by triangulation. The larger the number of independent locations from which the surveyor knows the distance and direction to the new point, the more precisely it is located.

Today operationism is no longer adhered to in the strict sense that Bridgman advocated. Now it is appreciated that some of the meaning of a theoretical concept may be defined by its relationship to a larger theory of which it is a part. Hunger, for example, may not be defined completely by any of the ways of measuring it, or even by all of them together. Some of its meaning may come from a theory of motivation requiring that hunger have certain properties. What we must remember about operationism, however, is to define carefully the terms we use so that their meaning is clear with respect to events in the world that can be observed objectively and with respect to the theories we develop to explain those events.

THE NATURE OF SCIENTIFIC PROGRESS

■ Paradigms

paradigm
a set of laws, theories, methods, and applications that form a scientific research tradition; for example, Pavlovian conditioning

Laypersons commonly believe that science progresses in a straightforward manner by accumulating knowledge, much as a building is built brick by brick. That this stereotype is mistaken has been shown convincingly by Thomas Kuhn (1962). Basic to Kuhn's thought is the concept of a **paradigm**—a pervasive way of thinking about a branch of science that includes all of the assumptions and theories that are accepted as true by a group of scientists. During what he calls normal science, nearly all scientists accept the same paradigm and work under its influence. Eventually, problems develop that cannot be explained without difficulty by the paradigm. These anomalies cause a crisis, during which other paradigms are created that compete with the original paradigm. A new paradigm will be accepted when it accounts more successfully for empirical data than did the old paradigm. According to Kuhn, the course of science is not steady progress toward a goal. Rather, it consists of phases of normal science, each dominated by a single paradigm, alternating with revolutions that install new paradigms that last as long as each paradigm is reasonably successful in accounting for empirical data.

Kuhn's concept has gained widespread acceptance among scientists because it captures the reality of conflict among competing theories and the often acrimonious debates that take place among scientific camps. His viewpoint also accounts for some proverbs about science, such as the idea that a theory is not rejected because it is disproved but because a better theory displaces it.

More recently, Larry Laudan (1977) has taken issue with some of Kuhn's ideas. Laudan emphasizes the problem-solving nature of science. He believes that theories are developed to solve both empirical and conceptual problems. A theory comes to be preferred over another when it solves more problems than the other. Kuhn, in contrast, says a theory is accepted when it accounts for more empirical data than its predecessor. Laudan cites his view—that the ability of a theory to handle a conceptual problem is a legitimate criterion for evaluating the theory—as a factor in scientists' preferring one theory over others. Often, Laudan states, conceptual problems that scientists consider important relate to concepts that do not actually enter into scientific theories. Social, ethical, and theoretical problems, for example, have been given weight by scientists in evaluating scientific theories.

Kuhn, on the other hand, believes that only empirical data can be used to evaluate theories. Therefore, much of what motivates scientists to prefer one theory over another must be considered irrational. Laudan's view seems to be more faithful to the way scientists actually go about their work. If conceptual problems legitimately influence the choice of theories, then the behavior of scientists can be considered rational in this regard.

SERENDIPITY

"Here [is] a first principle not formally recognized by scientific methodologists: When you run onto something interesting, drop everything else and study it" (Skinner, 1956, p. 223).

We said earlier that doing science does not involve mechanically applying a pat formula called the scientific method. Science is a creative activity that is as varied as the people who practice it. As Arthur Bachrach put it: "People don't usually do research the way people who write books about research say that people do research" (1962, p. vii). Capturing in a book exactly what doing research is like is difficult because what people write down as the way they do research is often different from how they really do it. One of the major ways in which experimental psychology books deviate from the reality of research is in not paying enough attention to the role of hunch and luck in research. Perhaps we are embarrassed to admit that our recognition rests on a stroke of luck. Perhaps it is impossible to teach people how to have hunches and follow them productively. We hope not, because those ideas are behind the term **serendipity,** a word often heard in discussions of research.

serendipity
the gift of finding valuable or pleasing things not sought for

Serendipity is defined as the gift of discovering desirable things that one was not searching for. The word comes from a Persian fairy tale, *The Three Princes of Serendip,* in which the characters were always stumbling onto things they were not looking for. Rather than attempting to list rules for developing the gift of serendipity, we will simply note that serendipity plays an important role in developing scientific ideas. A breakthrough in a problem often comes because the investigator notices something peculiar happening and becomes more intrigued with exploring that than pursuing the original line of investigation. B. F. Skinner's quotation at the beginning of this section describes the process of serendipity. In the article from which the quotation is taken, "A Case History in Scientific Method," Skinner describes how he used "accidents" and curiosity to lead him to his famous discoveries.

We will mention only two of the many important discoveries that were serendipitous. In the 1950s much interest developed in the functions of a part of the brain known as the reticular formation, the importance of which for behavior was just becoming apparent. James Olds (1973) was attempting to find out whether mild electrical stimulation to the reticular formation of rats would facilitate learning. Olds permitted rats with electrodes aimed at their reticular formation to explore a large enclosure. When they approached a certain place, he stimulated them with electricity. He noticed that the rats would return to the place where they received the stimulation, as if it were pleasurable to them. Eventually, with Peter Milner, he rigged up an apparatus by which the rats could press a bar to stimulate themselves. This self-stimulation was found to be an extremely potent reinforcer (Olds & Milner, 1954). This experiment gave rise to much research on the physiological basis for reward. Not incidentally, Olds's original electrode had missed the reticular formation and instead was located in the septal area, about 4 millimeters away.

A recent example of serendipity comes from the use of tail pinch in rats as an experimental model of stress-related behaviors. For some time scientists have known that certain kinds of stressors, such as electrical shock or presence of a rival male, would cause animals to engage in certain unrelated behaviors, such as sexual behavior or grooming. Seymour Antelman and others (for example, Antelman & Szechtman, 1975) showed that a nonpainful tail pinch reliably caused a wide range of behaviors, depending on the situation. On each of 4,000 rats they placed a padded tail clamp. Within a few seconds after placement, more than 95% of the rats began to eat, even though just before the experiment they had been given all the food they wanted. If the food was replaced by a palatable fluid, the rat began drinking. If a female rat was present, a male began copulating (Antelman & Caggiula, 1977). These tail-pinch-induced behaviors have been widely studied as models of stress-induced behavior, such as compulsive eating. The discovery of tail-pinch-induced behavior was a serendipitous finding. Antelman describes the process:

> The ability of animals to show eating (and other motivated behaviors as well) in response to the stress of mild (nonpainful) tail pressure was first described by Henry Szechtman and me in 1973. This phenomenon was found quite by accident while attempting to induce rotation in rats following drug treatment. One of our rats *not* showing the desired behavior was tail-pinched, since mild stress can often induce rotation in such

animals. This rat was on a cart with another animal and when pinched it did not rotate but instead began to lick the tail of the other animal each time the pinch was applied. When food pellets were substituted for the second animal, tail pinch caused stimulation-bound eating. At first we thought that tail-pinching-induced phenomena were related to the drug we had given. It soon became apparent that this was not the case. In the years since our discovery, thousands of undrugged animals have been tested and it is obvious that tail pinch can induce eating in almost 90% of them.

The technique is now regularly used in laboratories throughout the world and tail-pinch-induced obesity (demonstrated by Neil Rowland and me) has gained widespread acceptance as a model for stress-related overeating in humans. (personal communication, 1982)

SCIENCE AS A PROBLEM-SOLVING ACTIVITY

Science often has been described as a problem-solving activity. Psychological science is a way of answering the *why* or *how* of behavior. In this sense, we can see that psychology springs from the basic curiosity about the world that is in all of us. The earliest stages of psychological science sought answers to questions that occurred to every person: How do we gain knowledge of the world? How do we learn our way in unfamiliar places? As psychology developed, other questions began to emerge from the experimental situations that had been developed in response to earlier questions. In this way, existing theories suggested new findings, and new findings required changes in theories.

Psychology, as every other science, has developed areas of specialization that seem far removed from the initial questions. Whereas simple curiosity about the world may motivate the initial stages of research, problems arising from trying to fit theories to data become the second motivation for scientific activity. Of course, these stages are not distinct and separate. There is some primitive theory behind the simplest curiosity, and even the most sophisticated scientists can be motivated by simple curiosity.

Even when a science is no longer in its infancy, curiosity can strongly influence its direction. For many years after the behaviorist revolution of the early 1900s, problems about consciousness were pushed into the background of psychology. Then, with the rise of popular interest in consciousness and Eastern philosophy during the 1960s, psychologists began to look more closely at questions of consciousness. So we see that science is never totally immune to the curiosity and interest of the average person.

Not all problems spring from simple curiosity or from conflicts between theory and data, however. Another motivation for science is the need to solve practical problems. As Alphonse Chapanis points out: "The field of mental testing started with a problem put to a French elementary school teacher; the field of speech communication started from some problems raised and first attacked by telephone engineers; . . . and some of the best work in color vision has been done to construct a usable system of specifying colors for engineers, business, and industry" (1971, pp. 950–951).

Many of the important theories of psychology have developed from applied research. One of the most successful theories in recent psychology is signal-detection theory, which explains how people detect weak signals in the presence of noise. This theory was developed to understand such applied problems as how sonar operators react to targets. The theory has been applied successfully not only to many areas of sensory psychology but to memory and motivation problems as well.

Finally, we should point out that some scientific psychology has no interest in theory at all. Considerable research is devoted to problems that are purely practical, such as determining which teaching method is best or what advertising campaign will be most successful. The experimenters have no intention of testing a theory, only of finding out what method works best. Such research often gives rise to theories, nonetheless, as conflicting data are obtained and people try to make sense of them.

A NOTE ON PSYCHOLOGY AND SCIENCE

The view of science that we have presented in the first two chapters is the one that has guided many researchers and much of the history of modern psychology. The reader should be aware that some would say it is an ideal that is seldom realized in practice. Although many discoveries will be made that do not conform to that ideal, it is best to understand the dominant position in order to be able to evaluate other views of science that you will encounter.

✳ NUTS & BOLTS ✳

Meta-Analysis

What do you do when you are reviewing the literature in some area and are faced with two studies that report opposite results? Perhaps one study finds evidence that a certain psychotherapy technique is useful, and another one finds that it is not. If that is not bad enough, suppose 35 studies find the technique to be useful, and 23 conclude that it isn't. Reviewers sometimes used to rely on the *box-score method*: simply count the numbers of positive and negative studies, and declare the winner to be the side with the largest number of studies. But the box-score approach clearly has its limitations. For one thing, all studies are not of equal value. Some studies may have procedural flaws in them, others may have smaller sample sizes, and so on.

In the past, reviewers who wanted to go beyond the simple box-score method would use their judgment when they considered one study better than another, but the criteria they used could not always be stated in a straightforward manner, and the whole process was subject to the reviewer's biases. There was a need for a method of reviewing that would be more "up front" about how the review would be conducted and what biases would be operating.

meta-analysis
a set of methods for combining the results of many studies

These concerns have led to the development of a methodology called **meta-analysis.** The word *meta* implies taking a larger view of a topic—something like backing away for a better perspective. Meta-analysis is actually a group of methods that permit one to combine many studies with a variety of characteristics in order to reach a unified conclusion. Some of these methods permit one to estimate whether there is a bias toward publication of only those studies with positive results—the so-called *file-drawer problem.* If researchers have a tendency to publish studies that favor behavioral psychotherapy and put their nonsignificant results into a file drawer, then the literature will be biased in favor of studies supporting behavioral psychotherapy.

Other meta-analytic techniques permit one to give more weight to studies with fewer flaws, larger samples, or other relevant factors. All of the meta-analytic methods are somewhat technical, so we will discuss just one of them to provide an introduction to the area. In one of the first meta-analytic reviews, Mary Lee Smith and Gene Glass (1977) reviewed studies of the efficacy of different types of psychotherapy. Prior to 1977, there had been some box-score analyses of psychotherapy, including a famous review by Hans Eysenck (1952, 1965), that concluded that psychotherapy was no more effective than doing nothing at all. Smith and Glass took a different approach in their review. Rather than simply count which of nearly 400 controlled studies found statistically significant, positive effects of psychotherapy, they looked at the *size of the effect* produced by psychotherapy in each study.

The difference between effect size and statistical significance is crucial. It is possible for a study to find a large effect that is not statistically significant because there were too few subjects. Conversely, it is possible to find a trivially small effect that is statistically significant because an enormous number of subjects are studied. Turn to pages 279, 434, and 444 if you are not familiar with the statistical concept of power. Thus, statistical significance has limitations as a criterion in determining whether psychotherapy is effective.

Comparing effect sizes among different experiments requires one to have a common metric, or yardstick, to measure the outcome. The problem is that different experimenters often measure their results on different scales. Suppose some studies compared improvement after psychotherapy on a 10-point scale, whereas others used a 5-point scale. Because the scales differed among experiments, it might seem impossible to have a single measure of effect size. For example, if a study using a 10-point scale found a difference of 3 points between groups, and one using a 5-point scale found a difference of 2 points, you might wonder whether two points on the 5-point scale meant more or less than a 3-point difference on a 10-point scale.

But if we use the *variability* of the group that did not receive treatment, instead of the arbitrary scale, as the unit of measurement, we can compare different studies on a single scale. Suppose the untreated group in the study with the 5-point scale had a small standard deviation because almost all of that group scored 2, but the untreated group in the experiment with the 10-point scale were spread out on the scale. Dividing the difference between the treated and untreated groups in each study by the standard deviation of the untreated group would give a common metric by which to compare the two experiments. Figure 2.3 shows that almost all of the treated subjects in the experiment with the 5-point scale did better than the untreated subjects, whereas many of the untreated subjects in the other experiment did as well as the untreated ones. Therefore, we could conclude that the effect size is larger in the experiment that measured the results on the 5-point scale.

Smith and Glass measured the size of the effect of psychotherapy in terms of the standard deviation, or variability, of the results. When they did this, they found that the average client who received therapy was better off than 75% of those who did not receive therapy. This result is illustrated in Figure 2.4, which also shows that different kinds of therapy—psychodynamic, behavior modification, and systematic desensitization—all had about the same effect size with neurotic clients. Thus, Smith and Glass were able to compare many different studies using different scales and conclude that psychotherapy is effective, whereas previous reviews had come to the wrong conclusion.

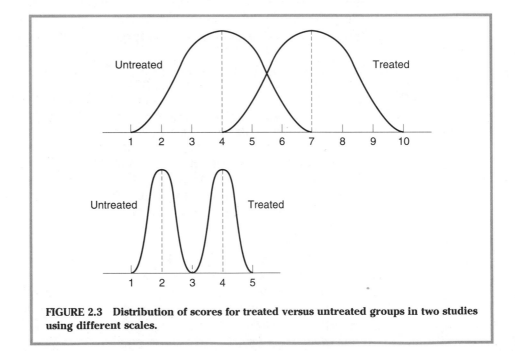

FIGURE 2.3 Distribution of scores for treated versus untreated groups in two studies using different scales.

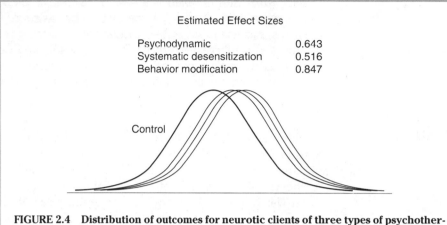

FIGURE 2.4   Distribution of outcomes for neurotic clients of three types of psychotherapy, compared with untreated controls. Source: "Meta-Analysis of Psychotherapy Outcome Studies," by M. L. Smith and G. V. Glass, September 1977, *American Psychologist, 32,* 752–760. Copyright © 1977 by the American Psychological Association. Reprinted by permission.

The Smith and Glass review had a major impact on the field. Now that the effectiveness of psychotherapy had been demonstrated, insurance companies began to pay the cost of treatment. In addition, the fact that therapies based on different theoretical foundations did not lead to different outcomes led researchers to focus on what therapists actually do and say when they deal with a client. Thus, we have the *process* approach to psychotherapy today.

The Research Question

Up to now you have been working on a general research problem. For example, why do people in large cities fail to help the victim of a crime? You have developed some ideas and you feel ready to test them. You must narrow down the larger research problem to a specific, testable question. You may want to test the idea that people in large groups feel less responsible for other individuals. Your hypothesis, which is a specific prediction of a relationship between variables, might be: As group size increases, the members feel less responsibility for the other people in the group.

The rest of the experimental process will be an empirical test of your hypothesis. It is essential that your hypothesis be as specific as possible. In the hypothesis about group size and responsibility, do you mean that the subjects will feel less concern for other persons, or do you mean that they feel just as concerned but they believe that someone else will do something? (See Darley & Latané, 1968.) The more precise you can be in stating the hypothesis, the better you can design a cogent and straightforward test of it. If the hypothesis is vague, the experiment is likely to be difficult to interpret. When the hypothesis is stated in vague terms, the temptation arises to develop a kitchen-sink design—to throw in every variable that might bear on the phenomenon. As you develop the hypothesis and then design the experiment, you must keep asking yourself "Exactly what am I trying to find out?" All efforts should be bent toward that question, and care should be taken to pare ancillary questions from the experiment unless the added cost of answering them is negligible. ❏

SUMMARY

1. Pseudoscience is activity that claims to be science but shows certain nonscience characteristics, such as a lack of objectivity or concern with measurement, nondisconfirmable concepts, a lack of formal logic and mathematics, isolation from the rest of science, lack of progress, attempts to answer ultimate questions, lack of precise definition of terms, definition of terms by exclusion, lack of lawful relationships among variables, lack of theoretical agreement, and the exaggerated importance of a few key people.

2. Scientists often follow these steps in studying a problem:
   a. Observe that there is a problem.
   b. Develop a rule of thumb that helps.
   c. Develop a more formal rule.
   d. Develop a theory.
   e. Make a prediction based on the theory.
   f. Test the prediction.

3. The goal of science is to understand the world.

4. Understanding the world can be broken down into two subgoals: the discovery of regularities and the development of theories.

5. Discovering regularities includes the description of behavior, the discovery of lawful relationships among aspects of behavior, and the search for causes.

6. Description of behavior is of crucial importance because it defines the subject matter for which laws are to be sought and theories developed.

7. Description can be thought of as creating the subject matter of science.

8. A law is a statement that certain events are regularly associated with one another.

9. John Stuart Mill proposed the method of agreement, the method of differences, and the method of concomitant variation to help in the search for the causes of a phenomenon.

10. Problems in applying Mill's methods can come from confusing coincidence with cause and overlooking a true cause.

11. The ultimate goal of science is the development of a theory to explain lawful relationships that exist in a particular field.

12. Broadly speaking, a theory is a set of statements about the relationships among variables.

13. More narrowly, a theory is a set of statements about relationships among variables that includes at least one concept that is not directly observed.

14. Theories and hypotheses must be capable of empirical testing.

15. Theories guide research and in turn are modified by research in a continuous cycle.

16. Theories should not be contrasted with facts; a theory remains a theory even if it is accepted as true.

17. Theories have three main functions in science: (a) organizing knowledge and explaining laws; (b) predicting new laws; and (c) guiding research.

18. A hypothesis is a statement that is assumed to be true for the purpose of testing its validity.

19. Operationism is the doctrine that scientific concepts must be tied to observable operations.

20. Although it is important to define theoretical concepts operationally, it is not held that an operational definition completely defines a concept.

21. Progress in science often involves a major shift in theories and assumptions, known as a paradigm shift, rather than a steady accumulation of knowledge.

22. Many discoveries in science come about by serendipity rather than the application of a certain formula for the scientific method.

23. Science can be thought of as an activity that is aimed at the satisfaction of curiosity or at the solution of theoretical or practical problems.

24. Meta-analysis is an approach to evaluating research literature that permits one to combine many different studies in order to reach a unified conclusion.

25. The research problem is narrowed down to one or more specific hypotheses that the research is designed to answer.

Suggestions for Further Reading

COOPER, H. M. (1989). *Integrating research: A guide for literature reviews*. Newbury Park, CA: Sage. This treatment of literature reviewing emphasizes psychological applications.

HACKING, I. (1981). *Scientific revolutions*. London: Oxford University Press. The introduction to this volume gives a concise statement of the basic propositions held by most philosophers of science prior to Kuhn. The article by Laudan contains a list of beliefs now generally held. The annotated bibliography is a valuable guide to the literature in the area.

HEMPEL, C. G. (1966). *Philosophy of natural science*. Englewood Cliffs, NJ: Prentice-Hall. This excellent brief introduction to the philosophy of science has a particularly good discussion of law, theory, and the nature of scientific explanation.

LIGHT, R. J., & PILLEMER, D. B. (1984). *Summing up: The science of reviewing research*. Cambridge, MA: Harvard University Press. Less technical discussion of the process of literature review than most treatments of meta-analysis.

MARX, M. H., & GOODSON, F. E. (Eds.). (1976). *Theories in contemporary psychology.* New York: Macmillan. This edited volume contains many of the classic papers on the philosophy of science as it relates specifically to psychological theories. The discussion is on a high level but is essential for serious students.

RADNER, D., & RADNER, M. (1982). *Science and unreason.* Belmont, CA: Wadsworth. An illuminating and entertaining account of some infamous pseudosciences and how they differ from science.

SALMON, M. H. (1989). *Introduction to logic and critical thinking* (2nd ed.). San Diego: Harcourt Brace Jovanovich. Contains a good discussion of Mill's methods of logical inference.

STANOVICH, K. E. (1992). *How to think straight about psychology* (3rd ed.). Glenview, IL: Scott, Foresman. Discusses some of the common misconceptions people have about the nature of psychology as a science.

⟫ A CASE IN POINT ⟪

Biorhythms

Biorhythm theory holds that three different cycles determine human performance: a 23-day physical cycle, a 28-day emotional cycle, and a 33-day intellectual cycle. Performance is better during the positive part of each cycle and worse in the negative part. Especially important, however, are "critical" days, when the cycle is changing from positive to negative. These cycles are fixed in duration and are triggered at birth. Therefore, it is possible to calculate the state of any person's biorhythm simply by knowing his or her birth date and the current date.

Biorhythm theory is the brainchild of Wilhelm Fliess, a surgeon and numerologist and a very close friend of Sigmund Freud, who proposed the 23-day and 28-day cycles in the 1880s. Later followers of Fliess added the 33-day cycle.

Biorhythms must not be confused with biological rhythms. It is well known that many different cycles occur in all living organisms, including humans. All known biological rhythms vary from individual to individual and from time to time within the same individual. These biological rhythms have been the subject of vigorous study, and their mechanisms are becoming understood.

The evidence for biorhythms comes from analysis of records of accidents, illness, death, and the like. No serious attempt has been made to link them to known biological rhythms or to study their physiological bases. Biorhythm theory does not make use of theoretical concepts from physiology or psychology to any extent. Research on biorhythms is not published in physiological or psychological journals.

Many studies are supposed to have shown that industrial accidents and the like correlate with biorhythms. One oft-cited study concerns a Japanese investigation of airline accidents that found accidents to be more frequent on negative and critical days. As a result, it is claimed that many firms use biorhythms to make assignments. Terence Hines

(1979) investigated these claims. Either he could not find the original studies or the reports did not give sufficient detail to permit him to evaluate the claims.

Hines also reviewed a number of well-conducted studies that failed to find any evidence for biorhythms. In spite of these negative studies, biorhythm theory has been neither modified nor abandoned.

REQUIRED: Decide whether you would consider biorhythms science or pseudoscience. Use the characteristics of pseudoscience listed in the chapter as a checklist. You may conclude that it has some aspects of science and some of pseudoscience. Defend your conclusions.

≡ READING BETWEEN THE LINES ≡

2.1 IMAGINE THAT ESP DOES OCCUR

One way to evaluate the hypothesis of ESP is to imagine what the world would be like if ESP existed. What does this exercise tell you about ESP? What goals and assumptions of science are violated in such a claim as the existence of ESP? ∎

2.2 REINCARNATION

Many people believe in reincarnation because they have recalled past lives under the effects of hypnosis. They may have had vivid recollections of being a soldier in the Trojan War or of being King Solomon's favorite concubine. How would you test such a claim? How would you suggest an alternative explanation? ∎

☑ EXERCISES

2.1 IDENTIFY FACTS, LAWS, AND THEORIES

After Ken left his dirty socks on the floor for the seventh time in the same week, Barbie went ballistic [_____ A _____].

"You always leave your socks on the floor [_____ B _____]. Men really want mothers, not partners [_____ D _____]. If I didn't pick up after you, the mice would be nesting in them [_____ C _____]. They can pile up until you can't cross the floor, for all I care [_____]."

REQUIRED: Assuming Barbie was not exaggerating, indicate the type of statements by putting the appropriate letter in each blank. Use each letter only once: (a) data, (b) law, (c) hypothesis, (d) theory. One blank should not be filled.

2.2 IDENTIFY FACTS, LAWS, AND THEORY

One theory of hunger motivation says that the brain acts as a feedback mechanism, something like a thermostat, that has a set point, or ideal weight, which our body strives to maintain. It is known that rats that are starved below the weight that they would maintain if they could eat whatever they want will quickly return to their free-feeding weight after the period of starvation. Likewise, rats that are fed a high-fat diet will reduce their weight after they return to their normal diet. After Juan read about these ideas in his psychology book, he remembered that the weight he had put on over the Christmas holidays went away after he returned to college.

REQUIRED:
   a. Identify a statement in the paragraph that refers to theory.
   b. Identify a statement that may be considered a law and explain how it relates to the theory.
   c. Identify one statement of fact. How is the fact explained by the theory?

2.3   OPERATIONAL DEFINITIONS

A researcher plans a study to determine the extent of hostility between factory workers and their supervisors. Supervisors are classified as either autocratic or democratic.

REQUIRED: Suggest possible operational definitions of hostility, autocratic, and democratic.   ❑

3

Variables

In Chapter 2, we discussed how scientists develop laws and theories to explain the phenomena they observe. In order to do this, we must move from general statements about broad classes of behavior to specific examples of that behavior. The phenomenon we want to study can be any event in all of its complexity and variety. When we begin to study the event experimentally, however, we must strip away some of this complexity. In a word, we take the phenomenon and turn it into one or more variables.

variable
aspect of a testing condition that can change or take on different characteristics with different conditions

A **variable** is some property of an event in the world that has been measured. Variables are attributes of phenomena and thus belong to the world. Reducing a phenomenon to variables focuses the researcher's attention on specific events out of the many that may be related to the phenomenon. In the example of coloring by nursery school children discussed in Chapter 2, the phenomenon of interest was that rewards make coloring less fun. In order to study this phenomenon, it was necessary to designate a certain class of events as the variable to be measured, ignoring other events. Lepper et al. (1973) studied the amount of time spent coloring, rather than how many times the children expressed delight in coloring or the expressions on their faces while they colored.

In this chapter, we will study some topics related to variables. First we will make several distinctions that are important for psychology among types of variables. Then we will discuss the concept of measurement.

Before we discuss types of variables, we must show how the variables of a study relate to the theoretical concepts, as discussed in Chapter 2.

Because the variables exist in the world, but the theory is a product of your imagination, you must make certain assumptions in order to relate the two. These assumptions are guy ropes that tie a theory to the real world. The variables are tangible: duration, frequency, or intensity of bar presses; items checked on a questionnaire; murders committed; books written. The theoretical concept is intangible: hunger, motivation, anxiety. The variables are related to the theoretical concepts by means of the operational definitions used to measure the concepts. Recall our discussion of operational definitions in Chapter 2.

Suppose your theory says that increasing anxiety will increase the affiliation motive. In order to test this theory, you must take the theoretical concepts of anxiety and affiliation motive and relate them to variables in the real world by means of operational definitions. The theory is an abstract statement. You must bring it down to cases. You can measure anxiety by the Taylor Manifest Anxiety Scale and affiliation by how close subjects sit to each other in the experiment. These two measures constitute the variables of the study. It is the scores on the variables of anxiety and distance apart that are related to one another as tests of the hypothesis. The relationship between the variables is taken as providing support for or against the particular theory that generated the experiment.

TYPES OF VARIABLES

In order to understand how variables are used and discussed in psychological research, you must understand several distinctions that are made among types of variables.

■ Independent and Dependent Variables

dependent variable
a measure of the behavior of the subject that reflects the effects of the independent variable

independent variable
the condition manipulated or selected by the experimenter to determine its effect on behavior

The most basic distinction among variables is between independent variables and dependent variables. The **dependent variable** is a measure of the behavior of the subject. In the language of stimulus-response psychology, it is the response. We call it the dependent variable because it depends (we hope) on the value of another variable (the independent variable). In Chapter 2, we said that one of the goals of science is to find lawful relationships among events in the world. It is between the dependent and independent variables that these relationships are sought.

The **independent variable** is one that is believed to cause some change in the value of the dependent variable. It is the stimulus of stimulus-response psychology. The term *stimulus,* in its most general use, is equivalent to a cause. According to the famous frustration-aggression law, frustration causes aggression. If we were interested in the effects of poverty on crime, we might apply the frustration-aggression law. We might consider poverty to be a source of frustration and thus a cause of crime, even though not every poor person becomes a criminal. Poverty could be a probabilistic cause if the percentage of poor people who commit crimes was found to be larger than the percentage of nonpoor who commit crimes.

The independent variable can often be thought of as what the researcher does to the subject, and the dependent variable as what the subject does back. Although this analogy is true in many cases, sometimes there are independent variables that the researcher does not manipulate. Examples would be poverty, in the previous example, or the sex, age, or intelligence quotient (IQ) of the subject. These independent variables cannot be controlled by the researcher. We will devote Chapters 7, 8, and 12 to studies that use such nonmanipulated independent variables.

Although it is useful to think of the independent variable as a cause and the dependent variable as an effect, this is not always as simple as it may seem. Sometimes we have trouble deciding which of two variables in a study is the cause and which is the effect. Suppose there is a relationship between violent behavior and television watching. We may have a hard time, though, deciding whether watching violent television programs causes violent behavior or whether a predisposition to violence causes people to watch violent shows. In such investigations, the identification of cause and effect is the whole purpose of the study. This problem is typical of the nonexperimental research discussed in Chapters 7 and 8.

The experimenter manipulates the independent variable to produce different values of it. It is common practice to speak of the different values as different **levels** of the independent variable. For example, an experimenter might reward some children for coloring and not reward others. In this simplest example there are two levels of reward: present and absent.

levels
the different values of an independent variable

■ Quantitative and Categorical Variables

The distinction that some variables are quantitative while others are categorical is easy to state, even though it may be difficult to apply to particular cases. A **quantitative variable** is one that varies in amount, whereas a **categorical variable** varies in kind. Examples of quantitative variables would be speed of response and loudness. On the other hand, pitch or turning left versus right in a maze would be categorical variables.

quantitative variable
one that varies in amount
categorical variable
one that varies in kind

Note that loudness is quantitative, whereas pitch is categorical. Tones differ in *amount* of loudness but *category* of pitch. This particular example involves a subtle distinction and is not based on a single criterion. For example, loudness is coded in the nervous system by amount of nervous activity, whereas pitch is coded (largely) by activity in different neurons. Another distinction, and an important one, is that pitch and loudness follow different laws in certain psychological scaling situations (Stevens, 1975). Many variables that the layperson considers to be categorical the psychologist discovers to be quantitative: introversion/extroversion, normal/neurotic, masculinity/femininity.

A variable can be categorical even though boundaries between categories may be fuzzy and classifying particular examples may be difficult.

For instance, colors can be classified into red, yellow, green, or violet, even though finer distinctions can be made within colors and some colors can be considered on the border, such as blue-green. Notice that color as a psychological variable is categorical, whereas the underlying physical dimension (wavelength) is quantitative. The same is true of pitch.

The distinction between quantitative and categorical variables can become important when we start to build theories. For example, theorists debate about taste, asking whether there are only four tastes—salty, sour, sweet, and bitter—or whether all tastes fall along a continuum, with the four basic tastes being merely convenient but arbitrary categories (McBurney & Gent, 1979). For the same reason, keeping in mind the distinction between quantitative and categorical variables is necessary in making graphs, as we shall see in Chapter 4.

■ Continuous and Discrete Variables

continuous variable one that falls along a continuum and is not limited to a certain number of values

discrete variable one that falls into separate bins with no intermediate values possible

Some quantitative variables can take any value on a continuum. They are called **continuous variables** because they are not limited to a certain number of values, such as whole numbers, or to discrete bins. In principle, you can measure latency, duration, or force of a bar press with any desired precision; in practice, the fineness of the measure is limited by the ability of the measuring instrument. **Discrete variables,** on the other hand, fall into distinct bins, as the word *discrete* suggests. The number of marriages contracted, murders committed, or books written are all discrete variables.

Although a variable may be continuous, its measurement is often discontinuous. Although height is a continuous variable, we generally measure it to the nearest inch. Similarly, knowledge of psychological research methods may be a continuous variable, but it is often measured by the number of items correct on a test, a discontinuous measure. This does not make knowledge a discrete variable, because it would be possible in principle to measure knowledge as finely as one wished.

apparent limits the point indicated by a number

real limits the interval defined by the number plus or minus half the distance to the next number

physical variable aspect of a testing condition that can be defined in physical terms

Because continuous variables are commonly measured in a discontinuous fashion, it is necessary to distinguish the real limits of a measure from the apparent limits. The **apparent limits** of a score on a test are an infinitely small point: a score of 1, 2, or some other whole number. But that score represents an estimate of the knowledge of the material, which is a continuous variable. The **real limits** are that score plus or minus half the distance to the next score: 0.5 to 1.5, 1.5 to 2.5, and so on. This distinction is important when one graphs data and performs certain statistical computations, as we will see in the next chapter.

■ Physical and Nonphysical Variables

Among independent variables, some are simple **physical variables,** such as the intensity of a light or the number of hours of food deprivation. It is easy

nonphysical
variable
aspect of a testing
condition defined
in terms of
behavior or
cognitive
processes

to construct a graph with one of these physical variables as the independent variable. Other independent variables, however, are **nonphysical variables**— ones not defined directly in physical terms. Some experimenters ask questions that involve the relationship between two nonphysical variables.[1]

Suppose you want to know how the preference for sugar relates to its sweetness. Preference is obviously nonphysical, but sweetness might seem to be a physical variable. Sweetness, however, can be measured only by tasting the substance. Preference and sweetness are both nonphysical dimensions and have different relations to concentration:

$$Sweetness = f(Concentration)$$

This is read "Sweetness is a function of concentration," where f stands for "a function of." For the time being, we can say that "is a function of" means there is a particular shape of curve on a graph that relates sweetness and concentration. (See Appendix E for a discussion of functions.)

Other letters, g and h, are used to indicate other functions—that is, other shapes of curves relating variables.

$$Preference = g(Concentration)$$

That preference and sweetness are different is shown by the fact that for most people sweetness increases as long as concentration increases. On the other hand, preference is greater for medium concentrations and decreases for concentrations that are stronger. The relation between sweetness and preference would be between two nonphysical variables.

$$Preference = h(Sweetness)$$

Sometimes kinds of variables are more difficult to distinguish. Many psychologically important independent variables cannot be specified by any physical stimulus or combination of known dimensions. For instance, what are the physical dimensions underlying the pleasantness of odors, the beauty of faces, or the hostility of an expression? In terms of the type of equations shown above, we would have to write:

$$Beauty = f(?,?,? \dots)$$

Such variables are obviously important causes of behavior, but they may defy precise physical specification.

---

[1] Of course, all variables are physical in the sense that they depend on some event in the physical world. We use the term *nonphysical* to refer to those variables that are not easily defined in physical terms (such as friendliness) or are measured only indirectly in physical terms (such as sweetness).

Some nonphysical variables operate via the subject's interpretation. The same event in the physical world may mean one thing to Subject A and another thing to Subject B. Remarks by the experimenter will be seen as friendly by one subject and condescending by another. The interpretation of the remark becomes a variable for the subject but is not under the control of the experimenter. In social psychology, therefore, an area of difficulty arises that may not exist for a researcher of visual perception who asks the subject whether a light is visible or not. In the visual perception experiment, the subject's interpretation of the situation is less likely to significantly affect the outcome. We will talk about subjective interpretation again under the topics of validity and conducting experiments.

MEASUREMENT

All of the types of variables we have been discussing must be measured on some scale. Often we don't give much thought to this process, assuming that it is obvious. However, when we say that a person is an 8 on a scale of 10, we are making assumptions about the scale on which the measurements are made. For example, would a 10 be twice as good-looking as a 5?

Students may shy away from the mathematics involved in measurement. Some may be uneasy about numbers, while others may be turned off because to them numbers make the subject drier and less human. We cannot escape entirely the mathematics needed to do experimental psychology. The reason is simple. As has often been said, an indication of the scientific progress of a field is the extent to which it states its laws quantitatively.

The ability to state laws quantitatively means that two things are true. First, the phenomenon is regular enough to make a reasonably precise statement of it. Data that are too variable can obscure any underlying lawfulness. It is true that many ingenious techniques exist to uncover the regularities that can lurk in data, but the scientist always strives to make the regularity of the phenomenon as apparent as possible so that the law can be stated precisely.

The second implication of stating a law mathematically is that the law is simple enough to write an equation describing it. If the law contains many qualifying statements and special conditions, it follows that the equation will be complicated in order to be accurate. Complicated equations are difficult to test. For this reason, scientists seek simplicity in the laws they use to describe their data. This fact is one of the reasons that Einstein's famous $E = mc^2$ captures the imagination: His theory is simple and elegant. In psychology, an example of an elegant law is Stevens's law of sensation magnitude: $R = kS^n$. This law says that R, magnitude of response, is equal to k, an arbitrary constant, times S, stimulus intensity, raised to a power, n. Stevens's law has spurred much research and has greatly influenced the field of sensory processes, in large part because of the elegance with which the law is stated.

■ What Is Measurement?

measurement
the process of
assigning numbers
to events or
objects according
to rules

Measurement is the assignment of numbers to events or objects according to rules that permit important properties of the objects or events to be represented by properties of the number system.

The key to the definition is that properties of the events are represented by properties of the number system. The rules by which the numbers are assigned to the events determine how useful the measurement is. For example, if we called every psychologically normal person a 0 and every disturbed person a 1, we would have done a kind of measurement: We would have assigned numbers to persons according to a rule. The rule permits us to count numbers of persons that fall into the two categories and to determine the percentage of abnormal personalities in the population.

We could not do much more with this set of numbers, however. The reason is that the particular measurement permits us only to express an all-or-nothing difference between people. It does not enable us to represent severity of abnormality, duration of problem, or other gradations. To do this, we would need to assign numbers according to a different rule. Perhaps we might use a scale of severity from 0 to 10, with persons falling along the scale according to their symptoms. Then we could say that one person was twice as disturbed as another or that the average level of disturbance in Group A was three times that of Group B.

■ Types of Measurement Scales

The rule by which you assign numbers determines the kind of conclusions you reach. For this reason, it is common to distinguish four types of measurement scales according to the rules by which numbers are assigned to objects or events.

Nominal Scales

nominal scale
a measure that
simply divides
objects or events
into categories
according to their
similarities or
differences

A **nominal scale** is one that classifies objects or events into categories.

Suppose that Ulf is a foreign exchange student in the United States. He is learning the English names for vegetables: asparagus, broccoli, corn, green beans, and peas. He must learn that fresh peas, frozen peas, and canned peas are the same vegetable whether they are steamed, creamed, or stir-fried. What Ulf is doing is learning a simple scale of vegetables that gives each example of a kind of vegetable one name and each member of other classes different names. We will develop this rather elementary example of a nominal scale as we progress to the other types of scales.

A nominal scale is the simplest kind of scale because its rule for assigning numbers (or other labels) to objects or events is the simplest. The rule is that objects or events of the same kind get the same number and objects or events of a different kind get different numbers. A nominal scale, as the name implies, is a classification system. Each individual event or object—in this case, vegetables—has been assigned to a class.

People sometimes think that a nominal scale is too primitive to be considered a proper scale. It seems to have little mathematics in it. In the vegetable example, in fact, words can be used instead of numbers to identify classes. Such a view overlooks the importance of classification for the development of science. As we discussed in Chapter 2, defining classes of behavior is the first step in developing laws of behavior.

Ordinal Scales

ordinal scale
a measure that both assigns objects or events a name and arranges them in order of their magnitude

An **ordinal scale** is one that ranks objects or events in order of their magnitude.

Suppose that Ruth's mother tells her there are five vegetables in the freezer and asks her to list them in the order of her preference for them, with 5 standing for the most preferred. Ruth might give her mother the following ranking:

5   peas
4   corn
3   green beans
2   broccoli
1   asparagus

We have an ordinal scale of Ruth's preference for vegetables. The rule for assigning numbers on an ordinal scale is that the ordinal position (rank order) of numbers on the scale must represent the rank order of the psychological attributes of the objects or events. Notice that the scale does not tell *how much more* Ruth prefers green beans to broccoli. Perhaps she loves peas, corn, and green beans but is totally indifferent to broccoli. The scale gives only the order of preference, not the difference in degree of preference among items.

Interval Scales

interval scale
a measure in which the differences between numbers are meaningful; includes both nominal and ordinal information

An **interval scale** is one in which the differences between the numbers on the scale are meaningful.

Suppose that Joel's mother says to him: "I know you like peas the best and asparagus the least. On a scale of 1 to 7, with 1 standing for asparagus and 7 standing for peas, how do you rate broccoli, corn, and green beans?" Suppose Joel gives the following data:

7.0   peas
6.5   corn
6.0   green beans

5.0   broccoli

4.0

3.0

2.0

1.0   asparagus

From these data, we are able to infer that Joel's liking of green beans is halfway between that of broccoli and peas. Also, there are 5 units of difference between green beans and asparagus but only 0.5 unit of difference between corn and green beans. Joel's mother knows more about his liking for vegetables than Ruth's mother does about hers. Joel's mother has developed an interval scale of his liking for vegetables. The rule for assigning numbers to events or objects on an interval scale is that equal differences between the numbers on the scale must represent equal psychological differences between the events or objects.

Ratio Scales

ratio scale
a measure having a meaningful zero point as well as all of the nominal, ordinal, and interval properties

A **ratio scale** is one that has a meaningful zero point as well as meaningful differences between the numbers on the scale.

Suppose that Susan's mother says to her: "If your feeling toward green beans is 10 on an open-ended scale, how do you feel about broccoli, corn, and other vegetables? If you are neutral about a vegetable, give it a zero. If you like one twice as much as you like another, give it a number twice as large. If you dislike a vegetable, give it a negative number. A rating of −10 would indicate that you disliked a vegetable as much as you liked green beans. You may use any number that seems appropriate; there is no upper or lower limit to the numbers you may use." Now suppose that Susan gives the following data:

30

20   peas
15   corn
10   green beans

 0   broccoli

−10

−20

−30

−40   asparagus

−50

The scale developed by Susan's mother contains the most information of the scales we have discussed. First, this scale has a meaningful zero point, which none of the other scales had. Therefore, we can know that Susan is indifferent to broccoli. Second, the ratios between numbers are meaningful. We can say that Susan likes peas twice as much as green beans or that she hates asparagus four times as much as she likes green beans. The rule for assigning numbers to events or objects on a ratio scale is that the ratios between the numbers on the scale must represent the psychological ratios between the events or objects.

■ Comparison of the Scales

As we go from nominal to ordinal, interval, and ratio scales, we are able to gain more information from the data. The nominal scale only gives information about whether two events are the same or different. The ordinal scale does that but also gives us a ranking on some variable. The interval scale conveys nominal and ordinal information and also allows us to make quantitative statements about the magnitude of the differences between events. The ratio scale contains all the information of the other three scales as well as conveying information about ratios of magnitudes. For this reason, we strive to make our scales of variables ratio scales if possible. Failing that, we try for an interval scale, and so on.

You may have noticed as we went along that each person's rating of the five vegetables was consistent with all of the others' ratings. In other words, knowing Susan's data on the ratio scale, we could derive all of the information in the other three scales. This was done purposely to show that the ratio scale is the most powerful scale, with the other scales being less powerful in the order interval, ordinal, nominal. Thus, Susan's mother knew the most about her liking for vegetables, and Ulf's hostess the least about his. Specifically, Susan's mother knows that she likes peas twice as much as green beans, she is indifferent to broccoli, and she dislikes asparagus twice as much as she likes peas. Ruth's mother, on the other hand, knows only her rank order of preferences, not the differences between them or the zero point. All that Ulf's hostess knows is that he knows one vegetable from the other.

Another way to look at the differences among types of scales is to ask "How could we have altered the assignment of numbers to the events without violating the rule governing the type of scale?" The ways that we can alter the assignment of numbers to individual events without distorting the scale are called *permissible transformations*. The permissible transformations become fewer as we go from nominal to ratio scales.

In the nominal-scale example, we could have called asparagus 1 and broccoli 2. Or we could have done the reverse. Or we could have labeled them 37 and 59. Any five numbers would do for the five categories. We would not have lost any information about Ulf's ability to identify the vegetables if we had changed the labels, because we were using the numbers only to put vegetables into classes.

With an ordinal scale, we can change the numbers in any way that preserves the order. We could have called Ruth's favorite vegetable 59, the second one 14, and the third 13. We would still know Ruth's order of preference for the vegetables.

We can do less to change the numbers of an interval scale because we must preserve the meaningfulness of the differences between items. But we can add or subtract a constant from all numbers, or we can multiply them by a positive constant. Thus, we could add 10 to all of Joel's answers or multiply them by 100 without changing any of our conclusions about his preferences for vegetables.

With a ratio scale, we can change little without distorting it. The only thing we can do is multiply all of the numbers by a positive constant. If we were to add a constant, we would destroy the significance of the ratios between numbers; we could no longer say that Susan likes corn twice as much as green beans.

Table 3.1 summarizes the points we have been making in this section. The types of scales are listed in order in the first column. The second column indicates the properties of the number system that must be represented in the rule used to assign numbers to events or objects. The third column gives the permissible transformations. The fourth column gives common examples of psychology scales.

TABLE 3.1 SUMMARY OF INFORMATION ON SCALES OF MEASUREMENT

SCALE	NUMBER SYSTEM PROPERTIES REPRESENTED BY ASSIGNMENT RULE	PERMISSIBLE TRANSFORMATIONS	EXAMPLE
Nominal	Similarities and differences	Any substitution of a number for another number that preserves similarities and differences, including all below	Types of defense mechanisms
Ordinal	Similarities and differences, rank order	Any change that preserves order among members, including both below	Preferences
Interval	Similarities and differences, rank order, magnitude of differences between individuals	Addition of a constant, multiplication by a positive constant	IQ
Ratio	Similarities and differences, rank order, magnitude of differences, ratios of properties between individuals, meaningful zero point	Multiplication by a positive constant only	Stevens's law of sensation magnitude

The various psychological defense mechanisms are good examples of nominal scales. No order of severity is implied by the names for the defense mechanisms: projection, denial, intellectualization, and so forth. Common examples of ordinal scales include any preference data of the sort we have already used in our discussion. IQ is a good example of an interval scale. The IQ tests are designed so that the amount of the differences between people can be meaningfully represented by the IQ score. However, IQ is not a ratio scale because it would be meaningless to say that a person with an IQ of 120 is twice as smart as someone with an IQ of 60. The most common example of a ratio scale is Stevens's scale, as in the example of Susan's liking for vegetables. She was told to use numbers to represent ratios of differences between vegetables.

Understanding the type of scale that the data are measured on is important so as not to draw incorrect conclusions. As we just noted, it would be meaningless to say that a person with an IQ of 120 is twice as smart as someone with an IQ of 60. Similarly, even though many teachers when computing grade-point averages consider an A to be worth 4 points, a B 3, and a C 2, no one would conclude that a person who received an A had learned twice as much as someone who received a C. In reality, there are relatively few variables in psychology that are measured on ratio, or even interval, scales. Therefore, we must know what kind of scale our data are measured on before we compare the magnitudes of differences between numbers.

■ Measurement and Statistics?

It is a widespread notion among psychologists that the scale on which a variable is measured determines the type of statistics that can appropriately be performed on the data. Thus, many hold that it is not appropriate to use the usual parametric statistics unless the data are measured on an interval or ratio scale. (Parametric statistics are those that make assumptions about the population from which the data are drawn—namely, that the population is normally distributed and each group has the same variance.) Parametric statistics include the usual Pearson correlation coefficient, the t test, and analysis of variance. Nonparametric statistics include various tests that are based on rank order of the data, or the sign of the differences between subjects.

Nonparametric tests are relatively little used because they lack power compared to the corresponding parametric test. The reason is technical, but in a nutshell, the parametric tests use all the information present in the data, whereas the nonparametric tests use only a portion of it.

Without going into the history of the controversy over scales and appropriate statistics, suffice it to say that the notion that parametric tests are limited in use to data measured on an interval or ratio scale originated with psychologists, and statisticians do not agree with it. Statisticians hold that it is appropriate to use parametric statistics on nominal, ordinal, interval, or ratio data (Gaito, 1980). Most psychologists have come to accept the position of the statisticians, although some statistics books written by psychologists still teach that the scale on which data are measured determines the appropriate statistics.

✳ NUTS & BOLTS ✳

Choosing the Levels of the Independent Variable

Many experiments involve only two conditions, such as presence or absence of a variable. In other experiments the number of conditions is strictly limited by practical or theoretical considerations. This section concerns experiments that call for several stimulus conditions. We can state four principles that apply to most such experiments.

First, the stimuli should cover as much of the range as practicable. Relationships between the variables will be better understood if the limits of the system are explored. Figure 3.1 shows how too short a stimulus range can be misleading. If the middle three stimuli were chosen, the experimenter probably would conclude that no relationship exists between the stimulus and the response. Adding more stimuli above and below the middle three, however, shows clearly that there is a U-shaped function relating stimulus and response. The middle three stimuli are not sufficient to provide an accurate picture of the functional relationship between stimulus and response.

The second principle is that the stimuli should be close enough together that overlooking any interesting relationship between the stimuli is unlikely. See Figure 3.2. Here the range of stimuli is wide enough, but the wrong conclusion could be drawn if the middle stimuli were not included.

The third principle is that when a subject is to experience all stimuli in a single session, at least seven stimuli should be presented if possible. If fewer than seven are experienced, subjects can identify and remember each stimulus. Then

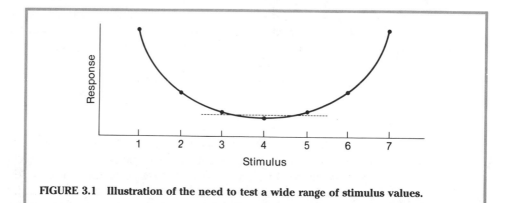

FIGURE 3.1   Illustration of the need to test a wide range of stimulus values.

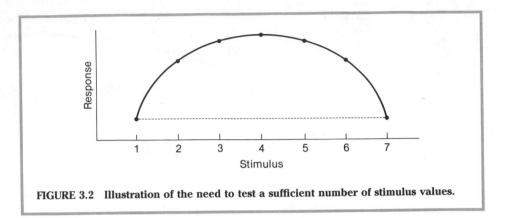

FIGURE 3.2   Illustration of the need to test a sufficient number of stimulus values.

responses may not be based on the stimulus itself but may be related to the memory of stimuli from previous trials. With seven or more stimuli, subjects respond to the stimulus itself because they are not able to identify it (Miller, 1956). Of course, using seven stimuli may not be possible because doing so may make the experiment too long.

The fourth principle of choosing stimuli concerns the spacing of quantitative variables—those that vary in amount along some continuum. If you plan to use only two stimuli, you simply pick the ones that seem the most appropriate. If you have more than two, you are faced with a choice of spacings. Should you make the intervals between stimuli equal, or should you use some other spacing pattern? You might wonder why you would ever use anything but equal intervals.

Suppose your experiment involves the effect of number of rat pellets on the speed a rat will run a maze. You want to use 1 pellet as the fewest and 81 as the most. You are going to have five groups of rats, each of which receives a different number of pellets. If you wanted to space the stimuli evenly, you would use 1, 21, 41, 61, and 81 for the various groups. However, you suspect that the difference in effect on the rat's running speed between 61 and 81 pellets may not be as great as the difference between 1 and 21. An alternative would be to space pellets evenly according to *ratios* between number of pellets, which would work out to 1, 3, 9, 27, and 81. Here each condition has three times as many pellets as the one before.

The difference in spacing is illustrated in Figure 3.3. Running speed is plotted as a function of number of pellets given as reinforcement. Notice that the difference in running speed between 1 pellet and 21 pellets is 2.75 units, whereas the difference between 61 and 81 is only about 0.25 units. If you had used the equal-difference spacing, you would have missed most of the "action," which occurs between conditions that present 1 or 21 pellets. On the other hand, by spacing pellets according to equal ratios, you have found equal effects on the running speed between each number of pellets used. Of course, this example was created so that this would be the case. Nonetheless, a great many

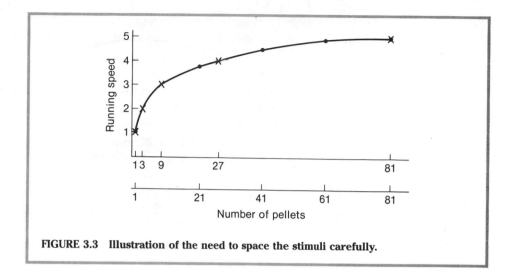

FIGURE 3.3   Illustration of the need to space the stimuli carefully.

stimulus dimensions—perhaps most—are such that most action takes place at the lower end of the scale. In these cases, stimuli should be spaced so that equal ratios fall between stimuli. This kind of spacing is also known as *logarithmic* spacing.   ❏

SUMMARY

1. A variable is some property of an event in the world that has been measured.

2. A dependent variable is a measure of the behavior of the subject.

3. An independent variable is one that is believed to cause some change in the value of the dependent variable.

4. The different values of an independent variable are called the levels of the variable.

5. Quantitative variables vary in amount, whereas categorical variables differ in kind.

6. A continuous variable is one that is not limited to a certain number of values.

7. A discrete variable is one that falls into a certain number of distinct bins.

8. The apparent limits of a number are the point indicated by the number itself; the real limits are the interval defined by the number plus and minus half the difference to the next numbers.

9. A physical variable is one that can be defined in physical terms. A nonphysical variable is one that cannot be so defined but must be defined in terms of behavior or cognitive processes.

10. Measurement is the assignment of numbers to objects or events according to rules that permit important properties of the objects or events to be represented by properties of the number system.

11. Four scales of measurement are distinguished according to the rules by which numbers are assigned to objects or events: nominal, ordinal, interval, and ratio.

12. A nominal scale is one that classifies objects or events into categories. Objects or events of the same kind get the same number, and different objects or events get different numbers.

13. An ordinal scale is one that ranks objects or events in order of their magnitude. The ordinal position of the numbers on the scale must represent the rank order of the psychological attributes of the objects or events.

14. An interval scale is one in which the differences between the numbers on the scale are meaningful. Equal differences between the numbers on the scale must represent equal differences between the events or objects.

15. A ratio scale is one that has a meaningful zero point as well as meaningful differences between the numbers on the scale. The ratios between the numbers on the scale must represent the ratios between the events or objects.

16. We are able to gain more information from the data as we progress from nominal to ordinal, interval, and ratio scales.

17. Knowing the type of scale that data are measured on is important so as to avoid drawing incorrect conclusions from the data.

18. Although many psychologists hold that parametric statistics may be performed only on variables measured on interval or ratio scales, statisticians do not agree.

19. The choice of stimulus values is guided by four principles:
    a. The stimuli should cover as much of the range as possible.
    b. They should be close enough together to prevent overlooking interesting effects between stimuli.
    c. In within-subjects studies, at least seven stimuli should be presented if possible.
    d. If the continuum is quantitative, the stimuli should be logarithmically spaced.

Suggestions for Further Reading

GUILFORD, J. P. (1954). *Psychometric methods*. New York: McGraw-Hill. This book contains a good discussion of scales of measurement as well as a mathematical introduction that covers much of the material in this chapter.

LEWIS, D. (1960). *Quantitative methods in psychology*. New York: McGraw-Hill. This text provides valuable mathematical background for this chapter.

STEVENS, S. S. (1951). Mathematics, measurement, and psychophysics. In S. S. Stevens (Ed.), *Handbook of experimental psychology*. New York: Wiley. The classic discussion of scales of measurement.

⫸ A CASE IN POINT ⫷

Class Size and Learning

State University is concerned about the effect of class size on learning. There are more students each year, but the legislature has not increased the instructional budget. The dean would like to find out if students in large classes learn as much as students in small classes.

Approximately 1,500 students take introductory psychology classes each term. The largest classroom available at State has 500 seats. The smallest classes generally have about 20 students. The psychology department will be able to staff eight sections of the course next term.

Professor Chips in the psychology department is coordinating the study. He believes that more highly motivated students will learn the same amount regardless of class size, because they will compensate for any differences in teaching methods or other factors by studying hard enough to learn the material. Less motivated students may learn less in larger sections. Mr. Chips will administer a standard test of motivation on the first day of class to all students and use the results to separate each class into highly motivated and less motivated students for the purpose of evaluating the data.

REQUIRED:
1. Decide how many sections of introductory psychology should participate in the study and what size each should be. (Assume that you have complete control over class size, within the limits on room size.)
2. Sketch a graph that shows the kind of data that Mr. Chips expects to find.

≡ READING BETWEEN THE LINES ≡

3.1   TESTING FOR INDEPENDENCE OF DIMENSIONS

Robert Hamm and James Mattson (1978) wanted to test whether stimuli to which an animal had been conditioned separately would have a combined effect when the stimuli were presented together. They taught rats in a Skinner box to press a plastic bar, causing the bar to be lit up from behind. The two dimensions were the intensity of the light and the rate at which it flickered. The intensity of the light on the bar could be either high or low, and the light could flicker either once per second or ten times per second. Can you think of a reason why light intensity and flicker rate might not be independent of one another?   ∎

☑ EXERCISES

3.1   IDENTIFY TYPES OF VARIABLES

A researcher administers an intelligence test to 30 college students. After gathering information on subjects' age, sex, height, weight, political preference, college major, career goals, and socioeconomic status, the researcher administers an attitude survey on current world issues to all 30 subjects.

REQUIRED: Identify examples of the following types of variables in the paragraph and the scales by which they would be measured:

a. discrete
b. continuous
c. categorical
d. quantitative
e. nominal scale
f. ordinal scale
g. interval scale
h. ratio scale

3.2   PORNOGRAPHY AND SEXUAL BEHAVIOR

Dolf Zillmann and Jennings Bryant (1984) studied the effect of viewing pornography on responses to pornography and other related matters. This exercise is based on a portion of their research.

A total of 80 male and 80 female undergraduates were randomly assigned to four groups. Three of the groups met weekly for several weeks. These three groups watched a different set of short films each week for six weeks. They evaluated each film for aesthetic quality, this evaluation being the supposed purpose of the study. One of the three groups saw six explicit pornographic films each week. The second group saw three pornographic films and three educational films. The third group saw only educational films. The fourth group did not meet during this period and so did not see any films.

On the seventh week, all subjects in the first three groups watched three different films. The first was a mildly erotic film, the second depicted explicit sex acts, and the third showed sex involving sadomasochism and bestiality. All subjects saw the same three films in the same order. On this week, the experimenters measured the subjects' heart rate and blood pressure before and after each film. They recorded the difference in these two responses from the first to the second measurement. They also recorded the subjects' reported enjoyment of the film and their reported repulsion by the film.

On the final week, all subjects—including those in the fourth group, which had not met up until then—were asked about (1) their assessment of the frequency of various common and uncommon sexual practices in the population, (2) their recommended punishment for rape, (3) their support of the women's liberation movement, (4) their attitude toward pornography, and (5) (for men) their callousness toward women.

REQUIRED: Identify the independent and dependent variables in the experiment. At least one of the independent variables has several different levels. It will help to specify these.

3.3   IDENTIFY VARIABLES

Following is an abstract of an article. Read it and answer the questions below.

The present research investigated the effects of counterfactual thinking on subjects' accident-related judgments. It was predicted that the availability of counterfactual alternatives for an accident would result in differential evaluation of incident-related victims and perpetrators. The results of two studies strongly supported this prediction. Specifically, subjects awarded more financial compensation to the victim of an accident when it was preceded by exceptional rather than routine circumstances. Similarly, under these conditions the accident perpetrators were deemed to be more negligent in their behavior and a harsher fine was leveled against them. (Macrae, 1992)

REQUIRED:
    a. What is (are) the independent variable(s)?
    b. What were the levels (conditions) of the independent variables?
    c. What is (are) the dependent variable(s)?
    d. Which sentence states a hypothesis?

3.4 IDENTIFY VARIABLES

The following is a slightly modified abstract of an article. Read it and answer the questions that follow.

Two experiments examined the effects of a number of motivated encoding strategies (anticipated interaction, friend comparison, and memory instructions) on the recall and cognitive organization of information about multiple target persons. As in past research on the effects of motivated encoding strategies on the cognitive processing of information about a single target, memory instructions produced the lowest levels of recall. However, in contrast to past research, no [other] instruction set produced evidence of higher cognitive [organization] of targets than [did] memory instructions. The results are discussed in the context of two alternative models of person memory—the associative network model and the elaboration model. (Sedikides, Devine, & Furman, 1991)

REQUIRED:
    a. What is (are) the independent variable(s)?
    b. What were the levels (conditions) of the independent variables?
    c. What is (are) the dependent variable(s)?
    d. Which sentence concerns a theory?

3.5 IDENTIFY INDEPENDENT AND DEPENDENT VARIABLES

The following questions are adapted from Walker (1982). For each of the following research reports, indicate the following:

    a. the independent variable(s)
    b. the dependent variable(s)

"A Rolling Stone Gathers No Moss"

Researchers took ten stones varying in color and size and rolled them down the stairs of their laboratory and then down a little slope on the laboratory grounds. None of the stones gathered any moss.

"I Know Which Side My Bread Is Buttered On"

Researchers gave a panel of 14 volunteers whole slices of bread with butter spread on only one side. No matter what kind of bread researchers used (white, whole wheat, or pumpernickel), all of the volunteers were able to identify which side of the bread was buttered. This was the case when the subjects were blindfolded, had their hands tied behind their backs, and had their noses pinched by clothespins.

"An Apple a Day Keeps the Doctor Away"

A panel of 10 volunteers was divided into two groups. Five of the volunteers were given an apple a day for 14 days. The other 5 were not given apples at all but were given other edibles. The researchers then instructed a doctor to approach each of the 10 volunteers every day. Researchers found that the doctor did successfully approach each of the 10 volunteers every day and that the apples did not keep him away. Whether the apples had been eaten or not, were being eaten at the moment of approach, or were hidden on the persons of the volunteers or at some distance away in metal footlockers, apples were completely ineffective in warding off the approach of the doctor.   ❏

4

Tabular and Graphical Description of Data

This chapter concerns the description of empirical data: analyzing and summarizing data in ways that make it possible to see the patterns that exist in them. This process includes presenting data in tables, graphs, and numerical summaries. The numerical description of data is well covered in most statistics courses, and most readers of this book will either have taken a course in statistics or be studying statistics together with research methods. Most statistics courses, however, discuss tables and graphs only incidentally to their discussion of numerical analysis of data. The purpose of this chapter is to discuss tables and graphs. A review of descriptive statistics is found in Appendix A.

One thing that psychology students quickly discover is that psychologists are constantly making tables and drawing graphs. A **table** is a display of data in numerical form in the rows and columns of a matrix. A **graph** is a representation of data by spatial relationships in a diagram. Graphs and tables help us to summarize data and understand the relationships between variables. The old saying that a picture is worth a thousand words often is literally true of graphs and tables. So you can see why it is imperative to be able to read and understand tables and graphs.

Most graphs used in psychology have two axes plotted at right angles to one another. Look at Figure 4.1 for an example of a basic graph. The horizontal axis is called the x-axis. The vertical axis is the y-axis. The x-axis is called the *abscissa,* and the y-axis is called the *ordinate*. A silly but simple way of remembering this is that when you say abscissa your mouth takes a

table
a display of data in a matrix format
graph
a representation of data by spatial relationships in a diagram

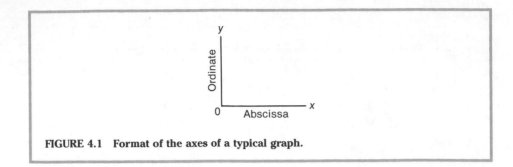

FIGURE 4.1   Format of the axes of a typical graph.

horizontal shape, and when you say ordinate it becomes vertical. Typically, the abscissa, or x-axis, represents the value of the independent variable, while the ordinate, or y-axis, shows the value of the dependent variable. Many other possibilities exist, as we will see. A graph may have two independent variables, or no independent variable. It is necessary to pay particular attention to what the axes of a graph represent.

TABLES AND GRAPHS OF FREQUENCY DATA

Supppose that Professor Carlton has given a 20-point test in his class, and finds that the students earned the following scores: 16, 12, 14, 17, 10, 17, 18, 17, 14, and 15. Before he can assign grades to the students, he needs to see how they did as a group. As you can see, it is hard to describe the data in their present format, because there is no order to them.

■   Frequency Tables

Before he goes any further, Professor Carlton decides to arrange the data in a table (see Table 4.1). In this table, the rows indicate possible scores on the test. The columns represent particular information about those possible scores.

The first column of the table is a list of all the possible scores from highest to lowest. The second column shows the upper real limits of the scores (see Chapter 3). The third column is a tally of the scores that were obtained by the students. Each score is noted by a slash. The fourth column is simply a numerical representation of the information in the third column: the number of students who obtained a given score. We will discuss other columns of this table later.

Each row gives information about a particular score. As one looks across the row that indicates a score of 15, for example, one sees how many students received a score of 15. Tables enable one to organize and display a

TABLE 4.1 Distribution of test scores

Score	Upper Real Limit	Tally	Frequency	Cumulative Frequency	Percentage	Cumulative Percentage
20	20.5		0	10	0	100
19	19.5		0	10	0	100
18	18.5	I	1	10	10	100
17	17.5	III	3	9	30	90
16	16.5	I	1	6	10	60
15	15.5	I	1	5	10	50
14	14.5	II	2	4	20	40
13	13.5		0	2	0	20
12	12.5	I	1	2	10	20
11	11.5		0	1	0	10
10	10.5	I	1	1	10	10
9	9.5		0	0	0	0

$N = 10$

$\Sigma = 150$

$\bar{x} = 15$

$Mdn = 15.5$

$Mode = 17$

considerable amount of information in a clear format. We will be looking at this table in some detail later, but for now we will move on to a graphical display of the same data.

■ Frequency Distributions

Next, Professor Carlton decides to make a graphical representation of his data. The particular kind of graph that Professor Carlton finds useful to describe his class's performance on the test is a **frequency distribution.** This is a graph that shows how many scores fall into particular bins, or divisions of the variable. The bins used here are the number of items correct on the test.

Figure 4.2 shows the same basic information as the table, but in a graphical format. The abscissa shows the various possible scores, and the ordinate shows the frequency of each score. Each bar, then, represents the frequency of a given score.

frequency distribution
a graph that shows the number of scores that fall in specific bins, or divisions of the variable

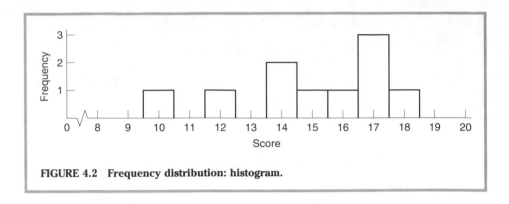

FIGURE 4.2   Frequency distribution: histogram.

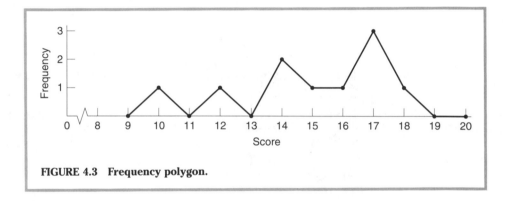

FIGURE 4.3   Frequency polygon.

histogram
a frequency
distribution in
which the
frequencies are
represented by
contiguous bars

**frequency
polygon**
a frequency
distribution in
which the
frequencies are
connected by
straight lines

Note that the bar that indicates a given score is centered on that score: the bar goes from half a unit below the score to half a unit above the score. Thus, for example, the bar that indicates a score of 15 extends from 14.5 to 15.5. Also note that the bar touches the bars representing the scores on either side, rather than being separated by a space. This use of contiguous bars represents the idea that the underlying variable we are measuring is continuous, rather than discrete. Although a student can only answer whole items, we believe that knowledge of the subject is continuous.

Both the table and the graph allow us to begin to see a number of characteristics of the data: the highest and lowest scores, the most common score, the shape of the distribution, and so on. A frequency distribution drawn with bars indicating the frequency at each particular score, as we have done, is called a **histogram.** Alternatively, we could have used a dot to represent the frequency at each score and connected these points with straight lines, as shown in Figure 4.3. This form of presentation is called a **frequency polygon.** Although both histograms and frequency polygons show the same information, and both are correct, generally a histogram is more informative when there are relatively few categories, as in Professor Carlton's

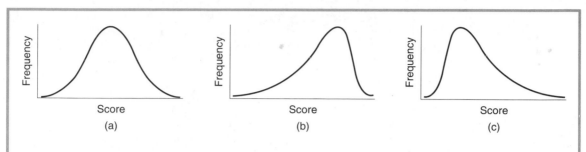

FIGURE 4.4   Normal and skewed curves: (a) normal distribution; (b) negatively skewed distribution; (c) positively skewed distribution.

test. When there are a great many categories, the data usually begin to approximate a smooth curve, and then the frequency polygon is clearer. The next three examples will use frequency polygons.

We are often interested in the shape of a frequency distribution. Many distributions are bell-shaped; that is, they are symmetrical, with most cases falling in the middle and fewer cases at either end (the tails). One particular bell-shaped curve is called the **normal curve** (see Figure 4.4a). This is a certain mathematical function that happens to describe many frequency distributions that occur in nature. The normal curve enters into a number of theoretical and practical statistical considerations.

normal curve
a bell-shaped curve described by a certain mathematical function

skewed
a distribution that is not symmetrical

If a frequency distribution is not symmetrical, but has a longer tail on one end or the other, we say that it is **skewed.** When the tail is to the low end of the distribution, it is said to be negatively skewed (Figure 4.4b); when the tail is to the high end, it is positively skewed (Figure 4.4c).

Notice that a frequency distribution is an exception to the usual type of graph in that the ordinate and abscissa do not represent an independent and dependent variable, respectively. The abscissa, or horizontal axis, of a frequency distribution represents values of a *dependent variable,* such as scores on a test. The ordinate, or vertical axis, represents *frequencies,* such as the number of individuals who obtain various scores on the dependent variable.

■ Cumulative Frequency Distributions

cumulative frequency distribution
a frequency distribution that shows the number of scores that fall at or below a certain score.

A frequency distribution indicates the number of cases at each score. A related distribution is the **cumulative frequency distribution** (see Figure 4.5). This distribution shows the number of scores that fall at or below a given score. Polygons are generally used to indicate cumulative frequency, as we have done, although histograms can be used.

Several points should be noted about the cumulative frequency distribution. First, note that the score is represented by its upper real limit, not the midpoint of the interval. For example, the line goes from a frequency

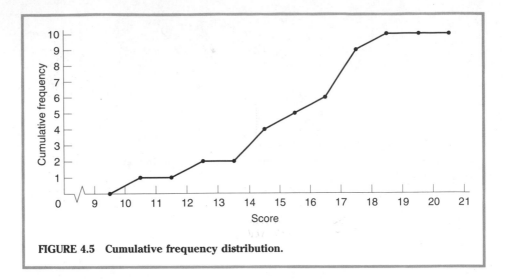

FIGURE 4.5   Cumulative frequency distribution.

of 0 at 9.5 to 1 at 10.5. The reason is that the upper real limit is the only point in the interval that is certain to include all scores that fall at or below the entire interval.

The second point that should be noted is that a graph of a cumulative frequency distribution always increases monotonically. That is, the graph either increases or stays horizontal as it goes from left to right, but never decreases. This follows from the definition of cumulative frequency: the number at or below a certain score can never be less than the number at or below a lower score. For example, if there are 5 cases at or below a score of 15, there must be at least 5 at or below 16.

Third, the shape of the cumulative frequency curve is generally *sigmoidal,* or S-shaped. The curve is horizontal at either end, and is steepest somewhere in the middle. If the distribution is skewed, as this one is, the steepest part of the curve will be toward the lower or higher end, because that is where most of the cases fall. Figure 4.6 shows a cumulative frequency distribution that represents a normal curve, one that is positively skewed, and one that is negatively skewed.

■ Percentiles

Look again at Table 4.1. Column 5 of the table gives the cumulative frequency, or the number of cases that fall at or below a given score. Column 7 converts these cumulative frequencies into cumulative percentages—the percentage of cases that fall at or below a given score. Looking at column 7, we find that 90% of the cases fall at or below a score of 17.5 and 60% fall at or below a score of 16.5. Therefore, the 75th percentile must fall somewhere in the interval of

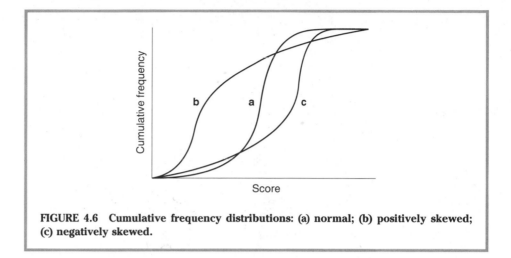

FIGURE 4.6   Cumulative frequency distributions: (a) normal; (b) positively skewed; (c) negatively skewed.

16.5 to 17.5; let's call it 17 for simplicity. Likewise, the 25th percentile is somewhere between 13.5 and 14.5; let's say it is 14.[1] Thus, the interquartile range is $17 - 14 = 3$.

Now we need to find the 50th percentile. Looking at column 7 and row 15, we find that 50% of the cases fall at or below a score of 15.5. Finding the 50th percentile in this example shows the importance of the concept of real limits. If you looked only at the midpoint of the interval—that is, the score—you might think that the 50th percentile should be 15, because 50% fall at or below a score of 15. Note, however, that 50% of the scores fall at 16 or higher. So, the median has to be between 15 and 16.

TABLES AND GRAPHS THAT SHOW THE RELATIONSHIP BETWEEN TWO VARIABLES

Frequency distributions only show one variable—the dependent variable—and a frequency. Other tables and graphs show the relationship between two variables. Some of these present individual data and others, group data.

---

[1] Although we have used the middle of the interval that contains the particular score to represent a percentile, it is possible to use linear interpolation to find the exact location within the interval that represents a particular percentile. For example, the 25th percentile falls in the interval of 13.5 to 14.5. From the graph we can see that the 25th percentile is actually in the lower part of the interval and could estimate the point graphically. Alternatively, we could set up an algebraic equation by which we could calculate that the 25th percentile is exactly 13.75.

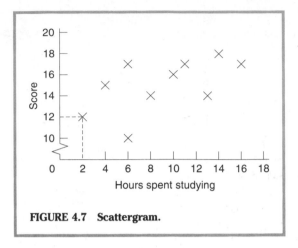

FIGURE 4.7   Scattergram.

■ Scattergrams

scattergram
a graph showing
the responses of
a number of
individuals on
two variables;
visual display of
correlational data

A **scattergram** is a graph that shows the relationship between two variables for a number of individual cases. Figure 4.7 shows the relationship between time spent studying and the grades earned by individual students in Professor Carlton's class. The abscissa indicates time spent studying, and the ordinate indicates grade on a test. Each symbol on the scattergram represents one individual student. By dropping a line perpendicular to the abscissa from a given point, we can read the number of hours an individual spent studying. By dropping a line perpendicular to the ordinate, we can read that same individual's grade on the test. We can see, for example, that one individual studied for 2 hours and earned a grade of 12. It is important to note that the scattergram shows the scores on two variables for each individual. By looking at the pattern of the individual data points, we can get an idea that there is some relationship between hours spent studying and test grade. We can determine the degree of the relationship and what the function is that relates the two variables by computing the correlation coefficient. (See Appendix A.) Scattergrams are commonly used to illustrate correlational data.

Although the abscissa of a scattergram often represents an independent variable and the ordinate, the dependent variable, as in this example, it should be noted that we often do not know which variable in a scattergram is independent and which is dependent. Sometimes both may be independent variables, or both may be dependent variables. Suppose you had a scattergram showing the relationship between the stickiness of the blacktop on the road in front of a hospital and the number of babies that die in the hospital on various days. Suppose also that the pattern of data points indicated that more babies died on days when the blacktop was stickier. You might wonder whether sticky blacktop killed the babies, or whether all of the ambulances rushing to the hospital made the blacktop sticky. Actually, hot weather makes blacktop sticky and also puts stress on babies. Thus, both variables on your scattergram would be dependent variables.

■ Tables with One Independent and One Dependent Variable

median split
a division of the subjects in a study into two groups of equal size on the basis of one of the variables

Rather than displaying individual data in a scattergram, as in Figure 4.7, we might prefer to display the same data in summary form. For example, we can do a **median split,** dividing the subjects into two groups of equal size, based on the number of hours studied. Then we can look at the average grade earned by those who studied the most, and those who studied the least. These data are shown in Table 4.2.

As with all tables, we have a matrix format. Notice that the independent variable, hours studied, becomes the columns of the matrix. The dependent variable, test score, becomes the elements of the matrix. We generally would not want to make a table just to show just two pieces of data. But we made this table to demonstrate that the values of the dependent variable become the elements of the matrix, and the values of the independent variable become the columns. So you might keep in mind that a table that shows a dependent variable as a function of one independent variable will have only one row. Tables become more complicated, and more informative, when there is more than one independent variable.

We could have more rows in this table, however. Suppose we want to show the variability of the data, as well as the mean. In Table 4.3, the two rows show different aspects of the same dependent variable: mean and standard deviation. Thus, although there is more than one row in this table, they both refer to aspects of the same dependent variable, score. Alternatively, if there had been more than one dependent variable, the different dependent variables could have become rows of the table. We might have measured the score on the test and the length of time spent taking the test, for example.

TABLE 4.2 TEST SCORE AS A FUNCTION OF HOURS STUDIED

	Hours Studied	
	Less than 10	10 or more
Mean score	13.6	16.4

TABLE 4.3 TEST SCORE AS A FUNCTION OF HOURS STUDIED

	Hours Studied	
Score	Less than 10	10 or more
Mean	13.6	16.4
Standard deviation	2.7	1.5

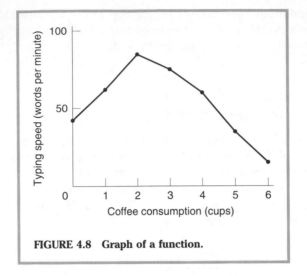

FIGURE 4.8   Graph of a function.

■ Graphs of Functions (Line Graphs)

Probably the most typical graph in psychology is the graph of a function. The ordinate represents some dependent variable as a function of an independent variable. Generally, functions that we graph involve a response that varies continuously with changes in the level of a quantitative independent variable. For example, we might graph the number of error-free words a person can type per minute as a function of the number of cups of coffee drunk during the previous hour. Figure 4.8 is a **line graph** that shows these hypothetical data. You can see that the speed of typing increases as the amount of coffee increases up to about 2 cups, after which more coffee is associated with slower typing speeds.

The fact that we have drawn lines between the data points implies that we could find a particular mathematical function that would describe the data if we tried to do so. (See Appendix E for a discussion of the mathematical description of functions.) Note that the data points in this graph are connected by straight lines. You should always connect data points by straight lines, rather than drawing a smooth curve through the points, unless you can write the mathematical equation that describes the curve. Drawing a smooth curve implies a particular mathematical function, and generally means that there is a theory that describes the exact shape of the function. Data points connected by straight lines indicate only an empirical, rather than a theoretical, function.

■ Bar Graphs

Bar graphs are used when the independent variable is categorical rather than quantitative. If the independent variable in an experiment is sex of subject, for

line graph
a graphic representation using lines to show relationships between quantitative variables

bar graph
graphic representation of categorical data in which the heights of separated bars, or columns, show the relationships between variables

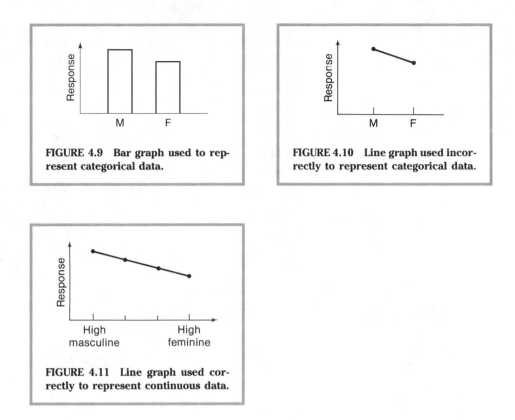

FIGURE 4.9 Bar graph used to represent categorical data.

FIGURE 4.10 Line graph used incorrectly to represent categorical data.

FIGURE 4.11 Line graph used correctly to represent continuous data.

example, the data can only be represented by a bar graph (see Figure 4.9). Because persons are either male or female, the independent variable is categorical; it is impossible to have data points that fall between the two points (M and F) on the abscissa. A line graph would be incorrect in this case, because it would imply the possibility of data points anywhere along the line (see Figure 4.10). On the other hand, if the independent variable is masculinity/femininity as measured by a test, drawing a line graph *is* possible because individual subjects could, in principle, fall anywhere along the abscissa (see Figure 4.11). Note that the individual bars on a bar graph are drawn so that they do not touch each other, emphasizing that they represent different categories of behavior.

RELATION BETWEEN FREQUENCY DISTRIBUTIONS AND OTHER GRAPHS

Recall that a frequency distribution differs from other graphs in that the ordinate represents a frequency, not the value of a dependent variable. Instead, the abscissa represents a dependent variable, such as number of correct responses on a test. However, frequency distributions and other graphs can often be related to one another.

Table 4.2 showed the mean number of correct responses as a function of number of hours studied. If we plot the two mean scores—13.6 for those students who studied less than 10 hours, and 16.4 for those who studied 10 hours or more—we have a graph of this function (Figure 4.12).

Figure 4.13 is a frequency distribution that combines the information in Table 4.2 (or Figure 4.12) with that provided by the scattergram in Figure 4.7. Compare Figure 4.13 with the frequency distribution shown in Figure 4.2. In Figure 4.13, we have superimposed two separate frequency distributions on the same axes. The boxes are shaded differently for the two groups: those who studied 10 hours or more, and those who studied less than 10 hours. The distribution looks a little different than it did in Figure 4.2 for two reasons: First, we have reversed the direction of the numbers on the abscissa. Second, data in the two conditions can overlap; see, for example, the two scores of 14, one from each group.

Figure 4.14 is a three-dimensional graph that combines the information

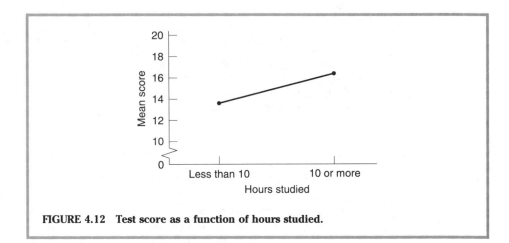

FIGURE 4.12   Test score as a function of hours studied.

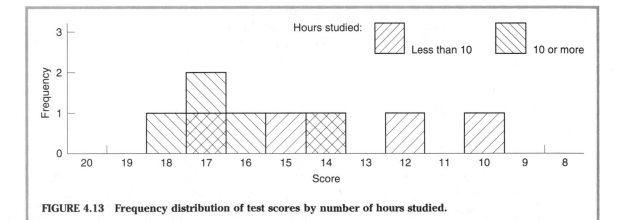

FIGURE 4.13   Frequency distribution of test scores by number of hours studied.

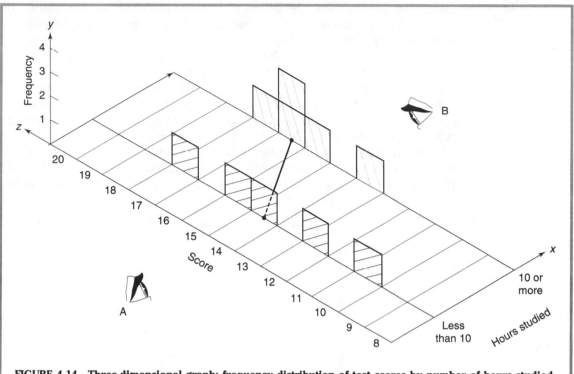

FIGURE 4.14   Three-dimensional graph: frequency distribution of test scores by number of hours studied.

from the two previous graphs. The x-axis represents hours studied, our independent variable. The z-axis represents the test score, which is the dependent variable. The y-axis, or vertical dimension, shows frequency, or how many students achieved each score. If we mentally rotate the graph so that we take Viewpoint A in the figure and look at right angles to the z-axis, the graph becomes identical to Figure 4.13. From this viewpoint, dimension x collapses and we have frequency (y) as a function of test score (z). Now if we rotate the graph again in our heads and look at it from Viewpoint B—that is, look down at the surface defined by the x and z dimensions—we see score as a function of hours studied (Figure 4.12). Thus, we see that frequency distributions are different from other graphs but can be related to them. Remembering this distinction will help you when you are reading graphs.

TIME-SERIES GRAPHS

time-series graph
a graph in which
the abscissa
represents time

A **time-series graph** is one in which the abscissa represents the passage of time.

Suppose an instructor who gives six tests in her course notices in the middle of the third test that a student's eyes are wandering to the paper of the person next to him. She moves the student to the front row and makes sure that the two students are separated for all subsequent tests. Because she kept a seating chart on the test days, she knows that the suspect sat next to the same person for the first three tests. Then she computes the percentage of identical answers on each test, as shown in Figure 4.15. This is an example of a time-series graph because the various tests took place over time in the order shown on the graph. From these data the instructor concludes that the student whose eyes were wandering had been copying answers from the other student, and she goes to the dean with her evidence.

Another type of time-series design in psychology is the cumulative record commonly used in operant conditioning research (see Figure 4.16). The abscissa shows time, as in all such graphs. The ordinate, however, shows

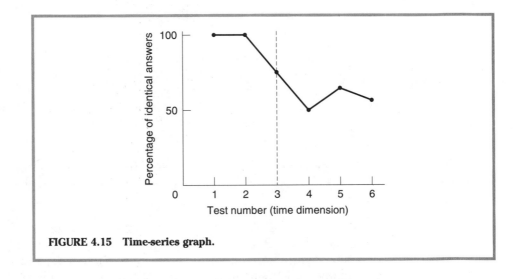

FIGURE 4.15   Time-series graph.

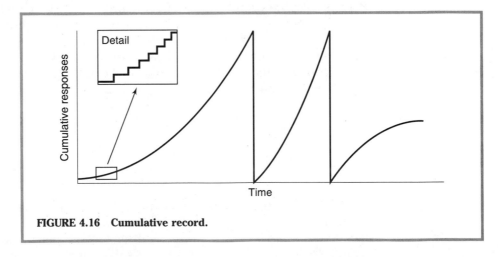

FIGURE 4.16   Cumulative record.

the cumulative number of responses since the beginning of the session. Each response causes the recorder to make a small vertical movement. If the detail of the graph were fine enough, you could see that each response made the pen move a step up and then move horizontally until the next response. (See detail insert.) The slope of the graph shows the *rate* of responding. When the animal is making no responses, the graph is flat because the pen does not move vertically as time passes horizontally. When the animal responds rapidly, the graph becomes steep. (The vertical line shows the recorder resetting to zero after reaching the top of the graph.)

Chapter 11 discusses a number of examples of research using time-series designs.

TABLES AND GRAPHS OF THREE VARIABLES

Almost all of the tables and graphs discussed so far have had only one independent variable. The graphs have had either a dependent variable or a frequency on the ordinate. Frequently, however, a study includes two (or more) independent variables.

Suppose we knew both the number of hours that Professor Carlton's students studied and their SAT scores, as well as their class test scores. Then we would have two independent variables and one dependent variable. The results might be laid out as shown in Table 4.4.

Two important types of graphs are used to represent the relationship among three variables: contour graphs and data maps. Because they are somewhat difficult to explain in the abstract, the best way to introduce them is to jump right in with a familiar example of the first kind, the contour graph.

■ Contour Graphs

Most people have used a topographical map to hike or to study geography. Figure 4.17 shows a map of two islands in the ocean. You may be able to tell

TABLE 4.4 MEAN TEST SCORE AS A FUNCTION OF HOURS STUDIED AND SAT SCORE

SAT SCORE	HOURS STUDIED	
	LESS THAN 10	10 OR MORE
1000 or more	15.3	17
Less than 1000	11	16

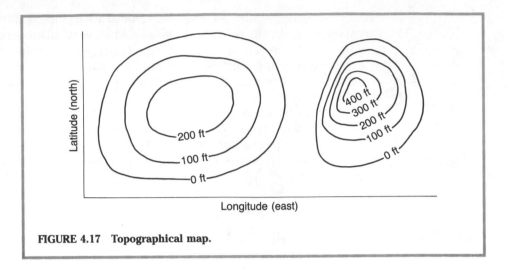

FIGURE 4.17   Topographical map.

without any help that the island to the west is larger and has a hill that is somewhat over 200 feet high. The smaller island to the east has a higher hill, over 400 feet, and the west side of that hill is much steeper than the other sides. If you can get that information out of the map, you are ready for contour graphs.

A topographical map represents three dimensions: longitude (east), measured along the abscissa; latitude (north), measured on the ordinate; and altitude, indicated by the contour lines. If we think of longitude and latitude as independent variables, and altitude as a dependent variable, the topographical map shows how altitude depends on (or varies as a function of) latitude and longitude. Each contour line goes through all contiguous points that have the same altitude. (It is possible for there to be two hills that are the same height, or two islands, as in this case.) Another way of saying this is that contour lines of a certain value show the location of all combinations of longitude and latitude that have the same value of altitude. Where the contour lines are farther apart along an axis, altitude is changing slowly as you move along the axis. When they are close together, the slope of the land is steep.

contour graph
a graph showing how a dependent variable changes as a function of two independent variables, one of which is on the abscissa and the other on the ordinate

A **contour graph** is also three-dimensional: The abscissa does not represent a dependent variable; instead, both the ordinate and the abscissa represent independent variables. A typical example of a contour graph used in psychology is Figure 4.18, which shows the effect of frequency and intensity of a sound on its loudness. There are two independent variables in this graph. The first is frequency in cycles per second, usually called hertz (Hz). (Differences in frequency are heard as differences in pitch.) Frequency is shown on the x-axis. Intensity, in decibels (dB), is shown on the y-axis. The dependent variable is loudness.

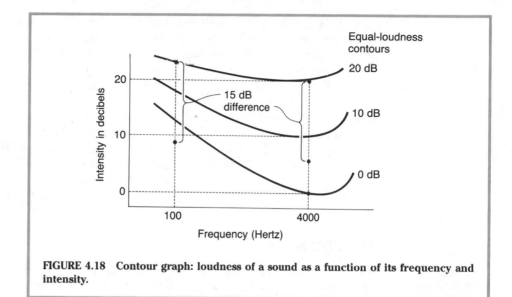

FIGURE 4.18   Contour graph: loudness of a sound as a function of its frequency and intensity.

It is important to realize that frequency and intensity are physical variables, whereas loudness is a psychological variable. (Note that the two physical variables have physical units—hertz and decibels, respectively.) The purpose of this graph is to show how loudness, the dependent variable, varies as a function of frequency and intensity, two independent variables. Another way of saying this is that the loudness of a sound depends on both the intensity and the frequency of the sound.

You probably know that we are more sensitive to sounds in the middle frequencies (about 4000 Hz) than we are to sounds of lower or higher frequencies. The bottom curve illustrates that fact: It shows the intensity required for sounds of various frequencies just to reach threshold. (Threshold is arbitrarily defined as zero loudness.) In other words, the bottom curve shows the locations of all combinations of frequency and intensity that produce a just-detectable sound. These points all have the same loudness, which we will call zero loudness. We can call this curve an equal-loudness contour for a loudness of zero.

The second curve shows another equal-loudness contour. What the experimenters did was raise the intensity of a 4000-Hz tone 10 dB above threshold. This tone obviously sounded louder than the zero-loudness tone. Then they found by experiment all combinations of intensity and frequency that sounded equally as loud as the 4000-Hz tone that was 10 dB above threshold. These points were connected by the curve labeled 10 dB on the graph. Now we have two equal-loudness contours: one for zero loudness and one for a loudness of 10 dB. The third curve is analogous to the second, this time for 20 dB above threshold.

This graph has a practical application. Stereo systems commonly have separate gain controls for treble and bass. (Some have equalizers that permit adjustments for a large number of frequency ranges.) This is because it is necessary to balance the treble and bass for the overall loudness level at which the system is played. If the treble and bass are balanced for a given loudness level and the overall loudness is reduced, the bass will be reduced more than the treble. You may have noticed this when your parents told you to turn down your stereo. At the lower level, the bass may be barely audible. Look again at the 20-dB equal-loudness contour in Figure 4.18. If you reduce the intensity of the 4000-Hz tone 15 dB below the curve, it has a loudness of 5 dB. If you reduce the intensity of the 100-Hz tone 15 dB below the curve, however, it can no longer be heard because it is below threshold!

■ Data Maps

data map
a graph showing
locations in space
that have some
characteristic; for
example, a map
of sensory areas
of the brain

A **data map** is a type of graph that represents locations in space that have a particular characteristic. Figure 4.19, for example, represents the sensory areas of the rat brain. The axes of the map are not shown, but the x-axis runs from front to back of the brain, and the y-axis runs from bottom to top. These conventions would be understood by readers of the map. Landmarks are shown to help interpret the map. The various areas indicated are those that have been found to respond with electrical activity when certain parts of the body are stimulated.

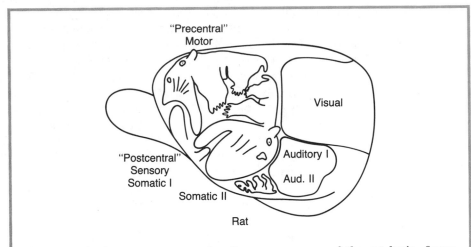

FIGURE 4.19 Data map representing the sensory areas of the rat brain. Source: "Organization of Somatic Sensory and Motor Areas of the Cerebral Cortex" by C. N. Woolsey. In *Biological and Chemical Bases of Behavior*, ed. H. F. Harlow & C. N. Woolsey (Madison, WI: University of Wisconsin Press, 1965). Copyright 1965 by University of Wisconsin Press. Reprinted by permission.

■ Graphs of Relations in Which the Data Points Are Pictures

Occasionally a graph of a function will be presented in such a way that the locations in the space are indicated by pictures. This type of graph is frequently used when two variables influence a behavior and the behavior can be illustrated by a picture. An example is given in Figure 4.20, which shows the response of a cat to the stimuli for aggression and fear. A neutral situation is indicated in the upper left-hand corner of the graph. Increasing stimulus for fear is indicated on the y-axis; increasing stimulus for aggression is indicated on the x-axis. (Interestingly, higher values of fear are shown as lower, rather than higher, points on the graph.) The behavior that results from each combination of fear and aggression is shown by a picture. The cat in the lower

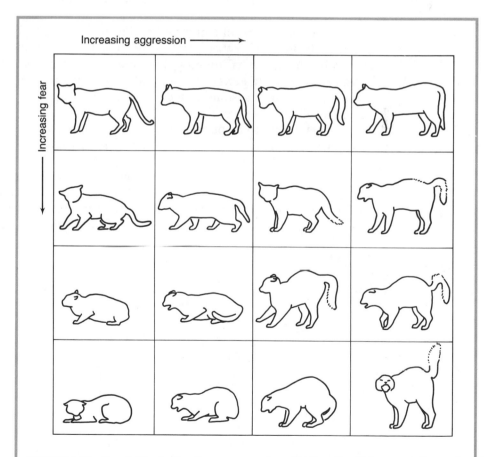

FIGURE 4.20   Graph illustrating the response of a cat to the stimuli for aggression and fear. SOURCE: "Verhaltensstudien bei Katzen" by P. Leyhausen, 1956, *Zeitschrift fuer Tierpsychologie, 2.* Copyright 1956 by Verlag Paul Parey. Reprinted by permission.

right-hand corner is the most afraid and the most aggressive, simultaneously. This sort of graph is very helpful when a behavior changes qualitatively as a function of two variables.

INDICATING VARIABILITY OF THE DATA IN A GRAPH

error bars
in a graph, vertical lines that indicate plus or minus one standard deviation of the data, or less frequently, the standard error of the mean

Oftentimes a researcher will want a graph to show the variability of the data, as well as the averages. This is commonly done by drawing **error bars** above and below a data point to indicate plus or minus one standard deviation, or sometimes the standard error of the mean.

Figure 4.21 is an example of a bar graph with error bars. Suppose we asked males and females to rate their liking of an action movie. We can see from the graph that males liked the movie more than females. The error bars tell us, in addition, that females were more variable than males in their responses.

Although error bars can be helpful, they also can be misleading. One standard deviation either side of the mean of a normal distribution will include 68% of the cases. How is it possible, then, that the error bar for females touches the origin of the graph—a rating of zero? That would imply that there should be some women who rate the movie less than zero, which is impossible.

box-and-whisker plot
a type of graph based on median and percentiles rather than mean and standard deviation

This problem can be resolved by using a different method for indicating the variability of the data. This technique, known as a **box-and-whisker plot,** is illustrated in Figure 4.22.

A box-and-whisker plot is based on median and percentiles, rather than on the mean and standard deviation. The box extends from the 25th to the 75th percentiles. A horizontal line through the box indicates the median (50th percentile). The lower line, or whisker, extends to the 10th percentile, and the

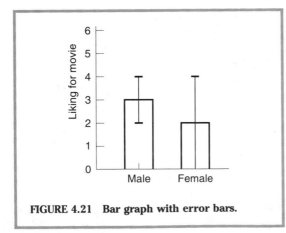

FIGURE 4.21   Bar graph with error bars.

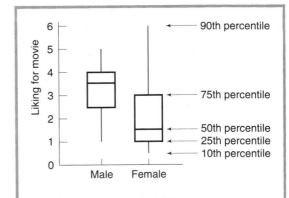

FIGURE 4.22   Box-and-whisker plot.

upper one to the 90th. It is clear from this graph that the two distributions are skewed: The median woman did not like the movie, but there were a few who liked it quite a lot. The reverse is true for the men. The box-and-whisker plot shows the skewness of the data very clearly, whereas the bar graph with error bars does not. Box-and-whisker plots are very useful whenever the data are skewed, as well as in other situations in which the median is appropriate for the data.

Box-and-whisker plots are seen more often in other disciplines than they are in psychology, but they deserve much more use in psychology. A little thought will reveal that they are useful for any type of graph we have discussed so far, including frequency data. Because the box-and-whisker plot is based on percentiles, it can be used in place of a frequency distribution.

PREPARING DATA FOR ANALYSIS

data reduction
the process of transcribing data from individual data sheets to a summary form

Beginning researchers are most likely to think about how to get their data ready for statistical analysis after the data have been collected and they are faced with a stack of raw data—the sheets on which they entered the subjects' responses. This can be a daunting prospect. If you do this, you will soon discover your first mistake: You should have decided exactly how you were going to handle your data—how to record them, how to prepare them for analysis, and which statistics to use—before you ever saw your first subject. This process of going from raw data to statistical analysis is called **data reduction.** It involves a number of steps.

■ Data Reduction

Let's assume that you have designed your study, including your hypotheses and all the procedural steps. You also know what type of statistical analysis you want to perform on your data. A number of practical matters must be dealt with in order to go from the subjects' responses to the statistical analysis. Because the actual details of data reduction will differ from one kind of study to another, we will give some general principles and one example.

The initial recording of the data is generally done on sheets that record the responses of a single subject. The data sheet should have spaces to record the date, time, researcher's name, condition (where appropriate, and nearly always in code), and any other necessary identifying information. (Most often, you do not want to record the subject's name on the sheet. If you need this information, you should identify the subject by number and keep the code in a separate place.) Do not count on the raw data sheet or the summary data sheet to remind you of the design and procedure of the study. This needs to be kept in another place, preferably a notebook. You will be amazed at the details of the study that you are sure you could never forget but that are lost forever if they are not written down.

If the data are collected as a questionnaire or in some other format that the subject, rather than the researcher, fills out, it may be desirable to place a column on the right-hand side of the data sheet into which the data can be transferred as a first step in data reduction. Each space in this column should be numbered to correspond to the column in the summary data sheet in which the data are to be recorded. Refer to the form for the Campus Security Survey in Chapter 8 for an example.

Next, the data are transcribed onto a summary data sheet. This should be, when possible, a single sheet that contains all the data from the study. Usually, the summary data sheet contains all of the data in a matrix format. In other words, the data are placed into a tabular arrangement in which the rows indicate subjects and the columns indicate independent variables. See Table 4.5, which shows hypothetical data from a study of reaction time. In one condition, subjects reacted as fast as possible to the appearance of any symbol on a computer screen. In another condition, they responded by indicating which symbol was shown out of a larger set of symbols. The former is known as simple reaction time and the latter, choice reaction time. There were two subjects, each of whom experienced five trials under both simple and choice conditions.

It is most convenient to have a given row of the matrix refer to the data on one particular subject and each column refer to one variable. The first column is simply the identification number of the subject. Thus, by looking in column 1, we see that the first ten rows all contain information about subject number 1. Columns 2 and 3 contain information about the independent variables. A 1 in column 2 indicates simple reaction time; a 2 indicates choice reaction time. The number in column 3 indicates the trial number: 1 through 5.

Column 4 gives the reaction time in milliseconds. Generally, all the data for a given dependent variable will appear in only one column (although that column may contain data from more than one variable). Thus, both simple and choice reaction-time data appear in column 4. You must look at column 2 to see whether the reaction time listed in column 4 is a simple reaction time or a choice reaction time.

The rows and columns of the matrix permit us to locate any particular reaction time. If we want to find out the value of the choice reaction time for the second subject on her third trial, column 1 tells us that rows 11–20 contain information about the second subject. Column 2 permits us to narrow our search to rows 16–20, which contain the choice reaction times for this subject. Then column 3 tells us that row 18 contains the data for the third choice reaction time for subject number 2.

In summary, even though the details of data reduction will differ a good deal from one type of study to another, the general idea is to put the data into matrix form.

TABLE 4.5 Hypothetical data from reaction-time study (MINITAB output, modified)

Row	ID	Simple = 1 Choice = 2	Trial	RT (msec)
1	1	1	1	390
2	1	1	2	405
3	1	1	3	691
4	1	1	4	2748
5	1	1	5	302
6	1	2	1	966
7	1	2	2	479
8	1	2	3	662
9	1	2	4	570
10	1	2	5	597
11	2	1	1	241
12	2	1	2	213
13	2	1	3	307
14	2	1	4	468
15	2	1	5	257
16	2	2	0	760
17	2	2	2	1292
18	2	2	3	588
19	2	2	4	337
20	2	2	5	447

■ Checking for Invalid Data, Missing Data, and Outliers

Once the data have been transcribed from the raw data sheets to the summary data sheets in matrix form, we can begin to analyze them. You might want to jump right into the inferential statistics you planned to do, but first we should take a preliminary look at them. It is possible that errors were made in transcribing the data to the matrix, or there may be some wild data that you might be justified in excluding. You could simply scan the data sheets, but most data sets are too big to scan efficiently. It is easiest to check for errors by looking at some preliminary statistics and graphs.

invalid data
data points that
fall outside the
defined range for
that variable

First, let's consider **invalid data.** Many times either the independent or dependent variables can take only certain values. The independent variable of simple versus choice reaction time, for example, can only take one of two values: simple or choice, which we have coded 1 or 2. Any other number is clearly an error. If the dependent variable were a rating on a 7-point scale, any value other than 1–7 would be invalid. If you have a sharp eye, you may have noticed in Table 4.5 that the trial number in row 16 is 0, which is invalid. There can be no trial 0.

missing data
empty cells in a
data matrix

Missing data are simply what the name implies. There may be a cell in the matrix that contains no data point. Perhaps a subject did not complete every part of the study. We would have missing data in this example if a subject made only four trials under one of the conditions. Missing data are common in questionnaires when a respondent skips an item or refuses to answer.

outliers
data points that
are highly
improbable,
although not
impossible

Third, we can have **outliers.** These are data points that are not invalid, but are highly improbable. Potential outliers can arise for two basic reasons. First, they may simply be extreme scores from a normal distribution. Recall that a normal distribution does not reach zero probability, but only approaches zero. Any valid score has some theoretical probability, however small. Generally, we do not want to exclude responses that actually come from the distribution of interest. Second, potential outliers can come from a different distribution than all the other scores. If we have a distribution of reaction times, an outlier could come from a distribution we might call " 'oops, I wasn't paying attention' responses." We do want to exclude such responses, as they are not true reaction-time responses. The best reason for excluding an outlier is obvious, gross failure to follow instructions. For example, a subject may fill out a questionnaire in a fraction of the time that the other subjects take, and give the same response to most of the items.

There are sophisticated statistical procedures for evaluating outliers (see, for example, Hawkins, 1980), but most researchers rely on informal analyses to exclude them. These informal methods include visual and numerical analysis of distributions to spot outliers. One criterion might be to eliminate any response that falls three or more standard deviations from the mean of the data.

We must emphasize that we do not eliminate wild data casually. It is all too easy to eliminate data in such a way as to bias the results in our favor. Wild data should be eliminated only after a process such as we have followed; then it is necessary to report that data were eliminated and the criteria that were used to do so. It is wise to perform the statistical analysis on all the data, including the wild data, and report what difference exclusion of the wild data made in the results. Not to do this can be an ethical violation. Elimination of data from analysis has resulted in ethical investigations of researchers.

Returning now to Table 4.5, we see that row 4 shows a reaction time of 2748 milliseconds, or nearly 3 seconds, which seems highly improbable to anyone familiar with reaction-time data. Row 17 also seems to stand out as

TABLE 4.6 PRELIMINARY SUMMARY STATISTICS ON REACTION-TIME DATA (MINITAB OUTPUT, MODIFIED)

	N	MEAN	MEDIAN	STDEV	MIN	MAX
ID	20	1.500	1.500	0.513	1.000	2.000
S/C	20	1.500	1.500	0.513	1.000	2.000
TRIAL	20	2.950	3.000	1.538	0.000	5.000
RT	20	638	474	563	213	2748

unusual, because it is the only other data point requiring four digits. We will keep these data points in mind as candidates for exclusion as wild data.

The simplest and most systematic way to search for invalid data, missing data, and outliers is to do some preliminary statistics on the matrix. Table 4.6 shows part of the output of one popular statistics package, MINITAB, as applied to these data. The rows of the table show the variables in the study. (These were the *columns* in our summary data matrix.) The columns are the various statistics on the variables.

There are many things one could look for in such a table. For example, it is possible that all the data for some variable were recorded in the wrong column. Errors like this are not rare, and can be caught by looking for obviously incorrect means. For example, if the mean ID were 638, instead of 1.500, we would suspect that we had recorded the reaction times in the ID column. No such error was made in these data, so we go on looking for other potential problems.

We can check for missing data by noting the numbers in the first column. Each row of this column (N) shows 20 data points; therefore, there are no missing data (2 subjects × 2 conditions × 5 trials = 20). If there were missing data, we would place a **missing data code** in the blank cell. Most computer statistical packages have a specified missing data code, such as an asterisk, that is used to indicate missing data. The computer will ignore that data point and adjust the number of cases accordingly.

The columns labeled MIN and MAX tell us the minimum and maximum score on each variable. The minimum value for trial shows up as 0.000, which we can recognize as invalid. The invalid data point is easy to fix in this example, because we can see that the 0 in row 16, column 3 had to be a 1. Note that we have found the invalid data point by looking at a fairly small summary table, rather than having to look through what could be a very large data matrix.

Now we are ready to consider whether the very large maximum reaction time of 2748 msec might be an outlier. The consideration of potential wild data points takes a little thought and effort. Perhaps the data are just skewed, and a few high values are to be expected. To check for possible skewness, we can

missing data code

a symbol, such as *, that is entered in a cell that has no data

TABLE 4.7 Histogram of simple reaction time (MINITAB output, modified)

Histogram of RT	Simple/Choice = 1	N = 10

Midpoint	Count	
200	2	**
300	3	***
400	2	**
500	1	*
600	0	
700	1	*
800	0	
900	0	
1000	0	
•		
•		
2700	1	*

TABLE 4.8 Histogram of choice reaction time (MINITAB output, modified)

Histogram of RT	Simple/Choice = 2	N = 10

Midpoint	Count	
300	1	*
400	1	*
500	1	*
600	3	***
700	1	*
800	1	*
900	0	
1000	1	*
1100	0	
1200	0	
1300	1	*

look at Table 4.6 and see that the mean reaction time is quite a lot larger than the median. This makes us suspect that the data are, in fact, skewed.

To look at the possible skewness, we can make a histogram of the data.[2] Tables 4.7 and 4.8 show histograms separately for simple and choice reaction time.

It is obvious that both distributions are skewed. When the data are skewed, one should consider a transformation to achieve symmetry (see Appendix F). Let us try a logarithmic transformation, which is probably the most commonly used transformation for this purpose. Tables 4.9 and 4.10 show the data after a log transformation. Here we can see that the data are now reasonably symmetric, with the exception of the one outlier: the value of 2748 msec for simple reaction time (which has a log of 3.4). We decide to do the rest of our analyses on the transformed data.

Now we are ready to consider the potential outlier. The value of 3.4 (the log of 2748) is 5.6 standard deviations away from the mean of its distribution (remember, all in logarithms). We know from tables of the normal distribution that a data point that actually belonged to a normal distri-

---

[2] Although this type of histogram looks different from the ones discussed earlier, and is found within a table, it is still a kind of graphical depiction of data.

TABLE 4.9 Histogram of simple reaction-time data after log transformation (MINITAB output, modified)

Histogram of Log RT	Simple/Choice = 1	N = 10
Midpoint	Count	
2.3	1	*
2.4	2	**
2.5	2	**
2.6	2	**
2.7	1	*
2.8	1	*
2.9	0	
•		
•		
3.4	1	*

TABLE 4.10 Histogram of choice reaction-time data after log transformation (MINITAB output, modified)

Histogram of Log RT	Simple/Choice = 2	N = 10
Midpoint	Count	
2.5	1	*
2.6	0	
2.7	2	**
2.8	4	****
2.9	1	*
3.0	1	*
3.1	1	*

bution would lie 5.6 standard deviations away from the mean only about one time in ten million. We can feel justified in assuming that this data point is, in fact, a wild point that can be eliminated. The subject was probably just not paying attention when the trial started. Our other potential wild data point was the value of 1292 msec for choice reaction time. When we look at the transformed data, we see that this point is actually only a little over one standard deviation from the mean, a very likely event. We will keep this data point.

We remove the one outlier from the data and treat that cell of the matrix as a missing data point. Table 4.11 shows the data after the correction of the incorrect data point and the replacement of the wild data with the missing data code.

Finally, it is prudent to recompute the summary data on the log reaction time, as shown in Table 4.12. Now we find that for both simple and choice reaction time the means are approximately the same as the medians. Further, the standard deviation of log reaction time is approximately the same for simple and choice reaction time. The closeness of the means and medians suggest that the data are normally distributed, and the similarity of standard deviations indicates similar variances (standard deviation squared). Thus, we are justified in proceeding with parametric statistics, which depend on the data being normally distributed with equal variance in each group.

TABLE 4.11 Hypothetical data from reaction-time study after correction and removal of wild data point (**MINITAB** output, modified)

Row	ID	Simple (= 1) Choice (= 2)	Trial	RT (msec)
1	1	1	1	390
2	1	1	2	405
3	1	1	3	691
4	1	1	4	*
5	1	1	5	302
6	1	2	1	966
7	1	2	2	479
8	1	2	3	662
9	1	2	4	570
10	1	2	5	597
11	2	1	1	241
12	2	1	2	213
13	2	1	3	307
14	2	1	4	468
15	2	1	5	257
16	2	2	1	760
17	2	2	2	1292
18	2	2	3	588
19	2	2	4	337
20	2	2	5	447

TABLE 4.12 Summary statistics on log reaction time after correction and removal of outlier (**MINITAB** output, modified)

Simple/ Choice	N	N*	Mean	Median	Stdev
1	9	1	2.53	2.49	0.16
2	10	0	2.80	2.77	0.17

■ Proceeding with the Analysis

At this point we should decide on our measures of central tendency and variability. We have computed both the mean and the median and have compared them. Because the data are now distributed reasonably symmetrically, we can be comfortable using the more powerful mean, rather than the median. Further, because the data not only are symmetrical but also have equal variance in both conditions, we can use the standard deviation as our measure of variability.

Finally, we should note that we have displayed our data visually as well as numerically, so we have a pretty good idea of our data. Now, finally, we are ready to perform inferential statistics on these data! We can summarize the components of data handling as follows:

1. Put the data into matrix form in a summary data sheet.
2. Do preliminary statistics and plots.
3. Check for invalid data, and make corrections.
4. Check for missing data, and replace with missing data code.
5. Check for wild data, and remove.
6. Check to see if the data are skewed, and consider a transformation.
7. Do descriptive statistics.
8. Choose measures of central tendency and variability.
9. Describe data numerically.
10. Describe data graphically.
11. Perform inferential statistics.

✳ NUTS & BOLTS ✳

Style Guide for Figures

Figures include bar graphs, histograms, line graphs, pie charts, scattergrams, drawings, charts, and photographs. The following guidelines concern figures other than drawings and photographs, which have specialized requirements. It is assumed that you will be drawing the figures by hand. If you use a computer to make your graphs, keep in mind that some software packages do not conform to APA guidelines.

1. Remember that the purpose of a figure is to communicate information. Plan the figure so that the reader will be able to understand clearly the information you are trying to convey.
2. Use graph paper for all graphs.
3. Use black pencil only. Do not use color, because journals generally do not reproduce color graphics.

4. Generally, graphs should be about two-thirds as high as they are wide.
5. Label both axes with the appropriate variables.
6. Provide a descriptive caption for each figure. Except in a final paper in APA format, when a figure goes on a separate page, you should place the caption below the figure.
7. If there are two or more types of symbols in a figure, label them or define them in a legend. The legend appears somewhere in the white space inside the figure.
8. All letters and symbols should be large enough to be legible when the figure is reduced in size. (A good test is to see if you can read your graph from about 15 feet away.)
9. Connect points using straight lines only. Do not draw curved lines unless they represent theoretical equations that you have computed.
10. If the lower left-hand corner of the graph is not the origin, and there is a possibility of misunderstanding, indicate that fact by a break in the axis. ❏

SUMMARY

1. A table is a display of data in a matrix format.
2. A graph is a representation of data by spatial relations in a diagram.
3. Most graphs in psychology represent two variables, and have two axes plotted at right angles to one another.
4. A frequency distribution is a graph that shows the number of scores that fall in specific bins, or divisions of the variable, rather than values of a dependent variable. It may be in the form of a histogram or a frequency polygon.
5. A cumulative frequency distribution shows the number of scores that fall at or below a certain score. They tend to be sigmoidal in shape and are useful for determining percentiles.
6. A scattergram shows the relationship between two variables for a number of individual cases.
7. A line graph is a graphic representation using lines to show relationships between quantitative variables.
8. Bar graphs are used when the independent variable is categorical; otherwise, line graphs are used.
9. Although frequency distributions are different from other graphs, they are related to them in that they represent different aspects of data that could be represented in a graph of a function.
10. A time-series graph is one in which the abscissa represents the passage of time.

11. Tables and graphs may represent two independent variables and one dependent variable.

12. Contour graphs are three-dimensional, and both axes represent independent variables. Lines on the graph indicate locations where the dependent variable has a constant value.

13. Data maps represent locations in space that have a particular characteristic.

14. Some graphs represent functions in such a way that values of the dependent variable are shown as pictures.

15. Variability of data may be shown graphically by error bars, which may indicate standard deviation or standard error, or by box-and-whisker plots, which represent percentile data.

16. Data reduction is the process of transcribing data from individual data sheets to a summary in the form of a matrix.

17. The summary data should be checked for invalid data, missing data, and outliers.

18. Before inferential statistics are performed, you should examine the data for skewness, calculate descriptive statistics, and represent the data in tables and/or graphs.

19. Figures should conform to the style described in this chapter and in the APA *Publication Manual*. Keep in mind that the purpose of a figure is to communicate information about your data.

Suggestions for Further Reading

Bowen, R. W. (1992). *Graph it! How to make, read, and interpret graphs.* Englewood Cliffs, NJ: Prentice-Hall. An elementary discussion of graphing with many specific hints and examples.

Cleveland, W. S. (1985). *The elements of graphing data.* Monterey, CA: Wadsworth Advanced Book Program. In spite of the title, a high-level discussion of graphing techniques.

Lewis, D. (1960). *Quantitative methods in psychology.* New York: McGraw-Hill. Valuable mathematical background for this chapter.

Mosteller, F., Feinberg, S. E., & Rourke, R. E. K. (1983). *Beginning statistics with data analysis.* Reading, MA: Addison-Wesley. An excellent introduction to statistics, with an emphasis on exploratory data analysis.

Tukey, J. W. (1977). *Exploratory data analysis.* Reading, MA: Addison-Wesley. Very practical introduction to dealing with data.

IIII➡ **A CASE IN POINT** ◀IIIII

Professor Smith's Slide Presentation

Professor Smith was about to present a paper on his research on food preferences at a psychology convention. As is customary, he gave an informal practice talk to the members of his department before going to the convention.

The slides that he presented are shown in Figure 4.23. Following is a description of the data on which they are based:

a. The ratings of preference, on a scale of 1 to 5, of ten subjects for four foods (1 = dislike intensely, 2 = dislike moderately, 3 = neutral, 4 = like moderately, 5 = like intensely).

b. Frequency distribution showing how many subjects liked one, two, three, or four of the sample foods. (The data in this figure cannot be verified from the previous one.)

c. Number of subjects who liked this many foods, or fewer (cumulative frequency of the same data as in b).

d. Professor Smith believed that the subjects had never had a chance to learn to like the foods they claimed to dislike. Therefore, he presented the most liked food and the least liked food to subjects alternately for lunch for six days, starting with the most preferred on day 1, the least preferred on day 2, and so on. He wanted to see if they would get tired of the most preferred, but begin to like the least preferred over the trials.

e. Professor Smith took pictures of their faces when they ate the various foods. He believed their expressions could be described in terms of two variables: pleasantness and fear. Combinations of these two variables produced four different facial expressions, which he labeled happy, sad, worried, and embarrassed and showed in schematic form.

After the talk, Professor Avuncular took him aside and suggested that he might make a better impression if he redid his slides.

REQUIRED: Redo Professor Smith's slides so that they better reflect the points he is trying to make. Pay attention to proper style.

≡ **READING BETWEEN THE LINES** ≡

4.1 "YOU CAN PROVE ANYTHING WITH STATISTICS"

In a televised speech to the nation in support of his tax-cut program, President Reagan used the graph shown in Figure 4.24 to convince viewers of the advantage of his tax proposal over that of the Democrats. The graph shows taxes paid by a typical family under the two proposals. He said, "The lines on the charts say a lot about who's really fighting for whom." ("That Numberless Presidential Chart," 1981). What is the problem in drawing conclusions

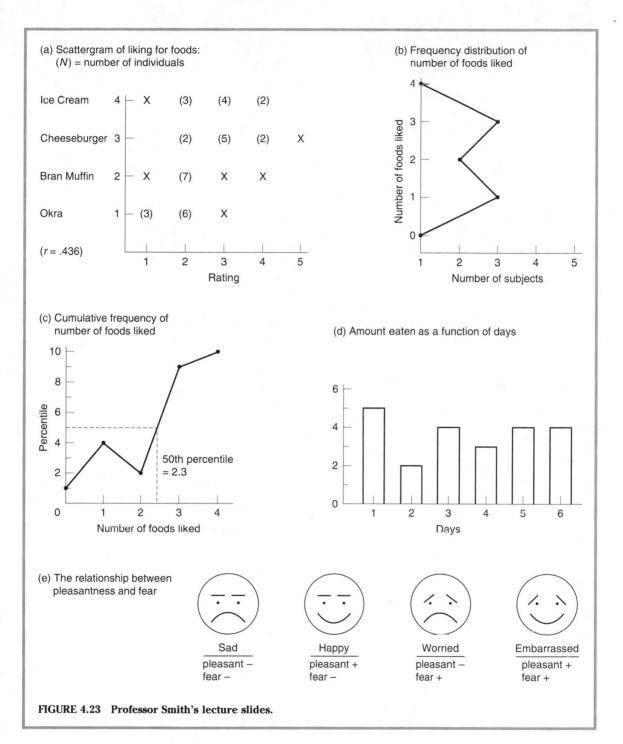

FIGURE 4.23   Professor Smith's lecture slides.

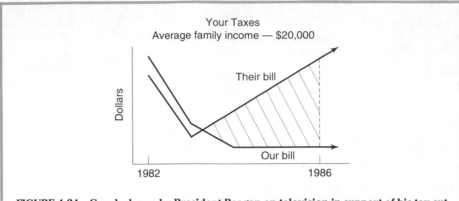

FIGURE 4.24   Graph shown by President Reagan on television in support of his tax-cut proposal. Souce: "That Numberless Presidential Chart," *New York Times,* 2 August 1981, p. F-17. Copyright © 1981 by the New York Times Company. Reprinted by permission.

from the president's graph? What is missing from the graph that makes it impossible to interpret?   ∎

✓ EXERCISES

4.1   GRAPHING WITH THREE VARIABLES

Robert Rescorla (1988) studied the effects of varying (1) the probability that shock (unconditioned stimulus) would occur during a signal (conditioned stimulus) and (2) the probability that shock would occur in the absence of the signal on (3) the strength of conditioning in rats. The data in Table 4.13 are adapted from his results.

REQUIRED:
   a. Identify the independent and dependent variables.
   b. Plot the strength of conditioning as a function of the probability of shock in the presence of the signal, with probability of shock in the absence of signal as a parameter.
   c. Describe in words the relationship among the variables.

OPTIONAL:
   d. Plot strength of conditioning as a function of probability of shock in the absence of signal, with probability of shock in the presence of signal as a parameter.
   e. Describe in words the relationship among the variables.
   f. Is the answer to **e** different from the answer to **c**? Why or why not?

TABLE 4.13 DATA FROM THE RESCORLA STUDY

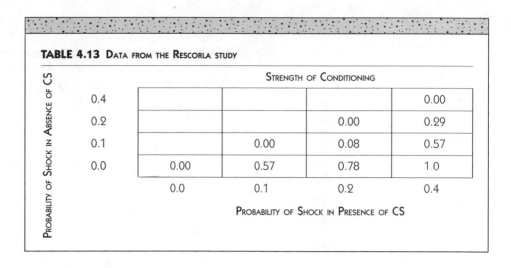

	STRENGTH OF CONDITIONING			
0.4				0.00
0.2			0.00	0.29
0.1		0.00	0.08	0.57
0.0	0.00	0.57	0.78	1.0
	0.0	0.1	0.2	0.4

PROBABILITY OF SHOCK IN ABSENCE OF CS (vertical axis)

PROBABILITY OF SHOCK IN PRESENCE OF CS (horizontal axis)

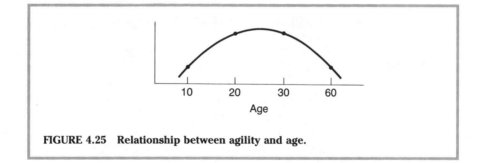

FIGURE 4.25   Relationship between agility and age.

4.2   GRAPH INTERPRETATION

Researchers have administered an agility test to a random sample of subjects ranging from 10 to 60 years in age. Figure 4.25 presents results from this study.

REQUIRED:

    a. What is the independent variable?
    b. What is the dependent variable?
    c. Explain the relationship between the dependent and independent variables.
    d. What kind of study was this?
    e. List five things that are wrong with this graph.

4.3   TYPES OF GRAPHS

Choose the most appropriate type of graph for each of the following situations:

    a. Professor Smith wants to make a graph showing the number of students who got various scores on a test.

b. The SAT publishes a graph showing how many people taking the test score at or below a certain score.

c. Brent makes a chart of the library on which he marks every seat occupied in the library during the course of a week.

d. The university publishes a graph showing how many students are in each major.

e. Debra wants to see if there is a relationship between the percentage gained by the stocks in her portfolio in 1991 and their price at the beginning of the year.

f. Scott makes a graph showing the combinations of oven temperature and baking time that cause his bread to come out with a nice brown crust.

g. Heather plots the percentage of people who volunteer to serve in her experiment as a function of the size of the class from which she recruits them.

4.4   GRAPH INTERPRETATION

Each of the following pairs indicates the type of variable that is on the ordinate (y) and the abscissa (x) of a graph, respectively. For example, "dependent, independent" means that the ordinate represents a dependent variable and the abscissa shows an independent variable. For each combination, choose the type of graph that could be indicated. Use each category only once.

a. dependent, independent
b. dependent, dependent
c. frequency, dependent
d. independent, independent

Alternatives: (1) grading distribution, (2) contour graph, (3) scattergram, (4) amount learned as a function of trials.   ❑

5

Validity

Most research is designed to permit the researcher to draw conclusions about cause-effect relationships among variables. As we discussed in Chapter 2, the ultimate goal is to develop a theory that explains the relationships found among variables. This chapter concerns the various problems that can threaten the validity of conclusions drawn by a researcher. By **validity,** we mean simply that the researcher's conclusion is true or correct—that it corresponds to the actual state of the world. You will probably realize that achieving the truth about the world is asking a great deal.

Some of the problems of validity threaten the conclusion that a cause-effect relationship exists among the variables at all; some threaten the theoretical explanation of the kind of relationship obtained. We will discuss, first, the various kinds of research validity and, second, the many threats to validity. In Chapter 6, we will consider the methods available to the researcher to control for these threats.

TYPES OF VALIDITY

Thomas Cook and Donald Campbell (1976) list four types of validity that must be considered in designing and evaluating a piece of research: internal validity, construct validity, external validity, and statistical validity.

119

■ Internal Validity

Internal validity is the most fundamental type because it concerns the logic of the relationship between the independent and dependent variables. An experiment has internal validity if there are sound reasons to believe that a cause-effect relationship really is present between the independent and dependent variables. In other words, the independent variable causes the dependent variable to change.

Suppose that you did an experiment on the effect of informational feedback on a motor learning task. Group A received a tone whenever they made the correct response; Group B did not. So far, so good. But you tested all of the subjects in Group A on Monday and all in Group B on Tuesday. Now, besides differing in feedback, the two groups also differed in the time of administration of the experiment. It is impossible to decide whether any differences in behavior should be attributed to feedback or to time of administration.

This experiment lacks internal validity because you cannot conclude that feedback caused the results. This problem is known as **confounding.** In this case, time was confounded with feedback because its possible effects were not tested separately from the effects of feedback. We say that time covaried with feedback. When some condition covaries with the independent variable in such a way that their separate effects cannot be sorted out, the two variables are confounded. You can easily imagine a number of potentially important variables that could affect performance on a motor skills task. The Monday could have followed fraternity rush weekend, with some of the subjects feeling the aftereffects. Perhaps on Tuesday the barometric pressure was high, or the experimenter had just learned that her boyfriend was going to join a commune. Notice that none of these confounded variables enter into any theory of motor learning, even though some of them might affect behavior.

Confounding is one of the biggest threats to validity in experimentation. Great care must be taken that no important variable is confounded with the independent variable. Much of Chapters 9 through 12 concerns techniques used to avoid confounding.

On the other hand, making sure that no other variable is confounded with the independent variable is not feasible. Among the possible confounded variables in the previous example is phase of the moon. Although some people have suggested that strange behavior occurs during a full moon, the evidence for this conclusion is weak. Most investigators therefore feel justified in ignoring lunar phase.

If day of the week is an important confounding variable but lunar phase is not, how do experimenters decide which variables to worry about? The fact is that many value judgments are made as the experiment is designed. For example, many taste researchers take care that no smokers serve as subjects or that no subjects smoke within one hour of the experiment. I used to eliminate smokers routinely from my taste experiments, in spite of the fact that no persuasive evidence existed that smoking affects sensation for college-age subjects. In one experiment that an undergraduate student and I did, we concluded that there was no discernible effect of smoking on taste thresholds in the college-age subjects we used. These results, together with the fact that other experiments in the literature are inconclusive, led me to quit paying attention to whether my subjects are smokers.

The problem of confounding is particularly acute in research in which the experimenter cannot control the independent variable—when subjects must be selected according to the presence or absence of a condition rather than having a condition assigned to them. Such variables are called **subject variables.**

subject variable
a difference between subjects that cannot be controlled, but can only be selected

A good example of a subject variable is sex of subject. Subjects cannot be assigned to one sex, but must be selected from preexisting groups. When sex of subject is one of the independent variables of an experiment, as it often is, we have a quasi experiment (see Chapter 12) and a much greater probability of confounding. Take, for example, the lively debate about the extent of the differences in psychological processes between men and women. This debate results from the greatly differing influences in our society on males and females that begin when they leave the hospital in their blue or pink clothes. All the innumerable experiences and the resulting learned attitudes and skills are confounded in the simple term *sex differences*. The extent to which these confounded variables contribute to the sex differences found in research is the crux of the sex-difference controversy. Similarly, in research on race and IQ we find many variables confounded with race that are known to influence IQ, such as parents' level of education, family income, and quality of available schooling.

■ Construct Validity

construct validity
extent to which the results support the theory behind the research

Construct validity concerns the question of whether the results support the theory behind the research. Is there another theory that would predict the same results?

Every study is designed to test some hypothesis; yet a hypothesis cannot be tested in a vacuum. Particular conditions of a study constitute *auxiliary hypotheses* that must also be true in order to test the main hypothesis. Suppose your hypothesis is that anxiety is conducive to learning. You may select your subjects on the basis of whether they bite their fingernails and test to see how fast they can learn to write by holding a pencil in their toes. If you find no difference in the rate of learning between groups, you might conclude that your hypothesis is false. However, you did not test just the one hypothesis that anxiety is conducive to learning. You also tested two auxiliary hypotheses: that fingernail biting is a measure of anxiety, and that writing with one's toes is a good learning task. If either of these auxiliary hypotheses is false, you could have found negative results.

How can you ensure construct validity? Actually, you cannot, but you can plan your research so that it is more plausible. In order to improve the validity of your experiment, you might have used the Taylor Manifest Anxiety Scale to classify your subjects on anxiety, and you might have used a more standardized learning measure, such as learning a list of unrelated words. These techniques, although not perfect, have been used many times. We have more faith that they are valid than we do for fingernail biting and writing with the toes.

Another example of the problem of construct validity can be taken from psychobiology. Destruction of a particular part of the brain will cause a rat to become obese if it is allowed to eat all it wants. Researchers initially believed that the rat was hungrier than normal as a result of the operation. Later they learned that the rat would eat more only if the food was palatable and if the rat did not have to work hard for it. The conclusion was that the rat really was not hungrier; it simply lacked the ability to tell when it had eaten enough.

Experiments that used destruction of part of the rat's brain as a way of increasing hunger, then, were actually decreasing satiety. Any research using this method to increase hunger in rats would lack construct validity, because the manipulation did not increase hunger as measured by other manipulations such as food deprivation. More recent work (Friedman & Stricker, 1976), in turn, has suggested that the injury to the brain may not be influencing either hunger or satiety directly but may be changing the rat's metabolism. The rat gains weight because it has a greater tendency to store fat, even if its food intake is restricted.

Construct validity is similar to internal validity. In internal validity, you strive to rule out alternative variables as potential causes of the behavior of interest; in construct validity, you must rule out other possible theoretical explanations of the results. In either case, you may have to perform another study in order to rule out a threat to validity. For internal validity, you may find it possible to redesign the study to control for the source of confounding. In the case of construct validity, you must design a new study that will permit a choice between the two competing theoretical explanations of the results. When the researchers suspected that rats with brain damage were not really hungrier, they designed tests to find out how the rats responded when the food was unpalatable or harder to obtain or when their exposure to food was limited. In each case, the brain-damaged rats ate less food than normal rats, making the hypothesis of greater hunger less tenable than the alternative theory.

■ Validity of Questionnaires and Tests

It is convenient to broaden the discussion of validity for the purpose of questionnaires and related instruments, for which the following types of validity are commonly defined: construct validity, face validity, content validity, and criterion validity.

construct validity
(of a test)
the property of a test that actually measures the constructs it is designed to measure, and no others

There are several ways to determine whether a test has **construct validity.** First, the test should actually measure whatever theoretical construct it supposedly tests, and not something else. A test of leadership ability should not actually test extraversion, for example. Second, a test that has construct validity should not only measure what it intends to measure, but it should not also measure theoretically unrelated constructs. A test of musical aptitude should not require too much reading ability, for example. Third, a test should prove useful in predicting results related to the theoretical concept it is measuring. A test of musical ability should predict who will benefit from taking music lessons, should differentiate groups who have chosen music as a career from those who haven't, should relate to other tests of musical ability, and so on.

The other kinds of validity discussed in relation to tests and measurement—face validity, content validity, and criterion validity—are actually different ways of talking about construct validity, although it is useful to give each one its own name for pedagogical purposes.

face validity
idea that a test should appear superficially to test what it is supposed to test

Face validity is the idea that a test should appear to any person to be a test of what it is supposed to test. Many a person who has been given a Rorschach has wondered what a bunch of inkblots have to do with personality. (Actually, projective tests have other serious problems of validity, besides face validity.) Face validity, however, is more a problem of public relations than of true validity. A test may have a high or low degree of validity regardless of its face validity.

content validity
idea that a test should sample the range of behavior represented by the theoretical concept being tested

Content validity is the notion that a test should sample the range of the behavior that is represented by the theoretical concept being measured. An intelligence test, for example, should measure general knowledge, verbal ability, spatial ability, and quantitative skills among others. An intelligence test that measured only spatial ability would not have sufficient content validity.

criterion validity
idea that a test should correlate with other measures of the same theoretical construct

Criterion validity is the idea that a valid test should relate closely to other measures of the same theoretical construct. A valid test of intelligence should correlate highly with other intelligence tests. It should also correlate with behaviors that are considered to require intelligence, such as doing well in school. If the criterion of an intelligence test is whether it correlates with how well a child is doing in school at the time the test is given, it is called *concurrent validity.* If the criterion of an intelligence test is how well the test can predict some future performance of the child, such as graduation from college, then it is called *predictive validity.*

Questions involving the various kinds of test validity are technical ones; for further discussion, refer to any standard text on tests and measurements (for example, Cronbach, 1990). As you can tell from this brief discussion, however, the concept of correlation is closely intertwined with that of validity.

A good test of leadership, for example, should not correlate too highly with a test of extraversion. On the other hand, a good test of intelligence should correlate highly with other tests of intelligence and with how a child performs in school.

■ External Validity

external validity
how well the findings of an experiment generalize to other situations or populations

External validity concerns whether the results of the research can be generalized to another situation: different subjects, settings, times, and so forth. Strictly speaking, the results of a piece of research are valid only for other identical situations: 18 sophomores at State University on a rainy 13th of April 1993 in a room with green walls and an experimenter with a beard. Such literalness is ridiculous, of course, but which variables are trivial to the validity of the experiment, and which are important?

In an influential experiment in perception conducted by McGinnies in 1949, subjects were asked to read words that were flashed on a screen. The results were interpreted as showing that a person's threshold for seeing taboo words was higher than the threshold for seeing ordinary words. Today researchers would interpret the data as reflecting subjects' reluctance to utter the "taboo" words rather than a truly higher perceptual threshold for them. We mention this experiment because of the particular taboo words used. You may be surprised and skeptical to learn that subjects would hesitate to say the words *belly, bitch,* and *rape* aloud in an experiment. We must remember, though, that this experiment was reported in 1949. The use of language in public has changed much since then. Today it is unlikely that the experiment would yield the same results. This experiment could not be generalized to today's world; it would lack external validity.

■ Statistical Validity

statistical validity
extent to which data are shown to be the result of cause-effect relationships rather than accident

Statistical validity is similar to internal validity. Here the question is: Was the observed relationship between the independent and dependent variables a true cause-effect relationship, or was it accidental? Or was the number of subjects so small that the results happened purely by chance?

As you may recall from your study of statistics, a statistical test only establishes that an outcome has a certain low probability of happening by chance alone; it does not guarantee that it was the result of a true cause-effect relationship. (See Appendix A.) Nevertheless, the use of inferential statistics is an essential way to judge the validity of a research outcome. For that matter, there is no way to guarantee any of the types of validity of a research result; all methods of judging validity simply increase confidence in the conclusion that has been drawn from research.

THREATS TO VALIDITY

We have been talking about kinds of validity. Now we will consider some problems that constitute threats to validity.

■ Threats to Internal Validity

In essence, guarding against threats to internal validity consists of learning to avoid the confounding of potentially important variables with the independent variable or variables of interest. The major sources of confounding will be considered in turn.

Events outside the Laboratory

Whenever an experiment is conducted in such a way that different experimental conditions are presented to subjects at different times, it is possible for events outside the laboratory to influence the results. If you studied the effects of success and failure on feelings of depression, and all of the subjects experienced the failure condition on Monday and the success condition on Wednesday, you can imagine that the results would be difficult to interpret if it rained on Monday. This situation may sound like a threat to external validity, but it is not. External validity assumes that there is no confounding within the experiment. Rather, it is concerned with important variables that might change between the time an experiment is conducted and when it is repeated another time.

Maturation

Subjects may change between conditions of an experiment because of naturally occurring processes. Certainly they get older. If the experiment involves a significant lapse of time, changes may occur in motor coordination, knowledge, and the like that could influence the results. Suppose you were interested in studying the effect of "Sesame Street" on children's reading skills. You would want to have a control for the improvement in reading that would occur over time in children not exposed to "Sesame Street."

maturation
a source of error in an experiment related to the amount of time between measurements

Maturation is a more critical problem in research involving children because they change more rapidly over time than do adults. Yet the fact that adults change with age is now becoming widely appreciated. Take, for example, a hypothetical long-term study of attitudes toward alternative lifestyles as a function of age. To separate out changes caused by shifting attitudes in society from changes in individual persons as a result of the aging process would not be easy. Chapter 12 contains a discussion of designs that are intended to separate the effects of maturation from experimental manipulations in studies of psychological development.

Effects of Testing

Simply being in an experiment or being tested will influence people's performance in a later experiment or administration of the test. The subjects may become sophisticated about the testing procedure or may learn how to take tests so that their later behavior is changed by the earlier experience. This phenomenon is similar to maturation in that the subjects are changed over time but is different in that the change is caused by the testing procedure itself, rather than by processes unrelated to the test.

Regression Effect

regression effect
tendency of subjects with extreme scores on a first measure to score closer to the mean on a second testing

This effect, one of the most insidious threats to validity, arises in many situations. The **regression effect** operates when there is less than a perfect correlation between two variables. Individuals who performed at the extremes on one test will tend to score closer to the mean on the other test.

The regression effect may occur when two different variables are correlated, such as SAT score and college GPA. It may also occur when the same variable is measured twice, such as when a student repeats the SAT. When two different measures are correlated, we are not surprised when the correlation is less than perfect. But we often get imperfect correlations when the same variable is measured twice. This situation arises when there is error associated with the measurement of the variable. Notice that when we say there is error in the measurement, we do not mean that recording errors are made. We mean that the test itself is not a perfect measure of what is being measured. For example, on a multiple-choice test students will make some lucky or unlucky guesses, resulting in a score that is not a perfect indicator of what they know.

The classic example of the regression effect is that of a teacher who notices that students who scored highest on the first test usually do less well on the second, whereas those who did the worst improve. The teacher often concludes that the ones who did well the first time rested on their laurels for the second test, while the ones who did poorly worked harder. In reality this is not what happened. Whenever **random error** exists in the measurement of a variable, individuals will deviate from their true score by chance. Some will be lucky; others will be unlucky. Many of the extreme scores, both high and low, will be more extreme than their true value. On the retest, the errors will tend to average out and the scores of these previously extreme individuals tend to return toward their true value, closer to the mean.

random error
that part of the value of a variable that can be attributed to chance

The regression effect can lead to some unfortunate conclusions. A parent may notice that praising a child for good behavior is followed by a decrease in the desired behavior, whereas the child's behavior improves after he or she is punished for bad behavior. If the bad behavior is unusual, generally it will improve anyway. The good behavior also may have been a random event that would decrease with or without praise. The parent wrongly concludes that praise is useless and that the way to teach children is to punish bad behavior and ignore good behavior.

Similar results may be found in experiments when subjects are chosen on the basis of a pretest, are given a treatment, and then are retested. The treatment is found to help the low-scoring subjects but to make the high-scoring subjects worse.

Selection

Many studies compare two or more groups on some dependent variable. Any bias in selecting the groups can undermine internal validity. In the next chapter, we will discuss the foolproof remedy of randomly assigning individuals to groups. Often this is not possible, however, particularly in research in which it is necessary to study existing groups. You can easily imagine that the local chapter of the Veterans of Foreign Wars would not be a good group to compare with the local chapter of the Society to Protect Baby Seals. Most people would not make as poor a choice as this. But would the Veterans of Foreign Wars from Detroit, Michigan, be a good choice to compare with the chapter from Tuscaloosa, Alabama? You must exercise care and ingenuity to choose or create groups that can be considered truly comparable.

Mortality

mortality
the dropping out of some subjects before an experiment is completed, causing a threat to validity

Even if there is no bias in selecting subjects and you are able to constitute groups that are the same in every respect, your study may be invalid if all subjects do not complete all phases of it. **Mortality** is a threat to validity because the subjects who drop out of a study may be different from those who complete it. Biases can result if particular kinds of subjects drop out.

Suppose you are studying two methods of behavior modification on weight control. Group 1 is given a diet to follow. In addition, they are to keep a diary of everything they eat, weigh all foods to the nearest gram, and estimate all calories consumed. Group 2 is simply given the diet to follow. You may reasonably assume that the subjects in the group with the more demanding tasks will be more likely to drop out. At the end of the experiment, that group will contain a higher proportion of highly motivated subjects who would, in turn, be more likely to succeed in losing weight. You then might falsely conclude that the first condition was more effective than the second.

Another example concerns whether intelligence declines with age in older persons. Here the difficulty is in obtaining equivalent groups to compare across age. If you use the same group at two different ages, some individuals will become unavailable the second time because of illness or death. If you consider only those people who are available on both occasions, you may find little or no decline. Are these the appropriate subjects on which to base your conclusion, or should you make a concerted effort to retest people who are now in hospitals and institutions for the aged? The harder you try to locate subjects for retest, the more likely you are to get people who will perform poorly because of sickness rather than old age per se. Thus, it is difficult to decide whether a true age effect on intelligence exists or whether all decline results from illness.

■ Threats to Construct Validity

Construct validity is perhaps the most difficult type of validity to achieve because of the indefinite number of theories that may account for a given lawful relationship. The general strategy for obtaining construct validity in a piece of research is to ask whether alternative theoretical explanations of the data are less plausible than the theory believed to be supported by the research. We will discuss two areas that pose threats to construct validity.

Loose Connection between Theory and Method

The experiment described earlier for testing the effects of anxiety on learning was an extreme example of a loose connection between theory and method. Nail biting is a poor method of measuring anxiety, and writing with the toes is likely to be a poor measure of learning. Much psychological research suffers from poor operational definition of theoretical concepts. In a previous chapter we gave the example of hunting and fighting in cats. We said that these two theoretical concepts would not be validly tested in a situation in which an example of one class of behavior was taken to belong to the other.

Take two examples of behavior that both might be called aggressive. We might say that Philip aggressively attacked his job of weeding the garden and that Willard showed aggression in deliberately being slow in carrying out his teacher's instructions. Philip's aggressive weeding may simply reflect his desire to get on with more interesting activities. Alternatively, someone familiar with the frustration-aggression law may conclude that he was showing displaced aggression. Perhaps his sister had provoked him to hit her and then had made the hitting appear to be his fault so that he had to weed as punishment. Willard's behavior, on the other hand, may be described by clinical psychologists as passive aggression.

Ambiguous Effect of Independent Variables

An experimenter may carefully design an experiment in which all reasonable confounding variables seem to be well controlled, only to have the results compromised because the subjects perceive the situation differently from the experimenter.

For example, some of my research has involved measuring taste thresholds to chemicals flowed over the outstretched tongues of subjects. The situation seemed perfectly straightforward to me. Occasionally, however, when the session was over a subject would say to me, "What was the experiment really about? You weren't interested in how all that junk tasted, were you?" What those subjects had done was conduct an experiment of their own instead of the one I thought I was conducting. Fortunately, in research of this type, the subjects' ideas about what is supposed to happen are not likely to influence the results that the experimenter is interested in.

Often, though, in psychological research the effect can be devastating. The classic example concerns a series of experiments conducted from 1924 to 1933 in the Hawthorne, Illinois, plant of the Western Electric Company.

Management wanted to study the effects of working conditions on productivity. Many factors such as lighting, length of working hours, and the like were varied. The results showed that changes in output bore little relation to working conditions. Output went up when lighting was *reduced,* for example. Overall, productivity increased throughout the period of the experiment regardless of working conditions. The accepted explanation of the now-famous Hawthorne effect is that the workers, who were separated from the rest of the plant and thus were aware that they were being tested, reacted to the knowledge that they were in an experiment rather than to the working conditions as such. The effect of the conditions caused the workers to conduct their own experiment, so to speak. Thus, the experiment that the researchers thought they were conducting was rendered invalid.

A more recent paper (Bramel & Friend, 1981) suggests another interpretation: Workers were suspicious of management and varied their output in order to maintain control over aspects of the working conditions that were important to them, such as work breaks. In any case, the independent variables have an ambiguous effect in this experiment.

Many experiments suffer from similar ambiguity. Whenever subjects are aware that they are participating in an experiment, their behavior may be different from their everyday behavior. A commonplace example is the reaction of people to having a movie camera directed toward them. The solution to this type of problem is to keep the subjects from becoming aware that they are participating in an experiment. We discuss the pros and cons of this technique in Chapter 7 when we discuss observational research.

The ambiguous effect of the independent variables results from the fact that any psychological experiment for which a subject has volunteered must be considered to be a social situation in which the subject has preconceived ideas about what is expected. Such ideas lead to several tendencies on the part of the subject. Perhaps the most prevalent is the **good-subject tendency.** That is, subjects act the way they think the experimenter wants them to act. They may deliberately feign a naive attitude about the expected results even though they can guess the true purpose of the experiment. Perhaps they have heard about the experiment or have learned of similar experiments conducted elsewhere. You may have observed this phenomenon among subjects recruited from introductory psychology classes in which many types of experiments are discussed. The subjects may pretend to be fooled by the instructions in order to be "good subjects."

Another kind of subject expectancy is the concern that the experimental procedure in some way measures the subject's competence. Some subjects are convinced that the experiment is a carefully disguised measure of intelligence or emotional adjustment. This expectancy gives rise to **evaluation apprehension,** in which subjects tailor their behavior to make themselves look as normal as possible. Another name for this problem is *social desirability.* Researchers who develop attitude scales take care to ensure that various responses appear equally socially desirable so that subjects will not damage the results by concealing their true attitudes.

good-subject tendency
tendency of experimental subjects to act according to what they think the experimenter wants

evaluation apprehension
tendency of experimental subjects to alter their behavior in order to appear as socially desirable as possible

Suppose you are conducting an experiment on the effects of pornography on sexual behavior. Subjects are asked to keep a diary of all sexual activity for a week before and after they are shown a pornographic movie. You can imagine that people would hesitate to volunteer information about deviant activities. Even if they were honest in their reporting, they might modify their behavior during the experiment in the direction of social desirability. You can see how evaluation apprehension will have the opposite effect of the good-subject tendency.

■ Threats to External Validity

Even if an experiment has internal validity, statistical validity, and construct validity, it may not be generalizable to other situations. There are as many threats to the external validity of research as there are dimensions along which one experiment can differ from another. We will consider the most important differences between experiments that may constitute threats to external validity.

Other Subjects

A common indictment of psychological research is that it uses mainly college students and white rats as subjects. The reasons psychologists rely on these two species is their accessibility to researchers and presumed representativeness. The problem is that millions species of animals exist, most of them insects. However, if you accept that psychologists are interested primarily in human behavior, then the attention to rats and college students is not as unfortunate as it might seem at first. The degree to which common principles of behavior operate across species is impressive. Many years ago Skinner (1956) presented data showing that the behavior of a pigeon, a rat, and a monkey under certain experimental conditions was identical in all important respects.

On the other hand, we must not assume that any animal can be substituted for any other in all situations. Keller Breland and Marian Breland (1961) give many examples of the need to choose the response one wishes to study and then to manipulate the variables, paying careful attention to the animal's natural behavioral repertoire. It is easy to teach a chicken to dance, for example, because dancing is similar to its normal behavior of scratching for food. You would not train a rat to dance, however, because dancing is not close to its natural behavior.

Human subjects should be chosen with equal attention to their representativeness relative to some larger population. If you are doing an experiment with college students on bargaining and negotiation, will the results validly predict what a secretary of state or a general would do?

Other Times

Would the same experiment conducted at another time produce the same results? We mentioned this problem earlier in introducing the concept of external validity. The "dirty word" experiment almost certainly lacks external validity today, at least as far as the original words are concerned. Many historical trends render particular research findings invalid, whether they concern use of language, attitudes toward foreign countries, or perception of deviant groups.

Other Settings

A pervasive problem that can hinder external validity involves the question of how the phenomenon observed in one laboratory can be related to a similar phenomenon observed in another laboratory or in the real world. Many psychologists have given up laboratory work altogether in favor of field research, or even armchair speculation, for this very reason. It is not easy to decide if a certain effect is simply a laboratory effect or whether it would survive transplantation to the world outside the laboratory.

Suppose that you are interested in whether letting students work at their own pace produces better learning than giving schedules, assignments, and tests. A school that would permit its students to be experimented on might be more open to innovation in general. Likewise, students, teachers, and administrators in such a school might respond more favorably to the self-paced condition than to the more regimented procedure. So your results may not be valid for more traditional schools.

■ Summary Note on Validity

Our review of the many threats to validity should make you aware of the kinds of problems that may arise in research. Not all of the problems discussed here will be as serious in all areas of psychology. From the examples we have used in this chapter, you may have surmised that the problems are acute in the social areas. It is true that most of the literature on validity has been contributed by social psychologists. An area such as visual perception is much less subject to these problems. As long as subjects have normal acuity and are not color-blind, one subject is much like another. Few visual experiments suffer from problems of validity.

In the next chapter, we will consider how to cope with the various threats to validity.

✳ NUTS & BOLTS ✳

The Social Psychology of the Psychology Experiment

Over the past three decades, much attention has been paid to the biases that can enter into an experiment as a result of the interaction between the subject and the experimenter. This concern comes from the realization that an experiment is a social situation with its own set of rules. Both the subject and the experimenter have expectations about how they should behave in an experiment. Earlier we discussed two threats to internal validity resulting from ambiguous effects of the independent variables: the good-subject tendency and evaluation apprehension. Here we will look more closely at the biases resulting from the interactions between subject and experimenter and suggest some ways of overcoming them.

Role Demands

role demands
subjects' expec-
tations of what
an experiment
requires them
to do

The subjects' knowledge that they are participating in an experiment constitutes a set of expectations about how they are to behave. These expectations are called **role demands,** or demand characteristics, of the experiment. In one experiment, I had subjects smell dirty T-shirts and judge them for unpleasantness and other attributes (McBurney, Levine, & Cavanaugh, 1977). Halfway through the series of shirts, one subject looked up and said, "You know, I don't believe I am doing this." Nevertheless, she continued. This illustration is just one of the apparently pointless and/or socially unacceptable behaviors that people will engage in when they believe that they are in a psychological experiment.

The role demands of an experiment can cause serious problems with interpreting the results. In hypnosis, for example, people have been concerned that they or others might be induced to perform antisocial acts while hypnotized. In one experiment, hypnotized subjects threw a concentrated acid at someone's face at the experimenter's request. (The person was protected by an invisible glass pane.) Interpretation of the results has been controversial. Did the hypnosis cause the compliance, or would nonhyp-notized subjects do the same thing? Martin Orne and Frederick Evans (1965) replicated the study using several new control groups. The experimental group was hypnotized and asked to throw "acid" at the assistant, which they did. One control group was instructed to pretend to be hypnotized. Five out of six of these faking subjects complied with the request to throw "acid." The subjects later said that they had thought that some safety precaution had been taken to prevent injury to the other person. Orne and Evans decided that no conclusions could be drawn about the likelihood of people performing antisocial acts under hypnosis because subjects could so easily be induced to perform the same acts without hypnosis.

One of the most extreme examples of the effects of role demands is the well-known Milgram study (1963), in which subjects were led to believe that they were delivering electric shocks to others over their vigorous protests. The subjects later said they did believe that the other person was being shocked. The fact that they were subjects in an experiment led them to engage in behavior that people have since found surprising and disturbing.

These role demands, together with the good-subject tendency, may cause subjects to play dumb about the purpose of the experiment even if they can figure out the hypothesis or see through a deception. Getting subjects to admit that they have learned the purpose of the experiment from someone else is difficult, because they don't want to make the experimenter feel bad.

Much ingenuity has been devoted to keeping the influence of role demands from undermining the validity of experiments. The most obvious and seemingly simplest solution is to deceive the subject about the experiment's purpose. A cover story is devised that provides a plausible rationale, and the true hypothesis is not revealed. This ploy often works but has several drawbacks, not the least of which involves ethics. In addition, developing a satisfactory cover story that will not affect the behavior being studied is often difficult. The story may cause subjects to behave in a way that interacts with the true hypothesis. Inevitably, too, subjects hear that many psychological experiments are not what they seem to be on the surface. This knowledge increases the difficulty of devising a believable cover story, and may even influence the results of experiments that do not use deception.

Another approach is to divide the experiment in such a way that part of the data are obtained in another setting. This design makes it less likely that subjects will put two and two together and surmise the hypothesis. For example, subjects are first given a test of anxiety. Later, those who scored either high or low on the test are requested to take part in an experiment without knowing the basis for their selection.

An additional method of counteracting bias is to use a measure that is unlikely to be influenced by subjects' guesses about the hypothesis. Some examples might be such nonverbal behavior as how close people sit to one another or whether they look a person in the eye. Finally, we will mention the tactic of keeping the subject unaware that an experiment is being conducted. Chairs may be rearranged in a public room to study the influence of seating arrangement on social interaction, for example. These and other methods of avoiding bias from role demands are discussed by Aronson and Carlsmith (1968).

Experimenter Bias

A large number of studies indicate that the experimenter can unintentionally bias the results of an experiment (Rosenthal, 1976). In one study, experimenters were given rats to train. Some were told that their rats had been specially bred for intelligence; others were told that their rats were particularly dull. Those experimenters who had the "bright" rats found faster learning than did the others (Rosenthal & Fode, 1963). The mechanism of the bias in this case was that the experimenters who had the "bright" rats handled them more than did those who had the "dull" rats. Some of these studies of bias have become controversial (Barber, 1976). Experiments were often designed to allow bias to operate freely. In some studies, evidence exists that the experimenters may simply have fudged the data rather than biasing them. Nevertheless, there is widespread agreement that an experimenter's biases can subtly influence experiments.

The effects of experimenter bias are so ubiquitous that a standard procedure in many disciplines is for the experimenter to be "blind" to the condition a subject experiences. This method of preventing experimenter bias is excellent and foolproof, but it is not always possible in a psychological experiment. In one experiment in my laboratory, we were interested in whether smokers had lower taste sensitivity than nonsmokers. Subjects were met by someone who asked them to empty their shirt pockets (to remove cigarettes or lighters) and who sent them on to the experimenter. Only after the experiment did we inquire about smoking habits. This technique was probably effective in most cases, but it could not make the experimenter blind to obvious tobacco stains or tobacco odor. Too, "blind" experimenters may devise their own hypotheses about experiments and thus unintentionally bias the subjects in the direction of their concocted hypotheses.

Another basic strategy for reducing experimenter bias is to standardize experiments as much as possible. In some experiments, testing subjects in all conditions at the same time may be possible. The various conditions can be induced by written instructions given to each subject. Or, if subjects must be tested individually, instructions can be tape-recorded so that each subject receives the same experience.

Variations on these basic strategies can be used in particular situations. Further discussion can be found in Aronson and Carlsmith (1968), Carlsmith, Ellsworth, and Aronson (1976), and Aronson, Brewer, and Carlsmith (1985).

❏

SUMMARY

1. A conclusion based on research is valid when it corresponds to the actual state of the world.

2. Four types of research validity are commonly recognized: internal validity, construct validity, external validity, and statistical validity.

3. An investigation has internal validity if a cause-effect relationship actually exists between the independent and dependent variables.

4. Confounding occurs when the effects of two independent variables in an experiment cannot be separately evaluated.

5. Construct validity concerns the question of whether the results support the theory behind the research.

6. Every experiment tests auxiliary hypotheses in addition to the main hypothesis. These auxiliary hypotheses are that particular conditions of the experiment are valid measures of the theoretical concepts the experiment is testing.

7. For questionnaires and related instruments, it is common to broaden the concept of construct validity to include face validity, content validity, and criterion validity.

8. External validity concerns whether the results of the research can be generalized to another situation: different subjects, settings, times, and so forth.

9. Statistical validity concerns whether the observed relationship is a true cause-effect relationship or whether it is accidental.

10. Threats to the internal validity of an experiment include events outside the laboratory, maturation, effects of testing, regression effect, selection, and mortality.

11. The regression effect occurs when subjects are tested on related measures and there is error in the measurement. Individuals who performed at the extremes on one measure will tend to score closer to the mean on the other.

12. Threats to construct validity include a loose connection between theory and experiment and the ambiguous effect of independent variables.

13. Among the problems that cause an ambiguous effect of the independent variables are tendencies for subjects to interpret conditions differently from the experimenter, as well as the good-subject tendency and evaluation apprehension.

14. Threats to external validity include problems arising from generalizing to other subjects, other times, or other settings.

15. Certain of these threats to validity are more prominent in particular types of research than in others.

16. Psychology experiments may be considered social situations with their own role demands that may interfere with the purpose of the study.

17. Ways of preventing role demands from biasing experimental results include inventing a cover story that deceives the subject about the purpose of the experiment, dividing the experiment in such a way that part of the data are collected in another setting, using measures that are unlikely to be influenced by the subject's expectations, and keeping the subject unaware that an experiment is being conducted.

18. Experimenter bias can be reduced by keeping the experimenter blind as to the conditions in the experiment or its purpose and by standardizing the procedure as much as possible.

Suggestions for Further Reading

Cook, T. D., & Campbell, D. T. (1976). The design and conduct of quasi experiments and true experiments in field settings. In M. D. Dunette (Ed.), *Handbook of industrial and organizational psychology.* Chicago: Rand McNally. This chapter is the standard source on validity.

⇒ A CASE IN POINT ⇐

The Effectiveness of Recitation Sections

Professor Morgan was interested in helping the less motivated students in his social-psychology class to learn the material. After the first test, he divided the class into high and low performers based on their test scores. Low performers were invited to attend special tutorial sessions. High-scoring students were not permitted to attend the extra sessions. In

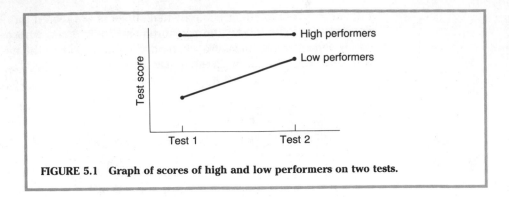

FIGURE 5.1   Graph of scores of high and low performers on two tests.

these tutorial sessions he covered the same material as in class, but he spent time discussing methods of studying, presented outlines of his lectures, and gave students hints on how to take notes.

On the second test, the experimental group (those who received the tutorials) improved noticeably. The control group did as well as they had on the first test. Professor Morgan concluded that his study proved that the tutorials improved the performance of less motivated students. The results are shown in Figure 5.1.

Professor Frass, however, had some doubts about the validity of the study. She felt that several problems made it impossible to conclude that the experimental condition was, in fact, responsible for the results.

REQUIRED: Prepare a memo that Professor Frass might send to Professor Morgan discussing the problems of validity in his study.

▮▶ A CASE IN POINT ◀▮

Cognitive Dissonance

Michael and Jennifer designed the following experiment as a project in their research-methods course. They wished to replicate the classical experiment on cognitive dissonance originally performed by Festinger (1957).

The basic plan of the experiment was that subjects performed a long and boring task of mating nuts and bolts. Then, the subjects were asked to tell other students who were outside waiting their turn to serve as subjects in the experiment how interesting the experiment had been. Some of the subjects were offered $1 for talking to the other students, and the others were offered $20. The subjects were to tell the other students that the task was actually fun and interesting.

Festinger's theory predicts that people who agreed to talk to other students for only $1 would experience "cognitive dissonance" because they would be telling the others that something was interesting when it was actually boring. One way to reduce the cognitive dissonance would be to change their opinions and decide that the task was actually interesting. Thus, the subjects who were paid $1 to tell the other students would later actually come to believe that the task was more interesting than would the subjects who were paid $20. (The subjects who were well paid would not experience cognitive dissonance because they had an obvious reason for doing what they did.)

Michael and Jennifer recruited their subjects from a social-psychology class whose instructor was very interested in Festinger's theory. After they ran the subjects in the nut-and-bolt mating task, they found that about a third of their subjects were grumpy and wouldn't even stay around long enough for the next phase in which they were going to ask them to talk to the waiting students. Of the ones who did stay, most acted polite, but made excuses why they couldn't do it. Because they were having difficulty getting subjects to agree to the next phase, they decided to get their quota of subjects in the $20 group before they started doing the $1 group. Their reason was that they were afraid that the term might be over before they finished their project, and they wanted to have at least some data so they could write up their project. They found that 85% of the subjects they asked to be in the $20 group of subjects agreed to do it; but only 25% of the subjects they asked to be in the $1 group ever agreed, and it took 20 minutes on the average to talk them into it. Most of those in the $20 group agreed right away.

Eventually, however, they found ten subjects who agreed to recruit others in the $20 condition, and ten for the $1 condition. Five of the $20 subjects were males, and two of the $1 subjects were males.

Because most of the subjects came from the same social-psychology class, Michael and Jennifer decided to measure the subjects' attitudes toward the experimental task by including the attitude survey on the final exam for the course. The professor agreed to let them add it onto the end of the exam. They found that six of the students who had been in the experiment didn't fill out the survey, but those who did said, on the average, that the experiment was very interesting and a valuable learning experience in relation to the course. Two of the remaining six subjects were tracked down and given the survey individually.

The average interestingness scores was 5.5 for the $20 group and 6.0 for the $1 group, on a 7-point scale.

Their research-methods professor was quite chagrined to read their report. He thought he had done a better job of teaching than was reflected in their project. He told them they had violated just about every type of validity mentioned in their text.

REQUIRED: Write Professor Jones's critique of the way they conducted their experiment.

≡ READING BETWEEN THE LINES ≡

5.1 DO YOUNGER INFANTS PREFER SIMPLER PATTERNS?

Wendy Brennan, Elinor Ames, and Ronald Moore (1966) showed infants cards with black-and-white checkerboard patterns on them. All cards were the same size, and the number of squares per card was either 4, 64, or 576. They found that 3-week-old infants looked longest at the simplest card, that 8-week-olds preferred the middle card, and that 14-week-olds preferred the most complex card. They concluded that there was a developmental trend in preference for complexity. Can you think of another interpretation of these results?   ∎

5.2 DO WOMEN FEAR SUCCESS MORE THAN MEN DO?

Matina Horner (1968; cited by Tresemer, 1977) had male and female college students write brief stories in response to the following verbal cue: "At the end of first-term finals, Anne [John] finds herself [himself] at the top of her [his] medical school class" (Tresemer, 1977, p. 32). Women saw the Anne version, and men saw the John version. Horner scored the resulting stories for themes that indicated a fear of success, such as social rejection ("everyone hates and envies her") and negative affect (feeling unhappy, unfeminine, guilty). Horner found that 62% of the women showed fear of success in their stories, whereas only 9% of the men did so. She interpreted her data as indicating that females had more fear of success than did males. Can you think of alternative hypotheses to account for these results?   ∎

☑ EXERCISES

5.1 FIND THE CONFOUND

Dr. R. A. Rabinoff, professor of physics at the Maharishi International University, claims scientific proof that transcendental meditation (TM) can influence the weather. According to Franklin Trumpy (1983–1984), the university was building a domed structure for the practice of levitation. They were rushing the construction throughout the cold Iowa winter and needed to pour concrete on days when the weather would permit.

According to the university's architect, the concrete was poured whenever the schedule called for it and was obtained from a company that supplied ready-mixed concrete. If the company agreed to supply the concrete the next day, the students at the university were instructed to meditate that evening for favorable weather.

According to Rabinoff, the weather was favorable six out of eight times that the students meditated, proving the effectiveness of meditation. Trumpy's analysis of the actual data for the area revealed that the weather was favorable on less than half of the days during the period covered by the project, showing that there was a considerable difference in the weather on the days when concrete was scheduled to be poured.

Let us assume that the data are statistically significant and that the results were not a fluke (a Type I error; see Appendix A).

REQUIRED: What possible source of confounding can you think of in this study? Is there some other variable that might explain the correlation between the practice of TM and the occurrence of good weather? (Hint: Think about the role of the concrete supplier. Remember that concrete tends to set up within a short time after it is mixed and thus cannot be stored for any length of time.)

5.2   THE *SPORTS ILLUSTRATED* JINX

Sports Illustrated magazine often puts outstanding athletes on its cover. It is widely believed that this exposure jinxes these athletes, because their performance often takes a nosedive afterward. However, this phenomenon is not limited to those who make the cover of *Sports Illustrated*. Between 1924 and 1986, only 8 National League batting champions and 13 American League batting champions repeated their feats the next year. Similarly, there have been 32 Cy Young Award winners between 1956 and 1986, and only 3 of them repeated the next year: Sandy Koufax of the Los Angeles Dodgers, 1965 and 1966; Denny McLain of the Detroit Tigers, 1968 and 1969; and Jim Palmer of the Baltimore Orioles, 1975 and 1976.

Besides a jinx, other causes of failure to repeat an outstanding athletic performance have been suggested: Perhaps the athletes are distracted by all the attention they receive, or they choke in trying to repeat, or they become complacent.

REQUIRED: What principle in this chapter can explain this phenomenon? Explain in detail how the principle applies to these situations.

5.3   IDENTIFY THE SOURCE OF INVALIDITY

An educational psychologist is asked to conduct a study to determine if class size has any effect on academic achievement. The psychologist identifies a large fifth-grade classroom in one inner-city school and a small fifth-grade classroom in another inner-city school. Principals from each school agree to participate in the study and select the teachers and classes. At the end of the school year, the researcher obtains achievement-test scores from students in both schools and compares the mean achievements of the two groups.

REQUIRED:
   a. Based solely on the preceding description, what threats to internal or external validity exist in this study? Explain.
   b. Can you think of an alternative method that would strengthen the internal and external validity of this study?

5.4   CONTROL AND VALIDITY

A psychology professor designs a study to determine the effects of using programmed learning materials as supplementary aids in an introductory experimental-methods course. She is interested in the amount of conceptual knowledge learned during a single semester. There are 104 students enrolled in four introductory experimental-psychology classes, and all four classes are taught by this same professor. Two of the classes are given the programmed learning materials, and the other two classes are not.

REQUIRED:
   a. Discuss whether it is necessary for the professor to use a pretest. What matters of control must be considered?
   b. Discuss whether this study has strong external validity.

5.5   FINDING THE SOURCE OF INVALIDITY

Ms. Hardnose and Mr. Goodheart are managers at Universal Widget, Inc. They make annual evaluations of their employees, but their evaluation methods are very poor. In fact, all differences in evaluations from one employee to another and from one time to another with the same employee are caused by random fluctuations. Ms. Hardnose fires all employees whose performance is unsatisfactory, whereas Mr. Goodheart usually gives them another try and works with them to help them improve. Hardnose finds that the replacements for the fired employees generally perform better than the ones fired. Goodheart finds that the unsatisfactory employees generally improve on their next evaluation. Thus, Hardnose has empirical evidence supporting her position that one should always fire someone who is doing poorly, while at the same time Goodheart finds empirical evidence that it pays to give unsatisfactory employees a second chance. How is this possible?   ❑

6

Control

In the previous chapter, we discussed the concept of validity and the various threats to the validity of research. In this chapter, we talk about ways of counteracting those threats to the validity of psychological research. First, we define the concept of control. Then we discuss, in turn, several general strategies for achieving control. Finally, we describe a number of specific control strategies.

THE CONCEPT OF CONTROL

control
providing a standard against which to compare the effect of a particular variable

Control is the other side of the validity coin. The heart of the experimental approach to knowledge is to ask the following two questions: (1) What are the threats to the validity of a contemplated piece of research? (2) What means are available to neutralize those threats? This approach is so basic that anyone who is acquainted with research has heard of control groups. Every experiment must have a control group. Right? Wrong.

It *is* true that you must have some method of countering every plausible alternative explanation of the results of your experiment. It is also true that this often involves the use of a group of subjects who do not experience the manipulation—that is, a control group—to serve as a standard against which to compare the effect of the variable of interest. Many experiments are performed, however, in which the use of a group that does not receive the independent variable makes no sense at all. Suppose you are interested in the effect of teaching methods on learning. You might arrange for some students to receive only lectures and others to receive only discussion. You conclude that one method of teaching was better than the other without having a group that never went to class.

We will define *control* as any means used to rule out possible threats to the validity of a piece of research. In psychology, the concept of control is used in two ways. The fundamental meaning of the term is that of providing a standard against which to compare the effect of a particular independent variable. If two experimental conditions differ on only one independent variable, then any difference between the two conditions following the treatment may be attributed to the operation of that variable. All other explanations are ruled out by the existence of the second, or control, condition.

Recall our discussion of Mill's methods for determining causes in Chapter 2. Following the method of difference, if two individuals differ on only one variable, then that variable may be considered to be the cause of the difference between the individuals. The concept of control is essentially a way of establishing that two individuals, or groups, or conditions, are identical except for the variable of interest. When that is the case, then the research is valid, and the method of difference can work.

This meaning of the term *control* is illustrated in Table 6.1. Two groups of subjects are tested on a dependent variable. Group 1 receives Treatment A; it is the **experimental group.** Group 2 receives no treatment; it is the **control group.** The control group serves as the basis of comparison for the experimental group. If the two groups were equal before the experimental treatment, then any postexperiment difference between them can be attributed to the treatment.

Although a control group is an effective way of achieving control of extraneous variables, it is not the only way. We said earlier that control can be achieved without a control group. Table 6.2 illustrates this point. We still have two groups, both of which are tested after receiving treatment. However, instead of Group 1 experiencing A and Group 2 experiencing the absence of A, both groups experience some value of A. As suggested previously, A_1 and A_2 could be two different teaching methods. Assuming the groups were equal before treatment, we can attribute any difference between Group 1 and Group 2 on the test to the difference between Condition A_1 and Condition A_2.

experimental group
subjects in an experiment who receive treatment
control group
subjects in an experiment who are like the experimental group in every respect except that they do not receive treatment

---

TABLE 6.1 USE OF A CONTROL GROUP

	TREATMENT	TEST
Group 1 (experimental group)	A present	Yes
Group 2 (control group)	A absent	Yes

TABLE 6.2 CONTROL WITHOUT A CONTROL GROUP

	TREATMENT	TEST
Group 1	A_1	Yes
Group 2	A_2	Yes

TABLE 6.3 USE OF A CONTROL CONDITION IN A WITHIN-SUBJECTS EXPERIMENT

ALL SUBJECTS	TREATMENT	TEST
Condition 1 (experimental condition)	A present	Yes
Condition 2 (control condition)	A absent	Yes

control condition a condition in an experiment that does not contain the experimental manipulation

within-subjects experiment research design in which each subject experiences every condition of the experiment

between-subjects experiment research design in which each subject experiences only one of the conditions in the experiment

Although we do not have a control group as such, each group serves as a control for the other. We have as much control in this situation as we did in the previous example, in which we had a control group.

Let us consider one further point. Instead of having different subjects experience each condition, in some experiments each subject experiences every condition. In such an experiment, instead of having a control group, we have a **control condition,** as illustrated in Table 6.3. When each subject experiences every condition, we say that each subject serves as his or her own control. An experiment of this kind is called a **within-subjects experiment** because the differences between conditions are tested within individual subjects. An experiment in which different groups of subjects experience different conditions is a **between-subjects experiment** because the differences between conditions are tested between different subjects.

A second meaning of the term *control* is distinct from the first but closely related—namely, the ability to restrain or guide sources of variability in research (Boring, 1954, 1969). This idea of experimental control is the one brought home so convincingly by the operant conditioning work of B. F. Skinner. When one has so limited the sources of variability in an experiment that the behavior becomes highly predictable, one has achieved experimental control. We are extremely impressed to observe a pigeon that has been trained to peck a key for food in the presence of a green light but not to peck in the presence of red. When the bird is well trained, the light virtually turns the bird on and off.

The two meanings of control are related in the following way. The primary meaning allows one to conclude that a dependent variable is associated with an independent variable and not with any other variable. The second usage facilitates drawing this conclusion by so limiting the number of variables operating in the situation and their range of values that the conclusion is clearer.

We can characterize the difference between the two meanings by use of the terms *control experiment* and *experimental control* (compare Sidman, 1960). When we have experimental control (secondary meaning), we have a much more sensitive situation in which to rule out alternative explanations of the experimental results (primary meaning).

Both meanings of the term *control* relate to the use of statistics in research. First, we use inferential statistics to evaluate the probability that a difference between experimental and control groups or conditions is likely to have arisen by chance alone. Second, we make enough observations or use enough subjects to reduce the variability of our estimate of the size of the experimental effect, and so make our statistical evaluation more precise.

The next section deals with the most important ways of achieving control in research. At the outset we should note that just as all types of threats to validity do not appear in all research, so it is not necessary or even possible to use every means of control in all research. The various methods of control are tools for psychologists to employ as necessary. Some will be used almost always, others less often.

GENERAL STRATEGIES

We will discuss three general strategies for achieving control in psychological research: using a laboratory setting, considering the research setting as a preparation, and instrumenting the response. Although these strategies are closely related, we will consider them separately for emphasis.

■ Control in the Laboratory

Laboratory research is generally preferred to field research. The reason is simple and has to do with what a laboratory is. We tend to think of a laboratory as a room with gray or black furniture, no curtains on the windows, tile floors, and workers dressed in white coats. Certainly, we are describing a typical laboratory, but the description has nothing to do with the essentials. Basically, a scientific laboratory is a place set up to allow the most appropriate control over variables of interest in the particular research. Thus, a social-psychology laboratory might well have rugs on the floor, curtains on the windows, pictures on the walls, and comfortable chairs—like any living room. Laboratory work in social psychology requires control over elements such as choice of subjects, beginning and end of social interaction, and freedom from distraction. If someone's home or a storefront building meets these requirements, such a setting might serve just as well or better than a sterile-looking room. The results of laboratory research depend entirely on the degree and type of control that is possible.

In Chapter 7 we will discuss some methods and advantages of field research. Here we will simply say that at times field research is preferable and at times laboratory research is preferable. Much social research is done in field settings because it is not possible or ethical to manipulate certain variables. Most people would frown on mugging subjects to learn what determines whether they will call the police. In some cases, the effect of a manipulation may not be realistic enough in the laboratory. Simulating a riot, for instance, would be difficult to do in a laboratory. But even those people who advocate field research agree that they must give up a degree of control and that problems of validity thus become greater. Field research is warranted when ethical or practical problems preclude the degree of control that would justify calling a certain research program a laboratory experiment. Laboratory research remains the ideal simply because the maximum control consistent with the nature of the problem is the ideal.

■ The Research Setting as a Preparation

One of the first questions to be answered in designing research is to decide what type of setting you want to use. You may be interested in learning what determines whether people will be cooperative or competitive. You could study how children play with toys, how basketball players pass to each other, or how salespeople decide who will help a customer. Any of these might be a good study. Another way to do research on cooperation is to use a situation called the prisoner's dilemma. The name comes from the situation in which two people have been arrested for involvement in a crime. If both of them refuse to confess, both will get a modest punishment. If both confess, they both get an intermediate punishment. If one confesses and the other does not, the one who confesses will be pardoned (rewarded) and the other severely punished. The dilemma arises because confession can lead either to reward or to punishment, with nonconfession also leading to punishment. This situation has been adapted to the laboratory, and much research has been done on the effects of the magnitude of rewards and punishments, relationship of the two people involved, and so forth.

The idea of a preparation is familiar to anyone who has studied biology. Researchers often use the giant nerve axon of the squid to study nerve conduction. Because the squid nerve is much larger than those in other animals, it permits biologists to do things that they cannot do with other nerves. The concept of a preparation is not as familiar in psychology, yet one of the researcher's goals is to choose the most suitable preparation for studying a given problem. Some of the most important contributions to psychology have been made by people who devised a new preparation for studying a given phenomenon. Perhaps the best example is that of B. F.

Skinner, who created the device that everyone, except Skinner, calls the Skinner box.

Before Skinner's invention, a number of devices had been used to study learning in small animals. Such study began with a maze patterned after the Hampton Court maze in England, one of those people-sized hedge mazes that were popular on large estates a few hundred years ago. Researchers soon realized that this first maze was too complicated for its purpose, so mazes were made progressively simpler until the T maze was designed. Later someone made a runway with no choice points at all and measured the speed at which rats ran the "maze." Then Skinner took a box, added a lever, and the rest is history. What his apparatus provided that others did not was simplicity, plus the opportunity for the rat to respond as often as it liked without waiting for someone to pick it up and return it to a starting point.

Skinner's seemingly small change made it possible to study *rate* of responding rather than *number* of correct turns or even *speed* in the runway. Having focused on an important dependent variable largely overlooked by others, Skinner went on to revolutionize the study of learning in animals. Thus, the Skinner box became one of the most important experiment preparations in psychology.

Preparation in this sense is involved in every experiment, but hardly ever is it spoken of that way in books on research design in psychology. Nevertheless, it is one of the most important considerations in designing research. Exactly which situation will provide the most powerful relationship between the variables of interest? No amount of sophisticated design or statistical analysis will make up for a poor choice of research preparation.

■ Instrumentation of the Response as Control

We have discussed the research setting as a preparation that allows the sensitive analysis of a phenomenon. Another important means of increasing the sensitivity of the research is to improve the measurement of the behavior being studied. Many researchers pay little attention to the response that will be measured, but here is where a little effort can pay big dividends. Just as certain preparations have become classic in psychology, so certain methods of measuring dependent variables have also had enormous impact. We have already mentioned the Taylor Manifest Anxiety Scale. The Minnesota Multiphasic Personality Inventory, the polygraph, and Stevens's direct psychophysical scaling methods are other excellent examples. These techniques have greatly improved the sensitivity of research in their respective fields. Many scientists devote their careers to developing and honing measuring devices. Most of these people do not intend to become methodologists but do so in order to evaluate more precisely phenomena of interest to them.

I have used the term *instrumentation* in discussing the task of improving response measurement. This use may seem strange because not all measurement methods employ mechanical means. The usage is deliberate, though. It calls attention to measuring devices as instruments for reducing behavior to numbers or to other forms convenient for data analysis. A characteristic of a good measuring instrument is that it takes the response out of the realm of casual observation and makes it reliable. Only in this way can we speak of measurement of behavior as objective, thus meeting the requirement of interobserver reliability necessary for science. Therefore, even a measure of a subjective state, such as the pleasantness of an odor, can be considered objective, provided the instrumentation of the response is adequate.

SPECIFIC STRATEGIES

■ Subject as Own Control

We are aware that each of us is unique and varies in many ways that could be important in an experiment. One of the most powerful control techniques is to have each subject experience every condition of the experiment. In this way, variation caused by differences between subjects is greatly reduced. The experimenter is wise to adopt the strategy of using subjects as their own controls whenever possible.

This control method is common in many areas of psychology, particularly sensation and perception. For example, if you are interested in the effect of adaptation to different concentrations of salt on the threshold for salt, using different subjects for each condition does not make much sense. The experimental manipulation is not likely to destroy the naivete of the subject, because the subject is unlikely to guess the purpose of the experiment even after experiencing it. In fact, the subject may not be aware that the experiment has different conditions. In addition, if enough time is allowed between conditions, there is not likely to be an important carryover between conditions. The subject will recover in a few minutes from the effect of adaptation to salt and will be ready to experience the next condition.

In many experiments, however, using subjects as their own controls simply is not possible. Once the subject has learned a problem by one method, learning the same problem again using a different method is impossible.

Another situation in which using subjects as their own controls is not feasible occurs when contrast effects exist between the conditions of the experiment, so that experiencing one condition may influence the response to another condition. These contrast effects, also known as order and sequence effects, will be discussed in Chapter 9. For now it is sufficient to note that there are situations in which conditions may affect one another. For instance, if magnitude of reward is the independent variable, subjects who experience a large reward first may respond less to a small reward than they would if only the small-reward condition had been received.

A more concrete example is provided by an experiment involving lifted weights. Suppose that you have two weights and each is lifted only once. You may think that you have controlled for order and sequence effects if half of the subjects experience one order (light, heavy) and the other half the opposite order (heavy, light). Let us suppose that there is a "true" response of 6 to the light stimulus and 8 to the heavy one, as determined in a between-subjects experiment in which each subject lifted only one weight. Now, if there were a contrast effect between the two weights that resulted in a doubling of the true difference in the responses when the weights were presented sequentially, the subjects who experienced light before heavy would give responses of 6 and 10, instead of 6 and 8. Those who experienced heavy before light would give responses of 8 and 4. The average responses for the two different orders would thus be 5 and 9, instead of 6 and 8, and the difference between the stimuli would appear to be 4, instead of the true difference of 2.

The type of effect we have just described is summarized in Table 6.4. Sometimes these effects can simply exaggerate an outcome that would occur between subjects, as in this example. Other times they produce outcomes that would not otherwise be found. The difference between using a within-subjects design and a between-subjects design can cause puzzling discrepancies in the results of experiments.

Returning to the lifted-weights example, we note that Harry Helson and his students (Helson, 1964), in their study of sequence effects in perceptual judgments, gave us the area known as adaptation-level theory. They found that a given weight would be called light or heavy depending on what other weights were presented along with it. Effects such as these can be studied only by using designs that permit contrast effects.

TABLE 6.4 THE PROBLEM OF CONTROLLING FOR SEQUENCE EFFECTS IN WITHIN-SUBJECTS EXPERIMENTS

WITHIN SUBJECTS

	STIMULUS	
ORDER	LIGHT	HEAVY
Light, heavy	6	10
Heavy, light	4	8
Average effect	5	9

BETWEEN SUBJECTS

	STIMULUS	
	LIGHT	HEAVY
"True" effect	6	8

In summary, you should consider using subjects as their own controls whenever three conditions can be met: (1) Using subjects as their own controls is logically possible. (2) Participating in all conditions of the experiment will not destroy the naivete of the subject. (3) Serious contrast effects between conditions will not be present.

■ Random Assignment

random assignment
unbiased assignment process that gives each subject an equal and independent chance of being placed in every condition

Another powerful control method is **random assignment** of subjects to conditions. The term *random assignment,* or *random allocation*, is used here in a specific sense: The allocation of subjects to conditions is random when each subject has an equal and independent chance of being assigned to every condition. The advantage of random allocation of subjects to conditions is that once subjects have been randomly assigned, the only way that confounding of subject-related variables with the experimental variable can occur is by chance.

At first glance, calling random allocation a method of control may seem improper because you appear to be throwing away a means of control and casting yourself on the mercies of chance. However, when you randomly assign subjects to conditions, you can be sure that only chance could cause the groups to be unequal with respect to a potential confounding variable. All sources of confounding variables are ruled out except as they become associated with the conditions by chance. Even if some variable is confounded with the independent variable by chance alone, assessing the likelihood of this happening is possible via statistical methods.

Modern statistical analysis provides numerous ways of testing whether experimental results are likely to have occurred by chance alone. These statistical methods rely completely on random allocation of subjects to conditions. In other words, statistical tests make estimates of the probability that purely random allocation of subjects to the various experiment conditions might have produced the results obtained. If the subjects are not assigned to conditions randomly, the statistical tests are not valid. One of the biggest "sins" in experimental psychology is to perform an experiment that cannot be analyzed statistically. The surest way to commit this error is to fail to assign subjects to conditions randomly.

Suppose you have already chosen your subjects from a population in some manner, and you have an experiment with two conditions. How do you decide which subjects will experience which conditions? There are many different ways of accomplishing this, but the following is a good way to do it.

The first step is to assign numbers to individuals. If you have 20 subjects, you assign numbers 1 through 20 to the individuals. Then go to a random-number table, such as the one in Table 8.1 (page 206). You could decide that the first subject would go into Group 1 or Group 2 depending on whether a 1 or a 2 came up first in the random-number table. This, however, would require you to go through many numbers, because only about one-fifth of the numbers in the table are 1s and 2s. (Of course, if you had more than two groups, it would be most efficient to consider the numbers in the table to be the number of the group.)

An alternative would be to consider Group 1 to be odd and Group 2 even. You would then put a subject into Group 1 if an odd number came up and into Group 2 if an even number came up. Turn to the random-number table on page 206 (Table 8.1). Because the first two columns appear to have been used, we might as well take column 3. The first four digits are all even, so the first 4 subjects will go into Group 2. Then there is one odd number followed by two more even numbers, one odd number, and then four more even numbers. By this time, we have allocated 12 subjects to conditions: 2 into Group 1, and 10 into Group 2. Because we want 10 per group, the last 8 must all go into Group 1. Does this sound like a random assignment—to have 8 out of the first 10 subjects go into Group 2 and all of the last 8 go into Group 1? It may not look random, but it was the result of a random process. Some researchers would be tempted to throw out this particular result as not representative and start over again, but the statistical model says we should go with it. (I would probably do another random assignment if I had some reason to believe that the numbers assigned to the subjects were systematic in any way—for example, if the assignment seemed to follow the order in which the subjects had signed up for the experiment.)

Using the procedure of randomization requires care. Students may be asked to volunteer for an experiment by signing up on a sheet for available times. The experimenter might be tempted to assume that the times are selected randomly and might place the first half of the students in one condition and the last half in the other. You can easily think of a number of ways in which the two groups could differ. The people who sign up for the early times may be more highly motivated to serve as subjects. On the other hand, all may have jobs requiring them to leave campus in the afternoon. The experimenter must randomly assign subjects to conditions *after* they have signed up.

Another example of a mistake in allocating subjects is to pull rats from a group cage and place the first batch selected in Condition A, the second batch in Condition B, and so forth. A little reflection will make it clear that the order in which the rats will be picked depends on their tendency to approach or avoid the experimenter's hand. This difference could be relevant for many experiments in learning, motivation, or social behavior. Table 6.5 summarizes the steps in a randomized-groups experiment.

■ Matching

matching
control procedure to ensure that experimental and control groups are equated on one or more variables before the experiment

Experimental precision can sometimes be improved by **matching** subjects on a pretest before randomly allocating them to conditions. When the subjects differ among themselves on an independent variable known or suspected to affect the dependent variable of interest, matching may be necessary. For example, suppose you are studying the effect of two different feeding schedules on weight gained by rats. You might expect that rats that were

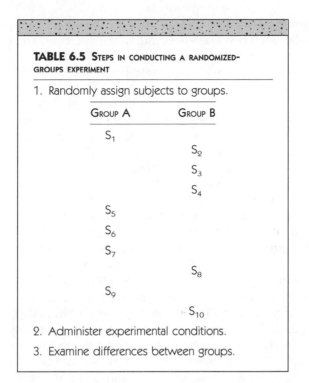

TABLE 6.5 Steps in conducting a randomized-groups experiment

1. Randomly assign subjects to groups.

Group A	Group B
S_1	
	S_2
	S_3
	S_4
S_5	
S_6	
S_7	
	S_8
S_9	
	S_{10}

2. Administer experimental conditions.
3. Examine differences between groups.

heavier to begin with would continue to gain more weight regardless of the schedule they were on. If subjects were allocated randomly to conditions, more of the heavier rats could wind up in one condition than in the other. By weighing the rats before the experiment, you can allocate them in such a way that the average weight in the two groups is the same.

The first requirement to justify matching is a strong suspicion that there is an important variable on which the subjects differ that can be controlled by matching. Further, you must believe that a substantial correlation will be present between the matching variable and the dependent variable. In our example of the weight-gain experiment with rats, you would find the two lightest rats and randomly place one in Group A and the other in Group B. You would repeat this procedure until you had paired off all the rats. If you found that, in fact, those animals that were initially heavier tended to gain weight regardless of the group they were in, you would have been justified in matching on weight. By correlating weight gain with starting weight, you would have found that weight gain correlated with beginning weight in spite of the effect of the variable of interest. On the other hand, if you found that there was little or no correlation, you would have wasted your effort in matching the subjects.

In fact, you can weaken your experiment by matching the subjects if the matching variable is not substantially correlated with the dependent variable. This effect results from the fact that the statistical test appropriate for a matched-groups design considers the data from pairs of subjects, while the randomized-groups test considers individual subjects. You can see that there are twice as many subjects as pairs of subjects, so the randomized test has more numbers to work with and therefore is more powerful.

A second condition necessary to justify matching is that it must be feasible to present a pretest to the subjects before assigning them to the conditions. For example, weighing rats before an experiment would be a simple matter, but giving an IQ test to every prospective student in an experiment on learning may not be feasible. The experimenter's time would probably be better used in simply testing more subjects, unless the IQ data can be obtained readily and ethically or unless the experiment is long enough to allow time for IQ testing.

Some bases for matching are better than others. Generally you try to match on the basis of some variable that has the highest possible correlation with the dependent variable. Normally the highest correlation is between the dependent variable and itself. In other words, if you are doing an experiment using reaction time, matching subjects according to their reaction times makes the most sense. You could present some practice trials and then allocate subjects to conditions based on their performance in the trials. On the other hand, if you are doing an experiment on learning and you want to control for intelligence, matching according to socioeconomic status (SES) would be a poor choice, even though there is some correlation between SES and intelligence scores. Your choice would be poor because the correlation between SES and IQ is weak. The slight control achieved by matching would be offset by the lower statistical power of a matched-groups design.

Let us emphasize a final point about the mechanics of matching. Even when you have matched your subjects, you must still randomly allocate the members of the pairs to conditions. If you have ten pairs of rats matched for weight, you must flip a coin or follow some procedure that will ensure that the members of each pair are allocated to groups randomly. Otherwise, your procedure for placing them into groups could introduce confounding. Table 6.6 summarizes the steps in a matched-groups experiment.

■ Building Nuisance Variables into the Experiment

nuisance variable
a condition in an experiment that cannot easily be removed and so is made an independent variable as a means of control

Another way to handle variables that cannot easily be removed from the experiment is to design the experiment so that these **nuisance variables** become independent variables in the study.

Suppose that your subject pool consists of both day-school and night-school students in introductory psychology. These people may differ in several ways that could relate to psychological variables. Night students may be older, may have more family and work responsibilities, and so forth. If you suspect that your subjects are dissimilar on some dimension related to day-versus night-student status, you have two choices. The first is to use only day or night students. This solution has the advantage of reducing the variability, but it also reduces the subject pool and the generality of the results. The second choice is to build a nuisance variable into the experiment.

TABLE 6.6 STEPS IN CONDUCTING A MATCHED-GROUPS EXPERIMENT

1. Administer pretest.
2. Rank subjects on pretest.

S_1

S_2

•

•

•

S_{10}

3. Form pairs on the basis of rankings.

S_1
S_2 } 1st pair

S_3
S_4 } 2nd pair

•   •
•   •
•   •

S_9
S_{10} } 5th pair

4. Randomly assign members of pairs to groups.

GROUP A	GROUP B
S_1	S_2
S_4	S_3
S_5	S_6
•	•
•	•
•	•
S_{10}	S_9

5. Administer experimental treatments.
6. Examine differences between members of pairs.

S_1 — S_2
S_4 — S_3
•
•
•

What is the average difference between pairs?

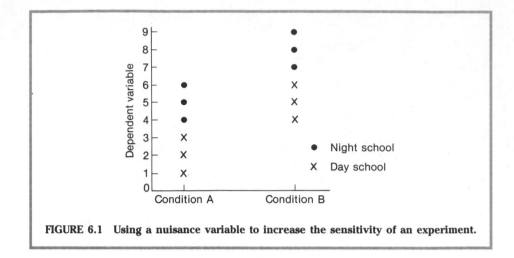

FIGURE 6.1   Using a nuisance variable to increase the sensitivity of an experiment.

Figure 6.1 shows the results of a hypothetical experiment in which night- or day-student status was designed into the experiment as a nuisance variable. If we do not consider day or night status, we find considerable overlap between the results of Conditions A and B. We might not be willing to conclude that the conditions had a differential effect on the dependent variable. (We are ignoring the possibility of using inferential statistics to help in this decision.) But let us consider day or night classes as a nuisance variable; that is, let us analyze the data separately for day and night students. We find now that no overlap exists between Group A and Group B for night-school students considered alone or for day students considered alone. We have increased the sensitivity of the experiment by building a nuisance variable into the study. Note that the nuisance variable need not have any theoretically important role in the experiment. We do not care why night-school students scored higher. On the other hand, the nuisance variable may suggest new theoretical questions for another experiment.

■ Statistical Control

Except for randomization, all of the control methods described so far can be classified as methods of achieving experimental control; they aim to reduce variability as much as possible. Sometimes these techniques can be spectacularly effective and a very few observations on a single subject can be used to draw firm conclusions. Usually, however, that old devil variability cannot be completely exorcised from the experiment. Then it is necessary to use **statistical control.**

statistical control mathematical means of comparing subjects on paper when they cannot be equated as they exist in fact

Statistical control in the broad sense is synonymous with inferential statistics, the branch of statistics that deals with making decisions in the face of uncertainty. Suppose you have a difference between two groups on some dependent variable in an experiment. Was the effect real, or did it happen by chance? The point behind the question is that statistical control is involved in designing an experiment. Are there enough subjects? How many trials should there be? Can the experiment as designed be analyzed properly by accepted statistical methods?

Such considerations are important enough to merit courses that specialize in the statistical analysis of experimental data. For now, because you are not taking such an experimental-design course, you will have to answer questions of statistical control with general knowledge about statistics and with advice from your instructor. Remember, too, that in the end the question of statistical control comes down to whether you and others believe the data. If you have enough subjects to look convincing, and if you have avoided the pitfalls discussed in this chapter, you probably have a good experiment. Although you may be fooled into thinking that some effect was caused by the independent variable when it was actually random—especially when you look at your own data—at this stage of your career you should aim to design an experiment that will convince yourself and others.

In the narrower sense, statistical control refers to a means of equating subjects on paper when they cannot be equated in fact. Suppose you are studying the effect on grades of two different teaching methods in the classroom. Because randomly constituting the classes is not feasible, you must work with existing classes. If the students in the two classes do not have the same average IQ, you will have a problem in attributing the difference in grades to the teaching methods. But if you know the relationship between IQ and grades in the class, you can find out how much the students' grades differed from what you would have expected, based on the prediction of the IQ/learning relationship.

This approach is illustrated in Figure 6.2, which represents the relationship between grades and IQ. Each data point represents a single subject, the X being placed at the intersection of the person's grade

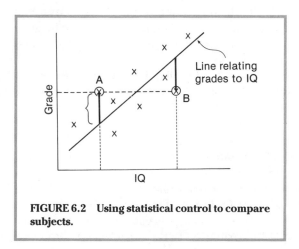

FIGURE 6.2   Using statistical control to compare subjects.

(measured on the y-axis) and his or her IQ (on the x-axis). The slanting line shows what grade would be predicted for persons having particular IQs. (In other words, it is the regression line predicting grade from IQ.) The data point circled and labeled A represents a single subject's position on the two axes. You can see that Subject A earned a higher grade than would have been expected from the relationship shown by the slanted line. Subject B, however, earned a lower grade than predicted by the line. Notice that both students received the same grade.

The basic idea of statistical control is that it enables you to compare students not on their absolute grade, but on the difference between grade and what would have been expected from the line predicting grade from IQ. Subject A would be scored as earning a grade of plus-so-many points and Subject B as earning minus-so-many points. You could conclude that A had benefited more from the condition than had B. This technique makes it possible to compare groups that are made up of subjects who differ on IQ. The technical term for this comparing process is analysis of covariance, a topic beyond the scope of this book. Be aware that this method is available as a means of controlling for variability in an experiment. You may refer to one of the standard books on statistics, such as Kirk (1982), for a description.

REPLICATION, REPLICATION

replication
repeating an experiment to see if the results will be the same

A method of control seldom described as such is **replication**—the repeating of an experiment to see if the same results are found the second time. Laypersons sometimes assume that once a result has been found by a scientific experiment, the conclusions are fixed permanently. The truth is that an experiment seldom stands by itself, particularly if the results are surprising. In fact, an unusual result remains in a kind of limbo until other experimenters have successfully replicated the experiment. If the same results are obtained by other experimenters, they become part of our scientific knowledge. If the replication is not successful, the supposed facts found in the original experiment are invalid and are forgotten. Many examples of this process have occurred throughout the history of psychology, as well as in the other sciences.

A particularly good example of how dubious phenomena get weeded out is provided by the history of research on transfer of memory by injecting material from a trained animal into an untrained animal. The line of research began with the finding that feeding trained planaria (flatworms) to untrained planaria resulted in a transfer of memory to the untrained worms (J. V. McConnell, 1962). Eventually a similar experiment was tried on rats (Babich, Jacobson, Bubash, & Jacobson, 1965), except that instead of feeding the trained rats to untrained ones, the experimenters injected extracts of their brains. The resultant finding created much interest in the scientific community because of its enormous implications for the mechanisms of memory and for the storage of information in the nervous system in general. A number of positive replications were published (see W. L. Byrne, 1970, for a review). However, it soon became clear that all was not well with this supposed phenomenon. Not all investigators could replicate the finding. Within a few years of the original research, an article was published by 23 authors from seven laboratories (Byrne et al., 1966) reporting that all of these scientists had failed to replicate the original finding. They stated their conclusions cautiously: "Our consistently negative findings . . . indicate only that results obtained with one method of evaluating this possibility are not uniformly positive" (p. 658).

In the intervening years, the phenomenon has not been firmly established in spite of continued work. One textbook (Cotman & McGaugh, 1980) summarizes the situation as follows: "In general the findings are extremely conflicting, and as a consequence no firm conclusions can be drawn. Research has not as yet specified either optimal or reliable procedures for producing a transfer effect. Further, it is not at all clear what type of molecule might be responsible for producing the effect. . . . Should such experiments be reproducible, it should be possible to determine the basis of the effects. At the present time, the memory transfer effect must be regarded as not yet convincingly demonstrated" (p. 313).

The history of the research on the transfer of training by injection followed a typical pattern. The first reports elicited a great deal of interest and many attempts at replication. Some of these attempts were successful, and the investigators naturally published their results. Those who did not find the effect were reticent about admitting their failures and, additionally, may have had difficulty getting negative results published. Enough negative results eventually accumulated, however, to overcome biases, and the literature began to reveal a preponderance of negative results. Such a scenario has occurred repeatedly in science, with the result that those research effects that are not repeatable are discarded.

Two types of replication are commonly distinguished: direct and systematic. Direct replication occurs when someone repeats essentially the identical experiment in an attempt to obtain the same results. Systematic replication occurs when Researcher B says, "If A's theory is correct, then the following should happen." Then B performs an experiment different from A's but based on it. If A's results and theory are correct, B should find a certain result.

Direct replication is seldom carried out because finding exactly the same thing as someone else did brings little glory. More specifically, it is difficult to get grants for replications, journals tend to avoid publishing such research, and professors who spend time replicating other people's work do not get promoted. Direct replication is usually attempted only when systematic replication has failed. Investigators then go back and repeat the original method more exactly in order to pinpoint the source of the difference in results.

Systematic replication is the usual way that experiments are replicated. Researcher B will do an experiment similar to Researcher A's but with different types of subjects, or with different values of the stimulus, or with different ways of operationally defining the theoretical concepts. All of these approaches are considered systematic replication. As long as results consistent with A's are found, A's original experiment is supported by B's work. You will notice that systematic replication tests external validity by using different subjects, species, or situations. Construct validity is tested when different ways are used to operationalize the theoretical concepts. Statistical validity is tested in all replications, both direct and systematic.

The need for replication is sometimes downplayed in favor of showing that a given result would be unlikely to occur by chance alone. Believers in ESP point out that particular experiments produced results that would have happened only once in billions of experiments by chance alone. The ESP believers' statistics are usually impeccable, but their understanding of the methods of science is faulty. Innumerable ways exist in which an experiment can fail to be valid, giving results that are due neither to chance nor to the particular hypothesis. Calculating long odds is impressive, but it is only one of a number of considerations in evaluating the experiment. Generally, experiments in ESP fail to replicate. Although believers in ESP may propose reasons for this failure, scientists will pay little attention to ESP until someone devises an experimental situation that gives consistent results in its favor. R. A. Fisher, who largely invented modern statistical methods, said, "Very long odds . . . are much less relevant to the establishment of the facts of nature than would be a demonstration of the reliability of the phenomena" (quoted by Crumbaugh, 1966, p. 527).

EXPERIMENTAL DESIGN AS PROBLEM SOLVING

The rest of this book consists largely of examples of good research design. We will not discuss all possible designs, for the simple reason that doing so would be impossible. Rather, we will give a list of designs for you to use as models in designing similar experiments of your own. Experimental designs should be tailor-made for each experimental problem. Sometimes an existing design will fit the problem perfectly. More often, alterations must be made. Therefore, it is better to create the design from the beginning.

Designing an experiment is a matter of solving particular problems of validity by the application of particular methods of control. When every problem has been solved, the experiment is designed. Then is the time to look in books on experimental design to see if your design can be analyzed according to accepted statistical procedures. To look in the books first is to get the cart before the horse and to forget that the essence of experimental design is solving threats to validity in the best way possible.

Two of the general strategies listed at the beginning of this chapter—using the setting as a preparation and instrumentation—are not usually discussed as such in experimental-design books. They are the guiding principles of design, however. Use the specific strategies we have discussed as tactics in applying these general principles.

THE ELEGANT EXPERIMENT

The goal of every scientist is to design the best possible experiment. How is such a concept put into practice, though? Do you keep testing more and more subjects until the conclusion is inescapable? Do you keep adding variables until every possible source of confounding is taken into account? I find the concept of the elegant experiment helpful in thinking about such questions. In everyday usage, the term *elegance* implies richness combined with tasteful simplicity. In mathematics, the term emphasizes simplicity. An elegant proof draws a powerful conclusion in the simplest possible way. This idea is what I mean by the elegant experiment: the simplest experiment that will make a clear and convincing test of a hypothesis.

It is possible to include so many variables in a study that not enough measures are made on any one to draw firm conclusions. It is possible to have such a complicated design that you lose sight of the forest for the trees. Consequently, it is important to realize that many trade-offs must be made in the course of designing an experiment and that this process requires hard decisions. Do you spend more time and effort at the outset testing pilot subjects and refining your experimental procedure? Or do you decide to test more subjects in the main experiment to make up for the uncontrolled variability? I cannot tell you what to do in any particular case. Paying careful attention to these questions, though, will result in experiments that are convincing tests of hypotheses.

In selecting the word *elegance,* I have deliberately chosen a term that has an aesthetic connotation. Designing experiments is an art that requires creativity and that reflects the tastes of the experimenter. Such activity can be both challenging and rewarding.

HOW TO USE THE REST OF THIS BOOK

By now we have an idea of what science is. We have talked about the basic principles of research design, as well as about the principles of validity and the basic means of controlling for threats to validity. We might stop here and tell you to begin designing your own research based on these principles. Obviously we have not done that, and for a good reason. Important as the principles are, probably no one could become a successful researcher by reading a book on the principles of research.

One learns to do research by studying examples of research and, better yet, by doing research. Scientific research is one of those activities that is best learned by working with someone who serves as a guide in a hands-on situation. In this respect, the way to become a scientist parallels the way an apprentice becomes skilled by working under the direction of an experienced person. The importance of this process can be seen in the many famous scientists who were students of other learned scientists. Firsthand experience in the laboratory of a good scientist has no substitute for learning how to do science. Myriads of attitudes, skills, and techniques are assimilated in such a situation. No book, including this one, can do more than serve as a pale substitute.

My goal in this book is to present those concepts that I spend the most time explaining when I talk with students about research. Although I cannot anticipate all questions, I have tried to answer those that are commonest and most important. Most of you will be taking a course in research methods. Your instructor, along with this book, will be guides as you learn to do research.

✳ NUTS & BOLTS ✳

Choice of Method

Once you have a question that you wish to investigate, you are faced with many decisions: what kind of subjects, what task, what apparatus, what kinds and values of independent variables? By the nature of this book, we must deal with these questions in a rather general fashion. Nevertheless, certain principles can be stated.

Your review of the literature will reveal standard tasks, apparatus, subjects, and so forth that are generally used in studying a certain problem. For practical and theoretical reasons, it makes sense to follow the standard practice as much as possible and to deviate only when there is good reason to do so. You may feel that a different task, for example, might be more appropriate. What you want to find out will dictate many of these choices. Recall our earlier discussion of the research setting as a preparation. You should make your choices of subjects, apparatus, and so forth with the following question foremost in mind: Which alternative will permit the most sensitive test of the hypothesis? Above all, you must choose a design that will yield data that you can analyze statistically.

Choice of Subjects

We will make only general statements about choice of subjects because many considerations are specific to particular studies.

The allegation that the college sophomore and the white rat have been studied too often is true. The reasons become obvious when you start to consider your own alternatives. If the problem lends itself to study with animals, and other experimenters have used the rat, those facts become good reasons for you to do so. Changing strains of rat or even the supplier of the rats can make comparing results between experiments difficult. In addition, using another species of animal may require you to solve new housekeeping problems. For example, can you keep another species of animal healthy in a laboratory?

If you are studying humans and you wish to use a population other than the college student, what problems will you face with recruitment and payment of volunteers, standardization of technique on the population, and so forth? Such considerations help to explain the extensive reliance on these two classes of subjects. Of course, if you have good reason to use a different population, a little care and effort in designing the study around other subjects often pays big dividends.

Selection of Subjects

Ethical and practical considerations enter into the selection process. With the exception of naturalistic observation and certain other types of research, the consent of the subjects must be obtained before they participate. We will discuss the ethics of research in Chapter 14, but meanwhile let us note that subjects in psychological research ordinarily should participate voluntarily.

Ideally, subjects should be a random sample of the population to which you wish to generalize the results of your study. For example, in order to generalize the results of an experiment on college students to the entire adult population of North America, the students ought to be a random sample of that population. Obviously they cannot be, but they should be at least a random sample of college students.

In actuality, most experiments on humans draw subjects from introductory psychology classes. Furthermore, subjects usually volunteer under coercion, for course credit or to meet a departmental requirement. Under these circumstances, you can see that students who sign up for experiments early in the term may be different from those who wait until the last week of class to volunteer. Even going into a class and asking for volunteers will produce a biased sample. For example, women are more likely to volunteer for an experiment when they are in the ovulatory phase of their menstrual cycle and less likely to volunteer when they are menstruating (Doty, 1975). If this variable were important in an experiment, atypical results would be found using women who volunteer spontaneously. The problem can be minimized by calling women randomly from a list of potential volunteers and asking them to come in at a particular time. In this situation they are less apt to participate differentially than if they have volunteered spontaneously.

Your college will likely have standard procedures for recruiting subjects. In fact, all details of the experiment must be approved by the appropriate authorities. You should follow these procedures carefully. For example, if all introductory psychology students must participate in a certain number of hours of experimentation as a course requirement, and if they are supposed to sign up through a central office, then going directly to the classroom to seek volunteers is not fair to other experimenters.

However subjects are to be recruited—in class, by poster, or through newspaper ads—make sure they know the exact building, room, date, and time of the experiment. You should give them a telephone number to call if they must cancel, and you should have their number in case you must cancel.

Random assignment of subjects to conditions is essential. You must decide in advance your procedure for achieving this. If the experiment is a between-subjects design, you should have a random order made up before the subjects arrive. Then you will follow the assignment as the subjects show up: the first one will receive the condition that is scheduled first, and so forth. Leave no room for subjectivity when you assign subjects to conditions. If subjects are to be tested in pairs, flip a coin to determine which one is assigned to which condition.

How many subjects should you test? There is a rational way of deciding how many subjects to use in an experiment, provided you know how much variability to expect in your data. In ordinary laboratory experiments, however, almost nobody uses this basis for deciding the number of subjects. The reason is simple and practical. Suppose that you wish to achieve a particular degree of precision in your results. Of course, the more subjects you have, the less the means of your data will deviate from their true values. The usual way of representing this error of measurement is called the standard error of the mean. The following equation shows how the standard error of the mean decreases with increases in the number of subjects:

$$\sigma_{\bar{x}} = \frac{\sigma_x}{\sqrt{N}}$$

In this equation, sigma represents the standard deviation of the scores and N is the number of subjects. You can see from the equation that in order to cut the standard error of the mean in half, you must double the square root of N. In order to double the square root of N, you must quadruple N.

How the number of subjects affects the precision of an experiment is illustrated in Figure 6.3, which shows how the standard error of the mean decreases with N. In this figure, we assume that the standard error of the mean is 1 unit when there are 10 subjects. In order to reduce the standard error to the mean to 0.5 unit, we must increase the number of subjects to 40. If we wish to reduce the standard error of the mean again by a factor of 2, to 0.25, we must use 160 subjects!

Thus, you can see that increasing the number of subjects does not decrease the error of measurement in a linear way. Doubling the number of subjects reduces the standard error of the mean by only 30%. (Not all experiments will use the standard error of the mean in data analysis, but the effect is the same for other statistics.) The law of diminishing returns operates. For this reason, most experiments will use about 10 subjects—or, if they have more than one condition, 10 subjects per condition. Observe how many subjects have been used in experiments similar to yours and how much precision was obtained. If you want more precision, ask yourself if using more subjects will make a significant improvement. If not, try to increase the precision of measurement experimentally.   ❏

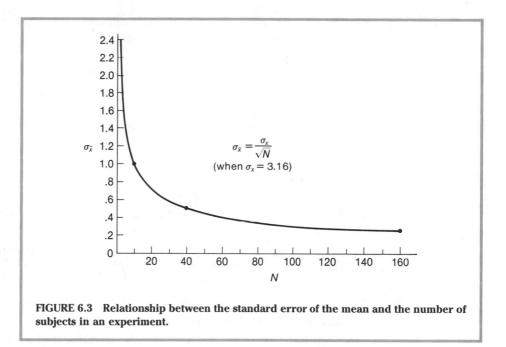

FIGURE 6.3 **Relationship between the standard error of the mean and the number of subjects in an experiment.**

SUMMARY

1. The fundamental meaning of the term *control* in psychology is that of providing a standard against which to compare the effect of a particular variable.

2. Experiments in which different groups of subjects experience different conditions are known as between-subjects experiments. Those in which each subject experiences every condition are known as within-subjects experiments.

3. The group in a between-subjects experiment that receives the treatment is called the experimental group; the group that does not receive the treatment is called the control group.

4. In within-subjects experiments, the condition that does not contain the experimental manipulation is called the control condition.

5. It is not necessary to have a control group or a control condition in an experiment as long as there is some group or condition that can serve as a comparison for the particular experimental manipulation.

6. A second meaning of the term *control* is the ability to restrain or guide sources of variability in research. This meaning is captured in the term *experimental control*.

7. There are three general strategies for achieving control in research: using a laboratory setting, considering the research setting as a preparation, and instrumenting the response.

8. Laboratory research is defined not by the use of a particular kind of room but by the ability to control the important sources of variability in the research setting.

9. The concept of a preparation emphasizes choosing the best possible research situation in which to test a hypothesis.

10. Instrumentation of the response refers to the means of measuring the dependent variables. Careful measurement renders responses objective and may even be thought of as creating responses.

11. Specific control strategies include using subjects as their own controls, randomizing, matching, building nuisance variables into the experiment, and using statistical control.

12. Subjects may be used as their own controls when doing so is logically possible, when serving in all conditions will not destroy their naivete, and when there will not be serious contrast effects between conditions.

13. The allocation of subjects to conditions is random when each subject has an equal chance of being assigned to every condition.

14. Matching may be used when there is an important variable on which subjects differ that is correlated with the dependent variable and where it is feasible to present a pretest to the subjects.

15. Nuisance variables that cannot easily be removed from the experiment may be controlled for by making them independent variables in the experiment.

16. Statistical control may be thought of broadly as synonymous with inferential statistics. More narrowly, statistical control involves equating subjects on paper by means of the analysis of covariance.

17. One of the most important means of control is the replication of an experiment. Direct replication is repeating essentially the same experiment. Systematic replication is doing a different experiment in which certain results should be found if the original experiment was valid.

18. Controlling the sources of invalidity is essentially a matter of solving problems. When the problems are solved, the experiment is designed. The goal of a researcher is to design the most elegant experiment that will answer the questions of interest and will deal with the problems of validity.

19. The choice of method is dictated by factors such as the exact hypothesis to be tested, the methods that are standard in the particular field, and practical considerations.

20. The number of subjects to be used depends on the size of the effect and the anticipated variability of the data. The power of the experiment increases proportionately with the square root of the number of subjects.

Suggestions for Further Reading

SIDMAN, M. (1960). *Tactics of scientific research.* New York: Basic Books. This book presents a classic discussion of experimental control from the Skinnerian perspective.

⟫ A CASE IN POINT ⟪

Vision in Babies

To illustrate the considerations involved in deciding on the number of subjects to test in an experiment, consider the following example. Professor Strauss studies vision in babies. She wants to find out if they can recognize their mother's face. Her experimental situation involves having a baby look at a pair of faces projected on a screen for 5 minutes. She measures how long they look at the mother's face compared with a control face. Previous studies have shown that if babies recognize their mother's face, they will look longer at the mother than at the control woman. From pilot work, Professor Strauss estimates that they will look 10 seconds longer at the mother's face. The standard deviation of time spent looking is 100 seconds.

Professor Strauss has a budget of $1,000 for this experiment. It costs her $10 to run a single subject. Her apparatus has some problems, however. She believes that a new projector would make the pictures much clearer, increasing the difference in the babies' viewing time for the mother's face to 20 seconds. A new projector would cost $250. Also, her method of recording the babies' preferences has some problems because it is hard to see where the baby is looking. An automatic recording device would reduce the standard deviation of the responses from 100 to 50 seconds but would cost $500.

Professor Strauss scratches her head and wonders what to do. If she uses her old equipment, she can run 100 subjects. If she buys both the projector and the recording device, she can run only 25. Of course, she could buy just one or the other. What should she do?

For this example, the t test is the appropriate statistic. The question then becomes what combination of effect size, standard deviation, and number of subjects will give the largest predicted t.

$$t = \frac{\overline{X}}{\sigma/\sqrt{N}}$$

Consider the effects of the various alternatives on this equation.

First, let us use our intuition. Increasing the effect size, decreasing the variability of the response, and increasing the number of subjects should all increase the predicted level of significance of the study.

Now, let us look at the equation and see how this works. Increasing the number of seconds that the babies look at the mother's face compared with the control face will increase the numerator, $\overline{X}$. So increasing the effect size will increase t. The denominator of the fraction is itself another fraction. The numerator of the bottom fraction is the standard deviation of the number of seconds by which the babies prefer the mother to the control. Decreasing the standard deviation will increase t because it affects the denominator of the main fraction. On the other hand, increasing the number of subjects will increase the value of t because it is the denominator of the lower fraction. Increasing the square root of N will decrease the value of the ratio $\sigma/\sqrt{N}$. Because this forms the denominator of the main fraction, t is increased.

Determining which alternative is best requires Professor Strauss to work out the value of t for each alternative.

≡ **READING BETWEEN THE LINES** ≡

6.1 BRAIN DAMAGE SOMETIMES PRODUCES OBESITY IN RATS

Lesions in a part of the brain known as the ventromedial hypothalamus have been known to produce obesity in rats. Some investigators, however, were unable to find the effect as reliably as others and proposed that the lesion itself did not produce the obesity. Rather, the scar tissue that resulted from the lesion stimulated a nearby area that actually controlled eating. Experiments were done to produce more or less scar tissue and, therefore, more or less irritation to the nearby area of the brain. These experiments showed that the manner in which the lesion was produced did not matter as much as which laboratory did the experiments. One group of investigators consistently found that the lesions produced obesity, while others tended to find no effect. Eventually, a simple difference in methods between the successful and unsuccessful experiments was found. Can you guess what it was?   ■

6.2 COGNITIVE AND AROUSAL FACTORS IN EMOTION

One of the most influential experiments in social psychology was conducted by Stanley Schachter and Jerome Singer (1962), who hypothesized that people experience particular emotions as the result of a cognitive interpretation of a physiological arousal. According to this hypothesis, the same arousal could be experienced, for example, as euphoria or anger depending on the person's cognitions.

The researchers tested their hypothesis by injecting subjects with a stimulating drug, then exposing them to a confederate who acted either euphoric or angry. The authors reported that the emotions of the subjects tended to match those of the confederate. Later the experiment was attacked in two separate research papers. Because the flaw in the experiment is not obvious, I will tell you that it has to do with replication.   ■

✓ **EXERCISES**

6.1 RANDOM ASSIGNMENT

You are designing an experiment in which 10 subjects will experience the experimental condition and another 10 will be given the control condition. A total of 20 subjects have signed up for the experiment. Randomly assign them to the two groups. Describe your steps.

6.2 READING A RESEARCH PAPER

Read the sample paper on pages 341–356 of the text, and answer the following questions.

INTRODUCTION

1. What problem, question, situation, or observation led to this study?
2. What theory is being tested, or what is the theoretical framework within which the work is developed (if it is explicitly mentioned)?
3. What hypotheses or predictions are made, or what will this study contribute to our knowledge of this problem?

METHOD

1. Subjects
   a. Who were the subjects?
   b. How were they selected?
2. Design
   a. What kind of study was this (true experiment, quasi experiment)?
   b. How many conditions were there, and what were they?
   c. Was this a between- or within-subjects design?
   d. How were subjects assigned to conditions (in case of a true experiment)?
   e. Were subjects run blind/double-blind?
   f. Was there a manipulation check (to see if the instructions were effective in setting up the appropriate conditions, in social psychological experiments)?
   g. What were the independent variables?
   h. What were the dependent variables?
   i. Were the subjects debriefed?
   j. Summarize the design.

RESULTS

1. Were any transformations performed on the data?
2. How were the results analyzed (what statistical analysis was used)?
3. Was the manipulation check effective (if applicable)?
4. Were the data collapsed over any independent variables, and if so why?
5. Summarize the major findings.

DISCUSSION

1. Were the hypotheses confirmed?
2. How do the findings relate to what is already known about the topic, or what are the implications of these findings?
3. What limitations do these findings have?
4. What future research is suggested by these results?   ❑

7

Nonexperimental Research, Part 1: Observational, Archival, and Case-Study Research

A s we saw in Chapter 6, experiments provide the most powerful means of studying behavior because they permit the greatest control, and hence the cleanest use of Mill's methods. Many questions cannot be studied experimentally, however. It would probably not be possible to study a student riot under controlled conditions. Even if it were possible, you certainly wouldn't want to attempt it.

As you can tell from the term, nonexperimental research is defined by exclusion: research that is not experimental. This requires us to define experiment before we go on. The distinction between experimental research and nonexperimental research is based on the degree of control that the researcher has over the subjects and the conditions of the research. Key words here are **manipulation** and **assignment** versus **observation.**

An experiment is a kind of investigation in which some variable is manipulated. The researcher has enough control over the situation to decide which subjects receive what conditions at what times. Suppose that you were interested in the differences in learning between students who only studied a book and students who read the book and also attended lectures. A researcher who is able to perform an experiment would set up the conditions (manipulate a variable) and assign subjects to them. As we will see in later chapters, this assignment of subjects to conditions makes it possible to determine with more certainty whether the differences between conditions actually caused any differences in behavior. If the researcher cannot assign subjects to groups but must only observe how

manipulation
in an experiment, the condition or variable assigned or presented to a subject

assignment
in an experiment, a subject experiences a condition or variable according to the experimenter's plan

observation
the record of a behavior

students in two already existing classes at a college learn according to the same two methods, we do not have a true experimental study. There are many other things that could have caused any differences in learning between the classes. For example, the students may have signed up for one class or the other on the basis of their preference for the instructor, or the teaching method, or the time of day. Any of these factors could cause differences in learning.

A second characteristic of nonexperimental research is that the data collection procedure often must forfeit some degree of control in return for obtaining the data. For example, we might decide to study public records that may be almost, but not exactly, in the form we desire. Or we might have to keep a questionnaire short in order to gain the cooperation of subjects.

correlational research
nonexperimental research that measures two or more variables to determine the degree of relationship between them

Nonexperimental research is often called **correlational research** because it seeks causes of behavior by looking for correlations among variables. (See Appendix A for a discussion of correlation.) The term is somewhat misleading, however, because all research is correlational to the extent that it seeks functional relationships between variables (compare Cook & Campbell, 1979). Calculating correlations among variables does not make the research correlational in the strict sense. We often compute correlations among variables in the truest of experiments. What makes research correlational in the loose sense is the inability to manipulate some variable independently. In correlational research, relationships are studied among variables, none of which may be the actual cause of the other. This is why all statistics books emphasize that "correlation does not prove causation." We prove causation when we can decide which variable caused the other, and this is best done in an experiment.

observational research
study method in which the researcher observes and records ongoing behavior but does not attempt to change it

Nonexperimental research is often a first step in starting to answer theoretical questions by empirical methods. Experimental research frequently is done as a follow-up to previous nonexperimental observations. For example, experimental research on physiological and behavioral factors in alcoholism has followed from the nonexperimental observation that alcoholism tends to run in families.

It is convenient to distinguish several varieties of nonexperimental research. The first may be called **observational research,** in which the researcher simply observes ongoing behavior. Examples are field observation of ducks from a blind or television monitoring of people in a store.

archival research
study method that examines existing records to obtain data and test hypotheses

The second category is **archival research,** in which existing records are examined in order to test hypotheses about the causes of behavior. For example, a researcher might study crime statistics in different countries to see if there is a relation between capital punishment and the murder rate.

case study
exploratory study of an existing situation as a means of creating and testing a hypothesis

The third category we will call the **case study.** This category is different from the others in that the research investigates a particular existing situation that comes to the attention of the researcher. The situation may be a practical problem that must be solved as soon as possible, or it may be an event that intrigues a researcher. An investigator might study the victims of a natural disaster to determine its effects on their psychological health. Case studies are typified by the varied nature of the methods used to study the problems.

survey
assessing public opinion or individual characteristics by the use of questionnaire and sampling methods

The fourth category of nonexperimental research is the **survey,** in which the subject is requested to cooperate by responding to questions. Nearly everyone has taken part in a survey. This chapter will consider observational, archival, and case-study methods. Chapter 8 will discuss survey research.

THE HERMENEUTIC APPROACH

Before we begin studying the various nonexperimental methods, we need to take a short detour to discuss what it is that scientists using these nonexperimental techniques are trying to accomplish. You may be inclined to wonder why this detour is necessary, because all psychologists try to understand behavior. And in fact, Chapter 2 discussed John Stewart Mill's methods of finding causes as a way of understanding behavior. The problem, however, is that causality is more difficult to determine in correlational research. It is often difficult to decide which variable caused the other, or whether both variables are caused by a third. (See Chapter 5.) This problem has led some social scientists to consider their task to be the discovery of the *interpretation* of a behavior, rather than the *causes* of the behavior. Another way to describe it is to consider it the search for *reasons* rather than causes. These social scientists have adopted the term **hermeneutics** to describe their methodology.

hermeneutics
the principles of interpretation of the meaning of a text

The concept of hermeneutics was borrowed from the field of biblical interpretation, where the task of the scholar is to find what the original meaning of the text was to the people to whom it was addressed. Psychologists who use the hermeneutic approach may try to interpret the meaning of a look exchanged between a couple, or a love note, or a part of a wedding ceremony. For example, consider that in the dining rooms of many American homes one of the chairs around the dining table has arms on it, whereas the others do not. The reason for this odd chair is to identify the father's place at the table, which in American culture has traditionally signified honor and power. None of this probably sounds unfamiliar to you, although the situation it describes might rub some of you the wrong way. We have used the hermeneutic method to understand why there is one odd chair. We *interpreted* the *reason* for the arms in terms of the *significance* it has for showing the father's position in the family. It would be much more difficult to explain the presence of the arms on the chair in terms of *cause* and *effect.*

As we proceed through this chapter, there will be some places where the traditional cause-effect approach seems more appropriate and others where the hermeneutic approach will be more natural.

OBSERVATIONAL RESEARCH

Observational research involves the recording of ongoing behavior without attempting to influence it. This method takes two general forms: naturalistic observation and participant-observer research.

■ Naturalistic Observation

naturalistic observation
observational research of subjects in their natural environment carried out so as to disturb the subjects as little as possible

unobtrusive research
another term for naturalistic observation, commonly used in the social sciences

nonreactive research
another term for naturalistic observation in the social sciences, emphasizing that the subjects are unaware that they are being studied

physical trace
unobtrusive measure of behavior that makes use of physical evidence

Naturalistic observation is research conducted in such a way that the subject's behavior is disturbed as little as possible by the observation process. You have probably seen films showing naturalists observing birds or other animals from within a blind—a device for screening the observers from the view of the animals being studied.

In the social sciences, naturalistic observation is often called **unobtrusive research.** The term *unobtrusive* simply refers to the effort that researchers make not to influence, or obtrude on, the behavior being studied. Still another term for naturalistic observation is **nonreactive research.** The term *nonreactive* emphasizes that the subjects are unaware that they are being studied, and therefore do not react to the presence of the observer.

Methods of observational research are as varied as the subject matter being studied. Researchers have been very ingenious in devising unobtrusive measures of behavior (for example, Webb et al., 1966). One broad category of unobtrusive measures is known as **physical trace** measures. These measures make use of physical evidence of some behavior. For example, researchers have recorded graffiti in school rest rooms to discover attitudes toward racial integration of the school, smudges on pages of library books to see which pages are most read, and grease prints on display cases in museums to see which displays are most interesting to children. Your instructor may look at the number of times the reserve readings for his course have been stamped for checkout to see if the class is studying the material. Incidentally, this example illustrates that the behavior of a group of individuals can sometimes be studied quite effectively by naturalistic observation even though it may be unethical to observe an individual's behavior. (It is illegal to obtain a person's borrowing record from a library.)

Although much has been made of the cleverness of social scientists in making use of physical traces of behavior, naturalists have for many years made use of scratches on trees to study territoriality in bears, droppings to study eating habits of owls, and similar physical traces of animal behavior.

Observational research has begun to play a more prominent role in psychology as more social scientists are becoming influenced by methods and theories of animal behaviorists. Traditionally, however, most psychologists have not made much use of observational methods. Perhaps the fact that psychologists and their favorite object of study are of the same species accounts for the difference. We tend to assume, often incorrectly, that we have a great deal of insight into the important categories of human behavior and their causes. Careful observation of naturally occurring behavior might suggest many fruitful hypotheses for research and might help prevent half-baked experiments.

An excellent example of the use of naturalistic observation is found in the work of Erving Goffman (for example, 1971). He has described such naturally occurring behavior as how people avoid bumping into each other on public sidewalks. He finds that people engage in rituals of looking at each other and giving signals to indicate their intention to pass on one side or the other. Many people would not be aware that they engage in these behaviors. Because Goffman's studies do not include the kind of objective records that would allow one to evaluate the generality of his findings, we should probably classify them as casual observation rather than strictly objective naturalistic observation. However, his insights have led other investigators to conduct more objective tests of his ideas. In a similar but looser way, investigators have turned to the writings of Shakespeare or Dostoyevski for hypotheses, which they then verify in a more rigorous fashion.

A particularly good example of how Goffman's suggestions have led to more rigorous work is provided by a naturalistic observation study by Peter Collett and Peter Marsh (1974). They placed a videotape recorder on the seventh floor of a building overlooking a busy pedestrian intersection. They recorded and later analyzed instances when two people met in such a way that both had to move in order to avoid collision. They noticed a striking difference in the way men and women maneuvered in passing. Men tended to turn so as to face the other person, whereas women tended to turn away. The differences were large. Of the men, 75% passed in the facing orientation, compared with only 17% of the women. Collett and Marsh hypothesized that the women turned away in order to avoid brushing the other person with their breasts. This hypothesis was confirmed by examining the frequency with which men and women held an arm across their bodies as they passed. Women used the arm cross more often than men, particularly in those instances when they were turned toward the other person as they passed. This occurrence was not related to whether they were carrying anything in their hands.

Another example of naturalistic observation is provided by Don Zimmermann and Candace West (1975). They were interested in whether patterns of conversational speech would reflect power and dominance between individuals. In particular, they were interested in looking for sex differences in interruptions and other turn-taking behavior in conversations. They tape-recorded conversations between sets of two persons in public places around a university, such as a coffee shop. They chose conversations that could be overheard easily in the normal course of being in a public place. They studied 10 female-female pairs, 10 male-male pairs, and 11 cross-sex pairs. Whenever possible, they obtained the permission of the conversationalists to use their recordings. Sometimes, however, people left before the researchers could approach them. All personal identifications were edited out of the transcripts of the recordings. (For a discussion of informed consent, privacy, and debriefing, see Chapter 14.)

Zimmermann and West found that 96% of interruptions in the cross-sex pairs were made by the males. These investigators decided to learn whether this finding was limited to the type of setting or to people who might be already acquainted. They conducted a laboratory experiment in which pairs of people were asked to chat and get acquainted "before the experiment begins" (1978). In five conversations between males and females, all of the males did more interrupting, with the men doing 73% of the interrupting on the average. The amount of interrupting was unrelated to which person talked first.

The Zimmermann and West research illustrates a typical and admirable progression in observational research from idea to naturalistic observation to laboratory. This move to the laboratory allows researchers to rule out sources of confounding that would occur in the original naturalistic situation. It also illustrates that observational research is not limited to field settings, but often occurs in the laboratory.

As we mentioned earlier, naturalistic observation has been a popular method with biologists. Perhaps the most famous examples of naturalistic observation come from scientists who work in ethology, the branch of biology that deals with the study of behavior. Although ethology is synonymous in many people's minds with naturalistic observation of animal behavior, ethology concerns itself with behavior as a product of natural selection and as a tool in studying the evolution of species. Much important ethological work is observational, yet an increasing amount of ethological work is conducted in the laboratory.

An example of naturalistic observation by ethologists is the work of Konrad Lorenz (for example, 1958) on the courtship behavior of ducks. Most people who watch ducks in a pond or zoo simply see a mass of random activity. After observing the behavior of ducks for countless hours and taking motion pictures, Lorenz was able to identify about 20 different specific behaviors. One of these is the grunt-whistle, described here for the mallard and pintail: "The male flick[s] its bill backward and upward through the water, throw[s] a shower of droplets toward the 'courted' bird, then rear[s] up and back in the water, and finally shak[es] the tail after settling back to the normal position. . . . A whistle is uttered during the display, followed by a low grunt" (Sharpe & Johnsgard, 1966, p. 263).

By studying these behaviors in many species of ducks, Lorenz was able to clarify the evolutionary relationships among them. The assumption is that species of ducks that share more specific behaviors are more closely related. The validity of the behavioral method is confirmed if the animals that share similar behaviors can be crossbred and the behavior of the resulting offspring studied. Behaviors that both parent species share should appear in the offspring, but behaviors that only one parent displays should be absent or present in a weakened or distorted form.

Roger Sharpe and Paul Johnsgard successfully crossbred mallard and pintail ducks for two generations. The second generation (F_2) offspring varied among themselves in the degree to which they resembled the two parent species. Some looked much like mallards and some looked mostly pintail, but the majority fell somewhere in between. Observation of the offspring showed that their behavior was closely related to their appearance: Those that looked mostly mallard showed mostly mallard behavior, and vice versa. According to the prediction, behaviors present in only one of the parent species were weakened or absent. Thus, the importance of heredity in behavior was demonstrated, and the predictions of ethological theory were confirmed.

The Sharpe and Johnsgard study is an interesting blend of observation and experiment. The researchers manipulated the genetics of the animals but did not present stimuli to them. They simply observed the natural behavior of their subjects after having created them to specification!

A final example of observational research illustrates the importance of having a coding system to aid in observation, and the amount of work that can be involved in developing one. Paul Ekman and Wallace Friesen have devoted many years to studying the expression of emotions in the human face (for example, Ekman & Friesen, 1975; Ekman, Friesen, & O'Sullivan, 1988). By a combination of observation and experiment, they have demonstrated that emotions are expressed by the face in the same way in different cultures, and are likewise interpreted universally.

An essential part of this research has been the development of a scheme to code the movements of the face, whether caused by emotion or other reasons, such as voluntary actions (Ekman & Friesen, 1976). Before their work, no one had systematically studied the effects of moving the various muscles of the face. Ekman and Friesen spent the better part of a year in front of a mirror, armed with anatomy texts and cameras. They taught themselves to move each muscle independently. (Remember trying as a child to move one eyebrow by itself, or learning to wink?) When they were able to move the intended muscle, they photographed the effect it had on the appearance of the face. Occasionally, when they were unable to determine which muscle was being moved, they had a neuroanatomist insert a probe into the muscle and record the electrical activity to be sure that the intended muscle was the one that moved.

As a result of their work, they were able to identify dozens of movements, which they called Action Units. These were mostly the action of a single muscle. For example, Action Unit 15 is the Lip Corner Depressor.

> The muscle underlying AU 15 emerges from the side of the chin and runs upwards attaching to a point near the corner of the lip. . . . [This action unit] pulls the corners of the lip down; changes the shape of the lips so they are angled down at the corner, and usually somewhat stretched horizontally; produces some pouching, bagging, or wrinkling of the skin below the lips' corners . . . ; may flatten or cause bulges to appear on the [end of the] chin, may produce depression medially under the lower lip. If the [furrow extending from . . . the nostril wings down to . . . the lip

corners] is permanently etched, it will deepen and may appear pulled down or lengthened. (Ekman & Friesen, 1976, p. 66)

Detailed descriptions such as these, along with photographs and other instructions, comprise the Facial Action Coding System (Ekman & Friesen, 1978). As you can imagine, the many Action Units can be produced in hundreds of combinations. Someone who wishes to code facial movements must spend many hours learning the coding system, and a considerable amount of time applying it to a sample of videotape.

The availability of the system for coding facial movements made it possible for Ekman, Friesen, and O'Sullivan (1988) to distinguish experimentally between truthful smiles and those that hid lies. In a nutshell, a truthful smile involves not only the corners of the mouth, but also the muscles around the eyes. In dishonest smiles, the muscles of the eyes may not move and muscles that signal negative emotions such as disgust or fear are activated.

Naturalistic observing has few hard-and-fast rules. Three that should be mentioned are careful recordkeeping, the use of a variety of types of measures, and care for privacy of the subjects. Careful recordkeeping is what separates naturalistic observation from casual impression formation. The observer should keep a record of all behaviors of interest and the times at which they occur. A check sheet may be used when all or most of the categories of behavior under observation are known in advance. This recording of information is facilitated by using movie cameras, videotape or audiotape recorders, or other devices. Many times using slow-motion or speeded-motion recording is helpful to make behavior patterns easier to see; stop-action recording can freeze critical moments. In the study of pedestrian passing, motion was frozen at the instant of passing. In the study of conversations, all tape-recorded utterances were transcribed to paper for analysis. Using a variety of measures helps to assure that the observations are representative and not dependent on one measure only. The concern for privacy will be discussed briefly in the section that follows, and at greater length in Chapter 14.

■ Participant-Observer Research

participant-observer research
observational research in which the observer participates in a group in order to record behavior

One kind of observational research that has yielded important results is **participant-observer research,** where investigators participate in naturally occurring groups and record their observations. One of the most famous of these studies was that of Leon Festinger, H.W. Riecken, Jr., and Stanley Schachter (1956), who joined a group that believed the world would come to an end at a certain time. Group members believed that they would be rescued by a flying saucer. The psychologists carefully observed interactions among group members and the effect the disconfirmation of their prediction had on their behavior. Surprisingly, when the world did not end, the group members began to be more open and less analytical about their beliefs. This research was instrumental in the development of Festinger's theory of cognitive dissonance, which predicts how people deal with conflicting beliefs. We should note that careful records and diaries are crucial in evaluating participant-observer studies because of the increased possibility of subjectivity in these situations.

When Is Participant Observation Appropriate?

The usefulness of participant-observer research is limited to certain types of situations (Jorgensen, 1989). It is most useful in studying a small group that is separated from the population as a whole, when little is known about a group, or when the group's activities are not generally available to public view. Groups studied in this way have included religious cults, nude beachers, criminals, hoodlums, and gays. The doomsday cult studied by Festinger and associates represents the type of situation to which participant observation is ideally suited.

Further, the researcher must be able to gain access to the group. For the study of a nude beach, it helps to be able to shed your inhibitions; to study an ethnic or racial group, it helps to be able to pass; to study a group of jazz musicians, it helps to be able to play an instrument.

Taking the Point of View of Those You Are Studying

Participant observation is characterized by the effort to view some behavioral activity from the viewpoint of an insider to a situation. The methodology must be open-ended, flexible, and opportunistic. The approach to theory is often hermeneutic, emphasizing interpretation and understanding. Some participant observers will take the role of a central participant because it would be impossible to learn much without doing so, as in studying the people who hang out in a bar in a poor section of town. Other times, a researcher can stay more in the periphery, as in studying an organization such as a church.

By definition, participating in a group leads to problems of objectivity. The researcher must strike a balance between taking the viewpoint of the group members and maintaining scientific objectivity. A researcher who is studying police officers tries to take the point of view of the officers. But he may find that his attitudes toward criminals, and toward society as a whole, start to match those of the police, who happen to be more prejudiced and authoritarian than the population as a whole. Researchers have been known to be converted by the religious cult that they were studying. Some researchers maintain their objectivity by regular contact with other researchers who "debrief" them about their experiences (Jorgensen, 1989).

Gaining Access to the Group

Sometimes it is possible to be open about the fact that you are there to study the group, as when a person openly enters a fundamentalist church for the purpose of research and is welcomed as a potential convert. This is known as undisguised participant observation. On the other hand, certain groups are hostile to the larger society and suspicious of anyone who shows an interest in them. Admitting that you are there to study them might result in your being kicked out or worse. Then the researcher would disguise his or her participant observation. In addition, it is often unrealistic to expect a researcher to inform each and every member of a group the first time they meet that she is there for the purpose of research. It would be highly artificial to begin every interaction with a new person by saying that you are a researcher. There is no hard-and-fast rule about whether to inform the group or not. It is best to be up-front where possible and to adopt a disguised strategy only when necessary.

Problems in Observational Research

Two important problems are present in participant-observer research. First, by entering the group, the observer by definition changes it to some extent. Therefore, the act of observing the behavior changes the behavior to be observed. A large group may not be influenced much by an observer's presence, whereas a small group may be influenced considerably. In general, participant-observer research is done in unusual groups that can absorb an observer whose presence would have little effect.

The second problem is the ethical question of invasion of privacy. Participant observers cannot always obtain informed consent from their subjects. Some researchers hold that participant-observer research is therefore always unethical. Others point out that professionals such as journalists are permitted to engage in this type of practice. They argue that if psychologists do not perform participant-observer research, they are withholding the application of psychological techniques and insights to important social problems.

Concern for the privacy of subjects is discussed in Chapter 14. Here we will only note that naturalistic observation may involve recording behaviors that, even though conducted in public, may still be of a private nature. In one study, a researcher feigned homosexuality in order to study the behavior of homosexuals. He gained their confidence by serving as a lookout in a public washroom while they engaged in sex. Later, having noted the license numbers of their cars, he obtained their identities from the department of motor vehicles by subterfuge. Then, in disguise, he joined a research team and interviewed his subjects as a public health worker (Holden, 1979). Although the investigator did not reveal the identities of the subjects and his conclusions are supposed to be sympathetic to homosexuals, he did obtain the data under false pretenses and subjected the persons he studied to risk. This study was later discussed at a conference on research ethics as a prime example of research that should not be conducted (Holden, 1979).

You should not get the impression that participant observation is done only on marginal groups. We have discussed examples in which there may be ethical problems involved in participant observation, but the method is applicable to the study of jazz musicians, athletes, college fraternities, and many other groups.

ARCHIVAL RESEARCH

archival data
factual information
in existing records

The term *archival research* refers to research conducted using data that the researcher had no part in collecting. **Archival data** are those that are present in existing records, or archives. The researcher simply examines or selects the data for analysis.

Archival research is appropriate in many instances. Data that bear on the hypothesis may already exist, and collecting new data would be wasteful. Or ethics or logistics may make it infeasible to conduct an experiment relating the variables of interest. In a moment we will consider archival research on suicides and sex crimes, both topics inappropriate for experimental research.

On the other hand, archival research has limitations. First, most archival data are collected for nonscientific reasons. Governments and private agencies collect the data for their own purposes, and such data often do not suit the purposes of the scientist. In order for archival data to be scientifically useful, the agency collecting the data must ask questions similar to the scientist's or must inadvertently collect data that are of value to the scientist. Second, because archival research is by nature carried out after the fact, ruling out alternative hypotheses for particular observed correlations may be difficult.

A researcher who relies on archival data is at the mercy of any biases that may have occurred in collecting the data. Police records are notoriously subject to bias. Many categories of crime are seldom reported to the police. Only one in four attempted rapes, for instance, is reported (Bureau of Justice Statistics, 1990). A 400% increase in attempted rapes would suddenly seem to have occurred if every one were reported. (About 65% of completed rapes are reported.) Police, in turn, use latitude in determining whether to record a particular incident as a criminal act or to look the other way. Accordingly, crime statistics can vary because of a crackdown motivated by an upcoming election or by individual officers' being concerned over their own efficiency ratings.

A successful use of archival research can be seen in David Phillips's analysis of motor vehicle fatalities (1977). Authorities have long suspected that many automobile fatalities are suicides rather than accidents. Phillips hypothesized that if suicides are triggered by reports of other suicides, then motor vehicle fatalities should increase just after publicized suicides. He studied all motor vehicle fatalities occurring in California during the week that followed the reporting of suicides on the front page of the state's two largest newspapers. Then he compared the fatalities with those in a control period in another year. He found a 9% increase in the number of fatalities in the week following the suicides, with a maximum increase of 30% on the third day after the stories appeared. By correlating the increase in fatalities following each story with the total circulation of all newspapers that covered the story, he showed that the publicity was responsible for the increase. Further analyses bolstered his conclusion that the increase was the result of the publicized suicides. Details were similar between the suicide stories and the types of accidents that increased following the stories. For example, if a murder/suicide was reported, there was an increase in multiple-fatality accidents (Phillips, 1979).

CASE STUDIES

Case studies comprise a category of research that is difficult to characterize with a simple definition. Because case studies often include the use of observation and archival methodologies, the distinctions among them are not always clear. Nevertheless, it is possible to say that case studies tend to involve an ongoing situation that presents itself for investigation. Yin (1989) defines a case study as "an empirical inquiry that: 1) investigates a contemporary phenomenon within its real-life context; when 2) the boundaries between phenomenon and context are not clearly evident; and in which 3) multiple sources of evidence are used" (p. 23). According to Yin's definition, it is the multiple approaches that distinguishes a case study from other nonexperimental methods.

Many case studies result from problems that present themselves to researchers as opportunities that must be grasped quickly or lost. Little time may be available for planning, and the study often must be conducted under difficult conditions. An example of case-study research is the study of "assembly-line hysteria" or "mass psychogenic illness" by Michael Smith, Michael Colligan, and Joseph Hurrell, Jr. (1978). In this phenomenon, which occasionally occurs in factories or schools, many people suddenly suffer such physical symptoms as headache, nausea, and blurred vision. Typically, the outbreak is triggered by a strange odor but investigation reveals no toxic substance that can account for the sickness. Colligan and his team at the National Institute for Occupational Safety and Health (NIOSH) investigated a number of such incidents, along with physicians and industrial hygienists.

After interviewing many people who experienced the symptoms and after administering a wide variety of psychological tests and comparing the results to a control group of workers who were not affected by the outbreak, the NIOSH team concluded that the main cause of mass psychogenic illness is physical or psychological stress in the workplace. This stress provides the setting for a potential outbreak. The trigger is a strange odor or other stimulus to which someone reacts with physical symptoms that increase the distress. For example, the person may begin hyperventilating, which causes dizziness. Someone then attributes the cause of the distress to the strange odor, and the symptoms quickly spread to other workers (Colligan & Stockton, 1978). Investigation showed that the affected workers had been experiencing more boredom, social isolation, and physical stress than had the unaffected workers.

This study of mass psychogenic illness is typical of case studies. The efforts of the NIOSH team were directed toward a practical problem. Cases appeared unpredictably and required prompt attention. A multidisciplinary team approach was used. Members of each discipline used several techniques to rule out various explanations and narrow down the possible causes. A special questionnaire was developed for use in succeeding cases. Other case studies are as varied as this one. In fact, one of the few generalizations possible about case studies is that it is difficult to generalize about them.

THEORY DEVELOPMENT AND TESTING IN OBSERVATIONAL AND ARCHIVAL RESEARCH

Owing to the ad hoc nature of observational and archival research, the process of theory development and hypothesis testing must be rather flexible. We are familiar with the model of hypothesis testing commonly used in statistical analysis of experiments, where the researcher states a null hypothesis and alternative hypothesis before the research is conducted. Hypothesis testing by this model involves attempting to reject the null hypothesis in favor of the alternative hypothesis. (See Appendix A for a discussion.) In observational research, however, the investigator may not even have particular problems in mind before beginning the research, let alone any specific hypotheses.

For this reason observational researchers use a more flexible, inductive process of developing and testing hypotheses (see, for example, Campbell, 1979). A hypothesis may be tentatively stated based on existing observations. Predictions are made based on the hypothesis, which are tested against new data. The hypotheses and theory are continuously modified to take account of new data. When a hypothesis is contradicted by the data, the hypothesis is abandoned or modified. When the data are what is predicted by the hypothesis, then confidence in the hypothesis is increased.

This cycle of hypothesis development, prediction, testing, hypothesis modification, and so on, illustrates a number of characteristics of science as stated in Chapters 1 and 2, particularly that concepts must be disconfirmable. Those that are not disconfirmable are not scientific. But some scientists tend to get so wrapped up in their ideas that they look mainly for evidence that confirms their hypothesis and ignore evidence that contradicts it. Any good researcher, but particularly those doing observational research, needs to be critical of his or her theory and look carefully for evidence that would disconfirm it. Philosophers point out that there are an unlimited number of incorrect theories that are consistent with any particular set of data. Evidence that seems to favor your theory also favors many other theories, all of which may be wrong. You know you have made progress when you have rejected an incorrect theory, but you have not necessarily made any progress if your data support your theory, because it may still be incorrect.

This process of hypothesis generation and modification is well illustrated in a study by Cressey (1971), who investigated men who were in prison for embezzlement. His study was a combination of observation (interview) and archival research. Cressey's first hypothesis was that embezzlers believed that what they had done was merely a technical violation, rather than a crime. It became evident from talking to a few men, however, that the embezzlers knew all along that what they had done was really wrong. After this first hypothesis was disconfirmed, his second hypothesis was that they embezzled when they had emergency needs that could be met by violating their trust and taking the money. He abandoned that hypothesis, however, when he found men who said they had had emergencies before that did not lead them to embezzle. Hypothesis number three was that they became embezzlers when they had incurred financial obligations that they felt they could not reveal to others, such as a gambling debt, that could be met by embezzlement. This hypothesis was abandoned, in turn, because some of the men did not need the money for actual obligations, but had a situation that could be considered a financial problem. For example, a man might be maintaining a mistress, which would incur a financial burden without being an actual obligation, like a debt. The fourth hypothesis, then, was that a person embezzled when he had a nonshareable financial problem that could be met by embezzlement. This hypothesis, too, had to be abandoned when he found some men who had fit this criterion at some earlier point but had not embezzled at that time.

Cressey's fifth, and final, hypothesis was that a person embezzled when he had a nonshareable problem that could be met by embezzlement *and* he could rationalize to himself that he was still a trusted person in spite of the illegality. An example might be a salesperson who receives an initial payment toward a new life insurance policy. Because the first payment largely goes to pay the salesperson's commission, he may convince himself that he can safely spend his share because the sale has been made and he will get it eventually anyway. The salesman would come to grief, however, if the client backed out of the sale, or if he could not come up with the cash to turn in to the company when he needed to deposit the first payment.

Cressey abandoned each hypothesis whenever he found a single case that contradicted it, and developed a new one. Eventually, he found that his final hypothesis covered all cases he could find. This method illustrates the ad hoc, cyclical nature of hypothesis testing and theorizing in observational and archival research. It may, however, raise too high a standard that cannot always be met. It is unusual to find a single explanation that will cover every single case of a phenomenon that one is trying to explain.

✱ NUTS & BOLTS ✱

Recording Methods in Nonexperimental Research

As we have seen, nonexperimental research encompasses a wide range of methods. This fact makes it impossible to provide a complete inventory of recording techniques used. It is important, however, to discuss recording methods in nonexperimental research because they present some challenges not present in experimental research. These problems stem from a number of factors. First, it may not be obvious to you what it is you should record because you don't know exactly what you are looking for. This is especially the case in naturalistic observation, participant observation, and case studies. Second, you may know what you are looking for, but not know how to define instances of it. This problem is particularly acute in archival research. We will discuss these two problems under the headings of field notes and content analysis, respectively.

Field Notes

Researchers using observation and case-study methodologies often start out with some general question in mind, but without specific categories of behavior defined. In fact, this characterizes much observational research.

Be systematic.   You should keep a notebook of all of your observations and interpretations of what you see. Checklists and other devices mentioned previously can help considerably. This documentation may sound like a daunting task, and it is. You may be so busy observing that you don't have time to take notes. Or you may be in a social situation where note taking would be impossible, either because it would inhibit the behaviors you are observing or because you are taking part in the situation. In such cases, you should write up your observations as soon as you leave the situation. You will be tempted to skimp on writing up your notes later because you are tired or you think you will remember what was important. If you think you wouldn't forget, just try to remember everything you did one week ago. What did you wear, eat, say, and do? Your notes should include as much detail as possible, including the time and the setting. Later on, the significance of these details may make sense in a way that they don't as you take the notes.

You may want to write your notes in stages. You can jot down brief notes as you work, and elaborate on them later at leisure. You may also need to develop shorthand codes to help in your note taking.

Be selective.   The problem of having too much to observe can often be solved by taking samples of behavior. Instead of watching television all day long for a week to observe the content of commercials, you might watch only the first batch of commercials after the top of the hour. Instead of watching all channels, you might focus on only one. Instead of watching everything that all of the children in a day-care center do for a whole day, you might watch for instances of one kind of behavior, such as fighting, or only those behaviors that are on your prepared checklist. Instead of watching all the children, you might focus on just one or two. Instead of watching constantly, you might record what they are doing at 10-minute intervals.

Make use of recording devices.   Nowadays, recording devices such as camcorders and tape recorders are cheap enough that most researchers can afford to record their observations electronically. The main problem is that you generally must review your records in real time; that is, it takes the same amount of time to review your tape as it did to record it. This problem can be reduced by viewing a videotape in fast-forward mode or employing a voice-activated audio tape recorder. In addition, there are commercial event recorders available that permit you to press defined keys to indicate particular events. In many situations, however, the problem is just the opposite: There is a great deal that happens quickly. In such situations, the tape can be played in slow motion to permit coding of subtle and transient phenomena.

Content Analysis

When dealing with textual or photographic materials, there is no need to take field notes, because the material is already in a permanent form. The problem remains, however, of deciding how to deal with what may be a large body of material. Suppose you are investigating the sexual content of magazines. How do you decide what to record? There are two basic approaches to content analysis. The first one is based on counting the frequency of some objective measure, such as frequency of certain sexual words. This is known as coding the **manifest content** of the text. Because it is relatively simple to count the number of times the word *kiss, love,* or whatever, appears in a body of text, the coding of manifest content is very reliable. There may be a problem, however, if words are used in different ways. The word *love* appears many times in a certain chapter of the Bible that has nothing to do with sex. You would draw the wrong conclusion about the point of the chapter if you just counted the word *love.*

The alternative method of analyzing the content of a text or photograph is coding its **latent content.** With this method, the researcher reads a passage of text, or looks at a photograph, and interprets the presence of a particular theme. That same passage of the Bible would easily be seen to be about what might be called brotherly love, rather than sexual love.

Because latent content analysis is inherently subjective, it runs the risk of being less reliable than manifest content analysis. It is a good idea to do both manifest and latent content analysis and compare the results. If the results turn out the same by both methods, you have strong evidence of the validity of your results. If they differ, you can look for the reasons why they differ.

Reliability of content analysis.   Whichever method of content analysis you use, there is a problem of reliability. If you use latent content analysis, one researcher might interpret the same passage differently from another. Even with manifest content analysis, there is the possibility of a coder's making mistakes when going through large amounts of data. Thus, it is important to use at least two coders in order to establish the reliability of your coding scheme. Various

manifest content
the content of a text or photograph as indicated by measuring the frequency of some objective word, phrase, or action

latent content
the content of a text or photograph as measured by the appearance of themes as interpreted by the researcher

techniques based on statistical correlation are available to quantify the reliability of coders and coding schemes.

Example of content analysis.   Rajecki, Bledsoe, and Rasmussen (1991) used content analysis to study personal ads in newspapers. ("Single White Female desires to meet professional male who enjoys dancing, long walks . . .") They were interested in discovering which ads were most successful in eliciting responses from readers. Categories that they coded were statements about looks (such as "attractive," "petite," "tall"), status (such as "affluent," "employed," "professional"), intelligence, sincerity, and age. These categories were based on previous investigations. The category "looks" was used to code information that other investigators had labeled "attractiveness," "appearance," "sexuality," or "physical status," because it was an inclusive category that encompassed all the others. Similarly, they chose "status" instead of "financial security," which a previous study had used, because it would incorporate social prestige ("career person," "gentleman," "professional") as well as material possessions.

Two of the authors coded all the ads independently. Then they got together and discussed all the ads until they agreed on the coding of each one. After the coding was complete, they sent a questionnaire to the advertisers through the newspaper asking about the results of their ads. They found that ads placed by younger women were more successful than those by older women. In contrast, ads placed by older men were more successful than those by younger men. The authors were surprised to find that advertisers who claimed to have good looks and high status did not receive many more responses than those that did not. They interpreted this finding as reflecting the fact that most of the ads contained such claims, so there was little information to be gained by considering looks and status.

The content analysis was an essential component of this study in that it defined the independent variables against which the outcomes were correlated.

Procedure

Procedure is different from method. Method is a broader term that encompasses all aspects of the study, including the logic of the design and the steps for carrying it out. Procedure refers only to the latter—what the researcher does in translating the design into action. The design, for example, may be an experiment with two conditions that are both experienced by each subject. Procedural concerns include whether each condition is tested on the same day or on different days. Procedure also involves instructions and how they are given, the debriefing, and so forth. Many details must be worked out in the course of translating a design into practice.

The step of going from design to procedure can be a difficult one for students, because it involves going from a logical plan in the mind to a practical plan of action in the lab. After the design is completed, you should develop a clear idea of the exact procedure—or protocol—you will follow. A **protocol** is a list of the exact steps needed to test a subject from start to finish. A written

protocol
list of all the steps that a subject goes through in a study

protocol is helpful for beginning researchers, especially so when more than one researcher will help run a given study.

The Pilot Study

pilot study
tentative, small-scale study done to pretest and modify study design and procedures

Once a protocol has been developed, you should do a **pilot study** to find the bugs in the procedure. Almost always there are some problems to be smoothed out. One of the researchers, your adviser, or a friend should be run through all steps of the study exactly as it will be carried out. Although the temptation to skip the pilot phase may be great, you should resist it. Nearly every experiment I have performed without testing some pilot subjects has been disappointing. Here is where a little effort can greatly increase the precision of a study.

Researchers with reputations for excellent design are often those who do extensive pilot research. Some researchers will not proceed to the main study until they have a good idea what they will find based on pilot work. This preliminary step is not always possible, but it is an aid to careful research. It also emphasizes that research is not a one-step process. When a pilot study has been done, followed by a main study that has been run once and replicated once or twice, the credibility of the finding is increased tremendously over a single study that was not preceded by pilot work. The phase in which the design is translated into procedure and then to a pilot study often takes longer than the study proper. You may have difficulty understanding what took all the time and effort. It is not unusual for the literature search and design phase of an undergraduate project to require three-fourths of the term. Running the subjects may take only a week.

The Proposal

proposal
preliminary statement outlining the literature review, statement of the problem, research design, and expected results and their significance

Your instructor may ask you to prepare a **proposal** before you proceed with your research project. This proposal is often called a *prospectus*. Proposals are required in various situations. Graduate students usually prepare proposals that are presented to the committee that oversees master's thesis or dissertation research. Proposals are also required by some agencies, including universities, before research is permitted in their institution. Thus, although the proposal is not logically necessary in designing research, it is often a practical necessity, and it has the advantage of getting the researcher to sit down and think through the issues before proceeding.

The proposal is a statement of everything necessary to evaluate the adequacy of the research before the research is conducted. As such, the proposal serves some of the same functions as does the published report that will result from the research. For this reason, you will find it convenient to follow the same outline and style in the proposal as in the final report (see Chapter 13). You may then be able to take much of the final report from the proposal, especially the introduction and the methods section.

The results section of the proposal indicates the expected results and the ways in which you intend to analyze and display them graphically. This function of the proposal is particularly useful. It is embarrassing to conduct a study and then find that you have to use some unconventional statistic to analyze the data simply because you overlooked an elementary design consideration. You can usually avoid this problem by deciding in advance what statistics you will use, obtaining advice when necessary.

The discussion section of the proposal is short and indicates the significance of your expected results. Both the results and discussion sections will need to be completely rewritten for the final report!

Although the proposal, when it is approved, serves as a sort of contract between the student and the adviser or committee, this does not mean that it must be adhered to slavishly. When a problem arises, as often happens, the researcher should solve it the best way possible, with the approval of the adviser or committee.

Guarding the Integrity of the Data

All of the care expended on designing and conducting a study is wasted if the data are compromised by carelessness in recording and handling. Before the study begins, the researcher must have a plan for recording and handling the data. A good procedure is to keep all data and other research details, such as dosages, stimulus settings, and the like, in a notebook. If loose sheets are used, they must be dated and identified in such a way that they can be replaced if any sheets become misfiled. Often it is convenient to reproduce a blank set of data sheets with spaces for all necessary information, so that nothing will be overlooked. Data should be placed in a file and kept in a secure place. They should never be carried around in a briefcase from which they can be lost. Too often data have been eaten by the dog, scribbled on by the baby, or left on the bus. Making photocopies of any data that must be taken out of the laboratory is a good practice.

Later the raw data will be transferred from the data sheets to a summary form. (See pages 103–105 on preparing data for analysis.) Preparing the format of the summary data sheet ahead of time is a good idea. The summary sheet should allow space for doing simple manipulations of the data, such as taking the logarithm and/or means, before the statistical analysis is performed. Any information necessary to recreate the summary data from the data sheets should be carefully recorded, such as the random order of stimuli that was used for each subject. Records of the study should be set up in such a way that another person could decipher the design and procedure from the records alone. Essential features of studies can be forgotten, especially if the researcher has conducted a number of them.

The data sheets should be kept for as long as anyone is likely to want to reanalyze the data. Although fraud in research is not a welcome topic, it does happen. The existence of original data sheets may be the only proof that the data were collected as claimed. The original data sheets should be delivered to an adviser or locked up after the data have been transferred to a tabular form, before data analysis is begun. This procedure protects the researcher from the temptation to fudge data to make them fit the hypothesis. (The raw data often do not permit ascertaining whether the hypothesis was confirmed.) Recording the original data in ink is advisable. A modicum of compulsiveness in guarding data is a good idea.   ❏

SUMMARY

1. Nonexperimental research has two main characteristics: No attempt is made to manipulate an independent variable, and the data collection procedure often must forfeit some degree of control.

2. Although nonexperimental research is called correlational research, all research is correlational in that it seeks to find relationships between variables.

3. Nonexperimental research methods include observational, archival, case study, and survey.

4. The hermeneutic approach to understanding behavior attempts to discover *reasons* for behavior, rather than *causes*. It is based on techniques of textual interpretation.

5. Observational research involves recording a subject's behavior without attempting to influence it.

6. Naturalistic observation involves recording a subject's behavior in such a way that the behavior is not disturbed by the process of making the observation. Other terms for this are *unobtrusive research* and *nonreactive research*.

7. Physical-trace research is a kind of naturalistic observation that makes use of physical evidence of behavior.

8. Participant-observer research is useful in studying small, little-known groups that are not generally open to public view. Observers join the group, take the point of view of the members, and record their observations.

9. Invasion of privacy poses an ethical problem in participant-observer research. A practical problem is the likelihood that the researcher may influence the group as well as observe it.

10. Archival research involves the examination of existing records. Advantages are that the data do not need to be collected by the researcher and that the research afforded may be on problems not amenable to experimentation. Disadvantages are that the researcher is limited to the types of questions asked by the agency that collected the data and by any biases present in the collection procedure.

11. Case studies are ad hoc studies of existing situations. They take many forms and cannot be neatly classified.

12. Theory development and testing are more flexible and inductive in observational and archival research than in experimental research.

13. Observational and case-study researchers must be systematic in making field notes, but often need to be selective in what they record.

14. Manifest content is the objectively measurable content of a text. Latent content is the content as interpreted by a researcher.

15. The procedure of a study consists of the steps taken to carry out the method and design of the study.

16. It is advisable to conduct a pilot study before doing the main study.

17. It is common practice to write a proposal, or prospectus, before beginning to carry out research.

18. The data should be carefully managed so that they can be understood long after the study is completed.

Suggestions for Further Reading

Jorgensen, D. L. (1989). *Participant observation: A methodology for human studies.* Newbury Park, CA: Sage. A thorough discussion of methods for participant-observer research.

Webb, E. J., Campbell, D. T., Schwartz, R. D., & Sechrist, L. (1966). *Unobtrusive measures.* Chicago: Rand McNally. This book contains thought-provoking discussions of observational and archival research, with emphasis on methods that do not cause the subjects to be aware that they are being studied.

Yin, R. K. (1989). *Case study research: Design and methods* (2nd ed.). Newbury Park, CA: Sage. Gives many examples of case-study research.

⫸ A CASE IN POINT ⫷

Suggestions for Nonexperimental Research

Important Guidelines

You may not use the telephone to collect data or recruit participants. (This is to avoid public relations problems. Properly done, the use of the telephone is not illegal or unethical.) Do not use the name of the university. Observe the APA ethics guidelines (see pages 372–381.) Do not break any laws, violate privacy, or do anything that will embarrass or annoy anyone. If you do a natural observation study, do not observe any behavior that is not normally observable in public. Obtain approval in advance from your instructor for any study you conduct. Be sure to follow any guidelines he or she may have. Thank anyone who cooperates in research.

Is Group Size a Function of Sex?

Sociobiology predicts that females will travel in larger groups than males (Burgess, 1984). At a shopping mall, observe same-sex groups of teenagers. Record sizes of groups. Analyze your data using the chi-square method. (Some problems of design you may encounter are defining group and teenager.) You might observe groups of various ages to see if there are trends.

Styles of Carrying Objects by Males and Females

Females tend to carry books and similar objects across the chest, whereas males tend to hold them in one hand at the side (Jenni & Jenni, 1976). At a shopping mall, observe methods of carrying as a function of sex. (Problems: How do you define small package? What about packages with handles? What is the appropriate statistic?)

Seat-Belt Use as a Function of Sex

At a stoplight, record your observations of the passengers in the first car in the nearest lane only. Do males or females use seat belts more often? You might hypothesize that females will conform more. (Problems: Since females are smaller, it may be more difficult to see the belt. Would seat-belt use differ between two-door and four-door cars, because of difficulty of reaching belts in two-door cars? Do men and women tend to drive the same type of car?)

Smoking as a Function of Whether Parents Smoke

Interview some friends about whether they smoke and whether their parents smoke. Your hypothesis might be as follows: Smoking is more likely if both parents smoke than if one smokes or if neither smokes. (Consideration: how to define smoking.)

Success in Quitting Smoking

Interview several former smokers. Ask how many times they quit and relapsed before succeeding. Did they use any program to help them stop, or did they do it on their own? (Considerations: how to define smoking, quitting, relapse.)

Cohort Effects in Smoking

Interview people of different ages about their smoking history. Find out how many never smoked and how many once smoked but have quit. At what age did the smokers begin? Look for trends as a function of when they were born. (Considerations: distortion of memory, social desirability.) If you study members of the same family, the data will not be independent.

⮕ A CASE IN POINT ⬅

Naturalistic Observation of Nonverbal Flirtation

You are a social psychologist who is interested in the development of romantic relationships. You would like to know whether the man or the woman tends to take the initiative in developing a relationship, and whether the initiative shifts over the early phase of a relationship. Researchers used to assume that the male takes the initiative. There is new evidence, however, that the female may tend to control the relationship early in the interaction. Later in the flirtation episode the male may initiate the escalation of more intimate behavior.

A previous researcher has classified behaviors into two categories: those that escalate the relationship and those that de-escalate.

ESCALATION

Gaze toward
Move closer
Open posture (relaxed, facing toward partner)
Positive facial expression (smiling, laughing, grinning)
Self-grooming (smoothing hair, thrusting chest, licking lips)
Brief touching (such as shoulder, arm, hand, hair, for a few seconds)
Continuous touching (such as holding hands, arm around shoulder, leaning on)
Intimate touching (kissing, hugging, rubbing, hand on sexual areas)

DE-ESCALATION

Gaze away
Move away
Closed posture (arms/legs crossed, facing away)
Negative facial expression (frowning, yawning, grimacing)

CONSIDERATIONS: There are a number of bars near campus that are frequented by young adults. Some are hotel lounges, some restaurants with bars, some strictly bars, and some have live entertainment.

You decide to observe heterosexual couples for a period of 15 minutes each. You would like to have 10 couples in both the early- and later-phase groups. Perhaps 10% of the couples will turn out to be married. You can spend five hours per night on Thursdays, Fridays, and Saturdays for four weeks.

You are concerned that the couples not notice that they are being observed, but you need to take notes of the behavior in order to be objective. You want to have two observers so that you can determine the interobserver reliability, but you are concerned not to appear to be together or be obviously communicating with each other. On the other hand, you need some method of signaling that will permit you to coordinate whom to observe, and when to begin and end. Further, you need to develop a protocol for deciding which couple to observe, and how to avoid spending time observing couples that may only interact for a minute or two.

After the observation period is over, you want to be able to discard data from married couples. The remaining couples are to be divided into early- and later-stage groups on the basis of how long they had interacted that particular evening. Some may have just met, and others may have been interacting for hours.

You are concerned about the ethics of observing behavior that may be intimate, but you understand that the couples realize they are in a public place.

REQUIRED: Design the study. Describe your procedure in detail, taking account of the preceding considerations. Provide mock data showing interobserver reliability, behavior of males and females, and behavior during early and later stages of interaction.

OPTIONAL: Describe what statistical analyses would be appropriate for these data.

The study on which this material is based is referenced in the Instructor's Manual.

☰ READING BETWEEN THE LINES ☰

7.1 AGGRESSION AND XYY MALES

Some males have a genetic abnormality that results in an extra Y chromosome. One study found that these XYY males, as they are known, were overrepresented in a prison population and concluded that the XYY condition caused persons to be overly aggressive. This finding gave rise to speculation and research into the possible causes of the apparent connection between the XYY condition and aggression.

One such study was conducted at the Boston Hospital for Women, which is connected with Harvard University. Between 1965 and 1975 more than 16,000 male infants born at the hospital were screened for chromosome abnormalities as part of a large study funded by the Center for the Study of Crime and Delinquency, a federal agency. Before giving birth the mothers were presented with a booklet that contained the following paragraph: "In this hospital all male infants are undergoing chromosome analysis. This new and simplified test allows the doctors to do an accurate screening examination of your baby's chromosomes and if any serious abnormalities are found, you will be so informed. It is hoped that in time this test . . . will become a universal test on all infants" (Chorover, 1979, p. 176). Another paragraph of the booklet referred to the chromosome test as a "service" and pointed out that there was no charge for it.

The study identified six male infants with the XYY condition out of the more than 16,000 babies tested. A pediatric psychiatrist visited the homes of all of the XYY children and informed the parents that "their children have extra chromosome material" and that the baby's pediatrician was "fully informed about the child's variation" (p. 186). What ethical and design problems can you find with this study?   ■

☑ EXERCISES

7.1 IDENTIFY TYPES OF NONEXPERIMENTAL RESEARCH

For each of the research questions presented below, indicate the following: (1) the type of research that would best answer the question; (2) an appropriate sampling method; and (3) the best method of collecting the data.

a. How do the minority groups at a certain university view the student counseling program?
b. What are the daily classroom activities of the children participating in the Head Start program in Allegheny County?
c. What trends exist in the growth of population in American prisons from 1900 to 1988?
d. What is the relationship between intelligence and creativity?

7.2 IDENTIFY POTENTIAL PROBLEMS OF VALIDITY IN A CASE STUDY

Mr. E was an elderly man who gradually began having problems in speaking and understanding speech. When he could no longer talk over the telephone, Mr. E was tested by a neurologist, but no brain damage was detectable at that time. Later Mr. E went to a speech clinic, which tested his hearing, speech, and intellectual function and made some recommendations for therapy. Eleven years into the course of his problem, his family called in a researcher who interviewed Mr. E and his family. She began to develop a history of his case based on her continuing interviews, their recollections, and his letters and personal notes. An autopsy performed when he died a year later found widespread evidence of brain damage, particularly in the speech areas (Holland, McBurney, Moossy, & Reinmuth, 1985).

REQUIRED:

a. Identify the different types of research that went into this case study.
b. What problems of interpretation are presented by the fact that the researchers did not begin their study until Mr. E's problem had progressed for 11 years?

7.3 NATURALISTIC OBSERVATION OF SHOPPERS

Market researchers have recently begun observing people shopping for new cars, using products such as laundry detergents, or eating ice cream at home. They may ask permission to snoop in their refrigerators or closets to see what things they contain.

REQUIRED: List some advantages and disadvantages that this type of research might have over surveys of consumer attitudes.   ❏

8

Nonexperimental Research, Part 2: Survey Research

Surveys are a widely used method of gathering scientific information. Often the purpose of a survey is simply to determine how people feel about a particular issue, such as gun control or the performance of the president of the United States. Other surveys may attempt to find out the effect of some event on people's behavior. For example, surveys conducted after the Three Mile Island nuclear accident attempted to determine who evacuated the area and for what reasons. In addition, surveys provide an opportunity to examine correlations among the subjects' responses and to look for possible patterns of cause and effect.

A major function of surveys is to dispel myths. One such myth is that women whose children have grown up and left home suffer a kind of depression called the empty nest syndrome. Lillian Rubin (1979) surveyed 160 women in this life situation and found that, rather than being depressed, virtually all of them experienced a sense of relief. Other surveys surprise us by indicating how widespread child abuse and wife beating are.

Because survey research is technical and complex, we will give only a brief overview here. Nevertheless, it is important to have an idea of the techniques because survey research is used so often.

HOW A QUESTIONNAIRE IS DESIGNED

Designing a questionnaire is a surprisingly complex procedure that involves a great many considerations. It shares many of the other considerations of research design in addition to the concerns that are inherent in any written or oral form of communication. Frequently researchers use existing questionnaires, rather than designing their own instruments. Not only do they avoid redesigning the wheel, but they are able to compare their results with those of previous studies using the same instrument. The *Mental Measurement Yearbook* series (for example, Conoley & Kramer, 1989) reviews many standardized tests, including some questionnaires. The *Measures of Social Psychological Attitudes* series (for example, Robinson, Shaver, & Wrightsman, 1991) reviews and lists a great many measures of subjective well-being, self-esteem, social anxiety, depression, and so forth. The considerations listed in the following sections will be helpful whether you design your own questionnaire or select a previously existing one.

■ Determine the Purpose of the Questionnaire

The first question to ask when designing a questionnaire is the same as for any research: What do I expect to accomplish? We mention this here because beginning researchers sometimes tend to design and administer a questionnaire without thinking through the purpose of doing the survey in the first place.

Suppose the students at your college are concerned about campus security. Someone might design and administer a questionnaire that shows that students are, in fact, concerned about the problem. This is not particularly useful information. What would be useful is information about what specific things could be done to improve campus security: increasing the frequency of patrols by police, providing an escort service, reducing the number of entrances to buildings, or installing an electronic security system, for example. In this way, the administration would know what changes would be acceptable to the college community, and be given some guidance in deciding how best to allocate resources to improve campus security.

open-ended question
one that the respondents answer in their own words
closed-ended question
one that limits the respondents to certain alternatives

■ Determine the Types of Questions

Survey questions can be divided into two basic categories: open-ended and closed-ended. An **open-ended question** is one that permits the respondents to answer in their own words. A **closed-ended question,** on the other hand, limits the respondents to alternatives determined in advance by the designers of the questionnaire. Each type of question has advantages and disadvantages. The open-ended question permits respondents to answer more completely and to reveal the reasoning behind their answers. Using open-ended questions makes it more likely that the questionnaire will discover something not anticipated by its designers.

On the other hand, open-ended questions are harder to code, because the answers are in narrative form. (See the discussion of content analysis in Chapter 7.) It is necessary to categorize responses in some way so as to be able to summarize the data. This must be done after the survey is complete, making data analysis a messy job and making it likely that you will have to break a cardinal rule of research: Decide in advance how you are going to analyze your data. In addition, open-ended questions require more effort of the respondents and are more difficult for less articulate respondents to answer.

The advantages and disadvantages of open-ended questions make them more useful for smaller and preliminary studies. Coding a small number of open-ended surveys may be manageable, whereas hundreds would not. In addition, trying out a preliminary version of a survey with open-ended questions can determine the range of likely answers, permitting you to standardize the alternatives into a closed-ended format that will be easier to deal with in the larger administration.

Closed-ended questions have complementary advantages and disadvantages to open-ended ones. They are easier to code and analyze, and there are fewer off-the-wall responses. The alternatives are presented to the respondents so they do not have to think as hard. The respondents do not need to be as articulate to formulate their answers as in an open-ended question.

The disadvantages of closed-ended questions are that the issues being studied may be too complex to reduce to a small set of alternatives, or the respondent may not agree with any of them, resulting in simplistic answers. They tend to put words into the mouths of respondents, suggesting alternatives that they might never come up with themselves. Furthermore, errors can creep into the closed-ended questionnaire: if a respondent misinterprets the question or a clerical error is made in coding the data, there may be no way to discover the fact. In order to reduce errors, many questionnaires require that each response be recorded in two places, so that they can be tested for consistency.

In summary, the flexibility of open-ended questions makes them more useful for small-scale and preliminary studies, whereas the standardization of closed-ended questions make them more suitable for large studies. Often, the two types of questions are mixed in a single study, when respondents may be offered the opportunity to expand on the answers to a closed-ended question. This permits the data to be coded and analyzed easily, but gives some insights into the reasons why the respondents chose the alternative they did.

■ Write the Items

We will outline some basic principles of questionnaire construction so that you will be aware of the major pitfalls.

Address a single issue per item. The principal concern is that the questionnaire items be unambiguous. Each item should address a single question and do so in a clear manner. The following item is ambiguous because it is double-barreled: "College students should receive grades in their courses because this prepares them for the competitive world outside of college." This item contains both an opinion about grading and a reason for grading. A person might agree with giving grades but disagree with the reason stated for grading students. It would be better to phrase the item, "College students should receive grades in their course work." Another item could address the desirability of preparing students for a competitive society.

Avoid bias. The next consideration is to write the question in a way that will not bias the results. Two members of Congress may survey their respective constituents on attitudes toward abortion. The first one's newsletter asks, "Do you believe in killing unborn babies?" The second one's newsletter asks, "Should women be forced to bear unwanted children?" Even if the people in the two congressional districts had identical attitudes toward abortion, the survey results could indicate dramatically opposite attitudes toward abortion.

Make alternatives clear. There is an especial need to write closed-ended questions in such a way that the options are distinctly different from one another and that they cover all of the possibilities. A philosopher would say that the answers must be **mutually exclusive** and **exhaustive.** Categories are mutually exclusive if no individual case could belong to more than one category at a time. The categories *undergraduate* and *graduate* are mutually exclusive, because you cannot be both at the same time. But *scholarship recipient* and *undergraduate* are not mutually exclusive: you could be both an undergraduate and receiving a scholarship.

For the categories to be exhaustive, all cases must fall into one or another of the alternatives. Using only *graduate student* and *undergraduate student* leaves out the possibility that someone has a bachelor's degree but is taking undergraduate courses to prepare for application to graduate school. We might define the category *nondegree student* for this type of individual. Because of the difficulty of thinking of all the alternatives, questions sometimes include the category *other*. This category should be used with care, however, because you are in trouble if *other* turns out to be a popular answer.

Beware of the social desirability tendency. Bias often enters when respondents perceive one alternative as more socially acceptable than the other—a phenomenon called **social desirability.** (See also Chapter 5.) Researchers avoid this problem by wording questions so that each alternative appears equally socially desirable. The question on abortion might be better structured as follows: "Women should be permitted to decide for themselves

mutually exclusive categories defined so that membership in one rules out membership in another

exhaustive categories defined so that all possible cases will fall into one of them

social desirability a characteristic of certain responses that causes people to choose that response even if it does not represent their true tendency or opinion

whether to continue a pregnancy." In order to balance out people's natural tendency to agree with any item, an experimenter might also include a question that presents the matter the other way: "Abortions should be restricted by law."

Some personality tests include a set of questions designed to detect if a person has a tendency to be overly influenced by social desirability. A collection of such items designed to detect dishonest responses is sometimes called a **verification key.** The MMPI, a widely used personality test, has a verification key called the "lie scale." One question on the lie scale might ask whether a person has ever stolen anything, no matter how small. Most people, to answer truthfully, would have to say that they had. People who say they have never done so would raise suspicions. These scales can be quite sophisticated, so that it may be hard to make yourself look better than you really are without scoring high on a lie scale.

verification key
a collection of items on a questionnaire designed to detect dishonest answers

Determine the format of the item.   Answers can take various formats, depending on the type of question, such as true/false, multiple-choice, or ratings. Often respondents are asked to indicate their degree of agreement or disagreement with a particular position. Such an item is known as a rating scale, often called a **Likert scale** after the person who made it popular. Rating scales are used a great deal because they measure the magnitude of opinion, not simply its direction.

Likert scale
a question that asks for a rating of the extent of agreement or disagreement with a statement; a rating scale

Attitudes elicited by questionnaire items are frequently measured on a seven-point scale. Seven categories of agreement are the maximum that can be distinguished on most dimensions. The item might be laid out as follows, with instructions for the respondent to circle the number that most closely corresponds with his or her attitude:

> Women should be permitted to decide for themselves whether to continue a pregnancy.
>
> Agree   Disagree
>   1   2   3   4   5   6   7

Often it is convenient to write branching items that permit the respondent to skip inappropriate questions and move through a questionnaire more efficiently. Box 8.1 gives an extended example of a branching questionnaire. This example is particularly useful because it has a number of branching points. In addition, note that the terms used—alcoholic beverage, drink, weekday, weekend—are carefully defined. Although these terms may seem clear to you, they need to be defined in this context because different people use them differently. Some people do not consider beer an alcoholic beverage, for example. Friday is usually defined as a weekday, but this questionnaire defines it as a weekend day because people often start partying on Friday.

BOX 8.1
DRINKING PORTION OF HEALTH BEHAVIOR QUESTIONNAIRE

1. How would you classify your intake of alcoholic beverages (beer, wine, or liquor such as whiskey, gin, vodka, scotch, bourbon, rum, cocktails, etc.)?
   A. [ ] I have never consumed alcoholic beverages →**SKIP TO QUESTION 9**
   B. [ ] I used to consume alcoholic beverages, but don't anymore →**SKIP TO QUESTION 9**
   C. [ ] I currently consume some alcoholic beverages

2. Which answer best describes how often you drink beer, wine, or liquor?
   A. [ ] less than once per week →**SKIP TO QUESTION 9**
   B. [ ] 1 or 2 times per week
   C. [ ] 3 or 4 times per week
   D. [ ] nearly every day
   E. [ ] every day

3. On how many weekdays (Monday, Tuesday, Wednesday, and Thursday) do you usually drink alcoholic beverages?
   A. [ ] 0 days →**SKIP TO QUESTION 6**
   B. [ ] 1 day
   C. [ ] 2 days
   D. [ ] 3 days
   E. [ ] 4 days

   NOTE: ONE DRINK IS EQUAL TO 1½ OZ. OF HARD LIQUOR, 5 OZ. OF WINE, OR 12 OZ. OF BEER.

4. When you drink on a weekday, how many drinks do you usually drink in a day? [|] number of drinks per day

5. What is the most you drink on a weekday? [|] number of drinks per day

6. On how many days of a weekend (Friday, Saturday, and Sunday) do you usually drink alcoholic beverages?
   A. [ ] 0 days →**SKIP TO QUESTION 9**
   B. [ ] 1 day
   C. [ ] 2 days
   D. [ ] 3 days

7. When you drink on a weekend, how many drinks do you usually drink in a day? [|] number of drinks per day

8. What is the most you drink in a day on the weekend? [|] drinks per day

9. [Questionnaire continues with other health behavior questions.]

SOURCE: From The Health and Nutrition Questionnaire [Form 105 (1–8), November 1986], The Treatment of Mild Hypertension Research Group. Reprinted by permission. For information on the study, please refer to "The Treatment of Mild Hypertension Study," by The Treatment of Mild Hypertension Research Group, July 1991, *Archives of Internal Medicine, 151,* 1413–1423.

■ Determine How the Data Will Be Analyzed

Another question to consider is how the questionnaire is to be scored and analyzed. Once again, this should be done in advance of collecting data for any research project. If you think that women will respond differently from men, commuters differently from dorm students, freshmen differently from upperclassmen, and so on, you need to include questions to permit the classification of students on these dimensions.

You also need to decide what statistics will be used. Will you be able to draw proper conclusions from the data? It is an excellent idea to devise the form on which you will code your data as a way of checking to see if your questionnaire is well designed.

ADMINISTERING THE QUESTIONNAIRE

■ Determine the Method of Administration

There are essentially four different modes of administering surveys: face-to-face, written, computerized, and by telephone. Each one has its advantages and disadvantages, as we shall see. The one that is best depends on the circumstances. For example, it might be a relatively simple matter to survey the members of a local fraternity face-to-face. The alumni of that fraternity, however, could best be reached by mail.

The typical survey tries to obtain responses from a large group of individuals who are difficult to locate and whose cooperation may be difficult to obtain. Frequently, however, questionnaires are administered as part of a program in which people come to an office or a laboratory on a routine basis. A questionnaire may be administered to all patients in a doctor's office or all participants in a large study, for example. In such situations, obtaining cooperation may be less of a problem. The following discussion largely assumes the usual situation in which finding and gaining cooperation of the subjects is a major consideration.

Face-to-face. Personal interviews have the advantage that the interviewers can establish rapport with the persons being interviewed. They can direct the attention of the respondents to the material and motivate them to answer the questions carefully. Interviewers may be able to notice when respondents seem to misunderstand a question, and explain its meaning. They can probe for more complete answers when a respondent gives a brief answer or one that does not respond to the question.

The main disadvantage of face-to-face interviewing is the flip side of its main advantages: the presence of the interviewer creates a social situation that may result in biased responses. Respondents may tell interviewers what they think they want to hear. The potential for interviewer effects is greater with face-to-face interviewing than with any other method.

Face-to-face interviewing also has several practical problems. First, interviewing is much more expensive than conducting telephone or mail surveys because of the need to travel to the respondents' locations. Second is concern for the safety of the interviewers. With so many people away from home during the day, it is often necessary to conduct interviews in the evening. Interviewers are understandably reluctant to go from house to house after dark. Finally, personal interviewing has the problem that it is more difficult to supervise the interviewers. It is not unheard of for interviewers to look at the list of addresses they are to reach, and decide to fake the data, thus saving themselves a great deal of travel and interview time.

Written responses.   Written administration of questionnaires can take several forms: they may be administered to a group, they may be dropped off at a location, or they may be mailed to the respondents.

Group administration is familiar to you if you have completed course evaluations in college. Group administration is very efficient of time and money, and can have a very high response rate if attendance by group members is high, as in a class. Drop-off administration is often done by an organization, such as a church, that has many members who attend a location over some period of time but may not all be present at one time. Copies of the questionnaire are dropped off in a particular location to be picked up at some later time. Mail administration is familiar to all. We constantly receive questionnaires in the mail, sometimes as part of another mailing or in a magazine.

The main advantage of written questionnaires is their low cost. There is no monetary cost of group or drop-off administration other than the duplication of the materials. Even postage is relatively cheap, compared to the alternative methods of administration. Except for group administration, respondents can complete the questionnaire at their leisure, and they have greater anonymity in their responses, reducing interviewer bias.

response rate
in survey research, the percentage of individuals in the sample who return the completed survey

The main problem with written questionnaires is **response rate.** We will discuss the consequences of different response rates later in this chapter. At this point, we will simply note that low response rates may invalidate the results because of differences between individuals who respond and those who don't. Drop-off and mail administration may have very low rates of responding, often less than 50%.

Written questionnaires have other drawbacks as well. There is no possibility of clarifying questions that might be misunderstood. Some individuals in the sample may be illiterate or have vision problems. It is impossible to determine how seriously the respondent took the survey. Perhaps a survey of attitudes toward consumer products intended for the person who does the household shopping has been given to a child in the family to fill out for the fun of it.

Computerized administration.   If the subject is already in the office or laboratory, it may be convenient to administer a questionnaire by computer. The computer has the advantage of being impersonal, so social desirability may be reduced. The computer is also absolutely consistent. The investigator can be sure that all the questions were asked in order, and none were skipped.

The computer can check for invalid responses and prompt the interviewer to recheck implausible answers, such as the presence of 20 children in the home. More important, the computer can control the sequencing and branching of questions so that, for example, people who do not drive will not need to be asked about how many miles they drive to work.

Telephone administration. The telephone is rapidly increasing in popularity as a method of administering surveys. The main advantage is low cost. Nowadays the percentage of people who can be reached by telephone is about as high as the percentage who can be reached by other means. Even unlisted numbers are not a problem when random-digit dialing is used. This method involves choosing an exchange and then randomly selecting the last four digits from a random-number table. Although it may take as many as five calls on the average to reach a working number that is a residence instead of a business, this may still involve less effort than other methods of administration. Also, telephone interviews can be conducted rapidly, without having to wait for interviewers to travel to many locations or for respondents to mail back their completed surveys.

Another advantage of telephone surveys is the possibility of using a computer-assisted interview. Although computer-assisted interviewing is by no means limited to telephone administration, it is probably most widely used in conjunction with the telephone. The interviewer reads the questions from a computer screen and types the answers onto the keyboard. This method has many of the previously noted advantages of computerized interviewing.

Finally, telephone surveys can be conducted from a central location where the interviewers can be supervised to assure that they administer the survey as it was designed.

On the negative side, telephone surveys are less anonymous than mail surveys and introduce the possibility of interviewer bias. It is more difficult to ask complicated or open-ended questions over the telephone than with a written questionnaire. Compared to face-to-face interviews, it is harder to establish rapport or to judge the degree of seriousness with which the respondent is taking the interview, and it is impossible to use visual aids.

On balance, however, the telephone is becoming the preferred method of survey administration because of the higher response rate and low cost compared to other methods. The factors that have contributed to this situation are social changes, such as more women working, and technological changes, such as the computer. Technological changes, however, may also make telephone surveys less desirable. The increasingly common practice of using answering machines to screen calls may render the telephone less effective for the purpose of conducting surveys, and the outlawing of random-digit dialing has been proposed.

■ The Problem of Response Rate

A principal concern with all methods of administering surveys is the problem of response rate. We are all bombarded by surveys from a great variety of sources; many of them are actually sales pitches disguised as surveys. Over a third of the American population may refuse to participate in surveys

(Neuman, 1991). Further, the response rate varies significantly among methods of administration. Surveys printed in magazines may have a 1% or 2% response rate. Mail surveys often have return rates between 10% and 50%, telephone surveys 80%, and face-to-face 90% (Neuman, 1991).

Magazines and radio stations often publish questions for their audiences to respond to. Obviously these broadcast surveys lack reliability. One station says, "Our poll is not a scientific survey but a rough estimate of the views of our listeners." All of the data come from people who are motivated to respond. Most people feel only moderately one way or the other about an issue such as gun control, but a few are strongly, perhaps violently, opposed. A survey with a low response rate will be biased in the direction of the more vocal persons.

The British magazine *New Scientist* polled its readers on their attitudes toward ESP (Evans, 1973). The results showed that 67% of those responding considered ESP to be either "an established fact" or a "likely possibility." This sounds like impressive evidence in favor of the scientific credibility of ESP until one discovers that the return rate on this questionnaire was only about 2%. People who believe in ESP would likely be more motivated to respond than nonbelievers, thus giving biased results.

The quality of the data is a direct function of the return rate. Most researchers require at least 50% and prefer 90%, although many will accept a lower rate if ways of increasing return rate are not practical. Refusal to cooperate, failure to return a questionnaire, or unavailability of target persons should be recorded. Possible biases thereby introduced should be kept in mind when the research is evaluated.

SAMPLING

■ Types of Samples

Surveys differ greatly in value according to how the respondents are sampled. We will discuss four types of samples: haphazard samples, purposive samples, convenience samples, and probability samples.

Haphazard samples.   Sometimes the surveyor has control over whom to sample but uses haphazard methods of obtaining people. A television station may send a crew out to interview 10 people on the street with instructions to include 5 women, 2 blacks, 3 teenagers, and 1 adorable little girl. These **haphazard samples** are almost worthless. Perhaps the most famous haphazard survey was conducted by the now defunct *Literary Digest,* which obtained respondents from telephone books and automobile registration lists. This survey predicted that Landon would win the 1936 presidential election over Roosevelt by a landslide. It overlooked the fact, however, that during the Great Depression people who could afford telephones and automobiles were more likely to vote Republican.

haphazard sample
population subgroup that the researcher uses hit-or-miss methods for selection

purposive sample
a nonrandom sample that is chosen for some characteristic that it possesses

Purposive samples. Frequently, researchers will base a survey on a sample that is chosen to meet some particular definition. A **purposive sample** is one that is selected nonrandomly but for some particular reason. A researcher may survey the opinions of the presidents of several leading colleges about desirable changes in the college curriculum. The opinions of these people may be more valuable than those that would be obtained in a random sample of all college presidents.

Purposive samples can almost be considered to constitute a population—for example, all presidents of leading colleges. In practice, of course, a researcher frequently does not have access to an entire population, even one as small as the presidents of the top 50 colleges, nor will there necessarily be agreement on which are the top 50 colleges. Nevertheless, a purposive sample is frequently preferable to a random sample.

The main problem with purposive sampling is that an error in judgment on the part of the researcher in selecting the sample may influence the results. A list of leading colleges made up by a researcher is more likely to contain the researcher's own college than would a list made up by someone at a different college. Another problem is that the presidents of leading colleges may not in fact know what the most desirable curriculum would be for students at the colleges that make up the majority of the population of colleges.

convenience sample
a nonrandom sample that is chosen for practical reasons

Convenience samples. Another kind of sample that is quite acceptable is similar to the purposive sample in that it selects a desirable group of people but differs in that it may not come close to sampling all of a population. This is the **convenience sample.** A researcher may want to study the effects of integration on social development in schoolchildren. There may be many appropriate schools to choose among, but it is much more convenient to study one in the researcher's own city. Even though such selection is not random, one would usually be willing to generalize the results to other similar schools and similar children. Most research in psychology is done using convenience samples: students enrolled in introductory psychology courses.

Probability samples. The most satisfactory surveys generally obtain their respondents in some manner such that the researcher knows the probability that any given individual will appear in the sample. Whereas the other three types of samples permit only subjective evaluation of the validity of the results, probability samples permit one to apply various statistics. Our focus, therefore, will be on probability samples.

■ Probability Samples and Random Selection

Most probability sampling methods rely on random sampling, although there are important exceptions, as we shall see shortly. Before we go further, therefore, it is necessary to discuss the concept of random selection.

Although you may have an idea of random selection, the concept is not a simple one. First, it is necessary to realize that the term *random* as used in science is a technical one, very different from our everyday use, where we might say that we picked the socks we wore today "at random." In that usage, *random* means you picked the first pair of socks that fell to hand; most likely it implies that you would wear those same socks much more than some of your other pairs. That would happen if you always replaced the laundered socks in the drawer on top of the previously laundered ones, and pulled them out again from the top of the pile.

As a first approximation, selection is random when it is controlled by chance alone. A common example is selecting a state lottery number. The authorities want to be sure that no one will be able to predict the number better than chance. Another way to define a **random sample** is to say that a selection process is random if every member of the population has the same probability of being selected and selection of one individual is independent of the selection of any other. The equal-probability-of-selection part may seem obvious, but the necessity of independent selection of individuals requires some comment.

> **random sample**
> a sample in which every member of the population has an equal and independent chance of being selected

Suppose John and Marsha, Bob and Carol, and Ted and Alice attend a party at which there are to be two door prizes awarded. If the host puts each couple's names on a slip of paper and pulls one paper out of a hat, then it is obvious that if John's name is chosen, Marsha's will be also. Marsha's selection, then, was dependent on John's (and vice versa). John and Marsha each had a one-in-three chance of winning, but because only both or neither could win, their selection was not random. On the other hand, if the host put the names on separate pieces of paper and pulled two names, then the selection would be random. Both John and Marsha would have a one-in-three chance of being selected, as before, but Marsha's chance of selection would not depend on John's.

This example is a bit contrived, but it is quite possible for structure to exist in some ordering of individuals. You may have been in a group that was being divided into two smaller groups by counting off. If people tended to sit together in pairs, then counting off would result in each member of the pair winding up in a different group. This may be the desired result, but it is not random. Random selection would result in some, but not all, pairs' being separated. Thus, any method of selection other than a true random method could result in some nonindependence between members of the groups.

The Sampling Frame

In order to take a probability sample of a population, it is necessary to define the population. Suppose that you want to take a survey of 10% of your research-methods class. The population in this case is the class. The class, however, contains some individuals who have not yet officially registered for the course or who will drop before the end of the term. You must develop a definition of the population for the purposes of the survey, and this may be different from the actual population. For example, you may define the population for the purposes of the study as those whose names appear on the official class roster as of a certain date. Any who have not yet registered will not be considered, even if they are attending class. The population that you will work with in the study is called the **sampling frame.** To take another example, the sampling frame for the purpose of studying the population of Allegheny County, Pennsylvania, would exclude those who are in jails or mental institutions.

Each individual that falls within the sampling frame is called an **element.** You would sample a number of elements from the sampling frame.

sampling frame
a population as it is defined for the purposes of selecting subjects for a study

element
individual member of a sampling frame

systematic sample
a probability sample that is not randomly selected

Systematic Samples

A **systematic sample** is a probability sample but not a random sample.

Suppose you wish to select a sample of 20 students out of your research-methods class of 80 students. Your first step would be to obtain the class roster from the instructor. Then it is necessary to identify each element. You could use the students' names, but this would require you to have some way of randomizing their names. Because it is much more convenient to work with numbers, you would identify each element by a number. If there were 80 students in the class, they would be numbered from 1 to 80.

If you were to choose every fourth name from the class roster, you would have a probability sample, because 25% of the class would have been selected. The sample would not be random, however, because those whose names were in positions 1, 5, 9, and so on, had a 100% chance of being selected, and everyone else had a zero chance. This method fails the equal-probability part of the definition of random selection.

Suppose, however, that you randomly chose which of the first four positions you started counting from. This method would meet the equal-probability-of-selection criterion, but it would still be nonrandom, because the very first choice would determine the selection of all subsequent elements.

It should be noted that although systematic samples are not random, they may be perfectly good for practical reasons. Taking every nth individual from a roster is much less work than the random method we are about to describe. If there is some structure to the list, as we have seen, the results will be nonrandom. For example, a list of couples might be structured such that the man's name always followed that of his partner. Choosing every 10th person on the list would result in the selection of all men or all women.

If the list has no structure to it, however, the results will be as good as random in practice. A list of names in alphabetical order is unlikely to have any structure that would affect a sample drawn by selecting every nth name. (If names were selected in bunches, however, structure could easily arise: Selecting all the M's would result in a high proportion of Scottish names that begin with Mc and Mac.) Therefore, systematic sampling is commonly done in survey research because it is so easy.

Simple Random Samples

Exactly how to select elements randomly from a population may require considerable thought and ingenuity. As we have seen, some methods that may

**simple
random sample**
group chosen from
an entire popu-
lation such that
every member of
the population has
an equal and
independent
chance of being
selected in a single
sample

seem random actually are not. The basic **simple random sample** is used when we believe that the population is relatively homogeneous with respect to the questions of interest.

Let us continue with the same example of selecting 20 students out of your class of 80. After you have obtained the roster and assigned each student a number as before, you would next obtain a list of random numbers. Random-number tables are available in many books about research methods and statistics. Or you can generate a list of random numbers with a computer. (A program to generate random numbers is given in the Instructor's Manual.)

Table 8.1 shows part of a matrix of random numbers. This table presents columns of one-digit numbers. For our example, you need numbers between

TABLE 8.1 PORTION OF A RANDOM-NUMBER TABLE

0	9	8	3	5	8	0	6	9	9
5	6	0	5	3	7	2	6	6	4
9	6	2	7	1	7	0	0	0	2
3	1	6	9	2	7	1	8	5	8
3	6	3	2	0	4	9	6	4	0
5	0	4	7	3	2	4	6	9	4
7	7	4	6	6	7	1	5	3	
0	9	3	0	8	0	6	6	4	
4	9	6	5	1	9	7	0	7	
5	5	6	6	5	3	8	4	5	
5	2	8	8	7	2	2	6	1	
1	4	0	5	4	4	8	2	5	
0	9	7	8	3	9	1	0	4	
5	9	5	8	4	5	8	9	8	
0	5	0	2	5	8	6	4	2	
6	6	6	7	8	7	2	7	9	
4	1	4	1	8	6	0	8	5	
7	1	1	2	0	4	2	5	2	
4	5	7	4	8	6	1	0	7	
5	4	6	2	7	2	2	9	8	
3	1	7	7	6	5	6	7		
1	5	5	2	2	2	4	5		
8	4	0	2	6	4	4	3		
6	7	8	5	1	5	0	8		
9	6	7	1	1	5	6			
1	6	2	5	8	7	9			
9	8	3	3	5	5	4			
3	6	6	5	9	6	3			
8	5	7	2	9	7				
8	1	9	3	4	2				
1	7	4	4	3					
2	9	8							

1 and 80. This requires that you have a list of two-digit numbers. To accomplish this, simply rule the table into two-digit columns. Next, go down the list of numbers, looking for numbers between 1 and 80. Each time you see one, write it down on a list until you have found 20 numbers. These become the identification numbers of the people who are selected for the sample. Occasionally a number will repeat before you have completed your sample. Simply ignore such numbers, because the people they represent are already in the sample. In this example, ignore the repeat occurrence of 31 and 9 (twice). Also ignore the numbers 84 and 96 (twice), because they are outside the desired range.

Stratified Random Samples

stratified random sample
a random sample in which two or more subsamples are represented according to some predetermined proportion, generally in the same proportion as they exist in the population

If you are surveying a population that has identifiable subgroups that are likely to differ markedly in their responses, you can improve accuracy by obtaining a **stratified random sample.** Suppose you know that the college has 55% men and 45% women and you have reason to believe that males and females may respond differently on your dependent measure. If you took a simple random sample, the ratio of males to females would probably not match the population exactly. By stratified random sampling you can ensure that the proportion of men and women in the sample matches that in the college population.

Stratified random sampling essentially treats the population as two or more separate subpopulations and creates a separate random sample of each. In this case, you take one sample from the female subpopulation and one from the male subpopulation. First you determine how many of each you need. Because you want your sample to contain one-fourth of the population of 80 students and have the same sex ratio as the population, you need one-fourth of the females and one-fourth of the males. If there are 48 females and 32 males in the class, you will require 12 females and 8 males. Next you number the females from 1 to 48 and select from the random-number table in the same manner as before. Then you number the males from 1 to 32 and repeat the process. Now you can be sure that the sample exactly matches the population with regard to sex ratio. The procedure is still random, however, because every member of the population had an equal and independent chance of being selected.

Sometimes stratified random sampling is used to *oversample* some subgroup of the population—that is, to purposely include some group at a greater frequency than it is represented in the population. Suppose you are interested in comparing the opinions of blacks and whites on some matter. You would want to include the same number of blacks and whites in the survey so as to get as reliable an estimate of the attitudes of blacks as of whites, even though blacks may constitute only 10% of the population. You would stratify on race and include 50% blacks and 50% whites in your sample. The sampling would still be random within the subpopulations.

Random samples can be extremely accurate. A sample as small as 1,000 individuals will allow a survey researcher to estimate within plus or minus 3.2% the attitude of a population as large as that of the United States (Weisberg & Bowen, 1977).

Cluster Samples

There are many populations that would be impossible or impractical to number. For instance, making a list of every person in the United States would be impossible. Even random sampling of all the students in a college may be difficult. Suppose there is no student directory. You may decide to obtain the students from classes. Rather than taking one-tenth of the students in each class, sampling every student in one-tenth of the classes would be more efficient. You would obtain a list of all classes at the college. From this list you would randomly select one-tenth of the classes to study. This method would produce a **cluster sample.** Even though the students that you sample by clustering would probably be more alike than those in a purely random sample (because students within classes are likely to be similar in background), the ease of obtaining the sample would permit you to study more individuals and therefore offset the disadvantages of not having a purely random sample.

cluster sample
group selected by using clusters or groupings from a larger population

If you wanted to make sure your sample contained the same proportion of students in particular categories as the college as a whole, you could stratify your clusters. You might separate the classes into sciences, humanities, and so forth, as well as into lower- and upper-division courses. Then you would randomly select one-tenth of the classes in each category.

A sophisticated form of cluster sampling is known as **multistage sampling.** Commercial polls, such as the Gallup Poll, use multistage sampling. First, they may randomly select several ZIP codes. From these ZIP codes, streets are selected randomly; from the streets, addresses are selected randomly. For practical reasons, it is common to select a number of individuals from within a given cluster.

multistage sampling
a form of cluster sampling in which clusters are further broken down by taking further samples from each cluster

An example of multistage sampling can be seen in a study of drug use among high school seniors in the United States. Lloyd Johnston, Patrick O'Malley, and Jerald Bachman (1991) first selected a number of geographical areas. Next they selected one or more high schools within each geographical area. Then they selected senior students within each high school. This method was much more efficient than trying to make a simple random selection from all high school seniors. It is likely that no single list of all such individuals exists. Even if it did, it would be very inefficient to try to study one or two students in a given school. Obtaining access to the students and administering the test is vastly more efficient in groups. In contrast to cluster sampling, this study used only certain students from each school. If they had studied all students in a given school, they would have had more individuals than they needed by the time they had obtained enough clusters to be representative of different types of schools and regions of the country.

Although cluster sampling is not as accurate as random sampling, because each stage of sampling introduces another source of sampling error, they can be very accurate: Cluster samples are able to determine attitudes with a margin of error of plus or minus 4% with a sample size of 1,000 (out of the entire U.S. population), compared with 3.2% for a simple random sample of the same size (Weisberg & Bowen, 1977).

Note on using random-number tables.   Strictly speaking, it is necessary to choose the place to begin using a random-number table in a random manner; otherwise, each member of the population will not have an equal chance of being selected. As you can see, this involves an infinite regress (an endless chain of steps), because how do you choose your random starting place? In practice, there are two ways in which researchers commonly handle this problem. The first way is to start by pointing blindly at some point in the table and starting at that point. The second, and preferable, method is to start at the beginning of the table and use any part of the table only once. This method is feasible if you have access to a computer to generate new lists as necessary.

■ Summary of Sampling Procedures

RANDOM SAMPLING

1. Define and identify the sampling frame.
2. Determine the desired size of the sample.
3. Compile a list of all members of the population, and assign each member on the list a number from zero to the required number.
4. Group the columns of digits according to the required number of digits—for example, three digits for numbers up to 999.
5. Arbitrarily select a number in the random-number table by closing your eyes and pointing.
6. If the selected number corresponds to the number assigned to any member of the identified population, that member is in the sample.
7. Repeat step 6 by running down the table until the desired number of subjects has been selected.

STRATIFIED RANDOM SAMPLING

1. Identify the sampling frame.
2. Determine the desired size of the sample.
3. Determine the subgroups, or strata, for which you want equal or proportional representation.
4. Identify each member of the population as a member of one of the subgroups or strata.
5. For each of the population subgroups or strata, assign each member a number from zero to the required number.

6. Use a random-number table to select the appropriate number of subjects from each of the subgroups or strata.

CLUSTER SAMPLING

1. Identify the sampling frame.
2. Determine the desired sample size.
3. Identify and list all appropriate clusters.
4. Assign all clusters on the list a consecutive number from zero to the required number.
5. Estimate the average number of subjects in each cluster of the population.
6. Determine the number of appropriate clusters by dividing the desired sample size by the estimated size of a cluster.
7. Use a random-number table to select the appropriate number of clusters.
8. Either select randomly from the clusters or use the entire cluster.

✳ NUTS & BOLTS ✳

Tips on Interviewing

As is the case with those who conduct any type of research, interviewers must be properly trained in order to avoid "slippage" between the protocol designed by the principal investigator and what actually takes place. Kornhauser and Sheatsley (1976) give a number of suggestions on conducting interviews.

The first principle is to create a friendly but professional atmosphere. A face-to-face interview may start with some pleasantry about the weather or the dog, but should get right to the point to avoid arousing suspicion. A telephone interviewer may start out by saying "Good evening, I am conducting a survey and would like to get some of your ideas. For instance, . . ." followed by the first question.

The interviewer should keep the interview on track, without getting into discussions of subject matter. The interviewer is basically a reporter, and should avoid giving any of his own opinions so as not to bias the results.

It is very important to read the questions exactly as written, otherwise different respondents will be answering essentially different surveys. The interviewer should not rephrase questions, even if the respondent is confused about the meaning of the words. Similarly, the questions must be asked in order, without skipping questions, unless a branching questionnaire is being used.

If a respondent gives an incomplete or too brief answer to an open-ended question, it is permissible to use probe questions to get the respondent to complete the answer. You might say "That's interesting; could you explain that a little more?" It is very important not to put words into the respondent's mouth. Usually it is safer to simply repeat part or all of the question.

Sometimes people will say "don't know" when they are reluctant to reveal their opinion or confused as to the meaning of the question. Then you might say, "Well, I just want your own opinion; no one actually knows the answer to many of these questions." The number of questions that elicit unsatisfactory answers can be reduced by careful writing and by piloting the questionnaire on a number of people before beginning the actual administration.

The responses should be written down verbatim while the interview is in progress; don't wait until it is over, because you will forget or give biased answers. People will be patient with a few pauses as you write. Then the whole questionnaire should be reviewed for omissions and errors immediately after the interview is completed, but before leaving or hanging up, if possible.

Obtaining True Answers to Questions

There are times when people may not give honest answers on questionnaires. For example, it is likely that people will be influenced by social desirability when answering questions about behaviors that are criminal, antisocial, or unusual. Research on the prevalence of drug use, tax evasion, or condom use would likely encounter this type of problem.

randomized-response method
a survey technique that encourages honesty by introducing a random variable that makes it impossible to identify whether an answer is true of a particular individual

A method that encourages honest answers is called the **randomized-response method** (Kolata, 1987). With this technique, the person answering the question is guaranteed anonymity because he or she uses some random device to determine how to answer. Suppose you want to know how many people cheated in a course last term. You ask the subjects a question that has a true or false answer and have them flip a coin. If the answer to the question is true (if they cheated), they are instructed to answer no, regardless of what the coin says. If the answer is false (if they did not cheat) and the coin is heads, they are to say yes. If the answer is false (if they did not cheat) and the coin is tails, they are to say no.

It can be shown that the actual probability of the behavior in question is given by the following equation:

$$P(T) = 1 - [2 \times P(Y)]$$

That is, the probability of the behavior is one minus twice the probability of a yes response.

Because the person answering the questionnaire is the only one who knows whether the coin was heads or tails, there is no way of knowing whether that answer is true for that person (whether the person actually cheated). Also, a person for whom the answer is true will always say no. (The cheaters will always say no.) Further, all of the people who say yes actually did not cheat.

There are two drawbacks to this procedure. First, the person answering the questionnaire must understand the instructions and believe that there is no trick to them. Second, because flipping a coin introduces randomness into the process, the results have more variability than a direct question. Nevertheless, the randomized-response method can be useful when one wishes to investigate a behavior about which people are likely to lie.   ❑

SUMMARY

1. Surveys are useful ways to determine the attitudes of people on particular questions, to determine the effect of some natural event, or to look for patterns of cause and effect among many variables.

2. Designing a survey is a complex procedure that shares components of research design and written communication.

3. The first step in designing a questionnaire is to determine its purpose.

4. Questions may be open-ended or closed-ended. Each has advantages and disadvantages.

5. Questions should address a single issue per item, avoid bias, offer clear alternatives, and take into account the tendency toward social desirability.

6. A common response format is the Likert scale, a rating scale that asks for amount of agreement or disagreement with the item.

7. Before collecting the data it is important to decide how the data will be analyzed.

8. Methods of survey administration include face-to-face, written, computerized, and telephone. Each has advantages and disadvantages.

9. Written surveys may be administered in groups, dropped off for individual completion, or mailed.

10. Most researchers require at least a 50% return rate before they consider a survey representative.

11. Surveys may use haphazard samples, purposive samples, convenience samples, or probability samples.

12. Random sampling has a particular scientific meaning and requires considerable care to perform.

13. The sampling frame is the population that is available and actually sampled. Each individual that falls in the sampling frame is called an element.

14. Probability samples include systematic samples, simple random samples, stratified random samples, and cluster samples. Systematic samples use a probability rule for sampling that is not random. Simple random samples are feasible only with relatively small populations. Stratified random samples permit the researcher to ensure that various segments of the population are represented proportionately in the sample. Cluster samples are commonly used with large surveys.

15. Interviewing is a complex skill that requires considerable training.

16. The randomized-response technique, in which it is impossible to identify whether an answer is true of a particular individual, can be used to reduce the social-desirability bias.

Suggestions for Further Reading

FINK, A., & KOSEKOFF, J. (1985). *How to conduct surveys: A step-by-step guide.* Beverly Hills, CA: Sage. A clear, practical guide to designing and conducting surveys.

FOWLER, F. J. (1988). *Survey research methods* (rev. ed.). Newbury Park, CA: Sage. A concise description of survey and questionnaire techniques.

JUDD, C. M., SMITH, E. R., & KIDDER, L. H. (1991). *Research methods in social relations* (6th ed.). New York: Holt, Rinehart & Winston. This book has several chapters devoted to nonexperimental techniques: observational methods, questionnaires and interviews, archival research, and sampling of individuals from a population.

NEUMAN, W. L. (1991). *Social research methods: Qualitative and quantitative approaches.* Needham Heights, MA: Allyn and Bacon. Helpful discussion of advantages and disadvantages of various types of questionnaires and other issues of survey design.

A CASE IN POINT

Campus Security Survey

On pp. 214–215 is a survey of campus security. Adapt it to your campus. Are the questions unambiguous? Do they cover the appropriate alternatives? What is the purpose of asking students to rank various aspects of campus life that they dislike in this survey? Should there be open-ended as well as closed-ended questions? In what order should the questions be? Are there any other items that should be included to classify respondents? How should the questionnaire be administered—by interview, to individuals or groups, by mail? How should the respondents be chosen—randomly, all students in randomly chosen classes, all students in the population? Will the questionnaire yield information that will be useful? What should be done with the information when gathered?

READING BETWEEN THE LINES

8.1 ORCHESTRA CONDUCTORS LIVE LONGER

A study found that orchestra conductors live longer than average and concluded that the life that conductors lead somehow enables them to live longer. The important factor could

CAMPUS SECURITY SURVEY

We are taking a survey of things about the campus that students like and dislike.

Are you a student at Pitt?

Yes _____ No _____ (If answer is no, STOP HERE and return the questionnaire.)

If answer is yes, please check the appropriate box.

Year in school:

1. Freshman ....[   ]
2. Sophomore ....[   ]
3. Junior ....[   ]
4. Senior..[   ]
5. Graduate/Professional..[   ]
6. Other ....[   ]   (1) _____

Sex:

1. Male [   ]
2. Female [   ]   (2) _____

What are your living arrangements?

1. Live in a Pitt dorm...[   ]
2. Live off campus, but within walking distance ....[   ]
3. Commute by car or public transportation.........................[   ]   (3) _____

Please list some things that you DISLIKE about the Pitt campus.

1. _____

2. _____

3. _____

4. _____

5. _____

6. _____

7. _____

Following are some things you may DISLIKE about the Pitt campus. Please rank them from 1, meaning dislike most, to 9, meaning dislike least. (Use each number only once.)

Not enough community activities _____   (4) _____
Not enough campus activities _____   (5) _____
Too far between classes _____   (6) _____

Parking problems _____   (7) _____
Concerns about personal safety _____   (8) _____
Difficulty in finding a place to relax between classes _____   (9) _____
Inconvenient library hours _____   (10) _____
Not enough restaurant choices _____   (11) _____
Not enough recreational facilities _____   (12) _____

Please answer the following questions on the accompanying scales.

I feel safe in walking on the campus at night.
   Agree 1 _____ 2 _____ 3 _____ 4 _____ 5 _____ 6 _____ 7 _____ Disagree   (13) _____

I expect to be a victim of a crime on campus this term.
   Agree 1 _____ 2 _____ 3 _____ 4 _____ 5 _____ 6 _____ 7 _____ Disagree   (14) _____

I am considering transferring to another school because of the likelihood of being a victim of crime.
   Agree 1 _____ 2 _____ 3 _____ 4 _____ 5 _____ 6 _____ 7 _____ Disagree   (15) _____

I feel safe inside campus buildings.
   Agree 1 _____ 2 _____ 3 _____ 4 _____ 5 _____ 6 _____ 7 _____ Disagree   (16) _____

My parents are concerned about my safety while I am at school.
   Agree 1 _____ 2 _____ 3 _____ 4 _____ 5 _____ 6 _____ 7 _____ Disagree   (17) _____

I feel that my safety is threatened most by students, as opposed to persons from off campus.
   Agree 1 _____ 2 _____ 3 _____ 4 _____ 5 _____ 6 _____ 7 _____ Disagree   (18) _____

Following are some possible ways of increasing campus security. Please rank them from 1, indicating most preferred, to 8, indicating least preferred. (Use each number only once.)

Involve local police in investigating campus crime _____   (19) _____
Increase patrols by campus police _____   (20) _____
Provide an escort service _____   (21) _____
Reduce the number of entrances to buildings _____   (22) _____
Require identification for entering buildings after
   a certain hour _____   (23) _____
Lock all buildings after a certain hour _____   (24) _____
Have a curfew for female students _____   (25) _____
Have a curfew for male students _____   (26) _____

Which of these alternatives, if any, would be UNACCEPTABLE to you?
(Be specific.) _____

If you have a suggestion that is not listed above, please list it here.
(Be specific.) _____

be remaining active throughout life, because maestros tend to retire late or not at all. Or it could be the effect of making music. Can you think of any other explanation for the longevity of orchestra conductors?   ■

✓ EXERCISES

8.1   CHOOSING RESEARCH METHODS
For each of the following research problems, choose the method that would be most appropriate for studying it: (1) questionnaire, (2) naturalistic observation, (3) participant observation, (4) experiment. Use each method once.

a. Relation of eating, talking, and restlessness during a movie to age, sex, size, and composition of groups in a movie theater.

b. Effect of altering seating arrangements in a library on the amount of studying, socializing, and sleeping done by patrons.

c. How a psychologist uses a psychotherapy organization as a cover for her authoritarian political agenda.

d. The relationships among age, income, and other demographic factors and watching rented videos at home.

8.2   THE EFFECT OF SAMPLE SIZE ON SAMPLING ERROR
Before doing this exercise, you should read the section of Appendix A on sampling distributions. This exercise is based on the computer program listed in the Instructor's Manual. The program takes samples from one of two populations. Both populations have what are called *rectangular distributions*. That is, the distribution has the same height at all locations, so a graph of the distribution will be rectangular. The mean of the first distribution is 17, and the standard deviation is 9.7 (see Figure 8.1a). The second distribution has the same shape and the same standard deviation, but its mean is 22 (see Figure 8.1b).

The computer program will draw samples of various sizes from the distributions. These samples are actually being drawn randomly by the computer from the population. So the first point to notice is that the sampling distributions will not conform exactly to the shape predicted by the theory. They will differ from the theoretical shape because of chance factors.

At first you will be given a sample of size 1; that is, a single individual will be sampled from the distribution. The values will be built up into a sampling distribution. Notice that the first sampling distribution will look more or less rectangular. Any difference between your distribution and a perfectly rectangular distribution is purely the result of chance.

Next, you will see another sampling distribution from a rectangular population with a mean 5 points higher than the first. It will overlap the first one. Where the distributions overlap, the data points will be indicated by a plus sign. Notice that if you were given a score based on a single individual you would not be able to predict very well which distribution it came from.

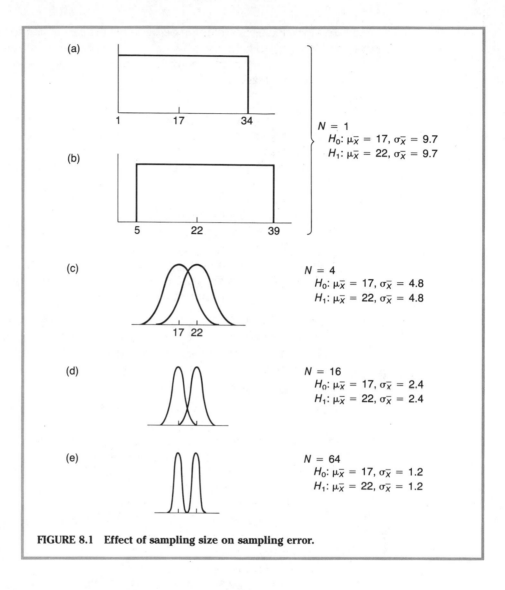

(a)

1   17   34

$N = 1$
$H_0: \mu_{\bar{x}} = 17, \sigma_{\bar{x}} = 9.7$
$H_1: \mu_{\bar{x}} = 22, \sigma_{\bar{x}} = 9.7$

(b)

5   22   39

(c)

17 22

$N = 4$
$H_0: \mu_{\bar{x}} = 17, \sigma_{\bar{x}} = 4.8$
$H_1: \mu_{\bar{x}} = 22, \sigma_{\bar{x}} = 4.8$

(d)

$N = 16$
$H_0: \mu_{\bar{x}} = 17, \sigma_{\bar{x}} = 2.4$
$H_1: \mu_{\bar{x}} = 22, \sigma_{\bar{x}} = 2.4$

(e)

$N = 64$
$H_0: \mu_{\bar{x}} = 17, \sigma_{\bar{x}} = 1.2$
$H_1: \mu_{\bar{x}} = 22, \sigma_{\bar{x}} = 1.2$

FIGURE 8.1   Effect of sampling size on sampling error.

The next two sampling distributions will be based on samples of size 4. (Figure 8.1c shows the theoretical shape of these distributions.) You will note two things about these distributions. First, they are beginning to look like normal (bell-shaped) distributions. Second, their standard errors are smaller. Because the sample size is four times as large, the standard error will be half as large. (As discussed in Chapter 6, the standard error is inversely proportional to the square root of N. The square root of 4 is 2, and the square root of 1 is 1.)

Successive pairs of distributions will have sample sizes four times as large as the previous pair, and thus will have standard errors half as large. Notice that the overlap between the distributions becomes less and less as sample size increases. (See Figures 8.1d and 8.1e.) The important point to be derived from this demonstration is that if you know that you have sampled from one of two distributions that have different means but don't know which one, your ability to guess which distribution your sample comes from increases as sample size increases.

REQUIRED:
  a. Define *sample mean, sampling distribution,* and *standard error of the mean.*
  b. How does the standard error of the mean vary with sample size? (Describe in words and with an equation.)
  c. What importance does the concept of sampling distribution have for doing experiments?

8.3 RANDOMIZED-RESPONSE QUESTIONNAIRE

The following exercise illustrates the randomized-response method of obtaining information about behaviors for which social desirability is likely to influence the results. This exercise should be done only with the supervision of your instructor. Administer the following questionnaire to two groups of students using the following control instructions and randomized-response instructions.

CONTROL INSTRUCTIONS
The purpose of this questionnaire is to determine the frequency of certain types of cheating. Please indicate which, if any, of the following you did during the last term. Your answers will be analyzed anonymously.

RANDOMIZED-RESPONSE INSTRUCTIONS
The purpose of this questionnaire is to determine the frequency of certain types of cheating. Please indicate which, if any, of the following you did during the last term.

  The procedure we are asking you to follow will make it absolutely impossible for anyone, including the person scoring the answers, to determine whether you actually cheated.
  1. Take a coin from your pocket and cup it in your hands.
  2. Shake the coin up and down for a while until you are sure that you cannot predict whether it is heads or tails. Then peek at it so that no one else can see it. Remember whether it is heads or tails.
  3. Read the next question.
  4. If the answer is TRUE, say NO, regardless of whether the coin is heads or tails.
  5. If the answer is FALSE and the coin is HEADS, say YES. Otherwise, say NO.
  6. Go back to step 2 and repeat the procedure until you have answered all of the questions.
If you have any questions, please ask the person administering the questionnaire.

CHEATING QUESTIONNAIRE
Answer the following questions with respect to *last term.*
  1. I used a crib sheet during an exam. (Y/N) _____
  2. I looked at someone else's paper during an exam. (Y/N) _____
  3. I received a copy of a test before it was given. (Y/N) _____
  4. I turned in a paper that someone else had written. (Y/N) _____
  5. I received help on a take-home exam. (Y/N) _____

6. I had someone else take an exam for me. (Y/N) _____
7. I turned in homework that someone else had done. (Y/N) _____

CODING THE ANSWERS

For the randomized response method, the true probability of cheating can be calculated by means of the following equation:

$$P(T) = 1 - [2 \times P(Y)]$$

That is, the probability of cheating is one minus two times the probability of a yes response. For example, if there were 23 yeses on the first question out of 54 students answering, then the true probability of cheating is

$$P(T) = 1 - [2 \times (23/54)]$$

or

$$P(T) = 1 - (2 \times .43)$$
$$= 1 - .86$$
$$= .14$$

The principal drawbacks to this method are that the instructions are more difficult to understand and flipping a coin introduces randomness, making the answers less statistically reliable.

QUESTION: Which is more important in this case, maximizing statistical reliability or reducing the effect of social desirability?

8.4   RANDOM SAMPLING

REQUIRED:

   a. Using the procedures outlined in this chapter, draw a random sample of size 10 from the population data set in Appendix C. List the identification numbers for each subject in the order obtained.

   b. Using the corresponding data in column A for each subject selected, calculate the sample mean and standard deviation.

OPTIONAL:

   c. Compare the sample mean and standard deviation with the population mean and standard deviation (listed in the Instructor's Manual). What do you conclude?

8.5   STRATIFIED RANDOM SAMPLING

REQUIRED:

   a. Using the procedures outlined in this chapter, draw a stratified random sample of size 20 from the population data set in Appendix C. Include 12 females and 8 males in your sample. List the identification numbers for each subject in the order obtained.

b. Using the corresponding data in column F for each subject selected, calculate the sample mean and standard deviation.

OPTIONAL:

c. Compare the sample mean and standard deviation with the population mean and standard deviation (listed in the Instructor's Manual). What do you conclude?

8.6   PROPORTIONAL ALLOCATION IN STRATIFIED SAMPLING

The population of undergraduate college students in a small state college is divided into four strata: 1,156 freshmen, 918 sophomores, 748 juniors, and 578 seniors. A sample size of 100 is to be selected, using stratified random sampling with proportional allocation.

REQUIRED: Distribute the sample among the four classes, or strata, using proportional allocation.

8.7   SAMPLE SIZE AND SAMPLE ERROR (MANUAL VERSION)

REQUIRED:

a. Draw 10 random samples of size 1 from the population data set in Appendix C. For each subject selected, list the corresponding data from column G.

b. Draw 10 random samples of size 4 from the population. For each subject selected, list the corresponding data from column G.

c. Calculate the mean for each sample selected in steps a and b.

d. Group the 10 sample means from steps a and b into side-by-side histograms. Which sampling distribution has less variability? Why?

e. The mean and standard deviation of the population are listed in the Instructor's Manual. What are the theoretical means and standard deviations for each of your sampling distributions? How do they compare with the actual data?   ❏

True Experiments, Part 1: Single-Factor Designs

As we saw in Chapter 6, a key concept in designing experiments is that of control. The experimenter seeks to control as many of the potential threats to validity as possible. When a sufficient number of these are under control, the study is a true experiment. A true experiment is one in which the experimenter has reason to believe that he or she has control over both the assignment of subjects to conditions and the presentation of conditions to subjects. When a study does not meet the requirements of a true experiment, it is called a quasi experiment. The word *quasi* means *as if* or *to a degree*. Thus, a quasi experiment is one that resembles an experiment but lacks at least one of its defining characteristics.

We will begin this chapter by defining true experiments and quasi experiments and discussing their differences. Then we will define the basic elements of a valid experimental design, mention some designs that should be avoided, and finally, describe some representative experimental designs.

TRUE EXPERIMENTS VERSUS QUASI EXPERIMENTS

true experiment research procedure in which the scientist has complete control over all aspects

In a **true experiment,** the experimenter has complete control over the experiment: the who, what, when, where, and how. Control over the who of the experiment means that the experimenter can assign subjects to conditions randomly. Recall that random assignment is preferred because it allows one to conclude that any other variable could be confounded with the independent variable only by chance. No other method of assignment of subjects to conditions permits such a conclusion. Control over the what, when, where, and how of the experiment means that the experimenter has complete control over the way the experiment is to be conducted.

quasi experiment
research procedure in which the scientist must select subjects for different conditions from preexisting groups

A **quasi experiment,** on the other hand, is an experiment in which the investigator lacks the degree of control over the conditions that is possible in a true experiment. The most important difference is that whereas it is possible to *assign* subjects to conditions in a true experiment, in a quasi experiment it is necessary to *select* subjects for the different conditions from previously existing groups.

For example, you may wish to study the effect of number of food pellets on the rate at which rats learn a maze. This situation would permit the design of a true experiment, because you could arbitrarily assign some rats to the large-reward condition and others to the small-reward condition. Assume that before the experiment the rats belonged to a homogeneous population of rats. For experimental purposes, you assign the rats to groups that you create according to your needs.

On the other hand, if you were interested in sex differences in detecting hidden figures, you would have to conduct a quasi experiment, because you cannot assign subjects to the two conditions, male and female. Here the researcher cannot create groups of males and females but instead selects members from preexisting groups.

Quasi experiments are sometimes called *ex post facto,* or after the fact, experiments because the experiment is conducted after the groups have been formed. In the case of a quasi experiment with sex as the independent variable, the experiment takes place long after the subjects become males or females. If you performed an experiment using preexisting classes of students, the two classes would be an ex post facto variable because the classes were formed before you did the experiment.

Another way to look at the difference between true experiments and quasi experiments is to note that in true experiments we *manipulate* variables, whereas in quasi experiments we *observe* categories of subjects. When we take two preexisting groups and consider a difference between them to be the independent variable, we are not manipulating a variable but simply labeling groups according to what we think is the important difference between them. The true difference between them for our experiment may be quite different from what we think it is. If we find that two different socioeconomic groups differ on some measure, the difference may be caused not by the socioeconomic difference itself but by cultural differences between the two socioeconomic groups. By calling the difference socioeconomic, we may obscure the fact that the difference is actually a difference in need achievement or perceived helplessness or religion.

When we present some independent variable to two preexisting groups, more is involved than measuring their behavior. We have the additional problem of not knowing whether the difference in behavior was caused by differences between the groups or by the independent variable. If we studied the effects of two different teaching methods on learning in two preexisting classes, we would not be sure whether any differences in learning resulted from the teaching methods or from preexisting differences between the classes.

A true experiment, then, permits the experimenter the greatest degree of control in ruling out alternative hypotheses, or alternative independent variables, as being the cause of the difference between two groups or conditions. This permits the most powerful use of Mill's method of differences (discussed in Chapter 2, and also in Chapter 5), because all other potential independent variables have been eliminated by randomly assigning subjects to conditions. A quasi experiment leaves open the possibility that other differences exist between the experimental and control conditions, and thus permits other potential differences to remain.

It is possible to have one experimental variable and one quasi-experimental variable in an experiment. For example, in studying the effects of two different teaching methods on classroom learning, we might be interested in whether slow learners differ from fast learners in their response to the teaching methods. The two teaching methods would constitute a true experimental variable, assuming we assigned students to sections, and the classification into slow and fast learners would constitute a quasi-experimental variable.

The degree of control that is possible varies from one type of investigation to another. The fact that we are discussing true experiments first does not mean that true experiments are necessarily better than other types of investigations. Rather, it reflects the fact that as the degree of control that the researcher can exercise decreases, the threats to the validity of the conclusions increase. Other things being equal, one would choose a true experiment over a quasi experiment and a quasi experiment over a nonexperimental method. Things are seldom equal, though. Many social-psychological phenomena are difficult to bring into the laboratory in a realistic fashion. Therefore, a field study may be preferable to an experiment, because the advantage of realism outweighs the loss of control. Nevertheless, you should try first to design a true experimental study and use the other designs only when you believe that the gain in validity will be worth the loss of control.

FACTORS, LEVELS, CONDITIONS, AND TREATMENTS

Up to this point, we have simply used the term *independent variable* to talk about what the experimenter manipulates in an experiment. Now we need to introduce some other terms that are often used in discussing independent variables.

factors
the independent
variables of an
experiment

The independent variables of an experiment are often called the **factors** of the experiment. Suppose we are doing an experiment on the effect of human handling and of the type of cage in which they are raised on the emotionality of rats. Rats would either be handled or not handled and raised either in a standard laboratory cage or in a large cage with lots of added items for the rats to play with. We would say that there were two independent variables: handling and type of cage. Handling and cage type, therefore, would be the two factors of this experiment. An experiment always has at least one factor, or independent variable; otherwise it wouldn't be an experiment! In order to have an experiment, it is necessary to vary some independent variable, or some factor.

level
in an experiment, a
particular value of
an independent
variable

Each of the two independent variables in our example would have two **levels.** A level is a particular value of an independent variable. An independent variable always has at least two levels, because if it didn't it wouldn't be a variable! The two levels of handling in this example would be handling versus no handling, and the two levels of cage type would be normal versus enriched. It is possible for an independent variable to have any number of levels, of course: The rats could be handled either 0, 10, 20, 30, or any other number of minutes per day, giving that many different levels of the independent variable of handling.

condition
a group or
treatment in
an experiment

The term **condition** is the broadest of the terms used to discuss independent variables. It refers to a particular way in which subjects are treated. In a between-subjects experiment, such as the present example, the experimental conditions are the same as the groups. Any one rat in this example was either handled or not handled, and was in one of two cage types. In other words, each rat experienced only one treatment or condition. In the present example, we might speak of a particular rat as being in the enriched, nonhandled condition or group. When it is possible for each subject in an experiment to experience every condition, then we speak only of various conditions, not groups, because there is only one group of subjects and that group experiences all conditions. There would be as many conditions as there are different ways in which subjects are treated. Thus, there could be many conditions in a complicated experiment.

treatment
another word
for a condition
of an experiment

Treatment is just another word for condition. You should be aware of this usage, however, as you may run across the term *treatment effect* in statistics. It is a statistical test of the effect of various conditions of the experiment.

SOME DESIGNS TO AVOID

In this chapter we will consider a number of examples of designs that are appropriate to the particular problem they address. However, before we consider good designs, let us look at some designs that should be avoided. These undesirable designs are weak in that they do not control for various

TABLE 9.1 ONE-GROUP POSTTEST-ONLY DESIGN		
	TREATMENT	TEST
Single group	Yes	Yes

alternative explanations of the results. They all fail to control for certain threats to validity discussed in Chapter 5.

■ The One-Group Posttest-Only Design

one-group posttest-only design
research design that measures the behavior of a single group of subjects after the treatment only

The **one-group posttest-only design** is a simple one in which a group of subjects is given a treatment and then tested on some dependent variable (see Table 9.1).

Suppose you wanted to test the effectiveness of est (Erhard Seminars Training), a program in which people attend a series of lectures and group activities, some of which are humiliating and exhausting. In order to evaluate the effect of the training, you decide to survey the participants. You find that most of them say that the experience was worthwhile and that they feel better about themselves than they did before the training. After a little reflection, you realize that the results of your survey are nearly worthless. Although the people report that they feel better than they did before the training, you have no measures of how they felt before. Therefore, you cannot determine if they changed. Furthermore, even if they did change, you have no assurance that the training itself caused this change. Perhaps the interruption in their routine caused the change. Or perhaps they would have felt better if they had gone to the movies for several evenings and then gone camping for a weekend.

Such a one-group posttest-only design leaves so many threats to validity uncontrolled that it is nearly worthless. Nevertheless, you can certainly recall people who have recommended a product or practice to you on the basis of their experience. Many people in everyday life, as well as some scientists, have used this design.

■ The Posttest-Only Design with Nonequivalent Control Groups

Suppose that you wanted to improve on the study of the effectiveness of est by comparing people who had taken the training with a control group who had not. You might try to find a group of people who matched the est group on as many variables as possible: age, income, education, and so forth. Table 9.2 illustrates this design. Although the design is an improvement over the one-group posttest-only design, it still has a serious flaw. The flaw is that the

TABLE 9.2 Posttest-only design with nonequivalent control groups

	Allocation of Subjects and Groups	Treatment	Test
Group 1	Any method that is *not* random	Yes (or A_1)	Yes
Group 2		No (or A_2)	Yes

nonequivalent control group
a group of subjects that is not randomly selected from the same population as the experimental group

control group is not equivalent in every way to those who took the training. The most important difference is that the test persons had selected themselves for the training and the control groups had not. Thus, we have a **nonequivalent control group** because the two groups were not randomly constituted from the same population.

A nonequivalent control group is better than no control group, but you would have to consider this study a quasi experiment at best, because the subjects were not randomly assigned to groups. The only way you could construct a control group that was equivalent to the est group would be to ask the est organization to provide a list of all people who applied for the training. Then you would randomly place half of them into a control group that would not be allowed to take the training.

■ The One-Group Pretest/Posttest Design

one-group pretest/posttest design
research design that measures the behavior of a single group of subjects both before and after treatment

Another way of improving on the one-group posttest-only design is to take a measure of behavior before the treatment that can be compared with behavior after the treatment. This approach is called the **one-group pretest/posttest design.** In the example of the est study, you might obtain responses of the participants before they took the training to compare with responses after training. Such a design is illustrated in Table 9.3. If you were to use this design in the est study, you would probably find a change in the subjects' reports of their moods, feelings of self-worth, and so forth. You would still have the problem of determining what caused the changes—the est training or some unrelated event. Even if the est procedure did cause the changes, you wouldn't know what aspect of it was responsible. You still wouldn't know if going to the movies for several nights followed by a camping trip might have been equally beneficial. The following example discusses these problems in the context of a different situation.

Suppose a company introduced a new work schedule whereby its employees put in four 10-hour days a week instead of five 8-hour days. If output increased, management would probably credit the new schedule. This conclusion represents an improvement over the one-group posttest-only design, because you know that a behavior change did follow the treatment. However, you have not considered other potential causes of the increase in output, and hence other threats to validity. Workers may have responded to

TABLE 9.3 One-group pretest/posttest design			
	Pretest	Treatment	Posttest
Single group	Yes	Yes	Yes

the attention paid them by management when the change was initiated. Or any number of events may have led to increased productivity: favorable weather conditions that allowed the workers to get to work on time, a change in seasons that made the plant more comfortable, or a favorable response to a new supervisor. These occurrences represent threats to internal validity: The change was caused by a variable other than the one management thought to be responsible. Threats to external validity could arise from the possibility that these workers are young and like long hours, whereas older workers might have preferred shorter days.

This study would have been better designed by forming two groups through random allocation of workers to different schedules so that one group would remain on the old schedule as a control group. This control would have eliminated the threats to internal validity. Random allocation of workers to two groups may not be possible, however. In that event, if the company had two plants, one could be switched to the four-day week while the other is kept on the five-day week. Productivity in the two plants could then be compared. This example is a nonequivalent-control-group design. Differences between the workers at the two plants or in the plants themselves may account for the results instead of the work schedule. The addition of a nonequivalent control group to a pretest/posttest design improves the control sufficiently that the design may be considered a quasi experiment. Chapter 12 will discuss a number of quasi-experimental designs.

THE BASIC ELEMENTS OF A VALID EXPERIMENTAL DESIGN

Chapter 5 discussed types of validity and the many threats to validity that exist, and Chapter 6 discussed methods of control that are available to improve the validity of an experiment. In this chapter, we begin to consider some specific experimental designs as examples of ways of achieving control over threats to validity. You should keep in mind a point made previously, that designing an experiment is an exercise in problem solving. When threats to validity are adequately controlled for, the experiment has been designed. At the same time you should realize that no design can rule out all threats to validity for all time. For example, as we said in Chapter 5, societal changes since the "dirty word" study was conducted have reduced the external validity of that experiment.

TABLE 9.4 Basic elements of good experimental design

	Allocation	Treatment	Test
Condition 1	*Either* random allocation of subjects to conditions *or* all	Yes (or A_1)	Yes
Condition 2	subjects experience both conditions	No (or A_2)	Yes

Even though there can be no perfect experiment, two particular elements of design provide control over so many different threats to validity that they are basic to all good experimental designs. They are (1) the existence of a control group or a control condition and (2) the random allocation of subjects to groups. Both of these methods of control were discussed in Chapter 6. (If the experiment is a within-subjects design, each subject experiences all conditions, so random allocation of subjects to conditions is not applicable. In such experiments, the subjects should experience the conditions either in random order or in counterbalanced order.)

These two basic elements of good experimental design are illustrated in Table 9.4, which represents a simple experiment with two conditions. If this is taken to represent a between-subjects experiment, then different subjects would be randomly allocated to the two conditions. This allocation assures that the groups will be equal in all respects, except as they may differ by chance. If this is a within-subjects experiment, then all subjects experience both conditions: A subject's behavior in one condition is compared with his or her behavior in another condition. Either way, we have reason to believe that the subjects in both conditions were equal to begin with, which enables us to compare their performance between experimental and control conditions. Any difference in behavior can be attributed to differences between the two conditions.

WITHIN-SUBJECTS DESIGNS

Recall that Chapter 6 discussed, as a specific strategy of achieving control, using a subject as his or her own control. Recall also that this strategy is desirable when the effect of one condition will not carry over to, or contaminate, the other condition or conditions of the experiment to a serious degree. The first group of designs we will discuss in this chapter makes use of this strategy. Because the same subjects experience all conditions in within-subjects designs, it is often necessary to exercise some ingenuity in controlling for possible carry-over effects.

■ Controlling for Order and Sequence Effects

In within-subjects experiments, because a subject experiences more than one experimental condition, the possibility exists that some variable may influence the data as a result of the repeated testing. Some of these possible variables are related to the subjects; others are related to the conditions of testing. The subjects may get fatigued during the session, or the first condition may be tested before lunch when subjects are hungry and the second after lunch when they are sleepy. Ordinarily, experimenters avoid within-subjects designs if they believe that order or sequence effects will be substantial. Then a between-subjects design is probably more appropriate.

order effects
changes in a subject's performance resulting from the position is which a condition appears in an experiment

sequence effects
changes in a subject's performance resulting from interactions among the conditions themselves

Before we discuss ways of controlling for these problems, let us note the distinction between order effects and sequence effects. **Order effects** are those that result from the (ordinal) position in which the condition appears in an experiment, regardless of the specific condition that is experienced. The best example of an order effect is the warm-up or practice effect that often occurs in experiments on learning. Whichever condition is presented first will show poorer performance than later conditions simply because the subjects have not warmed up to the task. **Sequence effects,** on the other hand, depend on an interaction between the specific conditions of the experiment. For example, in an experiment on judging the heaviness of lifted weights, there is likely to be a contrast effect such that a light weight will feel even lighter if it follows a heavy one, and vice versa. Order effects are more general and result from warm-up, learning, fatigue, and the like. Sequence effects are interactions among the conditions themselves.

The difference between order and sequence effects can be seen by referring ahead to page 231, where the six possible ways of ordering three different conditions, A, B, and C, are presented. Note that Subjects 1 and 3 experience condition C in the same ordinal position, namely third, and so have the same order effect for C. Subjects 2 and 3, however, both experience condition C following A, and so have the same sequence effect for C (with respect to A).

In general, one controls for order effects by arranging that each condition occur equally often in each ordinal position—first, second, third, and so on. Sequence effects are generally controlled for by arranging that each condition follow every other condition equally often. Note that these controls are not the same. You should also note that the various methods of controlling for order and sequence effects are effective only under certain conditions, which we will discuss shortly. However, if you are using a within-subjects design, you are wise to control as effectively as possible for order and sequence effects.

Two basic strategies are available for controlling order and sequence effects. The first, and preferable, one is to arrange the order of conditions in such a way that order and sequence effects are controlled *within subjects.* When this is not possible, you must control for order and sequence effects between subjects.

Within-Subjects Control of Order and Sequence

Controlling for order and sequence effects within subjects is possible when each subject receives each condition. Randomization can be used when each condition is given several times to each subject or when a sufficient number of subjects will be tested so that one particular sequence is unlikely to have much influence on the outcome. Experiments in learning or perception typically involve presenting each stimulus many times to the subject. The best procedure is to randomize the order of conditions for each subject. Although you might prefer to be told a magic number of subjects or repetitions that are sufficient for randomizing to be effective, this determination remains a matter for your judgment.

block randomization
control procedure in which the order of conditions is randomized, but with each condition being presented once before any condition is repeated

A useful variation on randomizing to control for order and sequence effects is **block randomization.** Block randomization means that the order of conditions is randomized, with the restriction that each condition is presented once before any condition is repeated. If there are four conditions and each one is to be represented twice, block randomization might give you the following sequence: BCAD, ADCB. Here each of the four conditions is presented once in random order within each of two blocks. Thus there is less chance that unwanted sequence effects would be produced by orders of the following type: AABDBCCD. Block randomization is particularly useful if you want to present each condition twice and your experiment requires two sessions.

reverse counterbalancing
method of control in which conditions are presented in order the first time and then in reverse order

When relatively few subjects will be tested and you have several conditions that can be presented only a few times, you must begin to exercise ingenuity. A typical example is the instance in which you have three conditions, each presented twice. In this situation, it is common to use **reverse counterbalancing** to control for order effects. The three conditions are presented in order the first time and then in reverse order. This technique is known as ABCCBA sequence, or ABBA for short. Counterbalancing works well when you suspect that the possible confounding variables will act in a linear manner over conditions. Figure 9.1 gives an example of ABCCBA order in which there is a linear effect. The order effect produces a large increase in the dependent variable that, since the effect is linear, averages out. The counterbalancing has done its job.

On the other hand, suppose a variable has a large effect in the early part of the experiment but a smaller effect later on. The best example is a warm-up, or practice, effect that may occur in the early part of an experiment and be less important later. Figure 9.2 shows an example in which there is a large practice effect. Here you can easily see that counterbalancing has not been effective in eliminating the order effect. One way of improving such an experiment is to provide enough practice beforehand that the practice effect is eliminated.

Note that counterbalancing may do an incomplete job of controlling sequence effects in an ABCDDCBA experiment: The B condition follows A once and C once but never follows D or itself.

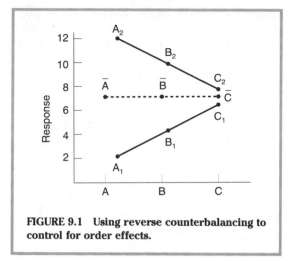

FIGURE 9.1 Using reverse counterbalancing to control for order effects.

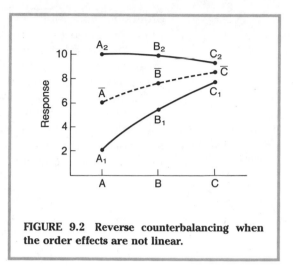

FIGURE 9.2 Reverse counterbalancing when the order effects are not linear.

Within-Groups Control of Order and Sequence

If presenting each condition enough times to randomize the order is not possible, or if counterbalancing within subjects does not seem appropriate, you must leave order and sequence confounded with condition *within subjects* and you must control for order and sequence *within groups*. For example, suppose you have three conditions and each one is to be presented only once to each subject. Then if you have six subjects, or $6N$ subjects, you can control for order and sequence in the following way:

SUBJECT	ORDER
1	ABC
2	ACB
3	BAC
4	BCA
5	CAB
6	CBA

Both order and sequence are completely counterbalanced within the group, because each condition occurs an equal number of times in each rank-order position and follows every other condition an equal number of times. Thus, you have controlled for order and sequence within a group of subjects, even though every subject experiences a biased sequence. The disadvantage of this method of counterbalancing is that as the number of conditions increases, the number of orders required increases geometrically. You have 2 possible orders of 2 conditions (AB and BA), 6 orders of 3 conditions (as in the previous example), 24 orders of 4 conditions, and 120 orders of 5 conditions! Even for only 4 conditions you would need 24 subjects to control for order and sequence.

It is possible to control for the order in which each condition occurs with fewer subjects than would be required by complete counterbalancing if you give up the requirement that each condition follow every other condition an equal number of times. You would be controlling for order, but not for sequence, of conditions. This type of incomplete counterbalancing is called the **Latin square** technique, after the ancient puzzle of finding ways to arrange a number of letters in a matrix such that each letter occurs once and only once in each row and column:

Latin square
control procedure in which each subject experiences each condition in a different order from other subjects

SUBJECT	RANK ORDER			
	1	2	3	4
1	A	B	C	D
2	B	C	D	A
3	C	D	A	B
4	D	A	B	C

If the letters represent conditions, the columns represent order, and the rows represent subjects, you are controlling for order effects with the Latin square counterbalancing technique.

A disadvantage of the Latin square technique is that sequence is not controlled for. Notice in the previous example that B always follows A, C always follows B, and so forth. Thus sequence is always perfectly confounded with order in this particular Latin square. If there were a contrast effect between conditions, this design would not control for it. However, you can control for sequence effects of the immediately preceding condition by using particular sets of Latin squares known as *balanced squares*. In the balanced Latin square, each condition is immediately preceded once by every other condition (W.A. Wagenaar, 1969), as in the following example:

SUBJECT	RANK ORDER			
	1	2	3	4
1	A	B	C	D
2	B	D	A	C
3	C	A	D	B
4	D	C	B	A

When you can assume that the contrast effects are primarily between pairs of conditions, the balanced Latin square will be effective.

The advantage of the Latin square technique over complete counterbalancing is that it permits greater flexibility in choosing the number of subjects to be tested. Instead of needing 24 or 48 subjects in a four-condition experiment, for example, you can use only 4 or 8. This advantage is great enough to outweigh the disadvantage of leaving small sequence effects uncontrolled.

We turn now to some representative within-subjects designs that offer typical solutions to the problems of validity and control discussed in Chapters 5 and 6. The designs presented here do not constitute all that are possible, because an indefinite number of designs exists. These designs are simply the most common solutions to common experimental problems.

■ Two Conditions, Tested within Subjects

two-conditions design
the simplest research design, involving only two conditions

The **two-conditions design** is the simplest possible true-experiment design, because it has only two conditions and each subject serves as its own control. This design is illustrated in Table 9.5. The two conditions are labeled Condition 1 and Condition 2, although one of them may be considered the experimental condition and the other the control condition. All subjects experience both conditions in counterbalanced order. In spite of its simplicity, this design is not used as often as one might expect, for two reasons. First, many experiments involve more than two conditions. Second, there is the possibility of carry-over effects from one condition to the other.

An experiment that serves as an example of this design is one by John Marshall and Philip Teitelbaum (1974) on the phenomenon of sensory neglect. Research has shown that damage to both sides of a small part of the brain known as the lateral hypothalamus produces a severe impairment of feeding and drinking. In addition to these motivational effects, there is interference with the ability to respond to sensory stimulation after this damage. Marshall and Teitelbaum were interested in the contribution of the sensory neglect to the motivational deficit.

Recall that the brain is approximately bilaterally symmetrical; that is, the left half is the mirror image of the right. Marshall and Teitelbaum destroyed the lateral hypothalamus on one side of the brains of 12 rats. When

TABLE 9.5 Two-conditions design, tested within subjects

	Allocation	Treatment	Test
Condition 1 (or experimental)	All subjects experience both conditions in counterbalanced order	Condition 1 (or experimental treatment)	Yes
Condition 2 (or control)		Condition 2 (or control treatment)	Yes

the rats had recovered from the operation, they were tested for their responsiveness to stimuli that were presented to one side or the other of their bodies. Visual, tactile, and olfactory stimuli were used. In all cases, the rats responded only when the stimuli were presented to the same side that had received brain damage. (Each side of the brain controls the opposite side of the body.) When the rats were stimulated on the opposite side, they did not respond.

Thus, from the design point of view, the unilateral damage allowed each animal to be used as its own control. One side of the brain was a control for the other, ruling out differences between subjects as a possible source of error. For example, one of the tests used was whether the rat would attack a mouse presented to the brain-damaged side. (Some rats will kill mice, and others will not.) By using each rat as its own control, the experimenters were able to say that all rats that were mouse killers attacked mice presented to the undamaged side of the brain but did not react to those presented to the damaged side.

■ Multiple Conditions, Tested within Subjects

**multiple-
conditions
design**
research design
that involves more
than two
conditions

Psychology experiments generally employ more than two conditions. The first reason researchers choose a **multiple-conditions design** is that seldom do they wish to ask a simple yes-or-no question. Usually they want to compare several variables or treatments for effectiveness. For example, the question may be which of three different types of psychotherapy is most effective.

A second reason for conducting multiple-conditions experiments is to determine the shape of the function that relates the independent and dependent variables. When experimenters want to know how brightness increases with intensity of a light, they present each of several intensities of the light to a group of subjects. From the responses to the various intensities, they can plot the relation between intensity and brightness. Each intensity is a condition of the experiment.

A third reason for doing multiple-conditions experiments is the presence of more than one rival hypothesis that must be ruled out. Suppose a child has a favorite toy that is fuzzy, colorful, and noisy. If you want to find out which of the three characteristics is responsible for the child's attachment to the toy, you could make up three versions of the same toy, as follows:

A   FUZZY, not colorful, not noisy
B   not fuzzy, COLORFUL, not noisy
C   not fuzzy, not colorful, NOISY

Toy A tests for fuzziness, B for colorfulness, and C for noisiness as the independent variable causing attachment. Because toys A and B are not noisy, they control for noisiness. Similarly, A and C control for colorfulness, and B and C control for fuzziness. To accommodate the three hypotheses, you would need three conditions (toys). Each toy serves as a partial control (condition) for the other hypotheses. In this example, we have varied three independent variables in a single experiment.

Most multiple-conditions experiments are between-subjects experiments, because it is often impossible or inappropriate to expose all subjects to the various conditions. Within-subjects experiments are fairly common, however.

One such experiment is a classic study by Fergus Craik and Endel Tulving (1975), which examined whether different strategies of processing words would affect memory. They flashed words on a screen. Before each word appeared, they asked the subject a question: "Is the word in capital letters?" or "Does the word rhyme with train?" or "Does the word fit in this sentence: 'The girl put the _____ on the table'?" Each of these questions was designed to induce the subjects to adopt a different strategy of processing the word. The first strategy focused on the visual properties of the word, the second on the acoustic properties, and the third on the semantic properties. Craik and Tulving theorized that each successive type of processing would induce greater "depth of processing." Their theory predicted that increasing depth of processing increases memory for words.

Each subject in their study experienced all three types of questions, making this a within-subjects design. The experimenters believed that subjects could adopt different strategies of processing on different trials. The various questions were the independent variables in the study. The questions were randomly varied for each trial. After the words were all presented, the experimenters unexpectedly gave the subjects a list that contained all of the words they had presented along with an equal number of words that they had not presented. They asked the subjects to indicate which words they recognized from the list. The percentage of words recognized varied as a function of the depth of processing induced by the questions. The subjects recognized only 18% of the visually processed words, but they recognized 78% of the acoustically processed and 96% of the semantically processed words.

Table 9.6 indicates schematically the general design of a multiple-conditions, within-subjects experiment.

TABLE 9.6 MULTIPLE-CONDITIONS DESIGN, TESTED WITHIN SUBJECTS

	ALLOCATION	TREATMENT	TEST
Condition 1	All subjects experience all con-ditions, in either random or counterbalanced order	1	Yes
Condition 2		2	Yes
Condition 3		3	Yes

BETWEEN-SUBJECTS DESIGNS

As indicated previously, there are many situations in which subjects cannot be used as their own controls because of the possibility of carry-over effects. As with within-subjects designs, between-subjects experiments may have two conditions, or more than two.

■ Two Conditions, Tested between Subjects

The experiment by Marshall and Teitelbaum described previously was a within-subjects experiment, because each rat served as its own control. This design may not be desirable when the possibility of large order or sequence effects is present. Such was the case in an experiment on the effect of anxiety on affiliation conducted by Stanley Schachter (1959). He hypothesized that inducing anxiety in people would cause an increase in their tendency to seek the company of others. He induced anxiety by telling subjects that they were to be connected to an apparatus that would deliver painful electric shock. After a lecture on the purpose of the research, subjects were instructed that they were to wait 10 minutes before receiving the shock. They filled out a questionnaire that asked whether they wished to wait alone or with other subjects. Subjects in the control condition were told they would receive mild, nonpainful shock. Otherwise, they were treated the same as the experimental subjects. Of the low-stress subjects, 33% indicated that they wished to wait with others, whereas 63% of the high-stress subjects preferred to wait with other subjects. Analysis of these data using chi-square is shown in Box 9.1.

You can see that this experiment had to be conducted as a between-subjects experiment. Once subjects had experienced one of the conditions, they would no longer be naive about the situation. In actuality, none of the subjects in either condition received shock. If they had been asked to serve again in the other condition, the instructions would not have had the same effect. Even if they had been shocked and then asked to participate again, they would have noticed the difference in instructions between conditions and would have begun to suspect the experiment's purpose. Only by having a separate group in each condition could Schachter test the effect of anxiety on the dependent variable.

■ Multiple Conditions, Tested between Subjects

The design of a multiple-conditions, between-subjects experiment is indicated in Table 9.7. An interesting example of such an experiment was conducted by Andrew Baum and Glenn Davis (1980). Their experiment is unusual in that it was a true experiment, with the experimenters having complete control over the independent variables, even though it was conducted partly as a field experiment and partly as a laboratory experiment. (Often field experiments must be run as quasi experiments because of practical complications.)

Baum and Davis wanted to study the effect of residential crowding on stress and social behavior. Through the cooperation of a college administra-

BOX 9.1

ANALYSIS OF THE RESULTS OF A TWO-CONDITION, BETWEEN-SUBJECTS EXPERIMENT BY CHI-SQUARE

Following is the analysis of the data from the Schachter (1959) experiment on the choice of waiting either alone or together by subjects who were expecting either high or low level of shock. Because each subject fell into one and only one cell of the table, analyzing these data by chi-square (χ^2) is appropriate.

INDUCED ANXIETY	NUMBER CHOOSING TO WAIT		
	WITH OTHERS	ALONE	TOTAL
HIGH	20	12	32
LOW	10	20	30
	30	32	62

1. Assumptions
   a. Every sample observation falls into one and only one category. (In this example, no subject served twice.)
   b. The sample observations are independent. (Although the subjects were run in groups, the author felt that the interaction among them was minimal.)
   c. N is large ($N = 62$).

2. Hypotheses
   a. H_0: Our null hypothesis is that there is no difference in companionship-seeking behavior between the high- and low-anxiety groups.
   b. H_1: Our alternative hypothesis is that there is a difference.

3. $\alpha = .05$

4. $\chi^2 = \sum_{ij}(E_{ij} - O_{ij})^2/E_{ij}$

5. Sampling distribution: $\chi^2(1)$
   $df = (R - 1)(C - 1)$
   $\quad = (2 - 1)(2 - 1)$
   $\quad = 1$

6. Look in a χ^2 table under $\alpha = .05$ and $df = 1$.
   $\chi^2.05 = 3.841$. If χ^2 calculated in step 7 is greater than 3.841, reject H_0.

7. Calculation of test statistic
   $\chi^2 = (15.48 - 20)^2/15.48 + (16.52 - 12)^2/16.52 + (14.52 - 10)^2/14.52 + (15.48 - 20)^2/15.48$
   $\quad = 1.32 + 1.24 + 1.41 + 1.32$
   $\quad = 5.29$

8. Since $5.29 > 3.841$, reject H_0. There is a significant difference between high- and low-induced-anxiety subjects in their companionship-seeking behavior.

TABLE 9.7 MULTIPLE-CONDITIONS DESIGN, TESTED BETWEEN SUBJECTS

	ALLOCATION	TREATMENT	TEST
Group 1		1	Yes
Group 2	Random allocation of subjects to groups	2	Yes
Group 3		3	Yes

tion, they were able to conduct the experiment in a women's dormitory. The dormitory had long corridors that subjected residents to frequent interaction, which was believed to cause stress. One dormitory floor was modified by converting three rooms in the middle of the floor into lounges that were separated from the rest of the floor by unlocked doors. Thus two shorter hallways were created, separated by this lounge area. Another floor was not modified. A third floor was shorter than the other two and had the same number of residents as had either half of the divided floor. This arrangement allowed the experimenters to study three floors: a long divided floor, a long undivided floor, and a short floor. Women were assigned randomly to the three floors. During the term the experimenters made a number of observations of hallway activity on the floors. An observer, who was not aware of the hypothesis of the study, spent a predetermined amount of time on each floor throughout the term. The observer's presence in the hallways was sufficiently unobtrusive that at the end of the term none of the women could identify him. (See also Box 9.2 on pp. 240–241.)

Although each hallway had equal activity, by the end of the term approximately twice the activity could be classified as social on the two short-hallway floors as on the long-hallway floor (see Figure 9.3). Whether doors were open or closed was also counted. About twice as many doors were open on the short-hallway floors as on the long-hallway floor.

Besides these observational results, another phase of the study involved behavior measured in the laboratory. Women were randomly recruited from the three floors to participate in an experiment ostensibly on impression formation. When each subject arrived at the laboratory, she was asked to wait for a few minutes in a room that contained a confederate. Observations were made of how many seats away from the confederate she sat and how many seconds she spent looking at her. After five minutes the experimenter returned and administered a questionnaire that asked the subject, among other things, how comfortable she felt at the moment. Then subjects took part in a dummy task and were debriefed. Table 9.8 shows that residents of the long-hallway floor sat farther from the confederate, spent less time looking at her, and felt more discomfort after having waited five minutes for the experimenter. These results are impressive, because the only manipulation was a change in the dormitory hallway length.

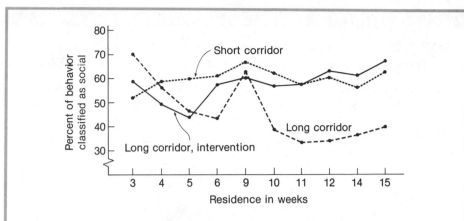

FIGURE 9.3   Percentage of hallway activity on dormitory floors rated as social. SOURCE: "Reducing the Stress of High-Density Living: An Architectural Intervention" by A. Baum and G. E. Davis, 1980, *Journal of Personality and Social Psychology, 38,* 471–481. Copyright 1980 by the American Psychological Association. Reprinted by permission of the publisher and authors.

TABLE 9.8 MEAN RESPONSES TO THE CONFEDERATE IN THE LABORATORY

DORMITORY DESIGN	SEATS AWAY FROM CONFEDERATE	FACIAL REGARD FOR CONFEDERATE (IN SECONDS)	DISCOMFORT AFTER WAITING
Long corridor	2.6_a	18.2_a	4.3_a
Long corridor, with intervention	1.9_b	50.3_b	2.8_b
Short corridor	2.0_b	52.0_b	2.7_b

NOTE: Discomfort was assessed on a 7-point scale, where higher values represented greater discomfort. Numbers with different subscripts are significantly different from one another ($p < .05$).

SOURCE: "Reducing the Stress of High-Density Living: An Architectural Intervention" by A. Baum and G. E. Davis, 1980, *Journal of Personality and Social Psychology, 38,* 471–481. Copyright 1980 by the American Psychological Association. Reprinted by permission.

BOX 9.2
ONE-WAY (MULTIPLE-CONDITION), REPEATED-MEASURES ANALYSIS OF VARIANCE (ANOVA)

The following example analyzes fake data that might have been obtained in the experiment on the effect of long and short hallways on amount of social activity in the hallways (Baum & Davis, 1980).

HYPOTHETICAL DATA ON AMOUNT OF SOCIAL ACTIVITY

CORRIDOR TYPE											$X_{i.}$ [†]
LONG	70	55	45	40	60	35	30	30	35	37	437
LONG, INTERRUPTED	60	50	50	55	60	55	55	60	58	65	568
SHORT	52	58	58	61	65	60	55	58	53	60	580

ANOVA, 3 groups, repeated measures ($I = 3$ corridor types, $J = 10$ observations per corridor, $N = 30$ observations)

1. Assumptions
   a. The population from which each sample is drawn is normally distributed.
   b. The variances of the three treatment populations are equal. (They have homogeneous variance.)
   c. The three samples and ten observations in each sample are randomly and independently drawn.
2. Hypothesis
   a. H_0: Our null hypothesis is that there is no difference in the activity observed in the three corridors.
   b. H_1: The alternative is that there is a difference.
3. $\alpha = .01$
4. Refer to the following table.

ANOVA: SUMS OF SQUARES CALCULATION FORMULAS

SOURCE	df	SS	MS	F
Between I	$I - 1$	$\dfrac{\sum_i X_{i.}^2}{J} - \dfrac{X_{..}^2}{IJ}$	$\dfrac{SS_{bet}}{df_{bet}}$	$\dfrac{MS_{bet}}{MS_{err}}$
Error (between J within I)	$I(J - 1)$	$\sum_{ij} X_{ij}^2 - \dfrac{\sum_j X_{i.}^2}{J}$	$\dfrac{SS_{err}}{df_{err}}$	
Total	$(I\,J) - 1 = N - 1$			

5. Sampling distribution, $F\,(2,\ 27)$. (F distribution with $V_1 = 2$ and $V_2 = 27$ degrees of freedom.)
6. Look in an F table under $\alpha = .01$.
   $F_{.01}\,(2,\ 27) = 5.49$. If the F calculated in step 7 is > 5.49, reject H_0.
7. Refer to the following table.

BOX 9.2 *(continued)*

ONE-WAY (MULTIPLE-CONDITION), REPEATED-MEASURES ANALYSIS OF VARIANCE (ANOVA)

ANOVA: DATA SUMMARY TABLE

SOURCE	df	SS	MS	F
Between corridor	$I - 1 = 2$	$\dfrac{846662}{10} - \dfrac{(1582)^2}{30} = 1242.1$	$\dfrac{1242.1}{2} = 621.05$	$\dfrac{621.05}{77.92} = 7.97*$
Error	$I(J-1) = 27$	$86770 - 84666.2 = 2103.8$	$\dfrac{2103.8}{27} = 77.92$	
Totals	29	3345.9		

* $p < .01$

8. Since $7.97 > 5.49$, reject H_0. The activity level in the three different corridors is significantly different.

---

† Note on dot notation:

In general, $X_. = \overset{n}{\underset{i}{\sum}} X_i = X_1 + X_2 + \cdots + X_n$

Dot notation is a useful, shorthand way to keep track of the sums and sums of squares in an analysis of variance. For example, suppose we have the following scores for two groups that experienced three different treatment levels:

I groups	*J* treatment levels			
	1	2	3	
Group 1	$X_{11} = 22$	$X_{12} = 50$	$X_{13} = 55$	$X_{1.} = 127$
Group 2	$X_{21} = 20$	$X_{22} = 51$	$X_{23} = 60$	$X_{2.} = 131$
	$X_{.1} = 42$	$X_{.2} = 101$	$X_{.3} = 115$	$X_{..} = 258$

In this example:

X_{ij} = the score in the cell in the *i*th row and *j*th column

$X_{1.} = X_{11} + X_{12} + X_{13} = 22 + 50 + 55 = 127$

$X_{2.} = X_{21} + X_{22} + X_{23} = 20 + 51 + 60 = 131$

$\underset{i}{\sum} X_{i.} = X_{1.} + X_{2.} = 127 + 131 = 258$

$\underset{i}{\sum} X_{i.}^2 = X_{1.}^2 + X_{2.}^2 = (127)^2 + (131)^2 = 33290$

$X_{..} = \underset{j\ i}{\sum\sum} X_{ij} = 22 + 20 + 50 + 51 + 55 + 60 = 258$

SUMMARY

1. In a true experiment, the experimenter has complete control over the experiment. A quasi experiment is one in which the experimenter lacks some degree of control. The most important difference is that in a true experiment the subjects are assigned to conditions, whereas in a quasi experiment the subjects are selected for conditions from previously existing groups.

2. The independent variables of an experiment are sometimes called factors, each of which has at least two levels.

3. The levels of the variables are sometimes called treatments or conditions.

4. Some designs to avoid are the one-group posttest-only design, the posttest-only design with nonequivalent control groups, and the one-group pretest/posttest design.

5. The two basic elements of good experimental design are the existence of a control group or a control condition and the random allocation of subjects to various conditions (for between-subjects experiments).

6. Order effects are those that result from the ordinal position in which the condition appears in an experiment, regardless of the specific condition that is experienced. Sequence effects are those that depend on an interaction between the specific conditions of the experiment.

7. Within-subjects control of order and sequence effects may be achieved by randomization, block randomization, or reverse counterbalancing.

8. When it is not possible to control for order and sequence effects within subjects, the Latin square technique may be used.

9. The simplest possible true experiment has two conditions tested within subjects. All subjects experience both conditions in counterbalanced order.

10. Multiple-conditions experiments are conducted when the hypothesis is not a simple yes-or-no question, when determining the shape of a function is desirable, or when multiple rival hypotheses must be ruled out.

11. Multiple-conditions, within-subjects experiments are common in perception research, as when one scales the brightness of different intensities of a light.

12. A between-subjects design is used when a significant interaction between conditions would occur if tested within subjects.

13. Multiple-conditions, between-subjects experiments are common in social psychology, as in the experiment on the effects of long and short hallways on social interaction in a dormitory.

Suggestions for Further Reading

For advice on true experiments, the best place to go is journals or books on particular research areas. Analyze the methods of actual experiments to see how problems of validity were controlled for in experimental situations.

IIII➤ A CASE IN POINT ◀IIII

Intensity of Tone and Reaction Time

Professor Stevens is designing an experiment to determine the effect of intensity of tone on reaction time. He believes that subjects will respond more quickly to more intense tones. He wishes to use five intensities of tone: 10, 30, 50, 70, and 90 dB.

He expects that there will be a practice effect, such that subjects will get faster over the first 20 or so trials. (A trial is a presentation of a single tone.) He is able to present a trial every 10 seconds. Subjects will be available for 1 hour, including the time taken in introducing them to the experiment, practicing, and debriefing. He estimates that he may be able to collect data for up to 30 minutes.

He has reason to believe that reaction time might differ between the left and right hand. It is likely that subjects are faster with their preferred hand. About 5% of subjects are left-handed, but left-handedness is more common in men than women. He has no theoretical interest in differences between left and right hand, the effects of handedness, or sex differences.

Professor Stevens wonders whether to use a within-subjects or between-subjects design. The within-subjects design would require him to decide which order of presenting the stimuli to the subjects would be best. If he used a between-subjects design, he would not have that problem, but he would require more subjects to complete the experiment.

If he uses a between-subjects design, each subject would experience only one intensity. He thinks that he would need at least 20 different subjects at each intensity to control for individual differences between subjects.

If he uses a within-subjects design, he could use reverse counterbalancing, a Latin square, random order, only increasing order or only decreasing order. He realizes that each one has certain advantages and disadvantages.

If he randomizes the order, or uses a Latin square, loud tones will follow soft ones, and vice versa, in an unpredictable manner. This might startle the subjects, causing them to be possibly faster on the loud tones, or slower, depending on whether the startle reaction is compatible with pressing the key on the computer. On the other hand, presenting the tones in a predictable sequence might make the subjects "tune out," or habituate to, the effects of intensity.

He believes that he needs a 100 trials per stimulus in the total experiment to obtain reliable results.

REQUIRED: Decide
     a. whether to do the experiment within or between subjects.
     b. what sort of order to use, if it is to be done between subjects.
     c. whether to control for hand and handedness, and if so, how.
     d. how many subjects to use.

Justify each of your decisions. Summarize your decisions by showing the total number of stimulus presentations and how they are distributed across subjects, in what order. (It is not necessary to list the exact order for all trials and subjects, just give the schema.)

Ⅲ➡ A CASE IN POINT ⬅Ⅲ

Psychological Reactance

Brehm's theory of psychological reactance (1966) predicts that people will desire an object more when some barrier is introduced that prevents them from obtaining it. Suppose that you want to test this theory with small children. Your specific hypothesis is that 2-year-olds will choose to play more often with toys that are visible but more difficult to reach than with toys that are equally far away but unobstructed. You have available to you the following resources.

SUBJECTS: There are 100 2-year-olds available from the files of the laboratory. Half are boys. Their mothers are willing to bring them in for an hour's observation. The expenses connected with observing the toddlers, including parking and paying the mothers, come to $10 per child.

APPARATUS: You have an observation room with a one-way mirror, and you have a reception room. There is a collection of toys available to use as choice objects. You know from earlier research that several of these toys are approximately equally preferred by 2-year-olds. You have clear Plexiglas available that would be suitable for making barriers that the toddlers could see through but that would make it more difficult for them to reach the toys.

PERSONNEL: Two female fellow students have volunteered to help you run the experiments. At the present time they are unaware of Brehm's theory or your hypothesis.

CONSIDERATIONS: You are inclined to test the toddlers with a pair of toys, one in plain view behind a barrier that they could easily get around and one that is an equal distance away without a barrier.

If you give instructions to the child, the order in which you show the toys might influence their desirability, because your holding one toy first might itself cause reactance by leading the child to think that you are trying to persuade him or her to take that one and not the other.

You have thought of three possible types of dependent variables. First, you could measure the amount of time spent playing with the toys. Second, you could measure which toy the child played with first. Third, you could measure the latency of playing with the toys.

Questions of design include whether to test both boys and girls, how many conditions to have, and whether to test each child on all conditions or to test different children on each condition.

Procedural questions include whether to have the mother in the room with the child, and if so, where she should sit and what she should be told. Should the child be put in a certain place to start? Should the experimenter go into the room with the mother and/or the child? What should the experimenter say to the child? Should the experimenter stay to observe the child or go outside? Who should record the data? Your budget for subjects is $500.

REQUIRED: Design the study. Include your hypothesis, method, and expected results. Justify your decisions, including why you rejected alternatives. Be sure to describe how you will analyze your data. Provide data sheets with mocked-up data. Make a table or graph of expected data.

OPTIONAL: What is the appropriate statistical analysis?
The experiment on which this case study is based is cited in the Instructor's Manual.

≡ READING BETWEEN THE LINES ≡

9.1 SUBLIMINAL SEDUCTION

In his popular book *Subliminal Seduction* (1973), Wilson Bryan Key describes many ways in which the advertising industry attempts, by subliminal advertising, to motivate people to purchase products. One example concerns an ad in *Playboy* for subscriptions to that magazine. The two-page spread shows a naked woman kneeling and holding a large Christmas wreath. Key says that of the approximately 100 men who had read the entire magazine, over 95 percent remembered seeing the ad. He states further that "over 70 percent specifically remembered the wreath, but could provide only vague ideas about the blonde's description. Over 40 percent of those who recalled the ad were not even certain that she was a blonde" (p. 40). Key's explanation for why the men remembered the wreath better than they remembered the woman is that the wreath was made of nuts, which on close inspection of an enlargement are seen to be drawn so as to resemble male and female genital parts. What alternative explanations can you think of for why the men would remember the wreath better than they remembered the woman? ∎

☑ EXERCISES

9.1 TWO INDEPENDENT GROUPS

An aspirin manufacturer claims that its brand of aspirin produces faster pain relief compared with the leading brand. To test this claim, a team of independent researchers identify 20 subjects who suffer from chronic headaches. Subjects are randomly divided into two groups of 10 each. One group receives Brand C aspirin, and the other group receives Brand E aspirin. Subjects in each group are given one aspirin when they experience a headache, and the researcher records the amount of time it takes before each subject experiences relief. The reported times are rounded to the nearest minute.

REQUIRED:
   a. *Option A:* Use Subjects 21–40 from the population data set in Appendix C. Subjects 21–30 use Brand C aspirin, and Subjects 31–40 use Brand E aspirin. Data for subjects using Brand C are in column C, and data for subjects using Brand E are in column E.

Option B: Using the procedures outlined in Chapter 8, draw a random sample of size 20 from the population data set in Appendix C. Randomly assign 10 subjects to the Brand C condition and 10 subjects to the Brand E condition. Data for subjects using Brand C are in column C, and data for subjects using Brand E are in column E.

b. Calculate the means of the two groups.

c. What tentative conclusions can you draw?

OPTIONAL:

d. Test the null hypothesis versus the alternative hypothesis at the .05 level of significance with the independent t test. Interpret the results.

9.2   TWO RELATED MEASURES

A research-methods professor has developed two equivalent forms of a test designed to measure students' conceptual knowledge of hypothesis testing. Both tests are intended to be equally difficult. On Monday, the professor administers both forms of the test to the population of undergraduate students enrolled in introductory research methods.

REQUIRED:

a. Option A: Use Subjects 11–20 from the population data set in Appendix C. Column A contains subjects' scores on Form A of the test, and column B contains subjects' scores on Form B of the test.
   Option B: Using the procedures outlined in Chapter 8, randomly select 10 subjects from the population data set in Appendix C. Column A contains the scores on Form A of the test, and column B contains the scores on Form B of the test.

b. List the corresponding paired scores on Forms A and B of the test for each subject selected.

c. Calculate the group means of the two tests.

d. What would you tentatively conclude?

OPTIONAL:

e. Test the null hypothesis versus the alternative hypothesis at the .05 level of significance with a related t test. Interpret your results.

9.3   MULTIPLE CONDITIONS

A number of recent commercial airline crashes are tentatively attributed to errors made by air traffic controllers. The Federal Aviation Administration (FAA) believes that a relationship exists between fatigue and errors made by air traffic controllers. To study the effects of fatigue on the performance of air traffic controllers, FAA researchers randomly select 25 air traffic controllers from the union roster; all subjects agree to participate in the study. The researchers randomly assign subjects to one of five groups of 5 individuals each. Subjects in each group are given a simulated vigilance task to perform on a radar screen after a designated number of hours at work. Listed below are the number of hours each group worked before performing the simulated task.

Treatment Group	Number of Hours of Work	Corresponding Columns in Population Data Set
1	0	B
2	2	D
3	4	E
4	6	F
5	8	G

REQUIRED:

    a. *Option A:* Use Subjects 40–64 from the population data set in Appendix C. Subjects 40–44 comprise Group 1, Subjects 45–49 comprise Group 2, Subjects 50–54 comprise Group 3, Subjects 55–59 comprise Group 4, and Subjects 60–64 comprise Group 5. Obtain each subject's score from the column corresponding to the treatment group as indicated above.

    Option B: Using the procedures outlined in Chapter 8, draw a random sample of 25 subjects from the population data set in Appendix C. Randomly assign 5 subjects to each of the five treatment groups, and obtain each subject's score from the column corresponding to the treatment group.

    b. Calculate and graph the group means.

    c. What tentative conclusions can you draw?

OPTIONAL:

    d. Test the null hypothesis versus the alternative hypothesis

$$H_1: \text{not all the means are equal}$$

at the .05 level of significance with a one-way analysis of variance. Present an ANOVA summary table, and interpret the results.   ❏

10

True Experiments, Part 2:
Factorial Designs

Up to now we have primarily discussed experiments in which the researcher studied the effect of one independent variable. Often, however, you will want to examine the effect of two or more variables in a single experiment. One reason is efficiency: As long as you are designing an experiment, building another independent variable into the design may not require much additional effort. But we have already seen a second reason for having more than one variable in a single experiment: There may be more than one alternative hypothesis to rule out, as in the fuzzy, colorful, noisy toy example in Chapter 9.

Suppose, for example, that the child did not like the toy at all if it was only, let us say, fuzzy. Instead, suppose that the child liked the toy only if it was both fuzzy and colorful, and was indifferent to a toy that was only fuzzy or only colorful. Our simple three-condition experiment would not be able to reveal that preference, because the only toy that was fuzzy was neither colorful nor noisy. There was no fuzzy, colorful, not-noisy toy presented. To solve this problem, we could design an experiment that included all possible combinations of these attributes in order to discover which combination the child preferred. Thus, the third reason for studying two or more variables in the same experiment is to reveal interactions among variables.

A **factorial design** is one in which two or more variables, or factors, are employed in such a way that all of the possible combinations of selected values of each variable are used. In the simplest case we have two variables, each of which has two values, or levels. This is known as a two-by-two (2×2)

factorial design
research design that involves all combinations of at least two values of two or more independent variables

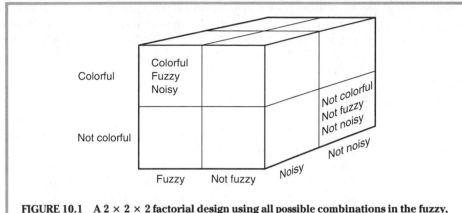

FIGURE 10.1 A 2 × 2 × 2 factorial design using all possible combinations in the fuzzy, colorful, noisy toy example.

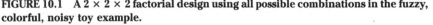

TABLE 10.1 A 2 × 2 FACTORIAL DESIGN

		FACTOR A	
		A₁	A₂
FACTOR B	B₁	A₁B₁	A₂B₁
	B₂	A₁B₂	A₂B₂

factorial design because of the two levels of each variable. The 2 × 2 design gives rise to four combinations, as shown on the front surface of Figure 10.1. (Table 10.1 also represents a 2 × 2 factorial design.) If there were two levels of one variable and three of another, we would have a 2 × 3 factorial experiment.

In the fuzzy, colorful, noisy toy example as discussed in Chapter 9 there were three conditions, which was the minimum number necessary to find out which attribute was responsible for the child's attraction to the toy. If we were to consider all possible combinations of these variables, we would need to consider 2 levels of fuzziness times 2 levels of colorfulness times 2 levels of noisiness equals 8 conditions. This 2 × 2 × 2 factorial design is illustrated in Figure 10.1. Such a design would permit us to determine if some combination of variables is responsible for the child's attraction to the toy, instead of one acting alone. For example, the child may like the toy because it is colorful and fuzzy, but be indifferent to a toy that is only colorful or fuzzy.

Of course, you can have as many factors and levels as you desire, but with increasing complexity you will require much more time to conduct the experiment. In addition, the large number of interactions to be considered taxes the mind, defeating the purpose of doing the experiment in the first place. Most experiments use two or three factors, with two to six levels on the various factors.

A SIMPLE FACTORIAL DESIGN

Suppose you are interested in the characteristics of a person that influence judgments of guilt made by a judge when that person is accused of a crime. You hypothesize that physical attractiveness of the accused may influence the judge. You also hypothesize that a smiling person may be judged less guilty than a person who displays a neutral expression. (This example is adapted from an experiment by Forgas, 1987. Data have been modified slightly for illustrative purposes.)

Thus, you are interested in two independent variables: attractiveness and facial expression. Your dependent variable is judgment of guilt. You could do two separate experiments, one in which you varied the attractiveness of the person being judged and another in which you varied his or her facial expression. The first experiment could be diagrammed as in Table 10.2. This table shows that the independent variable, attractiveness, has two values, or two levels: (1) unattractive and (2) attractive. The second experiment could be diagrammed as in Table 10.3, where we see that the independent variable of facial expression has two levels: (1) neutral and (2) smiling.

Now, suppose that you have the idea of studying the effects of the two different independent variables at the same time. You have two independent variables, each with two levels. This gives you four combinations of the various conditions, as shown in Table 10.4. The upper left-hand cell combines the first level of the variable of facial expression (neutral) with the first level of the variable of attractiveness (unattractive). This is indicated by the notation $A_1 B_1$, because you are combining the first level of Variable A with the first level of Variable B.

If you want to study the effects of the two variables of facial expression and attractiveness at once in a factorial design, you need to have one stimulus face that is attractive and smiling, one that is attractive and neutral, one that is unattractive and smiling, and one that is unattractive and neutral. Let us say that you had four different groups of subjects, each of which judged the guiltiness of one face after reading a description of an alleged crime. Your

TABLE 10.2 DESIGN OF AN EXPERIMENT ON ATTRACTIVENESS

ATTRACTIVENESS	
Unattractive	Attractive

TABLE 10.3 DESIGN OF AN EXPERIMENT ON FACIAL EXPRESSION

FACIAL EXPRESSION	
Neutral	Smiling

TABLE 10.4 DESIGN OF AN EXPERIMENT ON ATTRACTIVENESS AND FACIAL EXPRESSION

ATTRACTIVENESS (B)	FACIAL EXPRESSION (A)		ROW MEANS (EFFECT OF B)
	NEUTRAL (A_1)	SMILING (A_2)	
Unattractive (B_1)	A_1B_1 88	A_2B_1 24	56
Attractive (B_2)	A_1B_2 16	A_2B_2 32	24
COLUMN MEANS (EFFECT OF A)	52	28	

results might be as shown in Table 10.4. The number in each cell indicates the mean judgment of the face in that condition.

You can see that the data in the two left-hand cells are the judgments of Condition A_1—that is, the two neutral faces. The data in the two cells on the right-hand side are the judgments of Condition A_2—that is, the two smiling faces. Therefore, we can average the data in the two left-hand cells and find the average response to neutral faces to be 52, as shown below the left-hand column. Similarly, averaging the data in the two right-hand cells gives us the average response to the smiling faces, 28. Because 52 and 28 were obtained by averaging the columns of the table, they are called the column means. Looking at the column means shows us that neutral stimulus faces were judged to be more guilty than smiling faces, so we conclude that smiling reduces judged guiltiness.

The effect of attractiveness of the faces can be seen by looking at the rows of the table. The two upper cells show the judgments of Condition B_1, the two unattractive faces. The two lower cells show the responses to Condition B_2, the two attractive faces. Averaging across the rows, we find that the average judged guiltiness of the unattractive faces was 56, but the average for the attractive faces was 24. Because 56 and 24 are obtained by averaging across the rows of the table, they are called row means. From the row means we conclude that unattractive faces are judged more guilty than attractive faces.

MAIN EFFECTS

main effect
in a factorial experiment, the effect of one independent variable, averaged over all levels of another independent variable

At this point it is necessary to introduce the technical term **main effect.** Because this term can be misleading, we will say first of all that main effect does not mean the principal effect of a variable. It means simply the effect of a variable averaged over all values of another variable (or variables). We have already talked about main effects, except that before we simply called them the effects of facial expression and attractiveness. In other words, we found the main effect of facial expression by averaging effect of facial expression over the two levels of attractiveness when we looked at the column means. Similarly, we found the main effect of attractiveness by averaging the effect of attractiveness over the two levels of facial expression when we looked at the row means.

INTERACTIONS

The conclusions based on the main effects of the two independent variables are actually very misleading, however, and are incorrect if we do not qualify them. Compare the top two cells of Table 10.4 with the bottom two. Smiling does reduce the judged guiltiness of the unattractive faces (from 88 to 24), but it *increases* the judged guiltiness of the attractive faces (from 16 to 32). So the conclusion that smiling reduces judgment of guiltiness is true only for the unattractive faces. The correct conclusion is that an unattractive face is judged less guilty if it is smiling, but an attractive face is judged less guilty if it has a neutral expression.

interaction
when the effect of one independent variable depends on the level of another independent variable

This outcome is an example of an **interaction** between two variables. Two variables interact if the effect of one variable depends on the level of the other. We have an interaction here because the effect of smiling depends on attractiveness. Whenever it is necessary to say something like the following, you are looking at an interaction: The effect of smiling on judged guiltiness depends on the attractiveness of the faces; specifically, smiling reduces the judged guiltiness of unattractive faces but increases the judged guiltiness of attractive faces.

The concept of interaction is a difficult one for students to understand. We have presented it so far in the context of tabular presentation of data. Some people find the idea easier to understand when it is presented graphically. Figure 10.2 shows the same data as Table 10.4. Judged guiltiness

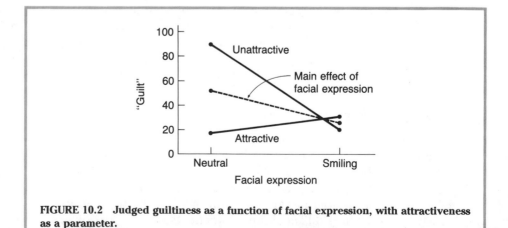

FIGURE 10.2   Judged guiltiness as a function of facial expression, with attractiveness as a parameter.

is plotted as a function of facial expression, with attractiveness as a parameter. The two solid lines show the effect of facial expression separately for attractive and unattractive faces. You can see that smiling decreases the judged guiltiness of unattractive faces but increases the judged guiltiness of attractive faces. This simply states the interaction, as we have already done. The dashed line shows the average effect of smiling on judged guiltiness, averaged over levels of attractiveness. This simply restates the main effect of facial expression. The main effect of facial expression is that smiling reduces judged guiltiness.

Now refer back to Table 10.4. You will notice that the table is completely symmetrical in its layout: The columns represent facial expression, and the rows represent attractiveness. We could just as easily represent attractiveness over the columns and facial expression over the rows; that is, we could simply rotate the table by 90 degrees. Similarly, in Figure 10.2 we could have plotted guiltiness as a function of attractiveness, with facial expression as the parameter, as shown in Figure 10.3. Here we see that the main effect of attractiveness is to reduce judged guiltiness.

We prefer graphical presentation of data where interactions are concerned for a simple reason: If the graphical representation of a factorial experiment shows curves that are not parallel, there is an interaction between the variables. The two curves in Figure 10.2 are not parallel; therefore, there is an interaction between facial expression and attractiveness. If you could slide one of the curves up or down so that it matched another, there would be no interaction, because they would be parallel; if you cannot slide them up or down so that they match, there is an interaction. This is true no matter how complicated the curve may be. Of course, small differences may be the result of chance, so statistical evaluation may be necessary.

Although we talked about the main effects in this example before we discussed the interactions, this was for pedagogical reasons. Whenever there

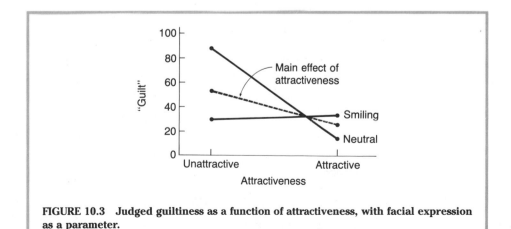

FIGURE 10.3 **Judged guiltiness as a function of attractiveness, with facial expression as a parameter.**

is an interaction in the data, the main effects cannot be interpreted without discussing the interactions. Some authorities hold that main effects are meaningless when interactions are present, but this seems extreme. It is true, however, that main effects can be misleading when interactions are present, as in this example.

■ Interactions When There Is No Main Effect

In our example, not only did we have an interaction in the data, but both independent variables showed main effects: Smiling and attractiveness both reduced judged guiltiness. It is entirely possible to have an interaction if one or the other independent variable has no main effect, or even if neither independent variable has a main effect.

We will first consider an example in which there is a main effect of one variable but another variable shows no main effect. Suppose that you are intrigued by the apparent contradiction between the following two proverbs: "Absence makes the heart grow fonder" and "Out of sight, out of mind." Certainly they appear contradictory, and they are often cited by psychologists as examples of the limitations of common sense.

You decide to do an experiment in which you study the degree of attraction between members of couples that are either near to each other or separated by some distance. Let us assume that you find the results shown in Table 10.5. From the column means you see that distance has no main effect on measured attraction. But you also suspect that whether the people are truly in love might make a difference in their mutual attraction. So you determine on some basis whether they are truly in love or are merely having a flirtation. The presence of a main effect of true love is shown by the row means in the table. Further examination of Table 10.5 reveals that there is an interaction between true love and distance: Attraction increases as a function of distance for members of couples who are truly in love, but it decreases for those who are only having a flirtation.

TABLE 10.5 RELATIONSHIP BETWEEN ATTRACTION WITHIN COUPLES AND DISTANCE

| | Distance | | Row Means |
TRUE LOVE	NEAR	FAR	(EFFECT OF B)
Yes	8	12	10
No	6	2	4
COLUMN MEANS (EFFECT OF A)	7	7	

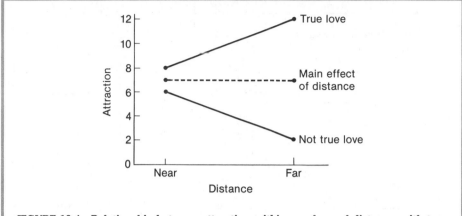

FIGURE 10.4 **Relationship between attraction within couples and distance, with true love as a parameter.**

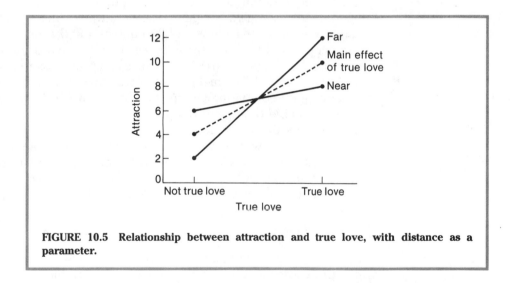

FIGURE 10.5 **Relationship between attraction and true love, with distance as a parameter.**

As it turns out, both proverbs are true, but under particular circumstances. Absence makes the heart grow fonder for couples who are truly in love; but out of sight, out of mind is the case for those who are not. In other words, there is an interaction between the two variables.

Let us now look at the graphical representation of the same data in Figure 10.4. Here we see again that distance increases attraction for the true-love condition but decreases it for the not-true-love condition. The fact that the lines are not parallel indicates the presence of the interaction. Furthermore, the dashed line showing the data averaged over the variable of true love indicates that there is no main effect of distance.

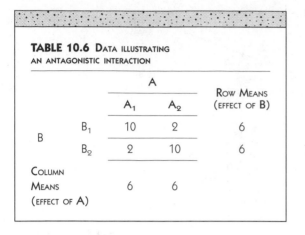

TABLE 10.6 DATA ILLUSTRATING AN ANTAGONISTIC INTERACTION

		A		ROW MEANS (EFFECT OF B)
		A_1	A_2	
B	B_1	10	2	6
	B_2	2	10	6
COLUMN MEANS (EFFECT OF A)		6	6	

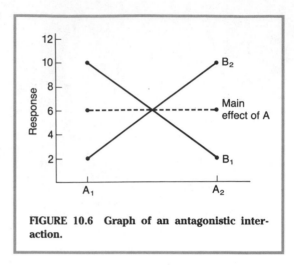

FIGURE 10.6   Graph of an antagonistic interaction.

Now let us replot attraction as a function of true love with distance as the parameter, as shown in Figure 10.5. Here we see that true love increases the attraction between members of the couples, but the increase is greater for distant couples than for near couples. In other words, there still is an interaction. (There had better be, because all we did was rearrange the same data we had before.) The main effect of true love is seen by the dashed line in the graph. By comparing Figure 10.4 with Figure 10.5, we can see that we have one variable (distance) that does not produce a main effect, and one (true love) that does produce a main effect.

A situation in which there is an interaction but no main effect is shown in Table 10.6. The row and column means indicate no main effect of either variable, A or B. Looking at the cells, however, shows that there is an interaction, as we can also see from Figure 10.6.

■ Types of Interactions

The type of interaction that we have been discussing so far can be called an **antagonistic interaction:** The two independent variables tend to reverse each other's effects. Distance had one effect under the true-love condition and the opposite effect under the not-true-love condition.

The interaction shown in Figure 10.7 can be called a **synergistic interaction,** because the higher level of B enhances the effect of A, and vice versa. This relationship is shown in the steeper slope of the line relating the dependent variable to A when B is larger. Figure 10.8 shows the same data replotted with B as the independent variable and A as the parameter. The same type of interaction is seen either way.

Figure 10.9 shows a **ceiling-effect interaction:** The higher level of B reduces the differential effect of A on the dependent variable. That is, Variable A has a smaller effect when it is paired with the higher level of B. Likewise in

antagonistic interaction interaction in which the two independent variables tend to reverse each other's effects

synergistic interaction interaction in which the two independent variables reinforce each other's effects

ceiling-effect interaction interaction in which one variable has a smaller effect when paired with higher levels of a second variable

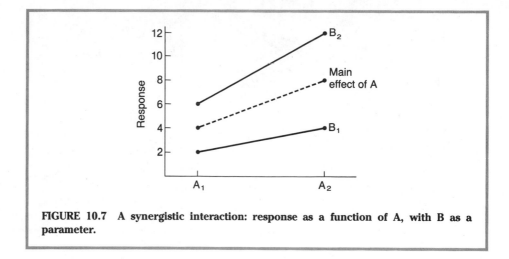

FIGURE 10.7   A synergistic interaction: response as a function of A, with B as a parameter.

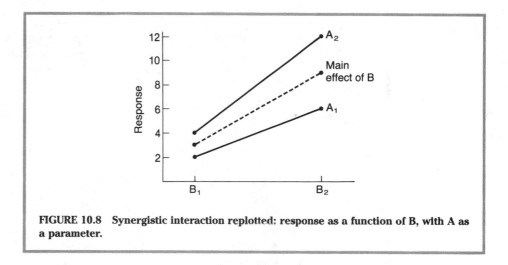

FIGURE 10.8   Synergistic interaction replotted: response as a function of B, with A as a parameter.

Figure 10.10, which shows the same data, Variable B has less effect when paired with the higher level of A.

All of these types of interactions are common in psychological research. Others are possible, but these are the principal kinds.

■ Transformations and Interactions

After what we have said about the importance of interactions, you may be surprised to learn that whether there is an interaction in a set of data may depend entirely on how the data are handled. Specifically, performing a transformation on the data can affect whether an interaction is found. Certain numerical transformations—such as taking the logarithm of all of

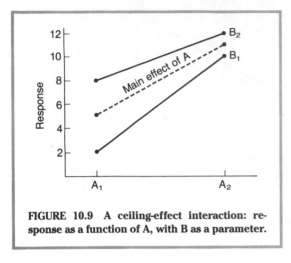

FIGURE 10.9 A ceiling-effect interaction: response as a function of A, with B as a parameter.

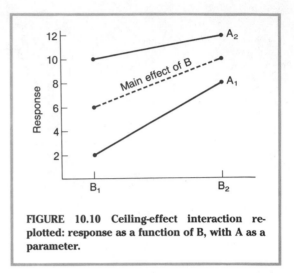

FIGURE 10.10 Ceiling-effect interaction replotted: response as a function of B, with A as a parameter.

the scores or taking the reciprocal of all scores—are commonly made on data. (See Appendix E.) Not only can a transformation remove an interaction from a set of data, but it may produce an interaction when the untransformed data did not show one, or even change the interaction from one type to another.

Consider Table 10.7. Suppose these data represent a measurement of latency. Perhaps rats were running an alley for food under two levels of hunger. Figure 10.11 represents the same data. The upper curve represents the low-hunger condition and the lower curve represents high hunger. From this figure we would conclude that an interaction existed between time to run the alley and hunger: Level of hunger had a bigger effect during early trials. We might also conclude that learning was rapid at first and tapered off after the first two trials.

Suppose, however, that we were to plot running speed instead of time. Recall that speed and latency are reciprocally related. Table 10.8 and Figure 10.12 show running speed as a function of trials, with hunger as a parameter. Now we find that the interaction is reversed: Level of hunger had a greater effect on speed during the later trials. Also, you might conclude that learning was slow at first and then speeded up.

How do we get out of this confusion? Before we try, let us be certain that we realize that the theoretical conclusions we reach about data may depend entirely on how we plot them. In other words, the presence or absence of an interaction and what form it takes depend on the type of transformations made of the data. An interaction exists only in a particular transformation of the data; it does not exist in the abstract, or even in a particular theory. If a theory predicts an interaction, it only does so together with a prediction (or an assumption) about how the data will be transformed.

Now, often there is a theoretical reason to prefer one transformation over the other. For example, we may have a theory of learning that says that

TABLE 10.7 RELATIONSHIP BETWEEN LATENCY AND HUNGER

		TRIALS		
		1	2	3
HUNGER	Low	100	32	10
	HIGH	32	10	3.2

TABLE 10.8 RELATIONSHIP BETWEEN RUNNING SPEED AND HUNGER (RECIPROCAL TRANSFORMATION OF TABLE 10.7)

		TRIALS		
		1	2	3
HUNGER	Low	0.01	0.031	0.1
	HIGH	0.031	0.1	0.31

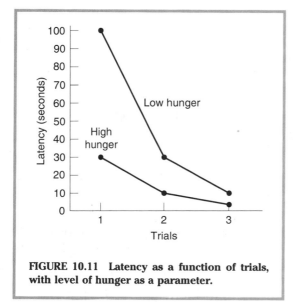

FIGURE 10.11 Latency as a function of trials, with level of hunger as a parameter.

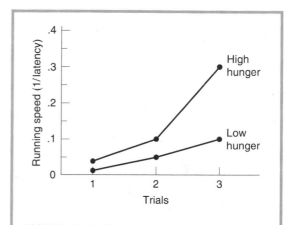

FIGURE 10.12 Running speed as a function of trials, with hunger as a parameter (reciprocal transformation of the data shown in Figure 10.11).

learning takes place at a constant rate in terms of the proportional improvement from trial to trial. This theory would lead us to prefer still another transformation: the logarithmic transformation. A logarithmic transformation will cause constant proportional changes in the response as a function of the stimulus to yield a straight line.

Table 10.9 and Figure 10.13 show the results of a logarithmic transformation. Here we see no interaction. We would conclude from Figure 10.13 that the rate of learning was constant and was the same for both groups of rats. Of course, it is circular thinking to prefer a transformation because of a theory and then use the data to confirm the theory. Other criteria exist for choosing which transformation to use. Usually, but not always, the transformation that produces normally distributed data with equal variability between conditions will be the preferred transformation for theoretical purposes as well. The point is to be aware of the problem and not draw conclusions about interactions out of ignorance.

TABLE 10.9 RELATIONSHIP BETWEEN LATENCY AND HUNGER (TABLE 10.7) AFTER A LOGARITHMIC TRANSFORMATION

		TRIALS		
		1	2	3
HUNGER	LOW	2.0	1.5	1.0
	HIGH	1.5	1.0	0.5

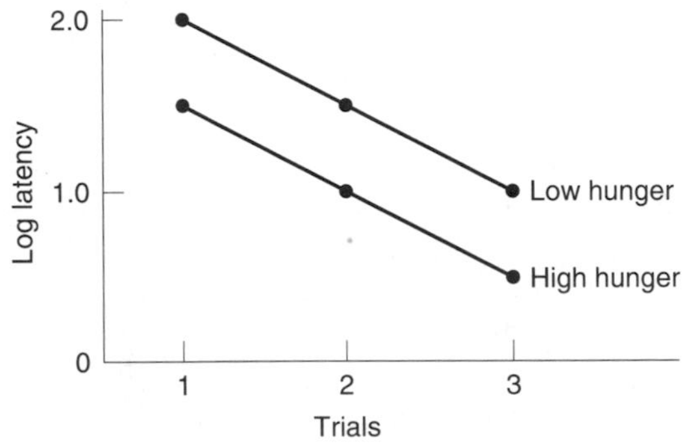

FIGURE 10.13 Latency as a function of trials with level of hunger as a parameter (Figure 10.11), after a logarithmic transformation.

WITHIN-SUBJECTS, BETWEEN-SUBJECTS, AND MIXED DESIGNS

Factorial experiments may be conducted either within subjects or between subjects, although between-subjects factorial designs may be more common. In fact, sex of subject, a between-subjects variable, is one of the most common variables in factorial designs. We will give examples of both within-subjects and between-subjects experiments, as well as a mixed design. A mixed factorial is one that has at least one within-subjects variable and at least one between-subjects variable.

Table 10.10 illustrates a factorial experiment in which Factors A and B are the two independent variables. Each independent variable has two values, or levels (for example, A_1 and A_2). The two levels of the two variables give us four possible combinations of the independent variables (A_1B_1, A_1B_2, A_2B_1, A_2B_2). Thus we have a 2×2 factorial design. If Table 10.10 is taken to represent a within-subjects experiment, then each subject experiences each condition. Table 10.11 shows the same information, indicating that the same group of

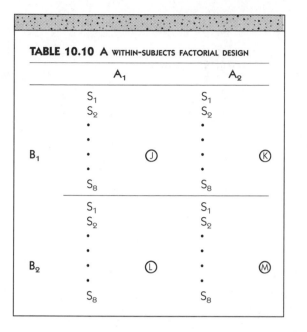

TABLE 10.10 A WITHIN-SUBJECTS FACTORIAL DESIGN

TABLE 10.11 POSSIBLE SEQUENCE OF CONDITIONS EXPERIENCED BY EIGHT SUBJECTS IN THE FACTORIAL EXPERIMENT ILLUSTRATED IN TABLE 10.10

SUBJECTS	1	2	3	4
S_1	J	K	L	M
S_2	K	M	J	L
S_3	L	J	M	K
S_4	M	L	K	J
S_5	K	J	L	M
S_6	M	L	J	K
S_7	J	M	K	L
S_8	L	K	M	J

subjects, eight in this case, experiences all conditions. The letters J, K, L, M stand for the four conditions, with J standing for the combination A_1B_1, and so forth.

Table 10.11 shows one way that eight subjects could experience the four conditions in counterbalanced order. Subjects S_1–S_4 together constitute a balanced Latin square, because each condition occurs once in each ordinal position and follows every other condition once (see Chapter 9). Subjects S_5–S_8 constitute another balanced Latin square. This example is only one way of showing how eight subjects could experience the four conditions. In this case, the experimenter winds up with eight responses to each of four conditions using eight subjects.

A between-subjects factorial design is illustrated in Table 10.12. This example is also a 2×2 design. Separate groups of eight experience each condition, thus requiring 32 subjects in order to get eight responses to each of four conditions. Table 10.13 shows another way of representing the information from Table 10.12.

A mixed factorial design is illustrated in Table 10.14. Variable A is the within-subjects variable, and Variable B is the between-subjects variable. Subjects either experience B_1, first with A_1 and then with A_2; or they experience B_2, first with A_1 and then with A_2.

Suppose that the A variable is two types of music and the B variable is sex. The dependent variable is degree of liking. Individual subjects would indicate their degree of liking for the two types of music, A_1 and A_2. Individual subjects, however, could only experience two conditions: Males (B_1) could rate their preference for music A_1 (Condition A_1B_1), and they could rate their

TABLE 10.12 A BETWEEN-SUBJECTS FACTORIAL DESIGN

	A_1	A_2
	S_1	S_{17}
	S_2	S_{18}
B_1	•	•
	•	•
	•	•
	S_8	S_{24}
	S_9	S_{25}
	S_{10}	S_{26}
B_2	•	•
	•	•
	•	•
	S_{16}	S_{32}

TABLE 10.13 BETWEEN-SUBJECTS FACTORIAL DESIGN (TABLE 10.12), IN SUMMARY FORM

SUBJECTS	GROUP
S_{1-8}	A_1B_1
S_{9-16}	A_1B_2
S_{17-24}	A_2B_1
S_{25-32}	A_2B_2

liking for music A_2 (Condition A_2B_1). Females would respond likewise (Conditions A_1B_2 and A_2B_2). An individual subject could not provide data in all four conditions.

The way the 16 subjects would experience the conditions is illustrated in Table 10.15. This particular example is actually a quasi experiment because sex is one of the factors. It was chosen, however, to show a situation in which you would have to use a mixed design because doing otherwise would be physically impossible. Mixed designs are also used when using the same subjects in all conditions is possible but not desirable. Suppose the A factor is two different sets of experimental instructions. The B factor might be the answer to two questions asked during the experimental session. The A factor would be studied better between subjects, but the B factor could easily be studied within subjects.

■ Advantages of Within-Subjects Designs

Comparing Tables 10.10, 10.12, and 10.14 shows one of the advantages of the within-subjects design. The within-subjects design requires only 8 subjects in order to obtain eight responses in each of the four conditions. The mixed design requires 16 subjects to obtain the same number of responses. The between-subjects design is the least efficient, requiring 32 subjects. When presenting each condition to every subject is possible, the within-subjects design should be considered, as long as order and sequence effects are not

TABLE 10.14 A MIXED FACTORIAL DESIGN

	A_1	A_2
	(WITHIN-SUBJECTS VARIABLE)	
	S_1	S_1
	S_2	S_2
	•	•
B_1	•	•
	•	•
(BETWEEN-SUBJECTS VARIABLE)	S_8	S_8
	S_9	S_9
	S_{10}	S_{10}
B_2	•	•
	•	•
	•	•
	S_{16}	S_{16}

TABLE 10.15 MIXED FACTORIAL DESIGN (TABLE 10.14) IN SUMMARY FORM, INCLUDING ORDER

GROUP	SUBJECTS	ORDER
B_1	S_{1-4}	A_1B_1, then A_2B_1
	S_{5-8}	A_2B_1, then A_1B_1
B_2	S_{9-12}	A_1B_2, then A_2B_2
	S_{13-16}	A_2B_2, then A_1B_2

expected. This choice is especially applicable if recruiting enough subjects is a problem.

■ Control in Within-Subjects Factorial Experiments

Within-subjects factorial experiments can require considerable ingenuity in order to control for order and sequence over both variables. A 3×3 factorial, for example, has nine conditions to consider, even if each one is only presented to a subject once. If there are multiple presentations of each condition, the situation can become very complex.

On the other hand, one of the variables may permit, or even require, that all of the conditions of one variable (A) be tested first under one condition of the second variable (B) and then tested under the other condition of the second variable (B).

Take, for example, an experiment on the effect of light adaptation on visual acuity. Suppose you wanted to measure the visibility of four targets (B_1, B_2, B_3, B_4) under both dark adaptation (A_1) and light adaptation (A_2). Varying the adaptation state between each pair of targets would be extremely time-consuming, because 30 minutes is needed to achieve a state of complete dark adaptation. Table 10.16 shows a sample design for such an experiment. The four targets are abbreviated 1234 and so forth. The order of stimuli (conditions of Variable B) has been block randomized for

TABLE 10.16 Design of experiment on light adaptation and visual acuity

	Dark Adapted	Light Adapted	Dark Adapted
S_{1-5}	2143, 4312 . . .	1342, 1243 . . .	
S_{6-10}		4123, 3214 . . .	3241, 1243 . . .

every subject, and the state of adaptation (conditions of Variable A) is reversed for half of the subjects. Often this type of control for order and sequence is successful.

SOME REPRESENTATIVE FACTORIAL DESIGNS

■ Factorial, Within-Subjects

An experiment by Joseph Stevens and Lee Rubin (1970) provides an elegant example of a within-subjects factorial design. Stevens and Rubin studied the size/weight illusion, a well-known effect in which large objects feel lighter than small objects when both have the same weight. You may have noticed that a large empty suitcase feels lighter than a full handbag even though both weigh the same. Table 10.17 provides a schematic of the essential features of the experiment. Subjects were asked to lift containers that varied in both volume and weight.

Figure 10.14 shows idealized data from the experiment. Apparent heaviness is plotted against physical weight, with volume as a parameter. You can see that containers having the same weight seem lighter the larger they are, thus showing the illusion. Because the curves are not parallel, you conclude that there is an interaction between volume and heaviness in the size/weight illusion.

TABLE 10.17 Simplified design of the Stevens and Rubin experiment

Weight	Size (Volume)		
	Small	Medium	Large
Heavy	X	X	X
Medium	X	X	X
Light	X	X	X

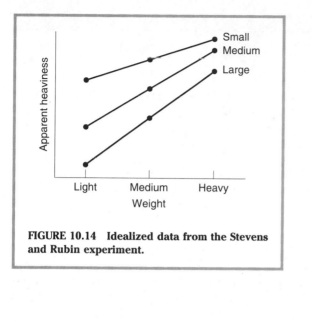

FIGURE 10.14 **Idealized data from the Stevens and Rubin experiment.**

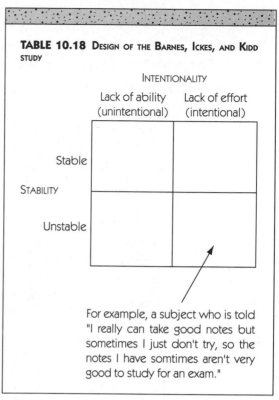

TABLE 10.18 Design of the Barnes, Ickes, and Kidd study

For example, a subject who is told "I really can take good notes but sometimes I just don't try, so the notes I have somtimes aren't very good to study for an exam."

■ Factorial, Between-Subjects

An interesting example of a between-subjects factorial experiment is provided by Richard Barnes, William Ickes, and Robert Kidd (1979). They studied the conditions under which students would give help in the form of lending class notes to a fellow student. They varied the intentionality of the need to borrow notes by having subjects say that they either lacked ability (unintentional) or had not put out the effort (intentional) to take good notes. They varied the stability of the need by having subjects say that they always (stable) took poor notes or sometimes (unstable) took poor notes. Thus they had a 2×2 design, with intentionality and stability of need varied between subjects. (In addition, sex of the subject and sex of the person making the request were included in the design for the purpose of counterbalancing these extraneous variables. These two variables did not produce any effects, so we will not consider them further.)

The design of the experiment is summarized in Table 10.18. As you might expect, more help was offered when the person making the request said that the reason for poor notes was lack of ability rather than lack of effort. In addition, the subjects were more likely to comply when the need was seen as stable rather than unstable. No interaction occurred between the two

BOX 10.1
A 2 × 2 Between-Subjects Factorial Analysis of Variance

This example analyzes fake data that might have been obtained by Barnes, Ickes, and Kidd (1979) in their study of helping behavior by students in the form of lending class notes.

| | INTENTIONALITY | |
STABILITY	UNINTENTIONAL	INTENTIONAL
Stable	4.4	3.6
	4.0	3.2
	4.5	3.7
	3.9	3.0
	4.6	3.8
	3.8	2.9
	4.7	3.9
	3.7	2.8
	4.8	4.0
	3.6	3.1
Unstable	3.7	2.9
	3.3	2.5
	3.8	3.0
	3.2	2.4
	3.9	3.1
	3.1	2.3
	4.0	3.2
	3.0	2.2
	4.1	3.3
	2.9	2.1

NOTE: Hypothetical data for ANOVA, 2 × 2 factorial, between subjects. ($I = 2$ levels of stability; $J = 2$ levels of intentionality; $K = 10$ subjects per cell; $N = 40$ observations.)

1. Assumptions
   a. The population from which each sample is drawn is normally distributed.
   b. The variances of the treatment populations are equal.
   c. The four samples and ten observations in each sample are randomly and independently drawn.

2. H_0: Our null hypothesis is that helping behavior is not affected by either the intentionality or the stability of the need.

3. $\alpha = .01$

4. Refer to the following table.

ANOVA: Sums of squares calculation formulas

Source	df	SS	MS	F
Between I	$I-1$	$\dfrac{\sum_i X_{i..}^2}{JK} - \dfrac{X_{...}^2}{IJK}$ *	$\dfrac{SS_I}{df_I}$	$\dfrac{MS_I}{MS_{err}}$
Between J	$J-1$	$\dfrac{\sum_j X_{.j.}^2}{IK} - \dfrac{X_{...}^2}{IJK}$	$\dfrac{SS_J}{df_J}$	$\dfrac{MS_J}{MS_{err}}$
$I \times J$ interaction	$(I-1)(J-1)$	$\dfrac{\sum_{ij} X_{ij.}^2}{K} - \dfrac{\sum_i X_{i..}^2}{JK} - \dfrac{\sum_j X_{.j.}^2}{IK} + \dfrac{X_{...}^2}{IJK}$	$\dfrac{SS_{I \times J}}{df_{I \times J}}$	$\dfrac{MS_{I \times J}}{MS_{err}}$
Error	$IJ(K-1)$	$\sum_{ijk} X_{ijk}^2 - \dfrac{\sum_{ij} X_{ij.}^2}{K}$	$\dfrac{SS_{err}}{df_{err}}$	
Totals	$(IJK)-1 = N-1$	$\sum_{ijk}(X_{ijk} - \bar{X})^2$		

*See note on dot notation, page 241.

5. Sampling distribution, $F(1, 36)$. (F distribution with $V_1 = 1$ and $V_2 = 36$ degrees of freedom.)
6. Look in an F table under $\alpha = .01$.
   $F = {}_{.01}(1, 36) = 7.40$. If the F calculated in step 7 is >7.40, reject H_0.
7. Refer to the following table.

ANOVA: Data summary table

Source	df	SS	MS	F
Between stability	$I-1 = 1$	$\dfrac{9620}{20} - \dfrac{(138)^2}{40} = 481 - 476.1 = 4.9$	$\dfrac{4.9}{1} = 4.9$	$\dfrac{4.9}{.20} = 24.5*$
Between intentionality	$J-1 = 1$	$\dfrac{9650}{20} - \dfrac{(138)^2}{40} = 482.5 - 476.1 = 6.4$	$\dfrac{6.4}{1} = 6.4$	$\dfrac{6.4}{.20} = 32.0*$
Stability × intention	$(I-1)(J-1) = 1$	$\dfrac{4874}{10} - 481 - 482.5 + 476.1 = 0.0$	0	n.s.
Error	$IJ(K-1) = 36$	$494.6 - 487.4 = 7.2$	$\dfrac{7.2}{36} = .20$	
Totals	$N-1 = 39$	18.5		

*$p < .01$

8. Since $24.5 > 7.40$ and $32.0 > 7.40$, we may conclude that helping behavior is significantly affected by both intentionality and stability of need. We also may conclude that no interaction is present between the two need variables.

BOX 10.2

A 2 × 2 MIXED FACTORIAL ANALYSIS OF VARIANCE*

This example analyzes fake data that might have been obtained by Bower, Gilligan, and Monteiro (1981) on the effect of mood on the recall of happy and sad facts.

MOOD	FACT RECALLED		MOOD	FACT RECALLED	
	HAPPY	SAD		HAPPY	SAD
	54	52		18	74
	56	51		19	77
Happy	58	50	Sad	20	80
	60	49		21	83
	62	48		22	86

NOTE. Hypothetical data for 2 × 2 factorial, mixed. ($I = 2$ mood levels; $J = 2$ fact types; $K = 5$ subjects per cell; $N = 20$ observations.)

1. Assumption
   The two samples of five subjects are randomly assigned to an induced-mood group (happy or sad).
2. Hypotheses
   a. H_0: Our null hypothesis is that mood has no effect on type of fact recalled.
   b. H_1: The alternative is that mood does affect type of fact recalled.
3. $\alpha = .01$
4. Refer to the following table.

ANOVA: SUMS OF SQUARES COMPUTATION FORMULAS

SOURCE	df	SS	MS	F
Between subjects				
Between moods at fact 1 (happy)	$I - 1$	$\dfrac{\sum_i X_{ij.}^2}{K} - \dfrac{X_{.1.}^{2\dagger}}{IK}$	$\dfrac{SS_2}{I-1}$	$\dfrac{MS_2}{MS_4}$
Between moods at fact 2 (sad)	$I - 1$	$\dfrac{\sum_i X_{i2.}^2}{K} - \dfrac{X_{.2.}^2}{IK}$	$\dfrac{SS_3}{I-1}$	$\dfrac{MS_3}{MS_4}$
Within cell	$IJ(K-1)$	$\sum_{ijk} X_{ijk}^2 - \dfrac{\sum_{ij} X_{ij.}^2}{K}$	$\dfrac{SS_4}{IJ(K-1)}$	

$\dagger$ See note on dot notation, page 241.

*For a more complete discusson of this analysis, see Kirk (1968, p. 266).

Within subjects

Between facts at mood 1 (happy)	$J - 1$	$\dfrac{\sum_i X_{1j.}^2}{K} - \dfrac{X_{1..}^2}{JK}$	$\dfrac{SS_6}{J - 1}$	$\dfrac{MS_6}{MS_9}$
Between facts at mood 2 (sad)	$J - 1$	$\dfrac{\sum_i X_{2j.}^2}{K} - \dfrac{X_{2..}^2}{JK}$	$\dfrac{SS_7}{J - 1}$	$\dfrac{MS_7}{MS_9}$
Facts × mood	$(I - 1)(J - 1)$	$\dfrac{\sum_{ij} X_{ij.}^2}{K} - \dfrac{\sum_i X_{i..}^2}{JK} - \dfrac{\sum_j X_{.j.}^2}{IK} + \dfrac{X_{...}^2}{IJK}$	$\dfrac{SS_8}{(I - 1)(K - 1)}$	$\dfrac{MS_8}{MS_9}$
Facts × subject within mood	$I(J - 1)(K - 1)$	$\sum_{ijk} X_{ijk}^2 - \dfrac{\sum_{ij} X_{ij.}^2}{K} - \dfrac{\sum_{ik} X_{i.k}^2}{J} + \dfrac{\sum_i X_{i..}^2}{JK}$	$\dfrac{SS_9}{I(J - 1)(K - 1)}$	

---

5. Sampling distribution: $F(1, 16)$ for between subjects and $F(1, 8)$ for within subjects.
6. Look at an F table under $\alpha = .01$.
   $F_{.01} = 11.26$. If the F calculated in step 7 (under within subject) is > 11.26, reject H_0.
7. Refer to the following table.

ANOVA: DATA SUMMARY TABLE

SOURCE	df	SS	MS	F
Between subjects				
Between moods at fact 1	1	$\dfrac{94100}{5} - \dfrac{(390)^2}{10} = 18820 - 15210 = 3610$	3610	385.1*
Between moods at fact 2	1	$\dfrac{222500}{5} - \dfrac{(650)^2}{10} = 44500 - 42250 = 2250$	2250	240*
Within cell	16	$63470 - 63320 = 150$	9.375	
Within subjects				
Between facts at mood 1	1	$\dfrac{146600}{5} - \dfrac{(500)^2}{10} = 29320 - 29160 = 160$	160	19.69*
Between facts at mood 2	1	$\dfrac{170000}{5} - \dfrac{(540)^2}{10} = 34000 - 25000 = 9000$	9000	1107.69*
Facts × mood	1	$63320 - 54160 - 57460 + 54080 = 5780$	5780	711.38*
Facts × subject within mood	8	$63470 - 63320 - 54245 + 54160 = 65$		8.125

*$p < .01$

---

8. Type of fact recalled *is* significantly affected by mood.

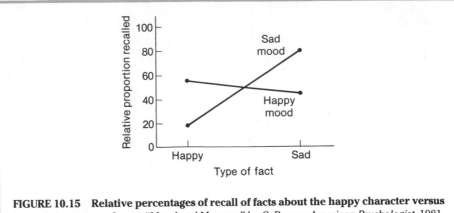

FIGURE 10.15 Relative percentages of recall of facts about the happy character versus the sad character. Source: "Mood and Memory" by G. Bower, *American Psychologist*, 1981, *36*, 129–148. Copyright 1981 by the American Psychological Association. Reprinted by permission of the publisher and author.

independent variables. This experiment is reproduced in Chapter 13 as an example of how to write an experimental report.

■ A Mixed Factorial Design

The next example of a factorial design has one between-subjects variable and one within-subjects variable and thus is a mixed factorial design. Gordon Bower, Stephen Gilligan, and Kenneth Monteiro (1981; Bower, 1981) studied the effect of mood on learning. They hypothesized that subjects would notice events in stories that matched their mood and would remember such events better than events that did not match their mood. By posthypnotic suggestion they made their subjects feel either happy or sad and then had them read a story about two men, Andre and Jack. Everything connected with Andre in the story is happy, but everything to do with Jack is sad. After the subjects finished reading the story, the experimenters asked them which character they identified with. Subjects identified with the character whose mood matched their own. The next day, when they were in a neutral mood, the subjects were asked to remember as much of the story as they could. The experimenters found that subjects remembered more facts connected with the character whose mood matched their own at the time they read the story. (See Figure 10.15.) The subjects' mood when reading the story was the between-subjects variable. Whether the facts were happy or sad was the within-subjects variable.

SUMMARY

1. A factorial design uses all combinations of two or more independent variables, each having at least two levels.

2. Factorial designs are employed when one wishes to study the joint effect of two or more independent variables.

3. A factorial design may save time by studying more than one condition per experiment, or it may be used when ruling out more than one rival hypothesis, or when one is interested in possible interaction between the independent variables.

4. In a factorial experiment, the main effect of one variable is the effect of that variable averaged over all of the levels of the other variable(s).

5. An interaction exists between two independent variables when (independent) Variable A has a different effect on the dependent variable when it is combined with one level of (independent) Variable B than with another level of B. If the graph of a factorial experiment has nonparallel lines, there is an interaction between the variables.

6. If there is an interaction, the main effect is uninterpretable unless the nature of the interaction is taken into account.

7. Types of interactions include antagonistic, synergistic, and ceiling effect.

8. The presence or absence of an interaction and the form it takes may be affected by transformations made on the data.

9. Factorial designs may be conducted as either within-subjects or between-subjects experiments, or they may be used in mixed experiments that have one within-subjects and one between-subjects variable.

10. The within-subjects factorial design requires the fewest subjects to achieve a particular degree of power, the mixed design the next fewest, and the between-subjects design the most.

11. The example given of a within-subjects factorial design was a study of the size/weight illusion, in which size and weight of lifted containers were the independent variables.

12. The example given of a between-subjects factorial design was a study of helping behavior by students in which the independent variables were the intentionality and the stability of the need to borrow notes for a class.

13. The example given of a mixed factorial design was a study of mood and memory in which the between-subjects variable was the mood of subjects when they read a story and the within-subjects variable was the happiness or sadness of facts in the story.

Suggestions for Further Reading

For advice on true experiments, the best place to go is journals or books on particular research areas. Analyze the methods of actual experiments to see how problems of validity were controlled for in experimental situations.

A CASE IN POINT

Within or Between?

You are interested in the role of mental images in memory. Your hypothesis is that children tend to use imagery more than adults do when they retrieve information from memory. In other words, you believe that to recall whether a tiger has spots, a child will first recall an image of a tiger, then look at the image and see that it has stripes instead of spots. An adult, on the other hand, might simply recall facts about tigers and know directly (without the use of images) that tigers have stripes.

You will use reaction time as the dependent variable. It is known that it takes longer to recall information from an image then to recall it directly.

Your first independent variable will be age. You have first-graders, fourth-graders, and adults available for your study.

Your second independent variable will be whether or not the subjects are instructed to use imagery in deciding whether an animal has a certain property. In the no-imagery condition, they will simply be asked to respond as quickly as possible whether, for example, a tiger has spots. They will be instructed to think about the properties of the whole animal, not just a part of it. In the imagery condition, they will be asked to form an image of the animal when they hear its name and then examine the image for the property in question.

REQUIRED: Design the study, and provide mock summary data in a table or graph. Decide which, if any, of the independent variables you would test between subjects and which, if any, you would test within subjects. Give the rationale for each of your choices.

CONSIDERATIONS: Your theory predicts that children will always tend to use imagery, whether you instruct them to or not. Adults, on the other hand, will use imagery when instructed to do so but may or may not use imagery when they are not instructed to do so. Therefore, you predict an interaction between age and instruction: Children will always be slow (because they will use imagery), but adults will be slow when they use imagery and fast when they don't. (It will help to graph your expected results at this point.)

You expect adults to be faster at this task than children, even when they use imagery.

In thinking about whether to study the imagery-versus-nonimagery variable within subjects, you realize that it may be inadvisable to randomize the order of conditions, because once a subject has received imagery instructions it may be difficult for him or her not to use imagery. Thus, there may be a sequence effect of imagery on the nonimagery condition.

On the other hand, you are not so concerned with how much slower the subjects will be in the imagery condition as with the interaction between age and imagery versus nonimagery. The prediction you are making is that adults will show a greater difference in reaction times between imagery and nonimagery conditions than children will.

There may be order effects between the first and second condition, regardless of which condition subjects experience first, because of either practice or fatigue.

The experiment on which this case study is based is cited in the Instructor's Manual.

≡ READING BETWEEN THE LINES ≡

10.1 THIRST IN BRAIN-DAMAGED RATS

Normal rats will respond to an intraperitoneal (into the body cavity) injection of salt solution with a marked increase in water drinking, in order to restore their normal salt balance. Blass and Epstein (1971) reported that rats with lesions of a part of the brain known as the lateral preoptic area did not drink in response to this stimulus. The result was not surprising in light of considerable other evidence that this brain area is involved in regulation of drinking in response to salt levels. Christopher Coburn and Edward Stricker (1978), however, suspected that another interpretation of the data might be possible. They knew that these brain-damaged rats also respond abnormally to other ways of making rats drink that should not have anything to do with the supposed function of the lateral preoptic area. First, they repeated the experiment of Blass and Epstein and found the same results. Then they showed that the brain-damaged rats responded normally to several other ways of changing salt balance. What might be some plausible explanations for the difference between the brain-damaged rats and the normal rats in their response to the intraperitoneal injections and the other ways of inducing thirst? ∎

☑ EXERCISES

10.1 FACTORIAL DESIGN

Professor Hyde studies the effects that two or more drugs have on animal activity when the drugs are administered simultaneously. She designs a study that involves two factors. Factor A consists of two levels of Drug A (3 cc, 6 cc). Factor B consists of two levels of Drug B (2 cc, 4 cc). The experimental subjects are white rats, and the dependent variable is amount

TABLE 10.19 DATA FROM THE STUDY OF THE EFFECTS OF TWO DRUGS ON THE ACTIVITY OF WHITE RATS

	B_1	B_2
A_1	1	11
	6	16
	3	11
	3	12
	5	14
A_2	6	11
	8	10
	7	9
	8	7
	4	9

of activity, as measured by the number of times each rat revolves an exercise wheel (in hundreds of revolutions, rounded to the nearest 100). The results of the study are given in Table 10.19.

REQUIRED:
    a. Calculate and graph the cell means.
    b. Is there an interaction between Factors A and B? If so, explain the nature of the interaction.
    c. Is there a main effect of Factor A? Explain.
    d. Is there a main effect of Factor B? Explain.

OPTIONAL:
    e. Analyze these data with a two-way fixed effects analysis of variance, using $\alpha = .05$ for all tests performed.
    f. Present an ANOVA summary table. What do you conclude?

10.2 READ AN ABSTRACT

The following is from the abstract of an article (Kernis, Zuckerman, & McVay, 1988, p. 535):

Subjects were led to attribute success on a two-person maze test either to their own actions (internal locus) or to the actions of their partner (external locus). Subsequently they worked either on another maze or on a completely different task. Performance on these tasks served as the . . . dependent measure. Level of self-awareness was manipulated by having half of the subjects work on the test task while facing a mirror. . . . Internal-success subjects performed better [than external-success subjects] when tested on the maze task, but worse when tested on a novel task. The self-awareness manipulation did not reliably affect performance.

REQUIRED:
    a. Is this a true experiment or a quasi experiment?
    b. Describe the design.
    c. Was there a main effect of locus (internal versus external)?
    d. Was there a main effect of task (maze versus novel)?
    e. Was there a main effect of self-awareness (mirror versus no mirror)?
    f. Was there an interaction? What kind of interaction was it?

10.3 READ AN ABSTRACT

The following is from the abstract of an article (Mollenauer, Bryson, & Phillips, 1991, p. 217):

After 5 weeks of voluntary wheel running . . . mice [of a certain strain] were significantly resistant to the sleep-inducing effects of [alcohol]. Sixty-four mice, 32 males and 32 females, were assigned to wheel (free access to a running wheel in the home cage) or no-wheel conditions. At the end of the training period, the animals were removed from the exercise cages and tested for sensitivity to [alcohol]. . . , assessed by [the time it took them to fall asleep]. Exercised animals [took significantly longer before they fell asleep and had] shorter duration of sleep time [after falling down]. Exercise caused a significant decrease in body weight in male, but not female, mice. The present results suggest that exercise training may be effective in reducing [alcohol]-induced sleep.

REQUIRED:
a. What was (were) the independent variable(s)?
b. What was (were) the dependent variable(s)?
c. What was the design of the study? (List each independent variable, and indicate the levels of each.)
d. Was this a true experiment or a quasi experiment, or partly both? Explain.
e. Was there a main effect of sex on time before the mice fell asleep?
f. Was there a main effect of running on time before the mice fell asleep?
g. Was there an interaction with regard to time to fall asleep? If there was, describe it.
h. Was there an interaction with regard to weight loss? If there was, describe it.

10.4 READ A DESCRIPTION OF A STUDY

Ilene Bernstein (1978) wanted to test whether the conditioning of taste aversion to novel foods experienced just before a gastrointestinal illness, known as the Garcia effect, occurred in humans. Children who were receiving chemotherapy were randomly assigned to three groups. Mapletoff is an unusual flavor of ice cream that the children would not have experienced before. Group 1 received Mapletoff ice cream and then chemotherapy. Group 2 received chemotherapy only, and Group 3 received Mapletoff ice cream only. Later, all three groups were given a choice of eating Mapletoff ice cream or playing with a game. It was found that 21% of Group 1, 67% of Group 2, and 73% of Group 3 chose Mapletoff.

REQUIRED:
a. What was the hypothesis?
b. What type of study was this?
c. What was (were) the independent variable(s)?
d. What was (were) the dependent variable(s)?
e. What was (were) the control group(s)?
f. What did it (they) control for?
g. What was the design?
h. What were the results?
i. What statistic would be appropriate?   ❏

11

Single-Subject Experiments

Up to this point in the book we have talked as if using groups of subjects were the only way to do research. It is true that most psychological research involves groups of subjects, but this approach is not the only way to do research. This chapter deals with strategies for achieving control in experiments using single subjects.

Research using single subjects not only is common, but has a long tradition. In fact, scientists have used single subjects in research for longer than they have used groups. Gustav Fechner, who some historians say is the founder of experimental psychology, worked extensively on individual subjects—himself and his brother-in-law. Beginning in 1860, Fechner invented the basic psychophysical methods that are still used today to measure sensory thresholds and discovered principles of psychophysics that are still taken seriously. Twenty-five years later, inspired by Fechner's work, Hermann Ebbinghaus did his experimental work on memory. Following Fechner's example, he used himself as his own subject. Wilhelm Wundt, who is credited with founding the first psychological laboratory in 1879, conducted experiments measuring various psychological and behavioral responses in individual subjects. Wundt's famous student, E. B. Titchener, espoused the use of introspection, which is the careful reporting of one's own experience. Because this procedure required a great deal of training, much of his work was done using one or a few individuals. Finally, I. P. Pavlov did his pioneering work on conditioning using individual dogs. The list of psychologists who relied on individual subjects is long and includes most of those working before about 1930, when modern statistical methods were developed.

These early researchers used single subjects in the time-honored scientific tradition. In any case, modern statistical methods did not then exist. Their solutions to the problems of reliability and validity were extensive observations and frequent replication of results. A traditional assumption of researchers doing single-subject experiments has been that individual subjects are essentially equivalent and that one should study additional subjects only to make sure that the original subject was not grossly abnormal.

The modern statistical methods that have become an integral part of present-day research grew out of a different tradition. A Belgian astronomer, Adolphe Quetelet, discovered that human traits followed the normal curve. From this he concluded that nature strove to produce the "average man" (Hersen & Barlow, 1976). The variability around the mean that is always found was considered to be a result of nature's failure to achieve the ideal average person in every case. The individual-differences tradition of Galton and Pearson grew out of this thinking. According to the individual-differences tradition, variability between subjects is inevitable. The task then becomes how to separate the effect of the experimental manipulation from this inherent variability. During the 1930s, statistician R. A. Fisher, a mathematician working on problems of genetics, invented many statistical methods such as the analysis of variance that have become standard in psychological research. These techniques dominated psychological research to such an extent that the single-subject tradition almost disappeared for several decades.

Nevertheless, certain psychologists continued to work in the single-subject tradition during that period, notably B. F. Skinner. Skinner disdained the use of statistics, claiming that he would rather study one animal for 1,000 hours than study 1,000 animals for an hour each. Skinner's philosophy of research is described in the classic book by Murray Sidman (1960). Sidman makes clear the difference in attitude between the single-subject approach and the groups approach to research. The single-subject tradition assumes that most variability in the subject's behavior is *imposed* by the situation and therefore can be *removed* by careful attention to experimental control. The individual-differences, group-research tradition assumes that much of the variability is *intrinsic* and should be *statistically controlled* and *analyzed*.

We cannot settle the debate between these two positions. Psychologists began using statistical methods to evaluate the results of experiments in which removing all sources of variability was not feasible. A set of data may look so regular that it is hard to believe that they could be the result of chance, especially when one has a large personal investment in getting a certain result. The use of statistics is one way to avoid being fooled into thinking that data are more reliable than they really are. On the other hand, using statistical methods does not guarantee that you will draw the right conclusion about the data; that is why we talk about Type I and Type II errors. In addition, we should note that employing single-subject methods is not completely incompatible with statistical analysis inasmuch as statistical methods are being developed to handle data from individual subjects (for example, Kratochwill & Levin, 1992).

ADVANTAGES OF THE SINGLE-SUBJECT APPROACH

Although we acknowledge that the group-comparison approach has a rightful place in psychology, we will point out several advantages of the single-subject approach. We should keep these advantages in mind whenever we are designing research.

■ Focusing on Individual Performance

Whenever data are averaged over many subjects, the possibility exists that the average picture is a distortion of the behavior of the individual subjects. Consider Figure 11.1. Suppose this represents a learning curve of a group of subjects on some task. Because the curve is a smooth ogive (S-shaped curve), we might conclude from the group data that learning was a gradual, continuous process. However, look now at Figure 11.2. This graph shows the individual data for the five subjects who make up the group in the previous graph. Here we get a different picture. Each subject learns suddenly, going from *no* to *yes* on a single trial. Subjects learn on different trials, however. Subject 1 goes from no on trial 6 to complete mastery on trial 7; Subject 2 goes from no on trial 9 to complete mastery on trial 10; and so forth. When the data of the whole group are averaged, though, the learning appears gradual. Although this example is extreme, it occurs fairly often in laboratory situations.

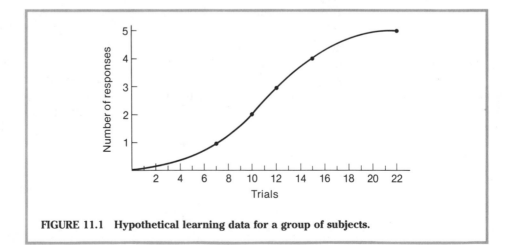

FIGURE 11.1   Hypothetical learning data for a group of subjects.

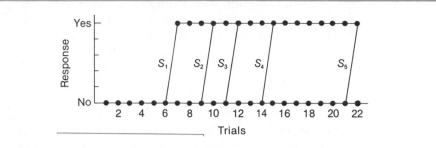

FIGURE 11.2 Hypothetical learning data for the individual subjects whose group data were shown in Figure 11.1.

■ Focusing on Big Effects

An experiment that employs large groups of subjects will be likely to discover that an independent variable has an effect even if the effect is a minor one. For example, given enough subjects, it might be possible to show that a clinical treatment produced improvement in 55% of the subjects, whereas 50% of the control subjects improved spontaneously. A therapist is not likely to adopt a treatment that shows such a marginal difference in success rate. The experiment would have little **clinical significance** even if it had plenty of statistical significance (Hersen & Barlow, 1976).

Some researchers in nonclinical situations feel this same reluctance. They would rather not spend time investigating the effects of variables that produce small effects but would rather find the powerful variables that produce large effects. Because the effect of a minor variable is less likely to be discovered in a single-subject experiment, the experimenter will not be distracted by it. In addition, the researcher can spend time reducing variability so that the effect of a given variable will be maximized, instead of spending time testing more subjects.

Statisticians use the term **power** to refer to the probability that a statistical test will find a significant difference when there actually is a difference in the population from which the data are drawn. The power of a test depends on the size of the difference that exists in the population and the size of the sample drawn from the population. Therefore, a researcher has two ways of increasing the probability of finding a significant result in an experiment: increasing the size of the effect or increasing the size of the sample (the number of subjects or the number of observations per subject). In Chapter 6 we discussed how increasing the number of subjects decreases the variability of the data. The other tactic, and the one favored by single-subject researchers, is to increase the size of the effect.

Suppose that you are interested in whether the students at Alma Mater College are smarter than those at Rival College. The larger the number of

clinical significance
the practical importance of a result

power
the probability that a statistical test will find a significant difference when a difference exists in the population

students sampled from each college, the greater the likelihood of finding a difference in intelligence between the groups. Eventually, if you include every student from both colleges, any difference you find is "statistically significant" because it is not based on a sample at all: you have measured the whole population. You are not performing an inferential statistic, but measuring the population value itself. This statement is true even if the difference between the students at the two colleges is barely measurable.

Suppose that two researchers work on the same problem, and each measures the correlation between the same two variables. Researcher A uses 10 subjects and finds a correlation of .765. Researcher B uses 50 subjects and finds a correlation of .361. Both researchers find that their correlations are significant at the .01 level. That is, there is 1 chance in 100 that the correlation either researcher obtained does not reflect a true correlation between the two variables in the populations studied. The question is, In which researcher's findings should you have greater trust? Should you put more confidence in Researcher B's results because more subjects were used?

The answer is that you should feel more confident with Researcher A's results, because the same level of significance was obtained with fewer subjects. Remember that each had the same probability that the results were spurious: 1 in 100. In order to get the same level of significance with fewer subjects, Researcher A had to obtain a larger effect. This fact is shown by A's having found a correlation that is larger than B's. The square of the correlation coefficient gives us the percentage of the variance in the data that is accounted for by the independent variable. Researcher A's correlation of .765 accounts for 58.5% of the variance, whereas Researcher B's correlation of .361 accounts for only 13% of the variance. Researcher A obtained a larger correlation, and the independent variable accounts for a greater percentage of the variance, even though fewer subjects were used. Researcher A must have had better control over the sources of variability in the study.

■ Avoiding Ethical and Practical Problems

Whenever research involves testing the efficacy of a treatment that is expected to benefit the participant, an ethical question arises over placing some participants into a control group that will not receive treatment or that will receive inferior treatment. In clinical psychology, this area is particularly touchy when the client's situation can be life-threatening, as with suicide-prone persons. One solution is to treat all of the participants but to evaluate them from a single-subject standpoint.

Another situation that calls for a single-subject experiment is when the researcher cannot locate enough subjects to constitute a group to study. Perhaps the researcher is testing the efficacy of a clinical treatment. If there are not enough people suffering from the same condition, subjects will have to be studied on a single-subject basis.

■ Flexibility in Design

An experiment on a group of subjects must be designed so that all subjects receive the same experience in order for them to be comparable. This necessity can result in a design that is not the best one for all subjects. In the course of an experiment on behavior modification, an experimenter may discover that a subject does not respond to a reinforcer that has worked on previous subjects. If the design is a single-subject one, the experiment can be modified on the spot by switching reinforcers or by altering the instructions.

Another problem that can be solved by a design modification is when a large change occurs in the subject's behavior that the experimenter suspects is caused by an outside event rather than by the experimental manipulation. The experimenter can immediately switch the conditions and see if the behavior changes correspondingly. A group experiment, on the other hand, would call for continuing all subjects in the same procedure and hoping that the outside events would cancel each other out.

DISADVANTAGES OF THE SINGLE-SUBJECT APPROACH

In contrast to the advantages of the single-subject approach, we should mention some of its disadvantages. If there were none, no multiple-subject experiments would ever be done!

First, some effects are small relative to the amount of variability in the situation. It may be impossible to control the other sources of variability sufficiently to observe the experimental effect in one subject. This is the reason why modern statistical methods were developed in the first place. For example, the only way to decide if having been abused as children causes adults to be child abusers themselves is to compare large groups of individuals. It is no surprise that group experiments and statistical analysis are discussed together so often. Statistical procedures for analyzing single-subject data are not as well developed.

Second, some experimental effects are by definition between-subjects effects. It is impossible to have a subject who simultaneously receives two opposite sets of instructions in a social psychology experiment, or who is taught the same material by two different methods.

BASIC CONTROL STRATEGIES IN SINGLE-SUBJECT RESEARCH

Just as there are standard ways of controlling for rival hypotheses in group experiments, there are standard strategies in single-subject experiments. We will discuss the most important of them. Others are discussed in Barlow & Hersen (1984).

■ Obtaining a Stable Baseline

When you are using a group design, you compare one group of subjects against another, or a group of subjects in one condition against the same subjects in another condition. The assumption that the groups were equal before the treatment is the basis of your attributing the effect to the manipulation rather than to something else. This assumption can be tested by statistically analyzing the differences between the groups. When you have only one subject, however, you must use a different strategy to compare outcomes between conditions. That strategy is to compare the behavior that occurs before and after the introduction of the experimental manipulation. The behavior before the manipulation must be measured over a long enough time span to obtain a stable **baseline** against which the later behavior can be measured.

baseline
the measure of behavior before treatment that establishes a reference point for evaluating the effect of treatment

Suppose that you want to measure the effectiveness of a treatment for anorexia nervosa, a disorder characterized by voluntary self-starvation. You would need to measure the patient's weight and food intake for a period of time before initiating the treatment in order to show that the weight was stable and that the patient had not begun gaining weight spontaneously. How long this baseline measure should be continued is difficult to say. The judgment of stability is a subjective one. However, the experiment would be useless unless it was evident that the patient had not begun gaining weight before the treatment. If the baseline behavior is not stable before treatment, a declining baseline may be acceptable if the treatment is expected to cause an increase in the behavior, and vice versa. For a patient with anorexia nervosa, a decrease in weight in the absence of treatment is not unusual and would constitute an acceptable baseline for comparison with a treatment. This example illustrates another consideration in obtaining baseline measures: Sometimes the existing condition is harmful to the subject, or even life-threatening, so that the goal of a stable baseline may be overridden by other factors.

■ Using the Withdrawal of Treatment (ABA Designs)

If you simply measure the baseline behavior and introduce a treatment, you will not know whether other variables may have produced the change in behavior. In fact, you would have the single-subject equivalent of the quasi-experimental design called the one-group pretest/posttest design. (See Chapters 9 and 12.) The inference that the treatment is the cause of the change is considerably strengthened if the treatment is withdrawn after a period of time and the behavior shows a return toward the baseline. This use of treatment withdrawal is often referred to as an **ABA design.**

ABA design
research design that includes a baseline period, a treatment period, and a subsequent withdrawal of treatment

Two principal problems are associated with an ABA design. First, the effect of the manipulation may not be fully reversible. If the treatment were a lesion of the brain that causes obesity, clearly it would be impossible to reverse the lesion. Or if a learning procedure causes a more or less permanent change in a subject's behavior, that too would not be reversible. In fact, many procedures are tested because a permanent improvement in a person's behavior is desired after the treatment is ended.

The second problem with the ABA design is that you may wish to leave the subjects in the new condition rather than return them to their original state. Treatments involving weight control, phobias, compulsive behaviors, and the like are typical examples. In such cases the experimenter may withdraw the treatment temporarily before the behavior change has reached the desired level. After the behavior shows some reversal of the trend toward improvement, treatment is reinstated. In any case, experimenters in behavior modification seldom end an experiment with the baseline, or withdrawal, condition. Rather, they reintroduce the treatment in order to produce maximum benefit for the client.

■ Repeating Treatments (ABAB Designs)

In the examples just discussed, the treatment was repeated after the withdrawal phase in order to leave the subject with the full benefit of the training. This repetition of treatment also has the advantage of providing another opportunity to evaluate the effect of the treatment. This kind of ABA design experiment in which treatment is repeated is called an **ABAB design.** Repeated presentation and withdrawal of a variable can produce strong evidence for the validity of the independent variable's effect. Anyone who watches a pigeon that has been trained in a Skinner box to respond in the presence of a light and not to respond in its absence is impressed by the control that the light exerts over the animal's behavior. The light appears to turn the behavior on and off as though by a switch.

An interesting example of an ABAB design is provided by the work of Edward Carr and Jack McDowell (1980). They wished to treat Jim, a 10-year-old boy who scratched himself so much that he caused sores on his body. Jim's behavior had begun when he got into poison oak, causing a dermatitis that lasted a few weeks. Three years later, however, Jim was still scratching himself. The first step in the experiment was to observe Jim's behavior in various settings. The observer noticed that Jim scratched himself mostly when other people were around. Carr and McDowell surmised that the scratching was an operant response reinforced by attention from his parents. This hypothesis was confirmed in a session in which an experimenter observed the family. In the first part of the session, the parents were instructed to ignore Jim's scratching. Then, for a period of time, they were to tell him to stop whenever he scratched himself. Finally, the session ended with another period in which they were to ignore his scratching. The experimenters found that Jim's scratching increased dramatically when he received social attention for it and that the scratching declined during the phase in which it was ignored (Figure 11.3).

Because Jim's parents were unable to ignore his scratching for long

ABAB design
an ABA design with treatment repeated after the withdrawal phase

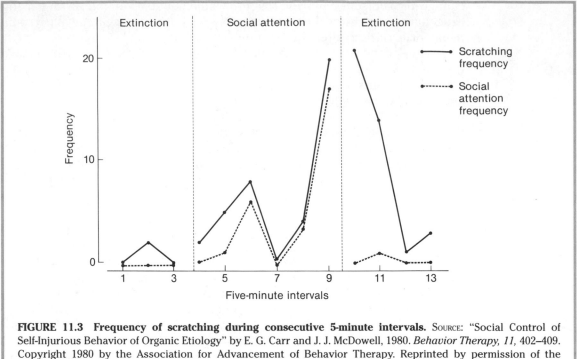

FIGURE 11.3 Frequency of scratching during consecutive 5-minute intervals. Source: "Social Control of Self-Injurious Behavior of Organic Etiology" by E. G. Carr and J. J. McDowell, 1980. *Behavior Therapy, 11,* 402–409. Copyright 1980 by the Association for Advancement of Behavior Therapy. Reprinted by permission of the publisher and authors.

periods of time, the experimenters decided to use a time-out technique. Whenever Jim scratched himself, he was sent to the utility room for 20 minutes. The condition is called time out from positive reinforcement because no reinforcement of social attention could occur while Jim was in the utility room. In addition, Jim was to receive a reinforcer of his choice (a trip to the science museum) at the end of any week during which the number of sores was reduced by two from the previous lowest number.

Figure 11.4 shows the number of sores on Jim's body over the 18-month span of the experiment. First was a baseline period that was kept brief because of the undesirable nature of Jim's condition. Then treatment proceeded for 2 months, during which the number of sores decreased dramatically. A natural reversal occurred when Jim's parents both lost their jobs and could not afford time or money for treatment. Following this 2½-month reversal, treatment was continued for a 4½-month period, after which no treatment was given for a 9-month follow-up period. You can see that the number of sores on Jim's body decreased steadily during treatment, increased during the reversal, and decreased again during the second treatment to a low level that continued after treatment was discontinued.

Interesting features of the design are that time-outs were given contingent on the behavior of scratching, but reinforcers were given

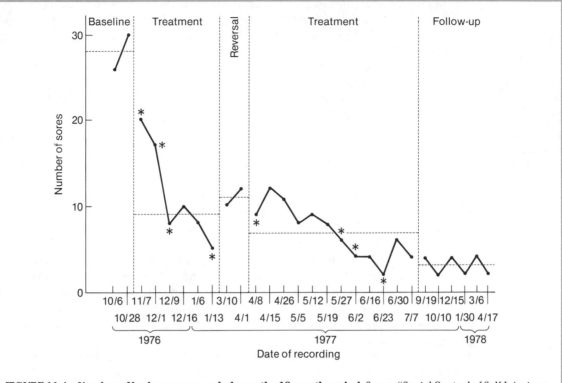

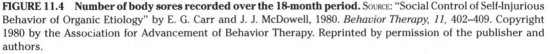

FIGURE 11.4   Number of body sores recorded over the 18-month period. Source: "Social Control of Self-Injurious Behavior of Organic Etiology" by E. G. Carr and J. J. McDowell, 1980. *Behavior Therapy, 11,* 402–409. Copyright 1980 by the Association for Advancement of Behavior Therapy. Reprinted by permission of the publisher and authors.

contingent on reducing the number of sores. In addition, progress of the treatment was monitored by recording the number of sores, which is only an indirect measure of the scratching behavior. Also, practical concerns dictated recording the number of sores on an irregular basis (the time axis of the graph is not measured in equal units), as well as the treatment reversal that occurred when Jim's parents lost their jobs. Neither of these features was likely to improve Jim's progress, yet the treatment was successful. In any case, the reversal strengthens the conclusion that the time-outs for scratching and/or the reinforcements for reducing the number of sores had an effect on the scratching behavior.

■ Changing Only One Variable at a Time

An important rule of single-subject research is to vary only one thing at a time. If two variables are changed simultaneously, it is impossible to decide whether the change in behavior was caused by one or the other, or by the two together. If there are two variables, called B and C, and the baseline condition is labeled A, then an acceptable sequence of presenting the conditions would be A-B-A-B-BC-B-BC. Notice that the conditions were presented in such a sequence that every condition was both preceded and followed by the same condition at least once and that only one variable changed at a time.

interaction design
single-subject research design that manipulates variables one at a time to determine their effect

The A-B-A-B-BC-B-BC design is often called an **interaction design.** Notice, though, that all possible combinations of B and C are not presented, because C is never presented alone (A represents the absence of B and C). Thus, it is not possible to assess the presence of an interaction as defined in Chapter 10. (Analyzing for an interaction requires at least a complete 2×2 factorial design.) What is tested by this procedure is whether C has an effect *in addition to* that of B alone.

Suppose that you want to know whether praise for making a correct response (C) has an effect on a child's learning in addition to the effect of a token reward (B). If you find that praise plus token reward has a greater effect than a token reward alone, you will have information useful for designing a learning situation for the child. However, you will not know the effect of praise when presented alone. Praise alone may have worked as well as the token reward plus praise. On the other hand, praise alone may have been ineffective. (Nothing except practical considerations prevents the use of C alone. The sequence would be A-B-A-B-BC-B-BC-C-BC, somewhat long for many situations.)

A study by Ansley Bacon-Prue, Ronald Blount, Connie Hosey, and Ronald Drabman (1980) provides a good example of an experiment that examines the effect of more than one variable. Bacon-Prue et al. wanted mentally retarded persons in an institution to make their own beds. First, they took baseline measures of the percentage of residents who spontaneously made their beds. Then they instituted a procedure to remind the residents each evening, when they were all together, to make their beds in the morning. As you can see in Figure 11.5, the instructions caused only a slight, temporary increase in bedmaking.

In the next phase, the experimenters placed photographs of the residents who made their beds on a given day on a conspicuously placed poster titled "The Bedmakers" that showed a picture of two made beds. The instructions continued to be given as well. Figure 11.5 shows that the percentage of made beds jumped suddenly and continued to increase thereafter. Next there was a second instruction-only phase, during which the percentage of made beds decreased steadily. A second instruction-plus-photograph phase reversed the decline.

Although this experiment involved changing only one variable at a time, Bacon-Prue et al. did not arrange that every condition was both preceded and followed by the same condition. In other words, the design was A-B-BC-B-BC, rather than A-B-A-B-BC-B-BC. Besides saving the time that would have been required for two additional conditions, the design is justified by the fact that the B condition (instructions only) did not have any permanent effect compared to the baseline condition. Therefore, there was no reason to return

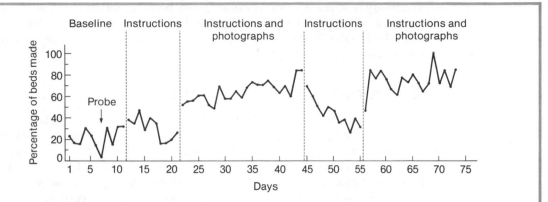

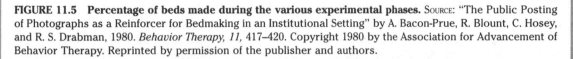

FIGURE 11.5   Percentage of beds made during the various experimental phases. Source: "The Public Posting of Photographs as a Reinforcer for Bedmaking in an Institutional Setting" by A. Bacon-Prue, R. Blount, C. Hosey, and R. S. Drabman, 1980. *Behavior Therapy, 11,* 417–420. Copyright 1980 by the Association for Advancement of Behavior Therapy. Reprinted by permission of the publisher and authors.

to baseline before introducing the additional manipulation (photographs). On the other hand, the results suggest that a photographs-only condition might have been worth trying. If it had been successful in maintaining the bedmaking behavior, it probably would have saved staff time and effort in the future. Then the design would have been A-B-BC-B-BC-C. An interesting aspect of this experiment is that it is a single-subject design applied to a large group of subjects.

■ Using Multiple Baselines

Another effective way to demonstrate that the manipulation caused the behavior change is to introduce the manipulation at different times for each of several different behaviors to see if the onset of behavior change coincides with the manipulation. For example, suppose a researcher is trying to determine if rewarding a retarded child for doing certain personal tasks is effective. If the researcher begins rewarding tooth brushing, face washing, hand washing, and hair combing all at the same time, it is possible that the presence of the experimenter, the attention received, or a spontaneous decision to turn over a new leaf was responsible for the change. The researcher, however, could begin rewarding only tooth brushing the first week, tooth brushing and face washing the second week, and so forth until, after four weeks, all behaviors were being rewarded. This sequence would make it possible to see whether the increase in behavior coincided with the reward.

multiple-baseline design
research design that introduces experimental manipulation at different times for different behaviors to see if behavior change coincides with manipulation

This design is known as a **multiple-baseline design.** The separate experimental baselines may be different behaviors in the same individual, as in this example, or the same behaviors in different individuals. A third possibility is to test the same behavior in the same individual but in different behavior settings. An example of this last approach will be given shortly. Multiple-baseline designs are especially useful if the behavior change with manipulation is irreversible.

■ Employing a Changing Criterion

Another way of showing that the manipulation caused the behavior change is to change the criterion for reward over time. After a baseline measurement, a reward can be given for meeting a lax criterion of the behavior. After the behavior stabilizes at that level, the criterion can be raised until the behavior stabilizes again, and so forth. If the behavior begins to change after each change in the criterion, then the conclusion that the reward is the cause of the improvement is rather convincing.

changing-criterion design
research design that introduces successively more stringent criteria for reinforcement to see if behavior change coincides with the changing criteria

Suppose that a child is unable to sit still in class. The teacher may reward the child for sitting still for 5 minutes at a time until the performance becomes stable. Then the criterion may be set at 10 minutes, later at 15, and so forth. The behavior at each criterion becomes the baseline against which to evaluate the effect of the manipulation at the next criterion. Like the multiple-baseline design, a **changing-criterion design** is useful when the behavior change is irreversible.

EXAMPLES OF SINGLE-SUBJECT DESIGNS

■ A Multiple-Baseline Design with Withdrawal of Treatment

As an example of a single-subject design, we will discuss an experiment conducted by Nirbay Singh, Maryan Dawson, and Paul Gregory (1980). They desired to stop a profoundly retarded 18-year-old female from hyperventilating. This problem, in which a person breathes too deeply, can have serious medical consequences. Several treatments had been attempted on the subject without success, including reprimand and medication.

Singh, Dawson, and Gregory decided to punish episodes of hyperventilation by briefly presenting ammonia (smelling salts) to the subject every time she hyperventilated. The design was a multiple-baseline design, with the withdrawal of treatment as a test probe. Baseline recordings were made for 5 days in each of four different settings (classroom, dining room, bathroom, and day room). Experimental sessions lasted 2 hours per day (30 minutes in each of four settings). During this time, all instances of hyperventilation were recorded but not punished. Then the baseline recordings were continued in three of the settings, and punishment was administered to any episodes of hyperventilation that occurred in the classroom. After 5 more days, punishment was instituted for episodes occurring in the dining room as well as in the classroom, and baseline recording continued in the bathroom and day room. After 5 more days, punishment was extended to the bathroom, and after another 5 days, to the day room.

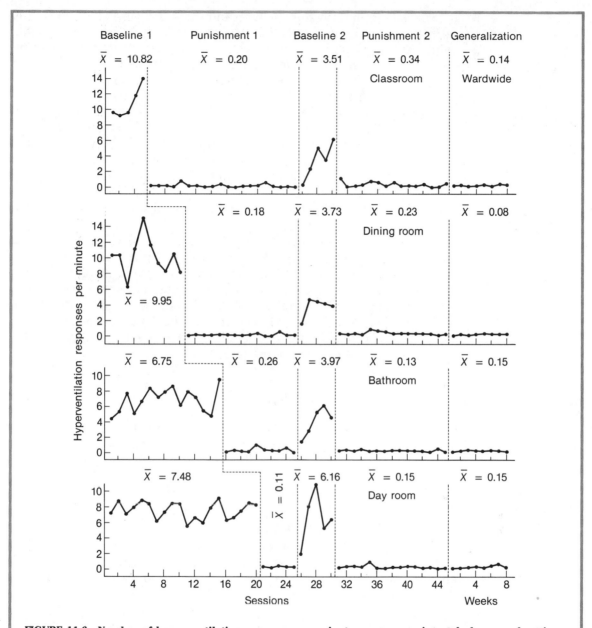

FIGURE 11.6 Number of hyperventilation responses per minute across experimental phases and settings.
Source: "Suppression of Chronic Hyperventilation Using Response-Contingent Aromatic Ammonia" by N. N. Singh, M. J. Dawson, and P. R. Gregory, 1980. *Behavior Therapy, 11,* 561–566. Copyright 1980 by the Association for Advancement of Behavior Therapy. Reprinted by permission of the publisher and authors.

The data from this experiment are indicated in Figure 11.6. You can see that frequency of hyperventilation did not decrease in any of the baseline conditions. In each situation, when punishment was initiated, however, hyperventilation decreased dramatically. After punishment had been continued for 5 days in the last setting, punishment was withdrawn but the episodes of hyperventilation were still recorded. You can see that the subject began hyperventilating again in all situations but ceased abruptly when punishment was reinstated. After 15 more days of punishment for any instance of hyperventilation in the four settings, the procedure was generalized. Instead of having one experimenter administer punishment in the four settings during a 2-hour session, all nurses in the ward were to administer punishment whenever they observed hyperventilation in any setting during an 8-hour day. This practice was instituted to consolidate and maintain the previous gains.

The study illustrates how to test the effectiveness of an experimental manipulation on a single subject in an unambiguous manner. Because the manipulation was instituted at four different times in four different settings, the researchers would have to have used four different alternative hypotheses to account for the decreases in hyperventilation that occurred. The increase in hyperventilation that occurred following the removal of punishment and the abrupt decrease when punishment was reinstated give further evidence of the effectiveness of the treatment.

■ Two Examples from Psychophysics

Our previous examples came from the Skinnerian tradition. The next two examples come from another major tradition employing single subjects: psychophysics. We mentioned earlier that Gustav Fechner, the founder of psychophysics, used single subjects extensively. This practice is still common in psychophysical experiments.

Visual Thresholds in Humans

Brian Wandell and E. N. Pugh, Jr. (1980) measured the threshold for detection of a flash of colored light seen against a background of a different color. They were interested in whether the color of the background made any difference in the threshold for the flash in their situation. Their theory predicted that it would not.

The threshold for detection of the flash was measured at each combination of several background colors and intensities. The flash was presented in one of two temporal intervals, and the subject was to guess in which interval it occurred. The intensity of the flash was varied from trial to trial depending on whether the subject had been correct or incorrect on the previous trial, thus giving a type of staircase method. A typical staircase sequence is shown in Figure 11.7. The intensity was increased after an error and decreased after two correct responses in a row. The staircase procedure

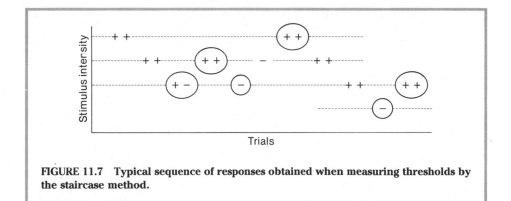

FIGURE 11.7   Typical sequence of responses obtained when measuring thresholds by the staircase method.

continued until 12 reversals in the staircase had been made. The threshold was taken to be the average intensity of the combined reversals. This procedure was repeated for each combination of background intensity and color.

No report is made of the order in which combinations were tested. This omission, common in psychophysical research, stems from the fact that the likelihood of finding significant order or sequence effects in such a study is minimal. Wandell and Pugh used two subjects in their experiment, a paid subject and one of the experimenters. This practice of using an experimenter as a subject is also common in psychophysical research inasmuch as the methods used make it unlikely that knowledge of the hypothesis will influence the outcome.

The design is a factorial experiment in that all combinations of selected background intensities and colors were used. It differs from most factorial experiments because it used only two subjects whose data were considered separately.

The results of the experiment for one subject are shown in Figure 11.8. The abscissa shows the intensity of the background against which the flash was seen. The ordinate shows the threshold for seeing the flash. Each curve is for a different color of background. In order to allow us to see the effects of the background color more clearly, the curves for each color background have been displaced vertically by 0.5 unit on the ordinate. In other words, each curve has been moved up by a certain amount so that the data from different curves will not overlap. The bottom curve shows what the data look like when they are not separated in this way. The curves drawn through the data points were derived from the pooled data.

From the curves the authors concluded that the color of the background did not affect the threshold for detecting the flash under their conditions. Note the impressive regularity of the data. The data points fit the line well with little variability. There is little doubt that Wandell and Pugh's conclusions are supported by the data. In addition, the data from the other subject were similar.

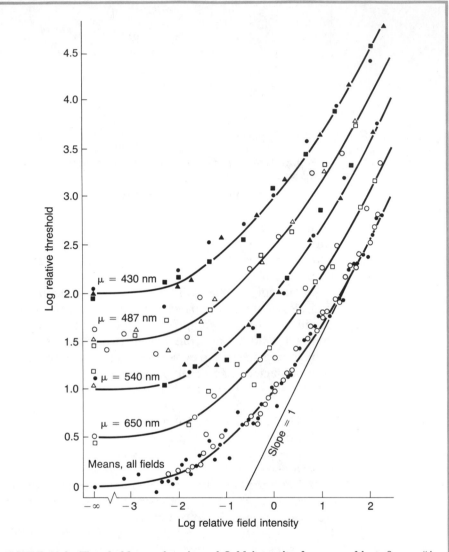

FIGURE 11.8 Threshold as a function of field intensity for one subject. SOURCE: "A Field-Additive Pathway Detects Brief-Duration Long-Wavelength Incremental Flashes" by B. A. Wandell and E. N. Pugh, Jr., 1980. *Vision Research, 20,* 613–624. Copyright 1980 by Pergamon Press. Reprinted by permission of the publisher and authors.

Visual Thresholds in Pigeons

Our previous example concerned vision, but the subjects were humans who could be instructed to look at a light, tell when they saw it, and so forth. Imagine trying to get an animal to give you information about what it can see! Nevertheless, one of the classic single-subject studies was conducted by Donald Blough (1956) on the dark-adaptation curve of the pigeon.

Blough used a variation of the familiar operant conditioning paradigm in which a pigeon pecks a key to obtain a reinforcement. He arranged two keys that controlled the intensity of light in the operant chamber. Pecking on the first key drove the intensity of the light lower. Pecking on the second key drove the intensity up and also led to occasional reinforcement. Blough wanted the birds to peck the first key until they could no longer see the light, then switch to the second key until they *could* see it, then go back to the first key, and so on. In this way the birds would drive the intensity of the light up and down across their visual threshold.

But how to get the pigeon to peck on the first key when pecking this key did not lead to reinforcement? Blough made use of the fact that animals will perform one task in order to have a chance to perform a second one that will lead to food. Being able to perform the second task becomes a reinforcer for performing the first one; it becomes a secondary reinforcer. So the birds will peck the first key in order to drive the light so low that they cannot see it, which signals them that they are then able to peck the second one for food.

The next question was how to keep the pigeons from simply pecking awhile at the first key and then switching to the second key even though they could still see the light. Blough's problem was that he wanted the pigeon to switch from pecking the first key and go to the key that drove up the light (and produced food) only when it could not see the light. But how could Blough know when the light was not visible to the pigeon? That was, after all, what he was trying to find out. He solved this problem in a most ingenious way: Every so often, pecking the first key would cause the light to go completely dark; only at such times was pecking on the second key reinforced. Therefore, Blough was sure that the pigeon would switch to the second key only when it could not see the light.

So, most of the time the bird would peck away on the first key until the intensity of the light was below its threshold and switch to the second key when it could not see the light. On those occasions when the pigeon was pecking on the first key and the light actually went completely dark, the pigeon would switch to the second key and get reinforcement.

In this way Blough was able to track a pigeon's dark-adaptation threshold and determine how it was affected by various manipulations. Notice that in this example the main questions of design did not concern control groups, counterbalancing, and the like, but did concern ways of achieving control over the pigeon's behavior. This is consistent with the positions of Skinner and Sidman that we discussed earlier.

SUMMARY

1. Experiments using single subjects have been performed for as long as psychology has existed.

2. The single-subject tradition assumes that variability is imposed by the situation and therefore can be removed by careful attention to experimental control. The individual differences group-research tradition assumes that much of the variability is intrinsic and should be statistically analyzed.

3. Single-subject research has several advantages over group research: focusing on individual performance that may be obscured by group research, focusing on big effects, avoiding ethical and practical problems in forming control groups, and permitting greater flexibility in design.

4. Averaging the data in group experiments may obscure individual performance because the average data may not resemble the performance of any single individual.

5. Group experiments that find small but significant effects may have little clinical or practical significance.

6. The term *power* refers to the probability that a statistical test will find a significant difference when there actually is a difference in the population from which the sample is drawn. A researcher can increase the power of an experiment by increasing the sample size or by increasing the size of the effect. The single-subject tradition prefers to focus on increasing the size of the effect.

7. Basic control strategies in single-subject research include obtaining a stable baseline, using withdrawal of the treatment, repeating treatments, changing only one variable at a time, using multiple baselines, and employing a changing criterion.

8. Withdrawal of the treatment is called the ABA design. Two major difficulties with the design are that the treatment may be irreversible or that the experimenter may wish to leave the subjects in the new state rather than return them to the original condition.

9. When treatment is repeated, the experiment is called an ABAB design. The ABAB design removes one of the objections to the ABA design in that it leaves the subject in the trained state.

10. When a single-subject experiment has several variables, only one variable should be changed at a time.

11. The A-B-A-B-BC-B-BC design is often called the interaction design, although it does not permit the testing for an interaction as defined earlier in this book. Every condition is both preceded and followed by the same condition at least once, and only one variable is changed at a time.

12. The multiple-baseline design is an effective way of demonstrating that the manipulation caused the behavior change. The manipulation is introduced at different times for different behaviors to see if the onset of behavior change coincides with the manipulation for each behavior.

13. The changing-criterion design introduces successively more stringent criteria for reinforcement over time. It is useful when the behavior change is irreversible.

14. The first example given of a single-subject experiment came from a clinical application of operant techniques to eliminate hyperventilation.

15. The second and third examples came from psychophysical research on color vision.

Suggestions for Further Reading

BARLOW, D. H., & HERSEN, M. (1984). *Single case experimental designs* (2nd ed.). New York: Pergamon Press. The emphasis in this book is on clinical research.
JOHNSTON, J. M., & PENNYPACKER, H. S. (1980). *Strategies and tactics of human behavioral research.* Hillsdale, NJ: Erlbaum.
SIDMAN, M. (1960). *Tactics of scientific research.* New York: Basic Books.

ⅢⅢ➡ A CASE IN POINT ⬅Ⅲ

Reducing Dangerous Behaviors in Infants

Infants and toddlers frequently injure themselves around the home with electrical devices and outlets, hot stoves, and the like. You are interested in testing a program for teaching parents to reduce such injuries by means of a variety of behavioral techniques: "childproofing" the home by removing dangerous objects from the baby's reach, giving positive attention to the infant for safe behaviors, and giving time-outs for unsafe behavior. A time-out is defined in this case as saying "No" and placing the baby in a playpen with only soft toys to play with until he or she remains for 10 seconds without crying.

You have 16 mothers of infants 10–12 months of age available from the files of the laboratory.

Sessions will take place in the infant's home. Some time will be needed with each mother to instruct her in how to childproof the home, how to pay positive attention to the baby, and how to administer a time-out.

CONSIDERATIONS: With 16 infants available, you have enough subjects for a complete $2 \times 2 \times 2$ factorial design, with two subjects per condition. Because you need to travel to the homes, it would take a lot of time to study all 16 infants. Some mothers may already have childproofed their homes, and some may already use positive attention and/or time-outs with their babies.

REQUIRED: Design the study. Decide whether a groups design or a single-subject design should be used. Should you study the three conditions separately or as one combined condition? If you study the conditions separately, how will you control for random events that might influence the data?

The study on which this case is based is cited in the Instructor's Manual.

☰ READING BETWEEN THE LINES ☰

11.1 ELECTRICAL INHIBITION OF AGGRESSION IN A CHARGING BULL

Jose Delgado (1969) received a great deal of publicity for a demonstration in which he entered an arena with a bull that had an electrode implanted in a part of the brain known as the caudate nucleus. The electrode was connected to a radio receiver attached to the bull's horn. When Delgado pressed a button, an electrical stimulus would be transmitted to the bull's brain. First, Delgado induced the bull to attack him. Then, while the bull was charging him, Delgado pressed the button, which caused the bull to turn sharply to one side and stop. Delgado claimed that he had stopped the charge by inhibiting the part of the brain that was involved with aggression. What other reason could account for the bull's sudden change of heart about goring Delgado?   ■

11.2 CLEVER HANS

In the early 1900s in Germany a sensation was caused by a horse that had amazing intellectual abilities. Although horses are not usually known for their intelligence, Mr. von Osten's horse Hans was able to add, subtract, multiply, and divide. Hans could tell all of the factors of a number and could even add fractions. He could tell the day of the week on which a certain date would fall. In addition, he had perfect pitch and could identify chords played on a musical instrument. If the notes played did not constitute a pleasing chord, he would indicate which notes should be removed. He could read German but not Latin or French. In short, Hans was able to do many things that a college graduate might well have trouble doing.

Hans answered questions by tapping with his hoof to indicate numbers and by moving his head for yes, no, and various directions. He demonstrated his ability to read either by choosing one card that contained the desired word out of several or by tapping to indicate the rows and columns of a specially prepared table of the alphabet. When asked a question, Hans would first nod if he understood or shake his head if he did not. No wonder he was called Clever Hans and was the subject of numerous newspaper and magazine articles. Hans was studied by many people, including zoologists, a circus manager, an animal behaviorist, a sensory physiologist, and a psychologist, all prominent in their fields. They concluded that no trick was involved and that Hans was genuine. What could these well-educated people have overlooked that would explain Hans's amazing abilities?   ■

✓ EXERCISES

11.1 IDENTIFY THE RESEARCH DESIGN

A teacher designs a study to test the hypothesis that positive reinforcement will improve the behavior of a hyperactive boy in her third-grade class. Figure 11.9 contains results from the study.

REQUIRED:

    a. Identify the design.
    b. Describe the initial baseline stability.
    c. What is the independent variable?
    d. What is the dependent variable?
    e. What is the effect of the independent variable on the dependent variable?

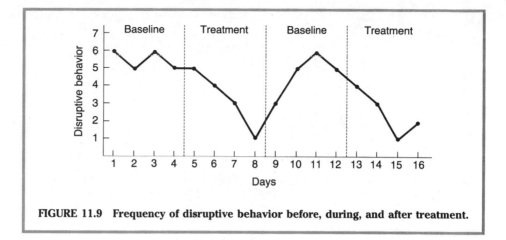

FIGURE 11.9   Frequency of disruptive behavior before, during, and after treatment.

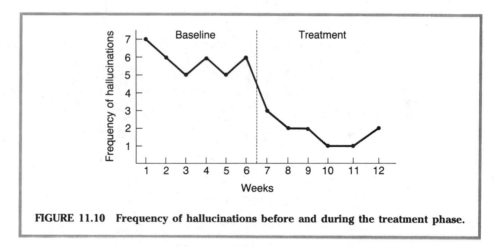

FIGURE 11.10   Frequency of hallucinations before and during the treatment phase.

11.2 IDENTIFY THE RESEARCH DESIGN

A psychologist designs a study to test a new drug that is supposed to reduce the frequency of hallucinations among schizophrenic patients. Figure 11.10 contains the results from the study.

REQUIRED:

    a. Is the baseline stable? Explain.
    b. What is the independent variable?
    c. What is the dependent variable?
    d. What is the effect of the independent variable on the dependent variable?
    e. What type of design is this?
    f. What major threat to internal validity is evident in this design?
    g. How could you modify this experiment in order to strengthen its
       conclusions?

12

Quasi Experiments

As you recall from Chapter 9, a true experiment is one in which the experimenter has complete control over the who, what, when, where, and how of the experiment. A quasi experiment, on the other hand, does not permit the experimenter to control the assignment of subjects to conditions. The example we gave of a quasi-experimental variable in Chapter 9 was sex of subject, over which the experimenter has no control. Thus when an experimenter uses sex as a variable in an experiment, the possibility exists that sex may be confounded with many other variables, such as differential learning experiences, parental expectations, and other cultural influences. This chapter deals with strategies that are useful in achieving control over the threats to validity found in quasi experiments.

In addition to not being able to control the who of an experiment, the experimenter in some instances cannot completely control the what, when, where, and how. Often data must be collected at a particular time or not at all. For example, an experimenter who wishes to study the effects of changing work schedules on productivity must do so when the management of the plant decides to make the changes. The problem with such an experiment is that productivity may already have been changing because of some outside variable. Similarly, the experimenter may wish to do parts of the experiment in certain ways but cannot because of practical limitations. Any of these considerations may lead us to regard a piece of research as a quasi experiment. The boundaries between true and quasi experiments are not always distinct. If the experimenter has good control over all aspects of the experiment, we can call it a true experiment. If enough compromise of experimental control takes place, the research is considered a quasi experiment.[1] When the experimenter has no control over the presentation of the independent variables but can only record what happens in a certain situation, we call the research nonexperimental.

The presence of uncontrolled or confounded variables reduces the internal validity of a quasi experiment but does not necessarily render it invalid. Recall that the presence of randomization in true experiments permits the strongest use of Mill's method of differences. Because quasi experiments lack randomized groups by definition, they also provide weaker application of the method of differences. The inability to randomly allocate subjects to groups reduces the internal validity of the experiment. The experimenter must evaluate the likelihood that the confounding variables are responsible for the outcome. This appraisal involves the use of the experimenter's judgment, as does the evaluation of all research.

On the other hand, the external validity of a quasi experiment may be higher than that of a true experiment done on the same problem, if the quasi experiment studies subjects or settings that are more appropriate to the question of interest than a true experiment could. For example, if you wanted to know the effects of changing the size of work groups in a widget factory on productivity, an experiment using college students working at solving anagrams would probably have little external validity.

In general, the true experiment is preferable to the quasi experiment, but many situations exist in which randomly assigning subjects to conditions is not possible. Then a quasi experiment is performed simply because doing it is better than doing no experiment at all. For example, does the disadvantage of using two preexisting classes to study the effects of different teaching methods outweigh the fact that it is virtually impossible to randomly constitute two new classes? The experimenter must weigh the costs and benefits of each choice made in designing a piece of research.

NONEQUIVALENT CONTROL GROUP DESIGNS

nonequivalent control group design
research design having both an experimental and a control group wherein subjects are not randomly assigned to groups

If both an experimental and a control group are part of an experiment but subjects have not been allocated randomly to the two groups, we have a **nonequivalent control group design.** Of the quasi experiments, this is the most typical. The problem with this design is in determining how to compare results between the experimental and control groups when they were not equivalent to begin with.

---

[1] We have adopted a broader definition of quasi experiment than Cook and Campbell (1976), who defined it as an experiment that does not permit random allocation of subjects to groups. Our definition includes lack of control over other aspects of the experiment, as does their discussion of particular quasi-experimental designs.

TABLE 12.1 NONEQUIVALENT CONTROL GROUP DESIGN WITH PRETEST AND POSTTEST

	Allocation of Subjects and Groups	Pretest	Treatment	Posttest
Group 1	Any method that is not random	Yes	Yes	Yes
Group 2		Yes	No	Yes

Recall the discussion in Chapter 9 of designs to be avoided. In the example of the company that wished to evaluate the effect of a new work schedule, we said that the study would be improved by having a second plant as a control group. Any change in productivity at the experimental plant that followed the switch in work schedule could be more confidently attributed to the new work schedule if a second plant showed no change over the same time interval. This example of a nonequivalent control group design with pretest and posttest is a typical quasi-experimental design. It is diagrammed in Table 12.1. Because the subjects were not randomly allocated to the two groups, we do not have good reason to believe that they were equivalent before the experimental manipulation was performed. Therefore, we must consider the likelihood that alternative hypotheses may account for the results. For example, the workers in the experimental plant may have been less experienced on the average than those in the control plant. Their increase in productivity may have been caused by the experience they gained between pretest and posttest. The control subjects, on the other hand, may already have been working at their maximum.

Quasi experiments that employ nonequivalent control groups with pretest and posttest may be interpretable or they may not. Whether they can be interpreted depends on whether the pattern of results obtained can be accounted for by possible differences in the groups or by something else in the experiment. The pattern of results we would like to see from this design is shown in Figure 12.1. Here the two groups showed the same performance on the pretest. The experimental group improved on the posttest, but the control group did not change. Although the experimental and control groups were not equivalent in all respects because they were not randomly constituted, their performances can be compared and the results interpreted because their behavior was the same at the beginning.

Figure 12.2 shows one kind of uninterpretable pattern of results. These results could be those of the factory study we just discussed. In this example, the experimental group improved but the control group did not. Notice that the control group was superior to the experimental group on both occasions. This difference could result from the operation of a ceiling effect. If it was not possible for the control group to perform any better, then we cannot attribute the improvement in the experimental group to the experimental manipulation.

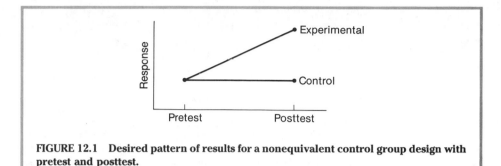

FIGURE 12.1   Desired pattern of results for a nonequivalent control group design with pretest and posttest.

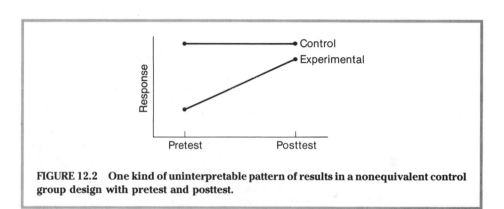

FIGURE 12.2   One kind of uninterpretable pattern of results in a nonequivalent control group design with pretest and posttest.

Another pattern of results that may be uninterpretable is shown in Figure 12.3. These results could represent a learning experiment in which the experimental group performed better than the control group on the pretest. Both groups showed improvement on the posttest, but the experimental group showed twice as much improvement. Can we attribute the difference in rate of improvement to the experimental manipulation? No, we cannot, because although the experimental group improved more, both groups showed the same proportional improvement. On the posttest, both doubled their previous performance. Their improvement likely was caused by maturation or some other variable that had nothing to do with the experimental manipulation. Recall our discussion of the effects of transformations on interactions in Chapter 10. These data could be transformed in such a way that both groups would show the same amount of improvement.

A pattern of results that usually is interpretable is shown in Figure 12.4. Here the experimental group was lower than the control group on the pretest but higher than the control group on the posttest. Finding a rival hypothesis for this pattern of results is difficult. You might suppose that the experimental subjects were as good as the control subjects to begin with and did worse on the pretest simply by chance. In that case, you would expect them to do the same as the control group on the posttest if the experimental manipulation

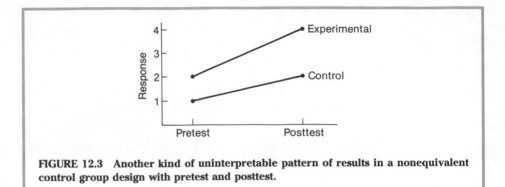

FIGURE 12.3 Another kind of uninterpretable pattern of results in a nonequivalent control group design with pretest and posttest.

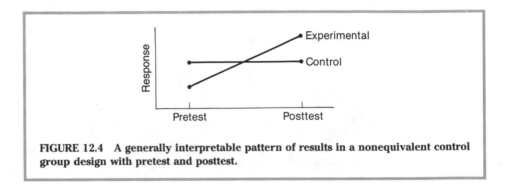

FIGURE 12.4 A generally interpretable pattern of results in a nonequivalent control group design with pretest and posttest.

were not effective. You would have no reason, however, to expect them to do better than the control group on the posttest by chance alone. Therefore, it is usually safe to conclude that a pattern of results such as those in Figure 12.4 shows the effectiveness of the experimental manipulation.

The two examples of the nonequivalent control group design that we will consider next are very different. The first is rather unconventional; the second is more typical.

■ Delayed Control Group Design

delayed control group design
nonequivalent control group design in which the testing of one group is deferred

A creative quasi experiment by David Marks and Richard Kammann (1980) illustrates the **delayed control group design.** These researchers were interested in studying the alleged psychic powers of Uri Geller, the Israeli magician. Among his many feats are spoon bending, mind reading, starting broken watches, and determining the contents of sealed envelopes. Because Geller, like most psychics, performs only when he is confident that he can convince anyone present, studying his methods is difficult. Marks and Kammann interviewed Geller under loose conditions and observed his routine but were unable to get him into their laboratory. They appeared to be stymied in their attempt to do a controlled study until Marks was on a radio talk show with Geller. Among the feats Geller achieved was to perceive two pictures through a sealed envelope (although he failed on a third picture).

After the show Marks retrieved the papers from the wastebasket. Marks and Kammann hypothesized that Geller had been able to perceive the pictures through the envelope by ordinary means. Later they showed the same pictures inside the envelopes to 48 students, who were asked to examine the envelopes and draw the picture without looking inside the envelope. On one of the pictures the students did a little worse than Geller and on another they did a little better, as rated by independent judges. Most revealing, perhaps, was the picture on which Geller failed. Not only did the students also fail, but their attempts looked strikingly like Geller's attempts.

From this experiment Marks and Kammann concluded that Geller uses ordinary sensory means to perceive pictures inside envelopes. Other conclusions are possible, of course. The students could also have extrasensory perception, but this conclusion is highly strained. At the least the results show that ordinary people can do essentially as well with the same materials and the same conditions as a person who claims to be a psychic. For the purposes of experimental design, the students constitute a nonequivalent control group for Geller. The fact that they did about equally well, when Geller would be expected to do much better according to the psychic hypothesis, makes it unlikely that he has any powers that the students do not also have.

null hypothesis statement usually saying that there is no real difference between the groups tested; treatment had no effect

Interestingly, the conclusion that he did not differ from the students constitutes an example of accepting the **null hypothesis,** or accepting the conclusion that the two groups are not different. Ordinarily scientists avoid drawing a conclusion on the basis of accepting the null hypothesis, because proving the nonexistence of some effect is theoretically impossible. When one performs a statistical test, one either rejects the null hypothesis, or fails to reject it. Any given experiment may not be sensitive enough to detect a real difference. Marks and Kammann were trying to prove that Geller was not psychic, which is equivalent to proving that there is no Santa Claus. However, one could conclude on the basis of their experiment that Uri Geller's abilities could not be distinguished from those of a naive student, or from a fraud. To be technically accurate, we might say that Marks and Kammann failed to reject the null hypothesis that Uri Geller was not psychic.

Because Marks and Kammann were interested only in testing whether Geller had psychic powers, they did no experimental manipulation and therefore no before/after comparison. Thus the experiment could be considered a simple after-only design.

■ Mixed Factorial Design with One Nonmanipulated Variable

The next example of a nonequivalent control group design is from an experiment on anxiety. Norman Endler (1977) wanted to test an interaction theory of anxiety. He believed that the state of anxiety was the result of a trait for anxiety that interacted with anxiety-provoking situations. Persons who were high on the anxiety trait would not be in the anxious state all the time

TABLE 12.2 DESIGN OF THE ENDLER STUDY

TRAIT ANXIETY	STATE ANXIETY	
	Low	HIGH
High	S_1	S_1
	S_2	S_2
	.	.
	.	.
	.	.
	S_{19}	S_{19}
Low	S_{20}	S_{20}
	S_{21}	S_{21}
	.	.
	.	.
	.	.
	S_{37}	S_{37}

but would respond more to certain situations than would other people. He tested this theory by administering a test of the anxiety trait to students. Those who scored high and those who scored low were placed in two groups. Then they were tested for their measured anxiety, or state, in a threatening situation: a major psychology exam. The measure of anxiety state was pulse rate. Two weeks later Endler tested the same subjects in a nonthreatening situation.

The design of this experiment is a mixed factorial because it has one between-subjects variable and one within-subjects variable. The between subjects variable is trait anxiety, because subjects were either high or low on trait anxiety. The within-subjects variable is situational anxiety, because subjects could experience both conditions at different times. The design is illustrated in Table 12.2. Endler found that students who were high or low on the anxiety trait, as measured by the questionnaire, did not differ in measured anxiety state in the nonthreatening situation. They did differ considerably, however, just before the test. The data are shown in Figure 12.5.

REGRESSION DISCONTINUITY DESIGNS

Researchers may want to evaluate the effect of an experimental manipulation of two groups that are known to differ to begin with. Some experimenters have attempted to evaluate such situations by taking into consideration that there is a correlation between the scores on the two variables over all subjects. Suppose that a manipulation is introduced following a pretest on one variable. Suppose also that some value on the variable is used as a criterion for the

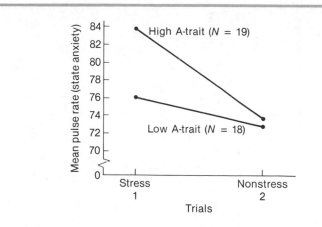

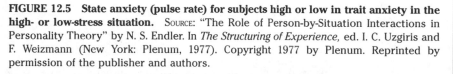

FIGURE 12.5   State anxiety (pulse rate) for subjects high or low in trait anxiety in the high- or low-stress situation.   Source: "The Role of Person-by-Situation Interactions in Personality Theory" by N. S. Endler. In *The Structuring of Experience,* ed. I. C. Uzgiris and F. Weizmann (New York: Plenum, 1977). Copyright 1977 by Plenum. Reprinted by permission of the publisher and authors.

presentation of the manipulation. Then the posttest is administered. We can plot the correlation between the pretest and the posttest for all subjects as in Figure 12.6. Note, however, that some value on the pretest was used as a criterion for assigning subjects to the experimental and control groups. Thus, we know in advance that the experimental and control groups are not equivalent. However, we have plotted a single regression line relating the pretest scores to the posttest scores. If the experimental manipulation had no effect, a single line would satisfactorily describe the data. If the manipulation did have some effect over and above the correlation between the pretest and the posttest, the effect would be seen as a discontinuity in the data at the value of the pretest that was used as the criterion. Then we would need two separate regression lines to describe the data adequately. Such an experiment is an example of a **regression discontinuity design.**

For example, suppose the dean of a college wants to know if recognizing students who have achieved high grades in one term will cause them to do better the next term (see Cook & Campbell, 1979). How would the dean evaluate the effect of seeing one's name on the dean's list when the two groups of students are by definition not equivalent to begin with? Let us begin by considering that a correlation in the grades between one term and the next is present for all students, not just the dean's-list students. We might look at the scatterplot of grades for all students in two successive terms to see if there is a break in the trend of scores at the dean's-list cutoff. Such a scatterplot is shown in Figure 12.7. The vertical line is the cutoff for the dean's list. The longer line below the cutoff is the best-fitting line for students who did not achieve the dean's list in Term 1. The shorter line to the right is the

regression discontinuity design

quasi-experimental design that uses a score on a pretest as a criterion for administering a manipulation whose effect is shown as a discontinuity in the regression line relating the pretest and posttest

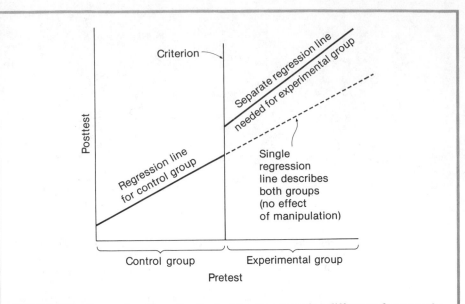

FIGURE 12.6   Regression discontinuity design when there is a difference between the experimental and control groups (solid line to the right of the vertical line) and when there is no difference (dashed line).

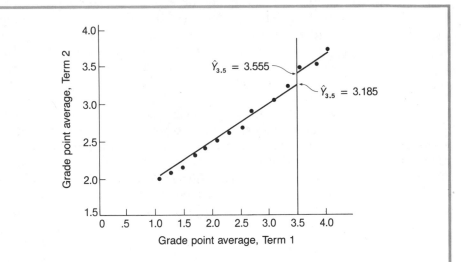

FIGURE 12.7   Relationship of grade point average in Term 2 to grade point average in Term 1 for students who did or did not achieve the dean's list in Term 1. Source: *Quasi-Experiments: Nonequivalent Control Group Designs* by T. D. Cook and D. T. Campbell (Boston: Houghton Mifflin, 1979). Copyright 1979 by Houghton Mifflin. Reprinted by permission of the publisher and authors.

best-fitting line for students who did appear on the dean's list in Term 1. The two lines are discontinuous; that is, the line for the dean's-list students falls above the other line at the cutoff. This occurrence is called a regression discontinuity because the two best-fitting lines, also known as regression lines, are discontinuous.

Although you may agree with the dean's conclusion that publishing the list of outstanding students had a beneficial effect on those students' next-term grades, such a conclusion has problems. Take a closer look at the actual data points in the figure. Notice that they seem to be curving upward throughout the whole range of scores. Perhaps, instead of breaking at the vertical line, the last three points simply reflect a trend that occurs throughout the range. A safer conclusion may be that these data do not show a regression discontinuity but that they fit a single curved line that goes through the entire range of scores. Regression discontinuity designs can thus be tricky to interpret. Unless the data points cluster tightly so as to form an obvious line, deciding exactly where the line should be drawn or what shape it should have may be difficult.

DESIGNS WITHOUT CONTROL GROUPS

Sometimes no control group can be obtained that can be considered comparable enough to be useful. Then a design that allows the same group to be compared over time can be used. We will discuss two such designs: the interrupted time-series design and the repeated treatments design.

■ Interrupted Time-Series Designs

In Chapter 9, when we discussed designs to be avoided, we said that measurement of a single group before and after the manipulation is not good design. One way to improve on the one-group before/after design is to consider the trend of the data before and after the manipulation, rather than simply comparing the average data before and after. For example, the manager of the plant that is changing its work schedule might keep a weekly record of output for the years preceding and following the change. Management could then look not only for average differences between the two periods but for trends that might appear. Seasonal changes or other cyclical changes in output may be important, as well as any overall trend toward higher or lower productivity that occurred around the time of the change.

interrupted time-series design
research design that allows the same group to be compared over time by considering the trend of the data before and after experimental manipulation

The ideal situation would be a flat and stable baseline before the change, followed by either an abrupt change to a new level or a gradual change to a new level. See Figure 12.8 for typical patterns. Evaluation of such time series is a difficult procedure that requires different statistical tools from those generally used for analyzing group data. **Interrupted time-series experiments** are similar in design and interpretation to many single-subject designs and to the nonexperimental methods, topics discussed in Chapters 7, 8, and 11.

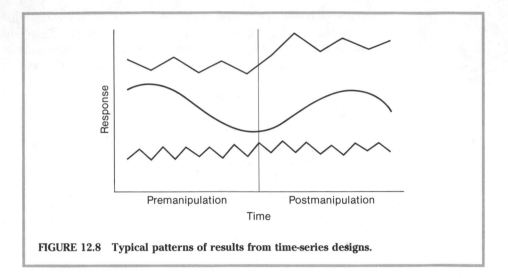

FIGURE 12.8   **Typical patterns of results from time-series designs.**

We will talk about two examples of interrupted time-series designs in this chapter. Because the authors of both studies examined existing records to obtain their data rather than manipulating some independent variable, the studies technically are examples of nonexperimental research rather than quasi-experimental study. Nevertheless, they present good examples of the advantages and disadvantages of interrupted time-series research. In addition, similar nonexperimental studies are commonly described under the heading of quasi experiments in books on design (for example, Cook & Campbell, 1979).

In the 1960s, a trend began in many Western countries, including the United States, toward greater availability of pornography. During the same period there was also an increase in the number of rapes reported in the United States. Many people have concluded that there was a causal relation between the two. You will recall, however, the problem that exists with Mill's method of concommitant variation: Correlation does not prove causation. During the same period there was also an increase in the number of television evangelists, for example. Although they have been blamed for many things, an increase in rape is not among them.

In order to conclude that pornography causes rape on the basis of trends in availability of pornography and the numbers of rapes, one would need to rule out a number of alternative hypotheses. It is possible, for example, that the increase in rapes was the result in a greater willingness of women and police to report incidents of rape. It is known that only a fraction of rapes are ever reported. Alternatively, population trends during that time led to an increase in the number of men in the age groups most likely to commit rape. These explanations would be threats to the internal validity of the study, because they would question the connection between the supposed independent variable, pornography, and the dependent variable, rape.

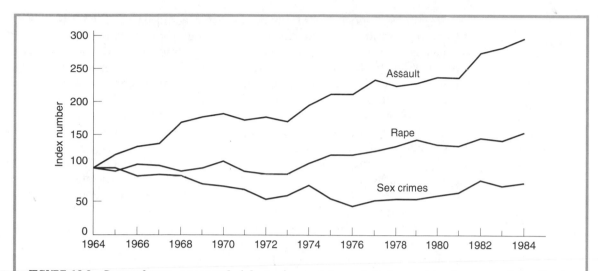

FIGURE 12.9 Cases of rape, nonsexual violent crimes, and nonviolent sex crimes known to the police in Sweden, 1964–1984. Indexes of offenses per 100,000 population. Index 100: rape = 7.7; violence = 126.4; sex crimes = 42.8. Based on official crime statistics for Sweden.   SOURCE: Reprinted from *International Journal of Law and Psychiatry, 14,* B. Kutchinsky, "Pornography and Rape: Theory and Practice? Evidence from Crime Data in Four Countries Where Pornography Is Easily Available," 1991, 47-64, with kind permission from Pergamon Press Ltd, Headington Hill Hall, Oxford OX3 0BW, UK.

Kutchinsky (1991) examined the statistics on rape in several countries from the mid-1960s to the mid-1980s. Although there was a marked increase in rapes in the United States during that period, there were only small changes in rates in Denmark and Sweden; West Germany actually had a decrease. The European countries can serve as controls for the United States because pornography became easily available in all these countries at about the same time. This suggests that it might be something other than pornography that caused the increase in the United States.

Because rape is simultaneously a sexual and a violent offense, it is possible to consider an alternative hypothesis: that rape increased as part of an increase in violent crimes. Kutchinsky compared the changes over time in the numbers of rapes, violent crimes other than rape, and nonviolent sex crimes in the same three European countries we have been discussing. Figure 12.9 shows the data for Sweden, which are similar to those for the other two countries. He found that nonviolent sex crimes actually decreased in all three countries, whereas violent crimes other than rape increased dramatically. Kutchinsky concludes that the increase in rape was part of the general increase in violent crimes during the period. If so, the increase in rapes was not due to pornography, unless the pornography was also responsible for an increase in muggings, murder, and other acts of violence. Although U.S. data were not available in all three categories shown in Figure 12.9, the increase in rape very closely paralleled the increase in assault, supporting the conclusion based on the three European countries.

Textbook discussions of any field present a snapshot of what is known at the time they are written. This fact is particularly relevant when it comes to discussing the results of research using time-series designs. Earlier editions of this book also used the possible relation of pornography and rape as an example of time-series designs, along with some of their problems. The passage of time and the collection of more time-series data have clarified some of the alternative hypotheses discussed in those earlier editions. The question is still controversial, however. The interested reader is referred to sources such as Green (1987) and Malumuth (1987).

Another example of an interrupted time-series design is Alexander Wagenaar's (1981a, 1981b) study of the effect on alcohol-related traffic accidents of raising the drinking age in Michigan. Michigan, along with many other states, lowered the drinking age from 21 to 18 in the early 1970s after the voting age had been lowered to 18 in all 50 states. The change was followed by a 35% increase in the number of alcohol-related crashes among Michigan drivers aged 18 to 20. Therefore, in January 1979 the state returned the drinking age to 21. Wagenaar wanted to know whether alcohol-related accidents had decreased following the change back to age 21 and whether this decrease could be attributed to the change.

Ordinarily one would want to make a series of observations both before and after the intervention to check for trends in the data, as mentioned previously. However, in this situation, the effects of raising the drinking age needed to be assessed as soon as possible for reasons of public policy. Therefore, Wagenaar did his study only one year after the change back to age 21. He found that in 1979 drivers aged 18 to 20 were involved in 26% fewer accidents that were reported by the police as "had been drinking" compared with 1978. This figure was the lowest in five years. Several alternative hypotheses would have to be ruled out, though, before one could conclude that the change in drinking age caused the decrease in accidents. For example, police officers might have changed their criterion for reporting that the driver in an accident had been drinking. Or the occurrence of an economic recession in Michigan and higher gasoline prices both might have reduced the amount of driving. Or the fact that the winter of 1979 had relatively mild weather might have made driving safer. In order to rule out rival hypotheses, Wagenaar compared data on accidents reported as "had been drinking" with other, similar data.

The first alternative hypothesis concerned a change in police officers' criterion for reporting drivers who "had been drinking." To test this hypothesis, Wagenaar compared the original data (drivers aged 18 to 20 who were in accidents in which the driver was reported as "had been drinking") with late-night, single-vehicle accidents involving drivers in the same age group. Of such accidents, 60% are known to be alcohol related, which means that statistics on these accidents would not be affected by police officers' judgments of drinking. Wagenaar found that these late-night, single-vehicle accidents had also decreased. The alternative hypotheses about the recession, the price of gasoline, and the winter weather were tested by

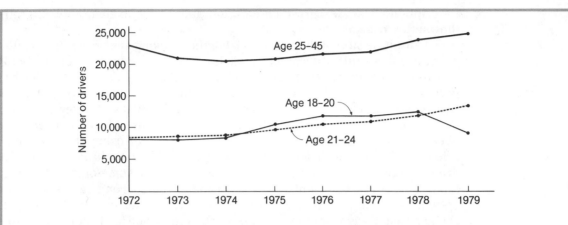

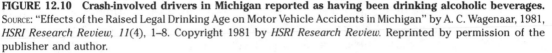

FIGURE 12.10 Crash-involved drivers in Michigan reported as having been drinking alcoholic beverages.
Source: "Effects of the Raised Legal Drinking Age on Motor Vehicle Accidents in Michigan" by A. C. Wagenaar, 1981, *HSRI Research Review, 11*(4), 1–8. Copyright 1981 by *HSRI Research Review*. Reprinted by permission of the publisher and author.

comparing the accident data for drivers aged 18 to 20 with data for drivers in age groups who were not affected by the change in the law (see Figure 12.10). The other age groups actually showed an increase in alcohol-related crashes.

A second test of the hypothesis that police officers might have changed their criterion for reporting "had been drinking" was possible by comparing single-vehicle nighttime crashes to similar daytime crashes for the 18- to 20-year-olds. It is known that fewer daytime crashes than nighttime crashes are alcohol related. Wagenaar found that both categories of crashes decreased after the change in the drinking age, but the nighttime crashes decreased twice as much as did the daytime crashes. A similar result was found by comparing crashes in which the police did not report that the driver had been drinking with those in which the police did so report.

Still it was possible that the results were caused by some factor other than a change in drinking age. Wagenaar therefore compared the Michigan results with data from another state that also raised the drinking age, Maine, and two that did not, New York and Pennsylvania. The results in Maine paralleled the Michigan results, whereas no change occurred in the accident rate in New York or Pennsylvania at the time that Michigan changed its law.

In addition to making the comparisons we have just discussed, Wagenaar used sophisticated statistical methods to test all conclusions. Together, the various comparisons make it reasonably certain that the change in the Michigan law did produce the decrease in number of traffic accidents. Because Wagenaar compared his group of 18- to 20-year-olds with several different groups that were not randomly assigned to conditions, his study is a multiple nonequivalent control group design. A complete description of the design would be a multiple nonequivalent control group time-series design.

Our discussion of the effects raising the drinking age on alcohol-related traffic accidents up to this point was written for the 1983 edition of this book, and there was little new material to add for the 1990 edition. The further passage of time has now made it possible to follow up Wagenaar's conclusions to see how valid they have turned out to be in the light of further evidence.

Another event in the interim contributed to the ability to answer the question of a possible relationship between drinking and crashes scientifically: A new federal law required all states to have a minimum drinking age of 21 in place by 1986 or face the loss of some of their highway funding. This law contributed to the raising of the drinking age in 26 states between 1976 and 1987, providing a much larger set of data to analyze. O'Malley and Wagenaar (1991) analyzed fatal crash data for 13 states for three years before and three years after they raised their drinking age to 21. They found a 15% decrease in single-vehicle, nighttime fatal crash rate for drivers under 21. The decrease for drivers 21 and older was only 5%. The first decrease was statistically significant, whereas the second was not. Thus, we see that Wagenaar's original conclusion in 1981 was correct, although we are much more confident of that now than we could be at that time.

■ Repeated-Treatment Designs

As the name implies, repeated-treatment designs attempt to improve the validity of the experiment by presenting the treatment more than once. The subject's response is measured before and after the introduction of a treatment, then the treatment is withdrawn and the whole process is begun again. Table 12.3 shows the general design. This design has an obvious limitation: The treatment must be one that can be withdrawn without causing complications in the analysis of data.

Suppose an instructor is going to give four hour-long tests in a course. She wants to find out if giving extra credit for turning in homework will improve grades on the tests. If she instituted the extra credit between the first and second tests, she would then have a pretest and a posttest to permit her to examine the effect of the treatment. In order to repeat the treatment, she would have to stop giving the extra credit after the second test (Posttest$_1$). The third test then could be considered Pretest$_2$, after which she would reinstitute the extra credit and look for improvement between Pretest$_2$ and

TABLE 12.3 A REPEATED TREATMENTS DESIGN

| Pretest$_1$ | Treatment | Posttest$_1$ | Withdraw treatment | Pretest$_2$ | Treatment | Posttest$_2$ |

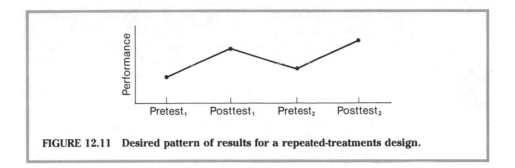

FIGURE 12.11   **Desired pattern of results for a repeated-treatments design.**

Posttest$_2$. This design might be a good one, except that the students would likely rebel at having the extra credit taken away. If the instructor went ahead with the plan anyway, the students might be demoralized enough that their performance would suffer on the later tests.

Figure 12.11 shows the pattern of results that is desired with a repeated-treatment design. Whatever change is found between Pretest$_1$ and Posttest$_1$ should be in the same direction as that between Pretest$_2$ and Posttest$_2$. It is desirable that there be a reversal in any previous trend of response between Posttest$_1$, when the treatment is withdrawn, and Pretest$_2$ to rule out the possibility that there would have been a continuous change in performance over the four tests regardless of treatment. Like the interrupted time-series design, the repeated-treatment design is one that is used in single-subject experiments (discussed in Chapter 11).

DESIGNS TO TEST DEVELOPMENTAL CHANGES

Many of the quasi-experimental designs we have discussed in this chapter have involved time as a variable, and others have involved nonequivalent control groups. There is an area of psychological research that has to deal with both characteristics: developmental psychology. We will use the development of the ability to program a VCR as a way of introducing the problems of developmental research design.

A few years ago when I bought my VCR, I decided to hook it up to play through the stereo system. After studying the manuals that came with the stereo amplifier, the TV, and the VCR for several hours, I gave up in frustration. Then I called my teenage nephew, who hooked it up in about 10 minutes without so much as a glance at the manuals. My chagrin at having to turn to my nephew was somewhat reduced when I learned that the average person cannot even set the time on his or her VCR. This led me to wonder about the developmental aspects of learning to program a VCR.

cross-sectional study
in developmental research, a study that tests different age groups at the same time

There are two simple approaches we could take to determining the effects of age on ability to program a VCR. We could do a **cross-sectional study,** taking samples of people at different ages and testing them for ability to program a VCR at the same general time. The advantage of the cross-sectional approach is that all of the age groups can be tested at the same general time. The disadvantage, however, is that the people at different ages were all born at different times, so age is confounded with date of birth. Because every group was born in a different year, there are likely to be **cohort** effects. A cohort is a group that has some characteristic in common, and so are treated as a group. Everyone born in 1980 could be considered part of the 1980 cohort. The 1980 cohort would have grown up with VCRs, whereas the 1950 cohort would have been in their 30s before such things even existed. It is likely that there would be a large cohort effect on ability to program a VCR.

To avoid cohort effects, you might do a **longitudinal study,** taking samples over time of people born in a certain year to see how many of them can program a VCR. The advantage of this approach is that all the people would have the same birth dates, and so there would be no cohort effects. There are two main problems with longitudinal studies—one theoretical, and one practical.

The practical problem is that the researcher has to wait years to complete the study as the cohort ages. Some longitudinal studies have gone on for many decades, during which time the researchers retire and new researchers take over the project.

The main theoretical problem with a longitudinal study is that it confounds age with time of testing. All the subjects would be aging together, but at the same time technology would be changing. It might be the changes in technology—not the changes in age—that caused any differences in ability to program a VCR. The technological changes are an example of **secular trends** that may influence the results of your study.

Thus, both designs have important sources of confounding. The longitudinal study confounds age with time. The cross-sectional study confounds age with date of birth. It is important to realize that there is no way to eliminate this confounding: It is logically impossible for a person born in 1950 to be 10 years old in 1990.

Considerable ingenuity has been devoted to developing research designs that help one to tease out the various results of this confounding. One such design is the **cross-sequential design.** This design tests individuals from two or more cohorts at two or more times. Suppose we take four groups of people, born in 1980, 1970, 1960, and 1950, and see what percentage of each group can program a VCR. Suppose also that we test them in the years 1990, 2000, and 2010. Let's say that we obtain the data shown in Table 12.4. Any row of the table shows the data for people with the same year of birth. The top row, for example, shows the data for the 1950 cohort. Any column of the table shows the data for people tested in a given year. The first column, for example, shows the data for all people tested in 1990.

We can see longitudinal trends by following the cohorts over time (see the horizontal arrow). We can see cross-sectional effects by looking at the people tested in a given year (vertical arrow). The cross-sequential design permits us to do something that neither a simple longitudinal nor simple

cohort
in research, a group that has something in common, such as age

longitudinal study
in developmental research, a study that tests individuals in a single cohort over the course of time

secular trend
a change that is taking place in the general population over time (the term has nothing to do with religion)

cross-sequential design
design used to help separate developmental, cohort, and secular effects

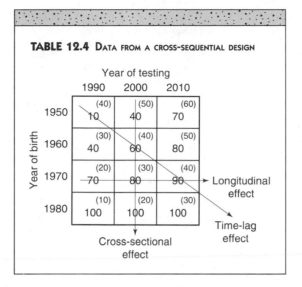

TABLE 12.4 Data from a cross-sequential design

	Year of testing		
Year of birth	1990	2000	2010
1950	(40) 10	(50) 40	(60) 70
1960	(30) 40	(40) 60	(50) 80
1970	(20) 70	(30) 80	(40) 90
1980	(10) 100	(20) 100	(30) 100

Longitudinal effect

Cross-sectional effect

Time-lag effect

time-lag effect
in a cross-sequential design, the effect resulting from comparing subjects of the same age at different times

cross-sectional study would permit: to see the effect of **time lag** on the ability to program a VCR. By looking down one of the diagonals we can see how many people of the same age can program a VCR at different times. Although the time-lag effect does not escape the problem of confounding, it helps to show the secular trend.

The longitudinal, cross-sectional, and time-lag effects can be seen by displaying the data from Table 12.4, as shown in Figures 12.12 through 12.14. Figure 12.12 shows the cross-sectional data by plotting percentage of people who can program a VCR as a function of age, with year of testing as the parameter. As you might expect from the anecdote about my nephew, the data clearly show that older people are less likely to be able to program a VCR than younger ones.

The picture is very different, however, when we look at the longitudinal data in Figure 12.13. Here the same data are plotted as a function of age, with cohort as a parameter. In other words, here we see the trend over age for people born in different years. These data show that the older cohorts learn faster, because the rate of change is steeper. The 1980 cohort doesn't show any learning at all in these data; it appears that they were born knowing how to program VCRs! (We can suppose that they learned very fast sometime between birth and age 10.) Actually, Figure 12.12 and Figure 12.13 are the same with the exception of how the data points are connected: Figure 12.12 connects the data points that represent the same year of testing, whereas Figure 12.13 connects those points that represent the same year of birth.

The explanation for the apparent contradiction between the two graphs can be seen by looking at the time-lag data. Figure 12.14 shows the percentage of people who can program a VCR as a function of year, with age as a parameter. This graph shows that there has been a very strong secular trend in ability to program VCRs. Thus, the cross-sectional data shown in Figure

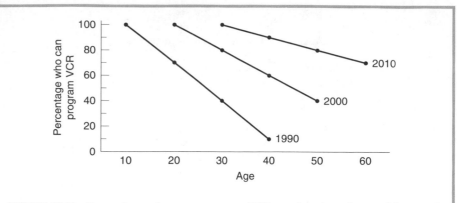

FIGURE 12.12   Percentage who can program a VCR as a function of age, with year of testing as a parameter.

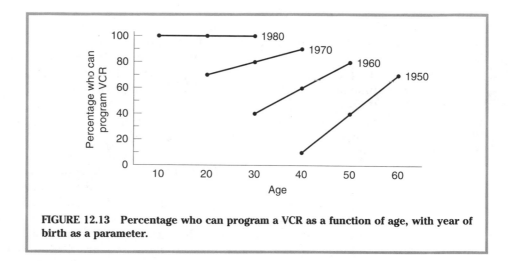

FIGURE 12.13   Percentage who can program a VCR as a function of age, with year of birth as a parameter.

12.12 could give the wrong impression because it does not highlight the fact that people of all ages are learning to program VCRs.

This example was concocted to show how longitudinal and cross-sectional studies could come up with opposite conclusions. A more common situation is one in which a cross-sectional study of, say, intellectual ability shows a decline with age, but a longitudinal study shows no change. The difference can be accounted for by recognizing that there has been a secular improvement in educational levels. A cross-sectional study will have younger people that are better educated than the older cohorts, resulting in higher intellectual performance. A longitudinal study, on the other hand, will follow the same person over time and find no decline in intellectual ability. A cross-sequential design will show the effect of increase in educational level by the time-lag effect.

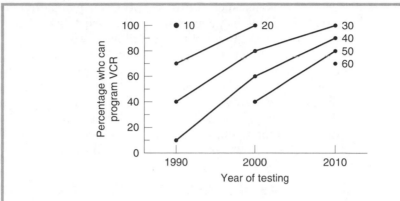

FIGURE 12.14 **Percentage who can program a VCR as a function of year of testing, with age as a parameter.**

PROGRAM EVALUATION

program evaluation

a set of techniques for determining the effectiveness of a social service program

Although we have emphasized the importance to research of developing and testing of theory, we have noted that some research is not driven by theoretical concerns, but is intended rather to determine some factual question. An important example of such an area of research in the social sciences is **program evaluation.**

Although private and public agencies have always provided social services, their effectiveness was not usually evaluated systematically until the mushrooming of federal government programs as part of the "Great Society" of the 1960s. When the government started spending millions of dollars to achieve social ends, there was understandable concern that the money be well spent. Now all programs that provide services supported by federal grants must be evaluated (Posavac & Carey, 1989).

How to go about evaluating a social program can be more difficult than would appear at first. Why not use the same techniques to evaluate programs that we employ in evaluating a company? You can ask what percentage of the market General Widget controls, how long their widgets last, or whether the company makes a profit. All of these indices can be used to evaluate a company operating in a competitive, market system.

These indicators do not work very well for social service agencies. In the first place, the agencies frequently do not operate in a competitive market: There is only one public school system in a given city. Second, their product is difficult to evaluate: Should you evaluate graduates by their scores on standardized tests, or by the percentage who go to college, or the percentage who are employed? Third, profit or loss is often irrelevant to program evaluation: If there were a profit to be made in providing a social service, a company would be providing the service in the first place.

For reasons such as these, program evaluation has developed as a specialized field that makes use of the expertise of psychologists, among other disciplines. Many of the techniques used in program evaluation have already been discussed in this book. They range across all the research methods from true experiments to archival research, with emphasis on quasi experiments and nonexperimental methods. As you can imagine, it would be difficult to evaluate a program such as an alcohol awareness intervention at a college by experimental techniques. Because of the wide variety of techniques employed, we have included program evaluation in this chapter after all the various techniques have been discussed.

■ Sources of Resistance to Program Evaluations

Program evaluation is unusual among types of research projects in the extent to which it is conducted in a social context. Generally the evaluators either work for the organization being evaluated or for the external sponsor of the program. In either case, the evaluation involves many people and affects many people. Further, the evaluation has the potential of making the people who run the program look good or bad, and can affect their futures very directly. These circumstances introduce a political dimension to program evaluation that is not present in most of the research methods discussed so far. People who feel threatened by the evaluation will actively or passively resist the process. Posavac and Carey (1989) discuss a number of potential sources of resistance to a successful program evaluation. We will discuss several of them here.

Fear that the program will be terminated. In the extreme case, a negative evaluation could result in termination of the program, although this seldom happens. Even in these days of "sunset laws," programs generally continue even in the face of negative evaluations as a result of pressure from people who benefit from the program. More often, programs are modified as a result of the evaluation. In any case, there may be resistance to the evaluation from people with a vested interest in the program, including its employees.

Fear of losing control of the program. Introduction of an evaluation procedure causes changes in the day-to-day operation of a program. The managers and personnel of the program may feel that they are losing control over their project. The evaluators should make clear that they are there to evaluate rather than control the program.

Fear that information will be abused. Some program personnel may fear that information generated by the program could shed a negative light on their individual performance. Successful evaluators will carefully distinguish between evaluation of the program and the individual personnel, and will work to build trust among the program personnel.

Fear that the wrong measures will be used.   The people working in the agency may believe that they have an understanding of the successful workings of the school or clinic that cannot be captured by a formal evaluation. The evaluator should try to integrate quantitative and qualitative measures into the final evaluation.

Belief that evaluation is pointless.   There is often cynicism about the worth of doing an evaluation because it may have no apparent effect on the program. This may be justified because the existence of programs is often subject to political considerations that are not directly related to their worth. Evaluations, however, often do accomplish their purpose.

Hopes that are too high.   Many times programs are begun with hopes of making dramatic changes in outcomes, whether dropout rate in school, drug rehabilitation, or whatever. When the program does not live up to these unrealistic expectations, personnel may resent an evaluation that is likely to find only a modest improvement over some alternative program. Frequently a new program is compared to some standard program of treatment. Usually the standard treatment will have some effect, or it would never have come into general use. It is necessary to reassure program personnel that the most successful program will not save the world.

■ Steps in Planning an Evaluation

Throughout this book we have discussed a number of steps in conducting research. The political dimension of program evaluation makes it necessary to be more systematic in planning an evaluation. Posavac and Carey (1989) list six steps in planning an evaluation. The following discussion is adapted from their list.

stakeholders
people in an
organization who
stand to gain or
lose by any
change in it

Step 1. Identify the stakeholders.   You need to spend some time finding out who the **stakeholders** in the program are. Stakeholders are those who have a vested interest in the program and stand to gain or lose by the outcome of the evaluation. The stakeholders in a college include students, faculty, alumni, trustees, administrators, and donors. All of these constituencies need to be consulted in important matters concerning the college. An evaluation that does not involve all the stakeholders in the planning phase is asking for trouble. Every stakeholder has some potential for sabotaging the evaluation.

Step 2. Arrange preliminary meetings.   Once the players have been identified, it is helpful to meet with them to discover the answers to several important questions: (1) Who wants the program evaluated? (2) Why do they want it evaluated? (3) What type of evaluation is desired? (4) What resources are available? (5) When do they want it completed?
    It makes considerable difference who wants the evaluation. The sponsors of the program need to be convinced that the evaluation would be

a good use of their dollars, and the program personnel need to be made comfortable with the idea of being evaluated. Ideally, both groups should see the evaluation as having potential benefit for them.

Different stakeholders may want the evaluation for different reasons. The sponsor may want to know how effective the program is; the personnel may want to know how to make it run more smoothly from their perspective; the administrator of the program may welcome the evaluation as a way of putting off making a difficult decision (let's form a committee and study it). The evaluators need to be sensitive to the political pressures that each stakeholder will be bringing to bear.

summative evaluation
an evaluation of the quality of a project, often after it is completed

formative evaluation
an evaluation of ways to improve a project while it is ongoing

The type of evaluation desired can differ from one stakeholder to another. The sponsor may want a **summative evaluation**—one that evaluates how effective the project is in meeting its goals. The sponsor may want to decide whether to continue the project or spend its money elsewhere. The project personnel, however, may prefer a **formative evaluation**—one that focuses on how the project can be improved.

The evaluators need to know what resources they have available to them. Will the program personnel be assigned to help them, or do the evaluators need to do all their own data collection? The resources available obviously impose a limit on the scope and quality of the evaluation that can be done.

It is also necessary to have a clear understanding of when the evaluation is needed. It may be that the sponsor wants the evaluation by a certain time in order to make a decision, but that deadline does not allow for the development of the proper methodology for the evaluation.

Step 3. Decide whether an evaluation should be done.   Although it might seem that this should be the first step, only after you have identified the players and met with them are you in a position to decide whether it is possible to evaluate the program. The stakeholders need to agree on what constitutes program success before the program can be evaluated. If the sponsor wants to reduce drinking by college students but the project personnel want to keep students from embarrassing the college by having loud parties that result in calls to the police, then there may be some differences in how the project should be evaluated.

Another consideration in deciding to proceed is whether the program is soundly based in theory. The program leaders may believe that providing information about the dangers of alcohol will be sufficient to reduce drinking, without considering the other factors that lead to drinking by college students, such as social pressure. Until the program is grounded in current knowledge of the problem it is addressing, evaluation may be a waste of time. Notice that the program evaluation does not test the validity of the theory underlying the program, it only concerns the effectiveness of the application of the theory. Nevertheless, if the program does not have a sound theoretical basis, it is not ready to be evaluated.

Step 4. Examine the literature. Evaluators tend to be generalists who evaluate many different types of programs. It is necessary to become familiar with the literature on evaluation in the field relevant to the program they are working on. What types of evaluation have been done in this area, and how successful were they? What methods were used, and how might they be adapted or improved upon? The methods of literature review discussed in Chapter 1 are useful here. Computerized databases are especially helpful in program evaluation because of the interdisciplinary nature of the field.

Step 5. Determine the methodology. We will say little about this important step because it concerns issues dealt with throughout this book: the measures, control and comparison groups, sampling methods, statistics, and so on. The one issue that should be mentioned is the general strategy of the evaluation: What is it exactly that you wish to evaluate? Is it the need for the program, the outcome of the program, the cost effectiveness of the program? The methodology will depend greatly on what you wish to evaluate.

Step 6. Present a written proposal. This step forces you to put in writing all the decisions in the previous step and permits the stakeholders to understand what is about to happen. There may be issues that need to be discussed further. The proposal might have an unrealistic timetable or make assumptions about resources that are contrary to fact. It is best to have these issues ironed out before the evaluation proceeds.

■ Two Examples of Program Evaluation

We will consider two examples of program evaluation to illustrate some of its problems and benefits. First, we will consider a case in which program evaluation failed because of organized opposition. Then, we will consider a more successful case.

Implementing Alcohol Guidelines in a University

Wittman (1989) describes the experience of a large state university that attempted to implement guidelines for the use of alcohol in its fraternities and sororities. The project began as a cooperative effort among representatives of the Greek system, an independent agency known as the Prevention Research Center, the Student Health Service, and another office of the university that worked with the Greek students.

The Student Health Center and the Prevention Research Center held a "kickoff" meeting to which a number of organizational representatives were invited, including all identified stakeholders. At the introductory meeting, it was explained that student representatives would be asked to accept a major share in planning the project, and that an evaluation would be built into the project.

The effort led to the formation of the Greek Alcohol Advisory Board, which developed a set of "Party Planning Guidelines" to reduce problems such as party crashing by high school students, a climate that encouraged drinking to intoxication, and the like. The GAAB, however, had little enthusiasm for the evaluation component of the project because it placed new responsibilities on students for enforcing university policy. More important, a vocal minority of the alumni advisers to the fraternities strongly objected to the evaluation. They objected to the design of the survey, complained that they had not been involved in planning the program, and feared that results might make the newspapers. The alumni advisers were successful in torpedoing the evaluation even after preliminary data had been collected for about a year on the first phase of the project. Wittman (1989) reports that the program is continuing at the university, and it seems to be successful on the basis of informal observations, although it is impossible to tell for sure.

The failure of this program evaluation can be attributed to several of the potential sources of resistance listed previously. Specifically, the alumni advisers were concerned that the program would change the relationship between the Greek system and the university, that the wrong kind of evaluation was being done, and that information from the evaluation could be abused. Although the developers of the program followed the steps suggested by Posavac and Carey by identifying the stakeholders and arranging preliminary meetings, it appears that they were not diligent enough in actually getting them involved. The organizers invited the alumni advisers to the preliminary meeting, but they apparently did not show up. Finally, and most significantly, relations between the university and the Greek community were already strained before this program was initiated, and the main issue was alcohol.

Preventing Pregnancy at a University

Fisher (1990) reports the results of a campaign to reduce pregnancies among undergraduate students at a large public university in Canada. For the five years prior to the start of the campaign, positive tests for pregnancy made by the Student Health Service were stable at a rate of about 10 per 1,000 female students. The university initiated a series of pregnancy-prevention lectures in the dormitories in 1983. The next year a specially developed videotape and booklet on prevention of pregnancy were added to the program. The pregnancy rate dropped to about 7 per 1,000 in the first year of the program and then dropped further the next year to 6.5, after which it remained at about the same low level for the three later years reported by Fisher. As a control for a possible secular trend in unwanted pregnancies, Fisher notes that the abortion rate for Canada remained steady during the period. (It was assumed that all pregnancies that resulted in tests by the Student Health Service were unwanted.) In addition, Fisher believes that the pregnancy rate measured by the Student Health Service was a reliable measure of the pregnancy rate because he sees no good reason to expect that the program would cause pregnant women to avoid the health service. The program was purposely designed to be nonjudgmental and to increase the likelihood that pregnant women would go to the Student Health Service. It is likely that the effect of the program was, if anything, larger than the measure indicates.

One reason that this evaluation succeeded where the previous example failed was that an outcome measure was already routinely available to the Student Health Service. Although not all women who suspected they were pregnant would go to the health service for a test, enough of them would go to give a good indication of the pregnancy rate.

SUMMARY

1. The boundaries between true experiments, quasi experiments, and nonexperiments are not sharp; the distinctions are based on the relative amount of control that the researcher is able to maintain.

2. Quasi experiments may be performed when a true experiment would be impossible or when the advantages of a quasi experiment outweigh its disadvantages.

3. The most common quasi-experimental situation is to have nonequivalent control groups. Such experiments are sometimes uninterpretable, depending on the pattern of results.

4. One example of the nonequivalent control group design was the delayed control group design employed to test the so-called psychic Uri Geller.

5. An example of a quasi-experimental factorial design was the study of anxiety. Trait anxiety was a quasi-experimental variable, and state anxiety was a true experimental variable.

6. The regression discontinuity design is used to study nonequivalent groups by considering the correlation between subjects' scores on the pretest and posttest. If the experimental treatment is given to those who meet some criterion on the pretest and if the treatment is effective, the regression line between the two variables will be discontinuous.

7. Interrupted time-series designs consider the trend of the data before and after some manipulation in a study with no control group. The ideal situation is to have a stable baseline before the manipulation, followed by an abrupt or gradual change to a new stable level.

8. Repeated-treatment designs improve on the validity of an experiment by presenting the treatment more than once. The ideal result is for each presentation of the treatment to produce a change in the same direction, with a reversal of the effect when the treatment is removed.

9. One prominent area of psychology that uses quasi-experimental methods is developmental, where time is a variable and nonequivalent control groups are used.

10. Longitudinal designs study the same individuals over time, but have the problem of secular trends.

11. Cross-sectional designs study individuals of different ages at the same time, but have the problem of cohort effects.

12. Cross-sequential designs attempt to get around the problems of longitudinal and cross-sectional designs by combining features of both. The time-lag effect compares subjects who are of a given age at different times.

13. Program evaluation is a set of techniques for evaluating the effectiveness of a social service program.

14. Some sources of resistance to program evaluation are fear that the program will be terminated, of losing control of the program, that information will be abused, or that wrong measures will be used; belief that evaluation is pointless; and hopes that are too high.

15. In planning an evaluation, the evaluators should identify the stakeholders, arrange preliminary meetings, decide whether an evaluation should be done, examine the literature, determine the methodology, and present a written proposal.

16. Formative evaluations are aimed at improving a program while it is ongoing; summative evaluations are of the quality of the program, often after it is completed.

Suggestions for Further Reading

CAMPBELL, D. T., & STANLEY, J. C. (1963). *Experimental and quasi-experimental designs for research.* Chicago: Rand McNally. This book is the classic reference on quasi experimentation.

COOK, T. D., & CAMPBELL, D. T. (1979). *Quasi-experimentation: Design and analysis for field settings.* Chicago: Rand McNally. This book updates the material in Campbell and Stanley, above.

CRONBACH, L. J., AMBRON, S. R., DORNBUSCH, S. M., HESS, R. D., HORNIK, R. C., PHILLIPS, D. C., WALKER, D. F., & WEINER, S. S. (1980). *Toward reform of program evaluation.* San Francisco: Jossey-Bass. A classic discussion of the issues.

POSAVAC, E. J., & CAREY, R. G. (1989). *Program evaluation: Methods and case studies* (3rd ed.). Englewood Cliffs, NJ: Prentice-Hall. An accessible discussion of the area.

SHADISH, W. R., COOK, T. D., & LEVITON, L. C. (1991). *Foundations of program evaluation.* Newbury Park, CA: Sage. Discusses differing approaches of major thinkers in the field of program evaluation.

ⅢⅢ➡ A CASE IN POINT ⬅ⅢⅢ

Bulimia in College Women

Bulimia is a very common eating disorder in women. It consists of episodes of binge eating alternating with fasting, strict dieting, or purging (by means of vomiting, diuretics, or laxatives). As many as 15% of college women may be seriously affected by bulimia.

You are a researcher who suspects that bulimia is partially controlled by social forces: Because women desire to match cultural norms of thinness, social pressure may influence women to engage in behaviors that they believe may help them achieve lower weight. This suggests to you that you might find evidence of social pressures for bulimia among groups of women.

SUBJECTS: There are two large sororities on your campus that are very popular with the same group of women. In talking with members of the sororities, you discover that Alpha seems to have more women who engage in bulimic behavior than Beta. You confirm this by giving a survey to the women in both sororities in the middle of April, before the term ends and the sororities close for the summer. Alpha women score higher on the Binge Eating Scale (BES; Gormally, Black, Daston, & Rardin, 1982).

MATERIALS AND MEASURES: Besides the BES scale, you can administer questionnaires to the women. Possible questions include height and weight (the ratio of weight to height can be considered a measure of deviation from ideal weight), popularity of the other women in the sorority, their perceived deviation from ideal weight, and the Rosenberg Self Esteem Scale (RSES). You can also physically measure height and weight. You can measure the popularity of each woman in the two sororities.

CONSIDERATIONS: You are concerned that the women who are recruited during the fall rush will be self-selected for bulimia to match the two patterns at the two sororities.

You are able to make your various measurements once per term for two more terms. You could make the fall term measurements shortly after fall rush. The spring wave of measurements could be any time from January through April. You are concerned that bulimia may be related to proximity of holidays and special occasions on campus.

Regression to the mean may be a problem because you have chosen your groups based on their differences on the BES, which is one of your possible dependent measures.

REQUIRED: Design a study to test your theory. Discuss how you will deal with the various considerations listed here. Specify the variables of the study, and indicate expected data. (Optional: Specify the statistical analysis you will use.)

The experiment on which this case is based is referenced in the Instructor's Manual.

ⅢⅢ➡ A CASE IN POINT ⬅ⅢⅢⅢ

Preventing Smoking in Adolescents

Cigarette smoking is a major public health concern because of its well-documented effects on health and because of the large numbers who smoke. It is very difficult for people to quit smoking, and most smokers begin as adolescents. Therefore, there has been considerable interest in preventing young people from beginning to smoke in the first place.

In spite of the importance of preventing smoking, programs to educate young people have not been notably successful. You are interested in developing and testing a program that would be successful. Research and common experience both indicate that peer pressure is an important factor in the onset of smoking. You believe that using slightly older students as counselors might be an effective method. In addition, you are aware of a technique called inoculation, in which people are exposed to pressure to conform to some behavior at the same time that they are given a means to counter the pressure. For example, a person may be shown an ad for cigarettes that has the implied message that women who smoke are more liberated. The inoculation technique would teach students to reason that a woman is not really liberated if she is addicted to tobacco. You suspect that the use of peer counselors and the inoculation technique will reduce the rate of smoking onset in seventh-graders.

You have the following resources at your disposal.

SUBJECTS: There are three schools whose principals are willing to let you test your program on their students. Central is located in the inner city and has the most problems with drugs and alcohol. Of the parents of students at Central, 50% are smokers. Greenfield is a suburban school. Drugs and alcohol are a problem there, but not as serious as at Central. Only 40% of Greenfield parents smoke. Millbridge is in a factory town that has fewer problems with alcohol and drugs than do the other two schools, but 45% of Millbridge parents are smokers.

APPARATUS: Your materials will be primarily printed matter, slides, and videotapes. There is a machine you can purchase that will measure exhaled carbon monoxide, which is present in the breath of smokers and those who breathe automobile exhaust. If you buy this machine it will use up half your budget, requiring you to test fewer subjects.

PERSONNEL: You have two assistants who can go to the schools to help run the program and analyze the data.

CONSIDERATIONS: You are inclined to combine the inoculation technique with peer counseling, because your main concern is to develop a program that works. On the other hand, if you had one group with peer counseling, one with the inoculation procedure, and one with both, you could assess the separate effects of the two variables.

You realize that in order to perform a true experiment you would have to randomize subjects to conditions. This would require, as a practical matter, that some students in any particular school would be in different conditions. You are concerned that students in different groups would talk among themselves and contaminate the effect of the different conditions.

Another possibility would be to use a nonequivalent control group design. You could use the three different schools as the groups. You are not sure which schools to use because of the differences among them. You wonder whether the school with the highest or the lowest rate of parental smoking should be the control group.

REQUIRED: Design the study. Include your hypothesis, method, and expected results. Justify your decisions, including your reasons for rejecting alternatives. Be sure to describe how you will analyze your data. Provide data sheets with mocked-up data. Make a table or graph of expected results. (Optional: What is the appropriate statistical analysis?)

The experiment on which this case study is based is cited in the Instructor's Manual.

≡ READING BETWEEN THE LINES ≡

12.1 ULCERS IN EXECUTIVE MONKEYS

In a famous study (Brady, Porter, Conrad, & Mason, 1958), pairs of monkeys received electric shocks. One of the monkeys in a pair received a shock when it failed to press a lever at least once every 20 seconds. The other monkey received a shock according to the behavior of the first monkey; its own behavior had nothing to do with the shock it received. The monkey whose behavior determined the shock was called the executive monkey. Before the experimenters placed the monkeys in the experiment, they gave them a pretest on their ability to learn the avoidance response. Those monkeys in each pair that learned more quickly were made the executive monkeys, and the ones that learned more slowly became the control monkeys. Brady et al. found that the executive monkeys tended to develop ulcers, whereas the control monkeys did not. Although this experiment became well known, other researchers were unable to replicate it. Can you think of any fault in the procedure?   ■

12.2 MEMORY FOR WORDS

The study of how words are remembered and later recalled is an active research area. One way this question is studied is by using the sentence verification procedure, in which subjects are asked whether statements such as "All robins are birds" are true or false. Variations in the speed of their responses between different pairs of concepts are taken to indicate how the words are related in memory. One theory says that the speed of response depends on how similar the concepts are to each other. Similarity is defined by how many characteristics the two concepts have in common. For example, a robin is a typical bird and so would share many characteristics with the concept bird: has feathers, sings, perches in trees, and eats berries. On the other hand, a penguin has fewer of these characteristics, even though it is a bird. Michael McCloskey and Sam Glucksberg (1979) tested this theory, using the sentence verification procedure. Their sentences were of the type "All As are Bs." In some of the sentences the words shared many characteristics: "All robins are birds" or "All oaks are trees." In other sentences the concepts shared fewer characteristics: "All penguins are birds" or "All mahoganies are trees." They found that subjects responded more quickly to the sentences containing the highly related concepts, supporting their theory. Can you think of anything else about the words that could explain the differences in reaction times?   ■

☑ EXERCISES

12.1 CLASSIFY A STUDY

This exercise is based on a study by Denenberg, Garbanati, Sherman, Yutzey, and Kaplan (1978). The following is from the abstract of the article:

> Litters were either handled or not handled between birth and weaning, and the weanlings were reared in either laboratory cages or enriched environments

between 21 and 50 days. When approximately 135 days old, animals within each of the four treatment groups had a right neocortical ablation, a left neocortical ablation, a sham operation, or no surgery. About 1 month later, all animals were given the open-field test for emotionality and exploratory behavior. (p. 1150)

REQUIRED:
a. Was this a true experiment, a quasi experiment, or a nonexperiment?
b. What was (were) the independent variable(s)?
c. What was (were) the dependent variable(s)?
d. How many conditions were there, and what were they? (Hint: It might help to diagram the conditions.)
e. Describe the design.

12.2 IDENTIFY THE DESIGN OF A STUDY

Reread the Zillmann and Bryant study described on page 80. Identify the design of the study and make a diagram of it. (Hint: There are actually three different designs for three dependent variables.)

12.3 DATA INTERPRETATION

Figure 12.15 shows the average classroom attendance of inmate groups enrolled in adult basic education classes in a certain correctional facility. Attendance is reported for the 18-month period before a "good time" law was passed and the 18-month period after the law was passed. The good time law allows inmates to earn three days a month off their minimum sentence for attending adult basic education classes.

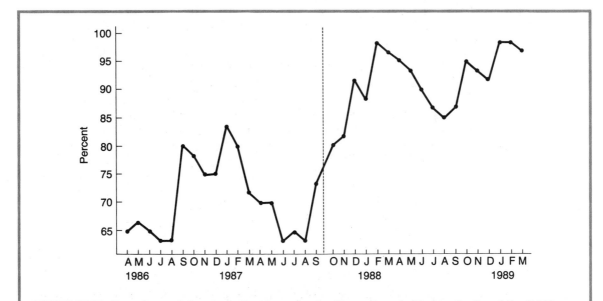

FIGURE 12.15   Percentage of classroom attendance for the 18-month period before the "good time" bill was passed and the 18-month period after the bill was passed.

REQUIRED:

    a. Is the baseline stable? (Hint: Look for seasonal trends.)
    b. What is the independent variable?
    c. What is the dependent variable?
    d. What is the effect of the independent variable on the dependent variable?
    e. What type of graph is this?
    f. Does the x-axis represent the independent variable? Explain.

12.4 IDENTIFY THE DESIGN OF A STUDY

Children who were trick-or-treating on Halloween were given an opportunity to steal candy from a bowl left in the entrance to a home. Some children came in alone, and others came in groups. The adult at the home randomly asked some of the groups or individuals their names and addresses, and others were not asked. More children in groups stole candy than children who were alone, and more anonymous children stole than the nonanonymous children. The effects of anonymity depended on group membership, being the greatest on children in groups. (Adapted from Diener, Fraser, Beaman, & Kelem, 1976).

REQUIRED:

    a. Was this a true experiment, a quasi experiment, a case study, or a survey?
    b. What was (were) the independent variable(s)?
    c. What was (were) the dependent variable(s)?
    d. What was the design of the study?
    e. What was (were) the effect(s) of the independent variable(s)?
    f. Was there an interaction? If there was, describe it in words.
    g. Suggest a variable that could have been confounded with group membership.
    h. Which statistic would be appropriate to analyze the data?   ❏

13

Reporting the Results

O f all the steps in the research process, the most crucial may be communicating the findings to others. The most perfect experiment in the world makes no contribution to science if the results are not reported to the scientific community. As we discussed in an earlier chapter, science is a social enterprise. It grows by the public discussion and assimilation of knowledge contributed by individual scientists.

Scientific communication takes place in different ways. We think of the article published in a scholarly journal as the standard form of scientific communication. This form is known as archival publication because these journals are publicly available in places such as libraries. Archival publication is the permanent record of science. As such, it clearly serves a vital function, but it is not the only way scientific findings are published.

Another important type of communication goes on informally over the telephone, by mail, by visits to laboratories, and at professional meetings. The people who communicate about their research in this way are said to form **invisible colleges**—informal networks of people with common scientific interests. It is through this informal communication that new ideas and results are usually first discussed. Published papers typically appear one or two years after the information is available to the invisible college. Informal communication not only allows scientists to keep up with what is happening in other laboratories, it also permits researchers to present their ideas in a tentative form before committing themselves in archival publications. For these reasons, it is important for scientists to be aware of the role of the

invisible college
informal communication network of persons having common scientific interests

invisible college and to become part of the one that operates in their area of research. Many a young scientist has been frustrated by the difficulties of "breaking into the club" by relying on archival communication. Therefore, we will discuss how to present findings at scientific meetings as well as via the standard article in an archival journal.

THE WRITTEN REPORT

In this section we will discuss the writing of a formal report as it is submitted to a scientific journal. We will follow the American Psychological Association format because it is used by most psychological journals as well as by other publications. Once you are familiar with APA format, it is convenient to work with. A full discussion appears in the *Publication Manual of the American Psychological Association* (1983), which you can refer to for details. Another way to learn how to prepare a paper for publication is to look through a recent issue of the journal that you wish to submit your paper to and study its format.

■ General

Writing a scientific report is not easy. From reading a few research articles, many students get the feeling that it should be easy: Just use a lot of big words and long sentences, stick with the passive voice, and above all sound dull and pompous. Sometimes these attributes, unfortunately, do characterize scientific writing. The purpose of scientific writing, though, is the same as that of all good writing: to convey a message clearly, concisely, and interestingly. It is true that scientific writing must conform to a certain format in the interest of economy. Yet every writer should try, within that format, to write as well as possible, and this takes effort. Many scientists with reputations as good writers testify that they must work hard to make their writing seem effortless.

Scientific writing, like other expository writing, aims to persuade as well as to inform (Sternberg, 1988). If you simply throw your results and theory down on paper and "let them speak for themselves," you will be disappointed with the outcome. Young scientists sometimes underestimate the importance of good writing in gaining acceptance for their ideas. Repeatedly in the history of science, the person who wrote more clearly and persuasively was remembered and the one who wrote poorly was forgotten.

In some respects, a scientific report is one form of presentation of an **argument.** Although we tend to think of an argument as a disagreement between two people, it has the technical meaning of a set of reasons that support a proposition that one wishes to prove. This proposition is known as the **thesis** of the argument. The term *thesis* is commonly used to refer to a scholarly paper, such as a master's thesis. It is helpful to think of your paper as a presentation of an argument in support of a proposition as a way of focusing your writing. Keep in mind what it is you are trying

argument
a set of reasons in support of a proposition
thesis
the proposition that is supported by an argument

to convince your reader of, and what support you are providing for your propositions.

The abstract is an overview of the entire argument. The introduction section gives the premises of your argument, the method section tells how you obtained your evidence, the results section presents the evidence itself, the discussion section draws the conclusion, and the references tell the reader where you got your premises.

We can capture the essence of good report writing in three words: clarity, brevity, and felicity. The first two terms are familiar; felicity means pleasing style.

Clarity.   The most important element of writing a scientific paper is to say exactly what you mean as directly as possible. You must look at each sentence and ask whether someone could mistake its meaning. Sometimes this approach means avoiding common usages, such as writing "hopefully" when you mean to say "it is hoped." Consider the following sentence: "Hopefully, the subjects followed the instructions." Does it mean that the author hopes the subjects followed the instructions, or that the subjects followed the instructions eagerly or full of hope? Eliminating such problems requires work and practice. Ask someone else to read a draft of your paper to suggest places where the meaning is unclear.

There are a number of words that are commonly misused in scientific writing; Sternberg (1988) has an excellent discussion of many of them. One pair of words is particularly troublesome in psychology because they are so similar, and their meanings can be confused. They are *affect* and *effect*. The problem is compounded by the fact that both can be either nouns or verbs. As a noun, *affect* means *emotion,* but as a verb it means *to influence. Effect* as a noun means *result* or *outcome,* but as a verb it means *to accomplish.* The meanings of the two as verbs are similar. If you say that the hurricane *affected* the demolition of the building, you mean that it influenced the demolition, which presumably was being carried out by workers. If you say, however, that the hurricane *effected* the demolition of the building, the hurricane accomplished the destruction by itself.

Brevity.   Next, work at brevity. Does every word, phrase, and sentence contribute to the paper? Years ago, research papers were long and discursive. Today, because of space shortage in journals, papers must be as brief as possible. Although the need for brevity can sometimes lead to an unfortunate terseness of style, brevity can also be an aid to good communication. Pascal once apologized to a correspondent, "I have made this letter longer than usual because I lack the time to make it shorter." Writers sometimes attempt to clarify by repeating instead of by revising material so that it is clear in the first place. Remember that your intended reader is a busy person whose time you are competing for. If you had an appointment with your reader in person, you would be careful not to waste his or her time.

Felicity. Felicity, or pleasingness of style, may seem out of place in scientific writing, but scientific reporting, too, needs liveliness and grace. Although many forms of humor are best avoided because they can distract from the message or even backfire, there is a place for wit. A well-known paper in vision research was entitled "What the Frog's Eye Tells the Frog's Brain" (Lettvin, Maturana, McCulloch, & Pitts, 1959). The title conveys the topic of the paper in such a way that people want to read it. This paper has become a classic in its field, helped in part by its catchy title.

■ Avoiding Sexism and Ethnic Bias in Writing

APA style reflects recent changes in our culture by requiring that authors avoid sexist language and ethnic bias in their writing. This is not easy to do. Long-lived attitudes and traditions have become built into our language. We have terms such as *manpower, mailman,* and *manhole cover.* It may be easy to replace *manpower* with *personnel,* and *mailman* with *letter carrier,* but it is harder to think of a replacement for *manhole cover.* It has been common to use the term *man* to refer to humankind: As teachers of English used to say with a wink, "man" embraces "woman." The pervasiveness of such sexist language can be startling when one runs across it in older writing, even in learned books and journals. Ethnic bias is also prevalent in scientific writing, as when particular groups are used to illustrate social problems that are common to all.

We will consider two common problems with biased language, following the discussion in the APA *Publication Manual* (1983). First is ambiguity of referent; the second is stereotyping.

Ambiguity of referent occurs when a masculine term is used when it is not clear that only males are in view. It is very common to read something like the following:

(Poor) The *subject* was asked to indicate *his* preference . . .

Unless the subjects were all males, this should be reworded to avoid the ambiguity by making clear that both sexes are being referred to:

(Preferred) *Subjects* were asked to indicate *their* preference . . .

When only one person is being referred to, it becomes somewhat awkward to avoid sexist language. Some writers solve this problem by creating another:

(Poor) The subject placed their preferred hand on the button.

Here the noun is singular and the pronoun is plural, but both refer to the same person. There is no simple solution to this problem. Without making the noun plural, there are two options. One is to indicate both sexes explicitly:

> (Preferred) The *subject* placed *his or her* preferred
> hand on the button.

The other is to alternate gender, one time saying *his* and another time, *her.* Neither of these is completely satisfactory: The first is wordier, and the second can be distracting.

Writing can stereotype people by choosing examples that imply limitations on sex roles, social status, and so forth, even though they may be accurate on a statistical basis. Although most professors are men, to refer to an unspecified professor as *he* implies that all are. The remedies are the same as those just discussed: Reword the sentence to make the noun plural so that you can use *they,* use *he or she,* or alternate usage.

In the matter of ethnic bias, one should avoid using terms that refer to ethnic status in such a way as to imply a difference, unless that difference is supported by evidence and relevant to the discussion. In addition, preferred ways of referring to ethnic groups change over time. One should be careful not to use a term that may have been acceptable at one time, but has been replaced by another. The appropriate term should be determined by the members of the group, not your own sense of style.

■ The Parts of a Paper

The parts of a paper are (1) title, (2) authors and their affiliations, (3) abstract, (4) introduction, (5) method, (6) results, (7) discussion, (8) references, (9) footnotes, (10) tables, (11) figure captions, and (12) figures. We have listed them in the order that they appear in a typescript submitted for publication in a journal. In the published form, the footnotes, tables, figure captions, and figures are placed appropriately throughout the paper.

Each part of the paper serves a specific function, which we will consider in order. As you begin to write a paper, consult a recent issue of the journal for which you are writing to see its style for a typical article.

On pages 341-356 we have reproduced an actual journal article (Barnes, Ickes, & Kidd, 1979) in the appropriate form for submission to a journal.[1] You should study this manuscript carefully for style. The circled numbers refer to paragraphs in the third edition of the *Publication Manual of the American Psychological Association.*

Following are some guidelines for typing the manuscript: Do not use erasable paper because it smudges easily and becomes messy. (If your typing is poor and you will make many mistakes, your instructor may accept a photocopy of a paper typed on erasable paper. A journal should receive an

---

[1] From "Effects of the Perceived Intentionality and Stability of Another's Dependency on Helping Behavior" by R. D. Barnes, W. Ickes, and R. G. Kidd, 1979, *Personality and Social Psychology Bulletin, 5*(3), 367–373. Copyright 1979 by the Society for Personality and Social Psychology, Inc. Reprinted by permission of Sage Publications, Inc.

original on standard bond paper. Probably the be⌐
computer or word processor, if available.) Leave wide
around. Double-space everything. Start every section ⌐
for the method, results, and discussion sections. Togeth⌐
tion, these sections form the body of the paper, whic⌐
through.

Title. The title is your chance to gain the attentioɪ   ᴛʜe desired
audience. It should convey the main idea of the paper in a few words. Include
key words that will catch the eye of a person scanning the table of contents
of the journal or that will come up on computerized searches of the literature.
Avoid words that do not contribute directly to the idea of the paper, such as
"An experimental study of . . . ."

Authors and their affiliations.   Authors are usually listed in order of the
importance of their contributions to the paper, although some authors prefer
an alphabetic or random listing. You will want to list your name in a form that
you will be comfortable with for the rest of your career, so as to avoid having
your work listed under several different names in bibliographic sources.

Abstract.   The abstract is a brief (100 to 175 words) synopsis of the
paper. It should summarize the problem, method, results, and conclusion, and
contain elements of each major part of a paper. The abstract must be
self-contained because it will be reproduced verbatim in *Psychological
Abstracts* and other publications. Because of its condensed form, the abstract
is the most difficult part of the paper to write and is often written last.

Introduction.   The introduction sets the stage for the rest of the paper.
First, state the general problem the paper deals with. Then briefly discuss the
relevant literature in a way that shows the present theoretical status of the
problem and places your experiment in context. Although you must
acknowledge the sources of the ideas you discuss, you do not need to give
a thorough history of the problem. Finally, state how your study will
contribute to understanding the problem. Indicate your hypothesis and
expected results.

Method.   The method section is the heart of the paper, and many
authors write this section first. Because the method section describes what
you did in the experiment, everything in this section should be stated in the
past tense. The method section has two purposes. First, having read your
method section, someone else should be able to repeat the experiment
exactly in all essential details. Second, another person should be able to judge
the validity of your conclusions by comparing them with the method section.
For example, in what exact ways did you induce a certain theoretical state,
such as hunger, in the subjects? How did you measure their responses? The
following subsections can be convenient for organizing the method section.

Subjects. Tell how many subjects you used and how they were obtained. Describe any characteristics of your subjects that are important to the study, such as their age, sex, or student status. In the case of animal subjects such as rats, you should name the strain and supplier as well as the species.

Apparatus. Indicate the materials used in the study, including the type of apparatus, and tell the values of stimuli.

Design. State the logic of the experiment, including the variables. (Example: "The design was a 2 × 2 factorial in which sex and instructions each varied between subjects.") State which variables were randomized, which were counterbalanced, and so forth. Tell what the dependent variables were.

Procedure. Although procedure does not need to be a distinct subsection from design, it is helpful to remember that the design is a logical construction in your head, whereas the procedure is a sequence of steps you followed in putting the design into effect. How were the subjects assigned to conditions? What instructions were they given? You may find it helpful to think of the design subsection as what you did and the procedure subsection as how you did it. Both aspects are fundamental to understanding the method.

Results. The main function of the results section is easy to state: What did you find? Results are usually described in the past tense. (Example: "The rats bar-pressed more when they were hungry.") First indicate any data transformations that you made before analyzing the data. Then state what you found. Usually you will refer the reader to a table or graph of the data. Indicate which results were statistically significant and what tests of significance you used.

A common problem in the results section is to get bogged down in describing the inferential statistics and lose sight of the results that you are trying to present. On the other hand, you should not spend time presenting results that were not statistically significant. Remember that the focus of the results section is on what you found; the statistics assure the reader that results are not likely to have been a fluke.

Usually you will summarize the results in either a table or a figure (a graph). Tables have the advantage of being economical of space, precise, and easy to coordinate with the statistical analysis. Figures, on the other hand, allow the reader to get a better idea of the size of the effects and any interactions among variables. My own preference is for figures because they seem to make it easier for the reader to grasp and retain the main features of the results.

Discussion. The discussion section builds on the results by interpreting them and relating them to the literature. The focus of this section is on the theoretical contribution of the study. Describe similarities and differences between your results and those of others. Do not introduce further data from your study unless they are incidental to a comparison with other published data. The following questions are appropriate to address: What weaknesses are there in your data? What qualifications must be made to your conclusions? What has your experiment contributed to the understanding of the problem stated in the introduction? Whereas the method and results sections are written in the past tense, conclusions are stated in the present tense. (Example: "Hunger increases bar-pressing rate.")

References.   The reference section contains the documentation of points made in your paper. It serves the essential function of tying your paper to the literature. Many readers will turn to the references immediately after reading the title and the abstract to see whom you cite. Be sure to reference all sources that you have drawn on for specific ideas. Remember, however, that the reference list is not a bibliography of background material not specifically cited in the text.

Footnotes.   A footnote is the appropriate way to provide a mailing address for reprints, acknowledge financial support or technical assistance, and the like. This type of footnote is not numbered and will appear in the journal at the bottom of the first page. Footnotes to the content of the paper should be avoided. When essential, content footnotes are numbered and will appear in the journal at the bottom of the page on which they are cited.

Tables.   Put data into a table when doing so will help make the data clearer than being strung out in lines of text. The best way to learn how to set

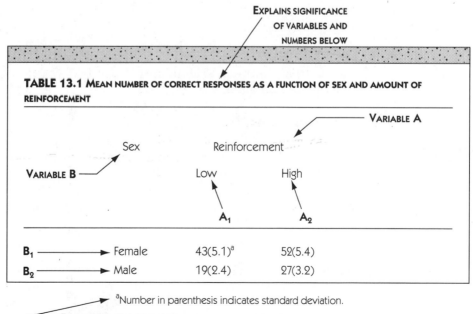

EXPLAINS SIGNIFICANCE OF VARIABLES AND NUMBERS BELOW

TABLE 13.1 MEAN NUMBER OF CORRECT RESPONSES AS A FUNCTION OF SEX AND AMOUNT OF REINFORCEMENT

VARIABLE A

	Sex	Reinforcement	
VARIABLE B		Low	High
		A_1	A_2
B_1	Female	$43(5.1)^a$	$52(5.4)$
B_2	Male	$19(2.4)$	$27(3.2)$

[a]Number in parenthesis indicates standard deviation.

FOOTNOTE EXPLAINS FEATURES THAT MAY NOT BE OBVIOUS.

up a table is to look in a journal to see how tabular material is handled. Table 13.1 shows a typical table and offers some suggestions. Tables should not duplicate material presented in the text or in figures. Indicate where a table should appear in the published paper by typing the following in the text:

Table 1 here

Figure captions. Each figure should have a caption that briefly describes the contents of the figure. The caption should be understandable by itself but should avoid repeating material from the body of the paper. Figure captions come after the tables and before the figures themselves.

Figures. Figures that are to be published in a journal should be professionally drawn. Many authors construct graphs using a computer, but it is important to be sure that the graphics package is capable of meeting APA style requirements. Frequently the standard, or default, choices in the graphics package must be altered to conform to APA guidelines. For unpublished papers, you may draw your own graphs in pencil on graph paper. Avoid color coding in graphs because colors do not photocopy. Different symbols should be used to indicate groups and conditions. Although the proportions of the graph will depend on the type of material, a rule of thumb is to make the ratio of height to width 3:4. If you draw the graph to fill a piece of 8½-by-11-inch graph paper and orient the horizontal axis along the longer side of the page, you will usually come out well. The axes should be clearly labeled. Make the symbols and lettering large enough that the figure can be read from a distance.

■ Documenting Your Paper

An essential feature of scientific writing is that certain types of statements must be documented.

What to Document

First, you must give credit to ideas that are other people's. Second, you need to show where your ideas fit into a larger framework. Third, your reader may want to know where to go for further information about the theory, methods, or data you discuss. It is not necessary to document statements that are common knowledge among your audience. For example, you do not need to document a reference to Pavlovian conditioning or Freudian theory. Beyond this generalization, however, one cannot give a clear rule on what to document. Perhaps one way of answering the question is to recall what it is like to read about scientific topics in popular literature. When scientific claims are made but not documented, readers who wish to learn more will be unable to do so. Who found this phenomenon? What methods were used? Under what conditions does it occur? What theories does it relate to? What do other scientists think of these ideas? All of these questions are unanswerable without documentation.

APA Style of Documentation

In APA style the authors of the work you are citing are named in the text, followed by the date of the publication:

> Jones and Smith (1993) found that . . .

Or you may say:

> Recent work (Jones & Smith, 1993) shows that . . .

Note that when the names appear outside of the parentheses you use the word *and,* but when they are inside the parentheses you use the ampersand (&). If there are two authors, always list both names whenever you cite their work in the text. If there are three or more authors, list all names the first time you refer to the work:

> Jones, Smith, and Brown (1993) found . . .

Thereafter, list only the first author, followed by et al. and the year of publication:

> Jones et al. (1993) found . . .

The reference list will contain an entry for each work cited in the paper. There must be no entries in the reference list that are not cited in the paper, and vice versa. A reference has four major parts: (1) author(s), (2) date, (3) title of article or book, and (4) publication information (including name of journal in the case of periodicals). Each part is separated by a period. Other information is separated by commas. For example:

> Miller, G. A. (1956). The magical number seven, plus or minus two: Some limits on our capacity for processing information. *Psychological Review, 63,* 81–97.

This particular example is of a journal article. The author data appear in the same form for all kinds of references (that have individual authors). Titles of books and names of journals are underlined (they will appear in italics in print), but titles of articles are not. The publication data may differ from one type of publication to the next, as the following examples show.

A reference to a journal article contains the following information: author(s), date, title, journal (underlined), volume (underlined), pages. Refer to the previous example for the appearance of a reference to a journal article.

Most journals number all pages of a volume consecutively even though each volume may have several issues. Some journals, however, begin each issue with page 1. For such publications it is necessary to give the issue number, as follows:

> Parks, A. B. (1990). Delinquency and social class. *Journal of Social Issues, 48*(3), 118–135.

The following information is given for a book: author(s), date, title (underlined), city in which it was published, publisher. Here is an example of a reference to a book:

> McBurney, D. H., & Collings, V. B. (1984). *Introduction to sensation/perception* (2nd ed.). Englewood Cliffs, NJ: Prentice-Hall.

Note that when the book is not published in a major city, you must give the state or country also. Note also that the publisher is identified as briefly as possible; nonessential words such as "Publishing Company" or "Inc." are eliminated.

When the work cited is an article or chapter in a book to which different authors have contributed, the book is considered an edited volume. The following information is given for an article or chapter in an edited volume: author(s), date, title of article or chapter, editor(s), book title (underlined) and article or chapter page numbers, city of publication, publisher. Here is an example of a reference to a chapter in an edited volume:

> Tooby, J., & Cosmides, L. (1992). The psychological foundations of culture. In J. H. Barkow, L. Cosmides, & J. Tooby (Eds.), *The adapted mind: Evolutionary psychology and the generation of culture* (pp. 19–136). New York: Oxford University Press.

Note that the editors' names and initials are listed in forward rather than reverse order.

These three forms are the most common types of references, but they are by no means all of them. Refer to the *Publication Manual of the American Psychological Association* for other examples.

■ Steps in the Publication Process

In this section we will describe the steps that a paper goes through in becoming an article in a typical journal. Our discussion will provide an overview of the publication process, rather than a detailed description. Refer to the APA *Publication Manual* for details.

Before you begin writing a manuscript for publication, you should decide which journal you are going to submit your paper to. Each journal may have slightly different requirements for style, length, and so forth that you should be aware of. Consult a recent issue of the journal for such information.

Use paper clip;
no cover

Short title, not the running head. Type the first two or three words of title on each page. This will allow editor to reassemble pages if they get separated. Do not use authors' names to identify pages.

The title page is page 1.

The maximum length of title is 12-15 words. Identify major variables. Note capitalization. Double-space everything, without exception.

Author's address at time research was conducted, not necessarily present address.

No more than 50 spaces, centered. This will go on each page of article.

Effects of the
1

(4.15)

(1.06) Effects of the Perceived Intentionality and Stability

of Another's Dependency on Helping Behavior

Richard D. Barnes and William Ickes

University of Wisconsin, Madison

Robert F. Kidd

Boston University

Running head: DEPENDENCY AND HELPING

(4.15)

New page

Do not indent abstract; type it in a single paragraph.

(1.07)

(4.16)

Set typewriter for a 5½ inch line; margins should be 1½ inches.

Period goes outside parentheses, unless entire sentence is in parentheses.

Length of abstract is 100-150 words.

Effects of the

2

Abstract

A field experiment was conducted to investigate the effects on help-giving of the perceived intentionality and stability of the cause of a dependent person's need. Subjects were asked to lend class notes to a caller whose need for help was described as due either to a lack of ability ("unintentional" dependency) or to a lack of effort ("intentional" dependency). The cause of the caller's dependency was also varied according to its perceived degree of stability (stable vs. unstable). As predicted, more help was elicited (1) when the caller's dependency was attributed to a lack of ability rather than to a lack of effort, and (2) when the dependency was seen as stable rather than unstable. The results are discussed in terms of theorizing which has attempted to relate outcome attributions to helping behavior.

Type the complete title at the beginning of the introduction. The introduction, which opens the main body of the paper, is not labeled.

Indent five spaces for every paragraph, including each footnote, figure caption, and table footnote.

Cite the source of ideas.

Abbreviations are sometimes used in parenthetical material (3.19).

Cite the source that you read.

Underlining indicates italics in printed version. Underline titles of publications. Otherwise, use italics sparingly. See 3.18 for rules.

Use correction fluid or tape and type over errors (4.07).

(4.17)

(1.08)

Effects of the

3

Effects of the Perceived Intentionality and Stability

of Another's Dependency on Helping Behavior

Previous research on the attributional determinants of helping behavior has been guided by Heider's (1958) distinction between "internal" and "external" causes. The results of a number of studies have indicated that more help will be given when a supplicant's dependency is attributed to an external cause (i.e., bad luck) than when the same dependency is attributed to an internal cause (i.e., laziness). For example, in an experiment by Schopler and Matthews (1965), subjects gave significantly more help when a subordinate's request for help appeared to be part of the planned experimental procedure (external locus of dependency) than when it appeared to be initiated by the subordinate himself (internal locus of dependency). Similarly, Berkowitz (1969) found that subjects worked harder on behalf of a fellow subject when his poor performance on a task was attributed to an error made by the experimenter than when it was attributed to his own mismanagement. And, as "real-world" support to complement these findings, Bryan and Davenport (cited in Berkowitz, 1969) reported that readers of the New York Times who contributed to 100 needy people during a Christmas season gave significantly more money to people whose dependency appeared to be externally caused than to those whose outcomes could be attributed to their own moral or psychological deficiency.

Although the simple distinction between an internal versus an external locus of dependency is an important one, recent theoretical developments have indicated that there is more to attribution than the internal/external distinction, and have stressed the need for multidimensional causal taxonomies

List all authors the first time they are cited. If there are five or fewer (3.87). List only the first, followed by "et al.," if there are six or more.

Abbreviation for "compare." Do not underline.

Use dashes sparingly.

Punctuation goes inside quotation marks at end of sentence, with few exceptions (see 3.34).

Effects of the

4

(cf. Horowitz, 1968). The first reformulation was proposed by Weiner et al. (1971). These authors noted that Heider's (1958) characterization of ability and effort as internal causes and task difficulty and luck as external causes implied a further division according to the degree to which each of these factors exhibits stability over time and situation. However, Weiner recognized that even a two-dimensional taxonomy was not sufficient to account for a number of important causal distinctions (Weiner, 1974).

To overcome some of the limitations, Rosenbaum (1972) proposed the addition of a third causal dimension--intentionality. In Rosenbaum's taxonomy, ability can be viewed as either a stable disposition or as a more variable facility. Similarly, the effort factor can take the form of a dispositional "trait" or a fluctuating, unstable "state." More importantly, Rosenbaum's scheme makes an explicit distinction between factors perceived to be under direct personal control (intentional factors) and those perceived to be under the control of other, more impersonal forces (unintentional factors). Although "controllability" might be a better term than "intentionality" in capturing the meaning of Rosenbaum's third causal dimension, we will employ Rosenbaum's terminology throughout this paper.

Following a review of the theoretical developments described above, Ickes and Kidd (1976) proposed a model to predict how the perceived stability and intentionality of a dependent person's outcome may affect his chances of being helped. It is usually assumed that a request for aid implies a failure on the part of the supplicant to independently satisfy his own needs. However, if the cause of his dependency is perceived as unstable, the potential helper may infer that the supplicant is at least sometimes able to take care of his own needs and so may question the degree to which help is really

Effects of the

5

required. From the potential helper's point of view, a supplicant whose

cause of dependency is unstable may be seen as in less need of help than a

supplicant who has no possibility of altering his outcome without additional

help.

With respect to the intentionality factor, Ickes and Kidd (1976) suggest

that the separation of effort and ability ascriptions on the basis of inten-

tionality may be an important element in the decision to help an unfortunate

other. For example, suppose you are downtown standing on a corner across

the street from a large electric sign showing the time. A man standing next

to you turns and asks you what time it is, and you tell him to look up at

the sign across the street. If his dependence on you is due to a lack of

effort, he might answer, "Would you read it for me? I can see that far,

but I'm not willing to try." However, if his dependence is due solely to

a lack of ability, he might answer, "Would you read it for me? I'm willing

to try, but I can't see that far."

In more general terms, if the supplicant's dependency is perceived as

due to a lack of effort (intentional), the outcome will be seen as one the

supplicant can control and the potential helper will not feel obliged to

intervene. However, if the outcome is perceived as due to a lack of ability

(unintentional), the outcome will be seen as one the supplicant cannot con-

trol and the potential helper will feel obliged to intervene on his behalf.

Thus, helping should vary according to whether the supplicant's dependency

is perceived as intentional or unintentional, with more help given in the second

case than in the first. (For an elaboration of the relationships among the

dimensions of internality-externality, stability-instability, and intentionality-

unintentionality, see Ickes and Kidd, 1975.)

For seriation see 3.31.

Do not begin a new page when a heading occurs. Center a main heading, but do not use all capitals. This paper uses only one level of heading. A second level of heading is typed underlined, flush with the left margin. If a third-level heading is needed, it is typed in the same style as a second-level heading, followed by a paragraph indented, followed by a period and two spaces, with the text following on the same line (see 3.30).

Use numerals for 10 and above, except to begin sentence (see 3.39).

Do not abbreviate "subject" or "experimenter".

Note spacing.

Use words for numbers 0-9, with certain exceptions (such as the preceding sentence). See 3.39.

Effects of the

6

In summary, it is proposed that when the perceived causal locus (internal/external) of a dependent person's outcome is held constant, helping will vary according to the perceived stability and intentionality of the outcome. The expected pattern of results would be two additive main effects indicating a greater degree of helping to the extent that the supplicant's dependency is seen as (1) stable rather than unstable, and (2) unintentional rather than intentional. A field experiment was designed to test these predictions.

(1.09)   Method

Subjects were 51 male and 54 female students enrolled in introductory psychology classes. The names and telephone numbers of these students were obtained from course rosters. Prior to being called, each subject was randomly assigned to one of the various experimental conditions within the constraints imposed by counterbalancing for the sex of the subject and the sex of the confederate.

The new dimensions of outcome attribution proposed by Weiner et al. (3.87) (1971) and Rosenbaum (1972)/stability and intentionality--were independently manipulated in a between-subjects design. The perceived causal locus of the caller's dependency was held constant so that it was "internal" in all conditions. Using Rosenbaum's classification scheme, an "unintentional" dependency was defined in terms of a lack of effort or motivation. Cross-cutting this intentionality manipulation, a relatively stable need or dependency was contrasted with a relatively unstable one. Thus, including the counterbalance variables, the complete design was a 2 x 2 x 2 x 2 factorial in which perceived intentionality, perceived stability, sex of subject, and sex of confederate were varied independently. There were either six or seven subjects in each cell.

Note periods and lowercase (3.25).

If exact instructions are crucial to the method, reproduce them as part of the procedure.

Indent long (four or more lines) quotations, but do not use quotation marks. Remember, double-space everything.

Effects of the

7

In an adaptation of a procedure developed by McFall and Twentyman (1973, Exp. IV), subjects in the present study were contacted by telephone between 6:00 and 10:00 p.m. three days before their final examination in introductory psychology. Using a carefully prepared script, the caller identified him/herself as another student in the same large (300-400) lecture section and expressed a need for help in studying for the final exam. After briefly describing the reason for (cause cf) his or her dependency, the confederate proceeded to make a series of five graded requests of the subject. These were structured in such a way that the cost of agreeing to help increased with each successive request. The script was as follows:

Hi, may I speak to _____? You're taking Intro Psych, aren't you? Well, I'm (Tony Freeman/Julie Pearson). I don't think you know me, but I'm in (professor)'s section, too. I don't know anyone else in the class, so I asked in the psych office for the class roster and got your name off of it. I hate to bother you, but I really need some help before the final.

I just don't seem to have the (ability/motivation) to take good notes. I really (try to/can) take good notes, but (sometimes I just can't do it/I just can't ever do it/sometimes I just don't try/I just don't ever try), so the notes I have (sometimes aren't/are never) very good to study for an exam with.

(Request 1:) Do you think I could take a look at yours?

(Request 2:) I think I'll need to fill in what I've missed since the last exam. I could come by your place tonight to look at them, okay?

Use a dash (two hyphens) to indicate a pause in thought (see 3.05).

Effects of the

8

(Request 3:) Actually, my notes are pretty bad, so I'll probably need to borrow yours for at least a day. Would that be all right?

(Request 4:) Great! Well, let's see -- I've got a paper for another class that's due tomorrow, so I can't pick them up tonight. Could I come by late tomorrow night [two days before the examina- tion]?

(Request 5:) I really don't know when I'll be through with them. Could you come by here to pick them up when I'm finished?

The script allowed for four variations in the perceived cause of caller's dependency: stable lack of ability, unstable lack of ability, stable lack of effort, and unstable lack of effort.

Although care was taken not to inform the confederates about the nature of the hypotheses under investigation, they could not be kept "blind" with respect to the experimental treatment which a given subject received.

Moreover, because the confederates may have developed their own hypotheses about how the subjects might be expected to respond, it was important to minimize the likelihood of their introducing a subtle bias into the tele- phone interaction.

A number of alternative solutions to this problem were considered, but as most were ultimately rejected as unfeasible, we attempted to counter the problem of bias in this particular paradigm by (1) holding to a minimum the differences in the wording of the scripts used in the various conditions, (2) repeatedly stressing to the confederates the need for experimental control in the comparability of presentation of each of the versions, and (3) conducting

Effects of the

9

three lengthy rehearsal sessions prior to the actual calling of subjects in which the confederates were required to "overlearn" the scripts to the point that they could be repeated in a standard, semi-automatic fashion. During these rehearsals, the confederates were carefully trained to use a similar pattern of inflection across the variable segments of the script.

After each request, the confederate noted on a response sheet whether or not the subject agreed to the request. Then, depending upon the subject's answer, the confederate either extricated himself or herself from the conversation or proceeded to the next request level. If the subject said "no" unequivocally to the first request, the confederate simply terminated the conversation by saying, "Oh -- Well, thanks anyway." If an ambiguous response was given, the confederate repeated the request and attempted to elicit a definite "yes" or "no." If the subject said "no" to any of the subsequent requests, or agreed to all of them, the confederate terminated the conversation and released the subject from any perceived obligation to help by saying, "Listen, this isn't going to work out. My schedule for the next few days is really messed up. Thanks anyway, okay?" (No notes were ever actually obtained from the subjects, and the subjects were never informed that the call was part of an experiment.)

1.10   Results

One problem presented by field experimentation is that of obtaining information about how participants perceived or interpreted the manipulation. Kidd (1976) has suggested that this problem may be dealt with by drawing a separate "manipulation check" sample from the same subject population, randomly assigning these subjects to the experimental treatments, inducing

Place question mark inside quotation marks when it is part of quoted material (see 3.07).

Period goes inside parenthesis when whole sentence is inside parentheses (see 3.07).

Effects of the

10

the manipulations, and then questioning these subjects about their perceptions

of and reactions to the manipulations. In line with this recommendation,

75 additional undergraduates, representing approximately equal numbers of

males and females taking introductory psychology, were called three days

before their final exams and questioned about their perceptions of the depend-

ency manipulations.

Data were obtained in the form of dichotomous responses, with "0"

and "1" assigned to the possible responses for a given manipulation check

question. As expected, subjects in the lack of effort treatment saw the

caller's failure to take good notes as due to a lack of effort rather than

to a lack of ability, χ^2 (1, N = 105) = 59.04, p < .001. The reverse pat-

tern of greater ability attributions than effort attributions was observed

in the lack of ability conditions. Likewise, subjects felt that the caller

had a chronic problem with note taking in the stable conditions, while in the

unstable conditions the caller's poor note taking was seen as occurring

"only sometimes," χ^2 (1) = 10.08, p < .005. There was no significant

interaction between the intentionality and stability factors.

The major dependent variable in the study proper was the number of the

five helping requests agreed to by the subjects over the telephone. A

four-way ANOVA for this measure revealed significant main effects for both

of the attribution factors (ps < .05) with no significant effects for sex

of subject, sex of confederate, or any of the interaction terms. For this

reason, the data were collapsed across the two counterbalance/sex variables

and analyzed in a 2 x 2 factorial design.

The results of this analysis took the form of the two additive main

effects predicted by Ickes and Kidd (Table 1). Significantly more requests

---

Handwritten marginal annotations:

The word "data" is generally used as a plural.

Use figures to express the actual numeral.

Describe the results, not the statistics.

Results are described in the past tense.

Chi square (χ^2) is the statistic; the degrees of freedom are indicated in parentheses; "p" refers to the significance level (see 3.54).

Identify any Greek letters by writing them in the margin and circling them.

Abbreviation for "analysis of variance." See 3.19, 3.27 for use of abbreviations.

Chi

"F" is the statistic for analysis of variance (3.54)

Indicate where tables and figures should be placed. Use arabic numerals for tables and figures, not roman (4.21).

Effects of the

11

were agreed to when the caller's dependency was attributed to a stable cause than when it was attributed to an unstable cause, $F (1, 95) = 4.40$, $p < .05$. Helping was also greater when the dependency was perceived as due to an unintentional lack of ability than when it was perceived as due to an intentional lack of effort, $F (1, 95) = 4.64$, $p < .05$.

Insert Table 1 about here

The same results were apparent when a chi square analysis was applied to the data. For this analysis, the range of possible helping responses was divided into two categories: no- or low-cost helping (0-2 requests agreed to), and high-cost helping (3-5 requests agreed to). This division is justified because (1) it exactly divides the range of possible responses in half; (2) it meaningfully contrasts low- versus high-cost helping, since the subject does not agree to relinquish physical possession and control of the notes until the third request and (3) this same request proved to be the natural breakpoint of the data in the McFall and Twentyman (1973) experiment.

The results of this analysis revealed that more subjects gave high-cost (vs. low-cost) help when the other's dependency was due to a stable cause (40 out of 51) than when it was due to an unstable cause (27 out of 48), $\chi^2 (1) = 5.56$, $p < .025$. Similarly, more subjects gave high-cost help when the other's dependency was due to an unintentional factor (40 out of 50) than when it was due to an intentional factor (27 out of 49), $\chi^2 (1) = 7.01$, $p < .01$. The interaction effect was not significant.

Effects of the

12

Discussion

The results of the present field experiment are consistent with Ickes and Kidd's attributional analysis of helping behavior. When the causal locus of a supplicant's dependency is held constant, the amount of help the person receives still varies according to the degree to which the cause of dependency is perceived to be stable and intentional.

In a given helping situation, of course, other factors may be expected to either combine additively or interact with stability and intentionality to affect helping behavior. The procedure used in the present study was in some ways unique in that it (1) held anticipation of future contact to a minimum, since the requests were made shortly before the final examination in the subjects' course; and (2) utilized a series of requests that escalated in cost to the subject, possibly producing a "foot-in-the-door" effect (Freedman & Fraser, 1966) that increased the level of helping in all of the experimental conditions. However, despite the possible influence of these other factors on helping, the present results clearly indicate that causal attributions made on the basis of stability and intentionality distinctions contribute significantly to observed differences in helping behavior. They also indicate that people make causal distinctions at a much more detailed level than that implied by a simple internal-external distinction.

1.11

Handwritten marginal notes:

In the discussion section compare the results to the literature.

Conclusions are given in the present tense.

Qualify conclusions, as appropriate.

Use ampersand (&) when reference is within parentheses (3.87).

Show what your study has contributed and how it has helped to resolve the original problem.

References start a new page.

Capitalize main words of journal title; underline title of journal or book (3.101).

Note space between initials in a name.

Capitalize first word following a colon in a title (3.11).

Indent second and following lines of a reference three spaces (4.18).

Use ampersand in references (3.87).

For an article in an edited book the editors' initials precede their last names.

Underline volume number of journal but not book. (Do not give the issue number unless the journal begins every issue with page 1.)

Note two-letter postal abbreviation (no periods).

Effects of the

13

References

Berkowitz, L. (1969). Resistance to improper dependency relationships. Journal of Experimental Social Psychology, 5, 283-294.

Freedman, J. L., & Fraser, S. C. (1966). Compliance without pressure: The foot-in-the-door technique. Journal of Personality and Social Psychology, 4, 195-202.

Heider, F. (1958). The psychology of interpersonal relations. New York: Wiley.

Horowitz, I. A. (1968). Effect of choice and locus of dependence on helping behavior. Journal of Personality and Social Psychology, 8, 373-376.

Ickes, W., & Kidd, R. (1976). An attributional analysis of helping behavior. In J. Harvey, W. Ickes, & R. Kidd (Eds.), New directions in attribution research (Vol. 1). Hillsdale, NJ: Erlbaum.

Kidd, R. F. (1976). Manipulation checks: Advantage or disadvantage? Representative Research in Social Psychology, 7, 160-165.

McFall, R., & Twentyman, C. (1973). Four experiments on the relative contributions of rehearsal, modeling, and coaching to assertion training. Journal of Abnormal Psychology, 81, 199-218.

Do not list any source you did not cite. This is not a bibliography.

Effects of the

14

Rosenbaum, R. M. (1972). A dimensional analysis of the per-

ceived causes of success and failure. Unpublished doctoral

dissertation, University of California, Los Angeles.

Schopler, J., & Matthews, M. (1965). The influence of perceived causal

locus of partner's dependence on the use of interpersonal

power. Journal of Personality and Social Psychology, 2, 609-612.

Weiner, B. (1974). Achievement motivation and attribution

theory. Morristown, NJ: General Learning Press.

Weiner, B., Frieze, I., Kukla, A., Reed, L., Rest, S., & Rosen-

baum, R. M. (1971). Perceiving the causes of success and

failure. In E. E. Jones, D.E. Kanouse, H. H. Kelley,

R. E. Nisbett, S. V. Valins, & B. Weiner (Eds.),

Attribution: Perceiving the causes of one's behavior.

Morristown, NJ: General Learning Press.

Acknowledgment footnotes will appear at the bottom of the first page of the printed article; they are not numbered. See 3.83 for a discussion of footnotes.

Effects of the

15

(3.83)   Footnote

This research was supported in part by National Institute of Mental Health Grant MH-26646 to William Ickes. The authors would like to express their thanks to Lori Schmitz and James Wacht for serving as the confederates in this study.

The tables follow the footnotes, one table per page.

Use arabic numerals.

Draw lines in pencil. (3.67).

If there are any figures, the figure captions begin on the next page, followed by the figures themselves, one per page. The figures are not paginated. Identification for each figure is handwritten on the back of the page.

3.59 – 3.70, 4.21

Effects of the

16

Table 1

Mean Number of Helping Requests Agreed To

Perceived Stability of Other's Outcome	Perceived Intentionality of Other's Outcome		
	Lack of Ability	Lack of Effort	
	(Unintentional)	(Intentional)	
Stable	4.27 (26)	3.48 (25)	3.88
Unstable	3.50 (24)	2.75 (24)	3.13
	3.90	3.12	

Note: Numbers in parentheses represent the N per cell.

Deciding which journal to submit a paper to is not always an easy task. You want your paper to appear in a journal with wide circulation. You will also want it to appear in a journal that is read by specialists in the area that the paper concerns. Other considerations include prestige of the journal and likelihood of acceptance. As you might expect, these last two considerations generally involve a trade-off. Two guidelines are helpful: First, choose a journal that has published other articles on the same topic. Second, choose the journal that you have cited most frequently in your reference list.

Before you submit your manuscript, consult a recent issue of the journal for the editor's address and double-check the requirements for submission. Prepare a cover letter addressed to the editor, giving the title of your paper and some details about it, such as the number of tables and/or figures. Tell the editor whether it has been presented at a meeting. Give your return address and your telephone number.

When the editor receives the manuscript, he or she reads it for an initial screening and sends it out for review, usually to two other persons in the field. After the reviews are received, the editor decides either to accept the paper as is (rarely), to accept it pending certain revisions, to reject it with the suggestion that it be resubmitted with certain revisions, or to reject it outright. The editor's letter gives an overall evaluation of the paper, interprets the reviewers' comments, and suggests how you should proceed. If you are going to revise the paper, you should study the comments of each reviewer. You need not accept each suggestion, but you must give a good reason if you do not. If a reviewer is completely off base, you may say so, carefully. In extreme cases an editor will get additional reviews if you can show that the reviewer did not do a competent job.

After you have revised the paper, print out a new copy of it. Resubmit it with a new cover letter that tells how you have accounted for the reviewers' comments. At this point the editor usually makes a final decision to accept or reject. Next you wait a considerable time, up to a year, while the article is scheduled into one of the journal's upcoming issues. This time period is sometimes referred to as "in press." The exact sequence of events varies from journal to journal, but the following is typical. You receive the copyedited version of your manuscript, with editorial changes in grammar, spelling, and style, but not in substantive matters. Any corrections you wish to incorporate should be made at this point. After the copyedited manuscript is returned to the editor and set in type, you receive page proofs, which show how your paper will actually look in the journal, along with your original manuscript. Read the page proofs carefully for typographical errors and compare them to your manuscript. Also check the beginning and end of each page to see that nothing is out of order or lost. Shortly after you return the page proofs, your paper appears in the journal. The whole process may take about a year. The editor usually requires about three months for the initial review process; after final acceptance, the publication delay may be another nine months. Many journals print a note indicating when a paper was accepted for publication. You may consult recent issues to estimate when your article will appear.

ORAL PRESENTATIONS

The oral presentation is an important means of scientific communication. Numerous regional, national, and international meetings are held each year in which the primary formal means of communication is the oral presentation of short research papers. For the student, presenting a paper toward the end of a course in experimental psychology is an excellent learning experience. Many regional student psychology conferences are also held, at which papers are given.

Although the parts of an oral presentation are the same as for a research report, simply reading the manuscript of a paper prepared for publication is a mistake. The oral format requires several changes. First, the paper must be shorter, because in the 10 or 15 minutes that are usually allotted, presenting all the material in a typical paper is physically impossible. Second, it is necessary to simplify the material in order for the audience to digest the ideas as they are presented. Third, written material tends to be boring to listen to. If you choose to write out your talk in order to feel prepared, focus on how it will sound when spoken. Then leave the written version at home or in your pocket and speak from an outline.

Organize your talk according to the main parts of a paper: introduction, method, results, and discussion. Make only one or two points in each section of the talk. Your introduction should set the stage in a few sentences. The method section should stick to the essential elements of design, assuming that your audience is generally familiar with how such research is done. Most of your time should be spent on the results. Be sure to emphasize the main findings. Keep the discussion section brief also, simply pointing out some of the implications of the research. Always summarize your results at the end.

Visual aids are a key element of any oral presentation. Ordinarily, visual aids are slides or overhead transparencies. In practice, it is surprising how often visual aids are the weakest part of a presentation. When you use slides, preview them to make sure they will be legible under the conditions that are typical of a convention. Also, see that they are not placed upside down in the projector. Complicated tables are not useful as slides because they are difficult to read, nor is typed material legible in slide format. If your talk is to a small group, you may choose to distribute a handout that describes the results.

Practice the talk in front of sympathetic peers. This technique helps you to know if you are on the right track, and it allows you to modify rough spots. An additional benefit is having most of the potential questions asked first by your friends instead of by strangers who may be less forgiving.

POSTER PRESENTATIONS

Posters have become a popular way of presenting research at meetings. The advantages are that people can browse among many posters, spending time on the ones that interest them, and can discuss the material in as much depth as desired with the author of the poster. Poster sessions are also ideally suited to class projects.

At meetings a vertical surface of 3 by 6 feet or 4 by 8 feet will be available for the presentation. You bring the parts of the poster and assemble it on the board with tacks. (See Figure 13.1.) Place a strip of paper across the top of the board with the title and the author's name in letters at least an inch high. Position the abstract of the paper in the upper left corner on a single sheet of paper. Place the rest of the material in columns so that people can read from top to bottom of one column, then move from left to right, without having to move back and forth. Type everything on a special large-type typewriter, or letter the material neatly by hand. Make all tables and figures about 8 by 10 inches. Keep in mind that your poster should be readable from a distance of several feet. Place copies of the paper or of the abstract in a pocket on the board so that interested persons can take one with them.

During the poster session, stand near the poster to answer questions and discuss the material with people who stop by. Many persons who have presented posters at meetings find they prefer the personal give-and-take of the poster format to the usual oral presentation.

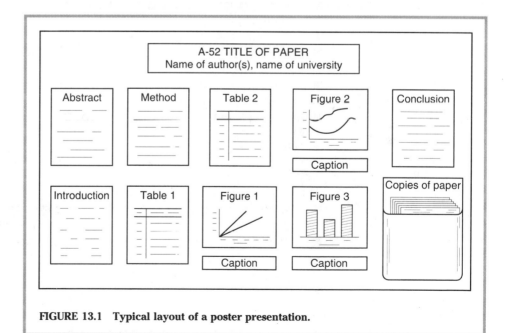

FIGURE 13.1 Typical layout of a poster presentation.

✳ NUTS & BOLTS ✳

Checklist for Evaluating Research Reports

This list was adapted from an article by Brendan Maher (1978).

ABSTRACT

- Does the abstract contain information from each major section of the paper: introduction, method, results, discussion?

INTRODUCTION

- Is there a review of the literature?
- What theory underlies this research?
- Is there a clear statement of purpose and/or hypothesis?

METHOD

- Is the method described with sufficient detail and clarity that a knowledgeable psychologist could replicate it based on the paper alone? Is the design clearly laid out?
- How were subjects obtained (randomly from what population, selected from what preexisting groups, volunteered from what group)?
- What biases might exist in selection (volunteering, atypical populations, and the like)?
- Were proper institutional and APA guidelines followed in obtaining subjects?
- Were subjects debriefed?
- What controls or control groups were used to control for which alternative hypotheses?
- If subjects experienced more than one condition, was order counterbalanced or randomized?
- Were the subjects run blind or double-blind?
- Were the dependent measures reliable and valid?
- Were there biases such as social desirability or role demands?

RESULTS

- Is there a clear description of the data?
- What statistical analysis was done; what were the significance levels of the various effects; were there any significant interactions?
- Of the effects that were statistically significant, which ones were large enough to be important or clinically significant?
- Are the figures and tables necessary (not redundant with the text)?
- Are the figures and tables easy to read, and are the captions clear?

DISCUSSION

- Does the discussion relate the findings back to the theoretical considerations raised in the introduction?

■ Have limitations in the data and their implications for the conclusions been considered?
■ Does the author try to explain away difficulties by ad hoc explanation?
■ Does the author avoid unfounded speculation?

REFERENCES

◢ Is each item in the reference list cited in the text, and vice versa?*

Reporting Statistics in the Text of a Paper

In writing your results, you should be careful to focus on describing the data, not the statistics. Nevertheless, you need to report certain information about the statistical tests you performed, particularly the significance level of effects you found. State that the effect of Variable X was significant, followed by the abbreviated name of the statistic, the number of degrees of freedom in parenthesis, the value of the statistic, and the probability—for example, $F(1, 14) = 4.2$, $p < .05$. Following is an example for the data in Box 9.2 on pages 240-241:

The short hallway had the greatest proportion of social behavior, 58.0%; the long, interrupted hallway had the next most, 56.8%; and the long hallway had the least, 43.7%. Analysis of variance showed that the effect of hallway was significant: $F(2, 27) = 7.97$, $p < .01$.

Other examples are given in the sample paper reproduced in this chapter. ❏

SUMMARY

1. Scientific communication takes place in many ways, including archival publication in scholarly journals and informal communication among groups of scientists known as invisible colleges.

2. Scientific writing can be considered one form of argumentation, which is the presentation of a set of reasons in support of a thesis, or proposition.

3. Most psychology journals follow the *Publication Manual of the American Psychological Association,* which should be consulted for detailed matters of style.

4. A scientific report requires the same attention to good writing as does any other form of written persuasion. Key concepts are clarity, brevity, and felicity.

5. Authors should be careful to avoid sexism and ethnic bias.

---

*Adapted from "A Reader's, Writer's, and Reviewer's Guide to Assessing Research Reports in Clinical Psychology," by B. A. Maher, 1978, *Journal of Consulting and Clinical Psychology, 46,* 835–838. Copyright 1978 by the American Psychological Association. Reprinted by permission.

6. Documentation is used in a paper to give credit to the work of other authors, to show the larger framework in which your ideas belong, and to point the reader to sources of further information.

7. References are cited in the text by author name and date of publication.

8. The reference list contains an entry for each work cited in the text, and no others.

9. The parts of a paper are (1) title, (2) authors and their affiliations, (3) abstract, (4) introduction, (5) method, (6) results, (7) discussion, (8) references, (9) footnotes, (10) tables, (11) figure captions, and (12) figures.

10. The title should convey the main idea of the paper in a few words.

11. The authors of your paper are listed in the order of the importance of their contributions.

12. The abstract is a brief summary of the paper and includes elements from the introduction, method, results, and discussion sections.

13. The introduction states the general problem the paper deals with, discusses the relevant literature, and states what the paper will contribute to the understanding of the problem.

14. The method section tells what you did in the experiment in such a way that another person can evaluate the validity of the conclusions of the study and can repeat it in all essentials. The method section describes the subjects, apparatus, design, and procedure.

15. The results section describes the results and their statistical analysis. Graphs and tables are described here.

16. The discussion section interprets the results and relates them to the literature. It states the contributions that the study makes to the understanding of the problem posed in the introduction, and it deals with any weakness in the data or any qualifications of the conclusions.

17. The steps in the publication process include choosing the journal, submitting the final manuscript along with a cover letter, revising the paper to account for reviewers' comments, resubmitting the paper, reviewing the copyedited manuscript, and reading the page proofs.

18. Oral presentations include most of the elements of the written paper in a simplified format. Practicing the talk before a sympathetic audience, preparing good visual aids, and speaking the paper rather than reading it are keys to a good presentation.

19. Poster presentations are an increasingly popular form of communication of results at scientific meetings. The various parts of the paper are placed on a vertical surface in such a way that they can be read from a distance of several feet. The author remains near the poster to discuss the results with passersby.

Suggestions for Further Reading

American Psychological Association (1983). *Publication manual of the American Psychological Association* (3rd ed.). Washington, DC: Author. This publication is an indispensable style guide for anyone writing in the field of psychology.

Barrass, R. (1978). *Scientists must write: A guide to better writing for scientists, engineers, and students.* London: Chapman and Hall/New York: Wiley. This book covers all aspects of scientific writing.

Rosnow, R. L., & Rosnow, M. (1992). *Writing papers in psychology* (2nd ed.). Belmont, CA: Wadsworth. Concise coverage of all aspects of writing in psychology.

Sternberg, R. (1988). *The psychologist's companion: A guide to scientific writing for students and researchers* (2nd ed.). New York: Cambridge University Press. Specifically covers psychology papers and APA style.

Strunk, W., Jr., & White, E. B. (1979). *The elements of style* (3rd ed.). New York: Macmillan. This short book, a classic in its field, concisely covers the essentials of good writing.

ⅠⅠⅠ➡ A CASE IN POINT ⬅ⅠⅠⅠ

On the following pages is a manuscript of an entirely fictitious paper. It contains many errors of style, grammar, and spelling, as well as some problems of design. Correct the paper, noting the design problems.

Behavior Modification: An Alternative to Drug
Therapy in Treating Hyperactive Children

ABSTRACT

The purpose of this study is to determine whether
application of behavior modification methods can be an
effective and safe alternative to amphetamine therapy
in the treatment of hyperactive school children. Sixty
elementary age school children who were identified as
hyperactive were randomly assigned to one of three
treatment groups. It was concluded that additional
research is needed to determine the generalizability of
the findings to larger groups and to non-special
education classes.

In recent years, the use of amphetamines in
treating hperactive children, has caused much
controversy and concern. According to some
researchers, an estimated 400,000 hyperactive school
children are presently being treated with these drugs.
Much of the public's concern has to do with the way in
which children are diagnosed. Many children, for
example, are being treated with amphetamines solely on
the recommendations of school authoritys. Despite the
fact that many teachers mistake the normal restlessness
of childhood for hyperkinesis. Anotehr cause for
concern stems from a lack of follow-up studies on the
long-term affects of amphetamines.

As an alternative to drug therapy, researchers
have begun to focus on behavior modification techniques
that are believed to be more safer and more effective
over time (Strong, 1974). Strong (1974) conducted a
two-year study with an autistic boy and found thast
positive reinforcement was significently more effective

than durg therapy in reducing facial grimacing. In
another study, this same researcher found token
reinforcement to be more effective then medication in
increasing adaptive behavior in retarded women.

Behavior modification techniques have also been
studied in classroom settings. Smith (1969), for
example, was able to reduce ina pprorpatie classroom
behavior of a ten-year old hyperactive girl by using
these techniques. In another study, Nixon (1969)
tested the effects of behavior modification in
increasing the "on-task performance" of 24 boys who had
been diagnosed as hyperactive by there teachers. In
the Nixon (1969) study, their was four treatment groups
which consisted of various reinforcement techniques and
control. Results of a one-way analysis of variance
indicated no significant differences between the
groups. Although it was reported that some of the
children in each gorup made great improvement in
staying on task in learning situations. The Nixon
study, however, contained possible sources of error:
(1) treatment groups only contained 6 subjects each;
(2) there were only 8 treatment sessions; (3) no
instruments were used to evaluate children's
performance; and (4) the children knew they were
participating in a study.

Widespread use of amphetamines in treating
hyperactive children may be a dangerous practice.
Moreover, behavior modification techniques have shown
to be just as effective in reducing hperactive behavior
in children in certain settings.

The sample group for this study will be selected
from the population of North Side Educational Center

for behaviorally disturbed, elementary-age children. Those children who were diagnosed as "hyperactive" or "hyperkinetic" by the school's psychologist were cosnidered the population. The stratified random sampling method is to be used to insure that children ages 6 through 12 were represented in the study.

METHOD

Subjects will be asisgned to three treatment groups. Each group will be pre-tested using the Swan Maze Test as the pre-test instrument and the Winsand Child Observation System as teh post-test instrument. AFter they were classified by age, subjects will be randomly asisgned to one of three treatment groups. During the semester, group 1 received amphatamine therapy, group 2 received behavior modification techniques, and group 3 received regular classroom instruction, thus serving as a control group. Each of the treatments took place in the regular classroom setting. The pre-test means revealed that the three groups were essentially equal at the beginning of the study (see figure 1). As figure 1 shows, levels of hyperactivity were extremely high in all three groups. At the end of the six month treatment period, all subjects were administered the Swan Maze Test. A one-way analysis of variance was used, to compare the post-test means of the three groups.

Results

It was found that the groups differed significantly ($F = 66.15$, $df = 2/57$, $p < .05$). At t-test comparison of the group means revealed that while the behavior modification and amphetamine therapy groups did not differ significantly, both treatment groups did differ significantly from the control group (See Figure 1). The control group maintained essentially the same level of hyperactivity during the treatment period (16.0 versus 15.7).

Insert Figure 1 about here

Discussion

The level of hyperactivity was reduced in both experimental groups from 15.8 to 5.9 and from 15.4 to 5.5 (See Table 1). Based on these results, it was concluded that behavior modification techniques and amphetamines treatment was equally effective in reducing hyperactivity in elementary-aged children.

Since this study utilized classroom groups of size 15, and teachers who had prior experience in handling behaviorally disturbed children, results cnanot be generalized to regular classroom situations. However, in vies of the results, it appears that research investigating the feasibility of using behavior modification techniques with larger groups of hyperactive children, and with regular elementary teachers, is warranted. If regular teaachers could be trained to recognize and modify some of the behavioral symptoms of hyperactivity, prhaps the widespread use of amphetamine drugs with these children could be minimized.

REferences

Smith, Judy L. (1972). The use of ritalin for treatment of minimal brain dysfunction and hyperkinesis in children, Baltimore: Simpson Publishers.

Ladd, E.G. (1971). "Pills for classroom peace?" Education Digest, 36, 1-4.

Nixon, S. B. (1965). Increasing the frequency of

attending responses in hyperactive distractable

youngsters by use of operant and modeling

procedures, Dissertation Abstracts, 26, 6517.

Woody, R. (1969). Behavior Problem Children in the

Schools. New YOrk: Appleton-Century-Crofts.

Figure 1. Means and standard Deviations for the

Behavior Modification, Amphetamine Therapy, and Control

groups on the Pre- and post-test measures.

	Amphetamine Therapy*	Behavior Modification*	Control*
Pre-Test			
Mean	15.4	15.8	16.0
SD	3.2	2.8	2.6
Post-Test			
Mean	5.5	5.9	16.9
	1.6	1.3	2.5

*n = 15

≡ READING BETWEEN THE LINES ≡

13.1 THE AUTHORITARIAN PERSONALITY

After World War II a group of researchers (Adorno, Frenkel-Brunswik, Levinson, & Sanford, 1950) were concerned to find the causes of anti-Semitism and German compliance with Hitler's policies. The researchers hypothesized that a personality type existed that lent itself to authoritarianism, antidemocratic beliefs, and racism. Using specially developed questionnaires, they gave tests of "authoritarianism" to a large sample of people. Those receiving especially high or low scores were interviewed about their childhood experiences. Persons with high scores more often were found to come from families with high status concern and repressive discipline procedures. According to the authors, children in these families learned to repress their faults and to project them onto minority groups. They also repressed feelings of anger and of hatred toward their parents, and these feelings also were projected onto the minority groups. Therefore, the authoritarian persons had a tendency to be prejudiced against Jews, blacks, and so forth and to show discrimination toward them.

Can you think of another explanation of the causes of the correlation between authoritarian attitudes and childhood experiences?   ∎

13.2 LIFE EVENTS AND ILLNESS
A large amount of research exists indicating that life events can cause illness. The life events may be of the kind that are obviously stressful, such as the death of a family member, or they may be desirable events, such as marriage, birth of a baby, or a new job. Many illnesses have been studied, including depression and schizophrenia. The studies ask people who have suffered the illness to list the life events they have experienced in a period before the illness. The control group of people who have not experienced the illness are asked the same questions. The results show that persons who suffered the illness had experienced more stressful life events than had the control persons. What problems of interpretation can you think of in such retrospective research?   ∎

☑ EXERCISES

13.1 REPORTING REFERENCES
Put the following information into APA-style references:
   a. Herkimer Alphonse Smith wrote a book entitled "The Psychology of Passing Exams." It was published by the Fullcourt Press, 3500 Forbes Avenue, Pittsburgh, PA 15213 on the 10th of July, 1993.
   b. Jones, A. P., and Riddle, R. A. "Knowns and Unknowns of Family Therapy" (1992). In Handbook of Group and Family Therapy, edited by A. D. Thurman and B. D. Munson (pp. 719-740). Grover Press: Boston.
   c. McBurney, Donald H. "Research Methods." (3rd ed.) Pacific Grove, California: Brooks/Cole Publishing Company, 1994.
   d. In his article, Science or Pseudoscience, John Neal provides a brief history of the role that introspection has played in science (1963). It is found on pages 25-42 of the New Age Journal of Psychology, volume 2.

13.2 REPORTING STATISTICS IN THE RESULTS SECTION
Describe the statistics from Box 10.1 on pages 266-267 as you would in the results section of a paper.

13.3 TABULAR VERSUS TEXTUAL PRESENTATION OF DATA
Read the following excerpt:

The mean reaction times reported for the 4 subjects were 5.7, 5.9, 4.9, and 5.3, respectively, for the low-resolution screen; 4.7, 4.6, 5.0, and 4.9, respectively, for the medium-resolution screen; 3.8, 3.6, 3.5, and 3.0, respectively, for the high-resolution screen; and 2.2, 2.4, 2.3, and 2.1 respectively, for the super-resolution screen.

REQUIRED:
   a. Present these data in a table.
   b. Give the table a brief but explanatory title.

OPTIONAL:
   c. In a sentence or two, describe the data in the table.

13.4 CLARIFY RESEARCH TITLES
Rewrite the following research titles to make them brief yet descriptive:
   a. "A Preliminary Investigation into the Effectiveness of the Key Image Method of Vocabulary Development in First-, Second-, and Third-Grade Primary School Children."
   b. "A Study Investigating the Relationship between Anxiety and Low Reading Achievement Scores."

13.5 IDENTIFY THE PARTS OF A RESEARCH REPORT
Prepare an outline of the major parts of a research report.

13.6 EVALUATE A RESEARCH REPORT
Use the checklist on pages 360-361 to evaluate a published report. (Suggestion: Choose a journal, such as *Personality and Social Psychology Bulletin* or *Psychological Science,* that publishes brief reports.)   ❏

14

Ethics in Research

The concern for ethics in psychological research may be seen as part of the historical trend in civil and human rights. Before World War II, research ethics were considered a matter for the individual researcher to worry about. However, the Nuremberg trials of Nazi war criminals led to a consciousness of the need for ethical controls in scientific research. In addition, the growth of all types of research, fueled by increasing government funding, prompted concern with research ethics. As a result, research ethics are in a state of rapid evolution. Some practices that were considered acceptable and routine 10 years ago are considered unethical today. For this reason we must present our discussion of research ethics as tentative, rather than chiseled in stone. What will be acceptable practice 10 or 20 years from now cannot be predicted.

THE APA ETHICS CODE

The American Psychological Association has developed an extensive document known as the "Ethical Principles of Psychologists and Code of Conduct" (1992). These principles cover all professional activities that psychologists engage in. A number of them, such as those on sexual harassment, nondiscrimination, and the like, concern all professional activities, not just research. Discussion of all of the statements that could bear on research would take us too far afield. We will quote those sections that are most directly relevant to ethical concerns in the conduct of research.

The APA ethics code represents the consensus of the psychology profession as to what is considered acceptable practice. The federal government, and certain other jurisdictions, however, have passed laws governing the conduct of research. In addition, the federal government requires institutions that receive federal funds to establish an institutional review board (IRB) to approve virtually all research on human subjects. As a student, you should consult your instructor, department chairperson, or school's IRB before you initiate *any* research in order to familiarize yourself with the applicable regulations on research. Depending on your institution's procedures, it may be necessary to obtain approval before doing class projects, directed research with a faculty member, or a project that you might initiate on your own.

1.04 Boundaries of Competence

(a) Psychologists provide services, teach, and conduct research only within the boundaries of their competence, based on their education, training, supervised experience, or appropriate professional experience.

(b) Psychologists provide services, teach, or conduct research in new areas or involving new techniques only after first undertaking appropriate study, training, supervision, and/or consultation from persons who are competent in those areas or techniques.

(c) In those emerging areas in which generally recognized standards for preparatory training do not yet exist, psychologists nevertheless take reasonable steps to ensure the competence of their work and to protect patients, clients, students, research participants, and others from harm.

1.05 Maintaining Expertise

Psychologists who engage in assessment, therapy, teaching, research, organizational consulting, or other professional activities maintain a reasonable level of awareness of current scientific and professional information in their fields of activity, and undertake ongoing efforts to maintain competence in the skills they use.

6.06 Planning Research

(a) Psychologists design, conduct, and report research in accordance with recognized standards of scientific competence and ethical research.

(b) Psychologists plan their research so as to minimize the possibility that results will be misleading.

(c) In planning research, psychologists consider its ethical acceptability under the Ethics Code. If an ethical issue is unclear, psychologists seek to resolve the issue through consultation with institutional review boards, animal care and use committees, peer consultations or other proper mechanisms.

(d) Psychologists take reasonable steps to implement appropriate protections for the rights and welfare of human participants, other persons affected by the research, and the welfare of animal subjects.

6.07 Responsibility

(a) Psychologists conduct research competently and with due concern for the dignity and welfare of the participants.

(b) Psychologists are responsible for the ethical conduct of research conducted by them or by others under their supervision or control.

(c) Researchers and assistants are permitted to perform only those tasks for which they are appropriately trained and prepared.

(d) As part of the process of development and implementation of research projects, psychologists consult those with expertise concerning any special population under investigation or most likely to be affected. (APA, 1992, pp. 1600–1608)[1]

■ Commentary on Responsibility

The decision to conduct research often presents a conflict between two sets of values. In general, the conflict is between (1) the commitment of the psychologist to expanding our knowledge of behavior and the potential benefit the research may have for society and (2) the cost of the research to the participants. It is not possible to resolve this conflict in terms of moral absolutes or by a set of prescriptions that will cover all cases. The conflict is faced continually by researchers, who must consider themselves responsible for deciding to conduct their research. Researchers who do not review ethical problems carefully are negligent toward society. From another viewpoint, a researcher who refrains from doing an important study because of an excessively tender conscience is also failing to keep a commitment to the same society that supports behavioral research with the hope that it will provide important social benefits.

The investigator—the person who is in overall charge of the research—has the greatest responsibility to see that ethical principles are followed. In most cases, students work in the capacity of experimenters or assistants under the supervision of the investigator. All persons working on a research project, however, should consider themselves bound by the APA ethics code, even if they are not professional psychologists or members of APA.

Investigators should discuss their research with colleagues and seek advice on the ethics of the research procedures. This helps to curb the bias we all have of thinking that our research is more important than it really is and that we are morally superior and therefore will act ethically. Most institutions have committees that review all research on human subjects. Before investigators begin any research, they should be certain that they are complying with institutional procedures. Students should initiate research

---

[1] These and all subsequent sections of the ethics code are excerpted from American Psychological Association, "Ethical Principles of Psychologists and Code of Conduct," 1992, *American Psychologist, 47,* 1597–1611. Copyright 1992 by the American Psychological Association. Reprinted by permission of the publisher.

only under the sponsorship of a faculty member, who is in turn subject to professional sanctions.

■ Commentary on Protection from Harm

Clearly it is impossible to avoid risk of harm entirely in behavioral research, because any new situation by definition is stressful and conceivably could be harmful. Some experiments, though, have subjected people to the threat of shock, to being told that they have latent homosexual tendencies, or to being locked in a room that appears to be on fire. Today these situations are considered unduly stressful. Stress in an experiment may be either physical or psychological. In judging the acceptability of stress, the researcher must assess how stressful the situation is likely to be compared with activities of everyday life. Would people willingly put themselves into this situation? What special groups must be considered, such as heart patients, epileptics, or borderline schizophrenics?

6.08 Compliance with Law and Standards

Psychologists plan and conduct research in a manner consistent with federal and state law and regulations, as well as professional standards governing the conduct of research, and particularly those standards governing research with human participants and animal subjects.

6.09 Institutional Approval

Psychologists obtain from host institutions or organizations appropriate approval prior to conducting research, and they provide accurate information about their research proposals. They conduct the research in accordance with the approved research protocol.

6.10 Research Responsibilities

Prior to conducting research (except research involving only anonymous surveys, naturalistic observations, or similar research), psychologists enter into an agreement with participants that clarifies that nature of the research and the responsibilities of each party.

6.11 Informed Consent to Research

(a) Psychologists use language that is reasonably understandable to research participants in obtaining their appropriate informed consent (except as provided in Standard 6.12, Dispensing With Informed Consent). Such informed consent is appropriately documented.

(b) Using language that is reasonably understandable to participants, psychologists inform participants of the nature of the research; they inform participants that they are free to participate or to decline to participate or to withdraw from the research; they explain the foreseeable consequences of declining or withdrawing; they inform participants of significant factors that may be expected to influence their willingness to participate (such as risks, discomfort, adverse effects, or limitations on confidentiality, except as provided in Standard 6.15, Deception in

Research); and they explain other aspects about which the prospective participants inquire.

(c) When psychologists conduct research with individuals such as students or subordinates, psychologists take special care to protect the prospective participants from adverse consequences of declining or withdrawing from participation.

(d) When research participation is a course requirement or opportunity for extra credit, the prospective participant is given the choice of equitable alternative activities.

(e) For persons who are legally incapable of giving informed consent, psychologists nevertheless (1) provide an appropriate explanation, (2) obtain the participant's assent, and (3) obtain appropriate permission from a legally authorized person, if such substitute consent is permitted by law.

6.12 Dispensing with Informed Consent

Before determining that planned research (such as research involving only anonymous questionnaires, naturalistic observations, or certain kinds of archival research) does not require the informed consent of research participants, psychologists consider applicable regulations and institutional review board requirements, and they consult with colleagues as appropriate.

6.13 Informed Consent in Research Filming or Recording

Psychologists obtain informed consent from research participants prior to filming or recording them in any form, unless the research involves simply naturalistic observations in public places and it is not anticipated that the recording will be used in a manner that could cause personal identification or harm. (p. 1608)

◾ Commentary on Informed Consent

The APA guidelines require researchers to "enter into an agreement with participants that clarifies the nature of the research and the responsibilities of each party" (6.10). This is to ensure that the participant is taking part voluntarily and is aware of what is about to happen. This agreement should be documented in writing. Depending on the nature of the procedures that are to be followed, it may be advisable to have the subjects sign a form that describes the procedures that will be followed and the potential risks involved. In most psychological research, however, the written protocol of the study constitutes sufficient documentation. Whether or not a signed form is required should be determined by consulting your department or institutional procedures.

Medical researchers have developed a concept of informed consent, according to which patients have the right to know exactly what is being done to them and for what reasons. The APA ethics code differs from this medical view of informed consent by saying that participants need only be informed of aspects of the research that might be expected to influence their decision to participate. The assumption of the APA ethics code is that subjects in psychological experiments ordinarily do not care what the hypothesis or purpose of the experiment is. For example, most subjects would want to know if their intelligence or mental health were being evaluated before they agreed to participate. On the other hand, the fact that an experiment concerns whether memory is scanned by serial or parallel processes would probably not influence their decision to participate.

6.14 Offering Inducements for Research Participants

(a) In offering professional services as an inducement to obtain research participants, psychologists make clear the nature of the services, as well as the risks, obligations, and limitations. (See Standard 1.18, Barter [With Patients or Clients].)

(b) Psychologists do not offer excessive or inappropriate financial or other inducements to obtain research participants, particularly when it might tend to coerce participation.

6.15 Deception in Research

(a) Psychologists do not conduct a study involving deception unless they have determined that the use of deceptive techniques is justified by the study's prospective scientific, educational, or applied value and that equally effective alternative procedures that do not use deception are not feasible.

(b) Psychologists never deceive research participants about significant aspects that would affect their willingness to participate, such as physical risks, discomfort, or unpleasant emotional experiences.

(c) Any other deception that is an integral feature of the design and conduct of an experiment must be explained to participants as early as is feasible, preferably at the conclusion of their participation, but no later than at the conclusion of the research. (See also Standard 6.18, Providing Participants With Information About the Study.) (pp. 1608–1609)

■ Commentary on Deception

So many experiments require subjects to be naive about the hypothesis that deceiving subjects about the true purpose of their research participation has almost become standard practice. The APA ethics code requires that a subject who has been deceived be provided with a sufficient explanation of the deception as soon afterward as feasible. Some researchers, however, feel that deception is always objectionable. They note that the prevalence of deception in psychological experiments is common knowledge among college students and that most subjects routinely assume that the story they are given at the beginning of an experiment is false. The effects of this pollution of the subject pool are not known.

Yet to forswear deception would rule out the study of many important questions. In order to handle this problem, some departments inform people at the time they join the subject pool that certain experiments in which they participate may use deception. Other experimenters have used role playing instead of deception to induce behaviors of interest. The subjects are asked to act as if they were in a certain situation or to tell what they would do in such a situation. The disadvantage of role playing is that it assumes that subjects can tell what they would do in a situation by just adopting a role. Evidence for this assumption is quite weak.

The simple term *deception* covers a wide range of actions on the part of experimenters. Relatively innocuous deceptions routinely involve setting up false expectations of the processes under investigation. More serious deceptions include giving subjects false information about their performance on a task. Some research has shown that the initial false feedback may be believed even after debriefing (Ross, Lepper, & Hubbard, 1975). Deception that presents subjects with a negative evaluation of themselves should be avoided.

6.16 Sharing and Utilizing Data

Psychologists inform research participants of their anticipated sharing or further use of personally identifiable research data and of the possibility of unanticipated future uses.

6.17 Minimizing Invasiveness

In conducting research, psychologists interfere with the participants or milieu from which data are collected only in a manner that is warranted by an appropriate research design and that is consistent with psychologists' roles as scientific investigators. (p. 1609)

■ Commentary on Privacy and Freedom from Coercion

The idea of freedom from coercion is part of the larger question of civil rights and the right to privacy in particular. The legal concept of a right to privacy is a development of the last hundred years or so. It is agreed that people have the right not to be disturbed, as well as the right not to reveal certain information about themselves. Although psychologists respect this right to privacy, it must be balanced against the welfare of society as a whole. The solution to many thorny social problems may require information that people are reluctant to reveal. How does one weigh the value to society of understanding and controlling the behavior of criminals and tax evaders against the rights of law-abiding citizens to be left alone? The reluctance of many people, particularly illegal aliens, to respond to the 1990 U.S. census is an indication of this tension. Although the Census Bureau stated that its information would not be made available to other government agencies, the Internal Revenue Service in particular, many people refused to answer the questions.

The experimenter must remember at all times that the subject is doing a favor by participating. The freedom to refuse to participate or to withdraw at any time without penalty should be made clear to the subject at the beginning of the research if it has not already been explained during the recruitment of subjects. The researcher should realize that many subjects are apprehensive about participating in research. The role demands of the situation, however, will cause them to tolerate considerable discomfort without complaint. This tendency on the part of the subjects increases the researcher's obligation not to exploit the subject.

The most likely problem of coercion that you as a reader of this book will face is the decision to use introductory psychology students as "volunteers." In many colleges, introductory psychology students are commonly asked to serve as research subjects as part of the course requirements. The APA guidelines require departments to alleviate the problem of coercion by allowing students extra credit for participation or by providing alternative means of satisfying the requirement. In favor of the research requirement is the educational value of serving in an experiment; unpublished data collected by the University of Pittsburgh Psychology Department indicate that most subjects enjoy their participation and learn something from it. Coercion may be subtle, however, if a student feels that participation may lead to a chance for a better grade. Most students do not seem especially concerned over this degree of coercion. In Pitt's experience, only about 1% of students who are required to participate either in research or in an alternative experience request the alternative. Serving as subjects appears to be as acceptable to them as other course requirements.

Issues of coercion become more serious if substantial sums of money are offered for participation or if subjects are induced to participate with promises to "improve your relations with the opposite sex" or "gain valuable insights into your personality." The APA's Ethical Principles (American Psychological Association, 1982) contains a list of guidelines for departments that wish to set up experimental participation requirements for students.

The concern for the privacy of the subjects continues after the data are collected. People who participate in psychological studies have the right to expect that their data will never be made public in a way that would permit their identification, unless they agree to such publication. Problems have arisen when researchers have written up actual cases in a thinly disguised fashion. In other instances, courts have subpoenaed information from social scientists about their clients or subjects who are involved in cases of alleged criminal activities. This situation is particularly problematic when a scientist has studied members of deviant groups or individuals who engage in illegal activity and has promised them confidentiality. Social scientists do not enjoy the legal protection that lawyers and physicians have against being forced to reveal information about their clients. In one case, a rape counselor was ordered to reveal information that the victim had given as part of the counseling process following the rape.

When data are coded, cases that involve sensitive material should be coded so that all information that would permit identification of the individual is destroyed. This process may not be possible in some types of case-study work because of the continuing nature of the data collection.

6.18 Providing Participants with Information About the Study

(a) Psychologists provide a prompt opportunity for participants to obtain appropriate information about the nature, results, and conclusions of the research, and psychologists attempt to correct any misconceptions that participants may have.

(b) If scientific or humane values justify delaying or withholding this information, psychologists take reasonable measures to reduce the risk of harm. (p. 1609)

■ Commentary on Debriefing

debriefing
the process of informing subjects after the session of the experiment's true purpose in order to increase their understanding and to remove possible harmful effects of deception

As soon as feasible after the individual subjects have completed their part in the experiment, they should be informed about the nature of the study, and have any questions answered and misconceptions removed. This process is known as **debriefing.** Debriefing is an extremely important part of the experiment. Subjects must be told the purpose and expected results of the experiment so that their experience has as much educational and personal value for them as possible.

When deception has been employed, the experimenter has a touchy situation. A blunt admission of deception can make subjects feel foolish, stupid, or abused. Because many investigators additionally use the debriefing to ascertain whether the deception was effective, their explanation requires great subtlety. In the first place, subjects, in an effort not to embarrass the experimenter, may be reluctant to admit that they saw through the deception. This response is part of the good-subject role that they tend to adopt. Second, the degree of awareness of deception varies greatly with the phrasing of the question. A simple "Any questions about the experiment?" may elicit no response, whereas "Was there anything that might lead you to suspect that the experiment was not exactly what it seemed on the surface?" is more likely to yield a statement indicating awareness of the deception. For this reason, any estimate of the effectiveness of the deception is highly uncertain.

Some investigators delay the debriefing so that other potential subjects will not learn the purpose of the study. In this case, the investigator may wish to take subjects' addresses and send them an explanation when the experiment is completed. This delayed debriefing is less effective because subjects may move away or may lose interest in the study over time.

6.19 Honoring Commitments

Psychologists take reasonable measures to honor all commitments they have made to research participants.

6.20 Care and Use of Animals in Research

(a) Psychologists who conduct research involving animals treat them humanely.

(b) Psychologists acquire, care for, use, and dispose of animals in compliance with current federal, state, and local laws and regulations, and with professional standards.

(c) Psychologists trained in research methods and experienced in the care of laboratory animals supervise all procedures involving animals and are responsible for ensuring appropriate consideration of their comfort, health, and humane treatment.

(d) Psychologists ensure that all individuals using animals under their supervision have received instruction in research methods and in the care, maintenance, and handling of the species being used, to the extent appropriate to their role.

(e) Responsibilities and activities of individuals assisting in a research project are consistent with their respective competencies.

(f) Psychologists make reasonable efforts to minimize the discomfort, infection, illness, and pain of animal subjects.

(g) A procedure subjecting animals to pain, stress, or privation is used only when an alternative procedure is unavailable and the goal is justified by its prospective scientific, educational, or applied value.

(h) Surgical procedures are performed under appropriate anesthesia; techniques to avoid infection and minimize pain are followed during and after surgery.

(i) When it is appropriate that the animal's life be terminated, it is done rapidly, with an effort to minimize pain, and in accordance with accepted procedures.[2]

6.21 Reporting of Results

(a) Psychologists do not fabricate data or falsify results in their publications.

(b) If psychologists discover significant errors in their published data, they take reasonable steps to correct such errors in a correction, retraction, erratum, or other appropriate publication means.

6.22 Plagiarism

Psychologists do not present substantial portions or elements of another's work or data as their own, even if the other work or data source is cited occasionally.

6.23 Publication Credit

(a) Psychologists take responsibility and credit, including authorship credit, only for work they have actually performed or to which they have contributed.

(b) Principal authorship and other publication credits accurately reflect the relative scientific or professional contributions of the individuals involved, regardless of their relative status. Mere possession of an institutional position, such as Department Chair, does not justify authorship credit. Minor contributions to the research or to the writing for publications are appropriately acknowledged, such as in footnotes or in an introductory statement.

---

[2] This section is essentially a condensed version of the APA guidelines for ethical conduct in the care and use of animals (American Psychological Association, 1985). They should be studied by any researcher using animals.

(c) A student is usually listed as principal author on any multiple-authored article that is substantially based on the student's dissertation or thesis.

6.24 Duplicate Publication of Data

Psychologists do not publish, as original data, data that have been previously published. This does not preclude republishing data when they are accompanied by proper acknowledgment.

6.25 Sharing Data

After research results are published, psychologists do not withhold the data on which their conclusions are based from other competent professionals who seek to verify the substantive claims through reanalysis and who intend to use such data only for that purpose, provided that the confidentiality of the participants can be protected and unless legal rights concerning proprietary data preclude their release.

6.26 Professional Reviewers

Psychologists who review material submitted for publication, grant, or other research proposal review respect the confidentiality of and the proprietary rights in such information of those who submitted it. (pp. 1609–1610)

■ Role of the Research Participant

The debate on research ethics has raised questions about the role that the subject plays in psychological research. According to the traditional view, the subject contributes behavior to the experiment in much the same way that a subject in a medical experiment might contribute a urine specimen. The very term *subject* is believed by some to imply that the participant is made an object of study and, necessarily, is dehumanized. This objectification is held to be a consequence of the traditional view of science that requires a separation between the observer/scientist and the observed/subject.

Another view of the research participant is popular with feminist and humanistic psychologists, who hold that the participant is a colleague who cooperates in providing the data. In some examples of this process, the participants take a role in designing the experiment and may have a degree of control over the conditions in which they are tested. Similarly, some psychologists have argued in the Marxist tradition that the participant should be considered part owner of the data by virtue of having helped to create them.

This view reminds us that the research participant may have valuable insights and suggestions that could improve the study. Another advantage of looking at the subject as a cooperator in the research effort is that the researcher becomes more sympathetic with the viewpoint of the participant. In addition, this viewpoint reminds us to treat the subjects with dignity and respect, and to make them know that they are doing the experimenter a favor.

Minority groups in particular have become resentful of being endlessly studied when they perceive that the only apparent result is to promote the careers of the already advantaged scientists.

On the other hand, although this view of research may increase cooperation on the part of the participant, it also increases the risk of sloppy experiments. The humanistic view of research is popular among parapsychologists and has led to many poorly conducted and uninter-pretable experiments. Although certain types of research may profit from the insights and opinions of the participants, the scientist bears the ultimate responsibility for the results and must make the final decisions about the research.

ETHICS OF ANIMAL EXPERIMENTATION

Not very long ago, opposition to animal research came only from fringe groups. Now there is a vigorous animal rights movement that would ban, or severely restrict, the use of animals in research. Although many people find the message of the animal rights movement appealing, it actually has serious implications for human welfare, as well as for the conduct of psychological research.

■ Animal Rights and Animal Welfare

animal rights
the notion that animals have the same sort of rights as people, includ-ing legal rights; not generally accepted

Because the term **animal rights** has become so widely used in connection with the use of animals in research, it is necessary at this point to make a distinction between "animal rights" and "animal welfare." Some authors have recently claimed that animals should have the same sort of rights as people, including legal rights (for example, Regan, 1983). According to this view, it is unethical to use animals for research, food, pets, recreation, work, or any other human-serving purpose. Ethicists, however, generally ascribe rights to members of a community that share moral standards and can be held to moral responsibilities. An individual who has rights has a moral claim on other members of the community to accept certain responsibilities with respect to that individual, who in turn takes on responsibilities. If an individual has the right of free speech, both the individual and other members of the community have the responsibility not to endanger (as by shouting "Fire!" in a crowded theater), defame, or unduly annoy one another (disturbing the peace). Animals do not belong to a moral community: You cannot take a dog to court for barking at night; a cat is not guilty of murder when it kills a bird.

If animals had the same sort of rights as people, we would be involved in murder by eating a hamburger, we would be guilty of slavery by keeping a dog as a pet, and we would be stealing when we collect eggs from a chicken. Although it is not impossible that some society might decide to give animals legal rights, ours does not.

animal welfare
the generally
accepted term for
concerns about
care and use of
animals

The generally accepted term to use in discussing the appropriate use of animals in research is **animal welfare,** or humane treatment of animals. As members of a moral community, *humans* are responsible for the welfare of animals that are under their care. Because mistreatment of animals reflects on the person who does the mistreating, it is called *inhumane* treatment. Although only a minority of those who would limit research on animals hold to the position that animals have the same legal rights as people, the term *animal rights* has become so widely used that it is necessary to make this distinction clear. The research community clearly supports humane treatment of animals, but rejects the notion of animal rights.

Some people raise an objection to this position on animal rights by pointing out that infants and individuals who are severely retarded, senile, or brain damaged are not capable of being held to the same moral standards as normal adult humans, and thus would not have rights according to that argument. First, it should be noted that not all humans have the same rights. Infants may not be elected president of the United States, and prisoners cannot vote. But, more important, we do make ethical distinctions on the basis of a larger class to which an individual belongs. No person under 35 years of age may be elected president, no matter how mature, and no nonhuman animal has legal rights, no matter how intelligent.

■ Speciesism?

speciesism
term used by
analogy with
racism and sexism
by those who
claim that it is
unethical to treat
animals differently
from humans,
particularly in
research

Another claim that needs to be discussed is that use of animals in research is a manifestation of **speciesism,** a term that was chosen to parallel racism and sexism. The claim is that researchers, as well as those who eat meat, wear animal products, and so forth, are guilty of discriminating against animals simply on the basis of their species membership. Although the concept has a certain plausibility, especially with those who eschew racism and sexism, it leads to a logical and ethical thicket. We can agree that it is wrong to discriminate against women or minorities on the basis of their gender or race because all humans share their essential humanity with us. But nonhuman animals are manifestly not like ourselves in certain important characteristics. To our knowledge, no monkey can contemplate its own mortality, and no cat has ever expressed moral ambivalence over killing a mouse.

Further, practical considerations require everyone to draw the line somewhere in the application of the doctrine of speciesism. Higher animals are like us in some respects, especially primates, dogs, and cats. But it is hard to consider a lobster just like us. For example, if we believe that doing research on a chimpanzee constitutes speciesism, what about ridding a house of termites, or inadvertently stepping on an ant while walking in the yard?

Finally, the concept of speciesism explicitly invokes the common evolutionary ancestry of all animals, including humans, and rejects any special moral status for humans. If that is taken seriously, then either a cat is guilty of speciesism when it kills a bird, or neither the cat nor the human is guilty whenever each does what it has evolved to do. There is no reason based on logic whereby the concept of speciesism can be used to support the inclusion of animals in our moral system instead of permitting humans to act like other animals (Stafford, 1991).

Although animal rights activists devote most of their concern and activities to the use of animals in research, it should be noted that research and teaching are responsible for less than 1% of animals killed annually by humans. And over 90% of those used in research are rats and mice (Miller, 1984). By contrast, more than 96% of animals killed by humans are used for food (Nicholl & Russell, 1990).

The animal rights activists also try to convey the idea that most animals used in research suffer pain. The fact is that about 94% of animal research involves no use of pain. Most of us have seen the gruesome pictures of research animals being operated on. What the pictures do not convey is that the animals have been anesthetized, and so are feeling no pain. The small number of animals that do experience pain in research are contributing to knowledge of human diseases such as arthritis that cause pain to millions of humans every day. The opposition to the use of animals in research cannot be justified by the amount of suffering that is being experienced by animals. The regulations on housing of research animals are more stringent than those for human habitation; and there is far more pain, abuse, and cruelty caused to animals by pet owners and farmers than by researchers (Miller, 1984).

There are compelling reasons to use animals in research. First, it should be noted that much animal research has led to an improvement in the welfare of animals themselves, from vaccines against feline leukemia, rabies, and distemper to nonlethal methods of pest control.

Second, although younger people find it difficult to appreciate the fact, there has been tremendous improvement in health care in the past century, much of it in the past few years. About 100 years ago, about 25% of the U.S. population died by age 25, and half were dead by 50. Today, only 3% fail to live to 25, and only 10% die by age 50 (Committee on the Use of Animals in Research, 1991). Research on animals has been essential to this progress. Some have suggested that we should substitute computer models, tissue cultures, bacteria, or even humans for animals in research and teaching. The simple fact is, however, that computers depend on the information and programs put into them. We often don't know enough about a process to be able to model it on the computer. Bacteria cannot be used to test systems that are found only in animals. Behavioral research in particular must be done on whole animals. And to test procedures on humans before testing them on animals would place many volunteers at grave risk. There simply is no substitute for live, intact animals in much research.

To eliminate or restrict use of animals in research would mean little or no progress against AIDS, Alzheimer's, cancer, arthritis, birth defects, traumatic injury, mental illness, and many other diseases and conditions that cause pain and suffering to millions of people each year. Whenever you see a picture of a lab animal that appears to be suffering, think of the millions of people who would continue to suffer dreadfully if there is no more medical progress.

Neal Miller (1985) has demonstrated how important behavioral research has been in this medical progress. To mention only two applications, behavioral techniques have made it possible to cure infants who suffer from a life-threatening condition that prevents them from keeping food down and to cure anorexia nervosa, another life-threatening eating disorder. Restricting the use of animals in research would bring this progress to a crawl.

Those who object that we should not use animals for research should consider that animals have been, and still are, used for work, for food, and as pets. None of these animals volunteers for these services. It may be useful to consider the research animals as draftees in a cause that helps society as a whole, much as men have historically been drafted for military service.

Finally, although the viewpoint presented here is the view of the great majority of scientists, we must acknowledge that ethics in general, and the ethics of animal experimentation in particular, is a difficult issue. There are many who are bothered by the use of animals in research, but do not want to restrict it altogether. The general position of researchers, like that of most people, is that it is permissible to cause a certain amount of suffering to a few animals to reduce the suffering of many millions of people. However, researchers have developed alternatives to the use of animals where possible and have been more careful in the use of their animals as a result of the increasing concern about animal welfare in our society.

■ The Case of the Silver Spring Monkeys

Perhaps no example of animal research has been more notorious among the proponents of animal rights than the work done by Edward Taub on deafferentation of the limbs of monkeys. Deafferentation is a surgical procedure whereby sensory information from parts of the body is prevented from reaching the brain by cutting particular nerves at the point where they enter the spinal cord. Taub was interested in discovering whether and how monkeys would learn to cope with loss of sensory information from their arms. His goal was to find ways of helping stroke victims cope with their losses.

In 1981, Alex Pacheco asked Taub for a job in his laboratory in Silver Spring, Maryland, claiming that he was thinking about a career in science and wanted to get laboratory experience to help him make up his mind. He did not tell Taub that he was president of People for the Ethical Treatment of Animals (PETA), a radical animal rights group whose goal is to end research on animals, or that he had been trained in guerilla-style antivivisection activities and had led demonstrations demanding that all animals in a certain facility be immediately released from their cages.

After working in Taub's lab for five months, during which time he never mentioned any deficiencies in the way the monkeys were being treated, Pacheco took photographs that appear to show cruel or unsanitary conditions. These photos have been widely distributed; it is likely that you have seen them. Later, in court, Pacheco admitted to staging at least some of the photos. Pacheco also brought a group of animal rights activists into the lab late at night to observe the conditions of the animals. These people filed affidavits highly critical of the lab.

Next, Pacheco, with the cooperation of other animal rights activists, induced the local police to raid the laboratory and arranged full media coverage, complete with press releases. What followed was a complicated set of circumstances and legal procedures. In brief, the monkeys were confiscated and given over to the care of PETA. Taub was charged with 119 counts of mistreatment of animals, his grant was withdrawn, and he was out of work for several years.

As a result of PETA's activities, many people have heard of the charges against Taub. What is not widely known is that Taub was eventually cleared of all 119 charges; the granting agency exonerated him in his treatment of the monkeys; and the relevant professional societies, including the American Psychological Association, also cleared him. Further details of Taub's experience can be found in Taub (1991).

The story of Taub's experience to this point would be important enough for what it indicates about the methods of the extreme animal rights activists. Recent events, however, add a most significant postscript to the story. As a result of PETA's activities, the Silver Spring monkeys were kept for many years after the scientists wished them to be sacrificed (Palca, 1991). In 1987, a group of researchers headed by Mortimer Mishkin secured permission to see what had happened to the monkeys' brains as a result of their longtime deafferentation. They found that the connections in the monkeys' brains had been reorganized to a degree far greater than had ever previously been suspected (Pons et al., 1991). These findings have far-reaching implications for treatment of patients with brain injury, including stroke.

In spite of these highly significant results, animal rights activists still vilify Taub and ridicule his research as not only cruel, but pointless. (I heard demonstrators who were attempting to prevent Taub from speaking to a scientific meeting compare him to the Nazi Dr. Mengele, who did sadistic research in the concentration camps.) Finally, Taub has since become employed at a university and has applied the results of his work with the monkeys directly to treatment of human stroke patients (Taub et al., in press). This application would not have been possible without the original work on the monkeys.

✳ NUTS & BOLTS ✳

Recommended Practices in the Use of Animals in Research

Pressure from animal welfare groups and pet owners has led to a tightening of practices in animal experimentation and to the promulgation of federal standards for the care of experimental animals. The days when researchers obtained their experimental cats and dogs by prowling the streets dragging a piece of meat are over. In general, acceptable practice in animal experimentation consists of ensuring that the scientific benefit of the study warrants whatever discomfort is caused and that the animals are kept in comfortable and sanitary conditions. Furthermore, the decision to use animals in an experiment involves a commitment to their care. Many species cannot tolerate the extremes of temperature common in academic buildings. Nor can animals be left uncared for during weekends or holidays. A researcher cannot initiate an experiment using animals without considering a host of logistical problems. For example, many people are allergic to rats. If a special facility with separate ventilation is not available, a number of people who share the building likely will suffer allergic reactions.

Ordinarily, a student who uses animals in research will be joining an ongoing laboratory with well-established animal care procedures. Most institutions have an animal care committee that oversees the operation of the animal facility. Such a committee is required for nearly all institutions that receive federal research grants. The U.S. Department of Health and Human Services (formerly HEW) has prepared a publication, *Guide for the Care and Use of Laboratory Animals* (1985), that summarizes guidelines for animal research. This document lists standards for food, sanitation, and health, including size of cage and recommended institutional policies on veterinary care and personnel. In addition, the document has a valuable bibliography on animal care and lists federal laws that relate to animal experimentation. Among recommended practices is the responsibility to make sure that the animals are kept in adequate-size cages and that they are warm, dry, and well fed and watered at all times, unless the experiment legitimately requires other conditions. Their health must be maintained, and they must be disposed of properly after the experiment. Any experiment that causes pain should employ anesthetics if possible. The animals should be as well cared for as would a pet. These provisions are not just idealistic notions. Much of the impetus for the restriction of animal research has come from pet owners.

These principles are summarized in another document (National Institutes of Health, 1986) that incorporates changes required by the Health Research Extension Act of 1985, Public Law 99-158.   ❏

SUMMARY

1. All psychological research should be guided by the APA ethics code.

2. The decision to conduct research often presents a conflict between the commitment to expanding knowledge and the potential cost to the research participant.

3. Although it is impossible to avoid all risk to research participants, researchers should consider whether people would willingly put themselves into such a situation in ordinary life.

4. There should be some documentation that shows that the subject gave informed consent to participate.

5. The APA position on informed consent differs from medical practice in that subjects need only be informed about aspects of the research that might be expected to influence their willingness to participate.

6. Although some researchers hold that deception is always objectionable, the APA code permits deception provided that the participant is provided with a sufficient explanation as soon afterward as is feasible.

7. Researchers should respect the right of privacy of their participants and be careful about the possibility of coercion.

8. Participants should be debriefed as soon after their part in the study as feasible.

9. Although the traditional and dominant view is that the researcher maintains control over the experimental situation and the subject in the interest of objectivity, humanistic psychologists consider the participant to be a colleague who cooperates in providing the data.

10. Acceptable practice in animal experimentation consists in ensuring that the scientific benefit of the study warrants whatever discomfort is caused to the animals and that they are kept in comfortable and sanitary conditions.

11. It is important to distinguish between the terms *animal rights* and *animal welfare*. Psychologists support the concept of animal welfare.

12. Most psychologists hold that there are compelling reasons to use animals in research.

13. The case of the Silver Spring monkeys illustrates many of the issues surrounding the use of animals in research.

14. Most institutions doing animal research have animal care committees that oversee the operation of animal facilities.

Suggestions for Further Reading

AMERICAN PSYCHOLOGICAL ASSOCIATION (1982). *Ethical principles in the conduct of research with human participants*. Washington, DC: Author. Ethical principles of research are presented, along with case studies and discussion of issues. Although the principles have been superseded by the 1992 statement, the discussion and case studies are still highly worthwhile.

BAIRD, R. M., & ROSENBAUM, S. E. (EDS.). (1991). *Animal experimentation: The moral issues*. Buffalo, NY: Prometheus Books. A reasonably balanced discussion of moral issues behind the use of animals in research. Provides arguments by representatives of both sides of the debate.

COMMITTEE ON THE USE OF ANIMALS IN RESEARCH (1988). *Use of laboratory animals in biomedical and behavioral research*. Washington, DC: National Academy Press. Discusses the benefits that have resulted from animal research, and addresses concerns for animal welfare.

COMMITTEE ON THE USE OF ANIMALS IN RESEARCH (1991). *Science, medicine, and animals*. Washington, DC: National Academy Press. An excellent summary of the case

for the use of animals in research, prepared for the Councils of the National
Academy of Sciences, and the Institute of Medicine.

Cook, S. W. (1986). Implications. In L. H. Kidder & C. Judd (Eds.), *Research methods
in social relations* (5th ed.). New York: Holt, Rinehart & Winston. This
excellent discussion is somewhat broader than the issues covered in the
APA principles.

Keith-Spiegel, P., & Koocher, G. P. (1985). *Ethics in psychology: Professional standards
and cases.* New York: Random House. This book provides commentary on
the APA ethics code and a number of cases that illustrate particular ethical
problems. These cases make worthwhile subjects for discussion.

Stolz, S. B., et al. (1978). *Ethical issues in behavior modification.* San Francisco:
Jossey-Bass. This book is the report of the Commission on Behavior
Modification of the American Psychological Association. It considers ethical
and legal issues surrounding behavior modification in outpatient settings,
institutions, schools, prisons, and society at large. The presentation is
balanced and well reasoned.

Williams, J. (Ed.). (1991). *Animal rights and welfare.* New York: Wilson. A collection
of reprints of popular articles on animal welfare. Balanced and accessible.

⟫ A CASE IN POINT ⟪

Professor D. Lemma and Informed Consent

Professor D. Lemma has developed a new method of therapy for depressed patients, based
on his theory of depression. Informal observation of several of his patients suggests that his
method is more effective than the current standard therapy for depression. He wants to
perform an experiment to test his therapy in which there will be three groups: a
no-treatment control group, a standard-therapy group, and the Lemma-treatment group.
Subjects in the no-treatment control group would be told that they are being placed on
a waiting list for inclusion in a later phase of the study. The two experimental groups would
be treated according to the respective methods.

Professor Lemma believes that it is necessary to assign subjects randomly to the three
groups in order to have a valid research design. He knows, however, that depressed
patients are at risk of suicide. He is concerned that some of his control subjects might
commit suicide while they wait for the treatment. Also, he is bothered by the fact that if
his new treatment actually is better than the standard treatment, he will be giving some of
the depressed subjects a treatment that is less effective than his new treatment.

Lemma's proposed protocol involves informing the subjects that they will be
randomly placed in the various groups. He knows, however, that research has shown that
many subjects in such experiments actually do not understand what randomization
involves, even when it is explained carefully to them (Appelbaum, Roth, Lidz, Benson, &
Winslade, 1987). These authors found that even though subjects are able to state the

principle of random assignment, they often simultaneously hold to the erroneous belief that the researchers will somehow manage to place them in the condition that will be best for them individually.

Professor D. Lemma is preparing to present his protocol to the institutional review board that must approve all experiments using human subjects at his university. He intends to argue that the use of a no-treatment control group is justified because he will be treating as many patients with this design as he would if there were no such control group: He can treat only 20 subjects in his study; he could not handle 10 extra subjects in the two treatment groups. So, the maximum possible number of depressed people will be treated. He intends to offer treatment to the control group after the experiment proper is completed.

Mr. Softheart is a nonscientist member of the IRB and is reading Professor Lemma's protocol in preparation for the IRB meeting. He thinks there should be only one group of subjects, who would all get the new treatment. The improvement shown by the subjects could be compared with that in other published studies. In any case, he is opposed to random assignment. He believes that subjects should be able to choose which treatment they prefer because one treatment might appeal to certain subjects and another might appeal to other subjects. Softheart is also afraid that the subjects in the control group will be even more depressed at being put on the waiting list than they were to begin with.

Dr. Caring is another member of the IRB and has also read the Appelbaum et al. article. She is concerned that subjects will not comprehend that a psychologist will sometimes put a subject in a condition that is not the best for him or her for scientific purposes. Caring holds that the subjects will believe that Lemma will have their own best interest uppermost in mind when assigning them to conditions.

Professor Weary is an anthropologist on the IRB. She believes that this business about informed consent is in reality a ritual whose purpose it is to legitimize the experimental procedure as much as to inform the subjects. She believes that it is sufficient to explain the procedure and not to worry too much about what the subjects really believe in their hearts. It is all right with her if the subjects all think they are getting what is best for them.

Professor Upbeat is in the education department. He wants Lemma to spend 3 hours teaching each participant the theoretical basis of randomness, with a mathematical treatment of probability and examples of coin flipping, until each one is able to understand the true nature of the process.

REQUIRED: Write the report of the IRB, including the main arguments for and against Lemma's proposed protocol, and your suggested solution. Cite the relevant parts of the APA ethics code.

ⅢⅢ➡ A CASE IN POINT ⬅ⅢⅢ

Doris Diligent and the Runaway Subject

Doris Diligent was a student experimenter in Professor Casual's laboratory. Casual was performing an experiment on the effect of failure at a certain task on subsequent performance of that task. Half of the subjects were to be given impossible anagrams to solve. The other half were to receive anagrams that had obvious solutions. After working on the anagrams for 5 minutes, the subjects were to be told that the time was up and that most subjects had solved them in the time allowed. Next they would be given another set of anagrams that had solutions. The dependent variable in the experiment was the number of problems solved in a given period of time. The subjects were not to be informed that the first set of anagrams was insoluble until afterward.

Doris asked how to go about getting approval from the institutional review board. Casual said that he felt that the research came under the category of "minimal risk" and that no IRB approval was necessary. This did not sound right to Doris, but she did not say anything.

Subjects were to be recruited from the class of one of Casual's colleagues, thus bypassing the necessity of going through the department's rather involved subject pool procedures. After the experimental sessions, those subjects who expressed an interest in learning about the experiment would be told about the deception. Casual said that in his experience most subjects just wanted to leave and get on to their next activity.

One day when Doris was running a group of four subjects, one subject became upset at his failure to solve the problems and said that he did not want to continue. Doris wanted the student to realize that the problems were impossible, but she could not say so in front of the other subjects. Before she knew what had happened, the student had left the room in a huff. She ran after him and tried to explain that the anagrams were insoluble and that he had no reason to be upset. When she put a hand on his arm to urge him to return, he threatened to call campus security and have her reported. He said that he had trusted her to tell him the truth; that it was just like psychologists to deceive people; and that he was fed up with this college and would probably change majors or even quit college.

By this time, Doris was upset and confused as to what she should do. She let the student leave and returned to her remaining subjects. After discussing the matter with her roommate, she decided not to tell Professor Casual about the incident and recorded the runaway subject as a no-show.

REQUIRED: List the violations of the APA ethics code that were involved in this situation. Cite specific sections.

OPTIONAL: What should Doris have done with the upset subject? What problems did she face in trying to prevent the subject from leaving? What should she tell the other subjects? Could this situation have been anticipated and thus prevented, and if so, how?

≡ READING BETWEEN THE LINES ≡

14.1 THE CAUSES OF CHILD ABUSE

The causes of child abuse have been a topic of experimental interest recently. Researchers have found that child abuse is reported more frequently in poor families than in middle-class or wealthy families. Some researchers believe that poor families do not abuse their children any more than do other social classes but that they are unable to cover up the abuse as well as middle-class and upper-class families. Leroy Pelton (1978) believes there may be political bias behind the objection to the class-differences theory of the amount of child abuse. Can you think why researchers would object to a conclusion that there is a class difference in the amount of child abuse?   ■

✓ EXERCISES

14.1 ETHICS OF AN EXPERIMENT

Reread the Zillmann and Bryant experiment described on page 80. Discuss the ethical issues involved in presenting pornographic movies to students. What are the ethical implications of the fact that the study changed students' attitudes toward pornography, rape, and women's liberation? What debriefing or postexperimental intervention would have been appropriate? Do you think debriefing or intervention would be effective in reversing the effects of the experience?

14.2 JOE EAGER AND THE DATING SURVEY

Joe Eager was a graduate student in social psychology at State University. He was taking a course in the psychology of social relations at the same time that he was a teaching assistant in an undergraduate research-methods course. He thought that a survey of dating and sexual experiences of his students would be a valuable and interesting example of questionnaires. He took it upon himself to develop, administer, and score such a questionnaire using the 15 students in his section.

Joe included an item in the questionnaire based on a theory he learned in his class. This item was designed to determine whether certain past experiences would predict various types of sexual activity. He did not discuss this hypothesis with the students either before or after they completed the questionnaire. The results were so interesting that he decided to publish a paper on them.

Sue Nice was embarrassed by the questions and said that she did not wish to participate. In front of the other students, Joe joked that Sue must have something to hide. Sue was so upset that she went to the department chair. She said that even though Joe had announced that participation was voluntary, she felt obligated to complete the form because she was afraid it would affect her grade.

REQUIRED: What ethical violations was Joe guilty of? Cite specific parts of the APA ethics code. Note that there may be other problems not specifically addressed by the ethics code.

14.3 IDENTIFY THE RESEARCHER'S RESPONSIBILITIES

A researcher designs a study to determine how truthful college students are in answering personality surveys. He designs the study in a way that makes it possible to detect certain lies that could not generally be detected under normal conditions. At the conclusion of the study, several subjects become furious when they learn that they have been deceived and caught in lies.

REQUIRED:
- a. Discuss the responsibility the researcher has to his subjects in this experiment.
- b. What steps or procedures would you take to meet this responsibility?

14.4 IDENTIFY THE RESEARCHER'S RESPONSIBILITIES

A researcher plans a study to determine the role of heredity and environment in determining individual differences in intelligence. As part of the study, he plans to administer an IQ test to a large sample of American Indians, blacks, and whites from all over the United States. He reasons that since most people do not understand the nature of research procedures and methodology, he needs to inform principals and teachers, but not parents and pupils, only about the general purpose of his research project. He decides that they need not be informed of such specifics as the IQ test to be administered, the number of students to be involved, and how, when, and where the results will be reported.

REQUIRED:
- a. Do you agree or disagree with the researcher's position? Explain.
- b. What responsibilities does the researcher have in conducting this study?

14.5 ETHICS OF ANIMAL RESEARCH

You are a professor whose research is on humans, although you have no objection to the use of animals in research. At a party you meet a person you would like to get to know better socially. This person is opposed to the use of animals in research. How would you defend animal research?

14.6 ETHICS OF ANIMAL RESEARCH

You are a professor who is opposed to animal research, although you have colleagues whom you respect who do use animals in their research. At a party you meet a person whose child is hospitalized with schizophrenia. What do you say to him when he asks you to justify your opposition to animal research?   ❑

15

Biases and Limitations of Experimental Psychology

W e have spent much of this book talking about what experimental psychology is and how psychology can be used as a method of gaining knowledge about human behavior. Before we end the book, however, we must temper our enthusiasm somewhat by discussing a few of the problems of psychological research. Science is, after all, a human activity and therefore subject to human failings. We should have a realistic idea of what science is and is not likely to accomplish.

Let us look at the place of science in relation to the fact that science has become one of the moral arbiters of our society. With the decline of the influence of traditional religions, psychologists have entered the priestly ranks in our culture. Psychologists are frequently interviewed in the media about all sorts of moral issues, from war to incest. A need for caution arises from the tendency of people to take scientific statements of how society does behave as indications of how it ought to behave. It is easy to conclude that because 85% of the population does something, it is right to do that particular thing. By documenting what is statistically common, we contribute to the definition of what is normal. A classic example of this phenomenon is the Kinsey report on sexual behavior, but this tendency is found in studies of everything from daydreaming to cheating on income taxes. This chapter will discuss some of the major limitations of research in experimental psychology.

BIASES

In Chapter 2 we emphasized the fact that science is a social enterprise. As such, science is subject to all of the types of human bias. Some of them affect the choice of problems to work on, the theories developed, and whether particular results are reported. We will consider the many sources of bias under two headings: those that cause science to be conservative, and those that lead science to have a liberal influence.

■ Science as Conservative

As is any social institution, science is conservative. Editors, reviewers, department chairpersons, and deans generally are older scientists who may be slower to change than younger ones. That new scientific ideas are adopted more readily by younger scientists is well known. Too, scientists sometimes refuse to change their positions on important theoretical issues, and thus it becomes necessary for a generation of scientists to pass before a new theory is firmly established.

Another source of conservatism is provided by the dependence of science on financial support. In the latter half of the 20th century, science entered a period known as "big science." In 1989, $142 billion was spent on research and development in the United States, of which 46% was supported by the federal government. In the same year, over $14 billion was spent on research at U.S. universities and colleges, 60% of which was federally supported (U.S. Bureau of the Census, 1991). The impact this federal spending has on psychological research is enormous. We can get some idea of its weight by noting how many journal articles report research supported by the government. For example, at least 83% of the articles published in the *Journal of Experimental Psychology: Human Perception and Performance* for 1991 were supported by government grants. The figure for the *Journal of Personality and Social Psychology* for the first half of 1992 was 60%. Many of these experiments required expensive equipment and facilities that would be beyond the reach of most universities, let alone individual researchers. The days of research conducted in spare time and funded out of the researcher's pocket are largely over.

The amount of money available for various categories of research is part of the congressional budget process and therefore is subject to political pressure. Many researchers keep an eye on the types of research that are being funded and direct their grant applications accordingly. In addition, the federal government puts out periodic Requests for Proposals on projects it wishes to fund. Although many of the steps in the review process involve peer review by nongovernmental scientists, the final steps include political considerations. The type of research that gets proposed and funded is subject to political pressure, even if the pressure exists only in the mind of the scientist who decides to slant a proposal to be relevant to aging, child abuse, education, or whatever is being funded at the time. One of the least subtle forms of pressure on scientists is fear of being ridiculed on the floor of the Senate if the research should be capable of sounding silly out of its proper context. As recently as 1992, individual research projects have been singled out in Senate debate as unworthy of being supported by the federal government simply on the basis of their titles.

Political considerations have rarely had a more chilling effect on research than in 1991, when Secretary of Health and Human Services Louis Sullivan canceled a research project on teenage sexual behavior. This study was to have focused on the behavioral factors that contribute to teenage pregnancy and sexually transmitted diseases, including AIDS (Moffat, 1991). At present, there is little basic information on adolescent sexual behavior, including the reasons teenagers ignore the risks they take, so it is difficult to know how to go about reducing the incidence of risky behaviors. Opposition to the project arose from conservatives who believed that it would encourage sexual activity on the part of adolescents. In fact, money that would have gone to the research project was transferred to a "just say no" teen pregnancy prevention program. Congressman Dannemeyer even offered an amendment to a bill that would have prevented the Department of Health and Human Services from ever supporting any national survey of human sexual behavior ("Sullivan Cancels Teen Sex Survey," 1991). These pressures have caused researchers to reconsider their commitment to pursuing research in this field.

Given that the major support for science is from the government, it is not surprising that there is a great deal of research on how to make people more productive and little on how to make work more meaningful; much research on how to exercise power over subordinates and little on what having power does to the wielder of power; a great deal of interest in the personality patterns of prejudiced people and little on the social conditions that lead to prejudice; more study of what is wrong with students who cannot read than of schools that do not teach; and so forth. It is easy to make a case that research is funded by powerful groups and organizations in order to further their purposes.

Similarly, the results of psychological research tend to be used to control certain groups. Mental patients receive behavior modification, hyperactive children receive drugs, and prisoners receive psychosurgery. In each case, a group of powerful people exists who find it necessary or desirable to control the behavior of others. Needless to say, mental patients and hyperactive children need help and society must protect itself against criminals. Yet psychologists should be aware that their work supports a social system that sometimes oppresses people.

In discussing the influence of the social context of psychology, Danziger (1979) points out that the very origin of psychology was dependent on the support of conservative forces.

> In the United States [as opposed to Germany] . . . control of university appointments, research funds, and professional opportunities was vested in the hands of either businessmen and their appointees, or politicians who represented their interests. If psychology was to emerge as a viable independent discipline, it would have to be in a form acceptable to these social forces. . . . Psychologists might become acceptable if they would reasonably promise to develop the technical competence to deal with [the problems of migration, urbanization, and industrialization]. (p. 35)

Let us not assume that scientists are swept along by forces beyond their control. As society members who have a stake in the status quo, scientists are often willing servants of power. Examples of these influences are not hard to document. Danziger quotes J. B. Watson as saying that "if psychology would follow the plan I suggest, the educator, the physician, the jurist, and the businessman would utilize our data in a practical way." Danziger suggests that "the reason his [Watson's] message found such immediate and massive resonance was that most American psychologists already accepted the premise that it was the business of their discipline to produce data to be utilized 'in a practical way' by educators, businessmen, and so on" (p. 38).

One of the less savory episodes of science in the service of vested interests is that of Samuel Morton, who in the middle 1800s systematically distorted data on brain size and on race to bolster the then-fashionable notion of white supremacy (Gould, 1978). A more recent example is provided by Sir Cyril Burt, the eminent British psychologist, who may have systematically concocted data over a long period of time to provide evidence that intelligence is largely inherited (Hearnshaw, 1979). Burt's data went unchallenged for years even though many suspicious clues were there to be noticed. Interestingly, it took a liberal, Leon Kamin, to do the work necessary to expose the conservative bias in Burt's work. We will discuss this case in the section on fraud later in this chapter.

■ Science as Liberal

Although we have a clear case for science as a conservative force, we can see that science may also have a liberal influence. In fact, many people intuitively see science as a force for change directed against established institutions. This view is almost true by definition because of the objective way science operates, as discussed in Chapter 1. Because science deals only with data that can gain the assent of every person, political and other orthodoxies are frequently challenged by science. In addition, the search for truth often leads to answers that are not palatable to society as a whole and to its powerful institutions in particular. Psychological research on the adverse effects of segregated education contributed to the Supreme Court's landmark desegregation decision in 1954. The fact that the struggle for desegregation is still going on decades later is testimony to the resistance of society to liberalizing influences, psychology among them.

Funding for research in social science was reduced during the Reagan era because social science was perceived to have a liberal influence. At the same time, funding for the natural sciences was increased. The ideological nature of the spending cuts was made clear in the arguments in favor of the cuts. Congressman John Ashbrook, for example, said:

> We have seen how scholarly works have been used to launch major new government policies or programs over recent years. It was a study on the learning abilities of schoolchildren that launched the nightmare of busing . . . . To avoid the risk of the government inadvertently aiding one side of an argument, many people, myself included, consider the best policy is for the government not to involve itself at all. (Association for the Advancement of Psychology, 1981, p. 3)

It has been argued that psychology is more radical than called for by the nature of science. Donald Campbell, whose work on validity we considered in Chapter 5, observes:

> Present-day psychology and psychiatry in all their major forms are more hostile to the inhibitory messages of traditional religious moralizing than is scientifically justified . . . . The religions of all ancient urban civilizations . . . taught that many aspects of human nature need to be curbed if optimal social coordination is to be achieved; for example, selfishness, pride, greed, dishonesty, covetousness, cowardice, lust, wrath. Psychology and psychiatry, on the other hand, not only describe man as selfishly motivated, but implicitly or explicitly teach that he ought to be so. They tend to see repression and inhibition of individual impulse as undesirable. (1975, pp. 1103–1104)

This bias comes through in the topics that are studied and the way they are studied. Campbell notes further: "Conformity or suggestibility to majorities and prestige figures has been extensively studied from the beginnings of experimental social psychology . . . but almost always as a popular character weakness" (p. 1107).

We could give more examples of issues on which psychologists have taken a more liberal or radical stance than prevailing public opinion, such as capital punishment, child welfare, and wife abuse. For this reason, those conservatives who believe that psychologists are a liberal influence are correct, whatever the merits of the particular issues.

LIMITATIONS OF SCIENCE

When we discussed the nature of science in Chapter 1, we said that science deals with phenomena upon which every person can agree. As we noted then, this premise limits the purview of science considerably. When Yuri Gagarin, the Soviet cosmonaut who was the first person to orbit the earth, returned from his historic flight, he said that there was no God because he had looked in the heavens and had not found him. To most people it is obvious that Gagarin's method was not suited to the purpose of finding God. In this section, we will discuss the limitations of science in obtaining knowledge. Some of these are essential limitations to the nature of science, and some of them are practical.

■ Essential Limitations

Yuri Gagarin's failure to find God in space is an example of the essential limitations of science. No matter how hard he looked, Gagarin would never find God from his spacecraft. He was using the wrong methods. Science must remain *agnostic* about questions that lie outside the realm of things on which every person can agree.

Science is agnostic not only concerning the existence of God but also about many questions of values. For example, a perennial political debate concerns whether tax rates should be directed more toward reducing the differences between the rich and the poor or toward providing incentives for people to work harder and thereby become richer. Psychology can discover that poverty leads to psychological distress and crime and that people will work hard for financial rewards, but it cannot tell which goal is more important. This question is one of values, and its answer must come from outside science. Lively debates take place in scientific organizations over the proper balance to strike between scientific objectivity and social responsibility. The decision of the American Psychological Association that its annual convention would boycott states that had not ratified the Equal Rights Amendment is an example.

Closely related to the fact that values lie outside of science is the idea that much of science is *culturally relative*. This concept is particularly true of the social sciences. Not only is the importance of a certain question a relative matter, but the framing of questions themselves is often relative. Years ago psychologists measured masculinity and femininity on various scales and studied the relationship of these traits to psychological adjustment and the like. It was assumed that males ought to be masculine and females, feminine. Then, in the 1970s, feminist psychologists proposed that every person should have a balance of both masculine and feminine traits and be more or less androgynous. The popular ideals of masculinity and femininity were seen as exaggerations of the norm, and it was held that a better-adjusted society would contain a higher percentage of androgynous persons. With a similar philosophy of cultural change, some psychologists specialized in assertiveness training for women and minorities. From another perspective, these psychologists might be viewed as encouraging defiance of legitimate authority. This type of problem, arising from cultural perspective, is common in many areas of psychology. Later developments have raised doubts about the scientific validity of the concept of androgyny (Mednick, 1989). Nevertheless, androgyny continues as a popular idea, or a bandwagon, as Mednick puts it.

Cultural influences on research can be seen in many areas of psychology. Recently, Charles McArthur claimed that the Strong Vocational Interest test, which for many years had been a widely used instrument to help people determine what occupations they were suited for, was withdrawn from use by its publisher as a result of political pressure from feminists (McArthur, 1992). He charged that psychologists were thus forced to use an unproven, and possibly inferior, alternative. You may refer to the later responses to McArthur in the same journal for an interesting discussion of the issue.

Science is also *incomplete*. We know only a tiny fraction of what there is to know, particularly in psychology. As one of the youngest sciences and one that deals with nature's most complex phenomena, psychology is more incomplete than other sciences that have existed longer. We must be humble about making claims for the truth of psychological principles because of the slender base on which many of these claims rest. It is interesting to look at psychology books of 50, 25, or even 10 years ago. We find that social psychology hardly existed before World War II and that cognitive psychology as we know it dates from about 1960.

Because psychological knowledge is so incomplete, it is therefore *tentative*. Science textbooks are continually being revised as new information is obtained. Many times it is not simply that more becomes known about a topic but that theories are developed in areas that did not previously have theories. Also, new theories replace older ones that have been found wanting. In Chapter 2 we discussed the idea that progress in science can take place by means of revolutions that overthrow earlier theories and install new ones. One example of an earlier theory that has been discredited is phrenology— the idea that one can judge personality and intelligence from the various bumps and protrusions on the head. It is sobering to realize that some of the theories we work on today will be cited in future textbooks as examples of obvious and amusing errors of an infant science.

An excellent example of the essential limitations in psychology is provided by the work of Lawrence Kohlberg (1981) on moral development. Following Piaget, Kohlberg sought to determine the course of the development of moral reasoning. He presented children with situations that posed a moral dilemma. By analyzing the reasons they gave for making particular moral choices, he found six stages of development, which may be grouped into three levels. The first level, preconventional morality, is characterized by the avoidance of punishment and gaining of concrete rewards. People in the second level, conventional morality, make decisions to gain approval of others and out of a sense of duty. People in the third and highest level have what Kohlberg calls postconventional morality. They make decisions based on agreed-upon rights and their own ethical principles. Kohlberg sees these stages as forming a ladder, with persons at a particular stage incapable of understanding the thinking of people at higher stages.

Kohlberg's theory has been criticized on several bases. Some have suggested that it represents a liberal, middle-class, secular, humanistic morality (Shweder, 1982). In fact, political conservatives do tend to score lower on Kohlberg's scale than do liberals. Gilligan (1982) took another approach. She argued persuasively that Kohlberg's theory is at best a theory of the development of morality in males. It is the case that Kohlberg based his theory exclusively on data from male subjects because hc found that females did not follow the same developmental pattern as males. Females tend not to "progress" to the third level but to remain at the level of conventional morality.

In her own research, Gilligan found that women are more concerned with the effects that their actions have on personal relationships and their responsibilities to others. They are less interested in abstract principles of right and wrong than are men. The importance these concerns have for women causes women to appear retarded on a scale of moral development that was developed by a man based on evidence from males.

As with the concept of androgyny, the positions of Kohlberg and Gilligan continue to be debated (Mednick, 1989). It will be interesting to look back at this debate from the perspective of history to see how dated this discussion will appear to be.

■ Practical Limitations

Certain problems remain unsolved not because of any essential limitation but for reasons outside the logic and methods of science. Perhaps the most important practical limitation of science is its *opportunistic* nature. Science progresses where the problems are easier, where techniques of study are available, and where financial support exists. Areas that are not blessed with these characteristics will remain backward. Consider the greater understanding we have of vision as opposed to olfaction. The eye is amenable to analysis by well-understood techniques such as optics, and there is money available for visual research because of the handicap that blindness causes. On the other hand, the olfactory system is difficult to study for many technical reasons, and anosmia, or "smell blindness," has not been considered to be serious. Many interesting theoretical problems in psychology wait for solutions, but they will not receive much attention as long as easier ones are present for which more financial support is available.

One major practical limitation of science is the *cost of research,* which stems from the size and complexity of many problems and the technical difficulties of research. Physics, for example, has progressed to the point where further advances require fantastically expensive apparatus, such as the superconducting supercollider that is now under construction in Texas, and which is a huge engineering project in itself. This one project will consume a major portion of the entire science budget of the country. Psychological apparatus has not reached that limit as yet, but the day may not be far off. Scientists who study the sense of balance and orientation would certainly like to have orbiting space laboratories to facilitate research under conditions of weightlessness. It is doubtful that such laboratories will ever be adequate to answer many questions that could be raised. Solutions to problems of abnormal personality may require the investment of more resources than our society is willing or able to provide.

Another practical limitation of science comes from the *complexity* of many problems. Traditional psychological theories are developed to account for the effect of one or two variables at a time on some behavior. When we discussed the idea of interactions, we saw how complicated it is to describe behavior with only two independent variables. Adding a third independent variable can make the interactions mind-boggling. In fact, a relatively new science that has developed to account for such complicated situations is known by the somewhat fanciful name of chaos theory.

Furthermore, traditional psychological theories are not intended to deal with situations in which the dependent variable can affect the independent variable via a feedback mechanism. In traditional theories the stimulus produces a response, and thus we have stimulus–response psychology. In many situations, however, the response can have an effect on the stimulus as well as vice versa. One simple example is the way we respond to the sensation of cold by turning up the heat in the house. Another example of a feedback system is the way you guide a forkful of spaghetti to your mouth. Your eye guides the motion of the hand (the response) by signaling to the brain any error in direction of the spaghetti (the stimulus). A game that is popular at some parties is for a blindfolded person to try to feed another person. When the person doing the feeding gropes about for the mouth of the person being fed, that person tries to correct for the error in aim of the feeder. Most of the food inevitably winds up splattered about. The reason this mess occurs, and is supposedly funny, is the lack of feedback that normally is present when one feeds oneself. This feedback permits correction of error so that the food reaches the mouth.

These and more weighty problems can be handled by a type of theory called systems theory. Systems theory has not had much impact on psychology yet for the reason that even relatively simple problems prove difficult to handle. Psychology therefore continues to deal with behavior according to theories that are known to be oversimplified and inadequate.

The results of interfering with the normal operation of a feedback system can be amusing, as in the feeding example, but they can be tragic when major social problems are dealt with in the same way. The likelihood always exists that a social change that seems desirable in itself will have unforeseen effects that may be dangerous. For example, giving Third World farmers pumps for their wells encouraged them to raise more cattle, which denuded the vegetation and made the land less productive than before. Politically conservative people believe that alterations in society based on scientific research too often lead to unforeseen and dangerous outcomes.

In summary, science is subject to a number of limitations resulting from the essential nature of science and from the practical nature of the problems that science must deal with. Awareness of the limitations of science should make us careful in making claims for science and should help put scientific knowledge in social perspective.

FRAUD

Fraud is an unpleasant topic that no one likes to talk about. But fraud occurs in science just as in all other human activity. Psychologists have long known that honesty is not a unitary trait. People may be scrupulously honest toward their employers but fudge on their income tax. An intriguing question is why fraud in science seems to strike us as so much worse than, say, fraud in banking. One answer lies in the nature of a scientist's data. Bank records can be verified in internal and external ways, but scientific data are creations that can easily be concocted. This means that often we are utterly dependent on the scientist's honesty for the truthfulness of the data. The role of honesty in science is not stressed, but we may say categorically that the honesty of the scientist is a prerequisite for the very existence of science.

Another reason that fraud in science seems so shocking is the priestly function that scientists serve in our society. Because of this role, we tend to expect scientists to have higher morals, and we are more apt to be scandalized when we find them to be human. Cases of fraud in psychology have not been many, but some have been spectacular.

In 1974, a scandal that rocked the field of ESP occurred in the parapsychology laboratory of J. B. Rhine. Walter Levy, a young physician and director of the Institute for Parapsychology in Durham, North Carolina, was caught cheating in an experiment. The experiment involved testing rats in an apparatus that was designed to allow them to use either precognition or psychokinesis (a kind of psychic ability) to increase the number of pleasurable brain stimulations they received. An assistant noticed that Levy seemed to be loitering needlessly about the automated apparatus. From a hiding place, the assistant and two others observed Levy during a session and saw him tamper with the apparatus. Suspicions confirmed, they rigged up a second recorder that would not be affected by the tampering. Later the first recorder showed the rats receiving stimulation 54% of the time, but the second one showed a chance level of 50%. Confronted with the evidence, Levy confessed and resigned. The scandal shook Rhine, who had considered Levy the best hope for the institute's future as well as for the field of parapsychology, because Levy's evidence had seemed the strongest yet for the existence of ESP.

The most spectacular case of apparent fraud in psychology was perpetrated by Sir Cyril Burt, an eminent British psychologist who was knighted for his work. He published much work on the IQs of identical twins reared apart. This work purportedly showed a high degree of correlation between twins and hence suggested that heredity was the dominant contributor to intelligence. About 1974, Leon Kamin noticed that the correlations reported were identical to the third decimal place in several different reports, over which the number of twin pairs supposedly increased from 15 to 53, a mathematical impossibility. This lead was followed up by a journalist, Oliver Gillie, who discovered that at least two of Burt's coauthors either did not exist or had never worked for him. Although leading scientists such as H. J. Eysenck defended Burt against "a determined effort on the part of some very left-wing environmentalists determined to play a political game with scientific facts" (Gould, 1979, p. 104), the consensus now is that Burt was guilty of a conscious fraud over the course of many years. Burt's life and career are the subject of a biography by Leslie Hearnshaw (1979). Although Hearnshaw began his work as an admirer of Burt's, he became convinced that Burt was undoubtedly a fraud. He attributes the deviation to serious setbacks in Burt's life: a marriage gone sour, the loss of his papers in the bombing of London, and a serious illness. These blows caused an exaggeration of a tendency to paranoia and led him to cheat as a way of vindicating his ideas (Hawkes, 1979).

A recent book by Robert Joynson has defended Burt against these charges (Joynson, 1989). Joynson was able to find some evidence for the existence of Burt's mysterious coauthors, and proposed explanations for some of Burt's apparent errors. If Burt's guilt or innocence is now in doubt, it provides another example of the importance of the role of social forces in the history of psychology.

Parallels between the Levy and Burt cases and with other famous frauds suggest that few scientists start out as frauds. They seem to cheat when early successes are followed by failure. The need to build on past successes, whether motivated internally or by external career pressures, can provide a strong temptation to cheat.

Recently, Stephen Bruening, a psychologist formerly at the University of Pittsburgh, pleaded guilty in federal court to falsifying research results on applications for federal research grants (Byrne, 1988). Bruening claimed to have studied the effects of the stimulant drugs Ritalin and Dexedrine on hyperactive children. His results had been cited widely and had influenced several states to change their regulations on treatment of hyperactive children. It turned out that he had studied far fewer children than he claimed and that he had not obtained the results he reported. Bruening, who had left the university before the fraud came to light, has been forced to abandon his research career, and the university returned approximately $136,000 of grant funds to the National Institutes of Mental Health. The Bruening case has resulted in considerable discussion of the manner in which universities and the granting agencies monitor research. Some have proposed that the federal government should audit research results, similar to the way that companies' records are audited.

Why are there so few frauds? The biggest factor seems to be the knowledge that successful experiments, particularly the more startling ones, frequently are replicated. This knowledge provides motivation for honesty. When word gets around that a certain person's experiment could not be replicated by several laboratories, that person loses credibility. Eventually the work is quietly forgotten, and the person fades into oblivion. The problem of fraud also points to the need for good recordkeeping so that an author's claims can be backed up with data sheets and protocols. Even though data sheets can be faked, they can be checked for internal consistency. Nevertheless, as we discussed in Chapter 6, replication is the ultimate test for the reality of a finding and thus is the ultimate deterrent to fraud.

THE RESPONSIBILITIES OF THE SCIENTIST

Our discussion of the biases and limitations of science was intended to provide perspective on our earlier discussion of the advantages of science as a way of gaining knowledge. It should not leave you with the feeling that science is so fraught with problems that you should shy away from it. Science remains one of the most magnificent achievements of civilization. This section will round out the chapter by considering the responsibilities of the scientist as a member of society.

Scientists are given many privileges. They are permitted to work on problems that they set for themselves under conditions that they control to a large degree. They are reasonably well paid and are accorded prestige. What responsibilities accompany these privileges? First must be the goal that society will be benefited by the work. Of course, much pure research has no apparent practical significance, and one can make a strong case for satisfaction of curiosity as a valid end in itself. Nevertheless, many disciplines have struggled with the problem of balancing the uncertain long-term benefits of their work against certain near-term dangers. Atomic physics is the classic example; gene splicing is the most recent. In psychology, debate has surrounded whether research on the genetic basis of intelligence should be done at all. What if particular groups were found to be genetically inferior in intelligence? Would it not be better if we did not know that? Most scientists have such strong commitment to the idea that knowledge is better than ignorance that they are willing to take the risks that new knowledge brings.

The role of free speech is crucial. Science flourishes only in an atmosphere of free exchange of ideas. When that atmosphere prevails, sufficient debate takes place that the necessary safeguards likely will be erected so that knowledge will be used wisely. Concerned scientists and lay watchdogs have so far been effective in preventing scientists from running amok. The principle of free speech also holds for scientists. They are free to study unpopular problems and propose unpopular ideas. It is up to their colleagues to refute these ideas in the open forum. Such considerations may seem hypothetical and far removed from testing rats in a Skinner box or college sophomores in a conformity study, but this philosophical arena is the larger context in which all scientists work.

Another responsibility of scientists is to educate the public about their findings. Some scientists feel that their work is done when it is published in a journal. Yet the support that society gives to science places a duty on the scientist to educate the public. It is no accident that many scientists divide their time between research and teaching. In addition, there is a long tradition of popularization of science by scientists themselves through public lectures, books, and the electronic media. Scientists must present their case directly to the public and respond to the public's concerns. For example, many psychologists feel that answering questions about pseudosciences such as parapsychology is beneath their dignity. That attitude, though, simply allows the pseudosciences to flourish and justifies the ivory-tower image of the scientist.

SUMMARY NOTE ON BIASES AND LIMITATIONS OF SCIENCE

We placed this chapter on the biases and limitations of science at the end of the book to balance out the enthusiasm and the promises we made for science at the beginning. In our concern to present a balanced view of science, however, we run the risk of leaving you with the wrong impression of the value and accomplishments of science. It is safe to say that science has been a spectacularly successful vehicle for human progress, and arguably more so than any other human institution. The contributions of science to our everyday life need no enumeration here. Even though psychology is one of the youngest sciences, it has made important contributions, from the very early work on problems of eyewitness testimony by Hugo Munsterberg to the recent work on the behavior of managers in organizations by Herbert Simon. These and many other investigations have resulted in immeasurable progress, not only economic, social, and political, but also intellectual.

It is likely that the contributions of psychology will be even greater in the future. Certain complex systems, such as piloting and traffic control of airliners, have become so complex that their functioning has become limited by the abilities of humans to process information. Evidence for this is the fact that human error is an increasingly large cause of plane crashes. For this and many other reasons, students such as you have a fertile and exciting field awaiting you.

SUMMARY

1. Because science is a human enterprise, it is subject to human bias. Some of these biases cause science to have a conservative influence, and some cause a liberal influence.

2. Science is conservative in the same way that any social institution is conservative, as well as in its dependence on financial support from society.

3. Much research done in colleges and universities is supported by the federal government and is subject to political pressure.

4. Individual scientists share the biases of their society and often perform research that supports the status quo.

5. Because science rests on observation rather than authority, it challenges political and religious orthodoxies and has a liberal influence on society.

6. Science has certain essential and practical limitations in achieving knowledge.

7. Essential limitations come from three considerations: Science must remain agnostic about questions that lie outside the realm of things on which every person can agree; science is culturally relative; science is necessarily incomplete and, therefore, always tentative.

8. Three considerations constitute practical limitations on science: Scientists often work on problems that seem capable of solution rather than the most important ones; some research is too expensive to conduct; some problems are too complex to study with present methods.

9. Fraud in science is a matter of serious concern because data are easily faked and scientists have so much influence in our society. Although not many documented cases of fraud have occurred in psychology, the Levy and Burt cases are instructive in their parallels.

10. The major deterrent to fraud seems to be the realization that important experiments are likely to be replicated.

11. The responsibilities of the scientist include having as the goal of research that society will be benefited by the work. One problem is justifying pure research that has uncertain future payoff against applied research that may be of immediate significance. Another problem is the risk that new knowledge presents to society.

12. Science flourishes only in an atmosphere of free speech, including freedom of inquiry into unpopular ideas.

13. Scientists have a responsibility to educate the public about the nature and results of scientific research.

Suggestions for Further Reading

Broad, W., & Wade, N. (1982). *Betrayers of the truth*. New York: Simon & Schuster. An important examination of fraud in science.

Hogan, T. T., & Emler, N. P. (1978). The biases in contemporary social psychology. *Social Research, 45,* 578–534. This article suggests areas of social psychology in which biases have affected research.

Vitz, P. C. (1977). *Psychology as religion: The cult of self-worship*. Grand Rapids, MI: Eerdmans. Although this volume deals primarily with personality theorists, it shows clearly the biases that influence how researchers approach their subject areas.

ⅢⅢ➡ A CASE IN POINT ⬅ⅢⅢ

Scientific Misconduct and Conflict of Interest

Professor Jaspers, a psychologist at Northern State University, has done a study that found that Dreckium contributes to the onset of Alzheimer's disease. Dreckium is a heavy metal commonly occurring in the soil that is taken up by certain vegetables and, when eaten, is concentrated in brain tissue.

Although it has been known for many years that Dreckium is toxic in large quantities, Jaspers's research found that it is harmful at much lower doses than previously believed. Publication of his study led to a determination by the Environmental Protection Agency (EPA) that Dreckium constitutes a public health threat, and has been instrumental in the outlawing by several states of the growing and selling of the offending vegetables.

Professor Weeble is a psychologist in the Psychology Department at Southern State University who has done a good deal of research on intellectual functioning in older adults, but he and Jaspers have not been fond of each other after Jaspers once wrote an unfavorable review of Weeble's research. Weeble served on the EPA committee that found Dreckium to be a health threat. At that time he thought some of the procedures in Jaspers's study were questionable. He couldn't figure out exactly how Jaspers had matched his high- and low-Dreckium subjects for education, socioeconomic status, and other variables that could be correlated with measured intelligence. Weeble wrote an article in which he questioned the validity of Jaspers's work. In that article, he suggested that the amount of money spent by the vegetable industry in changing over to production of different foods would better be spent on research to reverse the effects of Alzheimer's.

The Consolidated Amalgamated Vegetable Producers Association (CAVPA), which represents the interests of the vegetable industry, accuses Jaspers of being biased against the vegetable industry ever since his mother forced him to eat broccoli as a child. They note that Jaspers receives large fees for testifying in court on the dangers of Dreckium. They offer Weeble money to do research on Dreckium, and ask him to testify as a paid expert witness before a legislature that is considering weakening Dreckium standards. He accepts.

The Office of Research Integrity (ORI) at the National Institutes of Health (NIH) requires all universities that receive research grants from the federal government to have procedures in place to investigate allegations of research misconduct. Weeble next writes to ORI that he suspects that Jaspers had not properly reported how he did his study, and that the results may be invalid.

Congressman Diddle represents a farming district in Pennsylvania. He has been a keynote speaker before Consolidated Amalgamated's annual winter convention in Acapulco, Mexico. He also chairs a congressional committee that investigates waste and fraud in federal spending, and is particularly critical of what he sees as the lack of accountability in the use of NIH research grants.

ORI requests Northern State to investigate and report back.

Professor Berger is the Research Integrity Officer at Northern State. It is her responsibility to investigate accusations of research impropriety made against faculty at State. An internal investigation of Jaspers's work has already been conducted, but its report was inconclusive. Berger knows that Northern State has been criticized for covering up scientific misconduct in the past, and realizes that NIH could cut off all federal funding to

Northern if it is found that they do not properly investigate allegations of misconduct. Berger appoints a hearing board to investigate.

The chairman of the hearing board is Professor Marshall, the professor at NSU who knows the most about research on intelligence in older populations. She has known both Jaspers and Weeble for many years, having served on various committees with both, and having cited their research in her papers. After a long investigation that includes a complete reanalysis of Jaspers's data, the hearing board finds that Jaspers's results are valid, although a detailed reading of his original protocols shows that he did not accurately report exactly how he chose his subjects. Specifically, his criteria for placing subjects into the high- and low-Dreckium groups changed over time, so some subjects were included who, according to what he said in his published paper, should have been excluded, and vice versa. Nevertheless, the data from the disputed subjects did not alter the conclusions, because the statistical analyses were significant whether the disputed subjects were included or excluded. The board finds Jaspers not guilty of scientific misconduct, but concludes that he deliberately misrepresented his methods.

REQUIRED: You are the provost of NSU, one to whom all academic officials report, including Berger. Write a letter that is to be sent to all parties in the conflict. Deal with the various conflicts of interest. Discuss the role of free speech.

ALTERNATIVE: Arrange a panel discussion of the issues involved in this case, with a member of the class taking the role of each named person or agency. Each participant is to justify his or her actions while espousing the values of academic freedom, free speech, and fair play.

Note: This case study is entirely fictional.

≡ READING BETWEEN THE LINES ≡

15.1 THE LIBERATED FEMALE RAT

For many years researchers who studied sexual behavior in rats found that the male rat was the active partner, while the female was more passive. During these studies the rats were housed in small arenas that kept the animals close to each other. More recently, Martha McClintock and Normal Adler (1978) studied sexual behavior of rats in larger and more complex environments. They found that the female rat actually controlled the initiation and timing of sexual behavior by soliciting the male. What reasons can you think of for the failure of researchers to discover this fact for so many years?   ∎

☑ EXERCISES

15.1 SCIENCE AS LIBERAL

Describe several social issues on which the findings of scientists have had a liberal influence.

15.2 SCIENCE AS CONSERVATIVE

Describe several social issues on which the findings of scientists have been used to resist change. (You may be able to think of issues on which scientists have lined up on both sides.)

15.3 LIMITATIONS OF SCIENCE

List several theoretical or social problems that science may never be able to solve, and give reasons.

15.4 Look in the "News & Comment" section of *Science* for an example of the influence of the political process on the funding of scientific projects. What group or individual is attempting to influence the project? What is their special or vested interest in the matter?   ❑

Appendix A

REVIEW OF STATISTICS

We have found in teaching research methods that even when students have had a prior course in statistics, a review of some basic concepts is very helpful. We believe that this results from the technical and abstract nature of statistical thinking. The purpose of this appendix is to review some of the concepts from introductory statistics in a nontechnical way in order to provide some of the repetition needed to be able to understand them. Because there are so many different statistical tests, and they differ among themselves, you will need to refer to a book on statistics to select the appropriate tests and to find the formulas and steps for conducting them.

SOME BASIC TERMS

empirical data
facts derived from experience

First, let us review a few basic terms. Statistics is—this is not a misprint; statistics as a field is a singular word—an area of study having to do with interpretation of **empirical data.** This term needs some definition. The word *data* refers to facts. The word *empirical* means based on experience. So empirical data are facts that are obtained by observation or experiment. Now, these empirical data ordinarily exist in numerical form: The mean IQ of the population is 100; the average reaction time was 483 (milliseconds); and so forth. But it is important to note that not all numbers are empirical data. Mathematicians often talk about numbers in the abstract: Two plus two is four. These numbers are not empirical data because they

411

do not refer to a specific observation or experiment; they are true by definition.

[It is worth noting that *data* is a plural word. The singular form is *datum*. A datum is a fact, and data are a collection of facts. Scientists say "The data are such and such" rather than "The data is such and such." In common usage, it is often considered pedantic (picky) to treat the word data as plural, but scientific usage still favors treating data as a plural word.]

population
all members of some group

A **population** is the entire collection of individuals being considered: all people who live in the United States (the U.S. population), all students at State University, all college sophomores, all possible tosses of a pair of dice, and the like. Note from the last example that a population does not necessarily contain people or even animate objects. Nor is a population necessarily finite: You could toss dice forever and still be able to toss them some more. A **sample,** on the other hand, is a subset of the population: 100 randomly selected people who live in the United States, every 100th student at State University, 100 tosses of a pair of dice, and so on. Statistics deals sometimes with populations and sometimes with samples.

sample
a subset of a population

statistic
a quantity computed from a sample

A **statistic** is a quantity computed from a sample: The mean number of hours worked per week is a statistic if it is based on a sample of the students at State University. (This differs from the common usage in which a statistic is any sort of empirical datum: Drive carefully or you will become a statistic.) A **parameter** is a quantity computed from the population. The mean number of hours worked per week by students at State University would be a parameter if we had obtained the data from every student at the university. Note that the term *parameter* is used in statistics in a somewhat different sense than it is when one is talking about a function (see page 461). So a mean can be either a statistic or a parameter, depending on whether it is based on a sample of the population or the entire population. This distinction is signified in statistical notation: A statistic is identified by a Roman letter (the ones we use every day), whereas a parameter is identified by a Greek letter. Thus, the mean of a sample is usually indicated by $\overline{X}$, called "X bar," whereas the mean of a population is indicated by μ, the lowercase Greek letter *mu* (pronounced "mew").

parameter
in statistics, a quantity computed from a population

descriptive statistics
statistics that summarize a set of data

inferential statistics
statistics that help one to draw conclusions about populations

There are two main uses of statistics: to describe a particular set of data and to use data to draw conclusions about a population. These two uses correspond to the distinction between **descriptive statistics** and **inferential statistics.** We use descriptive statistics to summarize what was found in a set of empirical data. For example, we might have found that the mean reaction time was 483 ms when subjects had to respond to the presence of a single target and 621 ms when they had to respond differentially to one of two possible targets. If we try to draw a conclusion as to whether simple reaction time is shorter than choice reaction time in general, we need to use inferential statistics. Here we are trying to decide whether the mean of the population of simple reaction times is shorter than that of choice reaction times.

DESCRIPTIVE STATISTICS

The most common descriptive statistics are those that concern the average and the variability of a set of data, and those that describe the degree of relationship between two variables.

■ Measures of Central Tendency

A measure of central tendency is a single number that is used to represent the average score in the distribution. There are three common measures of central tendency: the mode, the median, and the mean. All three of them are actually a kind of average, although people commonly use the term *average* to refer to the mean, one of the kinds of averages. Some of the meanings commonly associated with the term *average* are: a number that is typical of all the scores, a number that is in the middle of the scores, and a number that represents all scores. Although all three meanings are true of each measure of central tendency, each measure best captures one of them, as we will see.

Mode

mode
the most common score in a frequency distribution

The **mode** is the easiest measure of central tendency to define: It is the most common score in a frequency distribution. The mode has the advantage of representing the most typical score. It also has the practical advantage of being the easiest to compute because it literally sticks out in a frequency distribution. We can see in data shown in Table 4.1 on page 85 that the mode is 17, having been earned by three students.

In a large distribution the mode will be fairly stable, but in a small data set such as the one we are discussing, the mode can bounce around considerably. For example, notice that if one student had earned a 14 instead of a 17, the mode would have changed by 3. The mode, therefore, is not very useful for small data sets. In large data sets, however, the mode is a good representation of the *typical* case. Another disadvantage of the mode is that it does not enter into any further statistical calculations. It is sort of a statistical orphan.

Median

median
The middlemost score in a distribution

The **median** is the middlemost score in a distribution. Computing the median requires one to rank-order the scores in a distribution from highest to lowest, and find the middle one. The following equation will tell you which score is the middle one:

$$\text{Middle Score} = (\text{Number of Scores} + 1)/2$$

For example, if there are 9 scores, the middle score is

$$(9 + 1)/2 = \text{5th score}$$

If there is an even number of scores, then there are two middle scores. In that case, the median is halfway between the two middle scores. For example, if there are 10 scores, the middle one is

$$(10 + 1)/2 = 5.5$$

You average the 5th and 6th scores to obtain the median.

For example, go back to Table 4.1 and find the median. We first count the number of scores and find that there are 10 scores. From the last equation we know that the median is halfway between the 5th and 6th scores. Counting up from the bottom, we find that the 5th score is 15 and the 6th score is 16. The average of these two, and thus the median score, is 15.5.

The median has the advantage that half the scores in the distribution fall above it, and half fall below it. Thus it is the *middlemost* score. It is not affected by how far other scores are from the median, only by how many scores fall above or below. Disadvantages of the median are that it requires ranking all the scores and counting to find the middle. This can be quite a chore in a large data set. Another disadvantage of the median is that its use in further statistical computations is somewhat limited, as we will see shortly.

Mean

The mean is the ordinary average that you learned to compute in grade school. As you recall, the mean is computed by adding all the scores and dividing by the number of scores:

$$\text{mean} = \Sigma \, X/N$$

or

$$\text{mean} = \text{sum of scores/number of scores}$$

The main advantage of the mean is that it makes use of all the information in the distribution. In other words, the mean is influenced by *the value of every score* in the distribution. (Note that all the scores are summed, and therefore enter into the value of the mean.) Thus, of the three measures of central tendency, it best captures the idea of the average as the quantity that *represents all the scores* in the distribution. The mode, by contrast, is not influenced at all by the other scores in the distribution; the median is influenced only by *how many* scores fall above and below it. A second advantage is that the mean is the basis of the most common and most powerful of the further statistical computations that we will discuss later.

Third, means of subgroups may be combined to obtain the mean of the entire group. If Professor Carlton has two sections of the same course, he can average the means of the two sections to get the mean of the whole course.[1] There is no way that medians of subgroups can be combined to get the median of the entire group.

The mean does have disadvantages, however. Precisely because it makes use of every score in the distribution, it is sensitive to the value of extreme scores, as we will see shortly.

Behavior of the Mean, Median, and Mode with Various Shaped Distributions

When the data are distributed symmetrically, the three measures of central tendency will be the same. When the data are skewed, however, they will be differentially affected. Refer back to Professor Carlton's test as shown in Figure 4.2. As is common with tests in college courses, the data are skewed to the left. Most students tend to do quite well, but a few fall at the low end of the scale. The mode is 17, the median is 15.5, and the mean is 15. This is what would be expected with a distribution skewed to the left: mode > median > mean. (Skewness to the right would produce the opposite order.)

The mode is not affected at all by the skewness of the data, because as we have seen, it is not affected by any other scores. The median is affected by the number of scores above and below it, so the skewness will pull it down somewhat. The mean, however, is lowest because it is affected by the distance of the low scores from the middle, as well as the number of them.

The effect of skewness on the various measures of central tendency can be seen by looking at Table A.1, which shows the same data that we have been talking about with the addition of a single outlier. Suppose that another student took the test late and got a very low score of 4. The mode is not changed by the addition of the score of 4. The median, however, has gone from 15.5 to 15, and the mean has gone from 15 to 14. These changes illustrate the differential effects of skew on the three measures of central tendency.

Professor Carlton will probably take the mode into account when assigning grades. He might decide to make the "A" cutoff at 18 because 17 was the most common score, and a lower cutoff would mean that an "A" would be the grade for the most common score. He will probably also take the median into account when trying to decide what he should consider the middle of the

---

[1] Provided each subgroup has the same number of cases, or the subgroup means are weighted by the number of cases.

$$\text{grand mean} = \frac{(\text{mean}_1)N_1 + (\text{mean}_2)N_2}{N_1 + N_2}$$

For example, if group 1 has a mean of 16 and 4 cases, and group 2 has a mean of 6 and 6 cases, the mean of all cases will be 10:

$$\frac{(16 \times 4) + (6 \times 6)}{10} = 10$$

TABLE A.1

Score	Upper Real Limit	Tally	Frequency	Cum Freq	%	Cum %
20	20.5		0	11	0	100
19	19.5		0	11	0	100
18	18.5	I	1	11	7.1	100
17	17.5	III	3	10	27.3	90.9
16	16.5	I	1	7	9.1	63.6
15	15.5	I	1	6	9.1	55.5
14	14.5	II	2	5	18.2	45.5
13	13.5		0	3	0	27.3
12	12.5	I	1	3	9.1	27.3
11	11.5		0	2	0	18.2
10	10.5	I	1	2	9.1	18.2
9	9.5		0	1	0	9.1
8	8.5		0	1	0	9.1
7	7.5		0	1	0	9.1
6	6.5		0	1	0	9.1
5	5.5		0	1	0	9.1
4	4.5	I	1	1	9.1	9.1
3	3.5		0	0	0	0

$N = 11$
$\Sigma = 154$
$\overline{X} = 14$
Median = 15
Mode = 17

"C" range. Because of the skewness and the outlier, he may decide that the median is the better choice than the mean for the center of the distribution. (On the other hand, Professor Carlton may not grade on the curve, and may pay no attention to these considerations! We are using this distribution simply to illustrate the behavior of kinds of averages, not professors.)

■ Measures of Variability

The second type of descriptive statistic is a measure of the variability of the data. Besides knowing the typical score, we generally want to know how much the data vary. Suppose you are a nonswimmer who wants to wade across a river that is 2 feet deep on the average. It makes a great deal of difference to you whether it is 2 feet deep all the way across, or whether it is 10 feet deep in places. There are three general types of measures of variability: those based on the range, those based on percentiles, and those based on the mean.

Range

The range is the simplest measure of variability: It is simply the difference between the highest and lowest score in a distribution. In Professor Carlton's class, the range was $18 - 10 = 8$ when the first 10 students were considered. When the late student took the test, the range became $18 - 4 = 14$. Thus, although it is simple to compute, the range depends completely on the two extreme scores. For this reason it is highly unstable, as we can see. The mode and range can be thought of together, then, as descriptive statistics that depend completely on a few individual scores rather than the entire distribution of scores.

Percentile-Based Measures

percentile
a score below which a certain percentage of the cases in a distribution fall. A percentile is a score, not a percentage.

Although we defined the median as the middle score, we could have also defined it as the 50th percentile. A **percentile** is a score in a distribution below which a certain percentage of the cases fall. The 50th percentile is the score below which 50% of the cases fall. That score is by definition the middle score in the distribution, or the median.

We can use any arbitrary set of percentiles to describe the variability of scores around the median, but the **interquartile range** is generally used. This statistic is defined as the 75th percentile minus the 25th percentile. The 25th percentile is called the first quartile (Q_1), the 50th percentile is called the second quartile, and so on.

interquartile range
measure of variability defined as the difference between the 75th percentile and the 25th percentile. It is a difference in scores, not percentages.

$$\text{interquartile range} = \text{75th percentile} - \text{25th percentile}$$
$$= Q_3 - Q_1$$

The interquartile range will include half the cases in a distribution. It has the advantage over the range that it is not affected by outliers.

A closely related measure of variability is the **semi-interquartile range.** It is simply half the interquartile range:

semi-interquartile range
measure of variability defined as half the interquartile range

$$\text{semi-interquartile range} = Q_3 - Q_1/2$$

The advantage of percentile-based measures of variability is that they better represent skewed distributions than do other measures. On the other hand, they are more cumbersome to compute, and they do not enter into further statistical calculations.

Variance and Standard Deviation

variance
the average of the squared deviations from the mean

The most commonly used measures of variability are the variance and the standard deviation. These measures are based on the mean. The **variance** (σ^2) is defined as the average of the squared deviations from the mean.

$$\sigma^2 = \Sigma (X - \overline{X})^2/N$$

TABLE A.2

X	$(X - \bar{X})$	$(X - \bar{X})^2$	X^2
16	−1	1	256
12	3	9	144
14	1	1	196
17	−2	4	289
10	5	25	100
17	−2	4	289
18	−3	9	324
17	−2	4	289
14	1	1	196
15	0	0	225
$\Sigma X = 150$	$\Sigma(X - \bar{X}) = 0$	sum of squares = 58	2308

$$\bar{X} = \frac{150}{10}$$

$$= 15$$

$$\sigma^2 = \frac{\Sigma X^2 - \dfrac{(\Sigma X)^2}{N}}{N}$$

$$= \frac{2308 - \dfrac{22500}{10}}{10}$$

$$= \frac{2308 - 2250}{10}$$

$$= \frac{58}{10}$$

$$= 5.8$$

Table A.2 shows how one would compute the variance. The first column contains all the individual scores. Below that column we see that the sum of all the scores is 150, and the mean is 15. The second column indicates how much each score deviates from the mean. Notice that the sum of these deviations is zero, as required by the definition of the mean. This tells you why we do not use the average deviation from the mean as a measure of variability: If the sum of the deviations from the mean is zero, the average deviation must also be zero.

The third column indicates the square of the deviation of each score from the mean. The square of a negative number is a positive number, so the sum of the squared deviations from the mean is greater than zero, and thus

sum of squares
the sum of the squared deviations from the mean

can be used as a measure of variability. The sum of the squared deviations from the mean is often called the **sum of squares.** The sum of squares is used to compute not only the variance, but many other statistics as well.

The formula we have given for the variance is simple to define and is useful to convey the idea of what the variance is, but it is somewhat cumbersome to compute because it requires one first to find the mean, then to subtract each score from the mean, and finally to square the deviation. Another formula, known as the computational formula, is more complicated looking, but is actually easier to use:

$$\sigma^2 = \frac{\Sigma X^2 - (\Sigma X)^2/N}{N}$$

The computational formula requires each score to be squared and then summed, as in the fourth column of Table A.2. The only other quantities required to compute the variance are the square of the sum of all the scores, and the number of scores.

The variance is useful mainly because it enters into other statistical calculations, such as the analysis of variance (ANOVA). It has the disadvantage that it is not scaled in the same units as the original scores, because it is expressed in terms of *squared* deviations from the mean. So the variance is analogous to a square foot, which cannot be used as a measure of distance. Fortunately, it is a simple matter to convert the variance into a measure of distance by taking the *square root* of the variance. The square root of the variance is known as the **standard deviation.**

standard deviation
the square root of the variance, a measure of variability in the same units as the scores being described

The standard deviation has the advantage, as already mentioned, that it is related to other commonly used statistical procedures. Therefore, it is widely used for this reason alone. Beyond that, it has the same advantages and disadvantages of the mean, on which it is based: It represents all scores, but it is also affected by outliers.

Choice of Measure of Variability

The range is not very useful because it depends completely on the two extreme scores. The interquartile range and the semi-interquartile range are useful in describing data when the median has been used as the measure of central tendency, and when the data are skewed. The variance and standard deviation are the most widely used measures because they relate to the mean and other common statistics. Even when the data are skewed, the variance and standard deviation can be used after certain data transformations that reduce skewness, as discussed in Appendix F.

■ Correlation and Regression

We said in Chapter 2 that one of the fundamental tasks of science is to establish that two variables are associated; for example, we may want to determine whether grades on a test are related to time spent studying. Statisticians have developed techniques to measure the strength of a relationship between variables.

Correlation

The most commonly used measure of relationship between variables is the Pearson correlation coefficient, usually referred to simply as the **correlation,** or r. The correlation is expressed as a number that can take any value between $+1.0$ and -1.0. Figure A.1 shows five scattergrams, or scatterplots, depicting different sorts of correlations between two variables, x and y.

In Figure A.1(a), there is a perfect correlation between x and y. The value of r is $+1.00$. Variable y increases with increasing values of x, and for any given value of x there is only one value of y. In other words, there is a perfect straight-line relationship between x and y. This is an example of a linear function, as discussed in Appendix E. An example of a correlation of 1.00 between two variables would be the relationship between weight in pounds and weight in kilograms. If you know someone's weight in pounds, you can predict perfectly his weight in kilograms, because one is a simple linear transformation of the other.

Figure A.1(b) shows another perfect correlation. There is a straight line relationship between x and y, but this time high values of x are associated with low values of y. The correlation here is -1.00. Examples of perfect negative

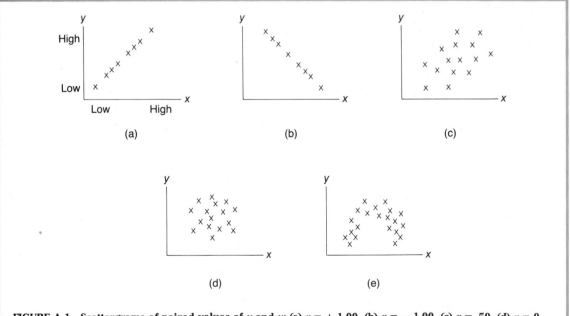

FIGURE A.1   Scattergrams of paired values of x and y: (a) $r = +1.00$, (b) $r = -1.00$, (c) $r = .50$, (d) $r = 0$, and (e) $r = 0$.

correlations are not common, but a trivial example would be the height of two ends of a seesaw.

Figure A.1(c) shows a more usual situation, in which there is a correlation between *x* and *y*, but the correlation is not perfect. High values of *x* tend to be associated with high values of *y*, but the data are scattered instead of falling exactly on a straight line. The correlation in this panel is about .5. There are many examples of such a correlation: height and weight of people, grades and time spent studying, education and income, and so forth.

Figure A.1(d) shows a situation in which there is no correlation between *x* and *y*. A value of *x* can be associated with any value of *y*, and vice versa. The correlation between the two variables is 0.00. An example of a zero correlation is eye color and income. People with each eye color are equally likely to be rich, poor, or in between.

It is important to note that the Pearson correlation coefficient is a measure of a linear (straight-line) function. It is entirely possible that there may be a close relation between two variables but the relation does not fit a straight line. If the data actually fit a curved line very closely, a straight line cannot make a good fit. As you can see, the data in Figure A.1(e) fit a curvilinear function closely. The correlation here is 0.00, because both low and high values of *x* are associated with the same values of *y*. Thus, if the data actually fit a curvilinear function, the correlation coefficient, *r*, will underestimate the amount of the relationship between the variables. There are other measures of correlation appropriate for curvilinear data.

Regression

It is an important property of the correlation coefficient that it measures how well you can predict the value of one variable when you know the value of the other. When the correlation is 1.00, prediction is perfect: If you know the temperature outside in degrees Celsius, you can predict the temperature in degrees Fahrenheit perfectly. When the correlation is 0.00, prediction is impossible: If you know a person's eye color, your prediction of her income will be no better than if you did not have that information.

regression
predicting the value of one variable from another based on their correlation

Regression is the technical term for the process of predicting the value of one variable from another. When we predict *y* from *x*, we use the familiar equation for a straight line:

$$y' = mx + b$$

The *y* has an apostrophe next to it and is read "*y* prime," to indicate that we are predicting *y* from *x*. The *m* is the slope of the line relating *y'* to *x*. (Refer to Appendix E for a review of linear functions.) The value of *m* depends on two things. The first is the correlation coefficient, *r*. Recall that if the correlation is perfect, the value of *r* is 1.00, and if there is no correlation, *r* is 0.00. Under certain conditions, *r* is the slope of the regression line predicting *y'* from *x*, and hence $r = m$. Return to Figure A.1 for a moment. Notice that the value of r is the same as the slope of the line drawn predicting y' from x in each case.

Now, what else goes into the slope of the regression line besides the value of r? Recall that we said that there is a perfect correlation between temperature in degrees Celsius and temperature in degrees Fahrenheit because one is a simple linear function of the other:

$$F = 9/5 \; (C) + 32$$

But the regression equation between the two, shown here, has a slope of 9/5 rather than a slope of 1.00. The difference in slope is due to the differing scales of measurement of the two variables. In fact, scale of measurement is all that differs between temperature in Fahrenheit and temperature in Celsius; otherwise the two are identical. So the slope of the regression line is a quantity that reflects both the correlation between the two variables and the scale of measurement of the two variables. The scale on which the two variables are measured is their variability, or standard deviation.

There is a mathematical procedure for determining the regression line, with which we will not concern ourselves. (It essentially involves computing the correlation coefficient.) The important thing to note is that when the correlation is perfect, there will be a slope of 1.00 between the two variables (when scaled in terms of their variability), and when there is no correlation, there will be a slope of 0.00. Values of r between 0.00 and 1.00 indicate differing slopes of the line predicting y from x.

The situation in which the correlation is 0.00 is very instructive. When there is no correlation between two variables, knowing the value of one does not help you to predict the other. If you know a person's eye color and want to predict his income, your best bet is to guess the mean income of the population. Your best guess would be the same number whether the person's eyes are blue, brown, green, or hazel. This simply puts into words the significance of a slope of 0.00 in the line predicting y from x: Always predict the same value for y no matter what the value of x.

Most of the time you will not see scattergrams in which the two variables are scaled in terms of their variability; they are usually plotted in terms of the units in which they are measured: IQ, GPA, centimeters, and so forth. Then the slope of the line predicting y and x will not be equal to the correlation coefficient.

Example of Correlation and Regression

Consider a group of 20 students who have taken the SAT and then attended college. Table A.3 shows their scores on the SAT and their first-year grade-point averages (GPAs). Figure A.2 shows the scattergram of their SAT scores plotted against their GPAs.

TABLE A.3

SAT Score	GPA
750	2.1
800	2.8
825	1.9
850	2.7
875	2.3
900	3.2
925	2.5
950	2.2
975	3.0
975	2.7
1025	3.3
1050	3.2
1075	2.7
1100	3.3
1125	3.0
1150	2.8
1175	3.8
1200	3.1
1250	3.5
1350	3.5

We find a correlation of .74 between SAT score and GPA. This is a fairly high correlation, and it suggests that we are justified in using SAT scores to select students for college, because the SAT score allows us to predict the first-year GPA. The regression line predicting GPA from SAT is

$$GPA' = 0.0022(SAT) + 0.61$$

This equation predicts that the GPA will increase by 0.0022 for every point increase in SAT score. (The difference between the slope of 0.0022 and the correlation coefficient of .74 is accounted for by the difference in the range of GPAs and SAT scores: GPAs range from 1.9 to 3.8, whereas SAT scores range from 750 to 1350.)

According to this equation, a student who has an SAT score of 1400 would be predicted to achieve a GPA of 3.7. A student with an SAT score of 600 would be predicted to achieve a GPA of 1.9, and a student with an SAT score of 0 would be predicted to earn a GPA of 0.61. (Actually, it is impossible to have an SAT score of 0, so strictly speaking, this prediction is outside the range for which the equation is valid.) Colleges use this information to select

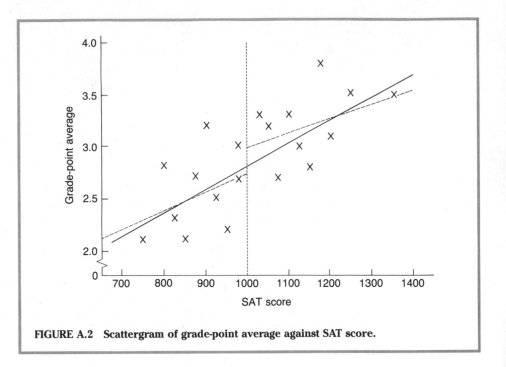

FIGURE A.2   Scattergram of grade-point average against SAT score.

students: They can use SAT scores to predict which applicants are likely to do better than others.

Variance Accounted For

It is an important property of the correlation coefficient that by squaring it we obtain a measure of the proportion of the variability in y that is accounted for by x. Now, there is a certain amount of variability in the scores on variable y and also on variable x. When there is a correlation between x and y, we can predict the value of y when we know x. Another way of saying this is that some proportion of the variability of y can be explained by the effect of x. If the correlation is 1.00, we have accounted for all of the variability in y when we know x, because the square of 1.00 is 1.00. If the correlation is 0.00, we have accounted for none of the variability in y by knowing x, because the square of 0.00 is 0.00.

When the correlation is other than 1.00 or 0.00, the proportion of variance accounted for is less than the value of the correlation. A correlation of .5 accounts for only .25 of the variance, because the square of .5 is .25. To account for half the variance, you need a correlation of .71, because .71 squared is .5.

This concept is important to remember because researchers sometimes are impressed when they find a correlation of .5 in their data. They need to remember that such a correlation accounts for only one-fourth of the variability in their data. Three-fourths of the variability in y is not associated with x.

goodness of fit
the degree to which data match the prediction of a regression line

The square of the correlation coefficient, r^2, is sometimes considered a measure of the **goodness of fit** of the data to the regression line. As r^2 approaches 1.00, the data fit the regression line better and better.

Effect of Truncation of Range

The size of the correlation coefficient is sensitive to the range of the variables measured. If you measure the correlation between two variables for a set of data that cover only part of the range over which the data vary, the correlation will be seriously underestimated. It is possible to think of the correlation as a measure of the pattern formed by the points around the line that relates the two variables. When the correlation is 1.00, there is no scatter and the data points form a straight line. When the correlation is 0.00, the data points make a completely unpredictable pattern. Now, when the correlation is somewhere in between these extremes, the points will form a sort of hot dog–shaped pattern. You can see from Figure A.1(c) that if you were to measure only the higher values of x, the pattern of y scores would be rounder than if you measured the entire range of x. That is, the pattern would look less like a good fit to a straight line the shorter it is. Therefore, the correlation between x and y drops when you consider only part of the range of x.

An example of this situation is given by the earlier case of the college that uses SAT scores as a basis for selecting students. Suppose there is a correlation of .74 between SAT score and first-year grade-point average (GPA). This correlation exists when you take into account all students who might apply to and attend this college. The college, however, has more applicants than it can admit, and it naturally wants to admit the best students it can. Suppose the college accepts only students who score at least 1000 on the SAT. If we consider the correlation between SAT score and GPA only for students who score at least 1000 on the SAT, we find that the correlation drops to .42. This is not an artifact of the way we have selected the particular data, because the correlation for those who fall below 1000 on the SAT is .41.

The drop in the correlation when the range is truncated is accompanied by a corresponding decrease in the slope of the regression line. The dashed lines in Figure A.2 show the regression lines for the two halves of the data considered separately. When the college accepts only students who score at least 1000 on the SAT, the slope of the regression line drops from 0.0022 to 0.0014. Using the regression line based only on those students who scored 1000 or better on the SAT, we would predict that a student scoring 1000 would achieve a GPA of 3.0 (instead of 2.8, based on the full range) and one who scored 1400 would achieve 3.5 (instead of 3.7). Thus the college's ability to predict GPAs from SAT scores decreases when the range is truncated.

The problem is that the college cannot admit students over the whole range just to determine the true correlation for all students who might be admitted. There isn't room for them, and the students with lower SAT scores will tend to do less well. But, if the college uses SAT scores as a basis for admitting students and tries to assess the ability of the SAT score to predict GPA, it will be underestimating the degree of the relationship between SAT score and GPA. The college may conclude that SAT score is not a useful predictor of college success because its correlation of .42 accounts for only 18% of the variability in college grades. In fact, if the college had admitted all students who took the SAT, it would have found that there was a correlation of .74 between SAT scores and grades and that SAT scores accounted for 55% of the variability in college grades.

INFERENTIAL STATISTICS

Now we turn to techniques for allowing us to draw inferences about the population from a sample drawn from the population.

■ Sampling Distributions

Suppose you knew that the mean IQ of the population was 100 and its standard deviation was 15. If you were to select a person at random and had to guess her IQ, you would probably guess that it was 100, because that is the mean of the population. You would not be greatly surprised, however, if that randomly selected person had an IQ of 70, or 130. After all, one person out of a population might have any score in the population. If you had a group of 100 randomly selected people, however, you would be very surprised if the mean IQ of the group were 70 or 130. If it were 70, you would probably guess that you had somehow selected a class of slow learners instead of a random sample from the population; if the mean were 130, you would likely think you had gotten the members of an honors class. This intuitive notion is related to the concept of a sampling distribution.

We know from descriptive statistics that we can describe a population by its mean and standard deviation. Now, suppose that we take samples from the population and measure IQ. These samples of IQ will vary from one to another. See Figure A.3, in which we have taken three samples of size 5 from the population.

We can do various things with these samples. First, we can find the means of the samples. Our three samples have means of 92, 99, and 104. We can also make a distribution of the means of the samples. This is a new distribution, a distribution of sample means, and it is not to be confused with the original population distribution. This distribution of the means of samples from a population is called a **sampling distribution.**

The sampling distribution has three important properties. First, it has the same mean as the original distribution. If the mean IQ in the population

sampling distribution
the distribution of means of samples from a population

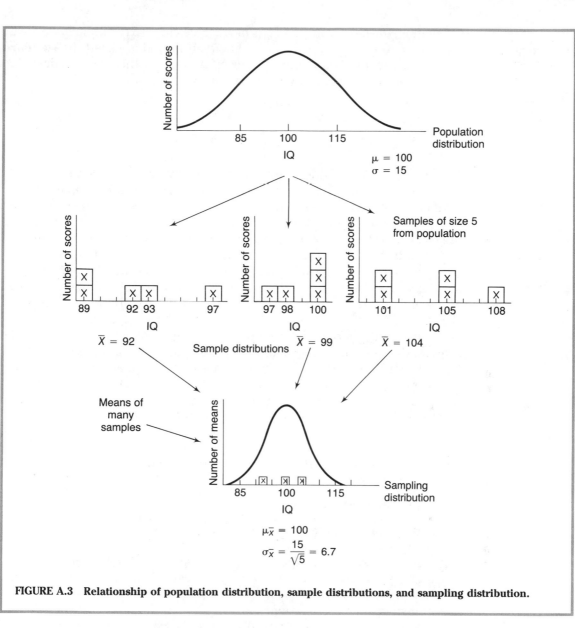

FIGURE A.3 Relationship of population distribution, sample distributions, and sampling distribution.

is 100, the mean of the sampling distribution will be 100. (The average sample you select will have a mean of 100.)

Second, the sampling distribution has a smaller standard deviation than the population distribution. The larger the size of the samples that are drawn from the population, the smaller the standard deviation of the sampling distribution. As noted previously, the larger the sample you draw from a population, the more you expect its mean to be close to the population mean. The standard deviation of the sampling distribution is called the **standard error of the mean.** The standard error of the mean is the standard deviation of the population divided by the square root of the sample size:

$$\sigma_{\overline{X}} = \frac{\sigma_X}{\sqrt{N}}$$

The standard error of the mean is thus inversely proportional to the square root of the sample size: The larger the square root of the sample size, the smaller the standard error of the mean. This is true because the square root of N is the denominator of a fraction. The larger the denominator of a fraction, the smaller is the value of the fraction. Therefore, increasing the square root of N by a factor of 2 will cut the standard error of the mean in half. Putting it another way, large samples will result in a smaller standard error of the mean because the means of large samples will be more similar to one another. The standard error of the mean of the sampling distribution in Figure A.3 is 6.7.

The third characteristic of the sampling distribution is that as the sample size becomes larger, the shape of the distribution approaches a normal distribution, regardless of the shape of the population from which the samples are drawn. The population distribution in Figure A.3 is normal because the distribution of IQ is normal. However, the sampling distribution will be normal no matter what the original population looks like.

Exercise A.1 on page 442 illustrates the concept of sampling distributions and shows the effects of changing sample size. Turn there now to see the effect of sample size on the shape and variability of sampling distributions.

■ Testing Hypotheses

We said in Chapter 2 that virtually all scientific research has the purpose of testing a hypothesis. Usually this will be a test of a theory-level hypothesis. But when we test such a hypothesis, we must state it in terms of a particular research hypothesis. The research hypothesis is more specific than the theory-level hypothesis because it must be stated in terms of the particular way the study was carried out.

In the Lepper et al. study discussed in Chapter 2, the theory-level hypothesis was that rewarding children for coloring would cause them to lose interest in coloring. The theory predicts only that rewarding children for coloring will cause them to lose interest in coloring. But we know that children lose interest in coloring for other reasons, such as boredom, fatigue, and lunchtime. For this reason, the experiment has to be designed to take these other factors into account. In the Lepper et al. study, the experimenters controlled for these other factors by having a control group that was treated exactly the same as the experimental group, except for the reward.

The difference between the theory-level hypothesis and the research hypothesis is that the research hypothesis must take into account other factors that the theory does not address. In this case, the research hypothesis was that the rewarded children would lose interest more than the control group.

Although we have stated the research hypothesis in terms of our study—that is, in terms of rewarded children and control children—we are not interested mainly in what our particular subjects do. We really want to know whether rewarded children in general will lose interest more than nonrewarded children in general. In other words, we are interested in a hypothesis about all possible children who are either rewarded or not rewarded for coloring. This is another way of saying that we are interested in a hypothesis about the population of children who are either rewarded or not rewarded for coloring, not just our samples of those populations.

When we have collected the data in a study, we need to analyze them statistically, to see which unobserved population they are most likely to have come from. (The logic of hypothesis testing is the same no matter what statistic you use. The arithmetic procedure differs with the statistic—*t* test, analysis of variance, and so forth. We refer you to a statistics book for the details.)

alternative hypothesis
statistical term for the research hypothesis

The statistical hypothesis is actually a restating of the research hypothesis into two different hypotheses. The first one is just the research hypothesis itself, but we are going to introduce a new name for it: the **alternative hypothesis.** It is generally written H_1 and is called "*H sub one.*" The reason for this term will become clear in a moment. In our example, the alternative hypothesis is as follows: Rewarded children lose interest more than do children who are not rewarded (the control condition).

null hypothesis
the hypothesis that is of no scientific interest; sometimes the hypothesis of no difference

The second hypothesis is the one that would be true if the alternative hypothesis were false. We call this one the **null hypothesis.** It is often written H_0 and is called "*H sub oh.*" It is called the null hypothesis because it is an "empty" hypothesis, of no scientific interest to you. You set up the null hypothesis strictly for the purpose of rejecting it. It is a "straw man" hypothesis. In our example, the null hypothesis is as follows: Rewarded children do *not* lose interest more than do control children.

Notice that the null hypothesis covers all possible exceptions to the research hypothesis. We could have stated the null hypothesis as follows: The control children will lose interest less than the experimental children, or they will lose interest to the same extent as the experimental children. In other words, either the null hypothesis is true, or the alternative hypothesis is true. Between the null hypothesis and the alternative hypothesis, you have covered all possible states of the world. A philosopher would say that the two alternatives are mutually exclusive and exhaustive.

The hypothesis that we are trying to prove is the alternative hypothesis. (Some people object to the term "proving the alternative hypothesis" because it implies that you have made the correct decision when in fact your decision may be incorrect. We will use the expression anyway, because we believe that everyone should realize that science never proves anything once and for all.) The way that we prove this hypothesis to be true is by a roundabout method of disproving the null hypothesis. If we have disproved the hypothesis that includes all possible outcomes that could happen if the research hypothesis is false, then the research hypothesis is left standing.

Now we know the reason for calling the research hypothesis the alternative hypothesis: The logic of the test is set up so that you try to reject the null hypothesis. When you have done that, all there is left is the alternative hypothesis, if you have set up the hypotheses properly. So the logic of hypothesis testing is to set up a straw man. When you have knocked it down, you have proven your research hypothesis.

Here is a tricky but extremely important point. Your alternative hypothesis is the one that you want to prove true. However, according to the logic of the statistical test, you cannot do this directly. You can only reject the null hypothesis, which leaves you with only one alternative: to accept the alternative hypothesis. If it turns out that your results are not statistically significant, then you fail to reject the null hypothesis. Thus, you must say that your alternative hypothesis was not accepted because you could not reject the null hypothesis.

The null hypothesis is often stated in the following way:

$$H_0: \mu_X \geq \mu_C$$

That is, the null hypothesis is that the mean of the population of those children who are rewarded for coloring is greater than or equal to the mean of the population of those who are not rewarded. The alternative hypothesis is then stated as follows:

$$H_1: \mu_X < \mu_C$$

directional hypothesis
an alternative hypothesis that predicts that the results of one condition will be greater (or less) than another, rather than a prediction that they will simply differ

one-tailed hypothesis test
statistical test of a directional hypothesis

two-tailed hypothesis test
statistical test of a nondirectional hypothesis

The alternative hypothesis is that the mean of the population of those who are rewarded for coloring is less than the mean of the population of those who are not rewarded for coloring.

In this example, the alternative hypothesis was that the experimental population had a lower mean than the controls. This is called a **directional hypothesis** because we predicted that the experimental subjects would differ in one particular direction from the control subjects. This gives rise to what is called a **one-tailed hypothesis test.** We are not interested in the case in which the experimental subjects might be higher than the controls in interest in coloring.

Sometimes we predict only that the two groups will differ from each other; we don't know which group will be higher. This is a nondirectional hypothesis, and it gives rise to a **two-tailed hypothesis test.** The null and alternative hypotheses in this case would be stated as follows:

$$H_0: \mu_X = \mu_C$$

$$H_1: \mu_X \neq \mu_C$$

That is, the null hypothesis is that the mean of X equals the mean of C, and the alternative hypothesis is that the mean of X does not equal the mean of C. We would use a two-tailed hypothesis if we predicted that the rewarded children would differ from the controls but our theory did not predict in which direction. When you do a two-tailed hypothesis test, you reject the null hypothesis if the experimental group is sufficiently higher or sufficiently lower than the control group.

■ Dealing with Uncertainty in Hypothesis Testing

One of the consequences of the fact that data are inherently variable is that we must be prepared to deal with uncertainty in making decisions about those data. Suppose the psychology department at your college wishes to evaluate the effectiveness of its undergraduate program. To do this, it requires all majors to take the psychology section of the Graduate Record Exam (GRE). We know that the mean score on the GRE is 500 for all students who take the exam. Suppose that the mean for the psychology majors at your college is 530. Does this prove that your college's psychology graduates are reliably better than the national average?

The fact that the group scored higher than the national average does not prove that the college's students are better than the national average. Although it may be that the college's program was responsible for the difference, it is not certain: The students in this year's graduating class may have been better than usual, or they may have been lucky on the test, or any of a number of other factors may have been responsible. So we are faced with a difference between our group and the population mean that we must interpret: Does an average score this high prove that your college's psychology majors are actually better than the national average? This average score will have its own sampling distribution: a sampling distribution of means. Our job is to decide whether the observed average score is likely to have come from the distribution of all possible samples of means from the population of scores on the GRE. So we need to make a decision based on this observed sample mean compared with the theoretical sampling distribution.

Type I and Type II Errors

Suppose that your college's psychology majors were actually the same as the average of the population of psychology majors. What would you expect to happen? This is the same as asking what is the null hypothesis. If we are studying the effectiveness of your college's psychology program compared with that of the average psychology program, we would say that our null hypothesis is that your college's psychology majors are no better than average:

$$H_0: \mu_X \leq \mu_0$$

Our alternative hypothesis is that your college's psychology majors are better than average:

$$H_1: \mu_X > \mu_0$$

These two hypotheses set up two possible states of the world: Either the mean of your college's psychology majors is better than the average for all psychology majors in the country, or it is not. Note that the two states of the world concern not the outcome of your single study but the outcome of all possible studies using exactly the same methods, type of students, and so on, that you did. In other words, the two states of the world are statements about whether your experimental hypothesis is true or false.

Corresponding to the two states of the world, there are two possible decisions you could make: Either your college's psychology majors are better, or they are not. These two sets of alternatives make it possible to consider four distinct situations. First, let us suppose that your college's psychology program is better. You might decide that it is better, or you might decide that it is not better. Second, suppose instead that the psychology program is not better. Here you could also decide that it is better or that it is not better. It is convenient to summarize these four possibilities in a 2×2 table (see Table A.4).

Looking at the table, you can see that if the program were better and you decided that it was better, you would be correct. You would also be correct if the program were not better and you decided that it was not better. Figure A.4 provides the same information in the form of a decision tree.

There are two ways of making errors. One kind of error occurs when the program is not better but you decide that it is. This is called a Type I error; you have rejected the null hypothesis when it is true. The other kind of error is to decide that the program is not better when it actually is. This is called a Type II error; you have accepted the null hypothesis when it is false.

TABLE A.4 FOUR POSSIBLE OUTCOMES IN MAKING A DECISION CONCERNING REJECTION OF THE NULL HYPOTHESIS

		Null hypothesis is true	Alternative hypothesis is true
Decision	Accept null hypothesis	Correct decision	Wrong decision: Type II error
	Reject null hypothesis	Wrong decision: Type I error	Correct decision (power of test)

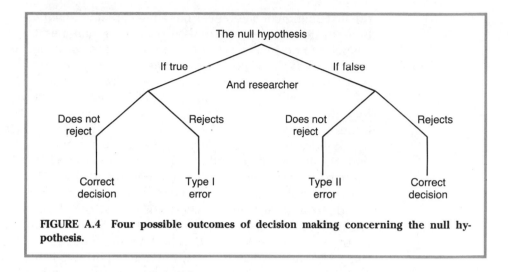

FIGURE A.4 Four possible outcomes of decision making concerning the null hypothesis.

Alpha and Statistical Significance

These four outcomes can be related to the sampling distributions of the means for the two situations. First, let us consider the sampling distribution of the means for the psychology majors when the null hypothesis is true. The curve in Figure A.5(a) shows the relative probability of getting any particular group mean. If the null hypothesis is true, the distribution of means will have a mean of 500 and a certain standard deviation (standard error). We can see that sometimes the mean will be higher than 500 and sometimes it will be less than 500.

Figure A.5(b) shows the distribution of means when the alternative hypothesis is true (when the program is better). Notice that on the average,

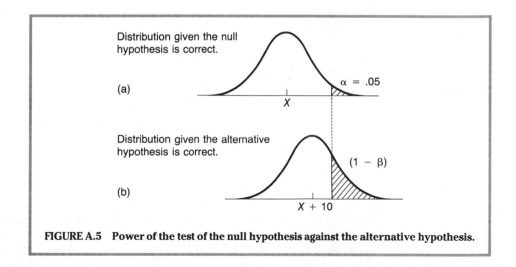

FIGURE A.5   Power of the test of the null hypothesis against the alternative hypothesis.

the distribution of differences has a mean that is 10 points higher. Most of the time the difference is greater than zero, but sometimes it is zero or less. What we need to do is set up a *criterion* on which to base our decision.

The way this is done is to decide how often we are willing to say that the program is better when in fact it is not. This is the same as setting a cutoff on the dimension of scores in Figure A.5(a) that will cause us to reject the null hypothesis a certain percentage of the time when it is true. This point is indicated by the vertical line that cuts through both curves in Figure A.5. The line divides the curve indicating the sampling distribution given the null hypothesis into two sections. The area under the curve represents the probability of various events given that the null hypothesis is true. The area to the right of the line cuts off a certain proportion of the curve. Suppose we decide to say that the null hypothesis is false and the alternative hypothesis is true whenever the mean score is greater than a certain amount, indicated by the vertical line. The section to the right of the line on the upper curve is the probability of deciding that the null hypothesis is false when in fact it is true. This is the probability of making a Type I error and is known as alpha. *Alpha is the probability of deciding that the null hypothesis is false when it is actually true.*

Usually, scientists prefer to make alpha a fairly small number, such as .05 or .01. The reason is that scientists believe that to decide that an experimental finding is true when it is not is a more serious error than it is to miss a true finding.

statistical significance
the probability that an experimental result happened by chance

Alpha is also called the level of significance of an effect, or the **statistical significance.** It is common to say that a certain experimental result was significant at the .05 level. This means that the effect was large enough that the probability that it happened purely by chance was .05, or 1 in 20.

Power

Looking now at Figure A.5(b), we find that the same criterion has divided the curve that represents the situation given the alternative hypothesis into two portions. The portion to the left is the probability of deciding that the null hypothesis is true when it is actually false. This is the probability of a Type II error.

The rest of the area under the curve showing the alternative hypothesis shows us another important probability: the probability of rejecting the null hypothesis when it is actually false. This is one minus the probability of a Type II error and is known as the power of the test. This is a very important probability: the probability of deciding that you have an experimental effect when you actually do.

Notice something about the two curves. You could decide to make your alpha, or probability of a Type I error, smaller by moving the line dividing the two curves to the right. However, by decreasing alpha, you would also decrease the probability of accepting the alternative hypothesis when it is true. In other words, you would decrease the power of the test.

There are three things that influence the power of a test. The first one is the value of alpha. The smaller your alpha level, the smaller your power. If you decide that you want to make it unlikely that you will make a Type I error, you must accept the fact that you will be more likely to make a Type II error.

The second thing that influences the power of a test is the size of your experimental effect. If you are able to make your psychology program much more effective, by giving the students more courses, better materials, higher motivation, or other advantages, you will increase their mean score. This will have the effect of moving the curve showing the alternative hypothesis to the right, making less overlap between the curves.

The third way to increase the power of a test is to increase the size of the two groups. This will have the effect of decreasing the variability of the sampling distribution, or the variability of the two curves in Figure A.5. This will also reduce the amount of overlap between them. Exercise A.1 is an illustration of this point.

■ Analysis of Variance

Analysis of variance (ANOVA) is a powerful statistical method for analyzing experimental data. It is a flexible but complex method that is adaptable to a great variety of experimental designs. These characteristics make ANOVA difficult to summarize and to understand. On the other hand, because ANOVA is so widely used, it is necessary to have an acquaintance with some of its basic concepts.

When one wishes to analyze the data of an experiment with only two conditions, a t test is appropriate. Whenever there are more than two conditions, however, a t test is not appropriate because a t test can compare only two groups at a time. If there were three conditions, it would be necessary to compare the first with the second, the first with the third, and the second with the third. This would result in three separate statistical tests. Performing several tests would give you more chances to reject a true null hypothesis, so you would increase the likelihood of rejecting the null hypothesis when it is actually true.

ANOVA was developed to make it possible to test the null hypothesis that there is no difference among a number of conditions. Suppose that an experiment tested the effect of three different doses of marijuana on motor coordination. The null hypothesis would be that there is no difference among the three doses:

$$H_0: \mu_1 = \mu_2 = \mu_3$$

The alternative hypothesis is

$$H_1: [\mu_1 = \mu_2 = \mu_3] \text{ is not true}$$

Note that the alternative hypothesis simply says that it is *not* true that all of the means are equal. It does not say that all of the means are unequal. In order for the alternative hypothesis to be true, it is necessary only that some combination of means is not equal to some other combination. For example, one situation that would make the null hypothesis false and the alternative hypothesis true could be that Conditions 1 and 2 differ significantly from Condition 3 in a three-condition experiment. It is entirely possible that neither Condition 1 nor Condition 2, considered alone, differs significantly from Condition 3, but that the subjects in Conditions 1 and 2 considered together differ significantly from those in Condition 3.

Any experiment that has more than two conditions must be analyzed by ANOVA instead of a *t* test. Very simply, any ANOVA tests the significance of a difference among several conditions in an experiment by making two different estimates of the variability that you would expect to find in the data given that the null hypothesis is true. If there is no true difference among the groups, each estimate of variability should, on the average, be the same. Let us see where those two estimates of variability come from.

Two Estimates of the Variability in the Population

Suppose that the null hypothesis is true. In that case, because the experimental conditions have no effect, you would predict that all of the individual data would have the same value. This value would be the mean of all the data, or the grand mean. Now, it should be obvious that all of the data would not be exactly the same, because chance factors are nearly always operating to introduce variability to the data. Therefore, individual data points will vary about the mean of their respective group. Just as the individuals will differ within a group, the means of the data from the various groups will not have the same value, for the same reason. Thus, the group means will vary about the overall mean in a random way.

We can think of the variability of the subjects within each group as one estimate of the variability in the population, and the variability of the means of the groups as another estimate of the variability of the population. Thus we have two different ways in which chance will affect the data in an experiment when there is no experimental effect (and the null hypothesis is therefore true): by producing differences between the means of the various conditions and by producing differences among the subjects within the various groups. These two ways in which chance affects the data provide the basis for doing ANOVA.

Figure A.6 represents the data from a hypothetical experiment in which motor coordination was measured in three different groups after the subjects experienced three different doses of marijuana. Figure A.6(a) represents the data from all of the subjects in the experiment. We see that there was some variability among the subjects, but we don't know how the variability relates to the conditions. In Figure A.6(b), we see one possible situation. All the subjects in a particular group had exactly the same data, and each of these

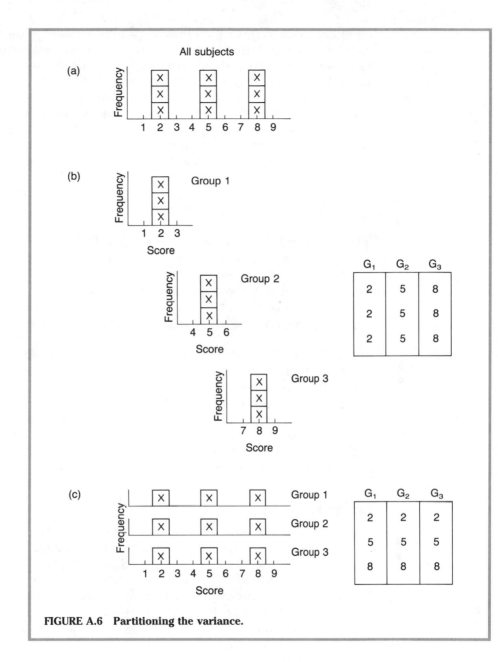

FIGURE A.6 **Partitioning the variance.**

groups differed from the others. Here there is variability among the groups but no variability within the groups. Figure A.6(c) shows another way in which the variability in the experiment could be distributed. Here all of the groups have exactly the same mean, and all of the variability is within the groups. This example is admittedly highly artificial. Ordinarily, of course, there would be some variability within, and some among, the groups. In our example, there was either no variability within the groups or no variability among the groups. The point, however, is that we have two ways of estimating the variability in the population: one based on the variability within the groups and the other based on the variability among the groups.

The differences among the means of the groups and the differences among the subjects within the groups give us two separate estimates of the variability in the population. Sometimes one estimate will be larger, and sometimes the other will be larger. On the average, however, they should be equal if the independent variable in fact had no effect. Consider a ratio of the between-conditions variability to the within-conditions variability:

$$\text{between-conditions variability/within-conditions variability}$$

This ratio is called F. The value of F will be 1.0, on the average.

(For the benefit of those who noted that we switched from talking about variability among groups to variability between groups, it should be acknowledged that *between* is grammatically incorrect because we are always comparing at least three conditions with ANOVA. Nevertheless, statisticians universally use between in this context, so we are stuck with it as a technical term.)

If the null hypothesis is false and there is an experimental effect, the between-conditions variability will be larger than expected, because the variability caused by the experimental effect will add to the random variability. Then the value of the F ratio will be greater than 1.0. The F ratio is central to ANOVA. Every ANOVA has at least one F ratio. The value of F obtained in the study is evaluated statistically against the value that would be expected to occur by chance alone. If the F ratio is larger than a certain value, the experimental effect is considered to be statistically significant.

Partitioning the Variance

There is one more concept we need to consider before discussing how to read an ANOVA summary table. The reason this technique is called "analysis of variance" is that ANOVA makes it possible to analyze all of the sources of variability in an experiment. In other words, there is a certain amount of variability in a set of data. Some of this variability comes from variability among the subjects: how people differ from one another regardless of the experimental conditions. Other variability in the data is caused by the experimental conditions: The independent variable caused the subjects to behave differently.

In a simple ANOVA there are two sources of variance: between-groups variance and within-groups variance. Return to Figure A.6. In Figure A.6(a), we see that there is a certain amount of variability among the subjects, but we don't yet know how much is between-groups variance and how much is within-groups variance. Figure A.6(b) shows a situation in which all of the variance is between groups and there is none within groups. Figure A.6(c) shows a different possibility, in which all of the variance is within groups and there is none between groups. Thus, in these highly artificial examples, we could say that all of the variance is either between- or within-groups variance. Ordinarily, of course, there would be some of each.

How to Read an ANOVA Summary Table

There are many different types of ANOVA, depending on the particular experimental design. You will need to consult a statistics book to be able to perform an ANOVA. Frequently, however, you will read a description of an experiment that contains an ANOVA summary table. Fortunately, you can read and interpret an ANOVA table without knowing how to perform the ANOVA. The purpose of this section is to help you understand such a table.

It is actually possible to decipher a great deal about an experiment from an ANOVA summary table. Consider Table A.5, which shows the analysis of a simple one-way ANOVA. The term *one-way* means that the experiment contains only one independent variable.

There are always at least two rows of information in an ANOVA summary table, one for each source of variance in the experiment. In addition, certain totals are shown. We see in this case that there is a row labeled "Between conditions." This row shows the information about the variance resulting from the different conditions, or levels, of the independent variable. The second row is labeled "Within conditions." This row indicates the information about the variance of the data within the conditions, or groups.

The columns indicate sum of squares *(SS)*, degrees of freedom *(df)*, means square *(MS)*, the *F* ratio *(F)*, and probability *(p)*. The sum of squares is a measure of the variability in the data. Some of the variance can be attributed to the experimental variable. This is the between-conditions

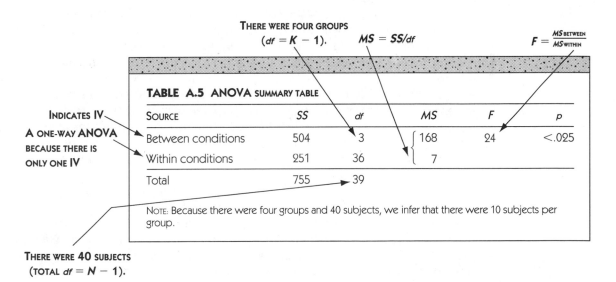

THERE WERE FOUR GROUPS
$(df = K - 1)$. $MS = SS/df$ $F = \frac{MS\,\text{BETWEEN}}{MS\,\text{WITHIN}}$

INDICATES IV

A ONE-WAY ANOVA
BECAUSE THERE IS
ONLY ONE IV

THERE WERE 40 SUBJECTS
(TOTAL $df = N - 1$).

TABLE A.5 ANOVA SUMMARY TABLE

SOURCE	SS	df	MS	F	p
Between conditions	504	3	168	24	<.025
Within conditions	251	36	7		
Total	755	39			

NOTE: Because there were four groups and 40 subjects, we infer that there were 10 subjects per group.

variance, which has a value of 504 in this example. The rest of the variance can be attributed to the variance within each condition. This is the within-conditions variance, which is 251 in this example. Notice that the sum of these values gives us the total variability in the experiment.

Degrees of freedom is a quantity that depends on the number of groups, subjects, and the like. The total degrees of freedom, 39 in our example, is 1 less than the number of observations; therefore, we can conclude that there were 40 observations in the experiment. Because this was a between-subjects experiment, and therefore each subject contributed one observation, we know that there were 40 subjects. The number of degrees of freedom between conditions, 3 in this example, is 1 less than the number of conditions; thus we know that there were four conditions. The mean square is the sum of squares divided by the number of degrees of freedom in the same row.

All of these figures are used to determine the value of F, which is the ratio of the mean square between subjects to the mean square within subjects. Remember that if there is an experimental effect, the variance attributable to the conditions (the mean square between conditions) will be larger than the variance attributable to the subjects (the mean square within conditions). If the F ratio is sufficiently greater than 1.0, it is considered significant. This is determined by looking in a table, or it may be printed out automatically by certain statistical programs.

ANOVA summary tables will differ in their structure depending on the design of the experiment. Certain things can always be counted on, however. First, there is a row in the table for each source of variance. Each independent variable is a source of variance. In the case of Table A.5, the first row indicates the independent variable. In a two-way ANOVA, both independent variables are sources of variance. The interaction between the two variables is also a source of variance.

Second, at least one of the sources of variance serves as an error term. The purpose of the error term is to form the denominator of the F ratio. In a simple ANOVA, such as the one summarized in Table A.5, the within-groups variance serves as the error term. The error term is generally in the last row.

Third, there is always at least one F ratio computed from two mean squares. The numerator of the ratio is the particular effect being tested—the between-groups effect (the effect of the independent variable), for example. The denominator of the ratio is the error term. Therefore, the F ratios in the table will usually be computed as the ratio of the mean square in one of the upper rows to the mean square in the last row.

Fourth, if there is a row with the word *subjects* in the label, we know that we have a within-subjects (repeated-measures) design. Table A.6 shows such a design. Here, the numerator of the F ratio is found in the between-conditions row, as before. The denominator of the F ratio (error term) is once again in the last row, but here it is called the residual. Because there are only three rows of information, we know that we have a one-way, repeated-measures

ANOVA. We can see that there were 30 observations, because there are 29 total degrees of freedom. Also, we know that there were three conditions because there are 2 degrees of freedom between conditions.

Table A.7 gives the summary information from another experiment. Here we see one row indicating the information for an independent variable A,

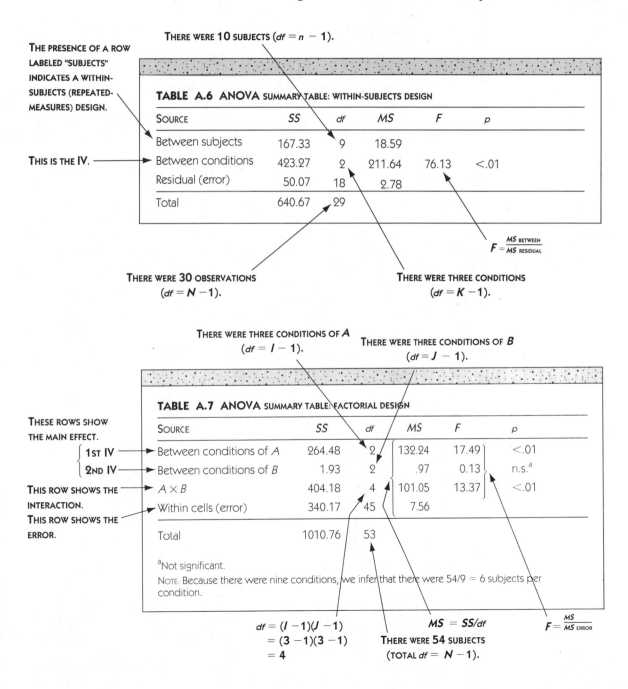

THERE WERE 10 SUBJECTS ($df = n - 1$).

THE PRESENCE OF A ROW LABELED "SUBJECTS" INDICATES A WITHIN-SUBJECTS (REPEATED-MEASURES) DESIGN.

THIS IS THE IV.

TABLE A.6 ANOVA SUMMARY TABLE: WITHIN-SUBJECTS DESIGN

SOURCE	SS	df	MS	F	p
Between subjects	167.33	9	18.59		
Between conditions	423.27	2	211.64	76.13	<.01
Residual (error)	50.07	18	2.78		
Total	640.67	29			

THERE WERE 30 OBSERVATIONS ($df = N - 1$).

THERE WERE THREE CONDITIONS ($df = K - 1$).

$$F = \frac{MS_{\text{BETWEEN}}}{MS_{\text{RESIDUAL}}}$$

THERE WERE THREE CONDITIONS OF A ($df = I - 1$).

THERE WERE THREE CONDITIONS OF B ($df = J - 1$).

TABLE A.7 ANOVA SUMMARY TABLE: FACTORIAL DESIGN

THESE ROWS SHOW THE MAIN EFFECT.

1ST IV

2ND IV

THIS ROW SHOWS THE INTERACTION.

THIS ROW SHOWS THE ERROR.

SOURCE	SS	df	MS	F	p
Between conditions of A	264.48	2	132.24	17.49	<.01
Between conditions of B	1.93	2	.97	0.13	n.s.[a]
A × B	404.18	4	101.05	13.37	<.01
Within cells (error)	340.17	45	7.56		
Total	1010.76	53			

[a]Not significant.

NOTE: Because there were nine conditions, we infer that there were 54/9 = 6 subjects per condition.

$df = (I - 1)(J - 1)$
$= (3 - 1)(3 - 1)$
$= 4$

THERE WERE 54 SUBJECTS (TOTAL $df = N - 1$).

$MS = SS/df$

$$F = \frac{MS}{MS_{\text{ERROR}}}$$

labeled "Between conditions of *A*," and a second row labeled "Between conditions of *B*." This tells us that there were two independent variables. This means that we have a two-way ANOVA and the experiment had a factorial design. With two-way ANOVA, we see a third row for information about the interaction between the two independent variables, labeled "$A \times B$."

■ The Significance of Significance

Let's suppose we have found that left-handed people with hazel eyes and free earlobes are better at repeating the Pledge of Allegiance backward and that the effect is significant at the .05 level. What does that mean? First of all, there is something that it does not mean: It does not mean that the results are important. Although in common usage that is exactly what the term *significance* means, results can be statistically significant when they have no importance at all.

First of all, results may be statistically significant even when an experiment has to do with the most trivial question imaginable, as in our little example. Second, given enough subjects, or observations, results can be statistically significant when the size of the effect is so minuscule that it has no practical importance. If you found that an alternative teaching method produced a one-tenth of one percent difference in course performance, you would not want to change your teaching methods. This concept is discussed further in Chapter 11.

Statistical significance means simply that your results have a certain low probability of having been the result of chance. When a result is significant at the .05 level, there is a .05 probability, or 1 in 20, that the result occurred when the null hypothesis was true—that is, when there was actually no effect. The level of significance is the same as alpha, or the probability of a Type I error.

☑ EXERCISES

A.1   HYPOTHESIS TESTING AND POWER

This exercise uses the computer program listed in the Instructor's Manual. The program takes samples from one of two distributions. The first distribution has a mean of 100 and a standard deviation of 16. The mean of the second is 101, and it has the same standard deviation. When you run the exercise, you will be presented with samples from either one distribution or the other; you will not know which.

Suppose you know that the mean IQ of the general population is 100 and the standard deviation is 16. (Actually it is 15, but 16 is more convenient for the program.) You also know that people with first names that have exactly seven letters have a mean IQ of 101 and the same standard deviation. Now, suppose you are told only the mean IQ of a sample of people, all of whom either have seven letters in their first names or have other than seven letters in their first names. Your job is to guess whether your sample has seven-letter names or other-than-seven-letter names.

Your best strategy is to guess 100 whenever the mean of the sample is less than

100.50. When it is equal to or greater than 100.50, it is at least an even bet that the sample is from the 101 population.

This exercise is an illustration of hypothesis testing. Your null hypothesis is that the sample came from the general population—those people who have names other than seven letters long and have a mean IQ of 100. The alternative hypothesis is that the sample came from the population of those who have seven letters in their names and have an average IQ of 101.

After each trial, the program will tell you whether you have made a correct guess or whether you have made an error. You can make a correct guess in two ways. First, you can guess that your sample comes from the general population when it does. This would be an example of correctly accepting the null hypothesis. Second, you could guess that the sample comes from the seven-letter-name population when it actually does. This would be an example of correctly rejecting the null hypothesis.

You could also make an error in two ways. You could guess that the sample came from the seven-letter-name population when it came from the general population. This would be a Type I error because you rejected a true null hypothesis. Alternatively, you could guess that the sample came from the general population when it actually came from the seven-letter-name population. This would be a Type II error because you accepted the null hypothesis when it was false.

You will see as you go through the exercise that you will sometimes make errors even when you make the best possible decision. This illustrates that hypothesis testing is a matter of probability—in this case, a probability of making certain kinds of errors.

At first you will be given the mean of samples of size 4; in other words, 4 individuals will be selected from the population. Later, you will be given the means of samples of size 400. As the sample size gets larger, the means of the samples will tend to be closer to the means of the populations from which they are sampled, and you will be able to make more accurate judgments. This illustrates the effect of sample size on the probability of making a correct decision.

The reason for this effect can be seen by examining the equation for the standard error of the mean. The standard error of the mean is the standard deviation of the distribution of sample means:

$$\sigma_{\bar{X}} = \frac{\sigma}{\sqrt{N}}$$

With a sample size of 4:

$$\sigma_{\bar{X}} = \frac{16}{\sqrt{4}} = \frac{16}{2} = 8$$

When the sample size is 400, the standard error of the mean is one-tenth as large:

$$\sigma_{\bar{X}} = \frac{16}{\sqrt{400}} = \frac{16}{20} = 0.8$$

The smaller standard error of the mean means that there is less variability in the means of your sample and so they tend to fall nearer the mean of the population. Thus, you are able to guess correctly which population you are sampling from more often.

statistical power
the probability of rejecting the null hypothesis when it is, in fact, false

This is an illustration of the concept of **statistical power.** Power is the probability of rejecting the null hypothesis when it is false, or the probability of deciding that you have an experimental effect when in fact you do. This probability is 1 minus the probability of a Type II error:

$$\text{power} = 1 - p(\text{Type II error})$$

In the IQ example, the probability of guessing 101 when it is in fact 101 is the power of your test. Power increases as sample size increases. The theoretical power of your decision is .52 when the sample size is 4, but it increases to .73 when the sample size is 400. (These numbers assume that you guessed that the sample came from the population with a mean of 101 whenever the mean of the sample was 100.5 or greater.)

The computer will print out your obtained power. Your actual power will differ from the theoretical power because the data are empirical data subject to chance factors. If your empirical data differ markedly from the theoretical values, you may want to repeat the exercise.

REQUIRED:
   a. What was your observed power when the sample size was 4? When it was 400?
   b. What else does power depend on?

A.2   SCATTERPLOTS

Professor Cora Late teaches psychological statistics to undergraduates at a large university. She believes that performance on statistics examinations is related to competence in algebra. She designs a study to test the hypothesis that students who are more proficient in algebra will do better in statistics. At the beginning of the term, she administers a 15-item algebra pretest to the population of undergraduates enrolled in her introductory statistics course. At the end of the term, she administers a 20-item comprehensive statistics examination to these same students.

REQUIRED:
   a. *Option A:* Use the first 20 subjects from the population data set in Appendix C. Column F contains the subjects' algebra scores, and column G contains the subjects' statistics examination scores. List the paired values of algebra and statistics exam scores for each of the 20 subjects.
   Option B: Using the procedures outlined in Chapter 8, draw a random sample of 20 subjects from the population data set in Appendix C. Column F contains the subjects' algebra scores, and column G contains the subjects' statistics exam scores. List the paired values of algebra and statistics exam scores for each of the 20 subjects.
   b. Construct a scatterplot of the paired values of algebra and statistics exam scores for each of the 20 subjects.
   c. Is Professor Late justified in her belief? Explain.

OPTIONAL:
   d. Calculate the Pearson correlation coefficient, *r,* for the obtained sample of paired raw scores.

e. Interpret the sign and size of r in terms of the scatterplot.
f. Determine the equation of the regression line for predicting statistics performance from algebra scores.
g. Plot the regression line determined in (f) on the scatterplot constructed
   in (b).
h. What statistics score would you predict for a student with an algebra
   score of 8?

A.3   IDENTIFY DIRECTIONAL AND NONDIRECTIONAL HYPOTHESES

A. $H_0: \mu_1 = \mu_2$ D. $H_1: \mu_1 \neq \mu_2$

B. $H_0: \mu_1 \leq \mu_2$ E. $H_1: \mu_1 < \mu_2$

C. $H_0: \mu_1 \geq \mu_2$ F. $H_1: \mu_1 > \mu_2$

For each of the following statements, identify the correct null hypothesis (A, B, or C) and
the correct alternative hypothesis (D, E, or F).

a. Introductory algebra students who are taught with hand-held calculators
   (Group 1) for a 15-week period will have different scores on tests of computational skills (taken without the use of a calculator) from introductory algebra students who are taught without calculators (Group 2).
b. New graduate male nurses whose orientation program utilizes a preceptor as
   a major component (Group 1) will exhibit higher performance levels than new
   graduate male nurses in a traditional orientation program (Group 2).
c. Kindergarten students who have a volunteer parent pool assisting their teachers (Group 1) in the classroom will show different achievement from kindergarten students whose teachers do not have extra assistance in the classroom
   (Group 2).
d. Students who receive key images, or pictures, with new vocabulary words
   (Group 1) will show greater acquisition and retention of the definition of
   words than will students who are left to their own strategies for learning new
   words (Group 2).

A.4   INTERPRET AN ANOVA SUMMARY TABLE

REQUIRED:

a. Complete the missing information in Table A.8.
b. Is this a one-way or a two-way ANOVA?
c. Was this a within-subjects or a between-subjects design?
d. How many levels of A were there?
e. How many subjects were in the experiment?
f. How many subjects were in each group?
g. Was the effect of A significant? If so, at what level?

TABLE A.8

Source	SS	df	MS	F	p
Between A	⬭	⬭	⬭	⬭	<.05
Within groups	1230	50	⬭		
Total	5166	54			

A.5 INTERPRET AN ANOVA SUMMARY TABLE

REQUIRED:

    a. Complete the missing information in Table A.9.
    b. Is this a one-way or a two-way ANOVA?
    c. Was this a within-subjects or a between-subjects design?
    d. How many levels of A were there?
    e. How many levels of B were there?
    f. How many subjects were in this experiment?
    g. How many subjects were in each group?
    h. Was the effect of B significant? If so, at what level?
    i. Was the interaction significant? If so, at what level?

TABLE A.9

Source	SS	df	MS	F	p
Between A	160	1	160	⬭	<.01
Between B	160	2	⬭	5	<.05
A × B	⬭	2	12	.75	n.s.[a]
Within groups	384	24	16		
Total	728	⬭			

[a]Not significant.

A.6 INTERPRET AN ANOVA SUMMARY TABLE

REQUIRED:

    a. Complete the missing information in Table A.10.
    b. Is this a one-way or a two-way ANOVA?
    c. Was this a within-subjects or a between-subjects experiment?
    d. How many levels of A were there?
    e. How many subjects were in the experiment?
    f. Was the F test significant?

TABLE A.10

SOURCE	SS	df	MS	F	p
Between subjects	162	9	◯		
Between A	456	2	228	◯	<.01
Residual	◯	◯	3		
Total	672	29			

A.7 INTERPRET AN ANOVA SUMMARY TABLE

REQUIRED:

    a. Based on Table A.11, how many subjects were there?
    b. How many independent variables were there?
    c. How many groups were there?
    d. Did each subject experience all conditions?
    e. Is this a one-way or a two-way ANOVA?
    f. Show where the value of F came from.
    g. Were the results significant at the .05 level?

TABLE A.11

SOURCE	SS	df	MS	F	p
Between conditions	504	3	168	24	<.025
Within conditions	251	36	7		
Total	755	39			

Appendix B

RANDOM-NUMBER TABLE

RANDOM-NUMBER TABLE

```
9 9 0 4 8 2 9 1 6 0 6 6 3 5 3 3 3 1 9 5 8 0 2 0 8 4
5 5 5 7 0 4 8 5 9 2 8 1 9 4 3 4 2 1 7 3 6 6 6 2 4 1
5 2 3 4 1 8 5 6 2 3 9 3 4 2 1 3 9 7 9 9 5 8 9 6 1
2 1 2 8 8 1 2 9 4 5 9 2 6 6 6 1 6 2 9 7 9 0 8 5 7 3
0 4 7 1 4 3 8 7 0 7 5 8 3 4 0 8 0 5 1 6 2 5 7 0 2 0
5 4 8 8 0 4 1 8 1 0 7 2 3 9 2 9 7 2 5 2 1 0 7 7 3 7
6 9 1 2 3 0 3 6 6 1 6 7 6 0 3 5 0 4 5 3 8 2 6 5 1 6
5 8 8 7 4 2 2 7 5 6 3 6 5 8 8 8 3 9 6 9 7 0 8 2 1 8
7 6 7 8 8 2 8 8 4 3 8 2 7 3 7 8 2 8 4 1 7 3 0 7 1 5
5 5 8 9 9 8 1 0 0 4 1 2 9 8 7 5 8 7 5 1 6 4 1 3 3 7
0 0 3 7 3 5 0 2 3 1 7 1 0 2 0 3 5 2 6 3 5 1 6 1 2 6
8 0 9 2 4 8 2 3 0 6 0 0 4 3 0 2 3 3 3 2 9 8 6 4 7 0
9 2 5 5 3 0 2 5 8 3 1 5 7 6 0 0 4 8 0 9 4 4 5 1 2 9
0 0 8 3 8 6 0 5 7 9 3 9 6 3 6 6 6 9 3 3 0 7 4 9 2 2
0 3 0 2 6 2 5 0 8 4 9 7 7 0 6 6 8 7 6 2 6 9 3 3 3 8
9 2 2 1 2 3 3 3 6 1 6 0 8 0 0 9 7 0 2 7 5 7 3 6 2 8
6 2 3 8 3 5 3 1 7 4 3 4 9 6 1 5 2 2 1 2 0 4 9 1 5 3
6 4 3 3 1 8 8 3 0 5 9 9 0 3 9 6 7 7 2 9 3 2 4 8 8 7
2 3 4 7 5 9 2 8 4 0 1 8 1 2 6 6 5 3 9 3 9 7 8 3 9 4
0 7 3 5 0 7 4 8 9 4 3 2 6 1 1 1 9 5 7 8 5 2 7 1 8 7
8 6 8 4 5 6 9 8 0 4 1 3 9 6 2 0 9 3 1 4 9 2 3 5 4 9
9 5 1 8 3 3 5 1 1 0 5 8 8 0 3 3 4 7 2 8 2 0 5 1 9 0
4 5 2 6 4 5 1 7 2 8 3 6 1 3 8 5 3 5 5 0 5 1 1 0 1 0
5 1 9 3 3 9 1 5 2 3 7 5 4 0 4 4 6 4 6 9 3 8 7 1 9 5
4 8 5 4 8 6 0 0 3 0 7 3 5 6 3 3 3 9 0 4 3 0 0 3 1 9
8 3 0 0 6 2 2 2 9 1 1 0 4 3 6 1 2 3 1 1 1 2 3 4 3 1
6 2 2 0 6 3 7 0 8 6 4 6 9 3 6 2 4 5 5 7 0 4 2 2 5 6
4 8 6 0 5 3 6 2 9 1 0 8 2 1 7 4 2 5 4 9 8 8 3 6 2 9
3 9 0 1 2 4 1 7 4 6 9 2 9 5 1 2 6 5 6 8 2 6 7 5 9 0
9 2 2 7 1 4 7 5 9 1 8 9 9 5 6 2 7 8 1 5 5 1 1 2 1 2
7 7 7 3 3 5 2 4 8 2 1 0 3 0 0 4 8 5 5 9 2 6 4 4 7 6
8 3 8 8 2 4 0 2 0 5 7 3 8 7 5 5 9 3 9 5 7 1 6 7 9 6
4 7 1 1 1 2 9 6 7 3 0 7 4 4 3 8 1 3 1 1 9 0 4 0 7 7
4 5 9 8 6 1 1 5 1 1 1 7 4 6 7 4 7 2 4 7 5 8 6 3 4 9
5 1 2 7 7 6 1 6 2 2 6 2 4 8 7 5 0 5 3 9 9 3 8 0 8 6
2 2 2 4 9 2 8 3 3 0 8 1 4 6 0 4 6 6 2 6 2 5 4 1 2 2
3 7 5 2 9 4 4 6 9 3 0 2 4 8 3 8 3 1 3 7 8 7 5 8 8 7
9 3 8 8 1 2 0 6 1 2 3 6 8 7 7 1 9 0 9 2 1 4 0 5 3 0
1 6 8 5 9 1 0 9 9 0 5 5 0 8 8 9 5 5 1 2 7 6 8 8 6 9
5 8 0 3 6 7 6 5 6 4 8 7 9 6 0 1 4 8 3 3 9 6 1 7 2 7
9 7 2 6 2 2 1 4 4 3 4 0 7 7 4 2 4 3 8 5 8 6 5 7 0 0
8 5 5 3 8 9 4 4 2 8 3 5 8 0 1 4 1 9 9 7 2 4 7 0 0 7
7 9 6 9 1 7 6 6 4 0 7 4 1 5 1 4 2 3 4 3 3 5 9 7 9 9
7 9 8 5 7 4 3 3 4 1 5 5 7 1 3 1 7 9 2 9 3 6 7 9 7 8
9 6 1 6 0 6 7 1 8 8 4 9 2 3 8 8 5 2 3 2 6 9 6 0 5 6
9 6 1 9 4 2 9 6 0 5 9 4 9 8 6 8 1 1 8 3 5 8 9 6 8 1
0 0 1 5 2 4 3 4 0 4 4 2 4 3 9 8 1 6 2 6 2 5 3 4 7 6
4 8 8 8 4 9 9 6 1 8 4 3 8 3 0 1 3 4 5 7 0 6 1 6 3 2
8 6 2 8 4 7 1 3 3 6 5 7 9 3 3 8 9 2 7 5 6 3 0 6 1 6
7 0 5 8 0 2 3 2 0 5 5 0 5 0 3 9 1 7 5 4 5 1 9 9 1 0
```

Note. The Instructor's Manual lists a computer program that will generate more tables of random numbers.

Appendix C

POPULATION DATA SET

This table represents a population of 64 individuals, identified in the column labeled ID by the numbers 1 through 64. Of these individuals, 29 are male and 35 are female, as indicated by M or F in the second column.

Columns A through G give values of seven different variables for these individuals. The data approximate a normal distribution and have a known mean and standard deviation. Data in columns F and G are correlated.

This data set is intended to be useful for exercises in random sampling, tabulating and plotting results of hypothetical experiments, performing statistical analyses, and interpreting data. Several exercises in various chapters refer to these data. Other exercises could readily be developed.

The means and standard deviations of the various columns and the correlation between columns F and G are given in the Instructor's Manual.

ID	Sex	A	B	C	D	E	F	G	ID	Sex	A	B	C	D	E	F	G
1	F	1	6	11	5	8	11	11	36	F	6	5	8	7	10	14	13
2	F	4	3	8	8	10	12	12	37	F	4	7	9	11	9	12	12
3	F	2	4	6	7	9	8	9	38	M	4	5	10	9	12	14	13
4	M	3	6	7	8	9	10	11	39	F	3	6	8	6	11	11	9
5	M	6	8	10	10	13	16	16	40	M	5	5	8	8	11	13	10
6	F	3	7	9	9	10	12	11	41	M	2	6	7	7	8	15	12
7	F	5	6	7	7	11	14	12	42	F	3	7	9	8	9	12	11
8	M	5	6	8	10	11	8	8	43	M	3	7	7	9	11	10	11
9	F	4	5	8	8	10	9	9	44	F	6	5	8	6	11	14	12
10	F	3	8	7	8	12	10	12	45	M	5	6	10	7	10	12	12
11	M	5	4	9	9	10	14	14	46	M	4	6	8	8	9	8	12
12	F	3	7	5	9	11	12	12	47	M	5	4	9	10	7	14	15
13	F	3	7	8	8	9	11	11	48	M	6	5	8	8	12	14	14
14	M	5	8	7	10	10	12	15	49	F	4	7	7	9	11	11	13
15	M	4	6	8	7	8	12	13	50	F	5	6	9	9	9	14	14
16	M	4	5	7	8	11	11	12	51	F	4	7	10	7	9	14	12
17	F	3	8	9	9	12	13	15	52	M	3	5	8	9	10	11	12
18	M	5	5	6	6	10	15	15	53	F	2	8	9	10	10	11	12
19	M	4	6	8	8	10	9	10	54	M	4	6	7	8	11	11	12
20	M	2	7	7	7	11	9	9	55	M	4	7	8	7	9	12	11
21	M	5	6	7	7	11	12	12	56	M	5	5	9	9	10	14	14
22	F	3	5	8	9	10	11	12	57	M	6	6	9	9	12	11	11
23	M	5	4	10	8	10	15	13	58	F	4	8	6	7	10	10	11
24	F	4	7	9	9	9	13	13	59	M	3	6	9	10	10	12	11
25	F	5	6	7	7	9	12	12	60	F	6	4	8	8	9	14	14
26	F	3	7	6	7	10	12	12	61	F	2	5	9	9	11	11	11
27	F	4	5	8	8	8	12	12	62	F	4	7	7	8	10	11	12
28	M	4	6	7	9	9	11	13	63	F	4	9	8	7	12	12	11
29	M	5	5	8	7	11	13	12	64	F	7	6	6	8	8	13	15
30	F	3	7	9	6	10	12	9									
31	M	2	6	6	6	9	13	15									
32	F	4	4	10	8	8	12	12									
33	F	5	7	7	6	10	12	11									
34	F	4	5	9	8	9	13	12									
35	F	3	6	8	8	11	12	6									

Appendix D

SUGGESTED ANSWERS TO "READING BETWEEN THE LINES"

1.1 GUNS DON'T KILL PEOPLE; PEOPLE KILL PEOPLE

The gun lobby assumes that people have free will and that they choose to kill. It follows from this that people who kill are different from ordinary people who would use a gun only in self-defense. The antigun lobby argues that the presence of a gun is a stimulus to use the gun. The two sides make different assumptions about the importance of determinism versus free will. One slogan might be: Guns turn people into killers. The gun control lobby's slogan, Guns don't die; people do, is less to the point but may be a better slogan because of its emotional appeal.

1.2 IS PRAYER EFFECTIVE?

Galton assumed that these groups would have the same longevity but for the effect of prayer. It is likely that being royalty is more stressful than being a scientist or a member of the gentry. Other factors could be hereditary weaknesses caused by inbreeding or simply the fact that royalty tend to be related to one another and therefore are not a random sample of the population. Ways of knowing used by Galton include logic and the scientific method.

2.1 IMAGINE THAT ESP DOES OCCUR

ESP challenges several basic limiting assumptions of science: that effects cannot precede causes, that we know the world only through the senses, and that mere thought cannot influence the world except via our bodies. If ESP did exist, most of human society as we know it would be impossible! There would be few secrets, and the daily lottery would be bankrupt. All banks would fail because their safes would be cracked by psychic means, and the stock market would cease to function. Most of these effects would occur even if only a few people had ESP and if it worked only part of the time. In addition, the various state lotteries that are conducted every day would not show the constant conformity to the laws of probability that they do. ESP violates the assumption of causality: If we can foretell the future, then effects (our knowledge) precede their cause (the events fore-told). ESP also violates the scientific goal of looking for regularities and laws: Most ESP experiments are aimed at finding an irregularity—something that cannot be explained by science.

2.2 REINCARNATION

The claim of reincarnation is virtually impossible to test, which seems to make it all the more appealing to some people. It is not hard to come up with alternative hypotheses, however. Hypnosis causes an increase in the ability to imagine scenes and events. Psychologists know that it is difficult to distinguish imagined events from real ones. The recall of past lives under hypnosis is just one example of the ability to imagine fictitious events. An interesting exercise is to relax and recall various scenes from your past, going back as far as you can. Then, imagine yourself 10 or 20 years from now. Most people can imagine the future about as vividly as they can recall the past. If you have little difficulty imagining what has not yet happened, what does that say about the ability to "recall" a past life? Although people may claim to be able to recall historical facts or to speak foreign languages that they could not have known in their present life, research shows that they are actually using bits of information they have learned by ordinary means in their present life which they remember by means of hypnosis.

3.1 TESTING FOR INDEPENDENCE OF DIMENSIONS

When the light flickered at a higher rate, more light was presented per unit time than when it flickered slowly. If each individual flicker of the light could not be detected by the rat, the light would appear as a steady light whose brightness would depend on the average intensity of the light per unit time. Therefore the fast flicker would appear brighter to the rats and the dimensions of flicker rate and intensity would not be independent after all, but confounded. There is evidence that 10 flashes per second would in fact appear as a steady light to a rat.

4.1 "YOU CAN PROVE ANYTHING WITH STATISTICS"

The y-axis is not labeled! The origin of the graph is actually $2,150 and the top of the graph is $2,400. Draw a rough sketch of what the graph would look like with an origin of $0 to see how much of a difference there was between the two proposals.

5.1 DO YOUNGER INFANTS PREFER SIMPLER PATTERNS?

Because all of the cards were the same size, the less complex cards had the largest squares. In other words, size of square was perfectly confounded with complexity. Miranda and Fantz (1971, in Fantz, Fagan, & Miranda, 1975) repeated the study but varied the number of squares independently of the size of the squares. They presented infants with cards that had 2, 8, or 32 black squares. The size of the squares was varied such that three of the cards had the same total amount of black area. These three cards constituted the replication of the earlier study. In addition, other cards were made in which size and number varied independently. The patterns used are shown in Figure D.1.

Considering only the three cards that were similar to the previous study, Miranda and Fantz found the same results as Brennan and Moore: There was a tendency for infants to prefer the simpler patterns when the size of the square was confounded with number. However, there was also a strong trend for the infants to prefer both larger squares, when number was held constant, and more numerous squares, when size was held constant. Therefore, if number is taken as a measure of complexity, even newborn infants prefer greater complexity to less. The previous experiments had pitted two strong tendencies against one another: preference for greater size and preference for greater complexity. In

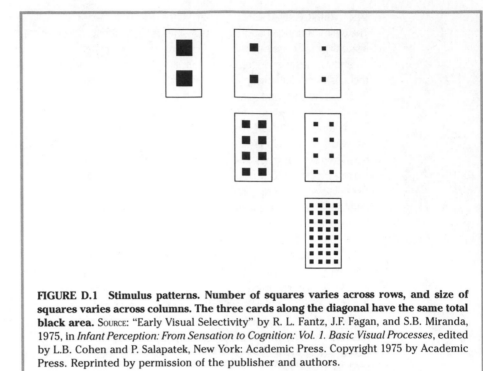

FIGURE D.1 Stimulus patterns. Number of squares varies across rows, and size of squares varies across columns. The three cards along the diagonal have the same total black area. SOURCE: "Early Visual Selectivity" by R. L. Fantz, J.F. Fagan, and S.B. Miranda, 1975, in *Infant Perception: From Sensation to Cognition: Vol. 1. Basic Visual Processes*, edited by L.B. Cohen and P. Salapatek, New York: Academic Press. Copyright 1975 by Academic Press. Reprinted by permission of the publisher and authors.

that situation the preference for size had won out. In another study, Fantz et al. found that older babies tended to be less controlled by pattern size and more by complexity alone, which would explain the apparent developmental trend toward greater complexity found by the previous investigators.

5.2 DO WOMEN FEAR SUCCESS MORE THAN MEN DO?

The subjects of the stories were in a situation that is highly sex stereotyped in our society: Most medical students are males. Women who show "fear of success" in this study may actually be showing fear of succeeding in a man's world. Imagine what might happen if the story were about a male nursing student who found himself the most popular member of his class (Tresemer, 1977).

When Horner's study was replicated using another profession, the results were reversed. Wood and Greenfield (cited in Tresemer, 1977) had male and female executives respond to the following verbal cue: "When Janet (Jeff) graduated from college, she (he) went on to get a graduate degree in business. Early in the spring quarter, she (he) is first in her (his) class to be offered a top management job" (p. 115). Of the men, 40% showed fear of success in their stories, compared with 30% of the women. It is possible that business executives see their jobs as less sex stereotyped than medical students see their profession. Or it may be that attitudes toward women having careers had changed in the eight years between the two studies. Or the difference may result from the fact that the earlier study used students and the later study used adults working in the profession. These examples are good case studies of the use of alternative hypotheses in interpreting data. See Tresemer (1977) for an excellent discussion.

6.1 BRAIN DAMAGE SOMETIMES PRODUCES OBESITY IN RATS
The successful investigators were using female rats, and the others were using males. Female rats consistently showed obesity after the lesions, whereas males showed it to a lesser degree (Valenstein, Cox, & Kakolewski, 1969).

6.2 COGNITIVE AND AROUSAL FACTORS IN EMOTION
The experiment had never been replicated until Christina Maslach (1979) and Gary Marshall and Philip Zimbardo (1979) published the results of their work. Maslach replicated the study but used posthypnotic suggestion to induce the state of arousal. Otherwise, the experiment was similar to the original. We may consider her experiment to be a systematic, rather than an exact, replication. Marshall and Zimbardo were prevented by their institution's human subjects committee from inducing the state of anger in their subjects, so their replication was a partial one. They produced the arousal using the original drug but induced only euphoria. Their control conditions were a placebo injection and a neutral confederate.

Neither experiment found evidence in favor of Schachter and Singer's hypothesis. Equally important, though, both papers assert that the data of the original experiment did not support Schachter and Singer's own hypothesis or conclusions. They claim that the original paper made inappropriate comparisons and drew conclusions on the basis of marginal effects. In rebuttal, Schachter and Singer (1979) point to differences in procedure between the original experiment and the replications and to other experiments that they consider similar enough to constitute replications. The dust probably will not settle for some time, but we can note how long it may take for an influential experiment to be replicated and how difficult it may be to decide when an experiment is similar enough to constitute a replication.

7.1 AGGRESSION AND XYY MALES
Stephan Chorover (1979) points out several problems with the study. First, the mothers were not told that the chromosome test was part of an experiment or that it was funded by an agency concerned with crime and delinquency. The experimenters implied that the chromosome test was part of the hospital's routine practice and that it was a service to the family. Second, the parents were told of their child's condition, which probably would have an effect on how they treated the child. They might consider that he had "bad seed" and was doomed to a life of crime, thus creating a self-fulfilling prophecy. Or, they might have been overly concerned with controlling his aggressive tendencies. The study was actually one on the effects of having the XYY condition *and* having the parents know that the child had the condition. A more adequate design would have included a group that was told that their child had the condition when the child did not. That design, of course, would introduce new ethical problems.

8.1 ORCHESTRA CONDUCTORS LIVE LONGER
People do not usually become conductors of major orchestras until they are middle-aged. So, in order to become a conductor it is necessary, but not sufficient, to live to middle age.

456   Appendix D

Therefore, it is not proper to compare the longevity of conductors with the standard mortality tables, which give the life expectancy of newborns. The proper comparison would be against the life expectancy of other middle-aged persons, which would be considerably greater than that of newborns. Another factor to consider is that in order to become a conductor, one must do more than live to middle age. One must be healthy and have enough vigor to achieve distinction in music. These factors would also predict longer-than-average life expectancy.

9.1   SUBLIMINAL SEDUCTION

A reader of that issue of *Playboy* would have seen many other pictures of naked women but few, if any, other wreaths. Therefore, the wreath would be a more distinctive stimulus than would one more naked woman. Without clothes, there are not many features that would distinguish one *Playboy* model from another. Certainly a blonde would not be unusual. The explanation in terms of subliminal perception of the fancied appearance of the wreath seems gratuitous in view of this explanation. Significantly, no reference to a scientific journal is given in which one might examine the evidence more closely. This case is typical of the rest of the evidence for subliminal perception cited in the book.

10.1 THIRST IN BRAIN-DAMAGED RATS

Coburn and Stricker proposed that the brain-damaged rats failed to respond to the intraperitoneal injections because these injections caused more stress than the other means of changing salt balance. There is evidence that rats with damage to this area of the brain are unable to react well to stress. In other words, these animals may have been too sick to drink. The other means of inducing changes in salt balance were not as stressful, and therefore the brain-damaged rats were able to respond normally. One consequence of this interpretation is that the lateral preoptic area may not be involved in the regulation of drinking in response to salt balance after all.

11.1 ELECTRICAL INHIBITION OF AGGRESSION IN A CHARGING BULL

Notice that the bull turned to one side when he stopped. The caudate nucleus is involved in the control of motor movements. The bull likely stopped because the involuntary movement to one side caused by the stimulation interfered with his charge. He may have been just as aggressively motivated as before but unable to carry out his intentions (Valenstein, 1973).

11.2 CLEVER HANS

Hans was picking up subtle cues from his questioners. Oskar Pfungst, a psychologist, found that Hans gave the correct answer only when the questioner knew the correct answer. Pfungst had one person think up a number and whisper it in Hans's ear. A second person did the same and asked Hans to add them up. Hans was at a complete loss in this situation. It was also necessary for Hans to be able to see the questioner. When blinders were placed on him, he struggled to view the questioner.

Pfungst knew by then that Hans relied on visual cues from the questioner, but what were they? Pfungst eventually noticed that all of the questioners made an extremely slight inclination of the head when a question was posed. This head movement caused Hans to start tapping. When Hans had made the correct number of taps, the questioner raised his head and Hans stopped tapping. Pfungst was able to cause Hans to start and stop tapping by merely moving his head without saying a word to Hans. So Hans was just an ordinary horse that had been well trained to respond to subtle visual cues.

Clever Hans was no isolated phenomenon. In addition to the potential for circus acts that such animals have, scientific interest has been created over whether chimpanzees are able to use sign language to communicate with people. Terrace (1979) concluded on the basis of his experiments that previous research that seemed to show that chimpanzees could communicate in this way was subject to the Clever Hans effect. Terrace's conclusions are controversial, but they show how difficult ruling out such subtle biases in research may be.

12.1 ULCERS IN EXECUTIVE MONKEYS

Because the animals were not randomly assigned to the executive position, it is possible that those that learned faster were predisposed to ulcers (Weiss, 1968, 1971). When Weiss replicated the study using the proper controls, he found that the executive animals developed *fewer* ulcers than the control animals. We should note that Weiss used rats instead of monkeys, so a possible species difference may exist. Nevertheless, the executive monkey study has joined the ranks of nonreplicable studies in the view of many researchers.

12.2 MEMORY FOR WORDS

It is not possible to assign words randomly to conditions in an experiment on memory. Some words are nouns, some are common, some are short, and so forth. Therefore, it is necessary to select words that meet particular criteria. Thus experiments on verbal memory are quasi experiments, according to our terminology. In any quasi experiment it is possible that another variable is confounded with the variable on which you are selecting. In this case, McCloskey eventually realized that the highly related words tended to be more familiar to the subjects as well: Robins and oaks are more familiar than penguins and mahoganies. McCloskey (1980) repeated his earlier study, this time measuring the familiarity of the words. He found that familiarity caused a large part of the effect he had previously found and had attributed to similarity. He was able to show, however, that similarity also played a role in the results, when familiarity was controlled.

13.1 THE AUTHORITARIAN PERSONALITY

Families with high levels of status concern and repressive disciplinary procedures tend to come from the lower social classes. They are less educated and more conservative. These values are passed along to their children through principles of social learning. Thus, the children learn to be prejudiced and discriminatory from their parents via such mechanisms as instrumental conditioning and modeling. This explanation is thought by many investigators to be more parsimonious than that of Adorno et al. Adorno et al. studied working-class people who generally have stricter child-rearing practices than the middle-class researchers. Racism is also a common attitude among working-class persons. Some researchers have suggested that the reason a correlation was found between authoritarianism and child-rearing practices was that the researchers had used a particular population in which these characteristics were common. According to this interpretation, authoritarianism is not a personality trait but a cultural norm.

13.2 LIFE EVENTS AND ILLNESS

The measurement of life events in retrospective research takes place, by definition, after the person has suffered the illness. Therefore it is impossible to measure the number of life events before the illness strikes. Having the illness is likely to influence the recall and interpretation of life events (Brown & Harris, 1978). People who are sad are known to recall more sad events from the past than are people who are not sad. In addition, people seek to find consistency among the events that happen to them. They are likely to reinterpret past events so as to provide some explanation of their illness. For example, one study found that mothers of Down's syndrome children recalled more emotional shocks during pregnancy than did mothers of normal children. The fact that the syndrome is caused by a chromosomal abnormality, however, makes it impossible that emotional stress during pregnancy could be the cause. The mothers must have searched their memories for stressful events that might explain the abnormal offspring.

14.1 THE CAUSES OF CHILD ABUSE

Pelton suggests that the idea that child abuse is unrelated to social class is politically convenient, both to mental health professionals and to politicians. The mental health professionals would like to see the problem of child abuse as part of their turf so they could benefit from funding available for the study and cure of child abuse. If child abuse is caused by poverty instead, the mental health profession receives no benefit. Politicians, for their part, may prefer to see child abuse as psychologically caused because that view permits them to seek a technological solution instead of resolving the more difficult causes of poverty.

15.1 THE LIBERATED FEMALE RAT

Most of the researchers were males who let their biases toward human females determine how they looked at the behavior of rats. Notice that McClintock is a woman. In the female rat, conception can occur only when the uterus is prepared by hormones that are triggered by sexual activity. Therefore the sexual behavior must be properly timed in order for a successful mating to occur. For this reason the female rat logically should be in control of the timing of sexual activity.

Appendix E

FUNCTIONS

We stated in Chapter 2 that one of the goals of science is to discover laws that describe regularities in behavior. Whenever we have a regularity of behavior, we have a functional relationship between two or more entities. We can say that one thing is related to another. This might be as simple as saying that amount learned is related to time spent studying. In general, when we say that there is a relationship between two entities, it is equivalent to saying that there is a mathematical *function* between the entities. For this reason, scientists in general, and psychologists in particular, strive to describe their results in terms of mathematical functions. These functions are more precise statements than simply putting the relationship in words. The mathematical function will say exactly in what way amount learned depends on time spent studying.

Although *straight-line,* or *linear,* functions are very common, many other functions are not straight lines. Suppose we say that a sociopath is a person who lacks a conscience. This statement can be put into a functional relationship,

$$y = 0 \text{ if } x \le 0$$
$$1 \text{ if } x > 0$$

where x represents amount of conscience, $y = 0$ indicates a sociopath, and $y = 1$ indicates a nonsociopath. This relationship is graphed in Figure E.1.

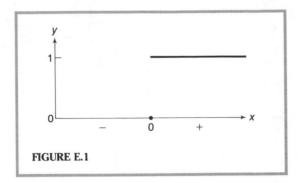

FIGURE E.1

Functions typically have *variables, constants,* and *parameters.* Variables were discussed in considerable detail in Chapter 3. For now, recall that a variable is a quantity that is free to take a number of values. Typically, x and y are used to represent variables.

DEFINITIONS

function
a mathematical
statement of the
relationship
between variables

What exactly is a mathematical function? For our purposes, we can say that a **function** is a relationship such that for every x in a domain there is one and only one value of y. This can be represented as

$$y = f(x)$$

This equation is read "y is a function of x." It simply puts into symbols the idea that there is a functional relationship between y and x.

There are many sorts of functions. One that you are familiar with is the equation for a straight line:

$$y = mx + b$$

In this equation, m is the slope of the line and b is the y intercept. Suppose $m = 2$ and $b = 3$. This equation is graphed in Figure E.2. A familiar straight-line function is the equation for converting temperature in degrees Celsius to degrees Fahrenheit:

$$F = \frac{9}{5}C + 32$$

constant
a quantity that is
fixed, such as pi

A **constant** is a quantity that is fixed. Common constants are π and e. The value of π is always 3.1415+, and e is always 2.7182+. Constants appear in functions such as the equation for the circumference of a circle:

$$c = \pi d$$

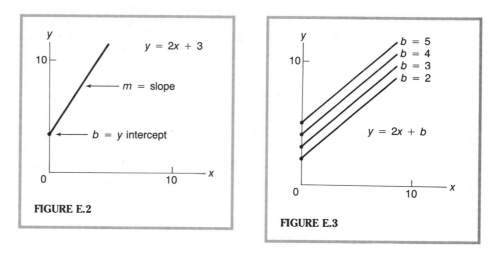

FIGURE E.2

FIGURE E.3

A parameter is less familiar and a little more difficult to define because it has an everyday use that is different from its mathematical meaning. In everyday usage, a parameter is a limit, as in "What are the parameters of this situation?"

As it is used in science, a **parameter** is a quantity that distinguishes among members of a set, such as among members of a family of functions. Consider again the equation

$$y = mx + b$$

parameter
a quantity that distinguishes among members of a set, such as among members of a family of functions

This equation represents all possible straight lines. They differ by their slopes and their y intercepts. The values of m and b determine which straight line we are talking about. Thus, m and b distinguish among members of the set of all possible straight lines; m and b are therefore parameters.

Notice that for a given straight line, m and b are not free to vary. When we write the equation

$$y = 2x + 3$$

we have determined a particular straight line; m and b cannot change without changing the line. But they are not constants, either. We can change b from 3 to, say, 4. This would define a new line with the same slope as before, but with a different intercept. Figure E.3 shows a set of functions described by the equation

$$y = 2x + b$$

The value of b varies from function to function, but it does not vary for a given function. For this reason a parameter is different from a variable, which takes on different values within a given function, and a constant, which never varies at all. It is common to refer to a set of functions like those in Figure E.3 as a *family of functions*. The family is related by the parameter, *b*.

SLOPES OF FUNCTIONS

We will take up the various types of functions in a moment. But first, in order to facilitate our discussion, we will talk about the slope of a line. Figure E.4 shows the simplest kind of function, a linear or straight-line function. We can find the slope of this linear function by taking any convenient segment of the line and determining the ratio of the change in *y* to the change in *x* for that segment. This can be expressed as follows:

$$\text{slope} = \Delta y / \Delta x$$

which is read "The slope equals the change in *y* divided by the change in *x*." The Greek letter *delta* (Δ) is used as a symbol for change. A horizontal line has a slope of zero because the change in *y* is zero. A 45° line has a slope of 1 because the change in *y* equals the change in *x*. The slope of a line may also be negative.

   Talking about the slope of a curved line is more complicated. It would be misleading to talk about the slope of the entire curve in Figure E.5, because the line is not straight. We can obtain the slope of the line at a given point, however, by drawing a straight line that is tangent to the curve at that point. Thus, we can see that the slope is shallower at Point A than it is at Point B. When the slope of a line is not constant—that is, when the line is curved—we say the curve accelerates. If the slope increases, as this one does, we say that it is is positively accelerated. Positive acceleration can be thought of as speeding up; negative acceleration is slowing down. Now we are ready to look at the various kinds of functions encountered in psychology.

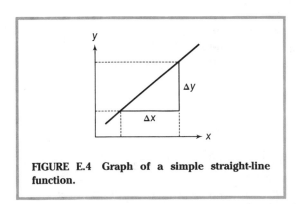

FIGURE E.4 Graph of a simple straight-line function.

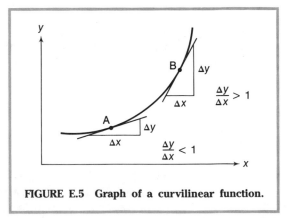

FIGURE E.5 Graph of a curvilinear function.

TYPES OF FUNCTIONS

Figure E.6 shows some common functions. Line A is a linear function such as we have already discussed. Because it has a positive slope, we call it a linearly increasing function.

Line B is curved in such a way that its slope increases as x increases. It is called a positively accelerated, increasing function. Curves like Line B are seen when the response grows more and more rapidly with increases in x. An example is the increase in apparent heaviness of an object with increasing weight. Doubling the weight more than doubles the apparent heaviness of an object.

Line C is a negatively accelerated, increasing function. Although y continues to increase with increases in x, the slope of the line decreases with increases in x. The growth in y becomes slower as x increases. Curves like Line C are common in psychology. For example, doubling the amount of light on a surface causes less than a doubling of the (apparent) brightness of the surface.

Line D is called a *sigmoid curve*. Sigmoid simply means S shaped. The dependent variable, y, starts out low, then increases until it levels off at a high value. In contrast, the *slope* of the line is almost zero at the low end, grows rapidly for a while, then *decreases* to almost zero at high values of x. Sigmoid curves are typical of learning data. During the early part of training, learning is slow, then it becomes rapid, until eventually the subject reaches some upper limit.

Figure E.7 is similar to Figure E.6. In fact, every type of curve shown in one figure is also shown in the other. The only difference is that all curves in Figure E.7 are *decreasing* instead of increasing. We have presented this figure to show that curves can be either increasing or decreasing and at the same time also be either positively or negatively accelerated. For example, Curve B in Figure E.7 is positively accelerated, decreas-

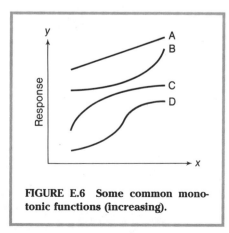

FIGURE E.6 Some common mono-tonic functions (increasing).

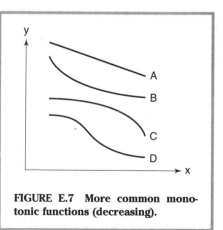

FIGURE E.7 More common mono-tonic functions (decreasing).

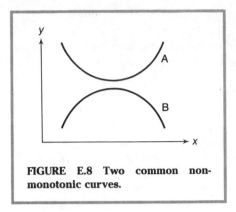

FIGURE E.8 Two common non-monotonic curves.

ing. Curve B in Figure E.6, on the other hand, is positively accelerated, increasing.

All of the curves in Figures E.6 and E.7 have one property in common: They all either increase or decrease over their entire range. They never reverse directions. A curve that never reverses direction is called *monotonic*. All of the curves in Figure E.6 are monotonically increasing curves. All of the curves in Figure E.7 are monotonically decreasing curves.

Figure E.8 shows some nonmonotonic curves. Curve A is a U-shaped curve. It first decreases, then increases with increasing x. In this curve, y might represent the discomfort caused when a room is either too cold or too hot. Curve B, an inverted U-shaped curve, is common in psychology. For example, it can be used to depict the effect of motivation on performance. Performance is optimal in the middle range of motivation but poor if motivation is too low or too high.

Appendix F

TRANSFORMATIONS

A **numerical transformation** is a rule for changing all the numbers in a set of data to other numbers in order to achieve some purpose. The general notation for a transformation is

$$x' = f(x)$$

where

$$x = \text{the original datum or number,}$$
$$x' = \text{the transformed number, and}$$
$$f = \text{the rule by which } x \text{ is transformed to } x'.$$

As an example, let us take the reciprocal transformation. To perform a reciprocal transformation, one takes the reciprocal of each original number. In other words,

$$x' = 1/x$$

In this example, $f(x) = 1/x$.

It is important to realize that there is nothing inherently suspicious in performing a data transformation. Suppose you were studying how rats learn to run down an alley to get food. You could record how long it takes to run the alley. This would be a measure of *duration*. On the other hand, you might be interested in how *fast* they ran down the alley. To obtain a measure of *speed,* you would divide the length of the alley by the time it took them to run it. Speed and duration are reciprocally related; that is, speed is a reciprocal transformation of duration:

$$\text{speed} = \text{distance/duration}$$

It is perfectly proper to look at the data either in terms of speed or duration. Which one you will choose will depend on considerations that we will take up shortly. But the point is that one measure is not more "real" or "natural" than the other. The data from an experiment do not come with a label saying "Handle these data only in their original form. Keep frozen. If transformed, do not re-transform."

TRANSFORMATIONS FOR STATISTICAL PURPOSES

Many statistical tests[1] make two assumptions about the way the data are distributed that must be satisfied in order for the test to be valid. The assumptions are (1) that the data are normally distributed and (2) that the variability of the data is the same for all conditions. These assumptions are often not justified for empirical data.

Consider Figure F.1, which shows hypothetical data from an experiment with three conditions. The data, which are displayed as box-and-whisker plots, are markedly skewed to the right (to the higher end). In addition, the variability of the data is different for each group. Thus, the data violate both assumptions underlying parametric statistics. Not to worry. We can perform a logarithmic transformation that will produce both a normal distribution and equal variance in all conditions. The result of transforming the data to logarithms can be seen in Figure F.2.

Figure F.2 shows the same data as Figure F.1, but the scale on the ordinate is the logarithm of the numbers, instead of the numbers themselves. (Next to the logarithms of the response there is another scale showing the response itself, but on the same logarithmic scale.) We can easily see that all the distributions are now symmetrical and have equal variance. The logarithmic transformation is often performed in order that a set of data will meet the assumptions of parametric statistics.

Whether or not a given set of data should be transformed for statistical purposes is a complex topic. Some statistical tests are "robust"; that is, they

---

[1]Those known as parametric statistics, including *t* tests and analysis of variance. Parametric statistics are the most widely used statistical methods. There are nonparametric statistics available that do not make these assumptions, but they are generally less powerful, and are therefore generally used only when the data markedly violate the two assumptions.

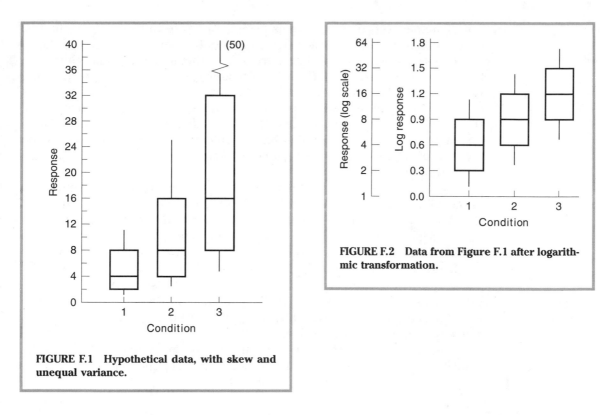

FIGURE F.1 Hypothetical data, with skew and unequal variance.

FIGURE F.2 Data from Figure F.1 after logarithmic transformation.

are not much affected by violations of their assumptions. Further, transformations of data can have consequences for the interpretation of the data (see pages 257–260). See also the discussion of handling data on pages 108–109.

TRANSFORMATIONS FOR THEORETICAL PURPOSES

Data are often transformed to permit tests of a theory. Frequently two theories will make different predictions about a given set of data. Take, for example, the theories of Fechner and Stevens about the way sensation magnitude grows with intensity of the stimulus. Fechner says that sensation magnitude is a logarithmic function of intensity; Stevens says it is a power function. The two theories are summarized in the following equations.

$$\text{Fechner: } S = n(\log I) + a \tag{1}$$
$$\text{Stevens: } S = a(I)^n \tag{2}$$

According to Fechner, then, sensation equals a constant, n, times the logarithm of intensity, plus a constant, a. According to Stevens, sensation equals a constant, a, times intensity raised to a power, n.

For some sets of data, Stevens's predictions are very close to Fechner's, and it is hard to choose which theory makes the better prediction. (This is by no means true of all sets of data; frequently the predictions of Fechner and Stevens will be markedly different.) Consider Figure F.3, which presents the predicted functions of Stevens and Fechner for how the (apparent) brightness of a light will increase with the physical intensity (measured, say, in watts) of the light. As you can see, the two theoretical functions are very similar in appearance. You can understand that it would be difficult to choose between Stevens and Fechner based on a given set of empirical data, particularly when they show some random error.

It happens to be the case that certain data transformations permit many nonlinear functions to be written in the form of a linear equation. And it is also the case that it is much easier to see whether a set of data fit that linear equation than whether they fit a curvilinear one. For these reasons, data transformations play a key role in choosing between different theoretical predictions. The basic strategy is to transform the data in ways predicted by the various theories to see which transformation results in a straight-line relationship between the variables. For example, the data in Figure F.3 can be transformed according to the different predictions of Stevens and Fechner, to see which best fit a straight line.

Fechner predicts that sensation magnitude is a linear function of the *logarithm* of the stimulus intensity. You can see that Equation 1 is in the form

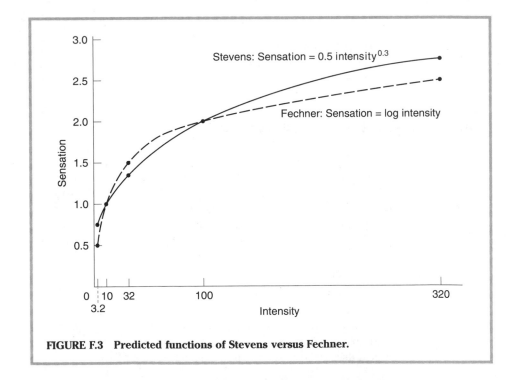

FIGURE F.3   Predicted functions of Stevens versus Fechner.

of a linear equation, where S corresponds to y and $\log I$ corresponds to x. So, in order to test Fechner's prediction we need to transform I to $\log I$. This has been done in Table F.1.

Figure F.4 tests Fechner's prediction by plotting the sensation magnitude against the logarithm of stimulus intensity. We can easily see that although the data fall close to a straight line as Fechner predicts, they deviate *systematically* from a straight line: They describe a concave-upward curve. Let's try Stevens's prediction.

Stevens predicts that the *logarithm* of sensation magnitude is a linear function of the logarithm of the stimulus intensity:

$$\log S = n(\log I) + \log a \tag{3}$$

TABLE F.1

I	$\log I$	S	$\log S$
320	2.5	2.8	0.45
100	2.0	2.0	0.30
32	1.5	1.4	0.15
10	1.0	1.0	0.00
3.2	0.5	0.7	−0.15

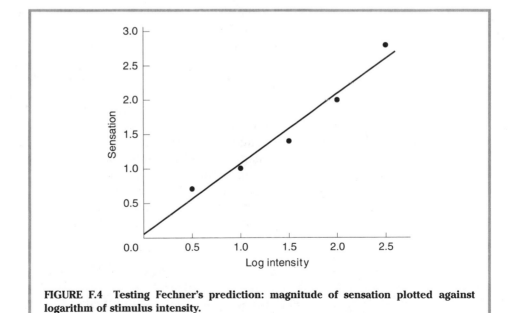

FIGURE F.4 Testing Fechner's prediction: magnitude of sensation plotted against logarithm of stimulus intensity.

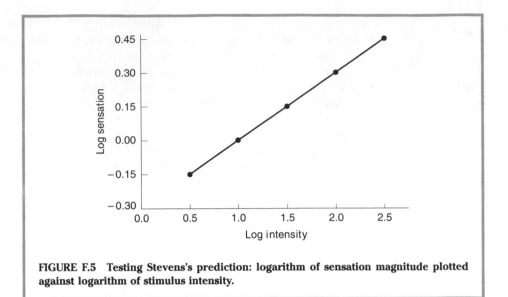

FIGURE F.5   Testing Stevens's prediction: logarithm of sensation magnitude plotted against logarithm of stimulus intensity.

This equation is another way of writing Equation 2. It is also in the form of a linear equation, but now log$S$ corresponds to y and log$I$ corresponds to x. In order to test Stevens's prediction, we not only need to transform I to log$I$, which we have already done, but transform S to log$S$. This has also been done in Table F.1.

Figure F.5 tests Stevens's prediction by plotting the logarithm of sensation magnitude against the logarithm of stimulus intensity. Here we see that the data fall exactly along the straight line. We can conclude that the data fit Stevens's theory better than they fit Fechner's.

To summarize, two theories made different predictions about a relationship between two variables. The two predictions appeared very similar when we considered the untransformed data. They became quite different, however, when we transformed the data according to the predictions of the two theories. Fechner's theory required us to take the logarithm of the stimulus intensity; Stevens's theory required us to take the logarithm of both sensation magnitude and stimulus intensity. The transformed data could then be tested for conformity to the theories.

It would be beyond our scope to discuss the various types of data transformations that are useful for the purposes of statistics and testing of theories. As implied by our two examples, the logarithmic transformation is the most common. We primarily want you to be aware of the possibility that a data transformation may be advisable. Transformations are discussed in more detail in certain statistics books and the manuals that accompany statistical packages. An excellent general review is given by Kruskal and Tanur (1978). Tukey (1977) and Mosteller, Feinberg, and Rourke (1983) have very useful introductory discussions.

Appendix G

KEY FOR IDENTIFYING APPROPRIATE GRAPHS AND STATISTICS

The following key will help you to decide which graphical and statistical procedures are appropriate for various kinds of questions, types of data, and experimental designs. The way to use it is to ask a series of questions, starting at the top. Each question is numbered at the left. On the right side of each line, you will find either the appropriate procedure or a number. If a procedure is listed, you have your answer. If a number is listed, look for that number on the left side of the page, where there will be another question. This will lead either to a procedure or to another number, and so on. You may have used keys like this one to identify flowers, insects, and the like. A key table is logically identical to a tree diagram, but permits many more branches without becoming impossible to represent on a single sheet of paper.

Key to Graphical and Statistical Procedures

1.0 PURPOSE OF PROCEDURE IS TO
1.1	Describe data	**2.0**
1.2	Make estimates about population means	**14.0**
1.3	Draw inferences	**15.0**

2.0 PURPOSE OF DESCRIPTION IS TO
2.1	Summarize data	**3.0**
2.2	Measure degree of a relationship	**13.0**
2.3	Make a prediction based on correlation coefficient	**linear regression**

3.0 TYPE OF SUMMARY DESCRIPTION DESIRED IS

3.1	Graphical	**4.0**
3.2	Numerical	**9.0**

4.0 PURPOSE OF GRAPHICAL DESCRIPTION IS TO DISPLAY

4.1	Categorical data	**bar graph**
4.2	Frequencies or numbers of cases	**5.0**
4.3	Quantitative data	**6.0**

5.0 PURPOSE IS TO SHOW FREQUENCIES OR NUMBER OF CASES

5.1	At particular values of a dependent variable	**frequency distribution**
5.2	At or below particular values of a dependent variable	**cumulative frequency distribution**

6.0 PURPOSE IS GRAPHICAL DESCRIPTION OF QUANTITATIVE DATA FOR

6.1	Two variables	**7.0**
6.2	Three variables	**8.0**

7.0 GRAPHICAL DESCRIPTION OF QUANTITATIVE DATA WITH TWO VARIABLES FOR

7.1	Individuals	**scattergram**
7.2	Functional relationships between variables	**graph of function**
7.3	Time as the independent variable	**time series**

8.0 GRAPHICAL DESCRIPTION OF QUANTITATIVE DATA WITH THREE VARIABLES WHEN THERE ARE

8.1	Two independent variables and one dependent variable	**contour graph**
8.2	Locations in two-dimensional space that have some characteristic	**data map**
8.3	Quantitative data that cannot easily be displayed numerically	**data points are pictures**

9.0 PURPOSE IS NUMERICAL DESCRIPTION OF

9.1	Typical case	**10.0**
9.2	Variability of cases	**12.0**

10.0 NUMERICAL DESCRIPTION OF TYPICAL CASE WHEN

10.1	Data are categorical	**mode**
10.2	Data are quantitative	**11.0**

11.0 DESCRIBE TYPICAL QUANTITATIVE DATA WHEN

11.1	Data are skewed, or you want the middle score	**median**

11.2	You want an average based on all the scores, or you plan to do further calculations, or you want to relate average to normal curve	**mean**
11.3	You want the most common score	**mode**

12.0 MEASURE OF VARIABILITY APPROPRIATE FOR THE
12.1	Mode	**range**
12.2	Median	**interquartile range, semi-interquartile range**
12.3	Mean	**variance, standard deviation**

13.0 PURPOSE IS TO MEASURE DEGREE OF A RELATIONSHIP WHEN DATA ARE
13.1	Ranks (ordinal)	**Pearson ρ correlation coefficient**
13.2	Ordinal, interval, or ratio	**Spearman *r* correlation coefficient**

14.0 ESTIMATES ABOUT POPULATION MEAN FOR
14.1	One group of subjects tested once	**confidence interval for the mean**
14.2	Two matched groups, or one group tested twice	**confidence interval for difference between means for correlated samples**
14.3	Two independent groups	**confidence interval for difference between means for independent groups**

15.0 PURPOSE IS TO DRAW INFERENCES WHEN DATA ARE
15.1	Frequencies in categories	**16.0**
15.2	Scores, quantities, or amounts	**17.0**

16.0 INFERENTIAL STATISTIC FOR FREQUENCIES WHEN
16.1	Data are distributed over levels of one variable, and you want to compare obtained distribution with hypothesized distribution	**chi-square test of goodness of fit**

16.2 Data are arranged in a two-way contin-
      gency table   **chi-square test of
                                                      independence**

___

17.0 INFERENTIAL STATISTIC FOR SCORES, QUANTITIES, OR AMOUNTS WHEN THERE ARE
17.1 One group of subjects   **18.0**
17.2 Two groups of subjects or two conditions   **20.0**
17.3 Three or more groups of subjects or con-
      ditions   **21.0**

___

18.0 INFERENTIAL STATISTIC ON QUANTITIES FOR ONE GROUP OF SUBJECTS
18.1 Hypothesis test for population mean   **19.0**
18.2 Hypothesis test for difference between
      means   ***t* test for correlated
                                                      samples**
18.3 Hypothesis test of strength of a linear rela-
      tionship between two variables   **significance of
                                                      Pearson
                                                      correlation
                                                      coefficient**

___

19.0 TEST HYPOTHESIS ABOUT POPULATION MEAN WHEN THE POPULATION STANDARD
DEVIATION IS
19.1 Known   **normal curve test**
19.2 Not known   ***t* test for
                                                      population mean**

___

20.0 HYPOTHESIS TEST, QUANTITATIVE DATA, TWO GROUPS OF SUBJECTS OR TWO
CONDITIONS, WITH
20.1 Matched groups or within-subjects design   ***t* test for correlated
                                                      samples**
20.2 Independent groups   ***t* test for
                                                      independent
                                                      samples**

___

21.0 HYPOTHESIS TEST FOR SCORES, THREE OR MORE CONDITIONS OR GROUPS OF
SUBJECTS, WITH
21.1 Three or more levels of one independent
      variable   **22.0**
21.2 Two independent variables   **23.0**

___

22.0 TEST HYPOTHESIS STATISTIC FOR THREE OR MORE LEVELS OF ONE INDEPENDENT
VARIABLE IN A
22.1 Between-subjects design   **one-way ANOVA**
22.2 Within-subjects design   **one-way, repeated-
                                                      measures ANOVA**

___

23.0 INFERENTIAL STATISTIC FOR TWO INDEPENDENT VARIABLES WHEN
    23.1 Both independent variables tested between subjects   **two-way ANOVA**
    23.2 Both independent variables tested within subjects   **two-way, repeated-measures ANOVA**
    23.3 One independent variable tested between subjects and one tested within subjects   **two-way, mixed-design ANOVA**

REFERENCES

ADORNO, T. W., FRENKEL-BRUNSWIK, E., LEVINSON, D. J., & SANFORD, R. N. (1950). *The authoritarian personality.* New York: Harper & Row.

ALLAN, W. (1975, JANUARY 10). UCLA scientist probes psychic events' reality. *Pittsburgh Press,* p. 5.

AMERICAN PSYCHOLOGICAL ASSOCIATION. (1981). Ethical principles of psychologists. *American Psychologist, 36,* 633–638.

AMERICAN PSYCHOLOGICAL ASSOCIATION. (1982). *Ethical principles in the conduct of research with human participants.* Washington, DC: Author.

AMERICAN PSYCHOLOGICAL ASSOCIATION. (1983). *Publication manual of the American Psychological Association* (3rd ed.). Washington, DC: Author.

AMERICAN PSYCHOLOGICAL ASSOCIATION. (1985). *Guidelines for ethical conduct in the care and use of animals.* Washington, DC: Author. (Reprinted 1986 in *Journal of the Experimental Analysis of Behavior, 45,* 127–132.)

AMERICAN PSYCHOLOGICAL ASSOCIATION. (1992). Ethical principles of psychologists and code of conduct. *American Psychologist, 47,* 1597–1611.

ANTELMAN, S. M., & CAGGIULA, A. R. (1977). Tails of stress-related behavior: A neuropharmacological model. In I. Hanin & E. Usdin (Eds.), *Animal models in psychiatry and neurology* (pp. 227–245). Oxford: Pergamon Press.

ANTELMAN, S. M., & SZECHTMAN, H. (1975). Tail pinch induces eating in sated rats which appears to depend on Nigrostriatal Dopamine. *Science, 189,* 731–733.

APPLEBAUM, P. S., ROTH, L. H., LIDZ, C. W., BENSON, P., & WINSLADE, W. (1987). False hopes and best data: Consent to research and the therapeutic misconception. *Hastings Center Report, 17*(2), 20–24.

Aronson, E. Brewer, M. & Carlsmith, J. M. (1985).   Experimentation in social psychology. In G. Lindzey & E. Aronson (Eds.), *Handbook of social psychology* (3rd ed.) (Vol. 2, pp. 441–486). New York: Random House.

Aserinsky, E., & Kleitman, N. (1953). Regularly occurring periods of eye motility, and concomitant phenomena, during sleep. *Science, 118,* 273–274.

Association for the Advancement of Psychology. (1981, August). Administration intensifies attack on social science research. *Advance,* pp. 3, 5.

Babich, F. R., Jacobson, A. L., Bubash, S., & Jacobson, A. (1965). Transfer of a response to naive rats by injection of ribonucleic acid extracted from trained rats. *Science, 149,* 656–657.

Bachrach, A. J. (1962). *Psychological research: An introduction.* New York: Random House.

Bacon-Prue, A., Blount, R., Hosey, C., & Drabman, R. S. (1980). The public posting of photographs as a reinforcer for bedmaking in an institutional setting. *Behavior Therapy, 11,* 417–420.

Barber, T. X. (1976). *Pitfalls in human research: Ten pivotal points.* New York: Pergamon Press.

Barlow, D. H., & Hersen, M. (1984). *Single case experimental designs* (2nd ed.). New York: Pergamon Press.

Barnes, R. D., Ickes, W., & Kidd, R. F. (1979). Effects of the perceived intentionality and stability of another's dependency on helping behavior. *Personality and Social Psychology Bulletin, 5,* 367–372.

Baum, A., & Davis, G. E. (1980). Reducing the stress of high-density living: An architectural intervention. *Journal of Personality and Social Psychology, 38,* 471–481.

Bernstein, I. (1978). Learned taste aversion in children receiving chemotherapy. *Science, 200,* 1302–1303.

Blass, E. M., & Epstein, A. N. (1971). A lateral preoptic osmosensitive zone for thirst in the rat. *Journal of Comparative and Physiological Psychology, 76,* 378–394.

Blough, D. S. (1956). Dark adaptation in the pigeon. *Journal of Comparative and Physiological Psychology, 49,* 425–430.

Boring, E. G. (1954). The nature and history of experimental control. *American Journal of Psychology, 67,* 573–589.

Boring, E. G. (1969). Perspective: Artifact and control. In R. Rosenthal & R. L. Rosnow (Eds.), *Artifact in behavioral research* (pp. 1–11). New York: Academic Press.

Bouchard, T. J. (1990). Genetic and rearing environmental influences on adult personality: An analysis of adopted twins reared apart. *Journal of Personality, 58,* 263–292.

Bower, G. (1981). Mood and memory. *American Psychologist, 36,* 129–148.

Bower, G. H., Gilligan, S. G., & Monteiro, K. P. (1981). Selectivity of learning caused by affective states. *Journal of Experimental Psychology: General, 110,* 451–473.

Brady, J. V., Porter, R. W., Conrad, D. G., & Mason, J. W. (1958). Avoidance behavior and the development of gastroduodenal ulcers. *Journal of Experimental Analysis of Behavior, 1,* 69–72.

BRAMEL, D., & FRIEND, R. (1981). Hawthorne, the myth of the docile worker, and class bias in psychology. *American Psychologist, 36,* 867–878.

BREHM, J. W. (1966). *A theory of psychological reactance.* New York: Academic Press.

BREHM, S. S., & WEINRAUB, M. (1977). Physical barriers and psychological reactance: 2-year-olds' responses to threats to freedom. *Journal of Personality and Social Psychology, 35,* 830–836.

BRELAND, K., & BRELAND, M. (1961). The misbehavior of organisms. *American Psychologist, 16,* 681–684.

BRENNAN, W. M., AMES, E. W., & MOORE, R. W. (1966). Age differences in infants' attention to patterns of different complexities. *Science, 151,* 354–356.

BROWN, G. W., & HARRIS, T. (1978). *Social origins of depression.* New York: Free Press.

BUREAU OF JUSTICE STATISTICS. (1990). *Criminal victimization in the United States, 1989: A national crime survey report, December 1990, NCJ-122024.* Rockville, MD: Justice Statistics Clearinghouse/NCJRS.

BURGESS, J. W. (1984). Do humans show a "species typical" group size? Age, sex and environmental differences in the size and composition of naturally occurring casual groups. *Ethology and Sociobiology, 5,* 51–57.

BYRNE, G. (1988). Bruening pleads guilty. *Science, 242,* 27–28.

BYRNE, W. L. (ED.). (1970). *Molecular approaches to learning and memory.* New York: Academic Press.

BYRNE, W. L., ET AL. (1966). Memory transfer. *Science, 153,* 658–659.

CAMPBELL, D. T. (1975). On the conflict between biological and social evolution and between psychology and moral tradition. *American Psychologist, 30,* 1103–1126.

CAMPBELL, D. T. (1979). "Degrees of freedom" and the case study. In T. D. Cook & C. S. Reichardt (Eds.), *Qualitative and quantitative methods in evaluation research* (pp. 49–67). Beverly Hills, CA: Sage.

CARLSMITH, J. M., ELLSWORTH, P., & ARONSON, E. (1976). *Methods of research in social psychology.* Reading, MA: Addison-Wesley.

CARR, E. G., & McDOWELL, J. J. (1980). Social control of self-injurious behavior of organic etiology. *Behavior Therapy, 11,* 402–409.

CHAPANIS, A. (1971). Prelude to 2001: Explorations in human communication. *American Psychologist, 26,* 949–961.

CHAPANIS, N. P., & CHAPANIS, A. (1964). Cognitive dissonance: Five years later. *Psychological Bulletin, 61,* 1–22.

CHARI, C. T. K. (1977). Some generalized theories and models of psi: A critical evaluation. In B. B. Wolman (Ed.), *Handbook of parapsychology* (pp. 803–822). New York: Van Nostrand.

CHOROVER, S. L. (1979). *From genesis to genocide.* Cambridge, MA: MIT Press.

COBURN, P. C., & STRICKER, E. M. (1978). Osmoregulatory thirst in rats after lateral preoptic lesions. *Journal of Comparative and Physiological Psychology, 92,* 350–361.

COCHRANE, P. (1978). Sex crimes and pornography revisited. *International Journal of Criminology and Penology, 6,* 307–317.

COLLETT, P., & MARSH, P. (1974). Patterns of public behavior: Collision avoidance on a pedestrian crossing. *Semiotica, 12,* 281–299.

COLLIGAN, M. J., & STOCKTON, W. (1978, January). The mystery of assembly-line hysteria. *Psychology Today,* pp. 93–99, 114–116.

COMMITTEE ON THE USE OF ANIMALS IN RESEARCH. (1991). *Science, medicine and animals.* Washington, DC: National Academy Press.

CONOLEY, J. C., & KRAMER, J. J. (EDS.). (1989). *The tenth mental measurements yearbook.* Lincoln: University of Nebraska, Buros Institute.

COOK, T. D., & CAMPBELL, D. T. (1976). The design and conduct of quasi-experiments and true experiments in field settings. In M. D. Dunette (Ed.), *Handbook of industrial and organizational psychology* (pp. 223–326). Chicago: Rand McNally.

COOK, T. D., & CAMPBELL, D. T. (1979). *Quasi-experimentation: Design and analysis issues for field settings.* Chicago: Rand McNally.

COOMBS, C. H., RAIFFA, H., & THRALL, R. M. (1954). Some views on mathematical models and measurement theory. *Psychological Review, 61,* 132–144.

COTMAN, C. W., & McGAUGH, J. L. (1980). *Behavioral neuroscience.* New York: Academic Press.

COURT, J. H. (1976). Pornography and sex crimes: A re-evaluation in the light of recent trends around the world. *International Journal of Criminology and Penology, 5,* 129–157.

COURT, J. H. (1984). Sex and violence: A ripple effect. In N. M. Malamuth & E. Donnerstein (Eds.), *Pornography and sexual aggression* (pp. 143–172). Orlando: Academic Press.

CRAIK, F. I. M., & TULVING, E. (1975). Depth of processing and the retention of words in episodic memory. *Journal of Experimental Psychology: General, 104,* 268–294.

CRESSEY, D. R. (1971). *Other people's money: A study in the social psychology of embezzlement.* Belmont, CA: Wadsworth.

CRONBACH, L. J. (1990). *Essentials of psychological testing* (5th ed.). New York: Harper Collins.

CRUMBAUGH, J. C. (1966). A scientific critique of parapsychology. *International Journal of Neuropsychiatry, 2,* 523–531.

DANZIGER, K. (1979). The social origins of modern psychology. In A. R. Buss (Ed.), *Psychology in social context* (pp. 27–45). New York: Irvington.

DARLEY, J. M., & LATANÉ, B. (1968). Bystander intervention in emergencies: Diffusion of responsibility. *Journal of Personality and Social Psychology, 8,* 377–383.

DEIKMAN, A. J. (1969). Experimental meditation. In C. T. Tart (Ed.), *Altered states of consciousness* (pp. 199–218). New York: Wiley.

DELGADO, J. M. R. (1969). *Physical control of the mind.* New York: Harper & Row.

DENENBERG, V. H., GARBANATI, J., SHERMAN, G., YUTZEY, D. A., & KAPLAN, R. (1978). Infantile stimulation induces brain lateralization in rats. *Science, 201,* 1150–1152.

DIENER, E., FRASER, S. C., BEAMAN, A. L., & KELEM, R. T. (1976). Effects of deindividuation variables on stealing among Halloween trick-or-treaters. *Journal of Personality and Social Psychology, 33,* 178–183.

DOTY, R. L. (1975). Influence of menstrual cycle on volunteering behavior. *Nature, 254,* 139–140.

EKMAN, P., & FRIESEN, W. V. (1975). *Unmasking the face: A guide to recognizing emotions from facial clues.* Englewood Cliffs, NJ: Prentice-Hall.

EKMAN, P., & FRIESEN, W. V. (1976). Measuring facial movement. *Environmental Psychology and Nonverbal Behavior, 1,* 56–75.

EKMAN, P., & FRIESEN, W. V. (1978). *Facial action coding system.* Palo Alto, CA: Consulting Psychologists Press.

EKMAN, P., FRIESEN, W. V. & O'SULLIVAN, M. (1988). Smiles when lying. *Journal of Personality and Social Psychology, 54,* 414–420.

ENDLER, N. S. (1977). The role of person-by-situation interactions in personality theory. In I. C. Uzgiris & F. Weizmann (Eds.), *The structuring of experience* (pp. 343–369). New York: Plenum.

EVANS, C. (1973). Parapsychology—what the questionnaire revealed. *New Scientist, 57,* 209.

EYSENCK, H. J. (1952). The effects of psychotherapy: An evaluation. *Journal of Consulting Psychology, 16,* 319–324.

EYSENCK, H. J. (1965). The effects of psychotherapy. *Journal of Psychology, 1,* 97–118.

FANTZ, R. L., FAGAN, J. F., & MIRANDA, S. B. (1975). Early visual selectivity. In L. B. Cohen & P. Salapatek (Eds.), *Infant perception; From sensation to cognition, Basic visual processes* (Vol. 1, pp. 249–345). New York: Academic Press.

FESTINGER, L., & CARLSMITH, J. M. (1959). Cognitive consequences of forced compliance. *Journal of Abnormal and Social Psychology, 58,* 203–210.

FESTINGER, L., RIECKEN, H. W., JR., & SCHACHTER, S. (1956). *When prophecy fails.* Minneapolis: University of Minnesota Press.

FISHER, W. A. (1990). Understanding and preventing teenage pregnancy and sexually transmitted disease/AIDS. In J. Edwards, R. S. Tindale, L. Heath, & E. J. Posavac (Eds.), *Social influence processes and prevention* (pp. 71–101). New York: Plenum.

FISHER, W. A., & BYRNE, D. (1978). Instrumentation and female indifference to arousing stimuli. *Journal of Personality and Social Psychology, 36,* 117–125.

FORGAS, J. P. (1987). The role of physical attractiveness in the interpretation of facial expression cues. *Personality and Social Psychology Bulletin, 13,* 478–489.

FOWLER, F. J. (1988). *Survey research methods* (rev. ed.). Newbury Park, CA: Sage.

FRIEDMAN, M. I., & STRICKER, E. M. (1976). The physiological psychology of hunger: A physiological perspective. *Psychological Review, 83,* 409–431.

GAITO, J. (1980). Measurement scales and statistics: Resurgence of an old misconception. *Psychological Bulletin, 87,* 564–567.

GILLIGAN, C. (1982). *In a different voice: Psychological theory and women's development.* Cambridge, MA: Harvard University Press.

GOFFMAN, E. (1971). *Relations in public.* New York: Basic Books.

GORMALLY, J., BLACK, S., DASTON, S., & RARDIN, D. (1982). The assessment of binge eating severity among obese persons. *Addictive Behaviors, 7,* 47–55.

GOULD, S. J. (1978). Morton's ranking of races by cranial capacity. *Science, 200,* 503–509.

GOULD, S. J. (1979, July). The father of Jensenism (review of Hearnshaw). *Psychology Today,* pp. 104–106.

GREELY, A. M. (1975). The sociology of the paranormal: A reconnaissance. *Sage Research Papers in the Social Sciences, 3* (Series No. 90-023).

GREEN, R. (1987). Exposure to explicit sexual materials and sexual assault: A review of behavioral and social science research. In M. R. Walsh (Ed.), *The psychology of women: Ongoing debates.* New Haven, CT: Yale University Press.

HAMM, R. J., & MATTSON, J. C. (1978). Additive summation following intradimensional discrimination training. *Journal of the Experimental Analysis of Behavior, 29,* 505–510.

HANSEL, C. E. M. (1966). *ESP: A scientific examination.* New York: Scribner.

HAWKES, N. (1979). Tracing Burt's descent into fraud. *Science, 205,* 673–675.

HEARNSHAW, L. S. (1979). *Cyril Burt, psychologist.* Ithaca, NY: Cornell University Press.

HELSON, H. (1964). *Adaptation level theory.* New York: Harper & Row.

HERNANDEZ-PEON, R., SCHERRER, H., & JOUVET, M. (1956). Modification of electrical activity in cochlear nucleus during "attention" in unanesthetized cats. *Science, 123,* 331–332.

HIBSCHER, J. A., & HERMAN, P. C. (1977). Obesity, dieting and the expression of "obese" characteristics. *Journal of Comparative and Physiological Psychology, 91,* 374–380.

HINES, T. M. (1979). Biorhythm theory: A critical review. *Skeptical Inquirer, 3,* 26–36.

HOLDEN, C. (1979). Ethics in social science research (news and comment). *Science, 206,* 537–540.

HOLLAND, A. L., MCBURNEY, D. H., MOOSSY, J., & REINMUTH, O. M. (1985). The dissolution of language in Pick's disease with neurofibrillary tangles: A case study. *Brain and Language, 24,* 36–58.

HORNER, M. S. (1968). *Sex differences in achievement motivation and performance in competitive and noncompetitive situations.* Unpublished doctoral dissertation, University of Michigan, Ann Arbor.

JENNI, D. A., & JENNI, M. A. (1976). Carrying behavior in humans: Analysis of sex differences. *Science, 194,* 859–860.

JOHNSON, M. (1976). Comments. *Journal of Parapsychology, 40,* 151–154.

JOHNSTON, L. D., O'MALLEY, P. M., & BACHMAN, J. G. (1991). *Drug use among American high school seniors, college students and young adults, 1975–1990,* (2 vols.). Rockville, MD: National Institute on Drug Abuse.

JORGENSEN, D. L. (1989). *Participant observation: A methodology for human studies.* Newbury Park, CA: Sage.

JOYNSON, R. B. (1989). *The Burt affair.* London: Routledge.

KAMIYA, J. (1969). Operant control of EEG alpha rhythm and some of its reported effects on consciousness. In C. T. Tart (Ed.), *Altered states of consciousness* (pp. 507–517). New York: Wiley.

KERNIS, M. H., ZUCKERMAN, M., & MCVAY, E. (1988). Motivational factors affecting performance: The importance of perceived locus of control. *Personality and Social Psychology Bulletin, 14,* 524–535.

KEY, W. B. (1973). *Subliminal seduction.* Englewood Cliffs, NJ: Prentice-Hall.

KIRK, R. E. (1982). *Experimental design: Procedures for the behavioral sciences* (2nd ed.). Pacific Grove, CA: Brooks/Cole.

Kohlberg, L. (1981). *The philosophy of moral development* (Vol. 1). San Francisco: Harper & Row.

Kolata, G. (1987). How to ask about sex and get honest answers. *Science, 236,* 82.

Kornhauser, A., & Sheatsley, P. B. (1976). Questionnaire construction and interview procedure. In C. Selltiz, L. S. Wrightsman, & S. W. Cook (Eds.), *Research methods in social relations* (3rd ed.). New York: Holt, Rinehart & Winston.

Kratochwill, T. R., & Levin, J. R. (Eds.). (1992). *Single-case research design and analysis: New directions for psychology and education.* Hillsdale, NJ: Erlbaum.

Kruskal, W. H., & Tanur, J. M. (1978). *International handbook of statistics.* New York: Free Press.

Kuhn, T. S. (1962). *The structure of scientific revolutions.* Chicago: University of Chicago Press.

Kutchinsky, B. (1973). The effect of easy availability of pornography on the incidence of sex crimes: The Danish experience. *Journal of Social Issues, 29,* 163–181.

Kutchinsky, B. (1991). Pornography and rape: Theory and practice? Evidence from crime data in four countries where pornography is easily available. *International Journal of Law and Psychiatry, 14,* 47–64.

Laudan, L. (1977). *Progress and its problems: Towards a theory of scientific growth.* Berkeley and Los Angeles: University of California Press.

Lepper, M. R., Greene, D., & Nisbett, R. E. (1973). Undermining children's intrinsic interest with extrinsic reward: A test of the "overjustification" hypothesis. *Journal of Personality and Social Psychology, 28,* 129–137.

Lettvin, S. Y., Maturana, H. R., McCulloch, W. S., & Pitts, W. H. (1959). What the frog's eye tells the frog's brain. *Proceedings of the Institute of Radio Engineers, 47,* 1940–1951.

Lorenz, K. Z. (1958, June). The evolution of behavior. *Scientific American,* pp. 67–78.

Maher, B. A. (1978). A reader's, writer's, and reviewer's guide to assessing research reports in clinical psychology. *Journal of Consulting and Clinical Psychology, 46,* 835–838.

Malamuth, N. M. (1987). Do sexually violent media indirectly contribute to antisocial behavior? In M. R. Walsh (Ed.), *The psychology of women: Ongoing debates* (pp. 441–459). New Haven, CT: Yale University Press.

Malamuth, N. M., & Donnerstein, E. (Eds.). (1984). *Pornography and sexual aggression.* Orlando, FL: Academic Press.

Marks, D., & Kammann, R. (1980). *The psychology of the psychic.* Buffalo, NY: Prometheus Books.

Marshall, G. D., & Zimbardo, P. G. (1979). Affective consequences of inadequately explained physiological arousal. *Journal of Personality and Social Psychology, 37,* 970–988.

Marshall, J. F., & Teitelbaum, P. (1974). Further analysis of sensory inattention following lateral hypothalamic damage in rats. *Journal of Comparative and Physiological Psychology, 86,* 375–395.

Maslach, C. (1979). Negative emotional biasing of unexplained arousal. *Journal of Personality and Social Psychology, 37,* 953–969.

McArthur, C. (1992). Rumblings of a distant drum. *Journal of Counseling and Development, 70,* 517–519.

McBurney, D. H., & Gent, J. F. (1979). On the nature of taste qualities. *Psychological Bulletin, 86,* 151–167.

McBurney, D. H., Levine, J. M., & Cavanaugh, P. H. (1977). Psychophysical and social ratings of human body odor. *Personality and Social Psychology Bulletin, 3,* 135–138.

McClintock, M., & Adler, N. T. (1978). The role of the female during copulation in wild and domestic rats *(Rattus norvegicus). Behaviour, 68,* 67–96.

McCloskey, M. (1980). The stimulus familiarity problem in semantic memory research. *Journal of Verbal Learning and Verbal Memory, 19,* 485–502.

McCloskey, M., & Glucksberg, S. (1979). Decision processes in verifying category membership statements: Implications for models of semantic memory. *Cognitive Psychology, 11,* 1–37.

McConnell, J. V. (1962). Memory transfer through cannibalism in planarium. *Journal of Neuropsychiatry, 3* (Supplement 1), 542–548.

McConnell, R. A. (1977). A parapsychological dialogue. *Journal of the American Society for Psychical Research, 77,* 429–435.

McGinnies, E. (1949). Emotionality and perceptual defense. *Psychological Review, 56*(5), 244–251.

Mednick, M. T. (1989). On the politics of psychological constructs: Stop the bandwagon, I want to get off. *American Psychologist, 44,* 1118–1123.

Milgram, S. (1963). Behavioral study of obedience. *Journal of Abnormal and Social Psychology, 67,* 371–378.

Miller, G. A. (1956). The magical number seven plus or minus two: Some limits on our capacity for processing information. *Psychological Review, 63,* 81–97.

Miller, N. E. (1984). Value and ethics of research on animals. *Laboratory Primate Newsletter, 23*(3), 1–10.

Miller, N. E. (1985). The value of behavioral research on animals. *American Psychologist, 40,* 423–440.

Moffat, A. S. (1991). Another sex survey bites the dust. *Science, 253,* 1483.

Mollenauer, S., Bryson, R., & Phillips, C. (1991). Voluntary exercise: Effects of ethanol-induced sleep in the C57BL/6J mouse. *Bulletin of the Psychonomic Society, 29,* 217–219.

Mosteller, F., Feinberg, S. E., & Rourke, R. E. K. (1983). *Beginning statistics with data analysis.* Reading, MA: Addison-Wesley.

National Institutes of Health. (1986). *Public Health Service policy on humane care and use of laboratory animals.* Bethesda, MD: Author.

Neuman, W. L. (1991). *Social research methods: Qualitative and quantitative approaches.* Boston: Allyn and Bacon.

Nicholl, C. S., & Russell, R. M. (1990). Analysis of animal rights literature reveals the underlying motives of the movement: Ammunition for counteroffensive by scientists. *Endocrinology, 127,* 985–989.

Nisbett, R. E. (1968). Determinants of food intake in human obesity. *Science, 159,* 1254–1255.

OLDS, J. (1973). Commentary. In E. S. Valenstein (Ed.), *Brain stimulation and motivation* (pp. 81–99). Glenview, IL: Scott, Foresman.

OLDS, J., & MILNER, P. (1954). Positive reinforcement produced by electrical stimulation of septal area and other regions of rat brain. *Journal of Comparative and Physiological Psychology, 47,* 419–427.

O'MALLEY, P. M., & WAGENAAR, A. C. (1991). Effect of minimum drinking age laws on alcohol use, related behaviors and traffic crash involvement among American youth: 1976–1987. *Journal of Studies on Alcohol, 52,* 478–491.

ORNE, M. T., & EVANS, F. J. (1965). Social control in the psychological experiment: Antisocial behavior and hypnosis. *Journal of Personality and Social Psychology, 1,* 189–200.

PALCA, J. (1991). Famous monkeys provide surprising results. *Science, 252,* 1789.

PELTON, L. H. (1978). Child abuse and neglect: The myth of classlessness. *American Journal of Orthopsychiatry, 48,* 608–617.

PHILLIPS, D. P. (1977). Motor vehicle fatalities increase just after publicized suicide stories. *Science, 196,* 1464–1465.

PHILLIPS, D. P. (1979). Suicide, motor vehicle fatalities, and the mass media: Evidence toward a theory of suggestion. *American Journal of Sociology, 84,* 1150–1174.

PONS, T. P., GARRAGHTY, P. E., OMMAYA, A. K., KAAS, J. H., TAUB, E., & MISHKIN, M. (1991). Massive cortical reorganization after sensory deafferentation in adult monkeys. *Science, 252,* 1857–1860.

POSAVAC, E. J., & CAREY, R. G. (1989). *Program evaluation: Methods and case studies* (3rd ed.). Englewood Cliffs, NJ: Prentice-Hall.

PUTHOFF, H. E., & TARG, R. (1974). Information transmission under conditions of sensory shielding. *Nature, 252,* 602–607.

RAJECKI, D. W., BLEDSOE, S. B., & RASMUSSEN, J. L. (1991). Successful personal ads: Gender differences and similarities in offers, stipulations, and outcomes. *Basic and Applied Social Psychology, 12,* 457–469.

RAO, K. R. (1977). On the nature of psi: An examination of some attempts to explain ESP and PK. *Journal of Parapsychology, 41,* 294–351.

REGAN, T. (1983). The case for animal rights. Berkeley: University of California Press.

RESCORLA, R. A. (1988). Pavlovian conditioning: It's not what you think it is. *American Psychologist, 43,* 151–160.

ROBINSON, J. P., SHAVER, P. R., & WRIGHTSMAN, L. S. (EDS.). (1991). *Measures of personality and social psychology attitudes.* San Diego, CA: Academic Press.

ROSENTHAL, R. (1976). *Experimenter effects in behavioral research* (enlarged ed.). New York: Irvington.

ROSENTHAL, R., & FODE, K. L. (1963). The effect of experimenter bias on the performance of the albino rat. *Behavioral Science, 8,* 183–189.

ROSENTHAL, R., & ROSNOW, R. L. (1969). *Artifact in behavioral research.* New York: Academic Press.

ROSS, L., LEPPER, M. R., & HUBBARD, M. (1975). Perseverence in self-perception and social perception: Biased attributional processes in the debriefing paradigm. *Journal of Personality and Social Psychology, 32,* 880–892.

ROWLAND, L. W. (1939). Will hypnotized persons try to harm themselves or others? *Journal of Abnormal and Social Psychology, 34,* 114–117.

RUBIN, L. B. (1979). *Women of a certain age: The mid-life search for self.* New York: Harper & Row.

SCHACHTER, S. (1959). *The psychology of affiliation.* Stanford, CA: Stanford University Press.

SCHACHTER, S., & RODIN, J. (EDS.). (1974). *Obese humans and rats.* Potomac, MD: Erlbaum.

SCHACHTER, S., & SINGER, J. (1962). Cognitive, social and physiological determinants of emotional state. *Psychological Review, 69,* 379–399.

SCHACHTER, S., & SINGER, J. E. (1979). Comments on the Maslach and Marshall-Zimbardo experiments. *Journal of Personality and Social Psychology, 37,* 989–995.

SEDIKIDES, C., DEVINE, P. G., & FURMAN, R. W. (1991). Social perception in multitarget settings: Effects of motivated encoding strategies. *Personality and Social Psychology Bulletin, 17,* 625–632.

SHAFFER, J. B. P. (1978). *Humanistic psychology.* Englewood Cliffs, NJ: Prentice-Hall.

SHARPE, R. S., & JOHNSGARD, P. A. (1966). Inheritance of behavioural characters in F. mallard × pintail *(Anas platyrynchos L. × Anas acuta L.)* hybrids. *Behaviour, 27,* 259–272.

SHWEDER, R. A. (1982). Liberalism as destiny. *Contemporary Psychology, 27,* 421–424.

SIDMAN, M. (1960). *Tactics of scientific research.* New York: Basic Books.

SINGH, N. N., DAWSON, M. J., & GREGORY, P. R. (1980). Suppression of chronic hyperventilation using response-contingent aromatic ammonia. *Behavior Therapy, 11,* 561–566.

SKINNER, B. F. (1950). Are theories of learning necessary? *Psychological Review, 57,* 193–216.

SKINNER, B. F. (1956). A case history in scientific method. *American Psychologist, 11,* 221–233.

SMITH, M. J., COLLIGAN, M. J., & HURRELL, J. J., JR. (1978). Three incidents of industrial mass psychogenic illness. *Journal of Occupational Medicine, 20,* 399–400.

SMITH, M. L., & GLASS, G. V. (1977). Meta-analysis of psychotherapy outcome studies. *American Psychologist, 32,* 752–760.

STAFFORD, T. (1991). Animal lib. In J. Williams (Ed.), *Animal rights and welfare* (pp. 40–48). New York: Wilson. (Reprinted from *Christianity Today, 34*(9), 18–23).

STERNBERG, R. J. (1988). *The psychologist's companion: A guide to scientific writing for students and researchers.* New York: Cambridge University Press.

STERNBERG, S. (1966). High-speed scanning in human memory. *Science, 153,* 652–654.

STEVENS, J. C., & RUBIN, L. L. (1970). Psychophysical scales of apparent heaviness and the size-weight illusion. *Perception and Psychophysics, 8,* 225–230.

Sullivan cancels teen sex survey. (1991, September/October). *Psychological Science Agenda,* p. 7.

TAUB, E. (1991). The Silver Spring monkey incident: The untold story. *Coalition for Animals & Animal Research Newsletter, 4,* 1–8.

TAUB, E., MILLER, N. E., NOVACK, T. A., COOK III, E. W., FLEMING, W. C., NEPOMUCENO, C. S., & CRAGO, J. E. (IN PRESS). A technique for improving chronic motor deficit following stroke. *Archives of Physical Medicine and Rehabilitation.*

TERRACE, H. S. (1979, JUNE). How Nim Chimpsky changed my mind. *Psychology Today,* pp. 65–76.

That numberless presidential chart. (1981, August 2). *New York Times,* p. F-17.

TRESEMER, D. (1977). *Fear of success.* New York: Plenum.

TRUMPY, F. D. (1983–1984). An investigation of the reported effect of Transcendental Meditation on the weather. *Skeptical Inquirer, 8,* 143–148.

TUKEY, J. W. (1977). *Exploratory data analysis.* Reading, MA: Addison Wesley.

U.S. BUREAU OF THE CENSUS. (1991). *Statistical abstract of the United States: 1991.* Washington, DC: U.S. Government Printing Office.

U.S. DEPARTMENT OF HEALTH AND HUMAN SERVICES. (1985). *Guide for the care and use of laboratory animals* (rev., NIH 78-23). Washington, DC.

VALENSTEIN, E. S. (1973). *Brain control.* New York: Wiley.

VALENSTEIN, E. S., COX, V. C., & KAKOLEWSKI, J. W. (1969). Sex differences in hyperphasia and body weight following hypothalamic damage. *Annals of the New York Academy of Sciences, 157,* 1030–1046.

WAGENAAR, A. C. (1981a, November). *Effects of raising the legal drinking age on traffic accident involvement of young drivers.* Paper presented at the American Public Health Association.

WAGENAAR, A. C. (1981b). Effects of the raised legal drinking age on motor vehicle accidents in Michigan. *HSRI Research Review, 11*(4), 1–8.

WAGENAAR, A. C. (1986). Preventing highway crashes by raising the legal minimum age for drinking: The Michigan experience 6 years later. *Journal of Safety Research, 17,* 101–109.

WAGENAAR, W. A. (1969). Note on the construction of diagram-balanced Latin squares. *Psychological Bulletin, 72,* 384–386.

WALKER, L. R. (1982, September). Empirical tests of famous sayings. *USAir,* pp. 64–68.

WANDELL, B. A., & PUGH, E. N., JR. (1980). A field-additive pathway detects brief-duration, long-wavelength incremental flashes. *Vision Research, 20,* 613–624.

WEBB, E. J., CAMPBELL, D. T., SCHWARTZ, R. D., & SECHREST, L. (1966). *Unobtrusive measures: Nonreactive research in the social sciences.* Chicago: Rand McNally.

WEISBERG, H. F., & BOWEN, B. D. (1977). *An introduction to survey research and data analysis.* San Francisco: Freeman.

WEISS, J. M. (1968). Effects of coping responses on stress. *Journal of Comparative and Physiological Psychology, 65,* 251–260.

WEISS, J. M. (1971). Effects of coping behavior in different warning signal conditions on stress pathology in rats. *Journal of Comparative and Physiological Psychology, 77,* 1–13.

WITTMAN, F. D. (1989). Planning and programming server intervention initiatives for fraternities and sororities: Experiences at a large university. *Journal of Primary Prevention, 9,* 247–269.

WORDEN, F. G. (1966). Attention and auditory electrophysiology. In E. Stellar & J. M. Sprague (Eds.), *Progress in physiological psychology* (Vol. 1, pp. 45–116). New York: Academic Press.

YIN, R. K. (1989). *Case study research: Design and methods* (2nd ed.). Newbury Park, CA: Sage.

ZILLMANN, D., & BRYANT, J. (1984). Effects of massive exposure to pornography. In N. M. Malamuth & E. Donnerstein (Eds.). *Pornography and sexual aggression* (pp. 115–138). Orlando, FL: Academic Press.

ZIMMERMAN, D. H., & WEST, C. (1975). Sex roles, interruptions and silences in conversation. In B. Thorne & N. Henley (Eds.), *Language and sex: Difference and dominance* (pp. 105–129). Rowley, MA: Newbury House.

ZIMMERMAN, D. H., & WEST, C. (1978). *Strangers when they meet: A study of same-sex and cross-sex conversations between unacquainted persons.* Unpublished manuscript.

NAME INDEX

SUBJECT INDEX